Management Accounting Standards for Sustainable Business Practices

Ionica Oncioiu
Titu Maiorescu University, Romania

Gary Cokins
Analytics-Based Performance Management LLC, USA

Sorinel Căpuşneanu
Titu Maiorescu University, Romania

Dan Ioan Topor
1 Decembrie 1918 University, Romania

A volume in the Advances in Finance, Accounting, and Economics (AFAE) Book Series

IGI Global
DISSEMINATOR OF KNOWLEDGE

Published in the United States of America by
IGI Global
Business Science Reference (an imprint of IGI Global)
701 E. Chocolate Avenue
Hershey PA, USA 17033
Tel: 717-533-8845
Fax: 717-533-8661
E-mail: cust@igi-global.com
Web site: http://www.igi-global.com

Library of Congress Cataloging-in-Publication Data

Names: Oncioiu, Ionica, 1972- editor. | Cokins, Gary, editor. | Capusneanu, Sorinel, 1975- editor.
Title: Management accounting standards for sustainable business practices / Ionica Oncioiu, Gary Cokins, Sorinel Capusneanu, and Dan Ioan Topor, editors.
Description: Hershey, PA : Business Science Reference, 2019. | Summary: “”This book explores various theoretical and practical approaches of management accounting and its impact on different areas of activity in the 21st century”--Provided by publisher”-- Provided by publisher.
Identifiers: LCCN 2019018095 | ISBN 9781799801795 (paperback) | ISBN 9781799801788 (hardcover) | ISBN 9781799801801 (ebook)
Subjects: LCSH: Managerial accounting.
Classification: LCC HF5657.4 .M366 2019 | DDC 658.15/11--dc23
LC record available at https://lccn.loc.gov/2019018095

This book is published in the IGI Global book series Advances in Finance, Accounting, and Economics (AFAE) (ISSN: 2327-5677; eISSN: 2327-5685)

British Cataloguing in Publication Data
A Cataloguing in Publication record for this book is available from the British Library.

For electronic access to this publication, please contact: eresources@igi-global.com.

Advances in Finance, Accounting, and Economics (AFAE) Book Series

Ahmed Driouchi
Al Akhawayn University, Morocco

ISSN:2327-5677
EISSN:2327-5685

Mission

In our changing economic and business environment, it is important to consider the financial changes occurring internationally as well as within individual organizations and business environments. Understanding these changes as well as the factors that influence them is crucial in preparing for our financial future and ensuring economic sustainability and growth.

The **Advances in Finance, Accounting, and Economics (AFAE)** book series aims to publish comprehensive and informative titles in all areas of economics and economic theory, finance, and accounting to assist in advancing the available knowledge and providing for further research development in these dynamic fields.

Coverage

- Comparative Accounting Systems
- Statistical Analysis
- Banking
- Evidence-Based Studies
- E-Accounting
- Investments and Derivatives
- Accounting information systems
- Economics of Risks, Uncertainty, Ambiguity, and Insurance
- Economics of Agriculture and Biotechnology
- Economic Indices and Quantitative Economic Methods

IGI Global is currently accepting manuscripts for publication within this series. To submit a proposal for a volume in this series, please contact our Acquisition Editors at Acquisitions@igi-global.com or visit: http://www.igi-global.com/publish/.

The Advances in Finance, Accounting, and Economics (AFAE) Book Series (ISSN 2327-5677) is published by IGI Global, 701 E. Chocolate Avenue, Hershey, PA 17033-1240, USA, www.igi-global.com. This series is composed of titles available for purchase individually; each title is edited to be contextually exclusive from any other title within the series. For pricing and ordering information please visit http://www.igi-global.com/book-series/advances-finance-accounting-economics/73685. Postmaster: Send all address changes to above address.

Titles in this Series

For a list of additional titles in this series, please visit: www.igi-global.com/book-series

Foreign Business in China and Opportunities for Technological Innovation and Sustainable Economics
Anna Visvizi (Deree – The American College of Greece, Greece) Miltiadis Lytras (Deree – The American College of Greece, Greece) Xi Zhang (Tianjin University, China) and Jie Zhao (Anhui University, China)
Business Science Reference • copyright 2019 • 284pp • H/C (ISBN: 9781522589808) • US $195.00 (our price)

Handbook of Research on Global Issues in Financial Communication and Investment Decision Making
Hasan Dinçer (Istanbul Medipol University, Turkey) and Serhat Yüksel (Istanbul Medipol University, Turkey)
Business Science Reference • copyright 2019 • 540pp • H/C (ISBN: 9781522592655) • US $365.00 (our price)

Behavioral Finance and Decision-Making Models
Tripti Tripathi (Jiwaji University, India) Manoj Kumar Dash (Khallikote University, India) and Gaurav Agrawal (Indian Institute of Information Technology and Management Gwalior, India)
Business Science Reference • copyright 2019 • 333pp • H/C (ISBN: 9781522573999) • US $215.00 (our price)

Global Challenges in Public Finance and International Relations
Deniz Şahin Duran (Tokat Gaziosmanpaşa University, Turkey) Yusuf Temür (Tokat Gaziosmanpaşa University, Turkey) and Doğan Bozdoğan (Tokat Gaziosmanpaşa University, Turkey)
Business Science Reference • copyright 2019 • 304pp • H/C (ISBN: 9781522575641) • US $225.00 (our price)

International Financial Reporting Standards and New Directions in Earnings Management
Jonas da Silva Oliveira (Instituto Universitário de Lisboa (ISCTE-IUL), Portugal) Graça Maria do Carmo Azevedo (University of Aveiro, Portugal) and Augusta da Conceição Santos Ferreira (University of Aveiro, Portugal)
Business Science Reference • copyright 2019 • 342pp • H/C (ISBN: 9781522578178) • US $225.00 (our price)

Throughput Accounting in a Hyperconnected World
Ionica Oncioiu (European Academy of the Regions, Belgium)
Business Science Reference • copyright 2019 • 362pp • H/C (ISBN: 9781522577126) • US $195.00 (our price)

Organizational Auditing and Assurance in the Digital Age
Rui Pedro Marques (University of Aveiro, Portugal) Carlos Santos (University of Aveiro, Portugal) and Helena Inácio (University of Aveiro, Portugal)
Business Science Reference • copyright 2019 • 404pp • H/C (ISBN: 9781522573562) • US $225.00 (our price)

International Firms' Economic Nationalism and Trade Policies in the Globalization Era
Harish C. Chandan (Argosy University, USA) and Bryan Christiansen (Global Research Society, LLC, USA)
Business Science Reference • copyright 2019 • 299pp • H/C (ISBN: 9781522575610) • US $215.00 (our price)

IGI Global
DISSEMINATOR OF KNOWLEDGE

701 East Chocolate Avenue, Hershey, PA 17033, USA
Tel: 717-533-8845 x100 • Fax: 717-533-8661
E-Mail: cust@igi-global.com • www.igi-global.com

Editorial Advisory Board

Table of Contents

Detailed Table of Contents

ABC method are presented by establishing the list of main activities, cost drivers, allocation of indirect costs, and determining unit costs. The theoretical aspects presented the basic national and international studies in the literature. The case study is based on data obtained from the energy company. The chapter ends with the authors' conclusions on the benefits of implementing EMA/ABC. This chapter contributes to the expansion of the theoretical and empirical framework of EMA and the methods used to implement it within various business companies.

Attila Szora Tamaş, 1 Decembrie 1918 University, Romania
Cristian-Marian Barbu, Artifex University, Romania
Ileana-Sorina Rakos, University of Petrosani, Romania
Alina-Georgiana Solomon, Dimitrie Cantemir Christian University, Romania

The issue of this chapter is to illustrate the aspects of planning, budgeting, and controlling green activities within an economic entity and their impact on the profitability of the entity. The objectives of this chapter are to present the strategic planning, budgeting, and control/controlling processes; the presentation of the principles underlying the budgeting; and the presentation of a case study on the elaboration of the budgetary process and the controlling of an economic entity in the manufacturing field. The chapter presents the types of integrated budgets and how to report the achievement of the objectives. By providing effective information on planning and budgeting, green controlling becomes an indispensable tool for any economic entity in monitoring and measuring performance. Thus, through the contribution made, a new theoretical and empirical framework is created by the authors, which facilitates the identification of new ideas, themes, and debates of other aspects encountered in the activity of the economic entities.

Traian Ovidiu Calotă, Titu Maiorescu University, Romania
Sorin-Adrian Robu, The Bucharest University of Economic Studies, Romania
Ionica Oncioiu, Titu Maiorescu University, Romania
Georgiana Burlacu, Valahia University, Romania

In the context of the monitoring of businesses through accounting, the profit and loss account is the component that reflects the performance of the enterprise, that is, the extent to which it has achieved its objectives in terms of profit. In the income statement, there are flows that determine the result, understood in principle as a variation in equity during a financial period. Defining the performance of an enterprise is different, depending on the interest of the users, on the principles, conventions, and accounting rules used to determine the outcome. This is what specialists in the field call accounting policies. This chapter examines the profit and loss statement in the context of scarce and expensive resources, which must be used efficiently. The results show that it is necessary for companies to determine efficiency indicators by comparing the effects obtained with the efforts and the resources consumed by the company and operated by the management.

This chapter presents, in a descriptive manner, the interrelation of the sustainability reporting concepts and the sustainability disclosure through internal and external stakeholders. The main objectives of this chapter are approaching the disclosure of environmental information, presenting the views of the stakeholders on the content and format of environmental reporting. The factors underlying the disclosure of the environmental information and the impact of these, including the views stakeholders on the content and presentation format of the environmental reporting, are presented and analyzed. A case study is also presented in order to highlight the disclosure and presentation of the environmental report of an industrial entity and the importance of the accounting information provided. This chapter brings a theoretical contribution to expand the knowledge on the environmental disclosure and reporting approaches. The authors' approaches remain open to the expansion of these issues at both national and international level and both in the academia and business area.

The chapter proposes an interdisciplinary perspective and explores from the theoretical and practical point of view approaches of management accounting and their impact on different companies in Romania. Also, the chapter examines the role of management accounting related to accounting and auditing and offers a number of new insights into management accounting. Romanian companies in the accounting, auditing, and tax consultancy fields use computer-assisted auditing techniques (CAAT) to find better solutions for generating profits, avoiding risks and improving the companies' business strategies. The chapter will help the academia, business environment, specialty organizations, and business analysts in identifying new trends in management accounting, building on existing research and new expert assertions.

This chapter highlights the results of a transversal study on the influences of managers' decisions on sustainable business models. The objectives of this chapter are presentation of business models and sustainable business models and a study on the influences of managers' decisions on the use of sustainable business models. Based on the internal and international literature, the authors present the concepts of

Creative accounting responds to the same issue faced by the management, but the answer lies at the boundary between the legal and de facto recording of the economic event, leaving accountants to create the entity's economic reality. The manager of the entity can choose from the multitude of accounting treatments and policies, the one that is most convenient and responds best to their own interests, which implies that the outcome may be convenient and not necessarily true. This chapter presents the implications and challenges of creative accounting on financial statements. The results show that the main controversy raised by the standards refers to the need for periodic reassessments and the possibility of choosing a method of measuring the value, which creates premises for the practice of creative accounting.

The responsibility of auditors is a controversial topic that has brought much debate amongst academics and experts alike in recent years. This chapter's aim is to set the framework in which audit reporting exists: part of the wider landscape of corporate reporting and the final fragment of the sphere of the financial statements audit quality. By using a general-to-specific deductive approach, the authors discuss the international and European perspectives on the process of financial statement audits, as well as the stakeholders or audit and audit reporting, in order to clearly define the regulatory space in which any changes in this field occur. The authors also discuss the theories that explain the process of audit reporting, with an emphasis on the lending credibility theory, the inspired confidence theory, and the sociology of education theory. The authors consider that these theories explain the improvements undertaken to improve the communicative value of the audit quality.

In the current business environment, the costing system used within the firms has prominent impact on strategic decisions. High-quality cost data significantly increases the quality of firms' strategic decisions. The activity-based costing system has failed to satisfy the needs of firms operating in the competitive economic environment. The time-driven activity-based costing system is the developed version of activity-based costing system. Time-driven activity-based costing system is one of the most sophisticated costing systems that enable firms to accurately calculate the cost of goods and services. Time-equations are used in time-driven activity-based costing system to estimate the time consumed by each activity. This chapter aims to discuss main dynamics of time-driven activity-based costing system and provides an illustration of this costing system in the manufacturing industry. The case study demonstrates that time-driven activity-based costing system is useful in calculating idle capacity cost.

Preface

Current modern companies, which are also the key factors of a global economy, are subject to increasing pressures to conduct their business in an environmentally responsible manner, due to social and environmental problems. Environmental damage caused by large companies; such as toxic waste, acid rain, deforestation, ozone depletion or global warming; can be reduced by taking appropriate measures and actions that can be translated into their sustainable business practices. Constraining companies to comply with environmental standards and eliminating environmental damage has been made more prominent in the last decade through regulatory organizations or governments that have imposed more severe rules and standards for companies to become more socially and environmentally responsible. In achieving their goals, companies need to find the means to deploy their businesses in a socially and environmentally sustainable way without sacrificing their economic performance (e.g., profits to shareholders and owners) and well-being.

By integrating multiple processes and methods, management accounting plays a key role in achieving a company's sustainability notably by providing reliable, relevant, accurate, and timely information to managers. With this information managerial decisions are well grounded. Improving long-term environmental performance can bring economic benefits to those companies that are innovative and environmentally sensitive, especially by integrating environmental information into their business strategies. On top of that, the context of the changes at the geo-political, legislative and environmental level, imposed the necessity to extend the area of scientific and academic research towards new approaches.

The title of this book, *Managing Accounting Standards for Sustainable Business Practices*, depicts different theoretical-methodological transversal or cross disciplinary approaches. The authors of the chapters propose practical solutions for the implementation of business concepts or practices aimed at enhancing the contribution to scientific development and the contribution of knowledge to serve the academic and business environment. The focus of authors on topical issues shows interest in connecting to the current effervescent state of the business environment that is continually adapting to sustainable development. Issuing soundly-based managerial decisions is based on robust information where leading providers of management accounting play a key role in establishing future business strategies and adapting to business, corporate image and reputation. For this reason, we believe that the content of this book is a solid starting point in identifying responses to the requirements of the business environment and all stakeholders in developing multilateral communication and interaction relationships whereby winning is mutual. The 15 chapters published in this volume are an invitation to explore sustainable business practices through the use of management accounting and other methods and tools needed to achieve sustainable development.

Some remarkable aspects of a Sustainability Balanced Scorecard and its implementation within an economic entity in the aluminum industry are presented by Gary Cokins and Sorinel Căpuşneanu, the authors of the first chapter, "Management Accounting: The Sustainable Strategy Map and Its Associated Sustainability Balanced Scorecard." The main objectives of this chapter are to present a Balanced Scorecard and integrate an additional fifth perspective into Sustainability Balanced Scorecard (SBSC), including some of its considerations and challenges. The authors identify the causes of SBSC's appearance and its conceptual-evolving treatments, some considerations stemming from the practical experience of specialists, but also some current and future challenges. The focus is on the implementation of the SBSC within an economic entity in the aluminum industry by presenting an original case study. It highlights the steps taken in designing and presenting the SBSC, including the architecture of the Strategic Sustainability Map used to translate the strategic objectives in the map of the entity and identify the performance indicators for each strategic objective. Based on strategic planning and a performance management system, Sustainability Balanced Scorecard helps to change the behavior of the company and its employees.

An interesting business perspective on the policies and benefits provided by implementing environmental managerial accounting in various areas of activity is revealed by Sorinel Căpuşneanu, Dan Ioan Topor, Dana Maria Constantin, Alexandru Manole and Mihaela Stefan Hint, the authors of the second chapter, "Environmental Management Accounting: A Business Perspective on the Policies, Analyses, and Benefits of Its Implementation." The objectives of this research are transposed into a case study based on the activity-based costing (ABC) method performed at an energy company. The implementation steps specific to the ABC method are presented by: establishing the list of main work activities, their cost drivers, and allocation of indirect expenses to calculate the costs of outputs (e.g., products and standard service-lines). A bonus is the calculation of the unit-level costs for each type of output. The case study is based on data obtained from the energy company. The chapter ends with the authors' conclusions on the benefits of implementing EMA/ABC.

The budgetary process of an economic entity is illustrated by Attila Szora Tamaş, Cristian-Marian Barbu, Ileana-Sorina Rakos and Alina-Georgiana Solomon, the authors of the third chapter, "Planning, Budgeting, and Green Controlling: The Budgetary Process of an Economic Entity." Here are emphasized the strategic planning, budgeting and control/controlling processes, the presentation of the principles underlying the budgeting; and the presentation of a case study on the elaboration of the budgetary process and the controlling of an economic entity in the manufacturing field. Also are presented the types of integrated budgets and how to report the achievement of the objectives. By providing effective information on planning and budgeting, green controlling becomes an indispensable tool for any economic entity in monitoring and measuring performance. Therefore, green control has been imposed as a necessary tool in substantiating decisions, being used to organize, manage and provide environmental data and information in physical and monetary units.

The Profit and Loss Statement in the context of scarce and expensive resources, which must be used efficiently, is presented by Traian Ovidiu Calotă, Sorin-Adrian Robu, Ionica Oncioiu and Georgiana Burlacu, the authors of the fourth chapter, "The Informational Value of the Profit and Loss Account in Line With International Accounting Standards." In the context of the monitoring of businesses through accounting, the profit and loss accounts are those revenue and expense components which reflect the performance of the enterprise, that is, the extent to which it has achieved its objectives in terms of profit. In the income statement, there are flows that determine the result, understood in principle as a variation in owner's equity during a financial period. Defining the performance of an enterprise is different, depending on the interest of the users, on the principles, conventions and accounting rules used to determine the outcome. This is what specialists in the field refer to as “accounting policies”. The results show that it is necessary for companies to determine efficiency indicators by comparing the effects obtained with the efforts and the resources consumed by the company and operated by the management.

In a descriptive manner, the interrelation of the sustainability reporting concepts and the sustainability disclosure through internal and external stakeholders is emphasized by Dana Maria Constantin, Dan Ioan Topor, Sorinel Căpuşneanu and Alexandru Manole, the authors of the fifth chapter, “Sustainability Reporting: Stakeholders and Reporting of Sustainability Accounting Information.” This chapter presents the approaching the disclosure of environmental information, presenting the views of the stakeholders on the content and format of environmental reporting. The factors underlying the disclosure of the environmental information and the impact of these factors, including the views stakeholders on the content and presentation format of the environmental reporting, are presented and analyzed. A case study is also presented in order to highlight the disclosure and presentation of the environmental report of an industrial entity and the importance of the accounting information provided. This chapter brings a theoretical contribution to expand the knowledge on the environmental disclosure and reporting approaches.

An interdisciplinary perspective and exploration from the theoretical and practical point of view approaches of management accounting and their impact on different companies in Romania is presented by Andreea Marin-Pantelescu, in the sixth chapter, “Financial Audit in Romanian Enterprises: Coming Across Tendencies, Profits, Further Tasks, and Improvement of Business Strategies.” Here are examined the role of management accounting related to accounting and auditing. This chapter offers a number of new insights into management accounting. Romanian companies in the accounting, auditing and tax consultancy field use computer-assisted auditing techniques (CAAT) to find better solutions for generating profits, avoiding risks and improving the companies' business strategies. Based on this, the management becomes the main actor in whose role the success or the failure of the business carried out through the company he leads is decided. Along with concepts such as controlling, auditing, or reporting, management accounting provides value with the decision making process.

A transversal study about the sustainable business practices made in Romania is realized by Mirela-Cătălina Turkeş, Dan Ioan Topor, Sorinel Căpuşneanu and Dana Maria Constantin, the authors of the seventh chapter, “Sustainable Business Practices and Their Influence on Managers Decisions: Transversal Study.” The objectives of this chapter are: (1) presentation of business models and sustainable business models, and (2) a study on the influences of managers' decisions on the use of sustainable business models. Based on the internal and international literature, the authors present the concepts of business models and sustainable business models as well as their typology. The types of sustainable business models are presented. The case study is focused on presenting the influences of managerial decisions on the sustainable business models of SMEs.

The dual nature of creative accounting has been intensely debated since its emergence in the Anglo-Saxon economies. The lack of a common accounting language, different accounting systems at international level, applied in different languages, international legislation harmonized more or less correctly, amidst a turbulent economic environment, left room for multiple interpretations and meanings. Ionica Oncioiu, Cristina Maria Ştefan, Valentin Radu and Georgiana Burlacu, the authors of the eight chapter, “The Effect of Accounting Manipulation on the Business Performances,” present the advantages of fair value in manipulating business performances by creative accounting, but there are voices that are challenging this concept because of its volatility and tendency to subjectivism, and also manipulating the models used to evaluate balance-sheet structures or profit and loss account. The results show that fair value was introduced by accounting norms in response to the deterioration of confidence in the financial statements and targets a new system for assessing the entity's assets and liabilities. Furthermore, the complexity of the economic life under the market economy competitively requirements have determined an increased role of information in the process of decision making. The quality of current and long-term decisions and implicitly the results obtained depend on the quality of the information.

In Chapter 9 dedicated to "Circular Economy and Circular Business Models in the Actual Global Ecological Context: Various Approaches," Dana Maria Constantin, Dan Ioan Topor, Sorinel Căpuşneanu and Hassan Danial Aslam synthesize some of the current issues of the circular economy and sustainable business models. Based on the international literature, the authors highlights aspects such as: the conceptual theoretical approaches of the circular economy and sustainable business models; interconnecting the principles of the circular economy; the difference between the linear and the circular economy; the circular economy and the sustainable development; the supply chain within the circular economy; possible business models of the circular economy; advantages and limitations in the successful implementation of the circular economy and supporting sustainability; other aspects of the circular economy and sustainability. The covered topics are based on the studies conducted by specialists and also present some authors' own opinions on the sustainable development and circular economy.

Seen as a reflection of the clear vision of some strong extreme leaders, the overall performance of the entity is achieved today against the backdrop of the Innovation process. The economic/financial value of the company is necessary to become the key element in any entity development strategy. However, it requires a comparative analysis of the entity with other market players or emerging markets. The author of the tenth chapter, "Perceiving the Value of the Company in Managing Business Risks: Evidence From Finland," Lavinia Essen, analysis the new research directions at the intersection between accounting and management, with the role of potentiating the important valorization of managerial culture and the implementation of an integrated system of performance indicators to accurately determine the value of a company. A decision-making process taking place on various organizational, operational and strategic levels needs to rely on data regarding the costs borne as well as other reliable analyses from within the organization, supplied by a managerial accounting process which must provide answers to the information needs signaled by the management of that company.

In the eleventh chapter, "Importance of Ethics and Education to Understand the Audit Mission," Melinda Timea Fülöp, George Silviu Cordoş and Nicolae Măgdaş bring forward the discussion of how the level of accounting and audit knowledge has an impact on how stakeholders understand the audit mission, the auditor's responsibilities and the message conveyed by the Audit Report, even when considering the new and extended reports. The preliminary results of this analysis indicate that audit education influences the audit expectation gap (the reasonableness gap). The results state that if measures would be taken to upsurge the stakeholder's levels of education in auditing and accounting, combined with new and revised standards, the audit expectation gap can be reduced. In this sense, the International Accounting Education Standards Board (IAESB) is an independent standard-setting body that serves the public interest by establishing standards in the field of professional accounting education that prescribe technical competence and professional skills, values, ethics, and attitudes.

The problem of financial statements conversion is brought out by Alin Eliodor Tănase, Dumitru Alexandru Stoica, Nicoleta Ileana Trăistaru and Monika Brigitte Sürgün, the authors of the twelfth chapter, "Important Managerial Controversies in Conversion of Financial Statements." The results show that the conversion of financial statements applies only if the entity whose financial statements are converted has a functional currency that is not a hyperinflationary economy. Functional currency has been defined as the currency of an entity's main economic environment. A group does not have a functional currency, but the functional currency is set at the level of each group entity. Determining each functional currency at each component of a group is made by looking at several factors. In this chapter, the conversion occurs when the currency in which the financial statements are prepared is different from the presentation, and the important managerial controversies are presented in conversion of the financial statements.

Creative accounting only responds to the same issue faced by a senior management team, but the answer lies at the boundary between the legal and de facto recording of the economic event, leaving accountants to cosmetize the entity's economic reality. The managers of the entity can choose from the multitude of accounting treatments and policies, the one that is most convenient and responds to their own interests, which implies that the outcome may be convenient and not necessarily true. In the thirteenth chapter, "Creative Accounting and Its Impact on Financial Statements," Gabriela Claudia Oncioiu and Alina Stanciu present the implications and challenges of creative accounting on performance. The results show that the main controversy raised by the standards refers to the need for periodic reassessments and the possibility of choosing a method of measuring the value, which creates premises for the practice of creative accounting. In any case, the leaders of the future need to understand the depth and impact of what managing change in organizational development means in their pursuit of performance.

In the fourteenth chapter, "The Concept of Corporate Reporting and Audit Quality," George Silviu Cordoş, Melinda Timea Fülöp and Nicolae Măgdaş discuss the theories that explain the process of audit reporting, with an emphasis on the Lending Credibility Theory, the Inspired Confidence theory, and the sociology of education theory; the connection between these theories and our research objective, as we consider that these theories explain the improvements undertaken to improve the communicative value of the audit quality. The responsibility of auditors is a controversial topic that in recent years has brought much debate amongst academics and experts alike. This research aim is to set the framework in which audit reporting exists: part of the wider landscape of corporate reporting and the final fragment of the sphere of the financial statements audit quality. By using a general-to-specific deductive approach, we discuss the international and European perspectives on the process of financial statement audits, as well as the stakeholders or audit and audit reporting, in order to clearly define the regulatory space in which any changes in this field occur.

In the final chapter, "Implementation of Time-Driven Activity Based Costing System in the Manufacturing Industry: Evidence From Turkey," Ahmet Özcan aims to discuss main dynamics of time-driven activity based costing (TDABC) system and provides an illustration of this costing system in the manufacturing industry. The case study demonstrates that time-driven activity-based costing system is useful in calculating excess and idle capacity cost. In the current business environment, the costing system used within the firms has prominent impacts on strategic decisions. High-quality cost data with accurate profit margin information significantly increases the quality of firms' strategic decisions. Time-driven activity-based costing system is an enhanced version of conventional rate-based activity based costing system when there is a need to calculate excess and idle capacity costs. Time-driven activity-based costing system is one of the most sophisticated costing systems that enable firms to more accurately calculate the cost of goods and services by excluding idle capacity. Time-equations are used in time-driven activity-based costing system to estimate the time consumed by each activity. But it also relies on capturing unit times or other equation inputs for major business processes. In many organizations, these simply are not available at the onset of the initiative.

This overview of this book highlights the fact that each chapter contains interesting elements whose potential and degree of interest open new directions for future research. Authorized analyzes indicate that accounting practices act as a mechanism to facilitate environmental management through: compliance with environmental legislation, stakeholders' communication, employees and management engagement, commitment to continuous improvement of environmental performance. Therefore, management accounting has a dual function in this respect: an environmental management facilitator and the benefit of an environmental management based on accountability.

Ionica Oncioiu
Titu Maiorescu University, Romania

Gary Cokins
Analytics-Based Performance Management LLC, USA

Sorinel Căpuşneanu
Titu Maiorescu University, Romania

Dan Ioan Topor
1 Decembrie 1918 University, Romania

Acknowledgment

Looking back, we wish to thank all the persons who made the publishing of the present volume possible: Jan Travers, Melissa Wagner, Erin Wesser, Christina Henning, Nicole Elliott, Kristina Byrne, Lindsay Johnston, Joshua Witman, Nick Newcomer, Jaimie Watts, Josephine Dadeboe, Jordan Tepper, Sean Eckman, Marianne Caesar, Colby Conway and many other IGI Global team members, reviewers, collaborators, and all the contributing authors: without your efforts and dedication this editorial project would have never been possible.

Chapter 1
Management Accounting:
The Sustainable Strategy Map and Its Associated Sustainability Balanced Scorecard

Gary Cokins
https://orcid.org/0000-0001-9832-0114
Analytics-Based Performance Management LLC, USA

Sorinel Căpușneanu
https://orcid.org/0000-0003-3799-3993
Titu Maiorescu University, Romania

ABSTRACT

This chapter illustrates some aspects of sustainability balanced scorecard and its implementation within an economic entity in the aluminum industry. The main objectives of this chapter are to present balanced scorecard and integrate the fifth pillar into sustainability balanced scorecard, including some of its considerations and challenges. The authors identify the causes of SBSC appearance and its conceptual-evolving treatments, some considerations stemming from the practical experience of specialists, but also some current and future challenges. The focus is on the implementation of the SBSC within an economic entity in the aluminum industry by presenting an original case study. It highlights the steps taken in designing and presenting the SBSC, including the architecture of the strategic sustainability map used to translate the strategic objectives of the entity and the performance indicators. Through the authors' contribution, a new conceptual-empirical framework is created to consider debate and aspects of sustainability encountered in the business environment around the world.

DOI: 10.4018/978-1-7998-0178-8.ch001

INTRODUCTION

Management of sustainable performance is one of the phenomena faced by the current business environment, and in particular, management corporations. The focus of management on profitability remains the main objective of any company, but it must also take into account the sustainability of social, economic and environmental aspects. Under these circumstances, managerial decisions need to be adjusted and strongly substantiated, considering the information required by internal and external stakeholders, including financial reporting. The information requirements of customers and other stakeholders (shareholders, investors, population, various regulatory organisms, etc.) are steadily increasing, and some companies face certain problems in implementing the concept of sustainability and environmental reporting. Due to the differences between performance management systems and their users, it can be considered as a current challenge. A key role in the process of globalization and the fulfillment of sustainability goals is the main actors, the companies. They are responsible for social and environmental issues, but also for creating wealth in an economy by creating new jobs. Environmental issues can become strategic influences on a company's image, profitability, competitiveness, markets and products and can affect its future in economic survival (Lansiluoto & Jarvenpaa, 2010).

Many of the implemented social and environmental management systems work only at the operating level, not being related to strategic planning and company management. Balanced scorecard presents an ideal solution for integrating environmental and social aspects into a company's management system, allowing for clarification of visions and strategies by translating them into viable actions. Due to the fact that it provides a feedback on the internal business processes and the external results of the actions, BSC is a continuous improvement tool for achieving strategic performance and results (Johansson and Larson, 2015). The main objectives of this chapter are: (1) *the presentation of the Balanced Scorecard evolution and its considerations,* (2) *the integration, evolution and challenges of the Sustainability Balanced Scorecard,* and (3) *the implementation of the Sustainability Balanced Scorecard within an economic entity in the aluminum industry.*

BACKGROUND

Balanced Scorecard (BSC): Evolution and Some Considerations

Balanced Scorecard philosophy is based on the cause-effect relationship that functions as a strategic management tool with four perspectives: financial, customer, internal processes and learning-growth. Kaplan and Norton (1996) defined the cause-effect relationship as a logical chain transforming intangible assets into corporal value by uniting management and the gap of indicators. All the objectives of each perspective are related to the cause-effect relationship. BSC has emerged in response to the limitations and shortcomings of traditional performance measurement systems due to inconsistency with fixed strategies, data overload and short-term guidelines (Kaplan, 1984; Johnson & Kaplan, 1987; Chandler, 1990; Ittner & Larcker, 1998; Neely, 1999). Specialists have introduced this concept as recognition of age-related challenges, in particular the need to integrate intangible asset measurement into management systems (Kaplan, 2010). In other words, a company's missions and strategies have been translated into a set of performance indicators, providing a framework for a strategic management and measurement system by interlinking the four perspectives.

Since its launch, Balanced Scorecard has evolved from a simple performance measurement tool to a performance management framework (Kaplan and Norton, 1996a) to a strategic management system (Kaplan & Norton, 2002).

As a performance management tool, specialists consider the BSC as:

- A structured tool to help measure and manage performance on the four key perspectives for any organization and that has a particular interest for stakeholders (Kaplan & Norton, 1992).
- A tool for assessing the expectations and demands of stakeholders that generate possible strategies to meet the requirements (Bieker, 2002).
- Provides a framework for performance measurement across the four perspectives (financial, customer, internal processes, and learning and growth) with financial and non-financial objectives (Horngren et al., 2010).
- By expanding its use as a strategic tool, the BSC is:
    - Instrument affecting decision-making by managers (Birch, 2010; Lipe & Salterio, 2000).
    - Strategic tool for reflection and implementation when the four perspectives are in full consistency with the organization's objectives and strategies (Chan, 2004).

As a result of its conceptual evolution, the BSC has made its mark by the theoretical developments of the specialists (Olve, 1999; Paladino et al., 2001; Neely, 2002), but also by its constant evolution based on practical experience (Lawrie and Cobbold, 2004). The BSC allows clear disclosure of the key factors for a high-performing, long-term financial and competitive performance (Kaplan & Norton, 1996b) and also allows managers to supervise performance, providing the organization with a clear way of communicating and strengthening the strategy (Epstein & Manzoni, 1998). According to specialists' studies, the BSC has some shortcomings. Thus, the BSC-specific cause-effect relationship is complicated and the company wishing to adopt the BSC must adopt a unique set of carefully selected and relevant indicators and units (Malmi, 2001). The BSC fails to address the crucial needs of all stakeholders by excluding the impact on the environment, human resources, community contributions and suppliers (Smith, 2005) and their elimination has been approved as essential to a company's survival and profitable development (Keating et al., 2008).

Hope and Sadness

The balanced scorecard, the methodology developed by Drs. Robert S. Kaplan and David Norton, recognizes the shortcoming of executive managements' excessive emphasis on after-the-fact, short-term financial results. It resolves this myopia and improves organizational performance by shifting attention from financial measures and managing non-financial operational measures related to customers, internal processes, and employee innovation, learning and growth. These influencing measures are reported *during* the period when sooner reactions can occur. This in turn leads to better financial results.

The balanced scorecard is one of the underpinnings needed to complete the full vision of the performance management framework. Will the adoption rate of the balanced scorecard find the same difficulty crossing the chasms encountered by activity-based costing (ABC) systems in the 1990s? It took many failures in ABC system implementations before organizations learned what ABC is and how to shape, size, and level the detail of ABC systems before organizations began to get them ready and right for use. Are balanced scorecard implementations going to travel down the same bumpy road?

Lack of Consensus

An early indication of trouble is the confusion about what a balanced scorecard is, and more confusion about what its purpose is. There is little consensus. If you ask executives whether they are using a balanced scorecard, many say they are. But if you next ask them to describe it, you'll get widely different descriptions. There is no standard–yet. Some executives say they have successfully transferred their old columnar management reports into visual dashboards with flashing red and green lights and directional arrows. Some realize a scorecard is more than that, and they have put their old measures on a diet, compressing them to a smaller, more manageable number of more relevant measures. Neither may be the correct method. But how does anyone know if those measures–the so-called key performance indicators (KPIs)–support the strategic intent of the executive team? Are the selected measures the *right* measures? Or are they what you *can* measure rather than what you *should* measure? And is the purpose of the scorecard only to better *monitor* the dials rather than facilitate the employee actions needed to *move* the dials?

Talk about balanced scorecards and dashboards seem to be appearing in business magazines, website discussion groups, and at conferences. Today's technology makes it relatively simple to convert reported data into a dashboard dial. But what are the consequences? What actions are suggested from just monitoring the dials? In the performance management framework, results and outcome information should answer three questions: What? So what? And then what? Sadly, most scorecards and dashboards only answer the first question. Worse yet, answering the "what" may not even focus on a relevant "what." Organizations struggle with determining what to measure.

Organizations need to think deeper about what measures drive value and reflect achieving the direction-setting strategic objectives of their executive team. With the correct measures, then organizations should strive toward optimizing these measures, and ideally be continuously forecasting their expected results.

Implementing too Fast and Skipping Key Steps

Why are so many people familiar with the term *balanced scorecard* but so few familiar with the term *strategy maps*? I believe the strategy map is orders of magnitude more important than the scorecard which is merely a feedback mechanism. Why do executives want a balanced scorecard but without a strategy map? One possible explanation is the mistaken belief that those vital few KPI measures, rather than the trivial many, can be derived without first requiring employee teams and managers to understand the answer to a key question: "Where does the executive team want the organization to go?" This question is best answered by the executive team's vision and mission–and they must point to the direction they want the organization to follow them to. That is the executive team's primary job–setting direction. The strategy map and its companion scorecard are important too, but their combination answers a different question: "How will we get there?"

Figure 1 illustrates a generic strategy map with its four stacked popular perspectives. Each rectangle represents a strategic objective and its associated projects or competencies to excel at plus their appropriate measures and targets.

Note that there are dependency linkages in a strategy map with an upward direction of cumulating effects of contributions. The derived KPIs are not in isolation but rather have context to the mission and vision. To summarize a strategy maps linkages from the bottom perspective upward:

Figure 1. Generic Strategy Map

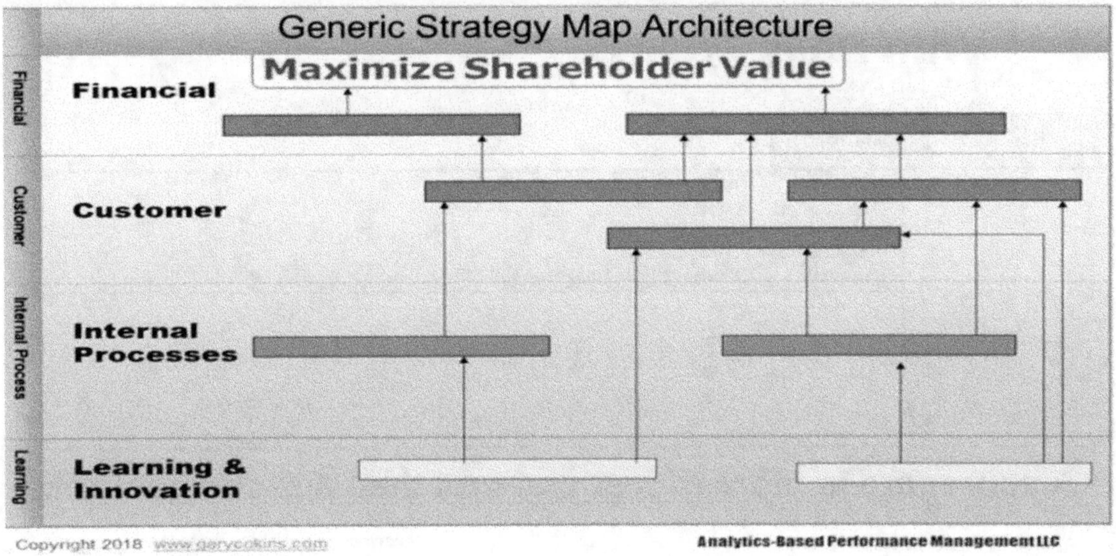

- Accomplishing the employee innovation, learning and growth objectives contributes to the internal process improvement objectives.
- Accomplishing the internal process objectives contributes to the customer satisfaction objectives.
- Accomplishing the customer-related objectives results in the achieving the financial objectives, typically a combination of revenue growth and cost management objectives.

The strategy map is like a force field in physics, as with magnetism, where the energy, priorities, and actions of people are mobilized, aligned, and focused. One can say that at the top of the map that is maximizing shareholder wealth (or for public sector organizations maximizing community and citizen value) is *not* really a goal–it is a result. It is a result from accomplishing all of the linked strategic objectives with cause-and-effect relationships.

The peril that threatens the success of this methodology is executive teams that are anxious to assign measures with targets to employees and hold them accountable. Executives typically skip two critical steps of involving the employees to gain their buy-in (and also commitment to the measures) to assure they understand the executive team's strategy, and the more critical prior step to identify the mission-essential projects and initiatives that will achieve the strategic objectives. The presence of enabling projects and initiatives goes to the heart of what distinguishes a strategic objective from just getting better at what you have already been doing.

Figure 2 illustrates ideally who should be responsible for which one of five elements of each strategic objective: the executive team or the managers and employees. Sadly, many organizations neglect the first two elements identified in a strategy map. They begin with the third column to select KPIs without constructing a strategy map. The performance management intelligence resides in the strategy map.

Strategy maps and their derived scorecard are navigational tools to guide the organization to *execute* the strategy, not necessarily to formulate the strategy. Executive teams are pretty good at defining strategy,

Figure 2. Who is Responsible for What?

Who Does What?

Measurement Period:	1st Quarter					
	Strategic Objective	Identify Projects, Initiatives, or Processes	KPI Measure	KPI Target	KPI Actual	comments / explanation
Executive Team	X	↕	↕	X		
Managers and Employees		X	X		*their score*	*X*
					<----- period results ------->	

A scorecard is more of a <u>social</u> tool than a technical tool.

but a high involuntary chief executive officer (CEO) turnover rate and the increasingly shorter tenure of CEOs are evidence of their failure to implement their strategy.

Measurements Are Far More a Social System Than a Technical One

Do not misinterpret me. Selecting and measuring KPIs are critical. You get what you measure, and strategy maps and scorecards serve a greater social purpose than a technical one (although information technology and software are essential enablers). Performance measures motivate people and focus them on what matters most.

Imagine if every day, every employee in an organization, from the cleaning person and janitor at the bottom of an organization to the CEO or managing director at the top, could answer this single question: "How am I doing on what is important?" The first half of the question can be easily displayed on a dial with a target; it is reported in a scorecard or dashboard. But it is the second half of the question that is the key– "on what is important"– and that is defined from the strategy map.

The risk and peril of the balanced scorecard involves the process of identifying and integrating appropriate cause-and-effect linkages of strategic objectives that are each supported by the vital few measures, and then subsequently cascading the KPIs down through the organization. KPIs ultimately extend into performance indicators (PIs)–operational performance indicators–that employees can relate to and directly affect.

The primary task of a strategy map and its companion balanced scorecard is to align people's work and priorities with multiple strategic objectives that, if accomplished, will achieve the strategy and consequently realize the end-game of maximizing shareholder wealth (or maximizing citizen value). The strategic objectives are located in the strategy map, not in the scorecard. The KPIs in the scorecard reflect the strategic objectives in the strategy map.

Debate will continue about how to arrive at the vital few KPIs for workgroups. Here are two approaches:

1. Newtonian-style managers, who believe the world is a big machine with dials, pulleys and levers to push and pull, find appeal in looking at benchmark data to identify which relevant and unfavorably large performance gaps should therefore be areas for their focus. They want to know, "What must we get better at?" The KPIs are then derived. Strategies are then deduced from recognizing deficiencies.
2. In contrast, Darwinian-style managers, who believe the organization is a sense-and-respond organism, find appeal in having the executive team design the strategy map by applying a SWOT (strengths, weaknesses, opportunities, and threats) approach. This approach begins with the executive team freely brainstorming and recording an organization's SWOTs. They then cluster similar individual SWOTs into strategic objectives with causal linkages in the strategy map. Following this initial step, the middle managers and core process owners are then tasked with identifying the few and manageable projects and core processes to improve that will attain the executive team's strategic objectives in the strategy map. After that step, then those same middle managers can identify the KPIs that will indicate progress toward achieving the projects and improving critical core processes. This latter approach not only assures that mid-managers and employee teams will understand the executive's strategy, about which most mid-managers and employees are typically clueless, but it further generates their buy-in and ownership of the scorecard and KPIs since these have not been mandated to them from the executives. (Of course, the executive team can subsequently challenge and revise their lower managers' selected projects and KPIs–debate is always healthy to do–but only after the buy-in and learning has occurred).

Scorecard or Report Card? The Impact of Senior Management's Attitude

Regardless of which technique or any other method is used to identify the KPIs, the KPIs ideally should reflect the executive team's strategic intent and not be reported in isolation disconnected, as typically the annual financial budget is disconnected from the strategy. This is the peril of the balanced scorecard. Its main purpose is to communicate the executive team's strategy to employees in a way they can understand it; and to report the impact of their contribution to attaining it. But starting with KPI definition without context to the executive's mission and vision denies this important step.

Research from Professor Raef Lawson when he was at the State University of New York, Albany, suggests that a major differentiator of success from failure in a balanced scorecard implementation is the senior management's attitude. Scorecard or report card? Will we use it for punishment or remedy? Do we work for bosses we must obey as if we are a dog– "roll over." Or do we work for coaches like on a sports team and mentors who guide and counsel us?

As an example, is senior management anxiously awaiting those dashboards so they can follow the cascading score meters downward in order to micro-manage the workers under their middle managers, acting like Darth Vader to see which of their minions may need to be cut off from their air supply? Or will the executives appropriately restrict their primary role and responsibility to define and continuously adjust strategy (which is dynamic, not static, always reacting to new insights) and then allow the empowerment of employee teams to select KPIs from which employees can actively determine the corrective interventions to align with the strategy?

The superior strategy map and scorecard systems embrace employee teams communicating among themselves to take actions rather than a supervisory command-and-control, in-your-face style from senior managers. An executive team micro-managing the KPI score performance of employees can be corrosive. If the strategy map and cascading KPI and PI selection exercise is done well and subsequently maintained, then higher-level managers need only view their own score performance, share their results with the employee teams below them, and coach the teams to improve their KPI and PI scores and/or re-consider adding or deleting KPIs or PIs. For the more mature scorecard users using commercial software, they can re-adjust the KPI and PI weighting coefficients to steer toward better alignment with the strategic objectives.

Why Not an Automobile GPS Navigator for an Organization?

The latest rage is to have a global positioning system (GPS) route navigator in our automobiles. As with most new technologies, such as when handheld calculators replaced slide rules or laptop computers emerged, a GPS is another gadget that is evolving into a must-have. They get you to your destination without a hassle and a comforting voice to guide you along the way. Why can't an organization have a similar device? It can. My belief is the refinement in usage of strategy maps and its companion balanced scorecard are becoming the GPS route navigator for organizations. For organizations the destination input into the GPS is the executive team's strategy. As earlier described, the executive team's primary job is to set strategic direction, and the "top" of their strategy map is their destination. However, unlike a GPS' knowledge of roads and algorithms to determine the best route, managers and employee teams must "map" which projects, initiatives, and business process improvements are best to get to the destination for realizing the strategy. In addition, when you are driving a car with a GPS instrument and you make a wrong turn, the GPS' voice chimes in to tell you that you are off track–and it then provides you with a corrective action instruction. However, with most organization's calendar-based and long cycle-time reporting, there is delayed reaction. The performance management framework includes a GPS.

Next, the organization as the automobile itself needs to be included. The motor and driveshaft are the employees with their various methodologies, such as customer value management and service delivery that propel the organization toward its target. Collectively, the many methodologies, including lean management and activity-based costing, constitute performance management as the organization's intermeshed gears.

But what important aspect of this automobile analogy is missing? Fuel efficiency. Performance management as a framework has arguably been around for decades (despite information technology (IT) research firms, like the Gartner Group and IDC, recently tagging this new name in the late 1990s). However, just like a poor performing car with some broken gears, tires out of alignment, and gunky lubrication will yield poor gallons per mile (or liters per kilometer), the analogy is poorly integrated methodologies, impure raw data, and lack of digitization and analytics results in poor rate of shareholder financial wealth creation. The full vision of performance management removes the friction and vibration plus weak torque to not only optimizes the consumption of the organization's resources–its employees and spending–but it also gets the organization to its strategy destination faster, cheaper, and smarter. The result? A higher shareholder wealth creation yield?

Finally, as earlier mentioned a strategy is never static but is constantly adjusted. This means the destination input to the GPS navigator is constantly changing. This places increasing importance on predictive analytics to determine where the best destination for stakeholders is located. How much longer do you want to drive your existing automobile when a performance management car with a GPS is now available to lift wealth creation efficiency and yield?

Failures Due to Arrogance, Ignorance, or Inexperience?

Some proposed management improvement methodologies, like the lights-out manufacturing factory touted in the 1980s, are fads that come and go. But the strategy map and its companion, the balanced scorecard for feedback, are most certain to be a *sustained* methodology in the long term–perhaps forever. It only makes common sense that executive teams provide direction-setting and employee teams then take the actions to "get there." Are these early twenty-first century missteps and misunderstandings in implementing the balanced scorecard due to arrogance, ignorance, or inexperience? I suggest it is due to inexperience.

Conflict and tension is natural in all organizations. Therefore it takes time among managers and employees to stabilize what ultimately is a behavioral measurement mechanism of cause-and-effect KPIs, to distinguish between KPIs and PIs; and to then get mastery with how to use both these types of measures to navigate, power, and steer as an integrated enterprise. As stated by the author Peter Senge, a thought leader in the field of organizational change management, the differentiator between successful and failing organizations will be the *rate*, and not just the amount, of organizational learning. Those intangible assets–employees as knowledge workers and the information provided to them–are what truly power the performance management framework.

How Are Balanced Scorecards and Dashboards Different?

There is confusion about what the difference is between a balanced scorecard and a dashboard. There is similar confusion differentiating key performance indicators (KPIs) from normal and routine measures that we can refer to as just performance indicators (PIs). The adjective "key" of a KPI is the operative term. An organization has only so much resources or energy to focus. To use a radio analogy, KPIs are what distinguish the signal from the noise–the measures of progress toward strategy execution. As a negative result of this confusion, organizations are including an excessive amount of PIs in their scorecard system that should be restricted to KPIs.

A misconception about a balanced scorecard is that its primary purpose is to monitor results. That is secondary. Its primary purposes are to report the carefully selected measures that reflect the strategic intent of the executive team, and then enable ongoing understanding as to what should be done to align the organization's work and priorities to attain the executive team's strategic objectives. The strategic objectives should ideally be articulated in a strategy map, which serves as the visual vehicle from which to identify the projects and initiatives needed to accomplish each objective, or the specific core processes that the organization needs to excel at. After this step is completed, then KPIs are selected and their performance targets are set. With this understanding, it becomes apparent that the strategy map's companion scorecard, on its surface, serves more as a feedback mechanism to allow everyone in the organization, from front-line workers up to the executive team, to answer the question: "How are we doing on what is important?" More importantly, the scorecard should facilitate analysis to also know why. The idea is not to just *monitor* the dials but to *move* the dials.

Vital Few vs. the Trivial Many

Michael Hammer, the author who introduced the concept of business process reengineering, described the sad situation of measurement abuse in his book, The Agenda: What Every Business Must Do to Dominate the Decade: "*In the real world ... a company's measurement systems typically deliver a blizzard of nearly meaningless data that quantifies practically everything in sight, no matter how unimportant; that is devoid of any particular rhyme or reason; that is so voluminous as to be unusable; that is delivered so late as to be virtually useless; and that then languishes in printouts and briefing books without being put to any significant purpose.... In short, measurement is a mess....We measure far too much and get far too little for what we measure because we never articulated what we need to get better at, and our measures aren't tied together to support higher-level decision making*" (Hammer, 2001). Hammer is clearly not hiding his feelings. But has the cure been worse than the ailment? Simply reducing the number of measures can still result in an organization measuring what it *can* measure as opposed to what it *should* measure. But to determine what you *should* measure requires deeper understanding of the underlying purposes of a balanced scorecard relative to a dashboard.

Scorecards and Dashboards Serve Different Purposes

The two terms–scorecards and dashboards – have a tendency to confuse, or rather get used interchangeably, when each brings a different set of capabilities. The sources of the confusion are:

- Both represent a way to track results.
- Both make use of traffic lights, dials, sliders, and other visual aids.
- Both can have targets, thresholds, and alert messages.
- Both can provide drill down to other metrics and reports.

The difference comes from the context in how they are applied. To provide some history, as busy executives and managers have struggled to keep up with the amount of information being thrust at them, the concept of traffic lighting has been applied to virtually any and all types of reporting. As technology has improved, more bells and whistles have been added; an example is the ability to link to other reports and to drill down to finer levels of detail.

The common denominator was the speed of being able to focus on something that required action or further investigation. The terminology evolved to reflect how technology vendors described what provided this capability. As a consequence, both dashboard and scorecard terms are being used interchangeably.

Figure 3 illustrates the difference between scorecards and dashboards using a taxonomy starting with all measurements in general. Scorecards and dashboards are not contradictory; they are used for different purposes.

At the top portion of the exhibit is the realm of scorecards. *Scorecards* are intended to be *strategic*. They align the behavior of employees and partners with the strategic objectives formulated by the executive team. In contrast, *dashboards,* at the bottom portion of the exhibit, are intended to be *operational*.

Some refer to dashboards as "dumb" reporting and scorecards as "intelligent" reporting. The reason is dashboards are primarily for data visualization; they display what is happening during a time period. Most organizations begin with identifying what they are already measuring and construct a dashboard dial from there. However, dashboards do not communicate why something matters, why someone should care about the reported measure, or what the impact may be if an undesirable declining measure continues. In short, dashboards report what you *can* measure.

In contrast, a scorecard does provide the information lacking in dashboards. A scorecard additionally answers questions by providing deeper analysis, drill-down capabilities, traffic light alert messaging,

Figure 3. Scorecard vs. Dashboard

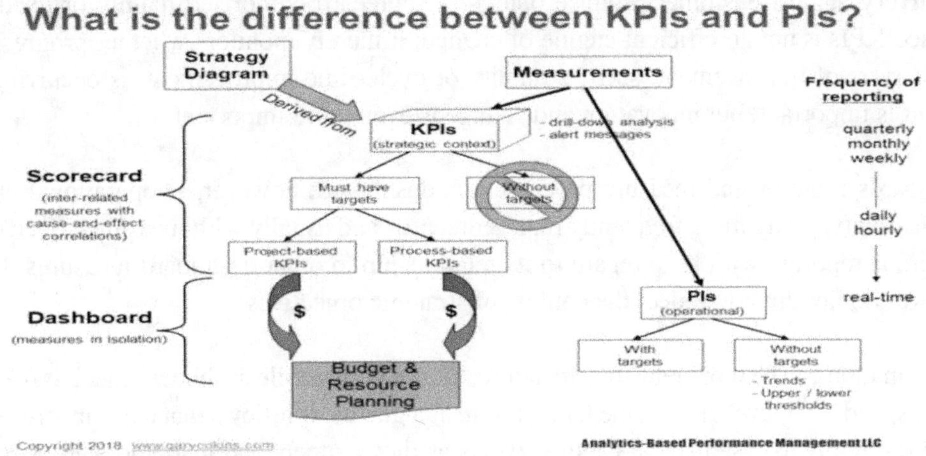

and forecasting for inferences of performance potential to determine motivational targets. Scorecards do not start with the existing data, but rather they begin with identifying what strategic projects to complete and core processes to improve and excel in.

The selection and validation of the correct or best KPIs is a constant debate. Statistical correlation interaction analysis among KPIs can determine the degree of influence and "lift" that various cascaded KPIs have on the higher level enterprise-wide KPIs–hence correlation analysis validates or improves the KPI selection. In addition this type of analysis can automatically uncover previously unknown statistical relationships that may suggest cause-and-effects and can be used for predictive power. You want to make changes based on anticipated targets and constantly refocused outcomes so that employees can proactively make changes before unexpected events occur that would require a much more expensive reaction. In short, scorecards report what you *should* measure.

Here are some guidelines for understanding the differences (Eckerson, 2006):

- Scorecards chart progress toward strategic objectives. A scorecard displays periodic snapshots of performance associated with an organization's strategic objectives and plans. It measures organizational activity at a summary level against pre-defined targets to see if performance is within acceptable ranges. Its selection of KPIs helps executives communicate strategy to employees and focuses users on the highest priority projects, initiatives, actions, and tasks required to execute plans. The adjective "key" differentiates KPIs from the PIs reported in dashboards.

Scorecard KPIs ideally should be derived from a strategy map rather than just a list of important measures that the executives have requested to be reported. Regardless of whether the Kaplan and Norton suggested four stacked perspectives are used or some variant, scorecard KPIs should have cause-and-effect linkages (e.g., statistical correlations). Directionally upward from the employee-centric innovation, learning, and growth perspectives, the KPIs should reveal the cumulative build of potential to realized economic value.

There are two key distinctions of scorecards: (1) each KPI *must* require a predefined target measure; and (2) KPIs should be comprised of both project-based KPIs (e.g., milestones, progress percentage of completion, degree of planned versus accomplished outcome) and process-based KPIs (e.g., percent on-time delivery against customer promise dates). A scorecard comprised mainly or exclusively by process-based KPIs is not an efficient engine of change; it merely monitors whether progress from the traditional drivers of improvement, such as quality or cycle-time improvement, is occurring. Process improvement is important, but innovation and change is even more important.

- Dashboards monitor and measure processes. A dashboard, however, is operational and reports information typically more frequently than scorecards and usually with measures. Each dashboard measure is reported with little regard to its relationship to other dashboard measures. Dashboard measures do not directly reflect the context of strategic objectives.

This information can be more real-time in nature, like an automobile dashboard that lets drivers check their current speed, fuel level and engine temperature at a glance. It follows that a dashboard should ideally be linked directly to systems that capture events as they happen, and it should warn users through alerts or exception notifications when performance against any number of metrics deviates from the norm or what is expected.

The caution I have for organizations that are paying more attention to their performance measurements involves (1) the linkage of scorecard KPIs to the strategy diagram (often referred to as a strategy map) and also to the fiscal budget (as well as rolling financial forecasts); and (2) the linkage of dashboard PIs selected to influence behavior that will ultimately result in achieving or exceeding the KPI targets. Strategy diagrams and the Budget are located in Figure 3 and are described below.

Scorecards Link the Executives' Strategy to Operations and to the Budget

A strategy diagram is located in the upper left of Figure 3. The exhibit denotes that KPIs should be *derived from* the executives' strategic objectives and plans. If KPIs are selected independent of the strategy, then they will likely report only what *can* be measured as opposed to what *should* be measured. Failure to execute a strategy is one of a chief executive officer's (CEO's) major concerns, and therefore KPIs should either reflect mission-critical projects and initiatives or core business processes that must be excelled at. (Hence there is the need for both project-based and process-based KPIs.)

The budget (and increasingly rolling financial forecasts) should be derived from the required funding of the projects (i.e., the nonrecurring strategy expenses and capital investments) and of the operational processes (i.e., the recurring operational capacity-related expenses that vary with driver volumes, such as customer demand).

A strategy is dynamic, never static, as executives appropriately shift directions based on their new insights and observations. Reliably accurate forecasting is critical for both strategy formulation and future resource capacity management. Hence, both the KPIs and the necessary funding to realize the strategic plans will continuously be derived from the "living" strategy diagram.

Dashboards Move the Scorecard's Dials

The organization's traction and torque are reflected in the dashboard's PI measures–the more frequently reported operational measures. Although some PIs may have pre-defined targets, PIs serve more to monitor trends across time or results against upper or lower threshold limits. As PIs are monitored and responded to, then the corrective actions will contribute to achieving the KPI target levels with actual results. Cause-and-effect relationships between and among measures underlie the entire approach to integrating strategy diagrams (formulation), scorecards (appraisal), dashboards (execution), and fiscal budgets (the fuel).

Strategy Is More Than Performing Better: It Involves Doing Different Things

A key to organizational survival involves differentiation from competitors. An important role of the executive team is to exhibit vision and constantly determine innovation to differentiate their organization from others. This explains a misunderstanding about strategic objectives. Some mistakenly believe the purpose of strategic objectives is to keep an organization adhered to a single, unbroken path. This is certainly not the case. As mentioned earlier, strategy is dynamic, not static. The purpose of strategic objectives in a strategy map is to re-direct the organization from the tyranny of maintaining the status quo. Strategy is about constant change. If an organization does not constantly change, then it is exposed to the competitors constantly converging to similar products, services, and processes. Differentiation is key to maintaining a competitive edge. Strategic objectives are about the changes an organization should make to maintain a competitive edge.

Dashboards and scorecards are not mutually exclusive. In fact, the best dashboards and scorecards merge elements from one another.

A simple rule is to use the term "dashboard" when you merely want to keep score as in a sports event, and use the term "scorecard" when you want to understand the context of key scores in terms of how they influence achievement of strategic outcomes. A scorecard's measures will be fewer in number–they are strategic and carry more weight and influence. In contrast, the number of dashboard measures could number in the hundreds or thousands–you still need a way to focus on the unfavorable-to-target ones fast for tactical action. However, action with respect to a single metric in a dashboard is less likely to change strategic outcomes as dramatically compared to when reported in a scorecard.

In general, scorecard KPIs are associated with the domain of the performance management framework. In contrast, dashboard PIs are associated with business intelligence.

Getting Past the Speed Bumps

I believe that the scorecard and dashboard components of commercial performance management software should have pre-defined KPIs. However, for the integrated software component that reports measurements, the vendor's software should deliberately come with a limited rather than a comprehensive selection of KPIs that are commonly used by each type of industry. The purpose of providing standard KPIs should only be to accelerate the implementation of an organization's construction of their scorecard/dashboard system with a jump-start.

The reason for *not* providing a comprehensive and exhaustive list of industry-specific measures is because caution is needed whenever an organization is identifying its measures. Measures drive employee behavior. Caution is needed for two major reasons:

1. Measures should be tailored to an organization's unique needs.
2. Organizations should understand the basic concepts that differentiate scorecards from dashboards and KPIs from PIs.

My interest is that organizations successfully implement and sustain an integrated strategic scorecard and operational dashboard system. Hence organizations should understand the distinctions described here. This is why I caution against simply using an out-of-the-box list of various industries' common KPIs and PIs–regardless of their source.

As with any improvement methodology, experience through use refines the methodology's effectiveness and impact. The plan-do-check-act (PDCA) cycle is a great practice for learning organizations. With improvement methodologies, it's difficult to "get it perfectly right" the first time. There will always be a learning curve. Many organizations over-plan and under-execute. With regard to KPI and PI selection, first learn the principles, and then apply them through selecting, monitoring, and refining the KPIs. Strategy maps and balanced scorecards are a craft, not a science.

Integrating Balanced Scorecard With Sustainability: Evolution of Sustainability Balanced Scorecard

Since BSC did not fully meet stakeholder requirements, it was necessary to introduce sustainability and add it either side by side or separately from the four perspectives of the BSC, thus developing a new system of scores (Figge et al., 2002a). The new SBSC system is based on the traditional perspectives to which the fifth (social or environmental) perspective has been added to address the company's strategic direction with sustainability management (Bieker, 2002; Hahn & Wagner, 2001).

By implementing the sustainability management strategy, with relevant financial and non-financial indicators and measurement procedures, comparisons can be made with other company's own systems. This may highlight different aspects of the annual reporting framework of sustainability performance or whether the company reveals more about the content of the selected and analyzed indicators. Some specialists believe that measuring of sustainability performance indicators can only be achieved in an integral form associated with the four traditional perspectives of the BSC (Bieker, 2002).

A problem is highlighted by performance measurement of non-financial indicators. For the accurate measurement of all the financial and non-financial indicators included in the SBSC, it is necessary to link all the sustainability pillars (Moller & Schalteggar, 2005). Such indicators include energy and resource consumption, water emissions, air emissions, solid waste production and disposal, product performance and aggregate environmental measures (Kaplan & Norton, 2004). Initially, the creators of BSC, Kaplan and Norton have warned companies about adding a fifth perspective, noting that it is essential that bindings penetrate into the organization as much as those of the four fundamental perspectives (Kaplan and Norton, 1996). Subsequently, stakeholder objectives should not be attached to the scoreboard through an isolated set of measurements (Kaplan & Norton, 2002) but should be incorporated into the strategy if other measurement and control systems cannot establish diagnostic requirements and compliance much more effectively than BSC (Simons, 1995).

In these circumstances, the authors have identified some reasonable circumstances that have allowed the creation of BSC's fifth perspective on social and environmental issues (Kaplan & Norton, 2004; Kaplan & de Pinho, 2007), such as:

- Highlighting the importance of sustainability issues for those companies with a high sustainability profile (oil, chemical industry, etc.).

- In the high allocation of resources for social and environmental responsibilities.
- The fifth perspective serves as a tool for focusing managers and employees' attention on social responsibility and the environment as a core corporate value.
- Sustainability and corporate responsibility are seen as a strategic imperative that creates a competitive advantage and not only as a means of improving operational efficiency.

In other words, measuring and managing sustainability today is seen as: "*Another critical process, customer relationship management, has once been at a stage similar to corporate sustainability today, before Kaplan and Norton launched the BSC in 1992*" (Laszlo, 2005). BSC and environmental performance concepts have been addressed in many scientific papers by specialists around the world: the ability to integrate BSC for environmental performance based on strategic goals of the company (Johnson, 1998); the starting point for integrating environmental and social aspects into the company's main management system (Radcliffe, 1999; Figge et al., 2002b); exploring the integration of BSC environmental factors and measures and how to update BSC with new measures (Nilsson & Olve, 2001); BSC variety depends on the success factors and social importance, environmental performance and general strategy of a company (Epstein and Wisner, 2001a); recognition of BSC integration capacity, but with regard to the correlation of any activity with the financial objective of the company or the exclusion of residents from some economic activities (Bieker & Waxenberger, 2002); using BSC to adapt to changes in globalization and the environment (Okcabol, 2007); the emergence of the Lubin-Esty sustainability model based on the basic platform of the Kaplan-Norton general model for strategy execution (XPP - Execution of the Premium Process) and the identification of an extended set of requirements and their consideration in the implementation of a sustainability strategy (Lubin et al., 2011).

Companies can choose to include environmental and social indicators in each of the four perspectives of the BSC or in the Fifth Perspective. The fifth perspective includes performance, social and environmental indicators that link to the other four perspectives. Various attempts to build BSC based on environmental and social components have been reported: environmental scorecard (e-BSC) and social scorecard (Zingales et al., 2002); integrating stakeholder requirements into the company's corporate management system to launch the operational ethics or integrity scorecard (ISC) (Bieker & Waxenberger, 2002); value-oriented sustainability management through balanced scorecard or SBSC (Figge et al., 2002a). SBSC helps companies integrate the three pillars of sustainability into a single management tool developed as an integral part of the European Corporate Sustainability Framework. A balance between external and internal stakeholders through 5 perspectives: customers and suppliers; financiers and owners; society and the planet; internal processes; employees and learning is proposed by Van de Woerd and Van der Brink (2004) and is called the *Responsive Business Scorecard.*

In the methodology of SBSC, 5 possibilities of social and environmental integration have been identified (Bieker and Gminder, 2001):

- Integration of one or two sustainability indicators into traditional BSC perspectives and with limited effects in practice or the so-called *partial BSC approach.*
- Adding the Fifth Perspective for Social and Environmental Sustainability at BSC, or *adding SBSC.*
- Integration of social and environmental aspects into top-level indicators in all four perspectives as facilitators of future success or the so-called *cross-cutting approach.*

- Integration of environmental and social aspects into all BSC perspectives, which could lead to a strong awareness of sustainability in companies or *total SBSC*.
- The *SBSC Shared Service Unit*, which has a limited impact on goal integration but is complementary to all four alternatives described above.

On the basis of the above, we note the consistency of specialists' studies to broaden the scope of BSC and sustainability, to develop SBSC for use for sustainability management, performance measurement, or planning.

Challenges of Sustainability Balanced Scorecard

Specialists identified a number of challenges for the SBSC: (1) whether the BSC is a strategy tool or strategy formulation and the related dual learning problem that is extremely important for integrating environmental issues into the long-term vision (Zingales et al., 2002); (2) the integration of other existing instruments in the BSC, besides the systemic approach (Bieker & Gminder, 2001) or the opening to the integration of various environmental reports, assessments and social audits regardless of the recognition of the benefits brought (Zingales et al., 2002); (3) the capacity to manage environmental and social indicators; (4) the size to manage environmental and social indicators by specialized organizations. Moving from the type of corporate culture to all levels of society also involves the passage of social and environmental responsibility. The degree of incorporation of responsibilities and the management of indicators could be achieved with the help of a specialized department simply called "Sustainability", idea which is supported and by other specialists (Laszlo & Zhexembayeva, 2011; Epstein & Buhovac Rejc, 2014).

SUSTAINABILITY BALANCED SCORECARD USED IN ALUMINUM INDUSTRY. CASE STUDY

A Strategic SBSC involves developing a system that identifies the links between organizational capacity, efficient business processes, customer value, stakeholder satisfaction, sustainable performance, and financial and market outcomes. Analysts, owners and investors perceive the organization as a financial system that provides return on investment, while customers and stakeholders perceive business products and services as a way of meeting needs and wishes at an appropriate price. Effective transformation of resources into results that can be sold to meet customer requirements is the concern of internal management and employees through internal processes. Branding operations made by the organization to meet customer and stakeholder requirements are also accomplished through internal processes and targeting sustainability including: greenhouse gases, water use, generated waste, and electricity used. Infrastructure, organizational culture, tools and technology used, knowledge, skills and IT systems needed to plan, design and deliver products and services to customers and stakeholders are highlighted through organizational capacity.

The Connection Between Strategy and Performance Measures

In a SBSC based on strategy, performance measures stem from business strategy, from the organization's vision, and from measuring outcomes in meeting established goals. The sustainability strategy must be integrated into the organizational planning and management process of the organization. Specialists emphasize the inclusion of sustainability in *strategic themes* (the major pillar of the strategy that directly supports the vision and mission of the organization) and *strategic objectives* of the organization. Viewed from the perspective of the 4 classic BSC perspectives, sustainability means:

- Financial perspective: maintaining business, keeping the business segment(s) on a certain market, creating an acceptable return for investors.
- Customer/stakeholder perspective: meeting customer requirements/increasing the number of satisfied consumers and respecting the safety and sustainability of the products/services provided.
- Internal processes perspective: the efficient management of materials, energy and waste.
- Organizational capacity perspective: creating a culture that exploits sustainability, reflected in the choices that employees make each day.

The strategic components of the strategic themes that contribute to creating the strategy for employees are called *strategic objectives*. In other words, strategic objectives are continuous improvement activities for each BSC perspective, and the union between them forms the strategic map indicating how the objectives work, the cause and effect of achieving the strategic outcomes of each strategic theme.

Referring to the economic entity under the case study, *its vision* is to continually improve the activities, processes, products and environmental performance. In order to translate this vision into sustainability-related objectives, they can be summarized as follows: conducting a strategic analysis with environmental centralization; identifying strategic objectives for environmental sustainability; operationalizing the objectives of strategic sustainability:

Strategic Analysis Focusing on the Environment

plays a key role in strategic planning. Environmental factors, internal factors and shareholder expectations were reviewed through a SWOT analysis (Table 1). Also, some potential opportunities have been identified but also the risks that grow with the environmental changes of the economic entity under analysis.

Identify Strategic Objectives for Environmental Sustainability

According to ICV (2011), there are four types of green and sustainable strategies: holistic green strategy, green production strategy, observation strategy and green compliance strategy. The economic entity in the aluminum industry subjected to our analysis opted for a green compliance strategy that requires compliance with legal minimum requirements. Schematically translating the vision of the economic entity in the aluminum industry into strategic objectives can be depicted using Figure 4. The strategic map adapted to strategic objectives is shown in Figure 5.

Operationalization of Strategic Sustainability Objectives

It is an important stage in control. The most appropriate instrument for integrating environmental sustainability objectives used by the economic entity in the aluminum industry is the Sustainability Balanced Scorecard (Figure 6). In the four perspectives (finance, customers, processes, learning and development) of SBSC, environmental sustainability issues have been directly integrated with relevant performance

Table 1. SWOT analysis

Strengths	Weaknesses
• Automated monitoring system for environmental factors; • system of intervention/prevention in case of accidental pollution; • environmental legislation and regulations contribute to improving the environmental conditions of the aluminum industry.	• the use of reduced environmental protection staff at the sector level (department, office) and with well-defined environmental tasks; • absence of a program for monitoring and transmitting information on the instantaneous values of the parameters on synoptic schemes or in the form of real-time diagrams.
Opportunities	**Threats**
• possibilities for updating the technologies and the high performance equipment; • the interest of shareholders and stakeholders in resolving environmental issues in line with the local action plan for sustainable development.	• the lack of effective support provided by the local government to the entity and the excessive control over it; • The willingness to communicate and resolve complaints from interested parties must be transparent.
Recommendations	
Participation in the adoption and application of EMAS; Continuous improvement of environmental activities, processes, products and performance; Continuous training and improvement of staff involved in EMA implementation; Enhance the relevance of selected indicators in assessing environmental performance according to the proposed environmental objectives and targets.	

Figure 4. Translating the mission and vision of the economic entity in the aluminum industry into strategic objectives

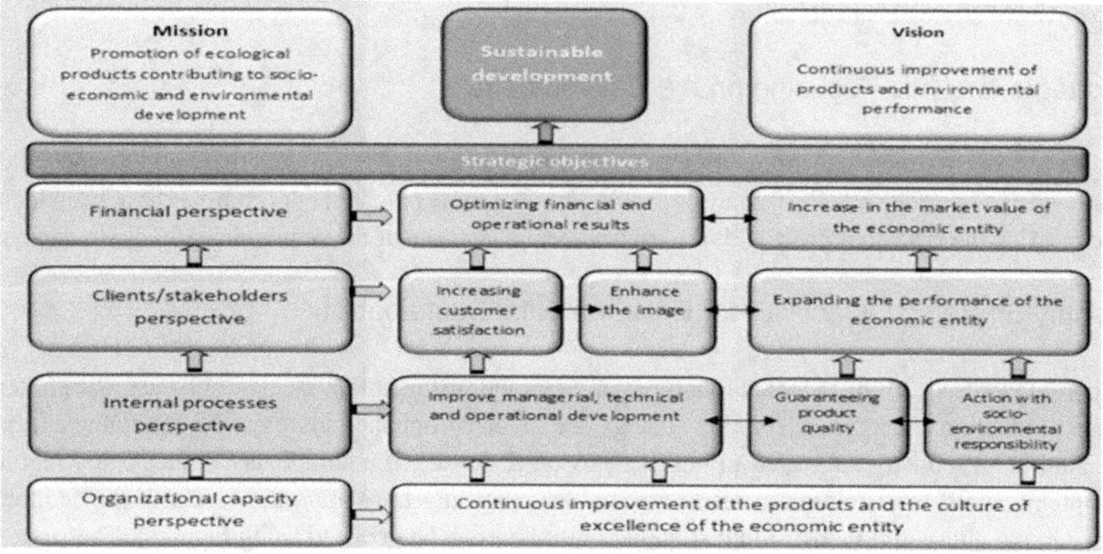

indicators, objectives and achievements. The Ecological Sustainability Strategy is anchored in the four known points of the BSC (Topor et al., 2017b): (a) identification of strategic goals for ecological sustainability; (b) defining the relevant sustainability performance indicators (according to the GRI guidelines), (c) agreeing the target values with an appropriate time reference, (d) adopting implementing measures to achieve the environmental sustainability strategy.

Figure 5. Strategic map of the economic entity in the aluminum industry

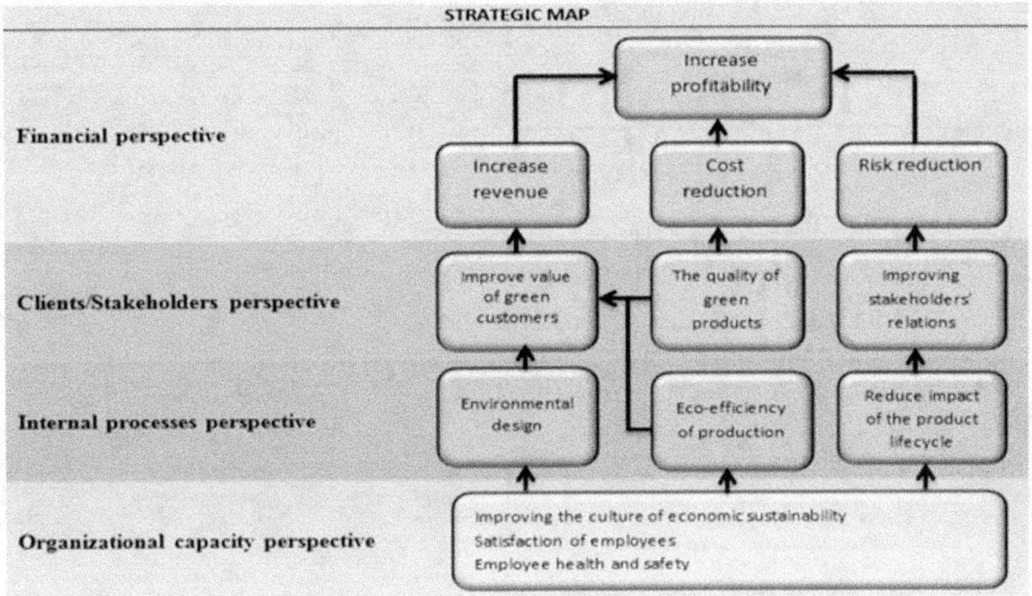

An effective implementation of a sustainability strategy is associated with change management, people systems, commitment of stakeholders and employees (Harmon et al., 2010). Sustainability Balanced Scorecard is a system where several existing models are combined to achieve a common goal to better understand and monitor the implementation of the strategy (Boerrigter, 2015). A well-executed sustainability strategy can indirectly create more profit, for example through an improved reputation. Companies that have adopted sustainability strategies, social and environmental issues will play a more important role in the Sustainability Balanced Scorecard.

Simultaneous transposition of social, economic and environmental goals into achievements helps companies to strengthen corporate sustainability. Thus, corporate performance becomes more sustainable and indicates the value of the business and the good direction of business-oriented environmental value and social management. Sustainability Balanced Scorecard also provides a powerful tool for integrated value management and sustainability. The decision to set up a Sustainability Balanced Scorecard is a bold, strategic one and will reflect at a certain moment the ability of a company to adapt to environmental requirements and measure its long-term performance. Based on strategic planning and a performance management system, Sustainability Balanced Scorecard helps to change the behavior of the company and its employees, causing them to think more strategically about organizing their activities.

SOLUTIONS AND RECOMMENDATIONS

Given the analysis and evaluation of the various BSC and SBSC considerations underlying the elaboration of this chapter, we propose to the specialists and to all those interested the following solutions for improving the topic addressed:

Figure 6. Complete Strategy-Based Sustainability Balanced Scorecard

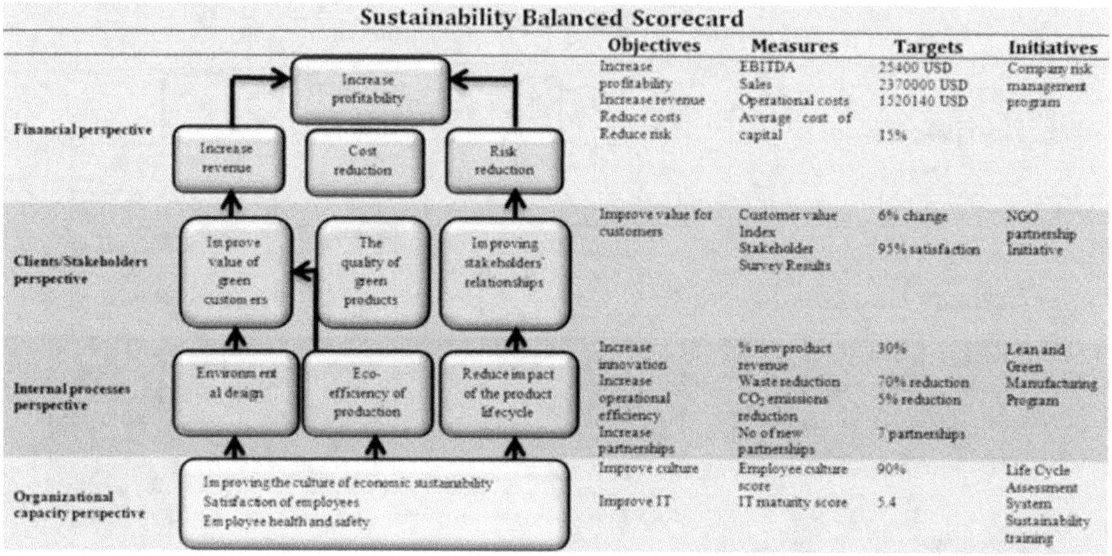

- Adopting and implementing Sustainability Balanced Scorecard due to its multiple benefits, such as: (1) clarifying the strategy and the framework for decision-making (Inamdar et al., 2002) or repositioning the organization to improve corporate responsibility (Epstein & Wisner, 2001b); (2) centering and alignment at all levels of the organization (Chang et al., 2008); (3) Increasing focus on customer service (Kocakülâh & Austill, 2007); (4) facilitating the shift from performance measurement to performance management (Gottlieb, 2008).
- The use of multi-instruments for the measurement of environmental performance necessary to substantiate environmental management decisions or to analyze environmental investments, including integrated reporting (Topor et al., 2016 and 2017a; Briciu et al., 2015, Căpuşneanu et al. 2015; Constantin et al., 2016; Martinescu & Căpuşneanu, 2009).
- The creation of new sets of synthesis documents specific to environmental management accounting, based on integrated use success stories from several environmental performance measurement tools, including the provision of non-financial information to stakeholders.
- Considering the concepts and case study presented, based on literature, we would like to recommend to the specialists and those interested in deepening and implementing the sustainability principles and the Sustainability Balanced Scorecard the following aspects:
    - Researching the impact of the different Sustainability Balanced Scorecard types on the environmental investment decision-making process.
    - Researching the role of knowledge in the relationship between the data provided by the SBSC and the decision-making process or the mediating role of knowledge of eco-efficiency on sustainability.
    - Developing and applying new indicators of eco-efficiency and creating new tools for measuring environmental performance.

- ◦ Extend the sustainability culture and BSC/SBSC to companies that have adopted or wish to adopt these tools along with other systems dedicated to performance management and performance measurement. This can be done by organizing training and information courses organized by specialists in the field.

FUTURE RESEARCH DIRECTIONS

Through the set goals and debates, we believe that the target of this chapter has been reached, addressing both business and academic specialists. The concepts presented and analyzed from the international literature are the synthesis of a considerable amount of representative information processed by authors covering the chosen topic, but there are other opportunities to quantify future research. The quantification of unexplored horizons is the future direction of research that can be centered on issues such as:

- Analyzing the possibility of adapting the principles of sustainability to managerial accounting methods and other instruments for measuring the environmental performance of companies.
- Analyzing the impact of the managerial decisions resulting from the adaptation of the principles of sustainability and environmental reporting to the company's environmental accounting.
- Analyzing the impact of financial and non-financial information on Sustainability Balanced Scorecard on internal management and stakeholders.
- Analyzing the possibility of using integrated reporting with direct effects on improving the measurement of eco-efficiency indicators of a company.

CONCLUSION

This chapter covers a wide range of topics, starting with the conceptual approaches of the Balanced Scorecard (BSC) and Sustainability Balanced Scorecard (SBSC) concepts, as well as the challenges posed by SBSC. As a strong point of this chapter we can mention:

- Presenting the evolution of the concepts of BSC and SBSC, making some considerations on the issues discussed in the literature and thus contributing to the widening of the conceptual framework and their understanding and application.
- Presentation of a case study on the creation of a Strategic Sustainability Map of a company in the aluminum industry and the development of a Sustainability Balanced Scorecard.

We believe that through our contribution on sustainability and Balanced Scorecard Sustainability the awareness has increased, launching new research and investigative assumptions and opening up new theoretical approaches to future theoretical and empirical approaches. This chapter remains open to all specialists interested in expanding knowledge about sustainability and the tools needed to measure environmental performance. The cooperation between various environmental regulators and business and academia specialists will contribute to the consolidation of sustainable business practices, to the creation of sustainable and sustainable business models to meet the information requirements of both internal management and stakeholders.

REFERENCES

Bieker, T. (2002). Sustainability Management with the Balanced Scorecard. *Corporate Sustainability, 5th International Summer Academy on Technology Studies, Deutschlandsberg, Austria, July 13–19, 2003, Conference Proceedings*, 17–34.

Bieker, T., & Gminder, C. U. (2001). Towards A Sustainability Balanced Scorecard. *Oikos PhD Summer Academy.* Retrieved from http://www.oikos-stiftung.unisg.ch/

Bieker, T., & Waxenberger, B. (2002). Sustainability Balanced Scorecard and Business Ethics: Developing a Balanced Scorecard for Integrity Management. In *Conference proceeding 10th Conference of the Greening of Industry Network*. Göteborg, Sweden: Greening of Industry Network.

Birch, C. (2000). *Future Success*. Prentice Hall.

Boerrigter, S. (2015). *The use of the Sustainability Balanced Scorecard Framework for Dutch SMEs as a tool for measuring the performance of their sustainability strategy.* 5th IBA Bachelor Thesis Conference, Enschede, The Netherlands.

Chan, Y. C. L. (2004). Performance measurement and adoption of balanced scorecards: A survey of municipal governments in the USA and Canada. *International Journal of Public Sector Management, 17*(3), 204–211. doi:10.1108/09513550410530144

Chandler, A. D. (1990). *The Managerial Revolution in Americas Business. Scale and Scope: The Dynamics of Industrial Capitalism*. Cambridge, UK: Belknap Press.

Chang, W., Tung, Y., Huang, C., & Yang, M. (2008). Performance improvement after implementing the Balanced Scorecard: A large hospitals experience in Taiwan. *Total Quality Management & Business Excellence, 19*(11), 1143–1154. doi:10.1080/14783360802323560

Eckerson, W. W. (2006). *Performance Dashboards: Measuring, Monitoring, and Managing Your Business*. John Wiley & Sons.

Epstein, M. J., & Manzoni, J. F. (1998). Implementing Corporate Strategy: From Tableaux de Bord to Balanced Scorecards. *European Management Journal, 16*(2), 190–203. doi:10.1016/S0263-2373(97)00087-X

Epstein, M. J., & Rejc Buhovac, A. (2014). Making Sustainability Work: Best Practices in Managing and Measuring Corporate Social, Environmental, and Economic Impacts (2nd ed.). San Francisco: Greenleaf Publishing Ltd.

Epstein, M. J., & Wisner, P.S. (2001a). Good Neighbors: Implementing Social and Environmental Strategies with the BSC. In *Balanced Scorecard Report* (pp. 5-6). Boston: Harvard Business School Publishing and Balanced Scorecard Collaborative.

Epstein, M. J., & Wisner, P. S. (2001b). Using a balanced scorecard to implement sustainability. *Environmental Quality Management, 11*(2), 1–10. doi:10.1002/tqem.1300

Figge, F., Hahn, T., Schaltegger, S., & Wagner, M. (2002a). The sustainability balanced scorecard – linking sustainability management to business strategy. *Business Strategy and the Environment, 11*(5), 269–284. doi:10.1002/bse.339

Figge, F., Hahn, T., Schaltegger, S., & Wagner, M. (2002b). The Sustainability Balanced Scorecard – Theory and Application of a Tool for Value-Based Sustainability Management. *Center for Sustainability Management.* Retrieved on February 12, 2008, http://www.strategyguide.org/

Gottlieb, G. (2008). Moving from performance measurement to strategy management at Brighamand Women's/Faulkner Hospital. *Balanced Scorecard Report, 10*(2), 11–13.

Hahn, T., & Wagner, M. (2001). *Sustainability Balanced Scorecard Von der Theorie zur Umsetzung.* Centre for Sustainability Management.

Hammer, M. (2001). *The Agenda: What Every Business Must Do to Dominate the Decade.* Crown Business.

Harmon, J., Fairfield, K. D., & Wirtenberg, J. (2010). Missing an opportunity: HR leadership and sustainability. *People and Strategy, 33*, 16-21.

Horngren, C. T., Forster, G., Rajan, M., Ittner, C., & Datar, S. M. (Eds.). (2010). *Cost Accounting: a managerial emphasis.* American Accounting Association.

ICV (Internationaler Controller Verein). (2011). *Internationaler Controller Verein e. V.* Green Controlling.

Inamdar, N., Kaplan, R., & Reynolds, K. (2002). Applying the balanced scorecard in healthcare provider organizations. *Journal of Healthcare Management, 47*(3), 179–195. doi:10.1097/00115514-200205000-00008 PMID:12055900

Ittner, C. D., & Larcker, D. F. (1998). Innovations in performance measurement: Trends and research implications. *Journal of Management Accounting Research, 10*, 205–238.

Johansson, A., & Larson, L. (2015). *A Standalone Sustainability Balanced Scorecard.* Institutionen för industriell ekonomi Blekinge Tekniska Högskola.

Johnson, H. T., & Kaplan, R. S. (1987). *Relevance lost: the rise and fall of management accounting.* Boston, MA: Harvard Business Press.

Kaplan, R. S. (1984). The evolution of management accounting. *The Accounting Review, 59*, 390–418.

Kaplan, R. S. (2010). *Conceptual Foundations of the Balanced Scorecard.* Working paper. Boston: Harvard Business School.

Kaplan, R. S., & De Pinho, R. R. (2007). *Amanco: Developing the Sustainability Scorecard.* Boston: Harvard Business School.

Kaplan, R.S., & Norton, D.P. (1992, January). The Balanced Scorecard – Measures that drive performance. *Harvard Business Review.*

Kaplan, R. S., & Norton, D. P. (1996a). Using the Balanced Scorecard as a Strategic Management System. *Harvard Business Review, 74*(1-2), 75–85.

Kaplan, R. S., & Norton, D. P. (1996b). *The Balanced Scorecard: Translating Strategy into Action.* Boston: Harvard Business School Press.

Kaplan, R. S., & Norton, D. P. (2002). *Partnering and the Balanced Scorecard.* HBS Working Knowledge. Retrieved from http:/hbswk.hbs.edu/item/3231.html

Kaplan, R. S., & Norton, D. P. (2004). *Strategy Maps*. Boston: Harvard Business School Press.

Keating, B., Quazi, A., Kriz, A., & Coltman, T. (2008). In pursuit of a sustainable supply chain: Insights from Westpac Banking Corporation. *Supply Chain Management*, *13*(3), 175–179. doi:10.1108/13598540810871217

Kocakülâh, M., & Austill, D. (2007). Balanced Scorecard Application in the Health Care Industry: A Case Study. *Journal of Health Care Finance*, *34*(1), 72–99. PMID:18972988

Lansiluoto, A., & Jarvenpaa, M. (2010). Greening the balanced scorecard. *Business Horizons*, *53*(4), 385–395. doi:10.1016/j.bushor.2010.03.003

Laszlo, C. (2005). *The Sustainable Company*. Washington, DC: Island Press.

Laszlo, C., & Zhexembayeva, N. (2011). *Embedded sustainability: The next big competitive advantage*. Sheffield, UK: Greenleaf Publishing.

Lawrie, G., & Cobbold, I. (2004). 3rd Generation Balanced Scorecard: Evolution of an effective strategic control tool. *International Journal of Productivity and Performance Management*, *53*(7), 611–623. doi:10.1108/17410400410561231

Lipe, M. G., & Salterio, S. E. (2000). The balanced scorecard; Judgmental effects of common and unique performance measures. *The Accounting Review*, *3*(3), 283–298. doi:10.2308/accr.2000.75.3.283

Lubin, D., Longsworth, A., & Russell, R. (2011). Sustainability Strategy Transforms the Enterprise. *Balanced Scorecard Report*, *13*(6), 1–6.

Malmi, T. (2001). Balanced scorecards in Finnish companies: A research note. *Management Accounting Research*, *12*(2), 207–220. doi:10.1006/mare.2000.0154

Moller, A., & Schaltegger, S. (2005). The sustainability balanced scorecard as a framework for eco-efficiency analyses. *Journal of Industrial Ecology*, *9*(4), 73–83. doi:10.1162/108819805775247927

Neely, A. (1999). The performance measurement revolution: Why now and what next? *International Journal of Operations & Production Management*, *19*(2), 206–228. doi:10.1108/01443579910247437

Neely, A. (2002). *Business Performance Measurement: Theory and Practice*. Cambridge, UK: Cambridge University Press. doi:10.1017/CBO9780511753695

Nilsson, F., & Olve, N.-G. (2001). Control Systems in Multibusiness Companies: From Performance Management to Strategic Management. *European Management Journal*, *19*(4), 344–358. doi:10.1016/S0263-2373(01)00036-6

Okcabol, F. (2007). Corporate and Government Accountability for Sustainable Environments: The Balanced Scorecard Approach. *Advances in Public Interest Accounting*, *13*, 151–175. doi:10.1016/S1041-7060(07)13007-8

Olve, N.-G., Roy, J., & Wtter, M. (1999). *Performance Drivers: A Practical Guide to Using the Balanced Scorecard*. New York: John Wiley & Sons.

Paladino, R.E. (2001). *Integrating EVA and ABM with the Balanced Scorecard.* In Balanced Scorecard European Summit 2001, Nice, France.

Radcliffe, M. (1999). Using Balanced Scorecard to develop Metrics for Sustainable Development. In *Conference Proceedings of Eighth International Conference of Greening of Industry Network: Sustainability: Ways of Knowing/Ways of Acting.* Chapel Hill, NC: The Greening of Industry Network.

Simons, R. (1995). *Levers of control: How Managers Use Innovative Control Systems to Drive Strategic Renewal.* Boston: Harvard Business School Press.

Smith, M. (2005). *The balanced scorecard, Financial Management.* Caspian Publishing.

Van Der Woerd, F., & van den Brink, T. (2004). Feasibility of a Responsive Business Scorecard - a pilot study. *Journal of Business Ethics, 55*(2), 173–186. doi:10.100710551-004-1900-3

Zingales, F., O'Rourke, A., & Hockerts, K. (2002). *Balanced Scorecard and Sustainability State of the Art Review.* Working Papers (65). Fontainbleu: CMER.

ADDITIONAL READING

Briciu, S., Căpuşneanu, S., Topor, D.I., Barbu, C.-M., & Ţepeş-Bobescu, A. (2015). Performance analysis of an entity from construction sector using dashboard, *Annals of the Constantin Brâncuşi University of Târgu Jiu, Economy Series*, 74-83.

Căpuşneanu, S., Ivan, R., Topor, D. I., Oprea, D.-M., & Muntean, A. (2015). Environmental Changes and their Influences on Performance of a Company by Using Eco-dashboard. *Journal of Environmental Protection and Ecology, 16*(3), 1091–1100.

Constantin, D.-M., Topor, D. I., Căpuşneanu, S., Barbu, C.-M., & Bogan, E. (2016). The monitoring of carbon monoxide air pollutant, as part of the air quality management. Case study: The Olt County, Romania. *Annales Universitatis Apulensis. Series Oeconomica, 18*(2), 27–34.

Martinescu, D.-M., & Căpuşneanu, S. (2009). Environment and environmental effects of pollution. Model of eco-dashboard - a tool for analysis of environmental management performances, *Metalurgia Internaţional, XIV* (12), Special Issue, Editura ştiinţifică F.M.R., 113-116.

Topor, D.I., Barbu, C.-M., Căpuşneanu, S., (Boca) Rakos, I.-S., & Constantin (Oprea), D.-M. (2016). Decisions based on environmental investments and sustainability, *Annals of the Constantin Brâncuşi University of Târgu Jiu, Economy Series*, 144-151.

Topor, D. I., Căpuşneanu, S., Constantin, D. M., Barbu, C. M., & Rakos, I. S. (2017a). ABB-ABC-ABE-ABM Approach for Implementation in the Economic Entities from Energy Industry. *Business and Management Horizons, 5*(2), 36–48. doi:10.5296/bmh.v5i2.12169

Topor, D. I., Căpuşneanu, S., & Tamaş, A. Z. (2017b). An efficient green control (EGC) encouraging environmental investment and profitability. *Journal of Environmental Protection and Ecology, 18*(1), 191–201.

KEY TERMS AND DEFINITIONS

Activity-Based Costing (ABC): An accounting method that identifies the costs of (indirect) activities and then allocates these costs to the products. Allocation of product costs to products is done through cost drivers.

Key Performance Indicators (KPI): Indicators that measures the efficiency of an organization in meeting key business objectives.

Plan-Do-Check Act (PDCA): Iterative approach used to continuously improve processes, products or services and to solve problems in four stages. It also requires systematic testing of possible solutions, evaluation of results, and implementation of functional ones.

Sustainability Balanced Scoreboard (SBSC): Balanced scoreboard that includes, besides the four perspectives (financial, customer, internal processes, and skills development) and fifth environmental perspective or Sustainability Pillar no. 5.

Sustainable Strategic Map (SSM): Translating an organization's strategies to the components or prospects envisaged in determining environmental performance.

SWOT: Method for analyzing and assessing the impact of strengths, internal weaknesses, opportunities, and threats from the external environment.

Chapter 2
Environmental Management Accounting:
A Business Perspective on the Policies, Analyses, and Benefits of Its Implementation

Sorinel Căpuşneanu
https://orcid.org/0000-0003-3799-3993
Titu Maiorescu University, Romania

Dan Ioan Topor
1 Decembrie 1918 University, Romania

Dana Maria Constantin
University of Bucharest, Romania

Alexandru Manole
Artifex University, Romania

Mihaela Stefan Hint
1 Decembrie 1918 University, Romania

ABSTRACT

This chapter provides a business perspective on the policies and benefits provided by implementing environmental managerial accounting in various areas of activity. The main objectives of this chapter are to present the evolution of the EMA and its policies, business analyses carried out by specialists, including the benefits of implementing the EMA. All of these objectives are transposed into a case study based on the ABC method performed at an energy company. The implementation steps specific to the ABC method are presented by establishing the list of main activities, cost drivers, allocation of indirect costs, and determining unit costs. The theoretical aspects presented the basic national and international studies in the literature. The case study is based on data obtained from the energy company. The chapter ends with the authors' conclusions on the benefits of implementing EMA/ABC. This chapter contributes to the expansion of the theoretical and empirical framework of EMA and the methods used to implement it within various business companies.

DOI: 10.4018/978-1-7998-0178-8.ch002

INTRODUCTION

The adoption by companies of cleaner or pollution prevention processes was due to: (1) internal pressures needed to use cleaner technologies, thus avoiding the costs of waste management, occupying a superior position on the national or international market; and (2) incentives to achieve corporate environmental performance that are being reviewed by investors, financial advisors, regulators and other stakeholders. In this respect, companies examine how external managerial reporting meets national and external social requirements and concerns. Environmental Management Accounting (EMA) is an essential tool in establishing an effective environmental management system. Considered a fundamental managerial tool, the EMA helps evaluate environmental efficiency alongside eco-labeling or life cycle analysis. Wide implementation and deployment of the EMA would have a major positive impact on companies in certain industries in terms of attitude towards environmental protection. If companies realized that waste treatment and disposal is less expensive than waste production, then companies would commit themselves to reducing costs by minimizing waste. This would motivate companies to strive to continuously improve their efficiency and profit levels and not just to comply with environmental regulations. This chapter aims at discussing the various conceptual approaches of the EMA, the evolution and policies to promote it on national and international level. Also, EMA implementation factors and EMA tools used for cost analysis and performance management will be analyzed. In addition to these issues, the advantages and disadvantages of EMA implementation will be addressed and analyzed through a case study of an energy company using the ABC method.

The main objectives of this chapter are: *(1) the presentation of EMA's evolution and promotion policies, (2) the analysis of EMA implementation factors and environmental reporting; (3) the presentation of EMA tools for cost analysis, investment appraisal and performance management; (4) analyzing the benefits and barriers of EMA implementation; and (5) presenting a case study on the implementation of EMA to an electric industry company using the ABC method.*

BACKGROUND

Environmental Management Accounting (EMA): Evolution

Coming from management accounting and developed from corporate accounting, Environmental Management Accounting (EMA) has experienced a dynamic evolution over the last 20 years. Environmental accounting (EA) comes from financial accounting under whose axis it develops and contributes to solving: environmental problems (Christmann, 2000; Fussel & Georg, 2000), insurance procedures (Dixon et al., 2004; Özbirecikli, 2007), financial performance (Gadenne et al., 2009, Moneva and Ortas, 2010) or practices of environmental information disclosure (Llena et al., 2007; 2009).

A lot of attempts to clarify the EMA concept have been made by specialists without achieving a concrete result due to the fact that EMA and EA are similar to subjects and tasks that overlap (UNDSD, 2001; Jasch, 2003; Bennett et al., 2003 Dillard et al., 2005; Cullen & Whelan, 2006; Jonäll, 2008; Eugénio et al., 2010; Collins et al., 2011; Bowen & Wittneben 2011). Another element of confusion was the ambiguous nature of the information to be measured (Alcouffee et al., 2008), since EMA accounts for environmental costs.

Some of the definitions given by EMA specialists emphasize issues such as: EMA is internal reporting (Burittet et al., 2002) which is related to organizational functions (Bennett et al., 2002) or data from financial accounting, cost accounting and material flow balances (Jasch, 2003) whose recipients are internal managers (Schaltegger & Burritt, 2000). Most EMA definitions focus on collecting information for internal management and for decision-making rather than externally reporting to audiences/ stakeholders. The clear limiting of the environmental information contained in EMA and EA was carried out by IFAC (2005), who issued a document that was accepted as a standard text by academics and practitioners. This delimitation also clarifies the views of specialists and other bodies dedicated to environmental issues, and it is accepted that EMA is a management system that reflects economic and ecological issues (Buritt et al., 2002; UNDSD, 2000; IFAC, 2005) in decision making process (by Beer & Friend, 2006).

EMA is the system that incorporates those methods and techniques for collecting, analyzing and providing physically sensitive environmental information (energy, water and materials) as well as financial information (covering environmental costs, earnings, environmental protection, etc.) neede by the company's leadership in the decision-making process. In other words, the EMA must provide information to decision-makers about material, energy, waste, water, or any other environmental sensitive material consumed and/or scattered in the production of goods or services. Specialist studies have indicated efforts to improve methodologies for defining and measuring costs, analyzing them, rethinking investment decision-making, and improving environmental performance. In this respect, some methodologies were adopted which did not use the EMA as a background but could provide a significant amount of information related to: waste accounting, Material Flow Cost Accounting (MFCA), Environmental Performance Indicators (EPI), Life Cycle Assessment (LCA), Life Cycle Costing (LCC), Full-Cost Accounting (FCA),Total Cost Assesment (TCA) or Material Flow Accounting (MFA).

Wastage Accounting has been recommended, supported and experimented on the basis of the UNDSD environmental cost classification methodology (Jasch 2003, Jasch, 2006b, Jasch et al., 2010). According to expert studies, physical data on the environment are extracted from the organization's operational records using Excel (Jasch, 2006b). This method does not take into account the costs of the externalities (social or environmental of the organization) and those outside the transactional system managed by EMA. Charging costs between different cost centers may depend on the appropriate allocation technique, depending on the type of industry and the nature of the product or process (Jasch, 2003).

Material Flow Costs Accounting (MFCA) The availability of EMA and the analysis of material and energy flows, including the impact of water and energy losses on the environment, was made using supply chain analysis and LCA to improve its efficiency (Viere & Schaltegger, 2007). Another study based on supply chain analysis revealed higher costs when producing a variety of organic products, but inventory costs could fall by applying an operational innovation (Seuring, 2001). The ability to delimit and load costs between different cost centers and the appropriate allocation technique is described in Cost Flow Accounting and the ABC method (Jasch, 2003).

Total Cost Accounting (TCA, Full-Cost Accounting FCA) The financial viability of environmental quality projects was analyzed using the TCA (FCA) and costs were classified into: direct costs, hidden costs, contingent passive costs and less tangible costs (Curkovic & Sroufe, 2006). Thus, the cost flows and average yields of environmental quality projects were determined, costs being detailed enough to assess the costs of externalities (Antheaume, 2004).

Environmental Performance Indicators (EPI) EMA is also used to evaluate CP projects, including design materials that occur in later periods (Staniškis & Stasiškienė, 2003). These CP projects contain a number of criteria specific to the impact of the environment and the pollution categories. CP evaluation covers organizational objectives, project evaluation, material balance, synthesis and environmental health control. The projects contain physical and financial performance indicators of the environment (EPI). Corporate Budgeting is a tool for managing and organizing management that is required to incorporate environmental impact, and can use eco-efficiency to create intelligible interpretation methods. This method was called Material and Energy Activity-BAsed Budgeting (MEABB) (Burritt & Schaltegger, 2001).

Further research by the specialists indicated that the EMA can be defined by three dimensions: the principal recipient (s), the main purpose(s) and the means (instruments, techniques and methods) (Spence et al., 2010; Waweru 2010). Thus, EMA can be defined as "the generation, analysis and use of financial and non-financial information to optimize the economic and environmental performance of enterprises and to achieve sustainable business" (Bennett et al., 2003). Another plausible definition is: "EMA is part of the SMA systematically using methods to report and control physical flows and associated environmental costs in order to optimize their environmental and economic performance" (Kaizer, 2017).

Most companies that have not implemented the EMA use EMS (Environmetal Management System) within SMA (Strategic Management Accouting) because EMS is not an accounting procedure and does not cover the scope of SMA or EMA procedures but helps management comply with the environment regulations (Darnall and Edwards 2006). The combination of SMA accounting procedures with the EMS environmental policy can be considered as a precursor or prerequisite for EMA but also as an insufficient substitute for it (UN, 2001).

Policies to Promote Environmental Management Accounting (EMA)

According to the opinion of the EMA specialists and organizations, the most common environmental policy instruments used are: regulatory, economic, information and social instruments (IISD, 1997; UNDSD, 2000; Bouma, 2000). It is the government that chooses the combination of viable tools to raise awareness of the political objective or issue, motivating the public and thus contributing to the goal of the promoted policy. Among the categories of EMA policy tools and activities most often promoted are: government regulations, voluntary adoption of standards and self-regulation, research and development of concepts and tools, dissemination of information, technical assistance, other incentives (United Nations, 2001).

Government Regulations allow EMA to explore or review issues related to: financial reporting regulations; National reporting rules for statistics; CERs, PRTRs or environmental reporting regulations; P2 Planning rules; EMS regulations; Business Licensing Requirements.

Voluntary Adoption of Standards and Self-Regulation of EMA requires collaboration and work with: different users/stakeholders of EMA, accounting associations, ISO/EMAS, GRI, bankers, insurance companies and other members of financial services to study the adoption potential/inclusion of EMA guidelines or requirements in these activities.

Research and Development of Concepts and Tools envisages the establishment of the EMA of: basic theories of concepts, definitions, guidelines and standards, methodological and empirical studies, curricula and training materials and specialized software programs.

Dissemination of EMA Information can be accomplished by: (1) guidance documents, articles in journals, empirical studies; (2) case studies on EMA best practices, successes and failures; (3) curricula and training materials; (4) specialized software; (5) organization of conferences, meetings, networking; (6) sponsorship campaigns, etc.

Technical Assistance provided to EMA users can be done either through training or by deployment assistance by a dedicated team.

Other Incentives used to promote EMA are related to: financial incentives (tax incentives, funding), regulatory incentives (authorization, review) and prizes.

A wide range of policies/programs are supported by governments to promote EMA concepts such as the Australian National Office of Local Government, the Austrian Federal Ministry for Environment, the Agency for Environmental Protection, Federal Environmental Agency, Japan Environment Agency, Netherlands national ministries, US EPA Office of P2 and Toxics, US EPA Office of Solid Waste, US Office of the President etc. There is a massive involvement of governmental organizations with non-governmental organizations, including individual firms, industry associations, financial institutions, accounting associations, universities, research and consultancy firms and NGOs in promoting EMA, through local and regional experience. The information provided by EMA proved itself to be useful both for internal management and for decision-making.

EMA can also be promoted through an EMA application whereby any initiative, program or environmental approach needs EMA information to be successful (pollution prevention, clean production, eco-efficiency, waste minimization, waste management). Any accounting or management system that is compatible with EMA data (e.g. EMS environment management system compatible with other accounting systems) may also be used.

Promotional policies or EMA programs include various methodologies and terminologies that relate to monetary data, data on physical flows, data related to external reporting. Further to the process of promoting the EMA, there are challenges related to the definition, cultural change and technical capacity of organizations.

Environmental Management Accounting (EMA): Analysis of Implementation Factors

In practice, EMA's level of implementation is reduced due to the gaps in the academic environment in terms of EMA knowledge and its potential to identify inefficiencies in a production process and to compare environmental costs resulting in environmental performance and higher economics (Christ and Burritt, 2013; Ván, 2012; Ferreira et al., 2010, Schaltegger et al., 2010; Burritt et al., 2009).

According to specialists' studies, there are several factors that can contribute to the successful implementation of EMA within a company. For example, support for higher management is crucial in the application of EMA (De Palma and Csutora, 2001) that helps transform it into a daily practice rather than just a one-time exercise. In the absence of the interests of external stakeholders, the resources allocated to higher management have been limited (Kumpulainen and Pohjola, 2008). Due to the group standardization of the management accounting system, top management is restricted from the point of view of the applicability of the EMA. It has to respect the internal regulations of the corporate group, making it more difficult for EMAs to apply especially to those companies that do not respect environmental policy. If the entire corporate group adopts the EMA unanimously, benchmarking can be used as a tool (Munkøe and Jasch, 2008).

The absence of strategic management and the existence of an "intuitive strategy" that does not present a structure by excessive attachment to the current strategy leads to the creation of resistance to change (De Palma and Dobes, 2010). It acts as a barrier to sustainable implementation, EMA's inclusion strategy within a company, as well as material inputs, regulatory and enforcement regimes, business environment stability (De Palma and Csutora, 2001). Practicing high prices of inputs encourages EMA implementation, while relaxed environmental legislation is a de-motivation factor for EMA implementation (De Palma and Csutora, 2001).

In conclusion, the factors contributing to the success of EMA implementation within a company are: support for superior management, strategic management, group internal regulations and policies, commodity prices, and environmental regulations.

Environmental Management Accounting (EMA) Tools for Cost Analysis, Investment Appraisal and Performance Management

EMA tools for cost analysis include: Life Cycle Assessment (LCA), Activity-Based Costing (ABC), Flow Cost Accounting (FCA).

Life Cycle Assessment (LCA) is a way of examining the environmental impact of a product or activity throughout its lifecycle (from raw material to disposal) (US EPA, 1995). Other authors have defined LCA as "a systematic process of assessing the lifetime costs of a product or service by identifying environmental consequences and assigning monetary value measures to these consequences" (Bennett and James, 1997).

LCA includes "identifying and quantifying energy and materials used and waste released to the environment, assessing their environmental impact and assessing opportunities for improvement" (US EPA, 1995). Production activities can affect the supply of natural resources and the quality of the environment, and therefore the negative environmental impact can occur at every stage of the product life cycle (US EPA, 1995). According to the opinion of other specialists, LCA should include an integral analysis of product life cycle costs, including both life cycle and life cycle, "from research to disposal, from cradle to grave" (Kreuze & Newell, 1994). In this way, LCA will generate data on environmental emissions and their effects, which in turn enable entities to identify pollution prevention opportunities.

Activity-Based Costing (ABC) is a suitable tool for calculating the total cost (Medley, 1997), which allows entities to allocate all costs, including environmental costs, cost centers and activity-based costs (Scavone, 2006). The following cost drivers can be used to allocate indirect costs (by environmental activities): the volume of emissions or waste, the toxicity of emissions and treated waste, the impact on the added environment (volume x inputs per volume unit), the volume of treated emissions and relative costs for dealing with different types of emissions (Schaltegger & Muller, 1997). The ABC method is one of the most effective tools for highlighting a company's performance with others such as: dashboard, balanced dashboard, cost-volume-profit analysis, etc. (Briciu & Căpuşneanu, 2010). The correct application of the ABC/ABM is the guarantee of the performance of an efficient management and the achievement of superior performance by the economic entities that want to be competitive under current conditions (Căpuşneanu & Martinescu, 2010; Cokins et al., 2012).

"Activity-based costs improve internal cost calculations by allocating typical costs found in indirect accounts to pollutant activities and products determined through quantitative life cycle assessment procedures," a link can be made between ABC and LCA (de Beer & Friend, 2006). Protected through cost-cutting strategies, some general costs (energy, water, waste disposal, and environmental staff salaries) are hidden by managers. The ABC method intervenes by identifying them and making them visible by creating more precise cost information not only for cost reduction or better pricing for products, but also for helping to prevent pollution (Bennet & James, 1997).

Flow Cost Accounting (FCA) consists of analyzing the material and energy flow (Staniškis & Stasiškienė, 2006) within a company and moving through a value creation (business) over a period of time (Gibson & Martin, 2004). The materials are divided into production stages and cost centers. Classical material flows are highlighted from raw materials to finished products following the chain of value added and logistics chain (scrap, damaged products, etc. that are non-ecologicaş and economically undesirable: solid waste, emissions) (UNDSD, 2001).

By incorporating the EMA, Flow Cost Accouting includes: "assessing cleaner plant production potential, preliminary estimate of waste generation costs, focusing on in-depth analysis of selected assessments (quantifying the volume and composition of different wastes, energy and emission streams, as well as a detailed understanding of the causes of these waste streams and energy and emissions) "(Staniškis & Stasiškienė, 2006).

The Total Cost Assesment (TCA) is a comprehensive financial analysis of a full range of cost and long-term savings, being part of the investment assessment and helping companies to prevent environmental pollution (US EPA, 1995; Medley, 1997). Total Cost Assessment is beneficial in evaluating an investment project and conducting a budget analysis. Environmental costs are included in the capital budget analysis, identifying the economic costs and cost-saving areas due to environmental pollution prevention.

Sustainability Balanced Scorecard (SBSC) is a performance management tool for a company using EMA and includes specific environmental indicators for each of the four perspectives or pillars (financial, customer, internal processes, development and skills). Specialists have defined SBSC as "a set of measurements that provide top managers with a quick but comprehensive view of business, including the effects of operational and environmental measures on different prospects, such as customer satisfaction, internal improvement, research and training, and financial perspectives and other aspects of business strategy "(Scavone, 2006). The integration of environmental indicators into SBSC aims to ensure that "measurement of financial performance is reflected by identifying environmental costs and their allocation to budgets" (Bennett & James, 1997). It has also been suggested by specialists the integration of management issues within SBSC as the only company management tool to align all corporate activities, especially those related to the environment, to implement corporate strategies (Figge et al., 2002).

Environmental Management Accounting (EMA) and Environmental Reporting (ER)

Accountancy plays an essential role in sustainability, emphasizing the potential of EMA implementation and company environmental reporting practices (Gray, 2010), facilitating the measurement of quantitative and qualitative environmental information, including the consequences of companies' strategies and actions on their financial performance (Hopwood et al., 2010). This is due to the fact that the impossibility of accurately measuring environmental information can prevent companies from generating relevant information (Burritt et al., 2002; Schaltegger et al., 2003). In this way, the company's commitment to the environment is considerably diminished, and there is no real interest in implementing the EMA. The claimed nature of EMA information as internal, confidential information influences the use of this information (Masanet-Llodra, 2006) for the decision-making process. In other words, the role of EMA is to support decision-making and external reporting (Frost & Wilmshurst, 2000; Burritt et al., 2002; Jasch, 2003; Schaltegger et al., 2003).

In order to defend apparent legitimacy, many companies have committed themselves to certain strategies of hiding environmental information and reporting positive information (Criado-Jimenez et al., 2008). Although the adoption of environmental accounting standards is increasing, the number of companies reporting environmental indicators is still low (Monteiro & Aibar-Guzman, 2010).

Benefits and Barriers to Implementing Environmental Management Accounting (EMA)

A decade ago, specialists noticed some possible benefits that a company could get from implementing EMA: helping to achieve a competitive advantage, greater cost efficiency, and improving relationships between image and customers (Godschalk, 2008). The value of a more structured accounting system contributes to increasing cost efficiency and improving environmental performance (Jonäll, 2008).

According to specialists' studies, the benefits of implementing EMA within a company are: cost reduction (Burrit & Saka, 2006; USEPA, 2000), lean innovation and the green supply chain (USEPA, 2000; Hendro et al., 2008), cleaner production (Burrit et al., 2009), better product prices and increased shareholder value (Staniškis & Stasiškienė, 2006). These benefits help to increase the company's reputation for launching ecological products on the outlets and running corporate activities with less harmful environmental effects. Experts have concluded that EMA allows companies to discover environmental costs that are often hidden in indirect costs and neglected by internal managers. Cutting costs, saving resources and better cost prices are obvious benefits for companies that have implemented the EMA.

Specialists have also identified other benefits of implementing the EMA, such as: (1) identifying environmental aspects of processes, (2) reducing raw material and energy consumption, and thus reducing costs, (3) accurately allocating costs (Jalil et al., 2016); (4) accurate tracking and identification of environmental costs (Christ & Burritt, 2013; Ferreira et al., 2010); (5) identification of high cost categories such as the cost of acquisition of materials from unproductive production costs (Jonäll, 2008). Successful adoption and deployment of EMA is hampered by the following barriers: institutional, financial and management (Olalekan & Jumoke, 2017).

IMPLEMENTING EMA WITHIN AN ELECTRICITY INDUSTRY

To implement EMA, we have chosen a Romanian power industry company to produce three main products: Display Line III, Apollo II, Low Intensity Beacon. The objectives of our case study were: *(1) identifying and analyzing environmental costs; and (2) the analysis of direct and indirect costs of the products executed (with and without including them in indirect costs).*

Objective 1: Identify and Analyze Environmental Costs

In order to improve environmental performance and to ensure a guarantee of managerial decisions, it is very important to identify correctly and recognize environmental costs. For the period under review, the investigating entity has agreed to conclude service contracts for the management of environmental operations (Table 1). Transferring responsibility for the management of packaging that has become waste within the national territory, from the beneficiary to the producer, in order to achieve the recovery and recycling targets, responsibilities which according to art. 16 paragraph 1 of the Law 249/2015 is the beneficiary's (ecological supplier 3R).

Table 1. Unitary tariffs for service provider

Type of Material		Unit Tariff per Tonne of Packaging Ron/T	Ecobonification per ton of Packaging Waste Ron/T
Paper and cardboard		**599**	**9.90**
Plastic	PET	699	9.90
	PE	649	9.90
	PVC	649	9.90
	PP	649	9.90
	PS	649	9.90
	Other	649	9.90
Glass		749	9.90
Metal	Steel	549	9.90
	Aluminium	849	9.90
	Other	549	9.90
Wood		649	9.90

Source: Own projection after annex of the contract

Depending on the type of material, the quantities of estimated packaging placed on the market by the investigated entity are shown in Table 2.

The quantities of estimated waste packaging to be managed individually by the investigated entity are presented in Table 3.

Transferring responsibilities for the collection, recovery and recycling of waste of electric and electronic equipments WEEE, as the calculation of the quantities, liabilities and costs of WEEE management depends on the quantities of EEE placed on the market. In this case, the supplier undertakes to report the number and type of products placed on the market according to Class 1 B of GD 448/2005 once a year as an estimate by 31 December of the preceding year for the following year, and then quarterly, at the latest 20 days from the end of a quarter for the previous quarter (CCR Logistic RO provider). Below we will exemplify the electrical and electronic equipment placed on the market and covered by the service contract (Table 4).

Table 2. Amounts of estimated packaging placed on the market by the beneficiary according to the type of material

Type of Material	Jan	Feb	Mar	Apr	May	Jun	Jul	Aug	Sep	Oct	Nov	Dec	Total
Paper and cardboard	0.12	0.12	0.12	0.12	0.12	0.12	0.12	0.12	0.12	0.12	0.12	0.12	1.440
Plastic	0	0	0	0	0	0	0	0	0	0	0	0	0
Glass	0	0	0	0	0	0	0	0	0	0	0	0	0
Wood	0	0	0	0	0	0	0	0	0	0	0	0	0
TOTAL	0.12	0.12	0.12	0.12	0.12	0.12	0.12	0.12	0.12	0.12	0.12	0.12	1.44

Source: Own projection after annex of the contract

Table 3. Estimate of the quantities of packaging waste that are to be managed individually by the beneficiary

Type of Material	Jan	Feb	Mar	Apr	May	Jun	Jul	Aug	Sep	Oct	Nov	Dec	Total
Paper and cardboard	0	0	0	0	0	0	0	0	0	0	0	0	0
Plastic	0	0	0	0	0	0	0	0	0	0	0	0	0
Glass	0	0	0	0	0	0	0	0	0	0	0	0	0
Wood	0	0	0	0	0	0	0	0	0	0	0	0	0
TOTAL	0	0	0	0	0	0	0	0	0	0	0	0	0

Source: Own projection after annex of the contract

Table 4. Estimation of electrical and electronic equipment placed on the market

Name of EEE in Annex 1B/H.G. 448/2005	Placed on the Market	
5. Lighting Equipment	**Tons**	**Number**
- Lighting apparatus for fluorescent lamps, excluding domestic lamps - Straight fluorescent lamps - Compact fluorescent lamps - High-intensity gas discharge lamps, including high-pressure sodium lamps and metal halide lamps - Low voltage sodium steam lamps - Other lighting or light-diffusing and controlling equipment, excluding filament lamps.		
Total	**5**	**4000**

Source: Own projection of the authors

In order to fulfill the legal obligations under H.G. 1132/2008, the beneficiary is required to report the quantities of batteries and accumulators placed on the market as follows: an estimate for batteries and accumulators placed on the market for the current year; quarterly quantities and types of batteries and accumulators placed on the market no later than 15 days after the closure of a quarter for the previous quarter (CCR Rebat RO supplier). In Table 5 we will present the types and quantities of batteries and accumulators placed on the market by the investigated entity.

We then identified the environmental costs for the company under review, over a period of time, namely 01.07.2018-31.07.2018, under the conditions of obtaining the products: (1) linear industrial projector

Table 5. Estimate types of batteries placed on the market by the analyzed entity

Types of Batteries and Accumulators See G.D. 1132/2008		Own Products				Imported Products	
		Total Quantity:		Of Which Exported:			
		Tons	Number	Tons	Number	Tons	Number
Industrial batteries (category 4)	4a Lead acid	-	-	-	-	-	-
	4b Cadmium Nickel (NiCd)	-	-	-	-	0.13	1
	4c Other	-	-	-	-	1.679	14.30
Total	-	-	-	-	-	**1.809**	**15.30**

Source: Own projection of the authors

Display Line III; (2) Apollo II; (3) Low Intensity Beacon, by collecting the third quarter environmental data according to Table 6.

In managerial accounting, the values of cost drivers for the three environmental cost identification activities for the specified period are presented in Table 7.

Next, the environmental costs for the three products analyzed were identified, knowing the weight of the products: Display Line III (3kg); Apollo II (4.52 kg); Low Intensity Beacon (6 kg), whose situation is shown in Table 8.

Objective 2: Analysis of Direct and Indirect Costs Related to Products

By Including Environmental Expenditure in Indirect Costs (Table 9)

Table 6. Service Providers and Inductors of Costs of Services Provided

No.	Supplier/Activity	Cost drivers Related to Environmental Activities
1.	CCR LOGISTIC SYSTEMS RO	Green stamp for quarter III/2018
2.	CCR REBAT RO	Services for waste battery management, quarter III/2018
3.	ECOLOGIC 3R	Service management fee for quarter III/2018

Source: Own projection of the authors

Table 7. Component of environmental costs related to the company in January-July/2018

<table>
<tr><th rowspan="2">No.</th><th rowspan="2">Supplier/Activity</th><th rowspan="2">Name of EEE According to Annex 1B/G.D. 1037/2017</th><th colspan="2">Cost Drivers
Quantities of EEE Manufactured in Romania, Including Assembled</th><th rowspan="2">Price Ron/ Piece Without VAT</th><th rowspan="2">Total Amount of Payment in Ron Without VAT</th></tr>
<tr><th>Nr. of pieces</th><th>Tons</th></tr>
<tr><td rowspan="2">1.</td><td rowspan="2">CCR Logistic System SRL</td><td>5.f.1. LED lamps</td><td>5229</td><td>14.433</td><td>0.3</td><td>1568.70</td></tr>
<tr><td>5.f.2. Other lighting or diffusing or controlling equipment</td><td>4768</td><td>6</td><td>0.8</td><td>3814.40</td></tr>
<tr><td></td><td>Total</td><td>-</td><td>9997</td><td>20.43</td><td>-</td><td>5383.10</td></tr>
<tr><td>2.</td><td>CCR Rebat RO</td><td>4.c. Other auto (cat.3 and cat.4)
4.c. Other tax management</td><td>1645
570</td><td>0.081
0.068</td><td>1261
-</td><td>102.14
1500</td></tr>
<tr><td></td><td>Total</td><td></td><td>2215</td><td>0.149</td><td>-</td><td>1602.14</td></tr>
<tr><td>3.</td><td>Ecologic 3R</td><td>Tax management services related to quarter III. 07. 08.09/2018</td><td>-</td><td>-</td><td>-</td><td>1,439</td></tr>
<tr><td></td><td colspan="2">Total cost of the environment</td><td>12212</td><td>20579</td><td>-</td><td>8424.14</td></tr>
</table>

Source: Own projection of the authors

Table 8. Composition of the environmental costs of the analyzed products over a determined period of time

No.	Supplier/ Activity	Name of EEE According to Annex 1B/G.D. 1037/2017	Cost Drivers						Price Ron/ Piece Without VAT	Total Amount of Payment in Ron Without VAT
			Quantities of EEE Manufactured in Romania, Including Assembled Related to the Products							
			Display Line III		Apollo II		Low Intensity Beacon			
			Nr. of pieces	Tons	Nr. of pieces	Tons	Nr. of pieces	Tons		
1.	**CCR Logistic System SRL**	**5.f.1.** LED lamps	300	0.9	65	0.293	1000	6	0.3	409.5
		5.f.2. Other lighting or diffusing or controlling equipment	-	-	65	0.293	-	-	0.8	52
	Total	-	300	0.9	65	0.293	1000	6	-	461.50
2.	**CCR Rebat RO**	**4.c.** Other auto (cat.3 and cat.4) **4.c.** Other tax management	300 300	0.9 0.9	65 65	0.293 0.293	1000 1000	6 6	- -	110.57 3592
	Total		300	0.9	65	0.293	1000	6	-	3702.57
3.	**Ecologic 3R**	Tax management services related to quarter III, 07, 08.09/2018	-	-	-	-	-	-	-	1439
	Total cost of the environment		**300**	**0.9**	**65**	**0.293**	**1000**	**6**	**-**	**5603.07**

Source: Own projection of the authors

Table 9. Situation of direct product costs

No.	Direct Expenses (Ron)	Display Line III	Apollo II	Low Intensity Beacon	Total
1.	Raw materials	36000	65000	56760	157760
2.	Direct pay	7200	15600	14400	37200
3.	Total direct expenditure	43200	80600	71160	194960

Source: Own projection of the authors

The Company presents the following indirect costs (including environmental costs) in the production of the three products (Table 10):

By applying the ABC method, the following activities and the specific cost drivers were identified (Table 11):

The cost drivers of the three products are shown in Table 12.

The allocation of indirect costs for each individual product is shown in Table 13.

The unit costs and unit results of the three products were then determined (Table 14).

As can be seen from Table 11, the Apollo II product is loss-making and is not a profitable product (-0.42%). The most profitable products are Display Line III (20.71%) and Low Intensity Beacon (29.89%).

b. not including environmental expenditures in indirect costs

Table 10. Situation of indirect costs related to products

No.	Indirect expences	Amount (R)	Cost Drivers
1.	Wages	95500	No. of employees
2.	Depreciation	21780	Surface (m^2)
3.	Other indirect expences (including environment)	30987	No. of working hours
4.	Total indirect expences	148267	-

Source: Own projection of the authors

Table 11. Identification of activities with cost drivers

No.	Activities	Cost Drivers		
		No. of Employees	Surface(m^2)	No. of Working Hours
1.	Launch and Receive Commands	2	10	378
2.	Storage of raw materials and materials	1	40	180
3.	Machine and equipment maintenance	3	30	528
4.	Production	28	400	5288
5.	Verification	2	15	364
6.	Storage of finished products	3	50	530
7.	Invoicing customers	3	15	530
8.	Dispatch	2	45	352
9.	Suppliers accounting	1	15	180
10.	Customer accounting	1	15	180
11.	Production accounting	2	20	352
12.	General accounting	3	30	530
	Total	51	685	9392

Source: Own projection of the authors

Table 12. Cost drivers for products

No.	Cost driver of Activity	Product			
		Display Line III	Apollo II	Low Intensity Beacon	Total
1.	Number of employees	10	28	13	51
2.	Surface	120	400	165	685
3.	Number of working hours	1702	5288	2402	9392

Source: Own projection of the authors

Next, we will analyze the profitability of products if environmental costs are not included in indirect costs. Considering the identification and recognition of environmental costs in the format presented by the company analyzed, we can conclude that environmental cost management and reporting is outsourced, reporting to service providers is communicated monthly and quarterly by an employee as appropriate,

Table 13. Share of indirect costs allocated to products

No.	Cost Driver of Activity	Allocation Coefficient	Product			
			Display Line III	Apollo II	Low Intensity Beacon	Total
1.	Wages	1872.54	18725.49	52431.37	24343.14	95500
2.	Depreciation	31.80	3815.47	12718.25	5246.28	21780
3.	Other indirect expences (including environment)	3.30	5615.40	17446.68	7924.92	30987
4.	Total indirect expences	-	28,156.36	82596.30	37514.34	148267

Source: Own projection of the authors

Table 14. Determination and analysis of the results of the three products

Indicators	Product			
	Display Line III	Apollo II	Low Intensity Beacon	Total
Direct expences (Ron) Indirect expences (including environment) (Ron)	43200 28156.36	80600 82596.30	71160 37514.34	194960 148267
Total expences (Ron)	71356.36	163196.30	108674.34	343227
No. of manufactured pieces	300	65	1000	1365
Unit cost (Ron/piece)	237.85	2510.71	108.67	-
Selling price (Ron/piece)	300	2.500	155	-
Unit result (Ron/piece)	+ 62.15	-10.71	+46.33	-
Rate of return (%)	20.71%	-0.42%	29.89%	-

Source: Own projection of the authors

so there is no Special service as a cost inductor activity falls into general accounting. Following the determination of the environmental values, the value result for the analyzed period is 8424.14 Ron, and the share of these expenditures in the total indirect expenditures is the following:

$$TEE = \frac{C_m}{\sum Ch_i} = \frac{8424.14}{30987} x100 = 27.18\%$$

In which: TEE = share of total environmental expenditure;

C_m = total environmental costs;

ΣCh_i = total indirect costs

There is a fairly significant share of environmental spending of nearly 30%.

Next, we will identify the impact of environmental costs on the production of the three products analyzed, as follows:

$$TEE = \frac{C_m}{\sum Ch_i} = \frac{5603.07}{30987} x100 = 18.8\%$$

In which: C_m = environmental costs of the three products analyzed.

From previous analyzes, the environmental costs of lighting products account for about 20-30% of the total indirect production costs, quite significant for a fixed period of time of one year. Next we will try to identify the profitability of products in case of diminishing the indirect costs with the value of the environmental costs, so we will get the following result:

$$\sum Ch_i - C_{m =} 30987 - 5603.07 = 25383.93 \text{ Ron}$$

In this case, the company records the following indirect costs according to Table 15:

The indirect costs in this case amounted to 142,663.93 Ron and the identification of the activities with the related cost inductors analyzed by ABC implementation is maintained as in the first analysis. Product-related cost drivers are shown in Table 9. Allocation of indirect costs (excluding environmental costs) per product is shown in Table 16.

In Table 17 the unit costs and unitary results of the three products were determined as follows.

Table 15. Analysis of indirect product costs (excluding environmental costs)

No.	Indirect Expenses	Amount (lei)	Cost Indicators
1.	Wages	95500	No. of employees
2.	Depreciation	21780	Surface (m^2)
3.	Other indirect expences (without environment)	25383.93	No. of working hours
4.	Total indirect expences	142663.93	-

Source: Own projection of the authors

Table 16. Share of indirect costs allocated to products

No.	Cost Driver of Activity	Allocation Coefficient	Product			
			Display Line III	Apollo II	Low Intensity Beacon	Total
1.	Wages	1872.54	18725.49	52431.37	24343.14	95500
2.	Depreciation	31.80	3815.47	12718.25	5246.28	21780
3.	Other indirect expences (without environment)	2.70	4600.02	14291.97	6491.94	25383.93
4.	Total indirect expences	-	27140.98	79441.59	36081.36	142663.93

Source: Own projection of the authors

Table 17. Analysis of the results of the three products

Indicators	Product			Total
	Display Line III	Waggy	Low Intensity Beacon	
Direct expences (Ron) Indirect expences (Ron)	43200 27140.98	80600 79441.59	71160 36081.36	194960 142663.93
Total expences (Ron)	70340.98	160041.59	107241.36	337623.93
No. of manufactured pieces	300	65	1000	1365
Unit cost (Ron/piece)	234.47	2462.18	107.24	-
Selling price (Ron/piece)	300	2,500	155	-
Unit result (Ron/piece)	+ 65.53	+ 37.82	+ 47.76	-
Rate of return (%)	21.84%	1.51%	30.81%	-

Source: Own projection of the authors

In this case, no product records losses. We will proceed to the comparative analysis (Table 18) of the three products in the two cases previously analyzed as follows:

The profit generated for the three products is: (300 pieces x 3.38 Ron/piece) + (65 pieces x 48.53 Ron/ piece) + (1000 pieces x 1.43 Ron/pcs.) = 1014 + 3154. 45 + 1430 = + 5598.45 Ron.

Following the identification of environmental costs in the company producing lighting equipment, on the example of the three products analyzed (Display Line III, Apollo II, Low Intensity Beacon), we can conclude that environmental costs could be expressed in value by highlighting the factors that caused them. Identifying and recognizing the environmental costs associated with products are important for making good management decisions to achieve the goals of reducing environmental costs but also to improve environmental performance. These costs take the form of production costs, in this case, and are entirely borne by the producing company.

During the analyzed financial accounting period, the total environmental costs were identified according to the three environmental cost activities, after the service providers, and represented a value of 8424,14 Ron, with a fairly significant weight, of about 30 percent of the total indirect costs. For the three products analyzed, environmental expenditures accounted for 18.8% of total indirect costs, i.e. Ron 5,603.07 for 1365 manufactured products. Environmental costs have been differentiated on each product by weight (kg), and costs vary according to their component raw material plus management fees under current environmental legislation.

Table 18. Comparative analysis of product results

No.	Product name	Unit result Ron/product		Resulting Recorded Differences (Ron/ Product)
		Environmental Costs Included in Total Indirect Costs	Environmental Costs not Included in Total Indirect Costs	
1.	Display Line III	+ 62.15	+ 65.53	+ 3.38
2.	Apollo II	-10.71	+ 37.82	+ 48.53
3.	Low Intensity Beacon	+46.33	+ 47.76	+ 1.43

Source: Own projection of the authors

The analysis highlighted the high importance of reducing the volume of waste, as well as the monitoring of environmental costs in products and environmental risks associated with the production process. At the same time, the analysis of these actions in the products in terms of management indicates an improvement of the environment, although in terms of performance they have generated quite a significant impact in the current conditions. We consider that the ABC method is an instrument in the service of the management of companies (Rof and Căpuşneanu, 2015). Maintaining an Activity-Based Costing (ABC) system goes beyond the fulfillment of the initial successful implementation factors to avoid factors that in some cases lead companies to abandon (sometimes temporarily) the maintenance of the system (Anghelache et al., 2009; Cokins & Căpuşneanu, 2011).

SOLUTIONS AND RECOMMENDATIONS

On the basis of the analytical construction of this chapter, we propose to the specialists and to all those interested the following solutions for the improvement of the topic addressed:

- The adoption and implementation of environmental management accounting (EMA) alongside other management accounting methods such as Activity-Based Costing (ABC/ABM) (Căpuşneanu, 2008; Topor et al., 2017b), Life Cycle Assessment (LCA), Flow Cost Accounting (FCA).
- Management of manufacturing companies should eliminate the EMA implementation barriers and base their claims on the information that best reflects the needs of environmental information and reporting (Topor et al., 2017a), especially by eliminating hidden costs (Briciu and Căpuşneanu, 2011).
- EMA offers long-term benefits that bring value and reputation to companies by providing them with competitive positions and performance improvements. Other EMA benefits are: improving customer relationships, developing green supply chains, making better prices for executed products, saving resources, and more.
- EMA offers the possibility to create new sets of synthesis documents specific to environmental managerial accounting, based on the integrated use successes from many of its methods.
- Considering the concepts discussed and the case study presented, based on the national and international literature, we would like to recommend to the specialists and those interested in deepening and implementing the EMA the following aspects:
    - Carefully analyzing the principles and EMA implementation factors that influence company cost management. It is necessary to set up an analysis and implementation team that will study all aspects necessary for the adoption and implementation of the EMA.
    - Researching the literature on the successful adoption and implementation of EMA along with other established management accounting methods (ABC, TCA, LCA, SBSC, etc.). Calling on competent bodies or specialized institutions can be viable solutions to ensure the successful adoption or implementation of EMA or EMS at company level.
    - Enhance EMA culture within companies that have adopted or want to adopt these systems along with systems dedicated to managerial accounting and environmental performance enhancing. The organization of training and information courses organized by specialists in the field are effective solutions to guarantee the implementation of the EMA.

FUTURE RESEARCH DIRECTIONS

Based on the objectives set at the beginning of the chapter, we believe that they have been reached, addressing both academia and the business community particularly interested in this topical theme. By compiling a large amount of information, processing and presenting them synthetically with national and international specialty studies, the chosen topic covered a fairly wide area, but there are some segments to quantify future research. In order to complete the subject presented by us, specialists and all those interested can open new research directions focused on:

- Analyzing the possibility of adapting the EMA/EMS to other management accounting methods.
- Analyzing the impact of managerial decisions resulting from adapting EMA/EMS to other managerial accounting methods across countries or continents.
- The analysis of the possibility of creating new instruments for monitoring and measuring performance based on EMA and SBSC and the ways to adjust or complete the decision-making process.

CONCLUSION

This chapter covers a wide range of topics, starting with conceptual approaches to environmental management accounting (EMA), environmental accounting (EA), environmental reporting (ER), and interconnections between these concepts. Also, other methodologies that can provide a large amount of information along with the EMA have been highlighted, such as: loss accounting, MFCA, EPI, LCA, LCC, FCA, TCA or MFA. The strengths of this chapter include the following:

- Complements some existing gaps in managerial accounting and the application of EMA within companies precisely through interpretations of conceptual approaches and theories debated, including their advantages.
- Analyzes the EMA implementation factors and EMA tools for cost analysis, investment assessment, and performance management within a company.
- Presents the conclusions of a case study on the implementation of EMA within a power industry company by applying ABC and highlighting environmental performance by excluding / disregarding indirect costs (by environmental activities).

We are of the opinion that through our contribution we have increased the level of knowledge and understanding of some less clear issues from the point of view of some companies, even from the academic environment, thus provoking new attempts to implement the EMA and opening up new directions for future research. This chapter remains open to future theoretical and empirical research and additions made by EMA implementation specialists. The degree of involvement of business and academics, including specialized bodies, will help identify effective and sustainable solutions to empirical EMA implementation practices within companies or organizations. Completing the theoretical and empirical framework of EMA can be achieved by developing partnerships between the above-mentioned actors, and collecting, processing and analyzing information will help identify the best solutions to guarantee the effectiveness of EMA implementation.

REFERENCES

Alcouffe, S., Berland, N., & Levant, Y. (2008). Actor-networks and the diffusion of management accounting innovations: A comparative study. *Management Accounting Research*, *19*(1), 1–17. doi:10.1016/j.mar.2007.04.001

Antheaume, N. (2004). Valuing external costs – from theory to practice: Implications for full cost environmental accounting. *European Accounting Review*, *13*(3), 443–464. doi:10.1080/0963818042000216802

Bennett, M., Bouma, J. J., & Wolters, T. (2002). The Development of Environmental Management Accounting: General Introduction and Critical Review. In M. Bennett & J. J. Bouma (Eds.), *Environmental Management Accounting: Informational and Institutional Developments. Eco-Efficiency in Industry and Science* (Vol. 9). Dordrecht: Springer.

Bennett, M., & James, P. (1997). Environment related management accounting: Current practice and future trends. *Greener Management International*, *17*, 33–51.

Bennett, M., Rikhardson, P., & Schaltegger, S. (2003). *Enviromental Management Accounting- Purpose and Progress*. Kluwer Academic Publishers. doi:10.1007/978-94-010-0197-7

Bouma, J. J. (2000). Environmental Management Systems and Audits as AlternativePolicy Instruments. In C. Knill & A. Lenschow (Eds.), *Implementing EU Environmental Policy*. Manchester, UK: Manchester University Press.

Bowen, F., & Wittneben, B. (2011). Carbon accounting. Negotiating accuracy, consistency and certainty across organisational fields. *Accounting, Auditing & Accountability Journal*, *24*(8), 1022–1036. doi:10.1108/09513571111184742

Burritt, R., & Schaltegger, S. (2001). Eco-efficiency incorporate budgeting. *Environmental Management and Health*, *12*(2), 158–174. doi:10.1108/09566160110389924

Burritt, R. L., Hahn, T., & Schaltegger, S. (2002). Towards a comprehensive framework for Environmental Management Accounting - Links between business actors and environmental management accounting tools. *Australian Accounting Review*, *12*(2), 39–50. doi:10.1111/j.1835-2561.2002.tb00202.x

Burritt, R. L., Herzig, C., & Tadeo, B. D. (2009). Environmental management accountingfor cleaner production: The case of a Philippine rice mill. *Journal of Cleaner Production*, *17*(4), 431–439. doi:10.1016/j.jclepro.2008.07.005

Burritt, R. L., & Saka, C. (2006). Environmental management accounting applications and eco-efficiency: Case studies from Japan. *Journal of Cleaner Production*, *14*(14), 1262–1275. doi:10.1016/j.jclepro.2005.08.012

Christ, L. K., & Burritt, R. L. (2013). Environmental management accounting: The significance of contingent variables for adoption. *Journal of Cleaner Production*, *41*, 163–173. doi:10.1016/j.jclepro.2012.10.007

Christmann, P. (2000). Effects of "Best Practices" of environmental management on cost advantage: The roleof complementary assets. *Academy of Management Journal*, *43*(4), 663–680.

Collins, E., Lawrence, S., Roper, J., & Haar, J. (2011). Sustainability and the role of the management accountant. *Research Executive Summary Series, 7*(14), 1-11.

Criado-Jimenez, I., Fernandez-Chulian, M., Larrinage-Gonzalez, C., & Husillos-Carques, F. J. (2008). Compliance with mandatory environmental reporting in financial statements: The case of Spain (2001–2003). *Journal of Business Ethics, 79*(3), 245–262. doi:10.100710551-007-9375-7

Cullen, D., & Whelan, C. (2006). Environmental mamangement accounting: The state of play. *Journal of Business & Economics Research, 4*(10), 1–4.

Curkovic, S., & Sroufe, R. (2007). Total QualityEnvironmental Management and Total Cost Assessment: An exploratory study. *J. Production Economics, 105*(2), 560–579. doi:10.1016/j.ijpe.2006.04.021

Darnall, N., & Edwards, D. Jr. (2006). Predicting the cost of environmental management system adoption: The role of capabilities, resources and ownership structure. *Strategic Management Journal, 27*(4), 301–320. doi:10.1002mj.518

De Beer, P., & Friend, F. (2006). Environmental accounting: A management tool for enhancing corporate environmental and economic performance. *Ecological Economics, 58*(3), 548–600. doi:10.1016/j.ecolecon.2005.07.026

De Palma, R., & Csutora, M. (2001). *Introducing Environmental Management Accounting (EMA) At Enterprise Level – Methodology and Case Studies From Central and Eastern Europe - A contribution of the UNIDO project "Transfer of Environmentally Sound Technology (TEST) in the Danube River Basin"*. Retrieved from http://unipub.lib.unicorvinus.hu/223/1/Robertacsutora.pdf

De Palma, R., & Dobes, V. (2010). An integrated approach towards a sustainable entrepreneurship – Experience from the TEST project in transitional economies. *Journal of Cleaner Production, 18*(18), 1807–1821. doi:10.1016/j.jclepro.2010.07.025

Dillard, J., Brown, D., & Marshall, R. S. (2005). An environmentally enlightened accounting. *Accounting Forum, 29*(1), 77–101. doi:10.1016/j.accfor.2004.12.001

Dixon, R., Mousa, G. A., & Woodhead, A. D. (2004). The necessary characteristics of environmental auditors:a review of the contribution of the financial auditing profession. *Accounting Forum, 28*(2), 119–138. doi:10.1016/j.accfor.2004.01.001

Eugénio, T., Lourenco, C. I., & Morais, A. I. (2010). Recent developments in social and environmental accounting research. *Social Responsibility Journal, 6*(2), 286–305. doi:10.1108/17471111011051775

Ferreira, A., Moulang, C., & Hendro, B. (2010). Environmental management accounting and innovation: An exploratory analysis. *Accounting, Auditing & Accountability Journal, 23*(7), 920–948. doi:10.1108/09513571011080180

Figge, F., Hahn, T., Schaltegger, S., & Wagner, M. (2002). The sustainability balanced scorecard - linking sustainability management to business strategy. *Business Strategy and the Environment, 11*(5), 269–284. doi:10.1002/bse.339

Frost, G., & Wilmshurst, T. D. (2000). The Adoption of Environment-related Management Accounting: An Analysis of Corporate Environmental Sensitivity. *Accounting Forum, 24*(4), 344–361. doi:10.1111/1467-6303.00045

Fussel, L., & Georg, S. (2000). The institutionalization of Environmental Concerns - Making the Environment Perform. *International Studies of Management & Organization, 30*(3), 41–58. doi:10.1080/00208825.2000.11656794

Gadenne, D. L., Kennedy, J., & McKeiver, C. (2009). An empirical study of environmental awareness andpractices in SMEs. *Journal of Business Ethics, 84*(1), 45–63. doi:10.100710551-008-9672-9

Gibson, K. C., & Martin, B. A. (2004). Demonstrating value through the use ofenvironmental management accounting. *Environmental Quality Management, 13*(3), 45–52. doi:10.1002/tqem.20003

Godschalk, S. (2008). Does Corporate Environmental Accounting Make Business Sense. *Ecoefficiency in Industry and Science, 24*, 249–265. doi:10.1007/978-1-4020-8913-8_13

Gray, R. (2010). Is accounting for sustainability actually accounting for sustainability and how would we know? An exploration of narratives of organisations and the planet. *Accounting, Organizations and Society, 35*(1), 47–62. doi:10.1016/j.aos.2009.04.006

Hendro, B., Ferreira, A., & Moulang, C. (2008). Does the use of environmentalmanagement accounting affect innovation? An exploratory analysis. *31stAnnualCongress of the European Accounting Association.*

Hopwood, A. G., Unerman, J., & Fries, J. (2010). *Accounting for sustainability: Practical insights.* Abingdon, UK: Earthscan. doi:10.4324/9781849776332

IISD (International Institute for Sustainable Development). (1997). *Website of the International Institute for Sustainable Development "Instruments for Change" project – a collaborativeproject of IISD and the United Nations Division for Sustainable Development (UNDSD).* Retrieved from http://www.iisd.ca/susprod/ compendium.htm

Jalil, M. H., Abar, M. N., & Dadashian, F. (2016). Environmental Management Accounting Model on the Basis of Environmental Management System in Leather Industry. *International Journal of Environmental Sciences and Development, 7*(1), 52–58. doi:10.7763/IJESD.2016.V7.740

Jasch, C. (2003). The use of Environmental Management Accounting (EMA) for identifying environmental costs. *Journal of Cleaner Production, 11*(6), 667–676. doi:10.1016/S0959-6526(02)00107-5

Jasch, C. (2006). How to perform an environmental management cost assessment in one day. *Journal of Cleaner Production, 14*(14), 1194–1213. doi:10.1016/j.jclepro.2005.08.005

Jasch, C., Ayres, D., & Bernaudat, L. (2010). Environmental Management Accounting (EMA) CaseStudies in Honduras An Integrated UNIDO Project. *Social and Environmental Accounting, 4*(2), 89–103. doi:10.22164/isea.v4i2.48

Jonäll, P. (2008). *Environmental Management Accounting (EMA), Management Accounting including Environmental Management – a literature review* (Master's thesis). University of Goteborg.

Kaizer, M. (2017). *The suitability of Environment Management Accounting (EMA) models applied by the German Mittelstand* (Doctoral thesis). The University of Gloucestershire.

Kreuze, J.G., & Newell, G.E. (1994, February). ABC and life cycle costing for environmentexpenditures. *Management Accounting*, 38-42.

Kumpulainen, A., & Pohjola, T. (2008). Success factors in developing EMA- Experiences from four follow-up case studies in Finland. *Environmental Management Accounting for Cleaner Production, Eco-Efficiency in Industry and Science, 24*, 477–490. doi:10.1007/978-1-4020-8913-8_27

Llena, F., Moneva, J. M., & Hernandez, B. (2007). Environmental disclosures and compulsory accounting standards: The case of spanish annual reports. *Business Strategy and the Environment, 16*(1), 50–63. doi:10.1002/bse.466

Masanet-Llodra, M. J. (2006). Environmental management accounting: A case study research on innovative strategy. *Journal of Business Ethics, 68*(4), 393–408. doi:10.100710551-006-9029-1

Medley, P. (1997). Environmental accounting – what does it mean to professional accountants? *Accounting, Auditing & Accountability Journal, 10*(4), 594–600. doi:10.1108/09513579710180833

Moneva, J. M., & Ortas, E. (2010). Corporate environmental and financial performance: A multivariate approach. *Industrial Management & Data Systems, 110*(2), 193–210. doi:10.1108/02635571011020304

Monteiro, S. M., & Aibar-Guzman, B. (2010). The influence of the Portuguese environmental accounting standard on the environmental disclosures in the annual reports of large companies operating in Portugal: A first view (2002-2004). *Management of Environmental Quality, 21*(4), 414–435. doi:10.1108/14777831011049070

Munkøe, L., & Jasch, C. (2008). Waste reduction program based on IFAC's EMA Guideline. *Environmental Management Accounting for CleanerProduction. Eco-Efficiency in Industry and Science, 24*, 379–394. doi:10.1007/978-1-4020-8913-8_21

Olalekan, I. O., & Jumoke, O. O. (2017). Identifying barriers to environmental management accounting practices: A comparative study of Nigeria and South Africa. *The Business and Management Review, 9*(1), 168–179.

Özbirecikli, M. (2007). A Review on How CPAs Should Be Involved in Environmental Auditing and Reporting for the Core Aim of It. *Problems and Perspectives in Management, 5*(2), 113–126.

Robkob, P., & Ussahawanitchakit, P. (2009). Antecedents and consequences of voluntary disclosureof environmental accounting: An empirical study of foodsand beverage firms in Thailand. *Review of Business Research, 9*(3), 1–30.

Scavone, G. M. (2006). Challenges in internal environmental management reporting in Argentina. *Journal of Cleaner Production, 14*(14), 1276–1285. doi:10.1016/j.jclepro.2005.08.011

Schaltegger, S., Bennett, M., Burritt, R. L., & Jasch, C. (2010). *Eco-efficiency in industry and science. Environmental Management Accounting for Cleaner Production* (5th ed.). Springer Science and Business Media.

Schaltegger, S., Burritt, R., & Petersen, H. (2003). *An introduction to corporate environmental management: Striving for sustainability*. Greenleaf Publishing.

Schaltegger, S., & Burritt, R. L. (2000). *Contemporary environmental accounting – Issues, concepts and practice*. Sheffield, UK: Greenleaf Publishing.

Schaltegger, S., & Müller, K. (1997). Calculating the true profitability of pollution prevention. *Greener Management International*, *17*, 53–68.

Seuring, S. A. (2001). Green supply chain costing: Joint cost management in the polyester linings supply chain. *GMI*, *33*(Spring), 71–80.

Singh, G., & Joshi, M. (2009). Environment managementand disclosure practices of Indian companies. *International Journal of Business Research*, *9*(2), 116–128.

Spence, C., Husillos, J., & Correa-Ruiz, C. (2010). Cargo cult science and the death of politics: A critical review of social and environmental accounting research. *Critical Perspectives on Accounting*, *21*(1), 76–89. doi:10.1016/j.cpa.2008.09.008

Staniškis, J., & Stasiškienė, Ž. (2003). Environmental Management Accounting for CP Investment Project Development. *Environmental Research, Engineering and Management*, *1*(23), 60–69.

Staniškis, J. K., & Stasiškienė, Z. (2006). Environmental management accounting in Lithuania: Exploratory study of current practices, opportunities and strategic intents. *Journal of Cleaner Production*, *14*(14), 1252–1261. doi:10.1016/j.jclepro.2005.08.009

UNDSD. (2001). United Nations. Division for Sustainable Development, Environmental management accounting procedures and principles. New York: UNDSD.

UNDSD (United Nations Division for Sustainable Development). (2000). *ImprovingGovernments' Role in the Promotion ofEnvironmental ManagerialAccounting*. Report and meeting document of First Expert Working Group Meeting, Washington, DC.

United Nations. (2001). *Environmental Management Accounting: Policies and Linkages. Economic & Social Affairs*. New York: United Nations.

United States Environmental Protection Agency. (1995). *Federal Facility PollutionPrevention Project Analysis: A Primer for Applying Life Cycle and Total CostAssessment Concepts*. EPA.

United States Environmental Protection Agency. (2000). *The Lean and Green SupplyChain: A Practical Guide for Materials Managers and Supply Chain managers to Reduce Costs and Improve Environmental Performance*. Washington, DC: Author.

Ván, H. (2012). *Environmental benefits and its statement in Environmental Management Accounting* (Doctoral thesis). University of Szeged.

Viere, T., Schaltegger, S., & Enden, J. V. (2007). Supply chaininformation in environmental management accounting–the case of a Vietnamese coffee exporter. *Social and Environmental Accounting*, *1*(2), 296–310. doi:10.22164/isea.v1i2.19

Waweru, N. M. (2010). The origin and evolution of management accounting: A review of the theoretical framework. *Problems and Perspectives in Management*, *8*(3), 165–182.

ADDITIONAL READING

Anghelache, C., Căpuşneanu, S., & Barbu, C.-M. (2009). Analysis over critical issues of implementation or non-implementation of the ABC method in Romania. *Theoretical and Applied Economics*, *12*, 57–62.

Briciu, S., & Căpuşneanu, S. (2010). Effective cost analysis tools of the Activity-Based Costing (ABC) method, *Annales Universitatis Apulensis. Series Oeconomica*, *12*(1), 25–35.

Briciu, S., & Căpuşneanu, S. (2011). The increase of performance of an entity by the conversion of the hidden costs, *Annales Universitatis Apulensis. Series Oeconomica*, *13*(2), 207–214.

Căpuşneanu, S. (2008). Implementation opportunities of green accounting for Activity-Based Costing (ABC) in Romania. *Theoretical and Applied Economics*, *1*, 57–62.

Căpuşneanu, S., & Martinescu, D. M. (2010). Convergence of ABC and ABM principles-Guarantee of a performant management. *Theoretical and Applied Economics*, *10*, 93–102.

Cokins, G., & Căpuşneanu, S. (2011). Sustaining an effective ABC/ABM system. *Theoretical and Applied Economics*, *2*, 47–58.

Cokins, G., Căpuşneanu, S., & Briciu, S. (2012). Accounting's shift to decision-based costing. *Theoretical and Applied Economics*, *11*, 31–44.

Rof, L. M., & Căpuşneanu, S. (2015). Increase the Performance of Companies in the Energy Sector by Implementing the Activity-Based Costing, *International Journal of Academic Research in Accounting. Finance and Management Sciences*, *5*(3), 139–148.

Topor, D. I., Căpuşneanu, S., Constantin, D. M., Barbu, C. M., & Rakos, I. S. (2017b). ABB-ABC-ABE-ABM Approach for Implementation in the Economic Entities from Energy Industry. *Business and Management Horizons*, *5*(2), 36–48. doi:10.5296/bmh.v5i2.12169

Topor, D. I., Căpuşneanu, S., & Tamaş, A. Z. (2017a). An efficient green control (EGC) encouraging environmental investment and profitability. *Journal of Environmental Protection and Ecology*, *18*(1), 191–201.

KEY TERMS AND DEFINITIONS

Activity-Based Costing (ABC): An accounting method that identifies the costs of (indirect) activities and then allocates these costs to the products. Allocation of product costs to products is done through cost drivers.

Electric and Electronics Equipments (EEE): In order to place electrical and electronic equipment (EEE) on the market, manufacturers are required to register with the National Manufacturer's National

Registry of National Environmental Protection Agency, receiving a registration number to be communicated to them by all commercial networks through which they are sold EEE.

Environemntal Management Accounting (EMA): It consists in identifying, collecting, analyzing, and using physical information (energy, water, and materials, including waste and energy, flows, and rates) and monetary information (environmental costs, earnings, and savings) for internal decision making.

Environmental Management System (EMS): A set of processes and practices that allow an organization to reduce its impact on the environment and increase its operational efficiency.

Material Flow Cost Accounting (MFCA): A tool used by manufacturing companies to improve the efficiency of their materials in order to save energy and costs by avoiding material losses (waste).

Chapter 3
Planning, Budgeting, and Green Controlling:
The Budgetary Process of an Economic Entity

Attila Szora Tamaş
1 Decembrie 1918 University, Romania

Cristian-Marian Barbu
Artifex University, Romania

Ileana-Sorina Rakos
University of Petrosani, Romania

Alina-Georgiana Solomon
Dimitrie Cantemir Christian University, Romania

ABSTRACT

The issue of this chapter is to illustrate the aspects of planning, budgeting, and controlling green activities within an economic entity and their impact on the profitability of the entity. The objectives of this chapter are to present the strategic planning, budgeting, and control/controlling processes; the presentation of the principles underlying the budgeting; and the presentation of a case study on the elaboration of the budgetary process and the controlling of an economic entity in the manufacturing field. The chapter presents the types of integrated budgets and how to report the achievement of the objectives. By providing effective information on planning and budgeting, green controlling becomes an indispensable tool for any economic entity in monitoring and measuring performance. Thus, through the contribution made, a new theoretical and empirical framework is created by the authors, which facilitates the identification of new ideas, themes, and debates of other aspects encountered in the activity of the economic entities.

DOI: 10.4018/978-1-7998-0178-8.ch003

INTRODUCTION

Within all economic entities, the planning, drafting and implementation of budgets and their control have become crucial in streamlining the use of tangible and intangible resources. In order to ensure an efficient and transparent management system for the use of all these resources, economic entities are directly interested in modernizing the process of drafting, implementing, controlling and reporting the budget, improving accounting records, implementing the control system and measuring the results obtained, as well as the creation of an integrated information system for management of all the company's available resources. In fact, any economic entity cannot actually start its activity without a program of activity and without a forecast of revenues and expenses for a period. As a forecasting document, the budget is compiled annually and can be compared to an entity's GPS, being the instrument that helps management to determine the amount of activity and resources needed, responsibilities on each organizational structure, and last but not least in management guidelines in the future, the ultimate aim being to obtain profit. Also, the budget is a tool for coordinating the various activities of an economic entity, being useful in measuring performance, promoting efficiency and preventing waste. The constant analysis of past performance allows management to make optimal strategic decisions and to produce better forecasts in the future. Thus, over the past twenty years, the concept of controlling has greatly developed, becoming a management function without which a modern entity cannot be conceived. At the national level, there is a tendency for the two control and controlling concepts to be considered similar, but controlling is a functional leadership concept that has the role of coordinating management planning, control and management in the direction of achieving the proposed objectives. Controlling develops the possible methods of informing all those responsible for the budgetary process to act in such a way as to achieve consistency between the proposed objectives, the means of achieving them and the results achieved. This chapter addresses various conceptual formulations on the planning, budgeting, control/controlling process, which then integrates into an empirical study.

The main objectives of this chapter are: (1) *the presentation of the strategic planning, budgetary and control/controlling processes; (2) the presentation of the principles underlying the budgeting; and (3) the presentation of a case study on the preparation of the budgetary process and the controlling of an economic entity in the manufacturing sector.*

BACKGROUND

Regarding the issues addressed, the national and international literature offers a considerable number of theoretical and practical studies related to the concepts of strategic planning, budgetary process, budget itself, control and controlling (Albu & Albu, 2003; Anthony & Govindarajan, 2007; Burlaud & Simon, 2003; Bouquin, 2006, 2008; Briciu et al., 2010; Căpuşneanu, 2006; Dragomirescu, 2010; Kerzner, 2001; Tabără, 2009). Anthony (1965) defines strategic planning as a means of formulating the strategy. According to Kerzner (2001), strategic planning is the process of developing and implementing decisions about the future direction of the organization, being vital to the survival of any organization because it helps companies adapt to the ever-changing environment applicable to all managerial levels and all types organizations. Wagner (1883) defines the budget as "a plan comprised of figures, in a sequence determined by a systematic object, about the likely inputs and outputs (incomes and expenses) in monetary terms or monetary values that occur in the economic management of a public body for a certain period of time." After Man and Rakos (2015), a budget is "a provision for income and expenditure over a specified period, an evolutionary and comparative picture of earnings and expenses to be incurred."

Researching the literature we discover that performance-based budgeting has emerged since the 1980s, the first countries to have applied research results in this respect are the USA, New Zealand, the Netherlands, Australia, the United Kingdom and Switzerland, and later Germany and Russia.

Strategic Planning, Budgeting and Controlling

In the last decade, the subject of planning, budgeting and green control has been debated not only by specialists and professionals in the field, but also by academics. The research was based on the in-depth study of scientific papers from international literature such as: Afonso (2008), Tanzi (1974), Robinson (2007), Olson et al., (1998), Diamond (2006), as well as autochthon literature such as: Ciubotaru & Hîncu (2015), Casian (2013), Stratulat (2002), Botnari & Nedelcu (2015), Veveriţă, (2013).

In 1991, the first attempt was made to regulate the budgetary process of an economic entity, regulation that over time has been improved by the Ministry of Public Finance. In 1995, through OMF no. 596/1995 were the first methodological norms referring to the way of drawing up the budget of revenues and expenditures by the autonomous administrations and the commercial companies with state capital, at the time the private ones were in a very narrow number. In May 2000, the Order of the Minister of Public Finances no. 616/28 March 2000, which provided for the methodological norms for the application by the economic entities with state capital of the regulations regarding the elaboration of the Income and Expenditure Budget in a unitary manner, was published. The respective order was published in the Official Monitor of Romania, part I, no.7 of 2000. By the aforementioned order, three major changes were made regarding the budgetary process, namely:

- For the first time reference is made to companies with private capital, the order targeting mainly state-owned companies, national companies, research and development institutes, etc., all of which are called economic agents.
- The budget structure containing a number of four situations compared to nine was simplified, as was the number of forms requested in 1995.

The economic agents were also encouraged to use their own forms in the elaboration of the Income and Expenditure Budget specific to their own interests related to the performed activity.

Strategic Planning

Strategic planning is the communication tool that provides the context in which the decisions and reasoning underlying them are made, and the reasons underlying a particular action are set out. Strategic planning helps managers have a vision of the future, not just the present and strategic planning and forecasting helps to improve the long-term performance of economic entities applying this concept. We can say that strategic planning is the process that best describes the direction an entity has, uniting staff to achieve common goals. It helps the entity to prioritize its actions, being a collective and participatory process involving both management and executive staff, without exception, as well as a series of consultations with internal and external stakeholders interested in the entity. Strategic planning highlights some fundamental aspects of the entity, focusing on day-to-day operations, to actions that can improve performance.

Strategic planning answers questions like: (1) What is the reason for the existence of an economic entity? (2) What are the main and secondary objectives of the entity? (3) What are the expectations of its customers? (4) How does it measure its performance based on which indicators? (5) How does all this information contribute to the improvement of the economic activity itself?

We can therefore outline the strategic planning objectives: (1) *identifying and prioritizing, for effective and efficient allocation of resources*; (2) *better communication between decision-makers, employees and stakeholders*; (3) *transparency of decision-making*; (4) *better empowerment of all employees at all hierarchical levels; and* (5) *improvement of performance within each departmental structure*. Specific objectives for the duration of planning are defined in the planning, and various action alternatives are designed to achieve different types of planning. Annual planning is based on detailed measures to be taken to achieve the objectives and how to quantify them. Within each department, a product and service plan are drawn up, on the costs, respectively on the revenue that will be collected, will lead to the results of the annual planning.

Forecasting and planning mean two different and complementary processes. Perspective is a process of knowledge, while planning seems to be a process of action. The system of budgeting within an economic entity is more than a set of forecasts. This is a set of short-term plans, referring to resource sharing and attribution of responsibilities. The following eight steps are important in the forecast: (1) reporting opportunities, depending on market, competition, needs, customers, strengths, weaknesses; (2) setting goals by answering questions such as: Where do we need to get? What and how do we need to accomplish?; (3) taking into account the premises, finding the answer to the question: In what internal or external environment will the entity's plan operate? (4) identifying alternatives: What are the most promising alternatives for achieving goals?; (5) Alternative/objective comparisons: Which alternative will give the greatest chance of reaching the goals, with the lowest cost and the highest profit? (6) direction selection: Select the course of action to be followed; (7) formulation of derivative plans: purchasing equipment, purchasing materials, hiring and training, development of new products; (8) budgeting: volumes, prices, costs, sales, operational expenses, other expenses.

Strategic planning also involves taking steps, as shown in Figure 1.

Figure 1. Strategic Planning

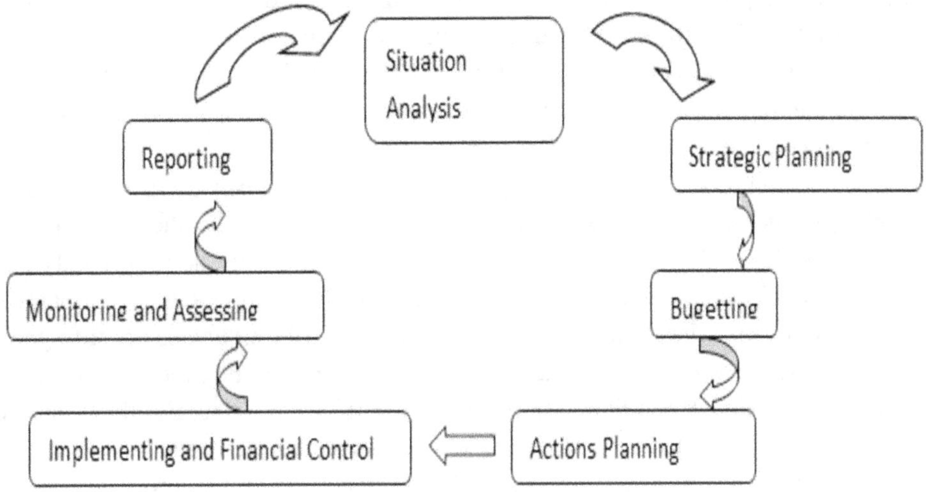

Budgeting

A budget is a planning tool needed to build a framework for the business and its finances. Combining past trends with realistic forecasts for the fiscal year, a budget provides a detailed picture of assets, realistic revenue expectations, and how they balance anticipated spending. Budgeting involves aligning all activities within an economic entity to all its objectives. The designation of the budget should be geared to its formal objectives, the *value objectives*. Practically, the shift between action and budget planning is fluent, as a fundamental planning of the values objectives as content could be possible, but only by a simultaneous planning of the necessary measures. Structuring and running the planning and budgeting system within an entity is the most important task of the control department. The method of issuing and analysing a budget must be addressed separately for the economic entities in the field of production and separately for the trade ones. This is due to the specific features of each domain. In production, cost budgets are usually issued through flexible calculations and planned costs.

The budget fulfils several functions as an instrument of managing an economic entity's economic activity, such as: (1) forecasting; (2) aggregation of economic and financial balance and (3) control. At the same time, the budget is an anticipatory tool that allows for the implementation of proactive development policies (the annual decline of strategic plans), but also a horizontal coordination tool - between different services and functions, and vertically (between managers and financial managers) that considers and harmonises the requirements and constraints of each. The budget provides the value dimensioning of objectives, revenues and expenditures, results from all management centres, and ultimately brings economic efficiency by comparing results with their budgeted level.

The budget allows for "clarifying responsibilities, performance, means and action plans in line with the actions of the various actors in the enterprise in the context of decentralization" (Dragomirescu, 2008). The budget thus appears as an important link to the functioning of an economic entity by means of which local actions are consistent with the overall performance of the entity. It is the quantitative expression of a pre-prepared activity over the period it refers to, highlighting "the management's vision of expectations for all operational activities within a specified period" (Dobrin & Badea, 2006).

Budget is a set of digital, realistic and voluntary predictions that translate the objectives of the economic entity (Bouquin, 2004). Throughout the year, the resulting figures must be analysed by comparison with those in the budgets. This is how new predictions are made based on new variables or variable levels at a given time in order to provide a basis for comparison under conditions close to the analysis period. From a financial point of view, the budget can be defined as a financial plan that includes revenue and expenditure over a given period, and from a non-financial point of view, the budget refers to the number of products, the number of employees, the number of new inputs on the market, etc. (Simionescu, 2015). Also, the budget can become a measure of performance.

All in all, the budgeting process includes budget forecasting and budget control. Forecasts are essential complementary of the management system. Thus, we can state that the short-term budget forecast is the detailed process, in the short term (one year) of the functional plans, activities and compartments of an economic entity. The concrete outcome of the financial forecasting activity is materialized in a series of instruments that take the form of documents that have different names according to the nature of the operations they reflect, the scope of the indicators they contain, the time horizon at which refers to: financial plan, income and expenditure budget, financial flow chart, etc. For the regular evaluation of the achievement of the scheduled objectives, the annual budget can be divided into budgets at shorter intervals, such as days, weeks, months, quarters, and semesters. The budget process must be seen as a milestone in the implementation of the long-term plan. Eco-budgeting is a tool that involves preparing a green budget separately in annual budgets.

For the unitary building of the budget system to the economic entities in the manufacturing industry, some elements should be taken into account, such as: delimiting the places of activity and integrating them into the budgetary system; the type and amount of resource consumption; selecting resource allocation criteria; the production capacity of the budget site; the volume of activity programmed and the mode of evaluation of the result of the activities; the volume of sales scheduled in the context of a competitive market; primary costs and calculation items; cost per unit of product; control and cost analysis; setting limits on responsibility for budget implementation; providing a database on hierarchical levels and good communication; integrating all data from the entity into an automatic data processing system. The organization of the budgetary process of an economic entity in the manufacturing industry considers the organizational structure, to the level of the workplaces, since the elaboration of the general budget is based on the partial expenditure budgets grouped in the general budget of the operating expenses. The Chief Accountant is responsible for fitting the level of budgeted costs.

Control. Controlling

By control, we can make the difference between what was planned and what was done, aiming at identifying the causes that led to differences and taking measures to diminish or eliminate the observed differences. Considered as process and way of thinking, *control* was set at the intersection between management and controller tasks. Regarding small and medium-sized entities, the control function is held by the management of the company or by the management of the accounting department. Within the large entities, a controller is appointed to check how each employee performs the service tasks. Controlling is a functional management system to coordinate information, planning, and budgeting to achieve goals and achieve optimal results.

The purpose of control within an organization is to strengthen the coherence and the consequences of the actions taken. Control also helps to achieve strategic goals over a given period and is part of the budgeting process. The *control capability* is given to the degree of influence a particular manager has on the costs, revenues and other similar items he is responsible for.

Controlling is also called the process of cross-organizing the activities of an economic entity. In the long term, it means a lifelong learning process through accumulation and exchange of experience. The system of planning and drafting the annual budget as part of an effective control system is based on the information provided by the management accounting. This has influenced people's behaviour by nature and mode of transmission of information, directed strategic decisions, and influenced the structure of the entity and its performance system. This type of accounting was mainly focused on the future performance of employees.

From the point of view of management accounting, within the economic entities, the budgetary system simultaneously performs four functions: (1) element of the management control; (2) planning means; (3) ensures the consistency of human resources, intentions and motivations; (4) pursuit of the objectives pursued. Regardless of how perfect an economic entity's strategy is, control of predictions is necessary to identify at a certain moment the causes that lead to certain deviations and to identify optimal corrective measures that can be taken in a timely manner. In the control activity and the comparison of forecasts and achievements for a correct analysis it is necessary to adjust the initial budget according to the performed activity, knowing that, depending on this activity, the variable expenditures are evolving, and the fixed expenditures remain constant.

Within the economic entities, the implementation of a green control system has emerged as a necessity as a result of the globalization and liberalization of the financial markets, the free movement of persons, information, capital, and last but not least, the application of internationally recognized standards and which must be understood in a unitary manner. At the beginning of the third millennium, in the practice of economic entities, the concept of controlling has greatly developed, becoming an extremely important management function within them, having the role of coordinating management information, planning and control, in order to obtain the expected results. In the last decades, controlling has been integrated in almost all sectors of activity. By applying controlling, managers ensure that the resources are obtained and used as efficiently as possible to achieve the objectives. The controlling departments are found in both classical industrial, commercial, financial and public institutions. Controlling is therefore a range of tasks that are carried out by different people, employed in economic entities, or which can be done by key and by management, without a particular person being appointed as a controller.

In small economic entities, the controlling function is held by the management of the entities, and in the case of large economic entities this function is held by a controller in charge of the controlling tasks. The goal of any entity is to have good management to implement public policies, programs and projects to achieve the mission of the entity through rational use of resources (so limited today) and at the same time meets the requirements of stakeholders. In the last years there is an interpenetration of the tasks of the manager with those of the controller, the latter attributing the role of management consultant, as shown in Figure 2.

The essential characteristic of controlling within economic entities is that it is a tool for both management and control oriented to results-oriented processes, aiming at the achievement of the goal of "3E" - economy, efficiency, effectiveness, according to the Figure 3. Controlling tools are based on a flexible data system that verifies the investments in the cost calculation, namely cost accounting, profit and loss account, investment account, as well as the formation of index systems and which are supplemented with strategic market. These tools are used both in planning, management and control, and in reporting. Fundamental control principles are defined by the significant control methods and tools that are essential to the planning and budgeting of economic and financial indicators.

Figure 2. Controlling - a connection between the tasks of the manager and the controller

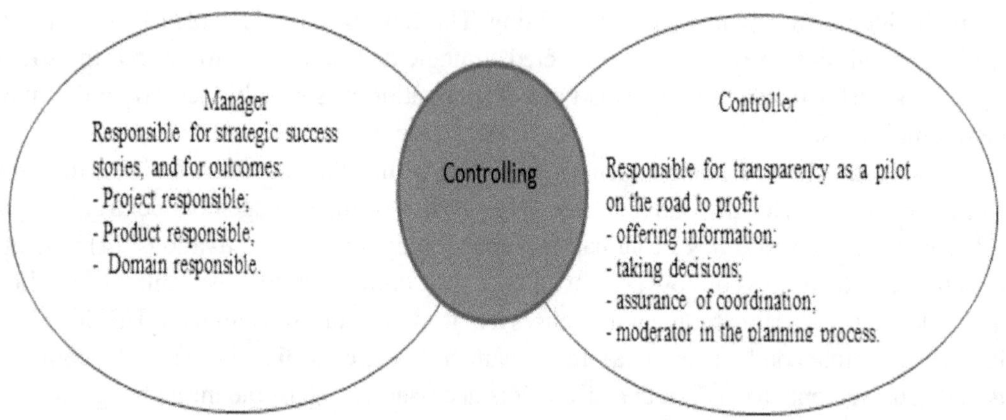

Figure 3. The 3E model for the performance-based budgeting concept

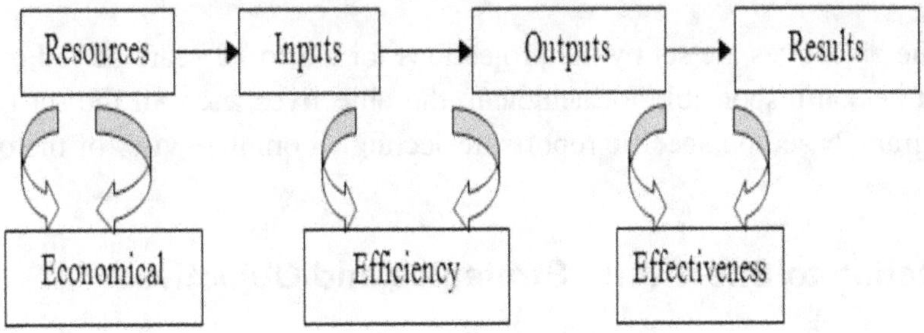

The organization and implementation of green controlling is specific to large-scale entities where, in addition to general controlling, emphasis is placed on the joint action between the information system and the planning system. Green control is primarily a computerized system for collecting, evaluating, and preparing for decision-making of environmental information.

Controlling is strategic radar for anticipating future developments and derivation of the subsequent strategy as well as for the operational management of the economic entity. The green control concept has a two-way objective: on the one hand, it measures and controls the effects of environmentally relevant actions on the financial side and, on the other hand, measures and controls the ecological effects of economic actions. IT provides the right and sustainable use and management of data. The integrative division of labour between controlling and environmental management ensures compliance with control standards and facilitates the provision of data by management from a single source. Economic entities around the world are increasingly concerned about the need to conduct their business so as to ensure minimal environmental degradation. The introduction of environmental objectives in decision-making and finance is the solution to these major management concerns. The environmental aspect is the consequence of a long process of understanding and awareness of the environmental issues generated by both production and consumption processes in the economic and life sectors in general. The financial impact of environmental damage is by no means neglected, and therefore economic entities need to provide information on the policies, objectives and environmental programs implemented, the costs they have incurred in the field and the environmental risks they face. Changing requirements of environmental regulations and increasing stakeholder pressure have led management to adapt to these requirements by effectively managing environmental costs, benefits and impacts, in terms of the sustainability of production processes. At the same time, the study of environmental issues has led to a semantic reconsideration of some vital concepts and issues, starting with the definition of production process, costs, profit, economic growth and continuing with those of economic and social development with rational and prudent - natural resources. Therefore, green control has been imposed as a necessary tool in substantiating decisions, being used to organize, manage and provide environmental data and information in physical and monetary units.

PRESENTATION OF THE PRINCIPLES BASED ON THE BUDGET DRAFTING

According to the specialists, the following principles should be considered in the elaboration of the budget system (Caraiani & Dumitrana, 2005):

Principles Relating to Long-Term Objectives

In the long run, the objectives are set by the projections for a 5 to 10 years period on process quality, market share, and person responsible for achieving the objectives, etc. All the set goals are grouped into a master program, based on specific reports, reflecting a complete view of the objectives as well as applied policies.

Principles Relating to Short-Term Strategies and Objectives

Top management sets short-term strategies and targets on sales and performance on human resources, materials, products and services. Functional budgets are prepared based on the organizational chart and the entity's defined functions being consolidated to obtain financial reports with reference to the financial position and performance of the economic entity.

Principles Relating to Staff Policy Interaction: Budget

It is very important that the person responsible for the Master budget management and the responsible persons who contribute to its realization is identified from the beginning. The budget manager is responsible for the good communication between all levels of decision-making and the coordination of the budgeting activity. In the preparation and implementation of the budgetary provisions, all the persons responsible for the budget are involved in a proactive manner, applying both the conceptual therapies and policies of participatory budgeting, as well as a free and full free communication between all the actors involved in the budget drafting and execution.

Principles Relating to the Actual Drafting of Budgets

General management has the task of setting clear objectives and levels that can be achieved by each responsible person in a realistic approach without prioritizing departmental goals more than the entity's goals. Meeting deadlines in presenting budget information is important in assessing both the performance of each manager and the realism of functional budgets. When implementing budgets, there must be flexibility, as budgets are seen as indicative tools and not as absolute truths, as over time changes take place in both the tax legislation and the production capacity of entities, consumer needs as well as the business environment.

Principles Relating to Budgetary Control

Budget officials have the obligation to verify budget estimates with actual results in order to detect and correct errors. Reconciliation involves delivering through a flexible budget estimates that can be automatically rectified to productive output changes. The variable budget, a cost control tool, is used to analyse the entity's performance, the causes of the differences between the actual and the budget are based on a value calculation process resulting in the analysis of the deviations through a selective management. We analyse favourable and unfavourable deviations that do not fall within the limits set by management, by applying selective management techniques. As a result of the control are the periodic reports on the performances that represent the essence of the functional accounting system. Based on the identified malfunctions, the solutions are identified and the data for the next budget cycle is adjusted.

CASE STUDY ON GREEN PLANNING, BUDGETTING AND CONTROLLING IN AN ECONOMIC ENTITY

For the analysis of the sources and the evolution of productivity in the manufacturing industry, an economic entity from the manufacturing industry was chosen. The entity has two main production sections: the section of machining (clothing and metal constructions) and the re-treading section (technical articles of rubber and plastics). The products obtained are metal spare parts, moulds, motorcycle chambers, tires, car chambers, rubber gaskets.

The objectives pursued through the budget system are: (1) designing flows in lei and foreign currency to control cash inflows and outflows and timely payments; (2) the transparency of all revenue and expenditure and the increase in the capacity to achieve profit; (3) providing resources to finance social-cultural actions; (4) the dimensioning of the realities of money with the employees, with the state budget, with the suppliers and with other natural and legal persons as creditors and debtors; (5) designing patrimony evolution by reflecting changes in its structure.

In order to predict the future of the entity's activity, procedures and techniques specific to the forecast are used. Today, software programs greatly ease the work of forecasting, planning, and budgeting. Tabular computing and spreadsheet programs allow rapid deployment of the various scenarios imagined by management.

The process of budgeting within the economic entity involves four steps, namely:

Stage 1: Preparation of the budget (free and total communication between factors (top-down and bottom-up) involved in budgeting by activity);
Stage 2: Assembling the budget (linking and assembling budgets by activity and applying the necessary corrections to achieve the goal and objectives of the entity);
Stage 3: Authorizing the budget (submitting for approval the final form of the budget, after negotiations at all hierarchical levels);
Stage 4: Budget monitoring (implementation of a budget tracking, measurement and control budgeting procedure).

The entity's budget consists of: *the operating budget, the cash flow and the budgeted balance sheet.*

The Operating Budget

It consists of: sales budget, production budget, marketing budget, administrative expenditure budget, etc. The projected balance sheet (financial budget) depends on many items in the projected profit and loss account. Thus, the logical starting point for preparing a main budget is the anticipated revenue account (the planned operating budget). Because the planned operating budget indicates the net effect of many interdependent activities, management needs to prepare several support budgets (for example: sales, production and procurement budgets), production budget, sales of goods, sales and administrative expenses.

Sales Budget

The basis of the budgeting process is the sales budget because it depends on the utility of the entire operating budget. This budget is a sales plan, divided by products and services expressed in physical and value units, which are expected to be sold during the projected time period. Also, at the basis of the budget is competition and market information, existing operational capabilities and contracts or sales agreements to customers. The sales budget involves estimating the volume of demand for the assets of the entity and determining if a realistic and achievable profit can be obtained on the basis of that demand. The sales forecast may involve either formal or informal techniques, or both.

The sales budget offers a comprehensive sales program and plans for a given period. It mentions the potential of sales in terms of quantity, values, period, product, etc. The sales budget is one of the major budgets, as it is the basis for preparing other types of budgets. In general, the sales manager prepares the sales budget with the assistance of sales supervisors, salespeople, market research officers and other salespeople. In order to prepare the sales budget, factors such as: product price trend, population trend, customer purchasing power, advertising degree, past sales, nature of competition, economic situation in the country, etc. are taken into account in preparing the sales budget.

The sales projection uses sales information or historic budget allocations that are expected to perpetuate in the upcoming period. The most useful sales projection methods are: the zero basis method (which considers the activity to be new and takes into account the concrete future conditions, sufficient of certainty and prudence), the incremental method (based on the coefficient when the target is fixed in advance, for example: 10% increase in sales or 5% increase in activity and budget allocation). The influence of material events may affect the trend of projections (e.g. capacity changes in the form of new investments or disinvestments), penetration into new markets, changes in sales volumes or activity, changes in pricing policy, introduction of new products or services, giving up some services.

Budget Network Solution Plan, Semester 1, Year 2018

The following information is known: sales prices for section (S1) 148 euro/piece, and for section (S2) 155 euro/piece. Receivables will be cashed 55% in the current month and 45% by trade effects with 30 days. Initial claims will be collected in January 2018. The production forecast takes into account the provision of a safety stock at the end of each month of at least 50% of the volume of sales for the next month. The forecast for sales for the first semester is shown in Table 1 and the sales forecast for 2018 is shown in Table 2.

Production Budget

This budget describes the number of physical units that need to be produced to meet inventory needs and sales needs. The inventory is considered as the stock at the beginning of the plan period and the end of it, the level of stocks in days and the speed of rotation of stocks in days. The main forecast of revenue generation resources - provided in the sales budget and those needed to cover the expenses to meet the objectives set out in the activity plan or programs is the production budget. There must be a balance between the sales budget and the production budget, because, on the one hand, production cannot be questioned without taking into account the possibility of selling the products obtained, and on the other

Table 1. Sales forecast for semester 1

No.	Explanations	U.M.	Month					
			January	February	March	April	May	June
1	Section (S1)	Pcs	2960	2880	2960	2920	2960	2960
2	Section (S2)	Pcs	2800	2960	2960	2960	2920	2960
Total out of which:		euro	1254400	1291200	1302400	1296800	1290400	1302400
3	Section (S1)	148	834400	847200	858400	852800	852400	858400
4	Section (S2)	155	420000	444000	444000	444000	438000	444000
5	TVA	19%	238336	245328	247456	246392	245176	247456
6	Value with VAT	-	3029264	1536528	1549856	1.543192	1535576	1549856
7	Current receipts	55%	1666095	845090	852421	848756	844567	852421
8	Trade Effects 30 Days	45%	1363169	691438	697435	694436	691009	697435

Table 2. Sales forecast for the year 2018

Explanations	Month						
	U.M.	January	February	March	April	May	June
Metalworking, Fabrication and Construction Section	piece	2960	2880	2960	2920	2960	2960
Re-treading, Technical Rubber and Plastics Articles Section	piece	2800	2960	2960	2960	2920	2960
Explanations	**Month**						
	U.M.	**July**	**August**	**September**	**October**	**November**	**December**
Metal Processing, Garments and Construction Section	piece	2800	2880	2920	2960	3000	2800
Re-treading, Technical Rubber and Plastics Articles Section	piece	2880	3000	2960	2880	2960	2720

hand the volume of sales cannot be estimated without account shall be taken of the production potential. At the same time, the production budget must take account of certain restrictions that occur within the entity (material inputs, skill levels, raw materials and materials, etc.). The stages of production budget production are:

Stage I: Staging of finished products obtained according to production schedule;
Stage II: Forecast - ante-calculation of production costs;
Stage III: Breakdown of budget provisions by quarters, months, sections, workshops, jobs.

The quantity of products to be produced is determined by the relationship:

$$Qf = Qv - Si + Sf \tag{1}$$

Where:

Qf = is the quantity of products to be manufactured;

Qv = the intended quantity to be sold;

Si = stock of products at the beginning of the period;

Sf = stock of products at the end of the period.

The condition of production planning is the optimal use of installed capacities and the efficient use of production factors. A single omitted restriction may lead to disruption of activity with implications for the entity's overall capacity. In order to organize production in optimal conditions and to observe all the restrictions, we invoke the operational research and especially the linear programming. Production budget can be produced either quantitatively or quantitatively and in value. The quantitative budget reflects the stocks of final products as well as the link between production and sales, and the value budget requires the calculation of the default cost of production.

The antecedence of costs consists of identifying direct product costs (materials, labour, machinery) and indirect costs (common and general maintenance, operation and administration of the entity). Direct spending on products includes direct materials, wages and direct social expenses; they are calculated according to the consumption of materials and labour expressed in the prices and labour tariffs in force. Indirect costs are allocated to products by means of successive allocation keys and lead to the formation of different stages of the unitary unit, factory, and full commercial cost.

In determining the default cost, the technical standards regarding the quantity of materials, the labour cost needed to execute a unit of the product, are to be known by the technical personnel. Labour technical standards are the times needed for production. Value standards are the means by which technical standards are assessed. The ante-calculation of costs makes it possible to produce four types of budgets derived from the production budget: the budget of consumed materials; direct labour budget; the market, the investment program, etc., the depreciation of machinery; general production expenditure budget. (Popescu, 2009).

These budgets which detail the production budget provisions are developed only in large entities with territorially dispersed production units and only if their necessity is justified. For example, salary planning is done in the last month of the base year, depending on the predictable increase in salary in the year, the minimum wage established by normative act, the quantitative and professional changes in the estimated workforce, etc. The value budget, as compared to the quantitative, assesses the programmed quantities with the pre-set cost of production; it can be elaborated according to the methodological norms regarding the budget of revenues and expenditures.

The production capacity and its calculation are determined on the basis of Table 3 and Table 4.

The initial stock situation is presented in Table 5 and the standard cost sheet for Sections 1 and 2 in Table 6 and Table 7.

Table 8 presents the production and finished goods inventory for the first semester and Table 9, the raw material and packaging inventory budget for the first semester.

Table 3. Production capacity of the economic entity

Operations	U.M.	Number of machinery	Number of shifts	Number hours/shift	Average no. of days/ month	Available capacity
Debiting	Hours-Machine	5	3	8	20	2400
Turning	Hours- Machine	14	3	8	20	6720
Finishing assembly	Hours-Machine	8	3	8	20	3840
Packing	Hours-Machine	5	3	8	20	2400
Total						**15360**

Table 4. Calculation of the production capacity of the economic entity

No	Explanations	Time standard	January	February	March	April	May	June
1	Production manufactured in section S1	2.00	3040	2920	2940	2940	2960	2880
2	Production manufactured in section S2	3.20	2880	2960	2960	2940	2940	2920
3	Capacity required for S1	hours	6080	5840	5840	5880	5920	5760
4	Capacity required for S2	hours	9216	9472	9472	9408	9408	9344
5	Theoretical capacity		15296	15312	15352	15288	15328	15104
6	Maximum capacity available		15360	15360	15360	15360	15360	15360
7	Unused capacity	hours	**64**	**48**	**8**	**72**	**32**	**256**

Table 5. Specification of initial stocks

Product Name	Amount (Pcs.)	Unit Price (euro/pcs.)	Euro Value
Section - manufacturing, clothing and metal constructions	1360	129.0	175440
Tire re-treading section, technical rubber and plastic articles	1400	141.0	197400
Total value of finished products			**372840**
Raw material M1 kg	10400	10	104000
Raw material M2 kg	6000	8	48000
Special Packages	4000	4	16000
Total material value	-	-	540840

The Procurement Budget takes into account the launch of orders with fixed quantities launched for two months of average consumption. The orders will be supplemented by 10% and will be launched as of January 2018. The additional orders are approximated by the addition of 100 kg. The orders are honoured in the month in which the order is placed. Monthly security stocks will necessarily cover the need for 50% next month's consumption. Payments to suppliers of raw materials are as follows: 40% of the debts in the following month; 60% of debts with promissory notes 60 days scandal. Payments to packaging vendors are made in the current month. The suppliers in the balance sheet 31.12.2017 are paid as follows: 50% in January 2018; 50% in February 2018. Table 10 presents the budget for supplies of packaging and raw materials. Table 10 presents the budget for supplies of packaging and raw materials.

Table 6. Standard account sheet for section S1

No.	Direct Material Explanations	U.M.	Standard Quantity	Standard Unit Price	Standard Value
1.	Direct materials				
1.1	Raw material M1	kg	5	10	50
1.2	Raw material M2	kg	3	8	24
1.3	Pack	pcs.	1	4	4
	Total direct material				78
II.	Direct labour plus social protection				
2.1	Debiting	hours	0.25	2	0,50
2.2	Turning	hours	1.00	4	4
2.3	Finishing assembly	hours	0.50	4	2
2.4	Packing	hours	0.25	4	1
2.5	Total direct labour		2		7.5
2.6	Social protection	40%			3
III.	Expenditure on administration	hours	2	20,00	40
IV.	Total Standard Cost				128.5
	Unit price per product/per unit				**140**

Table 7. Standard account sheet for section S2

No.	Direct Material Explanations	U.M.	Standard Quantity	Standard Unit Price	Standard Value
1.	Direct materials				
1.1	Raw material M1	tons	4	10	40
1.2	Raw material M2	tons	2	8	16
1.3	Pack	pcs.	1	4	4
	Total direct material				60
II.	Direct labour plus social protection				
2.1	Debiting	hours	0.40	2	0.80
2.2	Turning	hours	1.60	4	6.40
2.3	Finishing assembly	hours	0.80	4	3.20
2.4	Packing	hours	0.40	4	1.60
2.5	**Total direct labour**				**12**
2.6	**Social protection**	**40%**			**4.80**
III.	**Expenditure on administration**	**hours**	**3.2**	**20.00**	**64**
IV.	**Total Standard Cost**				**140.8**
V.	**Unit price per product/per unit**				**150**

Table 8. Production and finished product budget for semester 1

Explanations	U.M.	Month					
		January	February	March	April	May	June
Initial stock							
Section S1	Pcs.	1360	1440	1480	1460	1480	1480
Section S2	Pcs.	1400	1480	1480	1480	1460	1480
Manufacture							
Section S1	Pcs.	3040	2920	2940	2940	2960	2880
Section S2	Pcs.	2880	2960	2960	2940	2940	2920
Sales							
Section S1	Pcs.	2960	2880	2880	2920	2960	2960
Section S2	Pcs.	2800	2960	2960	2960	2920	2960
Final stock							
Section S1	Pcs.	1440	1480	1460	1480	1480	1400
Section S2	Pcs.	1480	1480	1480	1460	1480	1440
Final stock value	PU						
Section S1	128,50	185040	190180	187612	190180	190180	179900
Section S2	140,80	208384	208384	208384	205568	208384	202752
Total stock value		393424	398564	395996	395748	398564	382652

Table 9. Production and finished product budget for semester 1

Explanations	U.M.	Month					
		January	February	March	April	May	June
Initial stock M1	kg	10400	42080	15640	47500	21040	52880
Initial stock M2	kg	6000	23520	8840	26500	11800	29440
Inputs M1	kg	58400	-	58400	-	58400	-
Inputs M2	kg	32400	-	32400	-	32400	-
Consumption M1	kg	26720	26440	26540	26460	26560	26080
Consumption M2	kg	14880	14680	14740	14700	14760	14480
Final stock							
M1	kg	42080	15640	47500	21040	52880	26800
M2	kg	23530	8840	26500	11800	29440	14960
Raw materials stock value	EUR	608960	227120	687000	304800	764320	387680
M1	10 EUR/kg	420800	156400	475000	210400	528800	268000
M2	8 EUR/kg	188160	70720	212000	94400	235520	119680
The value of consumables	EUR	23680	23520	23600	23520	23600	23200
Stock value of packaging	EUR	16000	16000	16000	16000	16000	16000

Table 10. Budget for the supply of packaging and raw materials

Explanations	Specific Consumption	Month					
		January	February	March	April	May	June
Production manufactured in Section S1	Pcs.	3040	2920	2940	2940	2960	2880
Production manufactured in Section S2	Pcs.	2880	2960	2960	2940	2940	2920
Required packaging	1 piece /finished product	5920	5880	5900	5880	5900	5800
Value of packaging		23680	23520	23600	23520	23600	23200
VAT related to the purchase of packaging		4499	4469	4484	4469	4484	4408
Value of packaging with VAT		28179	27989	28084	27989	28084	27608
Required raw material M1	Kg/pcs	14880	14680	14740	14700	14760	14480
For S1 For S2	5 4	15200 11520	14600 11840	14700 11840	14700 11760	14800 11760	14400 11680
Required raw material M2	Kg/pc	14880	14680	14740	14700	14760	14480
For S1 For S2	3 2	9120 5760	8760 5920	8820 5920	8820 5880	8880 5880	8640 11680
Original stock M1		10400	36612	10172	36568	10108	36480
Consumption M1		26720	26440	26540	26460	26560	26080
Final intermediate stock M1		16320	10172	16368	10108	16452	10400
Order M1 for 2 months	2	52932	-	52932	-	52932	-
Retained M1 inventory		36612	10172	36568	10108	36480	10400
Original stock M2		6000	20532	5852	20528	5828	20480
Consumption M2		14880	14680	14740	14700	14760	14480
Final intermediate stock M2		8880	5852	8888	5828	8932	6000
Order M2 for 2 months	2	29412	-	29412	-	29412	-
Retained M2 inventory		20532	5852	20528	5828	20480	6000
Increased M1 order	10%	58400	-	58400	-	58400	-
Increased M2 order	10%	32400	-	32400	-	32400	-
Total orders value	**PU**	**843200**	**-**	**843200**	**-**	**843200**	-
For M1	10 EUR	584000	-	584000	-	584000	-
For M2	8 EUR	259200	-	259200	-	259200	-
VAT on purchasing raw materials	**19%**	**160208**	**-**	**160208**	**-**	**160208**	-
Value with VAT		1003408	-	1003408	-	1003408	-
Payments to 30 days	40%	401363	-	401363	-	401363	-
Payments to 60 days	60%	602045	-	602045	-	602045	-

The Budget for Direct Labour Costs takes into account the salary rates per operation and the time limits set for each product. Payment of salaries is done in the current month, and payroll taxes, 40% of wages are made in the following month. Indirect expenditure on wages and salaries will be predicted on the basis of individual standards. The salary cost budget is presented in Table 11.

The Direct Expenditure Budget includes the amount of materials required for existing production and in stock and is determined by the amount of material needed to produce a unit multiplied by the number of units planned. Also, this budget includes the direct productive workforce, i.e. the total number of hours directly required and the cost of the number of units in the production budget. The need for working hours can be changed when technological changes occur.

The Indirect Cost Budget includes the planned cost of indirect (auxiliary) production items. Costs are grouped into fixed and changeable variables, some of which can be identified per unit, and others as indirect production workforce estimated and distributed to the unit. Indirect variable costs are associated with direct costs to determine the allocation key or indirect variable cost rate. The situation of the indirect expenditure budget is presented in Table 12.

The Research and Development Expenditure Budget estimates indirect costs such as design costs, research expenses, documentation, prototype, etc.

The Administrative Expenditure Budget includes the estimated expenditures at the level of the administration of the economic entity being grouped into fixed and variable elements. Fixed assets include salaries of administrative personnel, depreciation of headquarters and related equipment, audit expenses, insurance expenses, suppliers, delegations, utilities. Variable items, such as the variable portion of managers' salary, change based on sales or performance criteria set or negotiated.

Table 11. Salary costs budget

Explanations			Month						Total
			January	February	March	April	May	June	
Production manufactured S1	Pcs.	Production budget	3040	2920	2940	2940	2960	2880	-
Production manufactured S2	Pcs.	Production budget	2880	2960	2960	2940	2940	2920	-
Direct Salaries for P1	7,5 EUR/ pc	-	22800	21900	22052	22052	22200	21600	-
Direct Salaries for P2	12 EUR/ pc	-	34560	34560	35520	35280	35040	35040	-
Total direct salaries	EUR	-	57360	57420	57572	57332	57480	56640	343800
Payroll due to the budget	EUR	quota 40%	22944	22968	23028	22932	22992	22656	137520
Indirect salaries	EUR	Adm. Expenses Budget	162048	162056	162076	162044	162064	161952	972240
Social protection due	EUR	40%	64820	64824	64832	64816	64780	64780	388896
Total salaries costs	EUR	-	307172	307268	307504	307124	306028	306028	1842456

Table 12. Budget of indirect costs for a normal activity of 20,640 hours/month

No.	Elements of Expenditure	VAT Generators	Standard Values	Unitary Variable euro/h
Production volume - activity hours			**15360**	
I.	**Fixed Indirect Station Expenses**		95040	
1.1	Personal: foremen, engineers salaries	Not	24320	
1.2	Expenditure on social protection	Not	60800	
1.3	Depreciation of buildings and section machinery	Not	4000	
1.4	Expenditure on inventory items	Yes	1920	
1.5	Thermic energy for heating	Yes	2000	
1.6	Expenditure on ventilation of sections	Yes	1120	
1.7	Office supplies, maintenance materials	Yes	880	
II.	**Variable production costs sections**	Yes	**15360**	
2.1	Repairs, revisions to fixed assets made by third parties	Yes	2304	0.15
2.2	Electricity for driving purposes	Yes	3072	0.20
2.3	Expenses with filters for environmental protection	Yes	2304	0.15
III.	**Mixed semi-variable spend**		**31216**	
3.1	Salaries of auxiliary workers	Not	9280	0.5
3.2	Related social protection	Not	3712	0.2
3.3	Expenditure on labour protection	Yes	8544	0.4
3.4	Energy, water, for administrative purposes	Yes	9680	0.5
IV.	**Fixed general administrative expenses**		**88800**	
4.1	TESA Personal Salaries	Not	56000	
4.2	Expenditure on social protection	Not	22400	
4.3.	Depreciation of buildings and other fixed assets of general interest	Not	4000	
4.4	Expenditure on inventory items	Yes	2000	
4.5	Thermic energy for heating	Yes	2000	
4.6	Telephone service charges	Yes	2000	
4.7	Office supplies, maintenance materials	Yes	400	
V.	**Fixed out selling expenses**		**84464**	
5.1	Salaries of sales staff	Not	36000	
5.2	Expenditure on social protection	Not	14400	
5.3	Depreciation of fixed assets	Not	5600	
5.4	Expenditure on inventory items	Yes	12000	
5.5	Thermic energy for heating	Yes	5400	
5.6	Telephone service charges	Yes	8200	
5.7	Office supplies, maintenance materials	Yes	2864	
Total indirect production costs			**307200**	

Expenditure Sales Budget refers to the planning of sales and distribution costs. Costs are grouped into variables and fixed ones, variables are changed according to sales volume (e.g. commissions, transport costs, suppliers, etc.) and the fixed ones remain constant (e.g. workers' wages, equipment depreciation in the marketing department, delegations, advertising).

Expenditure forecasts generally use three methods, namely: (1) percentage of sales or revenue (the percentage may be considered from the current situation or an average of the situation in the last months); (2) analytical method - takes into account the structure of costs (fixed, variable, semi-variable and their variation depending on sales or income); (3) the regression method (using the least squares method).

The financial statement of budget revenues brings together all operational budgets and other items in the financial budget that ultimately highlights the planned revenue of the economic entity.

Financial Budget

This budget includes the treasury budget and the budgeted cash flow situation. The Treasury Budget is a plan detailing the planned financial sources and their uses and also comprises five sections, namely: (1) cash available, (2) cash consumptions - payments, (3) excess or insufficiency of cash, (4) financing and (5) cash balance.

The *Available Cash Section* refers to the initial cash at the beginning of the plan period plus the expected cash to be obtained from sales. Since not the entire amount is instantly collected from sales, many transactions being made through bank wire transfers over a certain contractual period, an important issue is the way receivables are collected. To predict, a certain percentage of sales may be used.

The *Spending Section* shows us the planned cash outflows. Comparing the required cash with available cash indicates the excess/cash deficit. Depending on the policy of the economic entity, the minimum amount of cash that must exist in the bank accounts and the cashier is determined. If there is a positive difference, other payments such as credit, interest and investment rates may also be made, and if the resulting difference is negative, other sources of funding (e.g. short-term loans) should be found.

The *Finance Section* includes the loans made and the payment rates.

The *Cash Balance* shows the cash at the end of the budget period.

The *Budgeted Cash Flow Situation* uses the components of the treasury budget and investment budget.

Future projections of the economic entity are based on historical data and also calculated and planned financial data. The steps used in these projections are as follows:

Step 1: Correcting the operating profit from sales by the difference between direct and indirect costs is done through amortization and provisions.

Step 2: Corrected profit in step 1 is corrected again with the change in working capital requirement, i.e. current inventories, receivables and payables.

Step 3: The cash flow from financing is obtained by subtracting other contractual obligations or mandatory payments, such as: financial debt - loan rates, interest, lease rates, taxes and fees.

Step 4: The cash flow from the investment is obtained by subtracting the investments and purchases of equipment or other property from which amortization, capitalized interest and dividends have decreased.

Step 5: The cash flow at the end of the planned period is obtained by adding cash from the beginning of the period.

Any important action of the manager regarding the activity of the economic entity must be preceded by the drafting of the revenue and expenditure budget and the budgeted cash flow.

Planned-Budgeted Balance Sheet

The forecasted data in the cash budget and in the revenue budget are the basis for the financial statement preparation. The committed capital is taken from the historical situation plus the sources of the investments, taking into account the reapproval of the profit, whether dividends are paid or not, and whether or not the profit is retained for reserves.

The Revenue and Expenditure Budget is intended to control the entire business entity's activity by forecasting and tracking expenditures that can be covered by income or other sources, highlighting the funding possibilities of the entity's expenses. The budget is limited to the expenses required to earn revenue. The balance sheet of the economic entity is presented in Table 13.

The Investments Planned for 2018

In March 2018, equipment worth 108000.00 euro excluding VAT, 19% VAT will be purchased and put into operation? The supplier's payment is made in the following month. The normal service life is 6 years. The machine will replace an old one fully depreciated worth 50000.00 euros.

Sources of Financing

In the long run, a bank loan of 60000.00 euro can be repaid in five years at constant rates, payment of interest rates and interest at the end of each year. The depreciation plan is presented in Table 14.

Table 13. Balance sheet of the economic entity at 31.12.2017 (euro)

No.	Assets	Gross Amounts	Depreciation and Provisions	Net Amounts	No.	Liabilities	Amounts
1	Fixed assets	800000		320000	1.	Personal capital	**702840**
2	Current assets	**624840**		**624840**	1.1	Social capital	600000
2.1	Raw materials	152000		152000	1.2	Reserves	102840
2.2	Packing	16000		16000	1.3	The result of the exercise	
2.3	Finished product	372840		372840	2.	Debts	**242000**
2.4	Customers	80000		80000	2.1	Bank loans on medium term	
2.5	Availability	4000	480000				
				4000	2.2	Providers	80000
					2.3	Tax	26000
					2.4	VAT on payment	32000
					2.5	Debts to salaries budget	12000
					2.6	Payment Dividends	8000
					2.7	Short term bank loans	84000
	Total assets	**3924200**	**480000**	**944840**		**Total liabilities**	**944840**

Table 14. Credit depreciation plan

Explanations	Year 1 (2019)	Year 2 (2020)	Year 3 (2021)	Year 4 (2022)	Year 5 (2023)
Payment	12000	12000	12000	12000	12000
Capital	60000	48000	36000	24000	12000
Interest	3600	2880	2160	1440	720
Annuity	63600	50880	38160	25440	12720

For our application we consider that the loan is on 01.03.2018. Interest expense will be 3600:12 = 300 euros per month. In the short term, the entity has a credit line with a maximum limit of 50,000 euros for which interest is 15% per year. To adjust your treasury budget, we shall use the pay-out effects for which the discount rate is 12%. The tax rates owed by the company to the state budget are as follows: 19% VAT rate; profit tax rate 16%; share of the 5% dividend tax. The profit tax on the balance sheet is payable in April 2018. For the year 2018, the following anticipated amounts are paid to the profit tax account (Table 15). Table 16 presents the profit and loss account as at 30 June 2018 and Table 17 presents the depreciation plan for property, plant and equipment.

Budget of Investments

Each year, the economic entity also compiles the investment budget when forecasting the budget for the following year, since the creation and growth of an entity's value is not possible without investment. In this regard, the following are considered in the investment decision making process: the investment opportunity, the choice of the investment objective or project, the financing of the investment project.

In the process of making the investment decision it is necessary to take two steps, namely:

Step 1: Verifying the proposed investment is feasible by evaluating and selecting projects based on the following: Verifying the project's classification in the management strategy; assessing the cash flow generated by the investment project implementation by applying the most appropriate cost of capital as a discount or discount rate; the period of obtaining the profit and covering the cost of the investment; illustrating restrictions and assumptions; consideration of opportunity costs.

Step 2: Identifying the source and mode of financing the investment project. The investment decision is based on the following: (1) the geographical location (location); (2) environmental protection standards; (3) calculation of investment valuation indicators (repayment period, accounting profitability, net present value, internal rate of return, cost-benefit ratio, etc.); (4) social aspects (the attitude of the population); (5) risks associated with the investment (construction, handling, operating risk, country risk, market risk, foreign exchange risk, documentary risk, force majeure, etc.).

Table 15. Profit tax payments

Explanations	March 2018	June 2018	September 2018	December 2018
Payments to the profit tax account	10000	10000	10000	10000

Table 16. Profit and loss account at 30.06.2018

Nr. post	Explanations	Cumulative Amounts	Budget Source
	Income from the sale of finished products	5103600	B. Sales
	Income from stored production - destowage	9812	B. Production
	Final stock value - initial stock value		
a.	**Total revenue**	**5113412**	
	Expenditure on raw materials and packaging	2435040	B. Supply
	Direct labour including social protection	481320	B. Labour
	Fixed indirect production costs	570240	B. B. direct costs
	Variable production costs	45840	B. direct costs
	Half-variable costs	186528	B. direct costs
	General administrative expenses	532800	B. direct costs
	Fixed out selling expenses	506784	B. direct costs
	Expenses with depreciation of new entrants	18000	Budget investments
	Financial expenses, of which:		
	- medium-term interest rates	4800	Loan Plan
	- Expenses with discounts granted	308	B. treasury
b.	**Total current expenses**	**4781660**	
c.	**Gross result**	**331752**	
d.	**Tax**	**82936**	
e.	**Net result**	**248816**	

Table 17. Profit and loss account at 30.06.2018

Explanations	Values to be Assigned	Month						Total euro
		January	February	March	April	May	June	
Depreciation of old equipment	13600	13600	13600	13600	13600	13600	13600	81600
Depreciation of new section equipment	6000	0	0	0	6000	6000	6000	18000
Total of which:		13600	13600	13600	19600	19600	19600	99600
Depreciation of buildings and section machinery		4000	4000	4000	10000	10000	10000	42000
Depreciation of buildings and other fixed assets of general interest		4000	4000	4000	4000	4000	4000	24000
Depreciation of fixed assets		5600	5600	5600	5600	5600	5600	33600

Investments are not only in fixed assets, but also in current assets, for example in financial securities that bring a relatively rapid flow of liquidity. Also, managers in investment decision-making should take into account inflation, interest rate, exchange rate, stock market, uncertainty and risk. After designing all these budgets, the correlation between them must be checked, principally the cash flow associated with the investment proposal and the attractiveness of the cash flows compared to the cost of the proceeds. The investment budget of the analysed economic entity is presented in Table 18.

SOLUTIONS AND RECOMMENDATIONS

The major challenge for today's governments is to achieve a durable and sustainable development of the business environment, both nationally and internationally. In light of this, national and sub-national actors such as the Government, the Parliament and the territorial administrative units should play a pro-active role in addressing the sustainability and sustainability of the business environment. This should be debated at Senate Budget-Finance Commission to expand the fiscal space from the point of view of green planning and budgeting, as well as controlling. Also, in the context of increasing vulnerabilities due to resource depletion and climate change, institutional frameworks need to be strengthened to respond globally and locally to environmental challenges. Government is the body that will need to create the financial framework and strengthen it in terms of public spending taking into account the priorities and potential for sustainable and sustainable development of the Romanian business environment.

The concept of "green budgeting" is a specific instrument involving both the preparation of internal budgets of economic entities and an annual budget (state budget). Preparing green budget statements may be an opportunity to encourage proactive thinking among government departments on the sustainability and sustainability of the business environment. In order to put this concept into practice, cost-effective methods must be identified to make this option attractive for managers of economic entities.

Table 18. Investment budget

Explanations	Values to be Assigned	The Purchase Month	January	February	March	April	May	June	Total euro
Value of the investment excluding VAT		March 2018	0	0	432000	0	0	0	432000
VAT on investment		0	0	0	86400	0	0	0	86400
Total payments to asset providers	April 2018	0	0	0	0	518400	0	0	518400
Sources of financing for the bank loan	60000.00 euro	0	0	0	60000	0	0	0	0
Own sources	48000.00 euro	0	0	0	0	48000	0	0	0
Runtime in months	72	0	0	0	0	0	0	0	0
Deprecation of new equipment	Euro/ month	6000	0	0	0	6000	6000	6000	18000

FUTURE RESEARCH DIRECTIONS

We believe that the objectives set at the beginning of the chapter are achieved by presenting in both the synthesis and in detail the empirical study, the strategic planning, budgeting and control/controlling processes, the principles underlying the budgeting process and the elaboration of the budgeting process and conducting controlling at an economic entity in the manufacturing sector. The theme is considerably broad, which is why it can be deepened by going to modern budgeting methods that combine several types of budgets or methods, such as ABB, ABC, ABM (Căpuşneanu et al., 2011, Man et al., 2014, Topor et al., 2017) and continue with program budgeting, respectively budgeting on performance. Therefore, interested specialists can focus on topics centred on:

- "Output Budgeting:" Focusing on expenditure items.
- Budgeting on Performance: Focusing on the results obtained.
- Deepening Controlling Issues.
- Analysis of the impact of managerial decisions resulting from the application of the two methods.
- The possibility of creating new performance measurement tools based on the two proposed methods.

CONCLUSION

In conclusion, it can be said that there are no prescriptive solutions about the most appropriate organizational structure of an economic entity, there is no predefined optimal planning and budgetary framework and there is no standardized form of effective control. But one thing is certain: economic entities can achieve performance if they have a well-defined organizational structure, if performance standards are known by all committed staff and last, but not least, if there is an adequate control framework and assimilated by all staff of that economic entity.

The budgeting process contributes to improving the efficiency of the business as it implies the following: (1) careful planning activity and providing a flow of useful information for the management of the entity; (2) the participation of management and workers; (3) coordination and cooperation; (4) the existence of an effective accounting system; (5) detecting trends and deficiencies as early as possible to implement corrections; (6) delegation of authority; clearer division of tasks into posts; (7) control by responsibilities; (8) application of the exception management method; (9) the existence of an appropriate assessment system necessary for the comparison of the entity, the reporting of budgetary provisions and achievements; (10) ensuring effective communication; (11) adoption by the manager of remedies to remedy irregularities.

For the budgeting activity to be truly effective, it must be forgotten that it is just a forecasting process. Once approved, the budget *becomes law*, it must be tracked during its execution and, if necessary, modified depending on the changes made in relation to the initial assumptions. The manager will look at the evolution of the following behavioural factors: (1) if left to accentuate and multiply, people's problems can become the main cause of failure to meet budget targets; (2) if the employees understand the purpose of the budget, they will participate in its elaboration, to make their opinions (more reasonable budgets) more accurate and realistic.

REFERENCES

Afonso, A., Schuknecht, L., & Tanzi, V. (2008). *Income Distribution Determinants and Public Spending Efficiency,* ECB Working Paper no. 861.

Albu, N., & Albu, C. (2003). Instrumente de management al performanţei: Vol. 2. Control de gestiune. Economica Publishing.

Anthony, R. (1965). Planning and Control Systems: A Framework for Analysis, Division of Research. Harvard Business School.

Anthony, R., & Govindarajan, V. (2007). *Management Control Systems.* Chicago: Mc-GrawHill Irwin.

Botnari, N., & Nedelcu, A. (2015). Evaluarea performanţei financiare a întreprinderilor industriale prin prisma dimensiunilor de profitabilitate, rentabilitate şi creştere. *Economica, 3*(93), 49–59.

Bouquin, H. (2004). *Contabilitate de gestiune.* Iaşi: TipoMoldova Publishing.

Bouquin, H. (2006). *Comptabilité de gestion* (3rd ed.). Paris: Economia.

Bouquin, H. (2008). *Contrôle de gestion.* Paris: Presses Universitaires de France.

Briciu, S., Căpuşneanu, S., Rof, L. M., & Topor, D. (2010). *Accounting and management control. Tools for performance evaluation entity.* Alba Iulia: Aeternitas Publishing.

Burlaud, A., & Simon, C. (2003). Comptabilité de Gestion. Vuibert.

Căpuşneanu, S. (2006). *Contabilitate de gestiune. Studii aplicative şi teste-grilă.* Bucharest: Economică Publishing.

Caraiani, C., & Dumitrana, M. (n.d.). *Contabilitate de gestiune & Control de gestiune.* Bucuresti: Ed. InfoMega.

Casian, A. (2013). *Dezvoltarea sistemului de audit intern în instituţiile publice din Republica Moldova. In 60 de ani de învăţămînt economic superior în Republica Moldova prin inovare şi competitivitate spre progres economic. Materialele conferinţei ştiinţifice internaţionale* (pp. 35–38). Chişinău: ASEM.

Ciubotaru, M., & Hîncu, V. (2015). Evaluarea performanţelor bugetare din perspectiva ajustării managementului finanţelor publice din Republica Moldova la principiile europene. In *Rolul investiţiilor în asigurarea dezvoltării economice durabile în contextul integrării europene. Materialele conferinţei ştiinţifice internaţionale* (pp. 28–36). Chişinău: ASEM.

Diamond, J. (2006). *Budget System Reform in Emerging Economies: The Challenges and the Reform Agenda.* International Monetary Fund. Retrieved from https://www.imf.org/External/Pubs/ NFT/op/245/ op245.pdf

Dobrin, C., & Badea, F. (2006). *Gestiunea bugetară a sistemelor de producţie.* Bucharest: Economică Publishing.

Dragomirescu, S. (2008). *Controlul de gestiune - coordonator al organizaţiilor descentralizate. Volumul "Convergenţa economică şi rolul cunoaşterii în condiţiile integrării în Uniunea Europeană, Universităţii "Alexandru Ioan Cuza"*. Iaşi: Publishing.

Dragomirescu, S. (2010). *Controlul de gestiune în economia modern* (Doctoral thesis). Iaşi.

Kerzner, H. (2001). *Project Management; Systems Approach to Planning, Scheduling and Controlling*. New York: John Wesley and Sons.

Man, M., & Rakoş, I.-S. (2015). Cost-Based Budgeting - A Relevant Instrument for the Improvement of Mining Companies' Performances. *Proceedings of the 25th IBIMA Conference*, 2444-2458.

Olson, O., Guthrie, J., & Humphrey, C. (1998). *Growing Accustomed to Other Faces: The Global Themes and Warnings of Our Project*. Osaka: Second Asian Pacific Interdisciplinary Research in Accounting Conference.

Robinson, M. (2007). *Performance Budgeting Models and Mechanisms*. Retrieved from http://www.focusintl.com/RBM137-0230553567.pdf

Simionescu, M. (2015). *Analiza financiară a afacerii*. Retrieved from http://cantemir.ro/cursuriudc/1sem1/Master/

Stratulat, O. (2002). Principii de optimizare a cheltuielilor pe verigile sistemului bugetar. In Simpossia Professorum. Chişinău: ULIM.

Tabără, N. (2009). *Control de gestiune-delimitări conceptuale, metode, aplicaţii*. Iaşi: Editura Tipo Moldova.

Tanzi, V. (1974). Redistributing Income through the Budget in Latin America. *Quarterly Review. Indexes - Banca Nazionale del Lavoro*, *27*(108), 65–87.

Veveriță, E. (2013). Bugetarea pe programe în cadrul Ministerului Economiei şi Ministerului Agriculturii și Industriei Alimentare. *Chișinău: Centrul analitic independent "Expert-Grup"*, 23.

Wagner, A. (1883). Finanzwissenschaft. *Erst Thail, Leipzig*, *1883*, 221.

ADDITIONAL READING

Căpuşneanu, S., Topor, D., & Rof, L. M. (2011). General implementation stages of the ABC method in the Small and Medium-Sized Enterprises", International Journal of Academic Research in Accounting. *Finance and Management Sciences*, *1*(1), 43–50.

Topor, D. I., Căpuşneanu, S., Constantin, D. M., Barbu, C. M., & Rakos, I. S. (2017). ABB-ABC-ABE-ABM Approach for Implementation in the Economic Entities from Energy Industry. *Business and Management Horizons*, *5*(2), 36–48. doi:10.5296/bmh.v5i2.12169

KEY TERMS AND DEFINITIONS

Assessment: A periodic assessment of effectiveness, efficiency, impact, sustainability and relevance in the context of the stated objectives.

Effect: Intentional change or not due directly or indirectly to an intervention.

Effectiveness: The extent to which the objectives of an intervention have been or are expected to be achieved taking into account their importance.

Efficiency: A measure of the economic way in which resources/contributions (funds, expertise, time, etc.) are transformed into effects or outcomes.

Interested Stakeholders: All those who are interested (directly or indirectly) by an institution, its activities, and achievements. These may include clients, partners, employees, shareholders/owners, government, or regulatory bodies.

Intermediate Goal/Milestone: An activity used to identify significant events in a program, such as completing a major milestone. An activity indicated or highlighted as regards special monitoring of progress or completion.

Monitoring: A continuous function that uses the systematic collection of data with reference to the specified indicators to provide management and the main stakeholders interested in an ongoing intervention, indications of the extent to which the objectives are met and the use of the allocated funds.

Objective: A general statement of what will be done and of the improvements to be made. An objective describes an expected result or impact and summarizes the reasons why a number of actions have been taken.

Sustainability: Continuing the benefits of an intervention after it is completed. The likelihood of continued long-term benefits. The risk resistance of the net benefits over time.

Chapter 4
The Informational Value of the Profit and Loss Account in Line With International Accounting Standards

Traian Ovidiu Calotă
Titu Maiorescu University, Romania

Sorin-Adrian Robu
The Bucharest University of Economic Studies, Romania

Ionica Oncioiu
Titu Maiorescu University, Romania

Georgiana Burlacu
Valahia University, Romania

ABSTRACT

In the context of the monitoring of businesses through accounting, the profit and loss account is the component that reflects the performance of the enterprise, that is, the extent to which it has achieved its objectives in terms of profit. In the income statement, there are flows that determine the result, understood in principle as a variation in equity during a financial period. Defining the performance of an enterprise is different, depending on the interest of the users, on the principles, conventions, and accounting rules used to determine the outcome. This is what specialists in the field call accounting policies. This chapter examines the profit and loss statement in the context of scarce and expensive resources, which must be used efficiently. The results show that it is necessary for companies to determine efficiency indicators by comparing the effects obtained with the efforts and the resources consumed by the company and operated by the management.

DOI: 10.4018/978-1-7998-0178-8.ch004

INTRODUCTION

The main objective of any economic activity is considered to be the «performance», and this objective has proven to be quite difficult in regards of finding an example for it (Caylor, 2010). Recent studies have shown that in the financial information market, the "most" popular product is the profit and loss account because it shows whether or not the enterprise has achieved its basic objective of achieving an acceptable return (He et al., 2017; Hou et al., 2015). Undertakings have the possibility to add to the profit and loss account other items, rows, titles and subtotals when an International Accounting Standard requires it or when such a presentation is required for a true presentation of the financial results of the enterprise. The criteria to be respected in this case are the materiality threshold and the nature and function of the different components of income and expenditure.

In the context of the expansion of transnational companies, users of financial information are interested in the performance of the enterprise determined not on the basis of the accounting result but of the economic result (Jackson & Liu, 2010). This latter indicator cannot be accounted for by the profit and loss account because it has a more comprehensive structure than the accounting result, including items that do not translate through the profit and loss account. Users of financial information are interested in information that the profit and loss account cannot provide (Dennis, 2014). In order to meet their informational needs, decision-makers need to turn to new sources of information. That is why the accountancy profession is called upon to create new tools to remove the information limits of the financial statements. The statement of changes in equity and the cash flow statement are the "new products" of the accounting offer (Ball, 2013). The statement of economic outturn should include the effects of all transactions and events occurring during the year, whether or not related to current operations, and which have an impact on equity (excluding shareholder or associate and distributor contributions). Also, gains or losses accounted for during the year, realized or unrealized, exceptional or extraordinary, participate in the performance of the enterprise and should therefore be included in the statement of comprehensive income.

On the other hand, given that companies can choose their accounting policies within certain limits, the results obtained reflect their objectives and not the reality. In this situation, is the outcome credible and relevant? The objectives of accounting policies differ according to the size of the enterprise and the economic environment in which it operates (Ahrens, 2008). As an example, it is possible to mention the reduction of the published losses, the decrease of the taxable profit, the increase or decrease of the current result, the increase or the decrease of the profit to be distributed, the temporary arrangement of the accounting results in order to reduce the risk perceived by the financial environment.

Many of the reported deficiencies were corrected during the reform (Barth et al., 2008; Cahan & Sun, 2015; Lukka, 2010). Moreover, the principle "nothing is perfect, everything is perfect" also works in accounting. In our opinion, any accounting system, however modern, converging with International Financial Reporting Standards, will never be perfect, because the world economy and, implicitly, the national economy is constantly changing (Richardson, 2011). New trends, new informational needs are emerging, and they pose a challenge to the accounting system and an invitation to reflection for accountants (Chen et al., 2017). The present chapter intends to identify the construct of a set of factors that influence the Profit and Loss Statement in the context of scarce and expensive resources.

This chapter is structured in the following way: in the first section, the authors will introduce a radiography of the current situation regarding the profit and loss account in accordance with the Internation

Accounting Standard; in the second section, research methodology will be discussed; in the third section, the results of the study will be discussed; finally, the authors will argue the conclusions and will presented this paper's limitation.

BACKGROUND

Given the recent history of scandals involving accounting conduct, the credibility of the public accounting profession has dropped significantly, losing one of the core responsibilities of the professional accountant (Doukakis, 2014). More recent research in the field suggests that there is a growing interest in studying the ethical conduct of professional accountants (Li et al., 2017). Moreover, since the 1980s, several institutions have encouraged education in accounting ethics, and today it has come to the fact that it has been present in schools since the beginning of the accounting profession (Alzola, 2017). However, the accounting scandals that took place in the 2000s prove that greater emphasis is needed on the Profit and Loss Statement, but also on improving the codes of ethics (Bettner & Kate, 2013). Thus, it is noted that, despite the increased interest in this issue, there are certain deficiencies in the principles, virtues, values and rules that undermine the credibility of the accounting profession.

As the economy develops, the main interest point, performance-wise, shifts from revenue towards the profit described in the Profit and Loss Statement (Brown, 2010). This reflects the value fluxes that interacted with the increase or decrease of the wealth of the company at a certain period of time. So, the profit and loss statement highlighted the success of a company required for its survivability, or its failure to stay on the market.

As the financial markets are in continuous expansion, investors are becoming the privileged receivers of the financial information (Holthausen & Watts, 2001). In our opinion, in this case, the profit and loss statement becomes the main tool because it provides all the required information for the past and future performance evaluation, and also for the determination of the future cash flow risks. Also, based on the information reflected by the profit and loss statement, a pertinent analysis is created for the company's performance, a verity of indicators are calculated, either in a specific moment in time, followed by their interpretation trough comparisons, either throughout a longer period of time, but correlated with certain statistic procedures.

In continental accounting, the steps of finding the result of the exercise are in close connection with the company's revenue and cost structure, while the Administrative Intermediary Balances are calculated (Li, 2010). These indicators allow comparisons throughout time in the same company or between companies. The Administrative Intermediary Balances start from the idea believing that a company is a place of turning goods into other goods, entries in exits. These transformations are done by using production factors, labor, public capital (goods and collective services), financial capital without risk and financial capital with risk. The appreciation over informational risk depends on the skills of the individuals in charge of the processes to assess the informational impact on the financial statement, on the company's performance (Schleicher et al., 2010). In consequence, the analysis of the communication system and the dialogue frequency stand for a variable that can be used in appreciating the informational risk level, as the communication frequency is inversely proportionate to the risk level.

Accounting principles are another risk-generating element when we refer to their accidental or willful misuse. We continue to present a number of risks associated with the misapplication of accounting principles, namely: the risk of under-valuation of assets or expenses or over-valuation of equity and debt;

the risk of misreporting the financial position or economic performance of entities; the risk of evaluating financial results that does not provide a true picture; the risk of fallacious recognition of their balance sheets and evaluation; the risk of transferring uncertainties in another financial year; the risk of showing a low or increased performance by practicing creative accounting; the risk of providing accounting information that does not meet the qualitative characteristics (Chen et al., 2017).

From an accounting point of view, accounting risks may be risks associated with financial accounting, risks associated with managerial or management accounting, risks associated with the budgetary process, or risks associated with the measurement of financial performance.

Special attention is also given to the IASB because "information on an enterprise's performance, especially its profitability, is necessary to assess potential changes in the economic resources that the enterprise will be able to control in the future [...] which are useful in assessing the firm's ability to generate existing cash flows [...] and to formulate judgments about the efficiency with which the enterprise can use new resources " (Parker, 2012).

When preparing the financial statements, the management of the enterprise should analyze the firm's ability to continue its business. Financial statements must be prepared on a going concern basis, unless the management either intends to liquidate the enterprise or ceases business, or has no realistic alternative but to do so (Ramanna, 2008). If there is uncertainty about the business going on, it must be highlighted. Cases where the financial statements are not drawn up on the basis of accrual accounting must be highlighted alongside the basis on which they are prepared and the reason why the enterprise can no longer continue its business.

Potential risks associated with the organization and operation of the accounting department relate to the lack of clear responsibilities regarding the process of recording operations or keeping the accounting registers, non-updating of the data, the presence of errors, the absence of procedures or accounting policies, the absence of accounting monographs, documentary evidence for each accounting record, lack of periodic inventory of accounts, failure to separate the duties of persons in charge of debt and debt records, existence of tax calculation errors, non-provisioning where necessary, absence of internal control procedures, the access of too many users to the IT system, the lack of regular staff training, etc.

As a managerial process, financial-accounting risk management should be based on identifying, analyzing, evaluating and defining management, monitoring, review and communication procedures. According to Alzola (2017), the main risk management strategies refer to: emergency strategies for risks that may have significant but low-probability consequences and which aim at mitigating the consequences of risks to an acceptable level; preventive strategies, applicable to risks that have an increased production likelihood but relatively low impact; monitoring strategies aimed at ensuring the functioning of safety standards and addressing risks with low probability of occurrence and low impact; mixed strategies that consist of various combinations of previous strategies.

The flexibility of the provisions of the Fourth ECE Directive, concretized through the four models of presentation, as well as the possibility of choosing them by companies, is the expression of the conciliation of cultural differences between the countries of the European Union (Barth et al., 2014). French companies prefer the presentation of the profit and loss account in the form of an account, with the classification of expenses and incomes by nature, while Anglo-Saxon companies interested in meeting the information needs of investors prefer the drafting of the profit and loss account with the classification expenditure by function.

RESEARCH METHODOLOGY

In order to achieve the research objective, we resorted to the conceptual analysis of reviewing the purposes of the Profit and Loss Statement in line with the International Accounting Standards, as well as to its quantitative assessment. This analysis is based on the information discovered following the documentation process, by means of comparative research methods and critical analysis, supported by professional reasoning. We also analyzed, during the conceptual and empirical incursions, along with the risk related to socio-human factors (for example, communication process, formal and informal environment, human behavior), technical elements related to the Profit and Loss Statement.

The IASB's general framework provides for the preparation of the (profit and loss) account under the accrual accounting and consequently the release of cash flows through this document can only be achieved by processing the information contained therein, i.e. converting revenue and expenditure into receipts and payments (Barth, 2013). Financial statements prepared on the basis of accrual accounting respond to the information needs of users by providing information "not only about past transactions that generated revenue and payments, but also about future payment obligations and resources on future receipts and payments" (Byard et al., 2011).

The disclosure of US economic results is treated by the American Accounting Standard FAS 130 "Reporting Comprehensive Income" issued by FASB in June 1997. This accounting rule is opposed to all US companies preparing financial statements, except for those that do not have items that do not translate into the profit and loss account and therefore have a direct impact on equity (Baker & Bettner, 1997). Under this rule, items that do not transit through the profit account, but have a direct impact on equity, need to be detailed in a financial statement of similar importance to the others. The cumulative balance of these items should be presented in a separate line of equity, reflected in the balance sheet.

In order to avoid the double counting of elements (included both in the net result and in the economic outturn), FAS 130 allows some adjustments to the overall result of the last financial year (reclassification adjustments), such as adjustment of the economic outturn of the last financial year with the earnings on other investment titles that were included in the net result of the current exercise, but also with the other items of economic result in the form of dormant earnings during the year in which they were ascertained (Allen & Ramanna, 2013). Such adjustments may be presented in the financial statement of the financial result or in the notes.

According to the documentation made, the adoption of the Fourth Directive by the Member States of the European Union generated an abundance of profit and loss account models (Table 1). In countries like Belgium, France, Italy, Portugal and Spain, it is illegal for companies to publish their profit and loss accounts in a list format with the classification of expenses by function. Even among the countries that allow the use of the four models, there are different variants of their use. The UK has adopted all four models for the presentation of the profit and loss account. UK companies may opt to present the profit and loss account using a cost analysis either by function (costs are broken down into costs of sales, sales and administrative expenses), either vertically or horizontally or by nature (expenses materials, wage costs, external costs, depreciation costs) in a vertical or horizontal format. However, most accountants are not familiar with the profit and loss account model, vertically and horizontally, with the classification of expenditure by nature.

Looking at Table 1, we wonder why there are so many European countries that prefer to model their profit and loss account with their vertical or horizontal format analysis for their business companies.

Table 1. Models of profit and loss accounts throughout European states

	Function wise		Nature-wise	
	Vertical	Horizontally	Vertical	Horizontally
Austria	⑨	x	⑨	x
Belgium	x	x	⑨	⑨
Denmark	⑨	⑨	⑨	⑨
Finland	⑨	x	⑨	x
France	x	x	⑨	⑨
Germany	⑨	x	⑨	x
Greece	⑨	x	x	x
Ireland	⑨	⑨	⑨	⑨
Italy	x	x	⑨	x
Luxemburg	⑨	⑨	⑨	⑨
United Kingdom	⑨	⑨	⑨	⑨
Holland	⑨	⑨	⑨	⑨
Portugal	x	x	x	⑨
Spain	x	x	x	⑨
Sweden	⑨	x	⑨	x

⑨ Allowed by national laws x Banned

A first argument can be a historical accident. German influence has been reflected in French accounting since the Second World War by introducing an accounting plan. Subsequently, France influenced the development of the accounting plans in Belgium, Spain and Portugal.

The second argument concerns the simplicity and transparency of the "by nature" format, although it is more detailed than the "by function" format (Andon et al., 2007). The format "by nature" only requires the analysis of operating expenses, such as material expenses, external expenses, labor costs, and depreciation expenses. For companies having an object of activity, it is not necessary to use a method of allocating indirect costs. The transparency of this format is due to the fact that there are no internal company decisions to be made on the basis of the accounting data and the policies used to calculate the cost of sales and the gross margin (for example, the choice of the depreciation method). Most countries requesting a "by nature" presentation also have account plans (Chen et al., 2010). Their role is to require commercial companies to maintain account balances in accordance with the national accounts plan.

The tax authorities in those countries may use the profit and loss account as a starting point for the valuation of the liabilities tax on the idea that the link to the balance symbols is transparent (Damayant, 2013). Perhaps the most relevant argument in favor of using a "by-nature" format is that this model provides the information needed to compile macroeconomic statistics. For example, in France, where the state has always been involved in business, a privileged user of financial information justifies the choice of "by nature" format. By imposing this format, the state can obtain comparable information on the added value of all enterprises that aggregate gross domestic product and other derived statistical information.

In Romania, the classification of information in the profit and loss account was based on the criteria of the nature and heterogeneity of the economic and financial transactions carried out by the enterprise (Florou & Pope, 2012). The accounting reform, started after 1990, materialized in the Accounting Law no.82 / 1991 and the Implementing Regulation approved by H.G. no. 704/1993 introduces a profit and loss account, mainly inspired by the Fourth Directive of the European Economic Communities presented in a list form, with the structure of revenues and expenses by nature. This important evolutionary step was carried out in a context that had not existed until then, namely the transition from the model of the super-centralized economy of the communist type to the market economy. This explains the appearance of controversy over the fairness of the chosen model, but in our opinion, this variation corresponded to the informational needs of the main recipient, at that time, the state.

Regulations approved by O.M.F.P. no. 3055/2009 represented a reference point since they reflected the "accounting point of view" of the Romanian economy, in the new context in which Romania is a full member of the EU, but also with the obligation of full integration into this community, which implied, among others, the continuation of the process of implementing and applying the communal regulations. It also took into account the impact of the international regulations inherent in the globalization process, which, in the case of the consolidated financial statements, included the option to draw them up, according to the Regulations in line with EEC Directive VII - based on the International Financial Reporting Standards (IFRS).

As it can be seen from the comparative analysis performed, along with the accounting practices, management decisions also have a main purpose to present a different image of the result, but without changing the business situation (Soltani, 2014). The elastic nature of the outcome limits the informational value of the profit and loss account, which sometimes can be misleading. A profitable business is not necessarily an enterprise that has liquidity. Behind profitability, it hides serious treasury issues.

The profit and loss account provides information on the financial flows recorded by the enterprise at the end of the financial year in the form of profit and loss. From this explanation, one can deduced that cash profits also flow through the profit account. The answer is affirmative, in the conditions of a cash accounting, and negative, if an accrual accounting is practiced.

SOLUTIONS AND RECOMMENDATIONS

In support of the major impact that these regulations had in the respective stage of the accounting evolution, we propose the following solutions:

- A better delimitation of the financial statements of the entities according to the fulfillment of certain size criteria.
- The express statement of the treatment of accounting errors on the profit and loss account in the case of errors related to the current exercise, namely, on the basis of the retained earnings for errors made in previous years.
- Introducing a new section that provides users with general purpose financial statements and their informative needs, specifying the four main qualitative characteristics of the annual financial statements (intelligibility, relevance, credibility and comparability).

FUTURE RESEARCH DIRECTIONS

Through the goals set, this chapter has touched its target. The presented and analyzed issues are a synthesized part of the vast amount of information that has been developed by the authors to create the framework for underlining the importance of producing documents providing information in such a way that, regardless of the accounting model used, it is also useful for the quality of each user. Therefore, new directions of future research have been created, such as:

- Analyzing the impact of managerial decisions resulting from the adaptation of the accounting principles to other management methods.
- The assessment of the informational risk within a company can be made by assessing the reiterative frequencies of such events attesting the risk presence (for example, rectifying statements and reports).
- Analyzing the possibility of creating new tools for monitoring and measuring environmental performance/performance based on the principles of other managerial accounting methods or systems.

CONCLUSION

Controversies about the information reflected by the Profit and Loss Statement have been, and are still, generated by the difficulty of accurately determining the financial situation, as well as ethical and moral aspects related to the user-company relationship, the limit between research and accounting treatment, etc.

The freedom of choice of accounting policies by companies, which leads to an increase or a decrease in the result, is, in our opinion, one of the main information limits of the profit and loss account. We have also previously highlighted some creative accounting techniques, often in line with the laws and regulations in force, which we call the "accounting engineers". The valuation of output stocks, the capitalization of borrowing costs, the capitalization of post-commissioning expenses of tangible assets, the preferential choice of depreciation methods are just a few examples. Often used in times of crisis, we consider that these "blunts" of accounting results do not shade, cannot minimize the role and the informational value of the profit and loss account. This is because accounting engineering mitigates the company's difficult image, but not infinite.

Such an aspect is favored by the diversification and amplification of transnational transactions that are under the impact of different accounting and tax systems. Therefore, it is important to emphasize the importance of accelerating the process of fiscality and convergence at European level and ultimately at a global level, by adopting and applying a uniform standard.

Within this context, the management tends to omit in most of the cases that the contracting of accountancy services does not mean the outsourcing of risks for the beneficiary of such services. On the contrary, it may trigger new risks that must be taken into account. For example, the outsourcing of accounting services requires a concomitant understanding of the fact that they do not exempt the Board of directors/administrator from the liability of making sure that the services, once outsourced, are carried in a safe manner, in compliance with the current regulations, so that the risks be eliminated.

From an accounting point of view, unethical conduct can be masked fairly easily through creative accounting practices, in which professional accountants find accounting methods at the law limit so as to diminish the accounting result or present a more favoring outcome to the entity they belong to. However, in this case, the accounting approaches are law-based approaches. Thus, the question arises: are these practices evidence of ethical misconduct?

REFERENCES

Ahrens, T. (2008). Overcoming the subjective–objective divide in interpretive management accounting research. *Accounting, Organizations and Society, 33*(2), 292-297.

Allen, A., & Ramanna, K. (2013). Towards an understanding of the role of standard setters in standard setting. *Journal of Accounting and Economics, 55*(1), 1–66. doi:10.1016/j.jacceco.2012.05.003

Alzola, M. A. (2017). Beware of the watchdog: Rethinking the normative justification of gatekeeper liability. *Journal of Business Ethics, 140*(4), 705–721. doi:10.100710551-017-3460-3

Andon, P., Baxter, J., & Chua, W. F. (2007). Accounting change as relational drifting: A field study of experiments with performance measurement. *Management Accounting Research, 18*(2), 273–308. doi:10.1016/j.mar.2006.06.007

Baker, C., & Bettner, M. (1997). Interpretive and Critical Research in Accounting: A Commentary on its Absence from Mainstream Research||. *Critical Perspectives on Accounting, 8*(4), 293–310. doi:10.1006/cpac.1996.0116

Ball, R. (2013). Accounting informs investors and earnings management is rife: Two questionable beliefs. *Accounting Horizons, 27*(4), 847–853. doi:10.2308/acch-10366

Barth, M., Landsman, W., & Lang, M. (2008). International accounting standards and accounting quality. *Journal of Accounting Research, 46*(3), 467–498. doi:10.1111/j.1475-679X.2008.00287.x

Barth, M. E. (2013). Global comparability in financial reporting: What, why, how, and when? *China Journal of Accounting Studies, 1*(1), 2–12. doi:10.1080/21697221.2013.781765

Barth, M. E., Landsman, W. R., Young, D., & Zhuang, Z. (2014). Relevance of Differences between Net Income based on IFRS and Domestic Standards for European Firms. *Journal of Business Finance & Accounting, 41*(3-4), 297–506. doi:10.1111/jbfa.12067

Bettner, M., & Kate, K. (2013). Changes in annual reporting rituals of financial services firms in periods of market crisis. *International Journal of Critical Accounting, 5*(6), 577–593. doi:10.1504/IJCA.2013.059027

Brown, J. (2010). Accounting and visual cultural studies: Potentialities, challenges and prospects. *Accounting, Auditing & Accountability Journal, 23*(4), 482–505. doi:10.1108/09513571011041598

Byard, D., Li, Y., & Yu, Y. (2011). The effect of mandatory IFRS adoption on financial analysts' information environment. *Journal of Accounting Research, 49*(1), 69–96. doi:10.1111/j.1475-679X.2010.00390.x

Cahan, S. F., & Sun, J. (2015). The effect of audit experience on audit fees and audit quality. *Journal of Accounting, Auditing & Finance*, *30*(1), 78–100. doi:10.1177/0148558X14544503

Caylor, M. L. (2010). Strategic revenue recognition to achieve earnings benchmarks. *Journal of Accounting and Public Policy*, *29*(1), 82–95. doi:10.1016/j.jaccpubpol.2009.10.008

Chen, H., Tang, Q., Jiang, Y., & Lin, Z. (2010). The role of international financial reporting standards in accounting quality: Evidence from the European Union. *Journal of International Financial Management & Accounting*, *21*(3), 220–278. doi:10.1111/j.1467-646X.2010.01041.x

Chen, M., Qu, X., & Sun, X. (2017). Whose cost of equity capital reduces after IFRS convergence and why? Heterogeneity evidence from Chinese stock market. *China Journal of Accounting Studies*, *5*(1), 1–27. doi:10.1080/21697213.2017.1304539

Damayant, T. (2013). Who is afraid of Qualitative Research? A Compromise Accounting Research Failure in Improving Accounting Practices. *International Journal of Advances in Management and Economics*, *2*(2), 89-94.

Dennis, I. (2014). *The Nature of Accounting Regulation*. New York: Routledge.

Doukakis, L. C. (2014). The effect of mandatory IFRS adoption on real and accrual-based earnings management activities. *Journal of Accounting and Public Policy*, *33*(6), 551–572. doi:10.1016/j.jaccpubpol.2014.08.006

Florou, A., & Pope, P. (2012). Mandatory IFRS adoption and institutional investment decisions. *The Accounting Review*, *87*(6), 1993–2025. doi:10.2308/accr-50225

He, K., Pan, X., & Tian, G. (2017). Legal liability, government intervention, and auditor behavior: Evidence from structural reform of audit firms in China. *European Accounting Review*, *26*(1), 61–95. doi: 10.1080/09638180.2015.1100547

Holthausen, R. W., & Watts, R. L. (2001). The relevance of the value-relevance literature for financial accounting standard setting. *Journal of Accounting and Economics*, *31*(1-3), 3–75. doi:10.1016/S0165-4101(01)00029-5

Hou, Q., Jin, Q., Yang, R., Yuan, H., & Zhang, G. (2015). Performance commitments of controlling shareholders and earnings management. *Contemporary Accounting Research*, *32*(3), 1099–1127. doi:10.1111/1911-3846.12111

Jackson, S. B., & Liu, X. K. (2010). The allowance for uncollectible accounts, conservatism, and earnings management. *Journal of Accounting Research*, *48*(3), 565–601. doi:10.1111/j.1475-679X.2009.00364.x

Li, L., Qi, B., Tian, G., & Zhang, G. (2017). The contagion effect of low-quality audits at the level of individual auditors. *The Accounting Review*, *92*(1), 137–163. doi:10.2308/accr-51407

Li, S. (2010). Does mandatory adoption of international accounting standards in the European Union reduce the cost of equity capital? *The Accounting Review*, *85*(2), 607–636. doi:10.2308/accr.2010.85.2.607

Lukka, K. (2010). The roles and effects of paradigms in accounting research. *Management Accounting Research, 21*(2), 110–115. doi:10.1016/j.mar.2010.02.002

Parker, L. (2012). Qualitative management accounting research: Assessing deliverables and relevance. *Critical Perspectives on Accounting, 23*(1), 54–70. doi:10.1016/j.cpa.2011.06.002

Ramanna, K. (2008). The implications of unverifiable fair-value accounting: Evidence from the political economy of goodwill accounting. *Journal of Accounting and Economics, 45*(2-3), 253–281. doi:10.1016/j.jacceco.2007.11.006

Richardson, A. (2011). Myth, Paradigms and Academic Accounting Research: A Comment on Reading and Understanding Academic Research in Accounting. *Global Perspectives on Accounting Education, 8*, 67–77.

Schleicher, T., Tahoun, A., & Walker, M. (2010). IFRS adoption in Europe and investment-cash flow sensitivity: Outsider versus insider economies. *The International Journal of Accounting, 45*(2), 143–168. doi:10.1016/j.intacc.2010.04.007

Soltani, B. (2014). The anatomy of corporate fraud: A comparative analysis of high profile American and European corporate scandals. *Journal of Business Ethics, 120*(2), 251–274. doi:10.100710551-013-1660-z

ADDITIONAL READING

Ahmed, A., Neel, M., & Wang, D. (2013). Does mandatory adoption of IFRS improve accounting quality? Preliminary evidence. *Contemporary Accounting Research, 30*(4), 388–423. doi:10.1111/j.1911-3846.2012.01193.x

Ball, R., Li, X., & Shivakumar, L. (2015). Contractibility and transparency of financial statement information prepared under IFRS: Evidence from debt contracts around IFRS adoption. *Journal of Accounting Research, 53*(5), 915–963. doi:10.1111/1475-679X.12095

Fan, J. P. H., Li, J., & Zheng, G. (2016). Revisiting the bright and dark sides of capital flows in business groups. *Journal of Business Ethics, 134*(4), 509–528. doi:10.100710551-014-2382-6

Ozkan, N., Singer, Z., & You, H. (2012). Mandatory IFRS adoption and the contractual usefulness of accounting information in executive compensation. *Journal of Accounting Research, 50*(4), 1077–1107. doi:10.1111/j.1475-679X.2012.00453.x

KEY TERMS AND DEFINITIONS

Convergence of Accounting: The process by which accounting standards are developed in a manner that is able to lead to the same act or purpose, by showing the similarity of national, regional, international.

Cost: The money form of all material and labor expenses made by the company to produce and market material goods, execution works, and service works.

Decision: A person or group of persons' social and deliberate act defining the purpose and the objectives of a certain action, the directions and the ways to achieve that action, all of them determined, according to a certain need, by a process of obtaining information, deliberation, and assessment of the means and consequences of carrying out that action.

Economic Management: The achievement of the budget objectives with minimum costs so that when the activity is completed the revenue exceeds the costs, namely there is a profit that ensures a level of profitability as high as possible both at general level and by product, department, or service performed.

Financial Accounting Standards Board (FASB): Set up and develop generally accepted accounting principles.

Financial Management: A tool in the decision-making relating to the collection and analysis of information in order to increase the performance level of the economic entity.

Integrity: The prohibition amendment—by deleting or adding—or the unauthorized destruction of information; integrity refers to confidence in the data and resources of a system by which to manage information.

Chapter 5
Sustainability Reporting:
Stakeholders and Reporting of Sustainability Accounting Information

Dana Maria Constantin
University of Bucharest, Romania

Dan Ioan Topor
1 Decembrie 1918 University, Romania

Sorinel Căpușneanu
https://orcid.org/0000-0003-3799-3993
Titu Maiorescu University, Romania

Alexandru Manole
Artifex University, Romania

ABSTRACT

This chapter presents, in a descriptive manner, the interrelation of the sustainability reporting concepts and the sustainability disclosure through internal and external stakeholders. The main objectives of this chapter are approaching the disclosure of environmental information, presenting the views of the stakeholders on the content and format of environmental reporting. The factors underlying the disclosure of the environmental information and the impact of these, including the views stakeholders on the content and presentation format of the environmental reporting, are presented and analyzed. A case study is also presented in order to highlight the disclosure and presentation of the environmental report of an industrial entity and the importance of the accounting information provided. This chapter brings a theoretical contribution to expand the knowledge on the environmental disclosure and reporting approaches. The authors' approaches remain open to the expansion of these issues at both national and international level and both in the academia and business area.

DOI: 10.4018/978-1-7998-0178-8.ch005

INTRODUCTION

The *environmental and social accounting* researches have been replaced by the research on *sustainability reporting* (Sciulii, 2009). In these circumstances, accounting is no longer considered a mere technical practice, but a social and institutional practice (Miller, 1994) that involves and generates social and institutional pressures, determining entities to adopt certain measures and decisions on behalf of the legitimacy of these institutions (Hopwood & Miller, 1994). In the current business environment, the notion that no business is profitable and successful without the approval of stakeholders is considered a socially and ecologically responsible entity (Gray, 2010). The environmental information should help both the civil society and companies in knowing the environmental impact of the business decisions of the companies (Milne & Patten, 2001; Kuk et al., 2005). This information, especially provided through IT, helps the managers identifying the environmental risks, cost structure, and investment that their companies face. In order to meet and respect the environmental requirements of the International Organization for Standardization (ISO), the stakeholders considered that the most important way of communicating with the companies is through the accounting information provided by the annual report of the company (Fernando et al., 2010). Starting from the overall sustainability reporting framework, the concept of environmental reporting/sustainability reporting, sustainability disclosure, and stakeholders' views on the sustainability reporting are presented and analyzed. The main objectives of this chapter are: *(1) the evolutionary presentation of the concept of sustainability reporting and disclosure; (2) the presentation of the concept of stakeholders and their views on the content and format of the sustainability reporting; and (3) the presentation of a case study related to the sustainability reporting of an economic entity in the industrial field as required by the stakeholders.*

THE SUSTAINABILITY REPORTING AND THE IMPACT ON THE FINANCIAL PERFORMANCE

The concept of Sustainability Reporting has begun its development since the first environmental reporting in 1980 (IISD, 1980). Since the beginning, this concept has also had other approaches: *(1) reporting the corporate responsibility* (CRR) used for describing the performance, or (2) *the Triple Bottom Line reporting* (TBL) that highlighted three aspects: profit (economic), people (social) and planet (environment) (Elkington, 1998) indicating the company's commitment to the stakeholders. According to G3.1, the economic dimension of sustainability refers to the impact of the organization on the economic conditions of the stakeholders and on the local, national and global economic systems (GRI, 2011).

By reporting to the existing literature theories related to the sustainability reporting, there have been identified the following:

1. **The Stakeholder Theory:** Claims that '*the companies have a responsibility to a wide range of stakeholders such as creditors, customers, suppliers, employees, government, community, environment, future generations etc.*' (Freeman, 1984). Strengthening the relationship between the company and the society in which it operates is achieved through the use of integrated sustainability reports

and ignoring the stakeholders' interests can affect the company's public image and the financial performance (King, 2002).

2. **The Theory of Legitimacy:** *Refers to 'the condition that exists when the value system of an entity is in harmony with the value system of society'* (Lindblom, 1993). According to this theory, the long-term survival of a company is achieved only by respecting the norms and expectations of the society. The sustainability reporting reduces the risk of regulatory actions and boycotting from the stakeholders and strengthens the company's operating license (Patten, 1992, Deegan, 2000).
3. **The Agency's Theory:** Is based on the principal-agent relationship that exists between owners and administrators. The value of the investors risk increases significantly when the environmental information is not published by companies (Klerk & de Villiers, 2012) and this is reflected in the under-evaluation of the stock market shares. The sustainability reporting may reduce the risk perceived by the investors, may increase the market efficiency and reduce the capital cost of the company (Dhaliwal et al., 2011; Warren & Thomsen, 2012).

The positive effects between the sustainability reporting and the financial performance have been highlighted in the specialized studies as it follows: (1) the use of sustainability indicators has led to the increased ROA and reduction of the fines and penalties, as well as improved the relations with the stakeholders (Ngwakwe, 2009); (2) the cross-cutting analysis of the company has led to positive market reactions in the case of the high quality environmental reports produced by companies comparing to the lower quality reports (Guindry & Patten, 2010); (3) GRI-based sustainability analysis contributes to increase the market value of a company, reducing the asymmetry of information between the administrators and other stakeholders (Schadewitz & Niskala, 2010); (4) the alpha superiority of the sustainability leaders (SAM & Robeco, 2011); (5) the high degree of the sustainable disclosure is associated to the increase of the average sells of the companies (Ameer & Othman, 2012; Khaveh et al., 2012) or to the company's reputation for the interested stakeholder groups (Bayoud et al., 2012a); (6) the corporate responsibility reporting is relevant to the investment decision-making, also contributing to an increase in the share price and market value of the companies (Klerk & de Villiers, 2012); (7) the companies with high sustainability reporting are more competitive during time, overcoming the business partners, a fact reflected in both the capital market and the accounting performance (Eccles et al., 2012).

The negative or insignificant effects between the sustainability reporting and the financial performance of the companies have been highlighted in the studies of the specialists as it follows: (1) the negative impact of sustainability practices on short-term financial performance (Lopez et al., 2007); (2) the values of the shares of the agricultural companies decrease significantly in the short term, due to the increase in costs associated with the sustainability initiatives (Detre & Gunderson, 2011); (3) the sustainable management behavior of the company does not contribute to the decrease in value of the shares or to any other improvement, although the environmental performance has a positive effect on the company (Ziegler et al., 2002); (4) an insignificant impact of the economic performances of the companies that voluntarily submitted sustainability reports comparing to those that did not submit GRI sustainability reports (Buys et al., 2011); (5) an insignificant difference between the financial performance (monthly profitability of the portfolios) of the companies with high or low ESG rankings (SAM database) (Humphrey et al., 2012); (6) a poor significance of the relationship between the corporate social ratings (related to different stakeholders) and the financial performance (Venanzi, 2012).

SUSTAINABILITY DISCLOSURE

The sustainability disclosure has been and is a subject of great interest in the academic environment (Marston & Shrives, 1991), but also in the business environment. Issues related to improving the social welfare or protecting and preserving the environment have been largely ignored by the business community and by the political and institutional institutions until the emergence of the concept of sustainable development at the beginning of the 20th century. The business objective set by the companies, namely maximizing shareholder value, was replaced by a strategic change in the financial dimension by taking into account the environmental dimension and the stakeholders directly involved: stakeholders. As the trends in reporting non-financial information have increased, the interest of the companies, shareholders and stakeholders has also increased, as they have found that they can affect their long-term viability. The new objectives of the management approach were to disclose the environmental information in the annual reports. According to the specialists, some aspects of the social and environmental externalities require different reporting systems and flexible disclosure methods by which stakeholders can understand the behavior of the companies in economic and social areas (Clarkson, 1995; Fineman & Clarke, 1996; Henriques & Sadorsky, 1999; Post et al., 2002). In order to maintain or generate these values for the society, as well as for the companies, the interest in the disclosure of the non-financial information has increased on the basis of the organization strategy and business models (Mansor et al., 2017).

According to the opinion of the specialists, the disclosure of the accounting information addresses the corporate practices (disclosure, type and level of disclosure) and the factors affecting disclosure (corporate characteristics, governance attributes, ownership structure of companies) (Al Mosh & Mansor, 2018). Regarding the impact study of the company characteristics on the degree of disclosure of the environmental information, the results of the specialists indicated the following aspects: (1) the positive impact of the age and size of the companies on the level of social disclosure and the profitability is positively linked to the level of social and environmental disclosure (Bayoud et al., 2012b; Gray et al., 2000); (2) a positive relationship of the society's dimension to the voluntary disclosure of the environmental information (Grecco et al., 2013); (3) a positive impact of the age, size and type of the industry on the level of the social disclosure (Trencansky & Tsaparlidis, 2014; Akbas, 2014); (4) a negative relationship between the company size and the social disclosure (Nawaiseh et al., 2015) or between the age of society and the type of industry on social and environmental disclosure (Bani-Khalid, 2017); (5) a positive relationship between the size and age of society and the level of disclosure of the environmental accounting information (Nguyen et al., 2017); (6) a positive impact on the size of the company which is the determining factor in the social disclosure (Sánchez et al., 2017) or the voluntary disclosure (Khalid Ba, 2017).

Other specialists dedicated a complex analysis to the studies on government attributes and their results showed the following: (1) significant positive impact of the foreign ownership levels on the voluntary disclosure of environment information (Barako et al., 2006); (2) the importance of the role of foreign ownership and the ownership of blocks in influencing the voluntary disclosure (Alhazaimeh et al., 2014); (3) significant positive impact of the size of the audit firm on the voluntary disclosure (Albawwat & Basah, 2015); (4) positive relationship between the size of the Board and the voluntary disclosure (Akhtaruddin et al., 2009) and the frequency of the council meetings (Alhazmi, 2017), between the size of the board of the audit and the voluntary disclosure (social and environmental) (Rouf, 2011; Money-Khalid, 2017), between the board size, composition of the board, the audit committee and the voluntary disclosure (Samaha et al., 2015).

Other studies of the specialists have also revealed negative governance issues such as: (1) the absence of a relationship between the audit committee, board meeting, board size and the voluntary disclosure (Albawwat & Basah, 2015); between the Council's dimension and the voluntary disclosure (Elfeky, 2017); (2) the absence of a significant relationship between it and the type of audit company and the disclosure of environmental information (Dibia & Onwuchekwa, 2015); (3) a negative impact of the ownership structure on the sustainability communications of the state enterprises (Persson & Vingren, 2017) or the practices of disclosure of the corporate social responsibility (Juhmani, 2013; Alhazmi, 2017). All the negative influences were also found in the following studies: (1) a negative impact between the number of shareholders, ownership of the block, the foreign ownership and the voluntary disclosure (Albawwat & Basah, 2015); (2) a negative relationship between the owner of the blocks and the voluntary presentations, and the property governance is not linked to the voluntary disclosure (Juhmani, 2013).

THE ENVIRONMENTAL REPORTING. OPINIONS OF THE STAKEHOLDERS

The Identification of the Stakeholders and Reporting Content Required by Them

In order to prepare a sustainability reporting, the decision-makers need to know clearly which category of stakeholders they are addressing to. In this respect, a company must identify the stakeholders or actors to which they have to present the sustainability reporting and determine the exact content of the information to be reported to them in order to meet their information needs. From this point of view, the stakeholders consider that the information provided is incomplete. But who are the actors or stakeholders in finding out this environmental information?

Before presenting the categories of stakeholders, there has been consulted the specialized literature in order to find out what stakeholders are and how they are defined. The Stanford Research Institute introduces for the first time the term "*stakeholders*" and the specialists defined it as "*any group or person who may or may be affected by the company's goal*" (Freeman, 1984), the definition being later reviewed by referring to "*those groups without whose support the organization would cease to* exist" (Freeman, 2010). Other authors consider that stakeholders are: "*... individuals or groups who have or claim ownership rights, rights or interests in a corporation and its past, present, or future activities. Such claimed rights or interests are the result of transactions or actions taken by the corporation and may be legal or moral, individual or collective. The stakeholders with interests, claims, or similar rights can be classified as belonging to the same group: employees, shareholders, customers, and so on*" (Clarkson, 1995). Conceptual approaches of the stakeholders have been expanded and studied by many specialists whose significant contributions can be summed up as it follows: (1) aspects of stakeholder analysis and legitimacy (Mitchell et al., 1997); (2) the significance of the theory and the importance of the strategic dimension of the stakeholder relations from a managerial perspective (Donaldson & Preston, 1995).

Other specialists/bodies have identified the following categories of stakeholders: academics, employees and managers, NGOs, financial community, local community, regulators, legislators, competitors and business (clients, suppliers), shareholders, investors, government, media (DTTI, 1993; Azzone et al., 1996, Wheeler & Sillanpää, 1997; Bellantuono et al., 2016; Oncioiu et al., 2018). Various stakeholder typologies have been identified by specialists as it follows: (1) external categories vs. internal (Freeman,

1984); (2) primary categories vs. secondary or social and non-social (Wheeler & Sillanpää, 1997); (3) latent parts, waiting parts and final stakeholders (Mitchell et al., 1997); (4) voluntary vs. involuntary (Post et al., 2002).

The advantages given to a company by the above-mentioned stakeholders are: (1) the company can effectively identify and provide information on reporting situations to the target stakeholder segments; (2) the stakeholders are interested in the environmental performance reporting (Azzone et al., 1997). The stakeholders' information requirements for reporting on the company environmental performance focus primarily on the content of the document (disclosure of the environmental information) and the format of the data (how to present the information and how often it is reported). Based on the literature, an extraction of the information requirements of the stakeholders was carried out as it follows:

Academic Environment

Teachers in the academia environment want that by the information from the environmental reports to monitor trends over time, making public benchmarking and best practice examples from which it can develop reference standards for the environmental issues of the companies in the industry environment. Based on these stakeholders' requirements, the companies need to consider publishing information on the quantification of the environmental objectives and ensuring the credibility and permissibility of the comparability between the annual environmental reports. In addition, the companies need to specify in the current/future environmental reports, the company's legal dossier, the description of the company's management system, and the performance related to the established environmental objectives. The companies have a social responsibility towards the stakeholders to disclose the environmental information, to ensure transparency of the information and the decision-making on environmental actions. Regarding the format that companies need to adopt, the academia has spoken out for clear reports that regularly highlight some significant annual issues related to the current environmental policies, the environmental management systems, the performance and environmental protection spending on the basis of which to ensure the timeliness of the information. This information may take the form of graphics, tables or statistical formats, while the figures or graphs shall be accompanied by interpretative data analyzes, indicating the take-up of the (departmental) sources.

Employees

Taking into account the employee involvement in a company, they are interested in the consequences on the environment through the following aspects: education, responsibility, participation, transparency of the decision-making process. In this respect, the company will have to report the compliance with the environmental regulations, the environmental acquisitions, the recycling and the environmental risk assessment of the employees (Azzone et al., 1997). In addition, the employees also want to see some statistics issued by different departments on the environmental impacts, the waste recycling rates, and the degree of accountability for the environmental decisions. By ensuring the transparency of the decision-making process, the reasons that lead to the fulfillment or non-fulfillment of the company's environmental objectives can be reported. By reporting on the environment, the employees provide a feedback on the environmental policy promoted by the company where they work and through which the report can be continually improved. From the employees' point of view, the environmental report should be as simple as possible (in the form of graphs or diagrams explained in paper or electronic format), be accessible, be as frequent as possible and contain varied information on: the environmental activity of the department where it operates, the impact on the environment and the comparison of performance with other departments.

NGOs

The non-governmental organizations are more interested in the public accountability and environmental action, and these issues are mentioned in the company's environmental reports. These environmental reports should also contain significant information on the future sustainability policies and trends, as well as the efforts to recycle or recover waste and protect the natural resources. As other interested environmental stakeholders, the NGOs would like to see the data which: (1) clearly demonstrate the regulatory compliance and (2) detail the performance trends over time (Azzone et al., 1997). In other words, a company's goals need to be measurable and reflect the extent to which the company has helped solving the current environmental problems.

The NGOs want standardization of the reporting process because it can provide better comparability of information in similar or specific sectors. From the point of view of the NGOs, the environmental reports should be drawn up annually and should contain information on: the respecting the environmental regulations, the environmental impact assessment, the atmospheric emissions, and the life cycle assessment of products produced with environmental influences, the environmental policy promoted by the company, and the concrete achievements (range), the environmental performance data. The format required by the NGOs for reporting the environmental information aims a standardization that allows them to access and verifies the company both by the society and by the companies, for a long time and their availability to be permanent.

Financial Community

The financial community is divided into: investors (institutions and private) and creditors (banks and insurance companies). The first category, made up of investors, wants the company's environmental reports to contain information on: respect on the environmental legislation in force, standards and issues in violation of various legal aspects, fines, environmental penalties, environmental risk assessment and inclusion of an environmental management system (covering the environmental debt and the asset impairment). There is also added the evaluation of the expenses and the financial costs of the environmental projects, the life cycle of the products on the markets etc. The second category, made up of creditors, wants environmental reports to address, in particular, the unfavorable aspects of the companies or the problems they face, and which have an impact on the company's image, cash flow and company viability, i.e.: the environmental standards, the environmental statement of compliance, the asset impairment provisions, the liabilities for emergencies, the potential environmental costs and their impact on results, the company environmental policy statement, the synthesis of the environmental audits, the policies on the environmental accounts, the external environmental auditors report, the risk assessment (Azzone et al., 1997). Many of the categories in the financial community produce their own environmental reports on their own, taking into account the environmental impact and the investment decisions. The form of the environmental reports and their content accepted by the financial community is a matte one that takes into account the financial and non-financial information of the environment related to the company's activity.

Local Community

The local community of the local society and the employees of the local companies are interested in the environmental information from the environmental reports, especially in their geographical area. These information requirements refer to the assessment of the environmental performance, the environmental impact and any changes in the activity of the local companies. Specifically, the local community is interested in: (1) respecting of the legal regulations on the environment; (2) the pollutants, solid waste, energy consumption and the wastewater; (3) the environmental management system used by companies; (4) the environmental investments at local community level; (5) the company's future environmental strategies. Regarding the format, the local community would like the environmental report to take the form of a concrete brochure, written in accessible and less technical language, and to either sent to their homes, or choose the simplest, level site, saving distribution costs.

Regulatory Bodies and Legislators

Through documents issued by the lawmakers or regulators, the companies provide a strong feed-back to complying with the environmental information requirements. The environmental report provided is not just an information tool; it also becomes a communication tool between regulators and companies. Providing well documented and reasoned environmental reports creates added value that the regulators cannot obtain from other sources. The environmental report is also an instrument by which the companies demonstrate respect of the environmental legislation, but also the respect of the legal requirements and those of other stakeholders in environmental information. In this way, the companies become credible before the law and other stakeholders, the local community and customers/suppliers etc. From this point of view, the environmental report should contain those elements that signal the financial commitments, time and resources allocated to the current and future environmental issues. The environmental report becomes an assurance tool by which the companies comply with the environmental law and proves the continuity in its work, including that relating to the environmental investments. The format agreed by the regulators is that the information requirements of stakeholders are met.

Customers and Suppliers

Using the environmental report, the companies can show that its product is safe, reliable, and it is responsible, with reduced risks of the environmental degradation. The provider environmental practice and the environmental impact and responsibility are the concerns of the industrial customers to find them in the environmental reports. This information provided by the companies must be certified by the bodies which issue them in order to increase the credibility among the customers and suppliers alike. The customers/suppliers want the environmental report to include information on: (1) the company debt; (2) the compliance with environmental requirements; (3) the products do not present inherent risks of litigation; (4) the life cycle of products; (5) the waste recycle. Therefore, the companies should provide, in their environmental reports, information related to: (1) the compliance with environmental legislation (certification); (2) the environmental management system (objectives, audit, performance); (3) the recycle or disposal of the waste (presentation of dangerous substances to humans, presentation of transfer licenses); (4) the health and safety (assessments of various commissions responsible for public health).

From the point of view of the customers and suppliers, the format of the environmental report must be clear, concise and reflect past, present and future developments noted above.

CASE STUDY CONCERNING THE SUSTAINABILITY REPORTING OF ALUMINIUM INDUSTRY COMPANY

In the current context of the global warming and the attempt to limit the air temperature rise to 1.5°C, there are needed a number of conditions that involve both the natural (geophysical and environmental) aspects and the socio-economic environment, such as the technology identification and the economic policies in order to increase the pace of sustainability (IPCC, 2018). This association of the global warming with sustainability is mainly the result of the atmospheric pollution with the greenhouse gases resulting from the industrialization of the society (Constantin et al., 2019). Sustainability becomes achievable and effective when the approach is an integrated one, involving all the stakeholders and when the decision-making process is transparent (Mathur et al., 2014; Antwi-Agyei et al., 2017). The assessment and monitoring of the quality of the environment is the basic condition for the achievement of the environmental management of an industrial company (Constantin et al., 2016).

The Sustainability Report is the instrument for quantifying the quality of the environment, providing the company with the opportunity to implement the best measures for reducing and combating the environmental pollution, in order to achieve the environmental performance needed for sustainability (Constantin et al., 2019). Therefore, we would like to exemplify such a sustainability report for an aluminum industry company because of the high impact and risk for the health and medicine. The sustainability report is based on the quarterly data for the air and water pressure indicators, specific to the aluminum industry, but also for the time evolution of the noise at the workplace.

The aluminum industry company is working in an integrated system with core production, maintenance and repair departments, machinery and spare manufacturing, power and utilities departments, the commercial department, the IT sector, the transport department, the social sector etc. (Constantin, 2013). The company's basic activity is the production of the electrolytic aluminum and the processing in different forms (sheets, plates, strips), being also added the marketing in the domestic and foreign markets, the know-how, the packaging activities, the transports and services. The technological flow to obtain the primary aluminum using the electrolytic method and the transformation of the primary aluminum into finished products require the following sectors (Constantin, 2013; Topor et al., 2017): (1) the anodes sector for the production of the anodes necessary for the electrolysis process; (2) the electrolysis sector where the electrolytic aluminum is produced; (3) the foundry sector where the electrolytic aluminum turns into semi-finished products.

The monitoring of the environmental factors by the aluminum industry company ensures the compliance with the current legislation in order to prevent the environmental pollution and to ensure the environmental performance. This monitoring is provided by a specialist office. Also, at the level of each sector of activity, there are staffs responsible for the environmental protection, with well-defined tasks. The monitored environmental factors on which the sustainability report is based are:

1. **The Air Factor:** for which the following pressure indicators are used: emissions (monthly, mg/mc) of fluorine, sulfur dioxide, nitrogen dioxide and total powders. The sampling points are located in the three sectors: anodes, electrolysis and foundry.

2. **The Water Factor:** for which the following pressure indicators are used: emissions (monthly; mg/l) of the suspended solids, chlorides, chemical oxygen demand (CCO-Cr) and aluminum. The sampling points are for the technological water necessary for the production of the primary aluminum and the processed aluminum.
3. **The Noise:** The noise level (dB) emitted by various sources at the workplace is monitored as a result of the fact that it is an essential factor in the occurrence and maintenance of the high stress.

In order to reduce the impact on the environment, the environmental pressure values of the indicators are analyzed in relation to the emission limit values (ELV) established by standards or other national regulations. The VLEs emission limit values or the maximum admissible concentrations (MAC) are set out in the following documents:

- The MAPPM Order no. 462/1993 – Technical requirements for the atmospheric protection. The methodological norm for the determination of the emissions of the atmospheric pollutants produced by the stationary sources (Order 462/1993).
- Decision no. 352/2005 regarding the modification and completion of the Government Decision no. 188/2002 for the approval of some norms regarding the discharge conditions in the aquatic environment of the waste waters (GD 352/2005).
- STAS 10009-88 - Building acoustics. Urban acoustics. Permissible sound level limits (STAS 10009-88).

In achieving the sustainability report, the responsibilities are divided as it follows:

- The director of the Environmental Quality Monitoring Bureau is responsible for organizing the whole activity so that the operator staff can work in optimal conditions.
- The director of the Environmental Quality Monitoring Bureau reports the data recorded in the environmental report, approved by the company's management, to the institutions dealing with the environmental protection at local, regional and national level.
- The operational staff shall draw up, review and monitor the compliance with the sampling program and their chemical analysis in a correct manner and with the appropriate equipment.
- The operational staff draw up sampling sheets, analysis bulletins and the environmental report.
- The responsible for samples follow the compliance with the sampling program.

The sustainability report presents, in detail, the evolution of the pressure indicators on the above-mentioned median table, tables and graphs, relative to VLE or CMA values. Depending on these limit values; it is determined whether the pollution indicators are within the optimal value range or if they exceed the episodes of pollution and, implicitly, the environmental protection interventions at the company level.

The quarterly evolution of the environmental hazards in the aluminum industry in the year 2018 is presented for the anodes sector in Table 1 (the evolution of fluorine and sulfur dioxide in Figure 1, the evolution of nitrogen dioxide and total powders in Figure 2), for the electrolysis sector in Table 2 (the evolution of fluorine and sulfur dioxide in Figure 3, the evolution of nitrogen dioxide and total powders in Figure 4), for the foundry sector in Table 3 (the evolution of fluorine and sulfur dioxide in Figure 5, the evolution of nitrogen dioxide and total powders in Figure 6).

Table 1. The anodes sector (ELV according Order no. 462/1993)

Indicator/period	Quarter I	Quarter II	Quarter III	Quarter IV	ELV (mg/mc)
fluorine	0.67	0.59	0.54	0.58	5
sulfur dioxide	22.1	19.76	2.83	12.7	500
nitrogen dioxide	0.05	0.06	0.21	0.12	500
total powders	3.2	3.26	3.27	3.66	50

Figure 1. The quarterly evolution of fluorine and sulfur dioxide

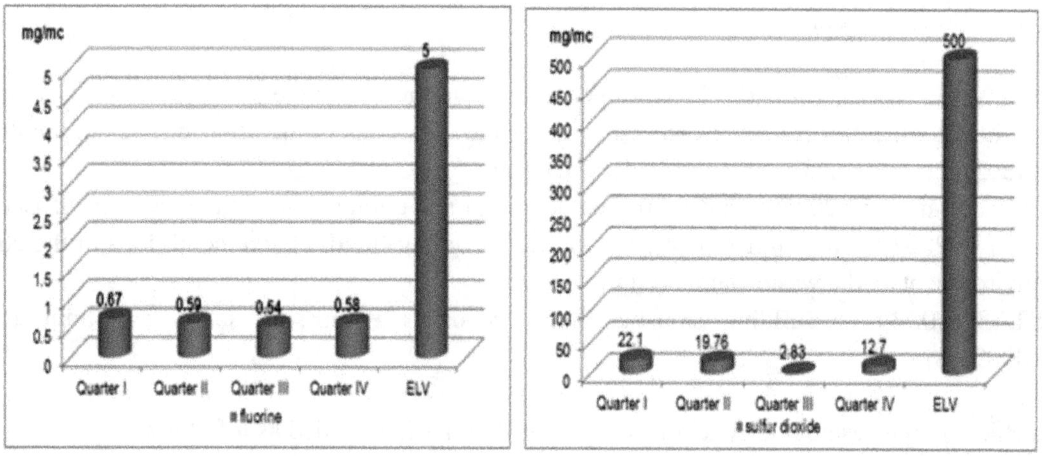

Figure 2. The quarterly evolution of nitrogen dioxide and total powders

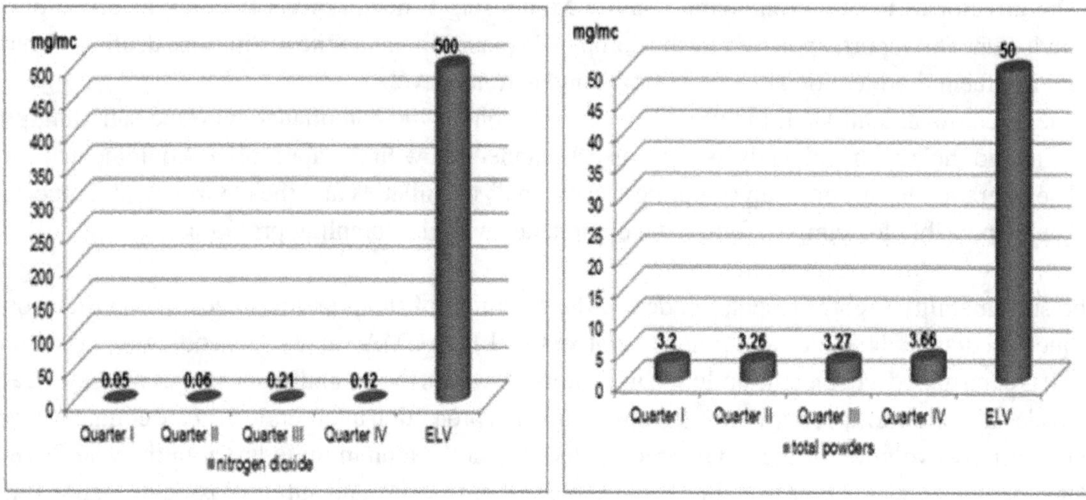

Table 2. The electrolysis sector (ELV according Order no. 462/1993)

Indicator/period	Quarter I	Quarter II	Quarter III	Quarter IV	ELV
fluorine	0.39	0.37	0.39	0.41	5
sulfur dioxide	14.43	16.43	15.35	7.26	500
nitrogen dioxide	0.19	0.18	0.08	0.12	500
total powders	9.46	7.82	7.19	7.27	50

Figure 3. The quarterly evolution of fluorine and sulfur dioxide

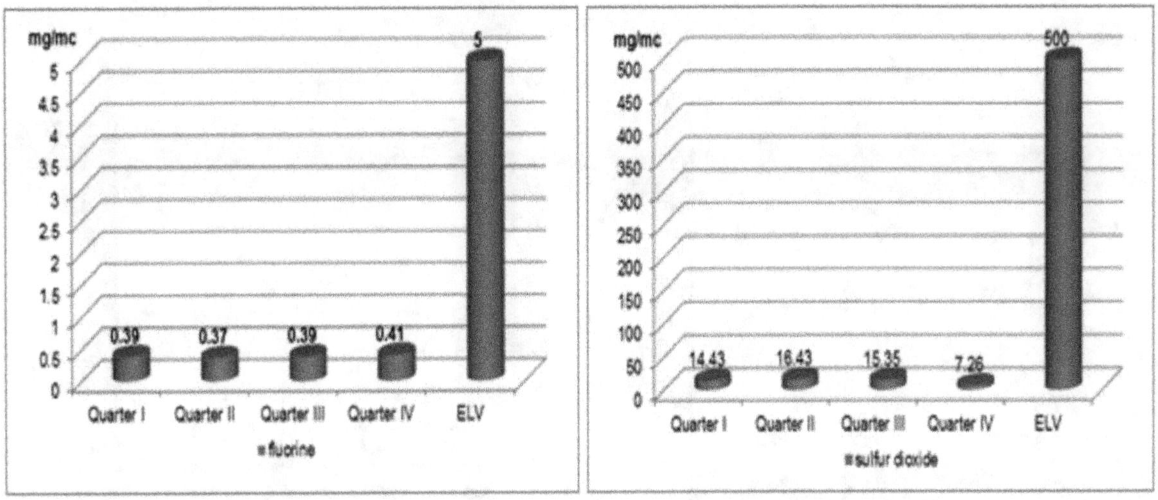

Figure 4. The quarterly evolution of nitrogen dioxide and total powders

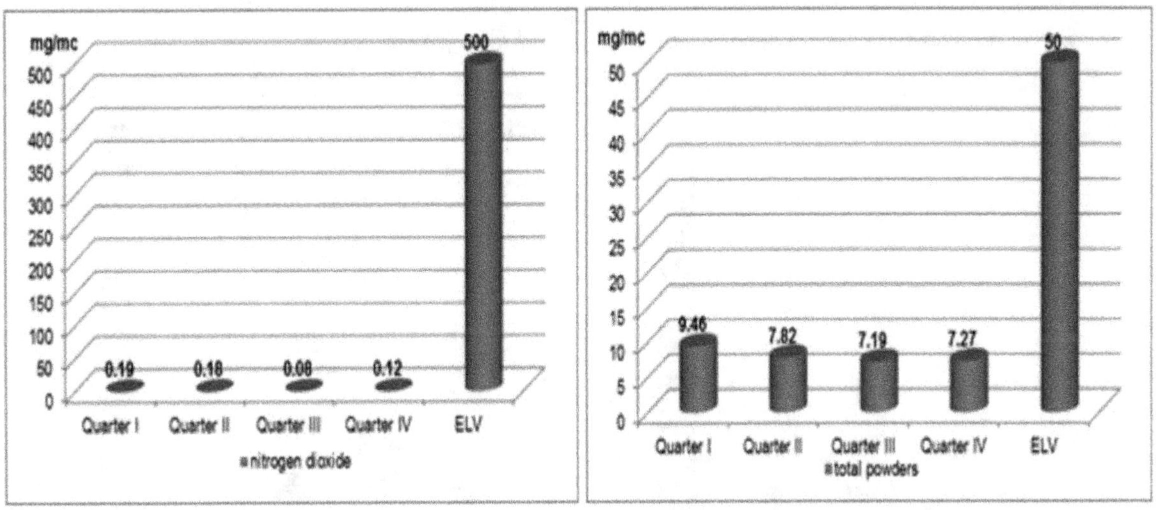

Table 3. The foundry sector (ELV according Order no. 462/1993)

Indicator/period	Quarter I	Quarter II	Quarter III	Quarter IV	ELV
fluorine	0.06	0.02	0.04	0.03	5
sulfur dioxide	0.6	1.48	1	1	500
nitrogen dioxide	0.7	0.72	0.53	0.6	500
total powders	0.46	0.48	0.38	0.42	50

Figure 5. The quarterly evolution of fluorine and sulfur dioxide

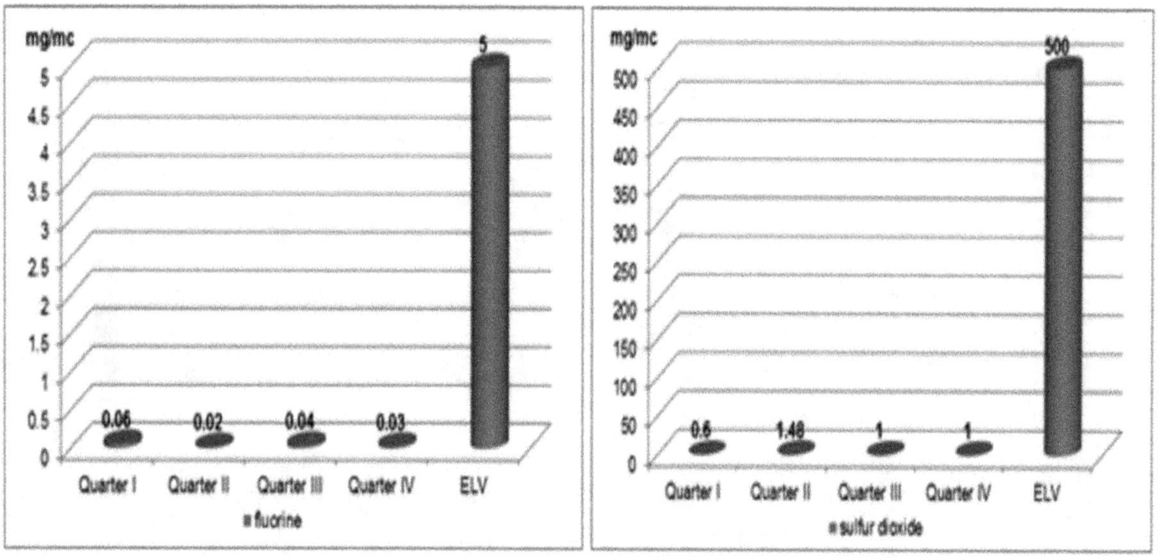

Figure 6. The quarterly evolution of nitrogen dioxide and total powders

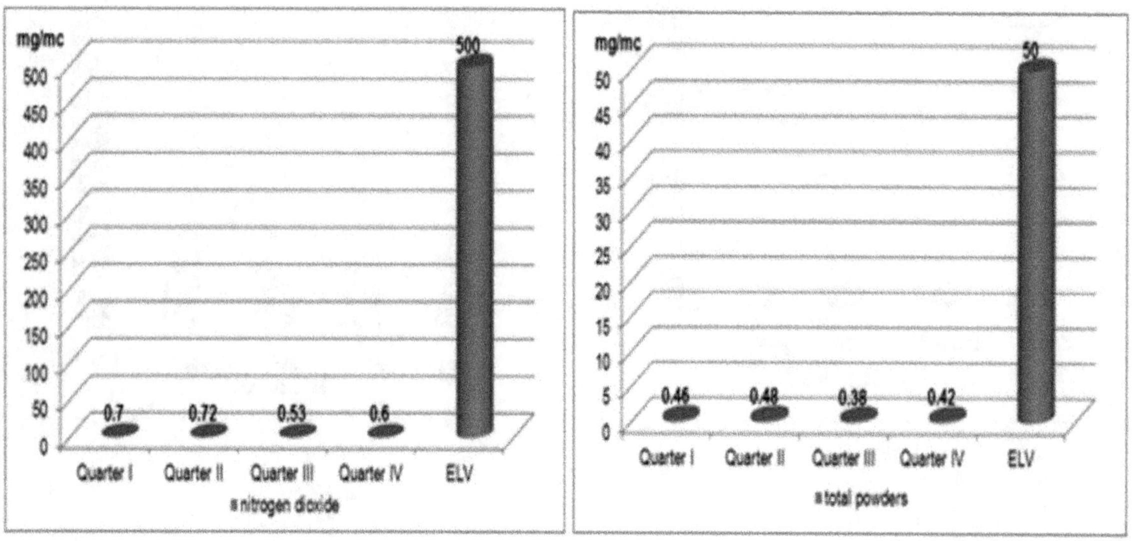

The Air Factor: Technological Emissions

The quarterly evolution of the environmental hazards in the aluminum industry in the year 2018 is presented for the primary aluminum in Table 4 (evolution of suspended solids and chlorides in Figure 7 and evolution of CCO-Cr and aluminum in Figure 8), for the processed aluminum in Table 5 (evolution of suspended solids and chlorides in Figure 9 and evolution of CCO-Cr and aluminum in Figure 10).

The Water Factor: Technological Water

The quarterly evolution of the environmental hazards in the aluminum industry in the year *2018* is presented for noise in Table 6 (evolution of noise on eastern side and western side in Figure 11 and evolution of noise on northern side and southern side in Figure 12).

Table 4. The primary aluminum (MAC according Decision no. 352/2005)

Indicator/period	Quarter I	Quarter II	Quarter III	Quarter IV	MAC (mg/l)
suspended solids	12.8	10.6	12.6	11.87	60
chlorides	141.12	120.53	116.98	138.84	300
CCO-Cr	21.2	19.41	20.32	18.22	125
aluminum	0.1	0.11	0.08	0.11	5

Figure 7. The quarterly evolution of suspended solids and chlorides

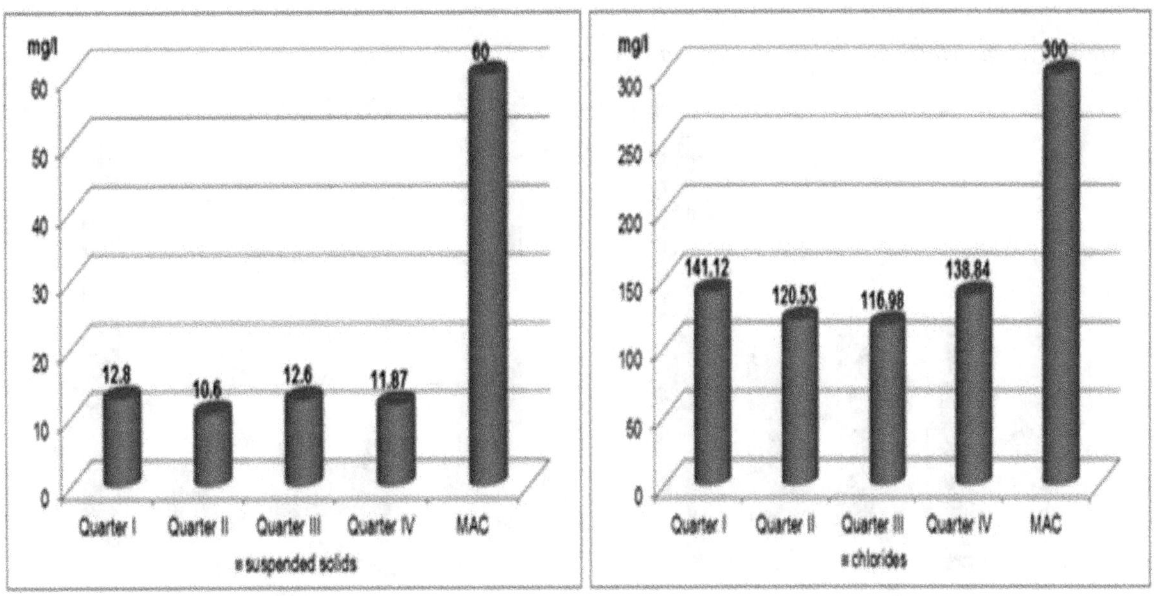

Figure 8. The quarterly evolution of CCO-Cr and aluminum

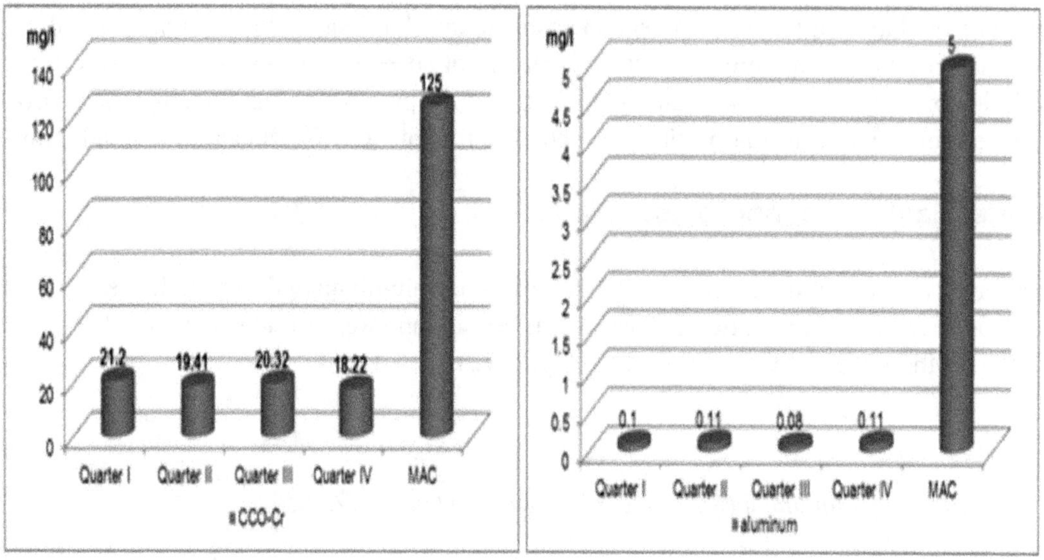

Table 5. The processed aluminum (MAC according Decision no. 352/2005)

Indicator/period	Quarter I	Quarter II	Quarter III	Quarter IV	MAC
suspended solids	32	31.4	30.8	29.6	60
chlorides	52.6	49.2	48	42.5	300
CCO-Cr	38	37	18	17	125
aluminum	0.57	0.31	0.31	0.3	5

Figure 9. The quarterly evolution of suspended solids and chlorides

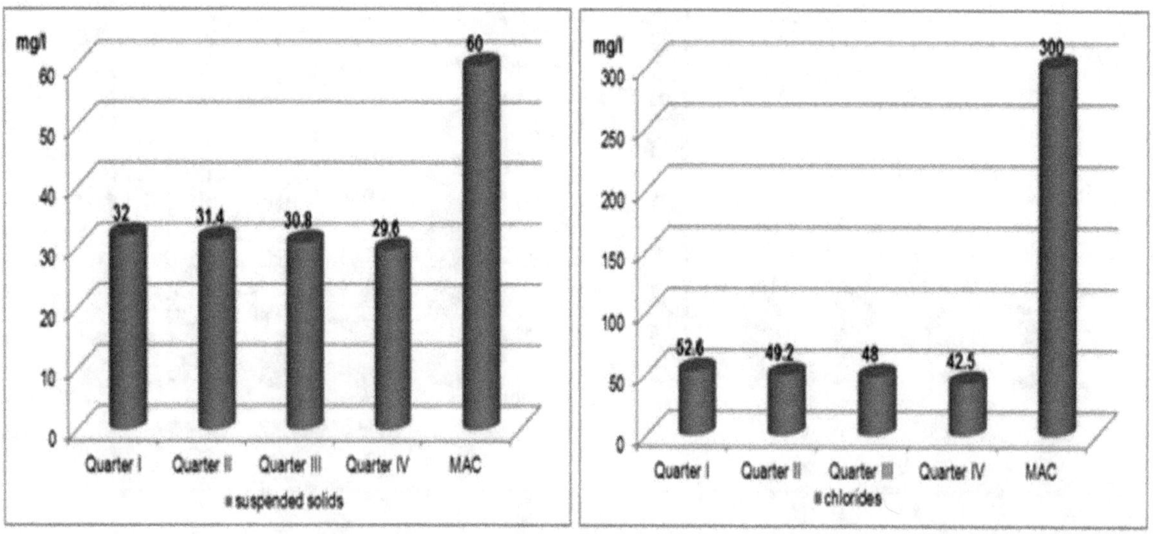

Figure 10. The quarterly evolution of CCO-Cr and aluminum

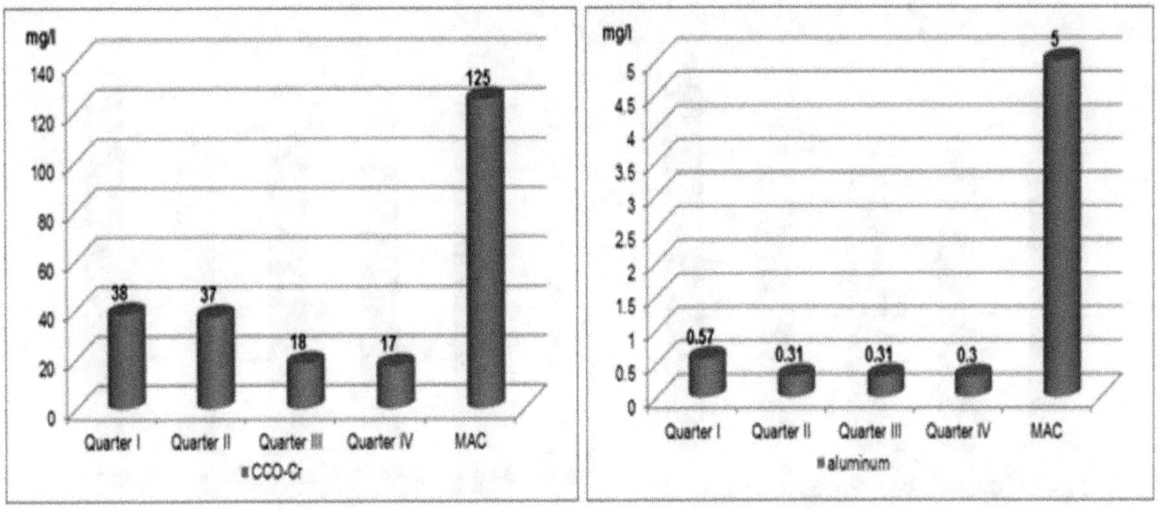

Table 6. Evolution of noise (MAC according STAS 10009-88)

Sampling direction	Quarter I	Quarter II	Quarter III	Quarter IV	LV (dB)
eastern side	52	51	52	51	65
western side	55	53	52	51	65
northern side	54	52	50	50	65
southern side	54	52	52	50	65

Figure 11. The quarterly evolution of noise on eastern side and western side

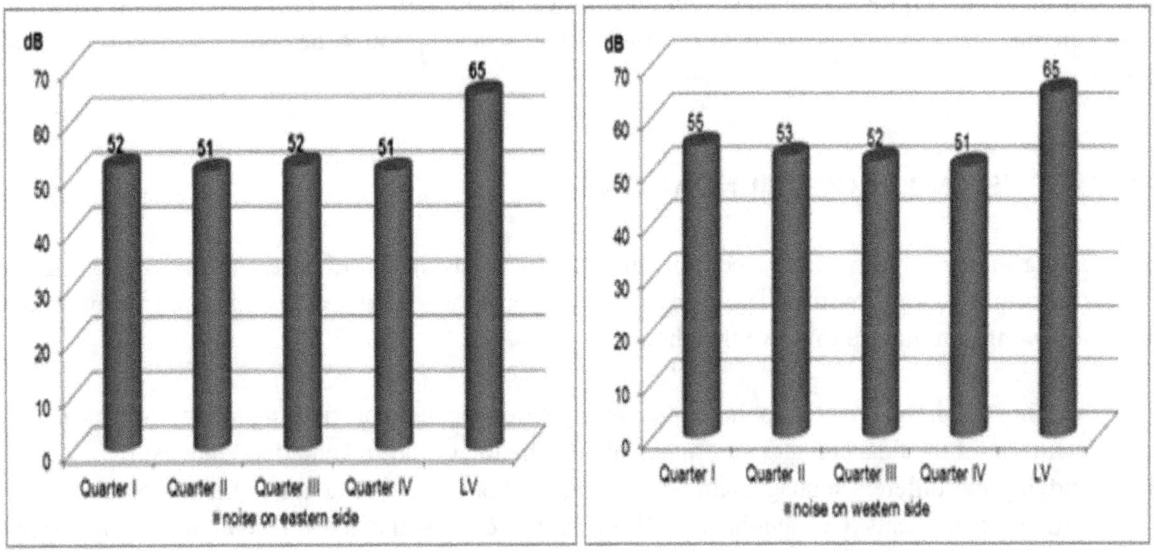

Figure 12. The quarterly evolution of noise on northern side and southern side

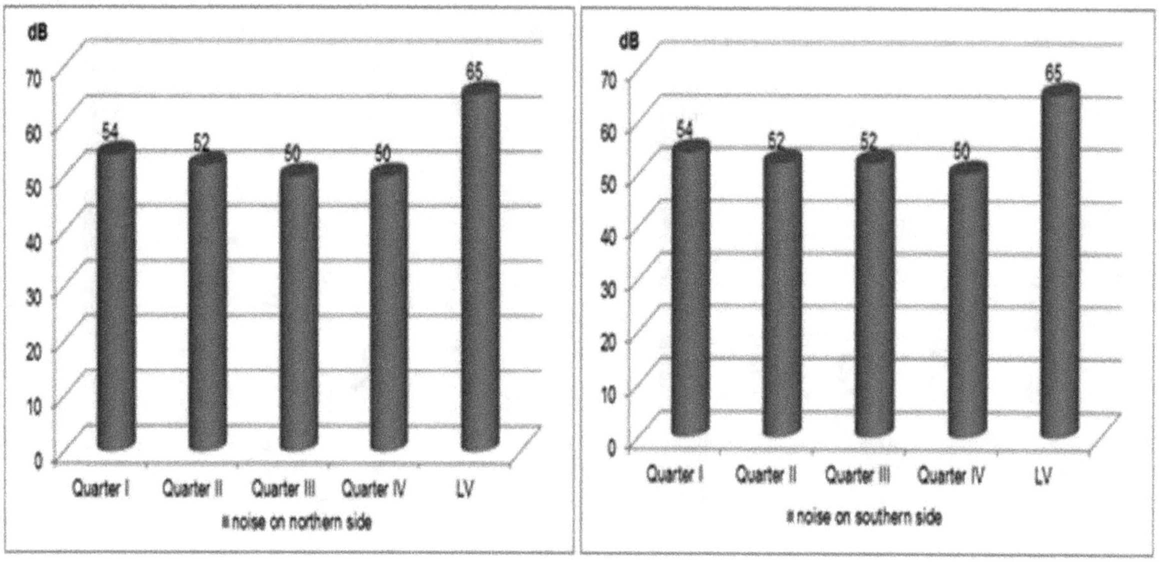

The Noise

In addition to the sustainability report at the company level in the aluminum industry, standardized sheets can be produced through which every operation in the technological process to be rendered. Thus, it is more easily to analyze if the company's environmental policy is appropriate for its sustainable development strategy. This document should also be seen as an additional tool for assessing the environmental performance. A proposal for such a sheet is shown in Table 7.

The sustainability report is a basic tool in delivering a qualitative environmental management in a company that wants to grow sustainably. It provides information on the state of the environmental quality at a given time, but also provides insights on how to improve and optimize the company's environmental policy.

SOLUTIONS AND RECOMMENDATIONS

Considering the constructive assessment of this chapter, focusing on the role and importance of the stakeholders in the corporate sustainability reporting, we propose to the specialists and anyone interested in the following solutions to improve this theme:

- Studying the drivers related to the sustainability reporting and contributing to the production and disclosure of the financial and non-financial information of the stakeholders' interest.
- Studying the different management accounting methods that can adapt to the sustainability reporting requirements (Constantin et al., 2019) and disclosing the non-financial information to the companies.

Table 7. Sustainability report model of aluminum company

<table>
<tr><th colspan="6">NAME OF THE COMPANY</th></tr>
<tr><td colspan="6">ACTIVITY PROFILE:</td></tr>
<tr><td colspan="6">PRODUCTION:</td></tr>
<tr><td colspan="6">PROCESS TYPE:</td></tr>
<tr><td colspan="6">INSTALLATION FUNCTION DATE:</td></tr>
<tr><td colspan="6">SPECIFIC ENERGY CONSUMPTION:</td></tr>
<tr><td>Month</td><td>Quantity of consumed fuel</td><td>Unit of measurement</td><td>Month</td><td>Quantity of consumed fuel</td><td>Unit of measurement</td></tr>
<tr><td>I</td><td></td><td></td><td>VII</td><td></td><td></td></tr>
<tr><td>II</td><td></td><td></td><td>VIII</td><td></td><td></td></tr>
<tr><td>III</td><td></td><td></td><td>IX</td><td></td><td></td></tr>
<tr><td>IV</td><td></td><td></td><td>X</td><td></td><td></td></tr>
<tr><td>V</td><td></td><td></td><td>XI</td><td></td><td></td></tr>
<tr><td>VI</td><td></td><td></td><td>XII</td><td></td><td></td></tr>
<tr><td colspan="6">Total consumed quantity:</td></tr>
<tr><td colspan="6">FUNCTION REGIME:</td></tr>
<tr><td colspan="6">EVACUATION INSTALLATIONS:</td></tr>
<tr><td colspan="3">Height of the chimney</td><td colspan="3"></td></tr>
<tr><td colspan="3">Diameter of the chimney</td><td colspan="3"></td></tr>
<tr><td colspan="3">Gas speed</td><td colspan="3"></td></tr>
<tr><td colspan="3">Temperature</td><td colspan="3"></td></tr>
<tr><td colspan="3">Gas flow through the chimney</td><td colspan="3"></td></tr>
<tr><td colspan="3">Number of chimneys for each source</td><td colspan="3"></td></tr>
<tr><td colspan="3">The geographic coordinates of the chimneys</td><td colspan="3"></td></tr>
<tr><td colspan="3">Height and width of the buildings near the chimney</td><td colspan="3"></td></tr>
<tr><td colspan="3">Distance of the buildings to the chimney</td><td colspan="3"></td></tr>
<tr><td colspan="3">The data on the depollution installations (if any and for which pollutant)</td><td colspan="3"></td></tr>
<tr><td colspan="3">Efficiency factor</td><td colspan="3"></td></tr>
<tr><td colspan="6">COOLING INSTALLATIONS</td></tr>
<tr><td colspan="3">Name of the cooling agent</td><td colspan="3"></td></tr>
<tr><td colspan="3">Quantity of the cooled products</td><td colspan="3"></td></tr>
<tr><td colspan="6">REINFORCED INSTALLATIONS</td></tr>
<tr><td colspan="3">Type of equipment</td><td colspan="3"></td></tr>
<tr><td colspan="3">The retention rate</td><td colspan="3"></td></tr>
</table>

- Studying the positive and negative impacts of the sustainability reporting on the size, type and sector of the company activities.
- Studying the practices of the corporate social responsibility (CSR) and the impact on the management decisions (Barbu & Căpuşneanu, 2012), on the investment (Topor et al., 2016) on the environmental information reporting to the society and stakeholders.

- Studying the different types of environmental reports, selecting the content and presentation format, taking into account both the stakeholders' requirements and the company's internal managerial requirements, including the degree of disclosure.

Based on the concept of sustainability reporting and the sustainability disclosure, but also on the presented case study, all based on the national and international literature, we recommend to the specialists and those interested in deepening this debated theme, the following issues:

- Carefully analyzing the maximum GRI and other rules dedicated to the sustainability reporting with direct implications for the environmental performance and financial companies (Martinescu & Căpuşneanu, 2009), but also on the society, taking into account the requirements of internal and external stakeholders.
- Researching the specialized literature on the chances of successful use of the templates dedicated to the sustainability reporting. Calling bodies or institutions specialized in sustainable development, particularly on the environmental reporting, can be a viable solution in order to ensure the successful use of the sustainability reporting, with positive effects on the environmental performance, the market image of the company and worldwide. Our recommendation focuses primarily on using the tools dedicated to the environmental sustainability reporting for the company (e.g. the Balanced Sustainability Scoreboard, the Integrated Dashboard), but also reporting other aspects of the sustainability to the stakeholders (various presentations in the literature).
- Expanding the culture of sustainability both within the companies (among the hierarchical levels and the other employees) that have adopted or plan to adopt performing environment management systems and among stakeholders. This can be done by organizing internal/external training courses and informing, organized by specialists in the field.

FUTURE RESEARCH DIRECTIONS

Through the objectives proposed and discussed within this chapter, we consider that our target has been reached; addressing the professional business and academics, as well as other organizations dedicated to the sustainability studies. By presenting these topics, there were covered and summarized several areas dedicated especially to the sustainability reporting and disclosure, but also to the impact of these on the accounting information and the financial performance of the companies. This leaves open a series of opportunities to quantify the future research, which we believe will contribute to fulfill the existing gaps in the literature and helping to clarify other aspects of sustainability reporting worldwide. In this respect, the future research directions can be directed towards:

- The analysis of the impact of the existing theories in the relevant literature on sustainability reporting.
- The analysis of the impact of the managerial decisions resulting from the sustainability reporting: the financial and environmental performance of the companies, the social performance, the company image, the stock market share of the companies, the increase/decrease of the environmental investments (Topor et al., 2017).

- The analysis of the possibility of creating new instruments for monitoring, measuring and reporting of the environmental performance (Căpuşneanu et al., 2015, Ivan et al., 2017, Constantin et al., 2019) and the ways of adjusting or completing the information content, internally (management) or externally (stakeholders) needed.

CONCLUSION

Through its content, this chapter covers several theoretical and methodological areas of the sustainability, starting with the conceptual approaches on the sustainability reporting and its impact on the company performance, and then continuing with the disclosure of its informational content by presenting the stakeholder views. As a strong point of this chapter, we can mention:

- Filling in some existing gaps in the sustainability and use of sustainability reports within the companies through the interpretations of the conceptual approaches and debated theories (stakeholder theory, legitimacy theory, agency theory).
- Presenting the impact of the sustainability reporting on the company performance, as well as presenting the case study of an aluminium industry company, through which the sustainability report is tailored to the needs of the stakeholders in the local community.

Through this analysis, we believe that we have contributed to the increase of knowledge in the area of sustainability, while also provoking new attempts to adapt and refine the ways of drafting, content and presentation of the sustainability reports. This chapter remains open to any future theoretical and methodological research of the sustainability specialists, including the business environment and the academic environment. The stakeholder engagement is also open because it can help explaining and conceiving new ways of addressing the information content of the sustainability reporting, thus, ensuring their effectiveness in the short or long term.

REFERENCES

Akbas, H. E. (2014). Company Characteristics and Environmental Disclosure: An Empirical Investigation on Companies Listed on Borsa Istanbul 100 Index. *Muhasebe ve Finansman Dergisi*, (62).

Akhtaruddin, M., Hossain, M. A., Hossain, M., & Yao, L. (2009). Corporate governance and voluntary disclosure in corporate annual reports of Malaysian listed firms. *Journal of Applied Management Accounting Research*, *7*(1), 1.

Al Amosh, H. A. M., & Mansor, N. (2018). Sustainability and corporate reporting: A review on environmental and social accounting disclosure, International Journal of Accounting. *Finance and Business*, *3*(8), 78–87.

Albawwat, A. H. (2015). Corporate governance and voluntary disclosure of interim financial reporting in Jordan. *Journal of Public Administration and Governance, 5*(2), 100-127.

Alhazaimeh, A., Palaniappan, R., & Almsafir, M. (2014). The impact of corporate governance and ownership structure on voluntary disclosure in annual reports among listed Jordanian companies. *Procedia: Social and Behavioral Sciences*, *129*, 341–348.

Alhazmi, A. N. A. S. (2017). *Exploring the factors and effects of Corporate Social Responsibility Disclosure in Saudi Arabia (in the area of accounting and finance)* (Doctoral dissertation). Nottingham Trent University.

Ameer, R., & Othman, R. (2012). Sustainability Practices and Corporate Financial Performance: A Study Based on the Top Global Corporations. *Journal of Business Ethics*, *108*(1), 61–79.

Antwi-Agyei, P., Dougill, A., & Stringer, L. (2017). Assessing Coherence between Sector Policies and Climate Compatible Development: Opportunities for Triple Wins. *Sustainability*, *9*(11), 2130.

Azzone, G., Brophy, M., Noci, G., Welford, R., & Young, W. (1997). A Stakeholders' View of Environmental Reporting. *Long Range Planning*, *30*(5), 699–709.

Azzone, G., Noci, G., Manzini, R., Welford, R., & Young, C. W. (1996). Defining Environmental Performance Indicators: An Integrated Framework. *Business Strategy and the Environment*, *5*(2), 69–80.

Bani-Khalid, T., Kouhy, R., & Hassan, A. (2017). The Impact of Corporate Characteristics on Social and Environmental Disclosure (CSED): The Case of Jordan. Journal of Accounting and Auditing: Research & Practice.

Barako, D. G., Hancock, P., & Izan, H. Y. (2006). Factors influencing voluntary corporate disclosure by Kenyan companies. *Corporate Governance*, *14*(2), 107–125.

Bayoud, N. S., Kavanagh, M., & Slaughter, G. (2012a). Corporate Social Responsibility Disclosure and Corporate Reputation in Developing Countries: The Case of Libya. *Journal of Business and Policy Research*, *7*(1), 131–160.

Bayoud, N. S., Kavanagh, M., & Slaughter, G. (2012b). Factors influencing levels of corporate social responsibility disclosure Libyan firms: A mixed study. *International Journal of Economics and Finance*, *4*(4), 13–29.

Bellantuono, N., Pontrandolfo, P., & Scozzi, B. (2016). Capturing the Stakeholders' View in Sustainability reporting: A novel approach. *Sustainability*, *8*, 379.

Buys, P., Oberholzer, M., & Andrikopoulos, P. (2011). An investigation of the economic performance of sustainability reporting companies versus non-reporting companies: A South African perspective. *Journal of Social Sciences*, *29*(2), 151–158.

Clarkson, M. B. E. (1995). A stakeholder framework for analysing and evaluating corporate social performance. *Academy of Management Review*, *20*(1), 92–117.

Constantin (Oprea), D.M. (2013). Relaţia climă – poluarea mediului înconjurător în arealul municipiului Slatina, Colecţia Pământul–Casa Noastră. Editura Universitară, Bucureşti.

Constantin (Oprea), D. M., Topor, D. I., Căpuşneanu, S., Barbu, C.M., & Bogan, E. (2016). The monitoring of carbon monoxide air pollutant, as part of the air quality management. Case study: Olt County, Romania. *Annales Universitatis Apulensis Series Oeconomica, 2*(18), 27–34.

de Klerk, M., & de Villiers, C. (2012). The value relevance of corporate responsibility reporting: South African evidence. *Meditari Accountancy Research, 20*(1).

Deegan, C. (2000). *Financial Accounting Theory*. Beijing: Mc Graw Hill.

Deloitte Touche Tohmatsu International (DTTI). (1993). *Coming clean - Corporate environmental reporting*. London: International Institute for Sustainable Development.

Detre, J. D., & Gunderson, M. A. (2011). The Triple Bottom Line: What is the Impact on the Returns to Agribusiness? *The International Food and Agribusiness Management Review, 14*(4), 165–178.

Dhaliwal, D. S., Li, O. Z., Tsang, A., & Yang, Y. G. (2011). Voluntary non-financial disclosure and the cost of equity capital: The initiation of corporate social responsibility reporting. *The Accounting Review, 86*(1), 59–100.

Dibia, N. O., & Onwuchekwa, J. C. (2015). Determinants of Environmental Disclosures in Nigeria: A Case Study of Oil and Gas Companies. *International Journal of Finance and Accounting, 4*(3), 145–152.

Donaldson, T., & Preston, L. E. (1995). The Stakeholder Theory of the Corporation: Concepts, Evidence, and Implications. *Academy of Management Review, 20*, 65–91.

Eccles, R. G., Ioannou, I., & Serafeim, G. (2012). *The impact of a corporate culture of sustainability on corporate behavior and performance (No. w17950)*. National Bureau of Economic Research.

Elfeky, M. I. (2017). The extent of voluntary disclosure and its determinants in emerging markets: Evidence from Egypt. *The Journal of Finance and Data Science*, 1–15.

Elkington, J. (1998). *Cannibals with forks*. Gabriola Island, BC, Canada: New Society Publishers.

Fernando, A., Albuquerque, F., & Almeida, M. (2010). As Matérias Ambientais, as Licenças de Emissão de Gases com Efeito Estufa e os Normativos Aplicáveis em Portugal. *Jornal de Contabilidade, 395*, 31–38.

Fineman, S., & Clarke, K. (1996). Green stakeholders: Industry interpretations and response. *Journal of Management Studies, 33*(6), 715–730.

Freeman, R. E. (1984). *Strategic Management: A Stakeholder Approach*. London: Financial Times Prentice Hall.

Freeman, R. E. (1984). *Strategic Management: A Stakeholder Perspective*. Boston, MA: Pitman.

Freeman, R. E. (2010). *Strategic Management: A Stakeholder Approach*. Cambridge, UK: Cambridge University Press.

Global Reporting Initiative. (2011). *Sustainability Reporting Guidelines*. Global Reporting Initiative.

Gray, R. (2010). Is accounting for sustainability actually accounting for sustainability. And how would we know? An exploration of narratives of organizations and the planet. *Accounting, Organizations and Society, 35*(1), 47–62.

Gray, R., Javad, M., Power, D. M., & Sinclair, C. D. (2001). Social and environmental disclosure and corporate characteristics: A research note and extension. *Journal of Business Finance & Accounting*, *28*(3-4), 327–356.

Grecco, M. C. P., Milani Filho, M. A. F., Segura, L. C., Sanchez, I. M. G., & Dominguez, L. R. (2013). The voluntary disclosure of sustainable information: a comparative analysis of Spanish and Brazilian companies. *Revista de Contabilidade e Organizações, 7*(17).

Guidry, R. P., & Patten, D. M. (2010). Market reactions to the first-time issuance of corporate sustainability reports: Evidence that quality matters. *Sustainability Accounting, Management and Policy Journal*, *1*(1), 33–50.

Henriques, I., & Sadorsky, P. (1999). The relationship between environmental commitment and managerial perceptions of stakeholder importance. *Academy of Management Journal*, *42*(1), 87–99.

Hopwood, A., & Miller, P. (1994). *Accounting as Social and Institutional Practice*. Cambridge, UK: University Press.

Humphrey, J. E., Lee, D. D., & Shen, Y. (2012). The Independent Effects of Environmental, Social and Governance Initiatives on the Performance of UK Firms. *Australian Journal of Management*, *37*(2), 135–151.

IISD. (2010). The State of Sustainability Initiatives Review 2010: Sustainability and Transparency. Berne, Switzerland: IISD.

Intergovernmental Panel on Climate Change (IPCC). (2018). *Special Report: Global Warming of 1.5°C*. Retrieved from https://www.ipcc.ch/site/assets/uploads/sites/2/2019/02/SR15_Chapter5_Low_Res.pdf

Juhmani, O. I. (2013). Ownership structure and corporate voluntary disclosure: Evidence from Bahrain. *International Journal of Accounting and Financial Reporting*, *3*(2), 133.

Khaveh, A., Nikhasemi, S. R., Haque, A., & Yousefi, A. (2012). Voluntary Sustainability Disclosure, Revenue, and Shareholders Wealth-A Perspective from Singaporean Companies. *Business Management Dynamics*, *1*(9), 6–12.

King, M. E. (2002). *King Report on Corporate Governance for South Africa 2002*. Institute of Directors in Southern Africa.

Kuk, G., Fokeer, S., & Hung, W. (2005). Strategic Formulation and Communication of Corporate Environmental Policy Statements: UK Firms' Perspective. *Business Ethics (Oxford, England)*, *58*, 375–385.

Lindblom, C. K. (1993). *The Implication of Organization Legitimacy for Corporate Social Performance and Disclosure*. Paper presented at the Critical Perspectives in Accounting Conference, New York, NY.

Lopez, M. V., Garcia, A., & Rodriguez, L. (2007). Sustainable development and corporate performance: A study based on the Dow Jones Sustainability Index. *Journal of Business Ethics*, *75*(3), 285–300.

Mansor, N., Jamil, A., & Bahari, A. (2017). Integrated Waqf Reporting System. *International Journal of Accounting. Finance and Business*, *2*(6), 155–166.

Marston, C. L., & Shrives, P. J. (1991). The use of disclosure indices in accounting research: A review article. *The British Accounting Review*, *23*(3), 195–210.

Mathur, V. N., Afionis, S., Paavola, J., Dougill, A. J., & Stringer, L. C. (2014). Experiences of host communities with carbon market projects: Towards multi-level climate justice. *Climate Policy*, *14*(1), 42–62.

Miller, M. (1994). Accounting as social and institutional practice: An introduction. In A. G. Hopwood & P. Miller (Eds.), *Accounting as Social and Institutional Practice* (pp. 1–39). Cambridge, UK: Cambridge University Press.

Milne, M., & Patten, D. (2001). Securing organizational legitimacy: an experimental decision case examining the impact of ED. *APIRA Conference*, 1-44.

Mitchell, R. K., Agle, B. R., & Wood, D. J. (1997). Toward a theory of stakeholder identification and salience: Defining the principle of who and what really. *Academy of Management Review*, *22*, 853–886.

Nawaiseh, M. E., Boa, S. S. A., & El-shohnah, R. A. Z. Y. (2015). Influence of Firm Size and Profitability on Corporate Social Responsibility Disclosures by Banking Firms (CSRD): Evidence from Jordan. *Journal of Applied Finance and Banking*, *5*(6), 97.

Nguyen, L. S., Tran, M. D., Nguyen, T. X. H., & Le, Q. H. (2017). Factors Affecting Disclosure Levels of Environmental Accounting Information: The Case of Vietnam. *Accounting and Finance Research*, *6*(4), 255.

Ngwakwe, C. C. (2009). Environmental responsibility and firm performance: Evidence from Nigeria. *International Journal of Humanities and Social Science*, *3*(2), 97–103.

Patten, D. M. (1992). Intra-industry environmental disclosures in response to the Alaskan oil spill: A note on legitimacy theory. *Accounting, Organizations and Society*, *17*(5), 471–475.

Persson, K., & Vingren, T. (2017). *Factors affecting the sustainability disclosures in Swedish State-Owned Enterprises as hybrid organizations* (Master thesis). Kristianstad University.

Post, J. E., Preston, L. E., & Sachs, S. (2002). Managing the extended enterprise: The new stakeholder view. *California Management Review*, *45*, 6–28.

Rouf, A. (2011). Corporate characteristics, governance attributes and the extent of voluntary disclosure in Bangladesh. *African Journal of Business Management*, *5*(19), 7836–7845.

SAM Research, & Robeco Quantitative Strategies. (2011). *SAM White Paper: Alpha from Sustainability*. SAM Sustainability Investing. Retrieved from http://www.robecosam.com/images/Alpha_from_Sustainability_e.pdf

Samaha, K., Khlif, H., & Hussainey, K. (2015). The impact of board and audit committee characteristics on voluntary disclosure: A meta-analysis. *Journal of International Accounting, Auditing & Taxation*, *24*, 13–28.

Sánchez, R. G., Bolívar, M. P. R., & Hernández, A. M. L. (2017). Corporate and managerial characteristics as drivers of social responsibility disclosure by state-owned enterprises. *Review of Managerial Science*, 1–27.

Schadewitz, H., & Niskala, M. (2010). Communication via responsibility reporting and its effect on firm value in Finland. *Corporate Social Responsibility and Environmental Management*, *17*(2), 96–106.

Sciulli, N. (2009). Sustainability reporting by local councils in coastal regions: An Australian study. *Asian Journal of Finance & Accounting.*, *1*(1), 76–86.

Trencansky, D., & Tsaparlidis, D. (2014). *The effects of company´ s age, size and type of industry on the level of CSR: The development of a new scale for measurement of the level of CSR* (Master Thesis). Umea University.

Venanzi, D. (2012). *Social Ratings and Financial Performance: An Instrumental Approach.* Available at SSRN 2188859.

Warren, J., & Thomsen, M. (2012). *The Case for Corporate Responsibility Reporting: Valuing and Communicating the Intangibles.* White Paper. OneReport, Inc.

Wheeler, D., & Sillanpää, M. (1997). *The Stakeholder Corporation.* London, UK: Pitman.

Ziegler, A., Rennings, K., & Schroder, M. (2002). *The effect of environmental and social performance on the shareholder value of European stock corporations.* Centre for European Economic Research (ZEW). Retrieved from http://www.eea-esem.com/papers/eea-esem/2003/342/paper.pdf

ADDITIONAL READING

Barbu, C.-M., & Căpuşneanu, S. (2012). The state and the corporate social responsibility. *Metalurgia International*, *XVII*(2), 141–145.

Căpuşneanu, S., Ivan, R., Topor, D. I., Oprea, D.-M., & Muntean, A. (2015). Environmental Changes and their Influences on Performance of a Company by Using Eco-dashboard. *Journal of Environmental Protection and Ecology*, *16*(3), 1091–1100.

Constantin, D. M., Topor, D. I., Căpuşneanu, S., & Anica-Popa, A. (2019). Throughput Accounting and Green Reporting: Decision Support for Enhancing Environmental Performance. In I. Oncioiu (Ed.), *Throughput Accounting in a Hyperconnected World* (pp. 94–119). Hershey, PA: IGI Global, USA.

Constantin, D. M., Topor, D. I., Căpuşneanu, S., Türkeş, M. C., & Anghel, M.-G. (2019). Green Reporting and Its Impact on Business Strategy: Computer Program for Evidence and Green Reporting. In I. Oncioiu (Ed.), Network Security and Its Impact on Business Strategy, 91-109, Hershey, PA: IGI Global, USA.

Ivan, O. R., Căpuşneanu, S., & Topor, D. I., & Oprea (Constantin), D.-M. (2017). The auditing of the eco-dashboard of a company in the aluminum industry and its impact on sustainability. *Journal of Environmental Protection and Ecology*, *18*(1), 399–409.

Martinescu, D.-M., & Căpuşneanu, S. (2009). Environment and environmental effects of pollution. Model of eco-dashboard - a tool for analysis of environmental management performances. *Metalurgia International*, *XIV*(12), 113–116.

Oncioiu, I., Căpuşneanu, S., Türkeş, M. C., Topor, D. I., Oprea Constantin, D. M., Marin-Pantelescu, A., & Ştefan Hint, M. (2018). The Sustainability of Romanian SME's and their Involvement in Circular Economy. *Sustainability*, *10*(8), 2761.

Topor, D. I., Barbu, C.-M., & Căpuşneanu, S., (Boca) Rakos, I.S., & Constantin (Oprea), D.-M. (2016). Decisions based on environmental investments and sustainability, *Annals of the „Constantin Brâncuşi" University of Târgu Jiu. Economy Series*, *I*(Special Issue), 144–151.

Topor, D. I., Căpuşneanu, S., & Tamaş, A. Z. (2017). An efficient green control (EGC) encouraging environmental investment and profitability. *Journal of Environmental Protection and Ecology*, *18*(1), 191–201.

KEY TERMS AND DEFINITIONS

Emission: Transfer of atmospheric pollution from the source to the free atmosphere.

Environment: The environment in which a company operates, including air, water, soil, flora, fauna, man, and relationships between them.

Environmental Performance: Results that can be measured by a company's environmental management.

Stakeholders: Groups interested in disclosing sustainable information contained in the company's sustainability report.

Sustainability: The current economic and social development without damaging the natural environment.

Sustainability Disclosure: Disclosure of the information contained in the sustainability report according to internal or external requirements (stakeholders).

Sustainability Report: (SR): Report on the environmental situation of a company based on environmental indicators.

Chapter 6
Financial Audit in Romanian Enterprises:
Coming Across Tendencies, Profits, Further Tasks, and Improvement of Business Strategies

Andreea Marin-Pantelescu
The Bucharest University of Economic Studies, Romania

ABSTRACT

The chapter proposes an interdisciplinary perspective and explores from the theoretical and practical point of view approaches of management accounting and their impact on different companies in Romania. Also, the chapter examines the role of management accounting related to accounting and auditing and offers a number of new insights into management accounting. Romanian companies in the accounting, auditing, and tax consultancy fields use computer-assisted auditing techniques (CAAT) to find better solutions for generating profits, avoiding risks and improving the companies' business strategies. The chapter will help the academia, business environment, specialty organizations, and business analysts in identifying new trends in management accounting, building on existing research and new expert assertions.

INTRODUCTION

Financial audit has the role of increasing the credibility of the information in the financial statements, by critically assessing it (Sharma et al., 2018; Tone, et al., 2018). The financial audit reviews the accounting and financial statements of the companies (Pagano et al., 2018).

The financial audit is used to express an independent opinion on the financial statements, designed to ensure and equally protect all users of the information they contain: investors, employees, unions, creditors, suppliers, clients, bankers (Fernandez, et al., 2018).

The financial information presents the risk of being less credible than it should. With a view to the legal and effective management of this risk, the financial audit analyzes the financial statements from

DOI: 10.4018/978-1-7998-0178-8.ch006

the perspective of the economic prevalence over the legal, which represents the extent to which the information is in accordance with the economic reality and not just with the existing legal framework (Talonen, 2016; Felicio & Rodrigues, 2015; Sling & Schaper, 2017).

The overall objective of the audit is to present fairly, in all material respects, a financial position and to issue an opinion according to which the economic operations are fair and in accordance with the law.

The financial audit fulfills the overall objective by achieving the following operational objectives: ensuring that the financial audit has taken into account all the risks associated with the audited entity; helping customers improve their internal audits by providing them with constructive advice on how to improve their financial statements in the future; checking the procedures used in the entity for accounting for the economic and financial operations, checking and analyzing the inventory results, ensuring that all operations were reflected in the appropriate supporting documents that were correctly and fully accounted and at the same time that there are no operations accounted repeatedly; checking that all asset and liability items recorded in the accounts are justifiable and verifiable; verifying the correctness of the recording in the accounting system and the correct reflection in the annual accounts (Meda Antal & Șumandea-Simionescu, 2015; Bruszas et al., 2018; Wang et al.; 2013; Ma et al., 2018; Johannsdottir, 2015).

The main objectives of this chapter are: *(1) the presentation of the specialized literature on financial insurance services (2) the analysis of the Romanian insurance market: both the evolution of the demand for insurance services in Romania and the analysis of the insurance services offer in Romania; (3) the presentation of the financial indicators of the leading financial audit firms in Romania; (4) the analysis of the benefits and barriers to implement a quality audit (5) the presentation of a case study on the implementation of the audit within a financial insurance firm.*

BACKGROUND

Financial services are provided by banks, credit card companies, insurance companies, finance companies, stock brokers, and investment funds. The financial services industry is relatively new, but certain parts of it, such as insurance coverage and banking services, go a long way in history. Insurances have arisen from the need to protect people and their assets against various unpredictable events such as accidents, illnesses and natural disasters. Ever since ancient times, people have been trying to find solutions to these problems (Dutta et al., 2019; Rizvi, 2013; Shi & Frees, 2010; Chen et al., 2018; Chang, 2018).

Zeyneloglu (2018) says that there is a strong link between consumer and financial insurer, trust and professionalism. Insurance companies have the opportunity to form natural and lasting relationships with consumers.

The insurance is concluded on the basis of a contract or obligation stipulated by law, whereby the insurance company undertakes in exchange for a sum of money, called the insurance premium to bear, the damages for the production of an event and to compensate the insured person (Axelsen et al., 2017; Shahzad et al., 2018; Chen et al., 2018).

The insurance is analyzed from a psychological, financial perspective, but also from a legal perspective. It can be defined from a psychological perspective as a sense of contentment, safety or psychological comfort based on covering the damage caused by the occurrence of unpredictable and unwanted events. From a financial point of view, we can state that insurance is created through a financial intermediary between insured individuals who pay quarterly insurance premiums and individuals or legal entities that need additional money (Brooks & Schophl, 2018).

In order to be useful, the insurance has to take a legal form, which can be materialized by a contract between the insured parties, therefore the insurance contract and the insurance law constitute important sources of rights and obligations in the field of insurance (Ionescu, 2010).

Technology advances, especially mobile phones, have revolutionized financial and insurance services and created new models to help both rich people and ordinary people. Insurances can be classified in several ways. Thus, the classification can show how many types of insurance do exist on this market and it is made according to several criteria, as follows:

The role of insurance has been thoroughly studied after the major global crisis (2007-2008) with its implications for the main states of the world. Studies have shown that it is extremely important to be insured during a financial crisis (Eling & Jia, 2018; Yang et al., 2017; Wei et al., 2011).

Mandatory insurances emphasize the principle of binding; they do not require the consent of the persons involved. Under these assurances, the rights and obligations of the parties are provided by law (Negru, 2006).

The optional insurance emphasizes the will of the insured person; this insurance is concluded on the basis of a contract between the two parties. Optional insurances can be completed in addition to the compulsory ones and give the insured persons the freedom to choose the risks they want compensated (Ionescu, 2010) (Figure 1). The life assurance has as its main purpose the provision of bank funds by the insurance company when an unpredictable event occurs that could endanger the insured person such as: illness, body injury, survival or death (Dobrin & Tanasescu, 2003). The insurance of goods have as purpose different material goods or values, owned by individuals or legal entities, which can be destroyed

Figure 1. Classification of insurance
Source: Adaptation after Ionescu R. (2010). Economia asigurărilor. Editura Universitară: Bucureşti

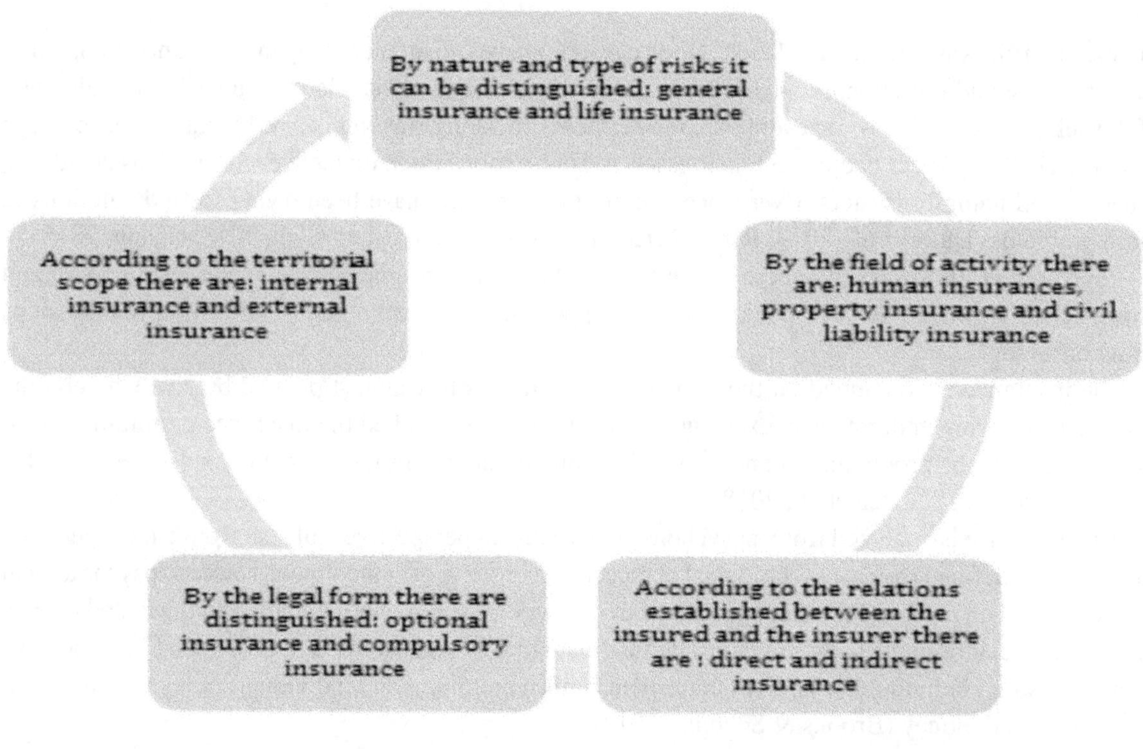

or damaged by various forces of nature or accidents. This category of insurance includes: insurance of buildings, constructions, machinery, electronic equipment, machinery and installations, animal insurance, insurance of goods, goods or other material values (Ionescu, 2010). The financial loss insurance covers losses caused by: loss of income, unforeseen expenses, loss of benefits, loss of market value other than those mentioned, as well as other financial losses or non-trade losses, according to the provisions of the insurance contract (Li et al., 2018; Aktas et al., 2019; Fischer, 2017).

The credit insurance is a form of insurance that is specific to a market economy, which is useful under the conditions of a developed credit system. Credit insurance has the role of helping traders or producers to face the risk of not paying the credit. This type of insurance focuses on risks at all stages of production, reaching even the distribution stage, with the exception of the sale to the final customer, which is covered by another category of insurance, namely the insurance of receivables. The internal credit insurance does not provide for the payment of a debit at maturity, the compensation being granted only if the creditor is not able to recover the loan due to the long-term buyer's default or the impossibility to pay it. Beginning with the 20th century, the audits are required by state, banks and shareholders, with the objective of avoiding fraud (Dobrin & Tanasescu, 2003; Zalata et al., 2018; Laptes et al., 2014; Carey et al., 2017).

The civil liability insurance is primarily intended to cover the damage caused by the insured to other persons, provided that the insured person responds according to the law. Those who suffer from accidents will be compensated by the insurer before the guilty persons are determined to pay. In our country, there are several categories of civil liability insurance, namely insurance of legal, professional liability, professional, carrier, manager, motor vehicle (by law), and the manufacturer (Brooks et al., 2019; Scholtens, 2017; Cumming & Groh, 2018; Narayan & Phan, 2019).

The civil liability insurance of motor vehicles (by law) covers both mandatory internal insurance for the damage caused to other persons by motor vehicle accidents, as well as external insurance, "green card", which compensates for any liability resulting from the damages to other people through the use of motor vehicles Pavlovic et al., (2016) and Santos, Favero and Distandio (2016).

Specialist Literature on Various Forms of Insurance

Life assurances can be defined as that form of insurance on the basis of which the insurer undertakes, in exchange for the sums received from the insured, to pay to the insured or insurance beneficiary a sum of money stipulated in the insurance contract in case of death or survival after exceeding the age stated in the contract. Life assurance covers the risk of death. The purpose of these insurances is the financial protection of the insured person's family, but it can also be used as a saving or investment. The contract period for this insurance is of minimum 3-5 years and may exceed 35-40 years.

Assuring survival: this type of insurance, the insurance company undertakes to pay the insured person the indemnities, provided that he is alive at the end of the contract. During the contract period, the insured person pays the insurance premiums, thus accumulating a sum of money in the possession of the insurer, an amount that the insured receives upon expiration of the contract. If the insured person dies before the expiration of the contract, the insurance company is exempted from the contractual obligations and has no obligation on the heirs of the insured person. In conclusion after the premature death of the insured person, the amounts paid by him during the contract remain to the insurance companies. This insurance has also a negative consequence, so in case of the death of the insured, the amount of money paid during the contract is lost, which does not foresee the spirit of saving. The management of the company chooses the maximum of shareholders' return as their goals (He et al., 2008; Elliehausen & Hannon, 2018 and Douglas et al., 2014).

The accident insurance protects people the consequences that may result from unforeseen events that may affect their life, ability to work or body integrity. In this case, the injured persons receive an indemnity either an amount fixed in the contract or several parts split to cover the medical expenses or the restoration of health. In the case of total permanent disability, the insurance company must pay the insured person the full amount or a part of it according to the degree of invalidity.

The rent insurance is a form of survival insurance by which the insurance company provides the insured person with the insured amount in the form of regular payments called rent. Payment of the rent is made either as soon as the contract begins or at a later date set by the insurance contract. The enhanced insurance is a method by which the dowry of a child can be provided gradually, either when the child is growing, when he/she marries or becomes financially independent. The birth insurance undertakes that in return for the insurance premium, the company will pay a sum of money to the insured person until a certain time stipulated in the insurance contract (Petrescu, 2005). Insuring marriage is when the insurer commits to pay a certain amount of money to the insured if he/she marries before reaching a certain age, which is set in the contract.

The health insurance has as its primary goal the elimination of poverty associated with incapacity for work caused by an accident or illness. By the health insurance, the insurer is obliged to reimburse all or a portion of the medical or pharmaceutical expenses if the insured person becomes ill. It is also possible for the insured to be compensated in case of permanent invalidity or temporary invalidity. For this, the insured person must pay regurarly a premium that will be charged to that company.

The insurance sale process begins with market prospecting and continues with customer contacting to establish a meeting where their needs are identified so that, on the basis of the acquired information, the solutions can be developed and the insurance product able to meet the customer's needs recommended. It then follows the meeting in order to show the client the recommended insurance benefits, and then the completion of the sale. Subsequently, our customers need our services so that the customer's advice will continue after the sale is completed. As part of a sales process, the steps taken to complete insurance are: prospecting, addressing prospective customers, phone contact, meeting information, sales meeting, resolving objections, and finalizing.

MARKET OF INSURANCE SERVICES IN ROMANIA: DEVELOPMENTS AND TRENDS CONCERNING THE DEMAND AND OFFER OF FINANCIAL INSURANCE SERVICES IN ROMANIA

"The insurance market is a framework in which insurance operations are carried out only on a contractual basis. In the insurance market there is an insurance claim coming from natural and legal persons wishing to conclude different types of insurance and the insurance offer coming from legal entities, namely organizations, specialized companies, which are authorized to operate in the field insurance and carry out such activity, of course, financially" (Ionescu, 2010). In the market economy, regardless of the country of origin or its degree of development, about the number of bidders and the number of applicants, is constantly changing. This feature also applies to the insurance market. In conclusion, the emergence of new insurance companies or other types of companies on the market takes place at the same time as the exit of other similar companies. Thus, these permanent changes prove that this market is not a closed market but a market in constant expansion (Negru, 2006).

The insurance offer comes from private insurance companies, private or public, from mutual insurance. Commercial insurance companies, whether private, state-owned or mixed-capital, seek profit-sharing and carry out their activities under the law. They have to respect the opinions and rules of the state body responsible for the supervision of insurance. (Ionescu, 2010)

The insurance market in Romania is characterized by a high level of concentration. During the year 2017, about 89% of the total gross premiums were realised by 10 insurance companies out of 31 companies providing insurance/reinsurance services at the end of 2017. In Romania, between 2013-2017, the number of insurance companies was steadily decreasing from 38 insurance companies at the end of 2013, to31 insurance companies at the end of 2017 according to the financial supervision authority. At the end of 2017 on the insurance market in Romania there were 31 insurance companies authorized by the financial supervisory authority, out of which 17 provided general insurance, 8 offered only life assurance and 6 provided various insurances (Figure 2).

On the total insurance market in Romania, the largest market share in 2017 had City Insurance SA 12.93%, followed by Allianz Ţiriac Asigurări SA, which held a quota of 12.66% and the third place is Euroins Romania Insurance Reinsurance SA with a share of 11.20%. At the end of the rankings out of the best 10 insurance companies, Generali România Asigurări Reasigurare SA ranked no. 8 with a market share of 6.32%, followed by Uniqa Asigurări SA with a market share of 4% and the last place is BCR Life Insurance Group SA with a market share of only 3.64% (Figure 3).

On the general insurance, the first 10 insurance companies received premiums in the amount of 7.7 billion lei, representing approximately 97% of the total of this insurance sub-group.

Figure 2. The evolution of the Insurance companies in Romania (number)
Source: Romanian National Insitute of Statistics adapted from Romanian Financial Supervisory Authority (2019)

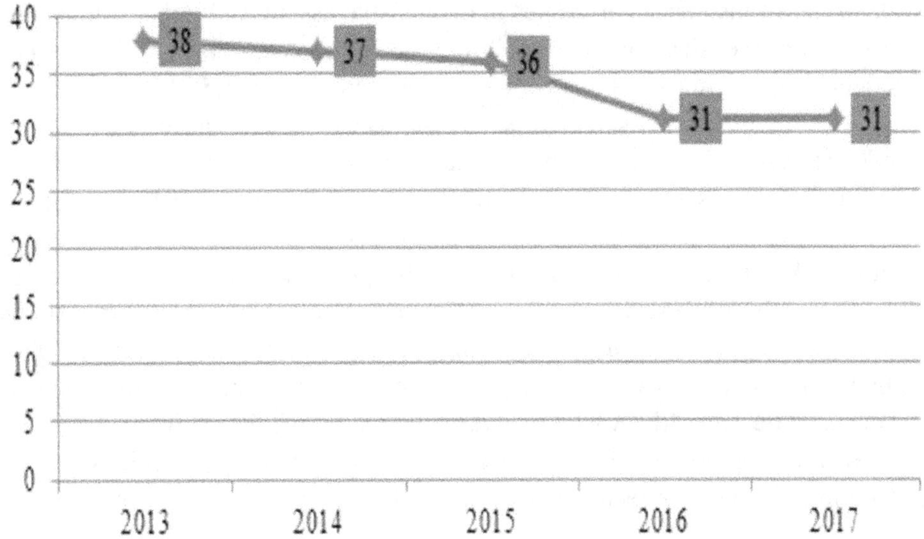

Figure 3. The market share of insurance companies in Romania in 2017. The market share of the Romanian Insurance Companies with the largest amount of gross written premiums in 2017.
Source: Romanian National Insitute of Statistics adapted from Romanian Financial Supervisory Authority (2019)

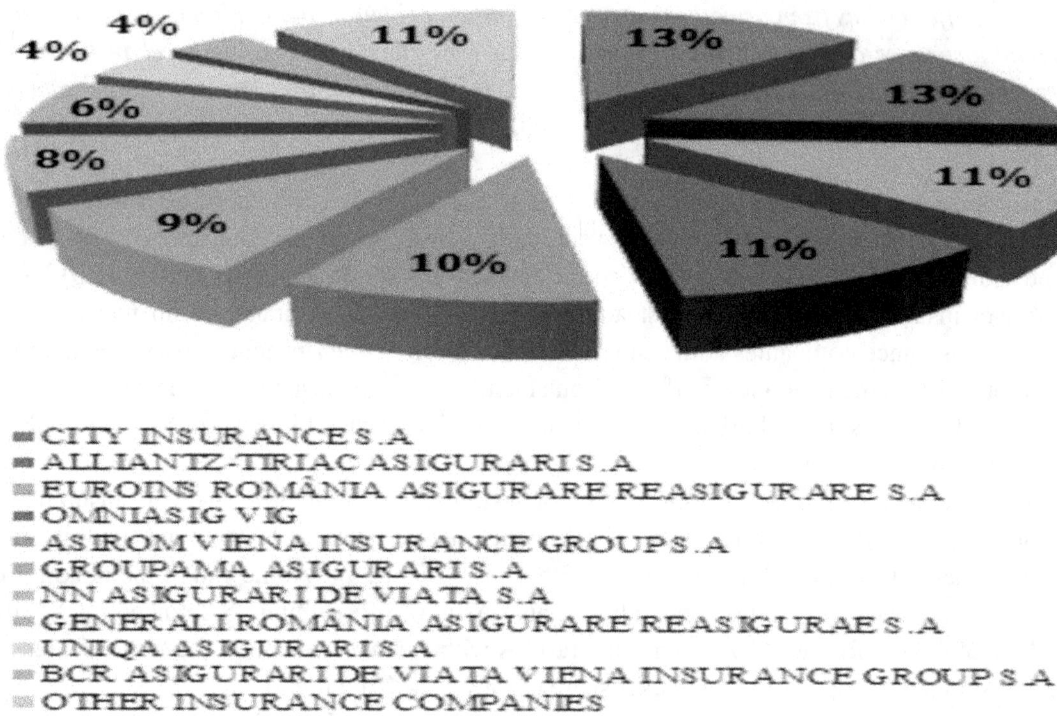

**For a more accurate representation see the electronic version.*

In Romania, general insurance sector, the largest market share at the end of 2017 had City Insurance SA with a share of 16.33%, followed by Allianz Ţiriac Asigurări SA with a market share of 14.22% and on the third place is Euroins Romania Insurance Reinsurance SA with a market share of 14.14%. At the end of the scale of the 10 insurance companies in the non-life assurance market, Uniqa Asigurări S.A is ranked no. 8 with a market share of 5.05%, followed by 9th by P.A.D. with a market share of 1.94% and Gothair Asigurari-Reasigurari S.A last with a market share of only 1.55%.

Concerning the life assurance market, the first 10 insurance companies have cumulated premiums of about 2 billion lei, representing about 95% of the total premiums earned in the life assurance segment. In Romania, in life assurance sector, the largest market share at the end of 2017 is owned by NN Life Insurance Company with a market share of 36.52%, followed by BCR Life Insurance Vienna Insurance Group SA with a market share of 17.49%, and on the third place is Ergo Asigurari de viata SA with a share of 7.57%. At the end of the scale out of the 10 insurance companies in the life assurance market, the company Generali Romania Asigurare Reasigurare SA with a market share of 3.30% ranked the 8th, followed by Uniqa Asigurari SA on the 9th place with a market share of 2.88% and the last place is Signal Iduna Asigurări Reasigurări SA with a market share of only 2.56% (Figure 4).

The insurance claim is represented by the occurrence of individuals and legal entities as insured persons in relation to their interest in the protection of certain goods, values, the integrity of individuals, against

Figure 4. Ranking of Romanian insurance companies according to gross written premiums for life assurance in 2017
Source: Romanian National Insitute of Statistics adapted from Romanian Financial Supervisory Authority (2019)

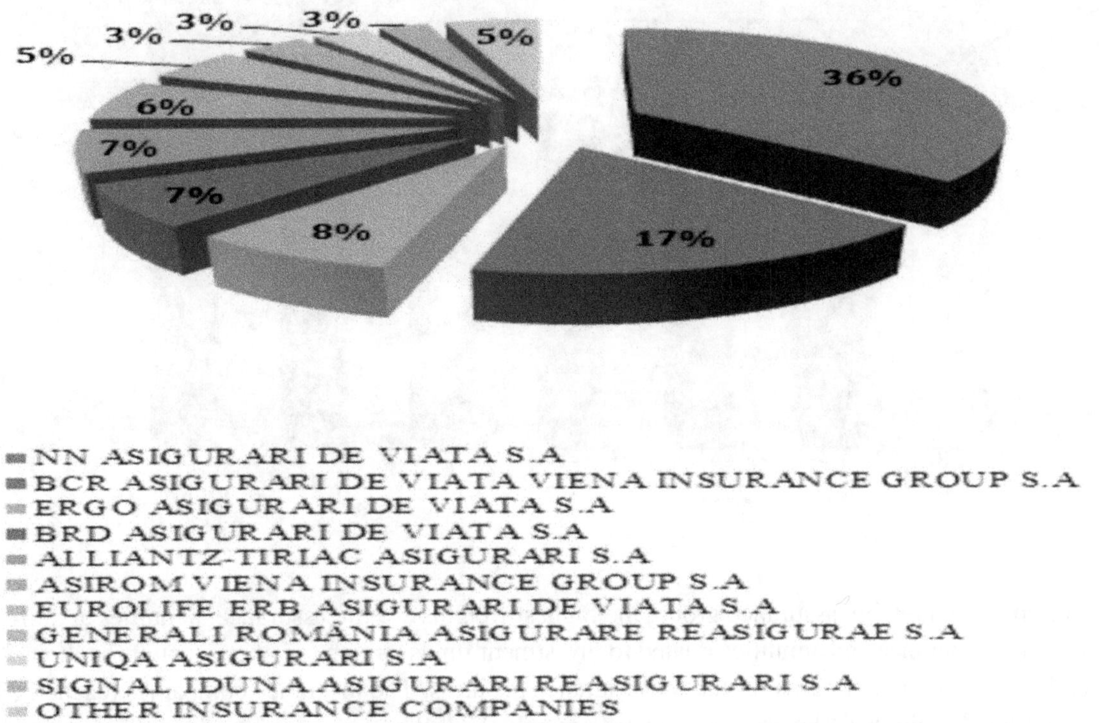

**For a more accurate representation see the electronic version.*

various risks that may affect them. The demand is integrated by consumers or insurance customers who need to cover a risk and are therefore willing to pay the appropriate premium.

The demand is defined as an expression of market needs and wishes that is conditioned by the buyer's available resources and the incentives received. The product demand is understood as a "physical or monetary quantity sold in a particular place and period". The insurance claim is materialized in insurance contracts concluded by different people at a given time. Regarding the investments of the insurance companies in Romania, they have risen significantly from year to year, reaching 14,234 million lei in 2016 (Figure 5).

In our country, the potential demand for insurance is higher than actual demand, which is lower due to a reduced economic culture and a lack of stable income that can give the buyer the certainty that he can pay the purchased insurance product. During 2017, according to the Financial Supervisory Authority, the insurance companies received gross premiums in the amount of 9.7 billion lei, increasing by 3.5% compared to 2016. In the category of general insurance during the year 2017 gross written premiums of about 7.7 billion lei were collected. Of the total premiums for non-life assurance, the highest amounts were civil liability insurance for the use of land vehicles - RCA, terrestrial vehicles excluding Casco railway material, fire and natural calamities.

In Romania, in the life assurance category, gross written premiums earned by insurance companies increased by 21% in 2017 as compared to 2016, reaching a value of approximately 2 billion lei. Of the

Figure 5. Investments of Romanian insurance companies (million lei)
Source: Romanian National Insitute of Statistics adapted from Romanian Financial Supervisory Authority (2019)

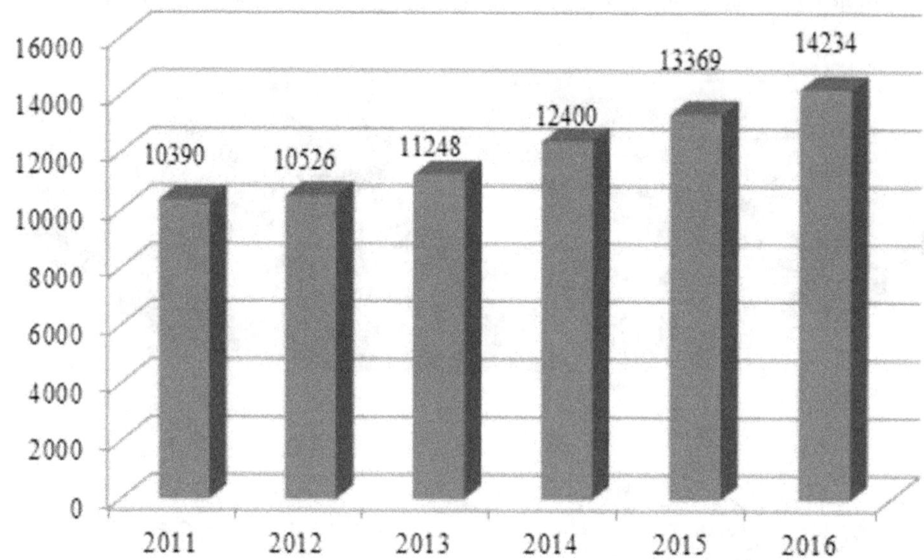

total premiums in the life assurance group, the highest weights are life assurance, annuities and life assurance, life assurance and annuities related to investment funds, which together account for about 96% of total gross written premiums for the life assurance business. The insurance companies reached 2017 gross written premiums in the amount of approximately 9.7 billion lei, increasing by 3.5% compared to 2016 so that the gross written premiums out of the general insurance are worth about 7.7 billion lei and the gross written premiums from the life assurance are in excess of 2 billion lei, thus there is a significant increase of this segment compared to the previous year.

The stabilization trend of the life assurance sub-group should be noted which increased significantly in 2017 compared to previous years. During 2017, the life assurance activity ratio in terms of the gross written premiums rose by 21%, rising compared to the lower levels recorded in previous years. At the level of the entire insurance market in Romania, the number of insurance contracts in force at the end of 2017 was approximately 14 billion lei, up 13% from the previous year. The number of insurance contracts in force at the end of 2017 for non-life assurance accounts for 87% of the total number of contracts. Both the number of contracts in force at the end of 2017 for non-life assurance and life assurance increased by 13% and 14%, respectively, compared to the same period of the previous year.

Within the framework of the general insurance during 2017, gross written premiums amounted to 7711459 thousand lei. The largest value was recorded by the motor liability insurance sub-group with a value of 4139970 thousand lei, followed by the sub-group of the non-railway vehicle insurance, other than the railway, with a value of RON 1755456 thousand. The lowest values were registered by the legal protection insurance sub-group with a value of 67 thousand lei. Concerning the life assurance, during the year 2017 gross written premiums amounted to 166947 thousand lei. The highest value was recorded by the sub-group of life assurance, annuities and supplementary life assurance of 1116592 thousand lei, followed by life assurance and annuities related to the investment fund with a value of 473969 thousand lei, health insurance has received bonuses amounting to 59438 thousand lei. The lowest values were collected by the sub-group of accident and sickness insurances amounting to 18548 thousand lei, followed by the sub-group of marriage insurance, birth insurance worth 900 thousand lei.

The German insurance company Ergo leaves Romania. The group announces that, although it has made a profit, the sales volume in Romania is too small. Ergo insurance Company emerges from several markets and, globally, businesses were in fact strongly affected by the end of their partnership with Unicredit Bank. The Italian bank sold its loans with insurance but decided to give up this model. As a consequence, the company no longer needed Ergo, because, from now on, it wants to enter into partnerships of this kind only in certain markets. The departure of the Germans does not leave their local businesses in the air: they will be bought by Generali Romania and Allianz Ţiriac.

Ergo had already asked the Financial Supervisory Authority for the agreement to sell RCA policies, and the notice is likely to be a positive one. Under these circumstances, Allianz Tiriac will remain non-life insurers, so with the RCA policies it can issue based on Ergo's business. On the other hand, Generali will take over all the life assurance business of the German company in Romania. Ergo sold insurance worth almost 47 million euros in Romania last year and net profit was half a million euros. Even so, compared with the global business of the Germans, the Romanian business was extremely small and represented only 0.3% of the total subscriptions.

THE ANALYSIS OF THE MAIN ECONOMIC-FINANCIAL INDICATORS IN AN AUDIT COMPANY IN ROMANIA

The Romanian company with the main filed of activity accounting and auditing and tax consultancy wants to keep confidentiality regarding its name for competitive reasons. The company has J40 /6775/ 1995 registration number at the Romanian Trade Registry.

"D" is the brand under which tens of thousands of independent firms from around the world collaborate to provide customer service in the following areas - audit, consulting, financial consulting, risk management and fees. In Romania, the services are provided or supported by D Audit. "D" is one of the largest professional services companies on the Romanian market and provides audit services, tax advisory services, legal services, financial advisory and consulting services, risk management services, outsourced services solutions technology consultancy and other related services.

Through more than 263,900 members of member firms, operating in more than 150 countries, "D" provides its clients with services in the following areas: audit and related services, tax consultancy, financial consulting, risk management. Worldwide D revenues in fiscal year 2017 amounted to $ 38.8 billion. Next, the evolution of the main economic and financial indicators of the company, referred to as "D" for confidentiality considerations, for the Romanian market will be presented (Table 1).

The annual average rare = (the annual average index -1)*100

The annual average index $\bar{I} = \sqrt[n-1]{\frac{y_n}{y_1}}$

Where,

n = number of years of the series

y_1 = the indicator in the first year of the series

Table 1. Financial-accounting analysis of "D" audit company in Romania over 5 years of economic activity, 2013-2017 (In lei)

	2013	2014	2015	2016	2017	*Annual average rate*
Fixed assets	1628903	1582726	1351407	1656460	2549939	*11.86%*
Current assets	30410020	33649202	39514856	34572357	35603989	*4.02%*
Total Assets	32038923	35231928	40866263	36228817	38153928	*4.46%*
Total Capital	11666087	12158319	14913042	10862938	9651821	*-4.63%*
Net turnover	63156225	70035832	78536942	78656318	84395110	*7.52%*
Total income	66158826	71100294	79898709	80389371	86194600	*6.84%*
Total expenses	59494168	65091651	71151431	68821938	76937729	*6.64%*
Gross Profit	6664658	6008643	8747278	11567433	9256871	*8.56%*
Net Profit	5478750	4992233	7254723	9581451	7697780	*8.87%*
Number of employees	213	236	274	270	292	*8.21%*
Labour productivity	*296508*	*296762*	*286631*	*291320*	*289024*	*-0.64%*
Economic profitability	*17.10%*	*14.17%*	*17.75%*	*26.45%*	*20.18%*	*4.22%*
Financial profitability	*46.96%*	*41.06%*	*48.65%*	*88.20%*	*79.75%*	*14.16%*
Commercial profitability	*8.67%*	*7.13%*	*9.24%*	*12.18%*	*9.12%*	*1.26%*
Cost-effectiveness	*9.21%*	*7.67%*	*10.20%*	*13.92%*	*10.01%*	*2.10%*

Source: Authors' calculations based on the tour operator's financial and accounting information using the economic efficiency formulas and the formula of the annual average rate. Romania Ministry of Public Finance (2019). http://www.mfinante.gov.ro/agenticod.html?pagina=domenii; 1 EURO = 4.7410 Lei according to BNR (Romanian National Bank).

y_n = last-run indicator of the series

Formula we used
Where:

r= profit rate,
PT = total net profit (absolute value),
CA = net turnover,
At = total assets,
K = used capital,
C= costs.

Relative indicators refer to the rate of return that can be of several types: commercial (R_c), economic (R_e) and financial (R_f). Labor productivity(W_L) = Net CA / Number of employees.

Analysis of Results for 2013-2017

After identifying all the figures in the "D" Financial Audit Company's profit and loss account, we can observe the following trends: fixed asset increases of 11.86% for the 5 years of economic and financial analysis (2013-2017), as well as increases in assets circulation of 4.02%. For the total assets of company "D" there is an increase of 4.46%, in 2017, the total assets of the audit company had the value of 38,153,928 lei. Going further in analyzing the trends of the company "D" a decrease in the total capital of about 4.63% can be noticed because a significant part of it was used for investment and development by the financial audit company.

The company's net turnover is up 7.52%, an extremely favorable and positive aspect, full of beneficial effects for the company's growth. For the year 2017, the company had a net turnover of 84,395,110 lei.

Both total revenue and total expenses are increasing from year to year, which means that this company is fully expanding on the Romanian financial services audit market. Regarding revenue, we have had an average annual growth rate of 6.84% over the 5 years of analysis (2013-2017) and the average annual growth rate of 6.64% for the company's total expenditure over the same period (2013-2017).

In terms of gross profit and net profit, the "D" financial audit firm has considerable increases for both indicators. These show the prosperity and freshness of the company. The growth-based vision of profit and reinvestment of profits is a winning choice for this company. As the figures speak for themselves, gross annual growth is 8.56%, and for the net profit (which remains after the state tax) the annual average growth is 8.87%. In 2017, the company had a net profit of 7,697,780 lei.

We go further in the analysis and reach the average number of employees of the firm. Thus, the average number of employees of the company increased by 8.21% during the period 2013-2017, which highlights the development of the company. If in 2013 the company registered 213 employees, in 2017 the number of employees reached 292 with growth prospects for the years 2019-2020.

For the labor productivity indicator that reports net turnover to the number of employees, we have a slight decrease of 0.64% for the entire 2013-2017 period. Employees are productive and their productivity is 289,024 lei / employee in 2017. Due to stress factors that affect workload and labor productivity, we had a slight decrease in total economic indicator of labor productivity.

Rates of return are all on the plus side, quite seldom seen on the Romanian financial market. We went into the analysis the economic profitability of the company that posted an average annual growth rate of 4.22%. If in 2013 the company had an economic rate (net profit on total assets) of about 17.10%, the economic rate increased in 2017 to 20.18%.

The second rate of return is the financial one, which brings the company's capital to the forefront. That is, net profit attributable to total capital. We are seeing an increase of 14.16% for the five years of economic and financial activity. It is a good thing, positive, favorable, and the tendency is prosperity and development, with an ascending trend. Company "D" had a financial return of 80% in 2017. The rate of return is a relative amount that expresses the extent to which the capital in its entirety brings profit. Profit and rate of profitability reflect the results of the enterprise's activity at all stages of the economic circuit. The different models used to express the rate of profitability have different informative power, reflecting the efficiency of the different sides of the enterprise's economic activity. Capital-based indicators predominantly express investor interests, while indicators built on consumed resources predominantly express the interests of managers of the economic unit.

Thus, the rate of return on equity, known in the international theory as "return on equity", allows the assessment of the efficiency of equity investments of shareholders and the opportunity to maintain them, calculated as a ratio between the net result of the financial year and the total capital. This rate is a relevant indicator in assessing the market position of the company. Increased remuneration of invested capital provides easy access to financial resources due to the confidence of current owners to reinvest in the enterprise and potential investors - holders of financial resources available for placements; and the future development capacity of the company.

The rate of commercial profitability (the ratio of the result obtained and the net turnover) shows how much the audit services offered by the company "D" are valued on the market. As the market dictates the trend, and the company under review has positive business rates, increasing from year to year, we can deduce that there is adequate management that has led to a quality of company resource management. It is fully appreciated on the market and valuable by the figures presented in Table 1. Thus, in 2017, the rate of commercial profitability was 9.12%, with an average annual growth rate for the period 2013-2017 of about 1.26%.

The Cost-effectiveness for "D" is 9.21% in 2013 and 10% in 2017. In the literature there are opinions that the optimal cost-effectiveness rate ranges from 9% to 15%. It is exactly the range in which all cost-effectiveness rates for the "D" company are found.

Following the analysis, I highlighted the high importance given to the economic and financial analysis indicators, which I calculated according to the data obtained from the profit and loss account of "D", available by the Ministry of Public Finance (2019), Unique identification number (CUI): 7756924.

ANALYSIS OF THE BENEFITS AND BARRIERS OF IMPLEMENTING A QUALITY AUDIT

"D" company offers consultancy and audit on the financial services market in Romania. For the company, a quality audit means to respect the ethics and values of the company, and to present the truth of the economic and financial statements in the profit and loss account, in the company's business portfolio, in the contracts with the clients. Collaboration is the key to success. Thus, the responsibility for conducting quality audits of financial statements lies with the auditors. However, the quality of the audit is best achieved in an environment where there is support from, and appropriate interaction among the participants in the chain of financial reporting.

According to ISQC 1 (International Standards on Quality Control), audit firms should establish a quality control system that provides for a firm a reasonable insurance, useful for its use and for its staff, in order to comply with the applicable professional standards and legal and regulatory requirements and the reports issued by the firm or the mission partners correspond to the circumstances. The results obtained include the reports and information formally drawn up and presented by one party to the other, as well as the results obtained from the audit process, which are not usually obvious to those outside the audited organization. For example, they may include improvements in the entity's financial reporting practices and internal control over the financial report that may result from the auditor's findings.

During the audit, the auditor will also carry out a series of ample communications with the management. Many of these communications are informative, but sometimes the auditor may decide, or the board may require the auditor to formalize its observations in the form of a written report.

The audit strengthens the credibility of financial reporting and can lead to an improvement in the quality of financial reporting. For example, the audit may result in management's action to modify the draft financial statements. These changes may be quantitative or qualitative in nature, such as clarifying the disclosures in the notes to the financial statements. Although these changes are not usually transparent to users, faced with what they perceive as high-quality financial statements, users can invoke a quality audit. And the opposite could also be true, for example, dealing with financial statements that contain arithmetical mistakes, inconsistencies and unclear information, in the absence of a stand-alone audit report, users can conclude that a poor quality audit has been performed.

PRESENTATION OF A CASE STUDY ON IMPLEMENTATION OF THE AUDIT IN A FINANCIAL SERVICE COMPANY

"D" set up a financial audit company in 2017 in the financial services sector, and wants to keep its confidentiality. Below I will show you what was good and what needs to be done in the insurance product portfolio based on the "D" financial audit report.

The "As You Want" insurance was one of the products analyzed and audited by "D". What was found? First of all, "As You Want" is an insurance that gives the client control over the program he or she benefits from. This insurance package provides flexibility by constantly adapting to consumer needs and requirements, including a wide range of benefits that can be changed to turn the product into a suitable insurance for anyone. The following risks are covered under this insurance package: death from any cause, total accident disability, accident and illness hospitalization, accident and illness surgery, fractures and burns from accident, serious illness, top protection.

The strenghts of the "As You Want" assurance perceived by the company's clients were: flexibility, transparency, simplicity, financial protection against the risks that may arise, and protection for the future. According to the audit firm, the motivations to purchase a life assurance are related to individual and family protection, protection against unforeseen expenses, saving for the period of the pension, but also a sense of feeling safe offered by a planned long-term protection.

"As You Want" provides a modular protection plan, which includes the company's payment of an insured amount of up to 1 million lei in the unfortunate case of death of any cause of the policy holder. In case of permanent disability or fracture and burn injury, the company provides a benefit of up to 500% of the insured amount, and for accident or surgery, it offers the same benefit, which can go up to 35,000 lei. If the client chooses for the insurance the investment component "As you wish" he can benefit from investment methods created specifically for his needs and desires, so he can also benefit from bonuses for happy events (admission to college, marriage, the birth of a child, etc.) that may occur or in the case of loyalty bonuses.

The "As You Want" insurance has been audited and is considered to be a good product for the Romanian insurance market today. The figures reported were: 84% of all customers claimed that this type of insurance is suitable to their needs; 89% of the compensation paid to the clients was for the benefits of hospitalization and surgery; 41% of the amounts paid to customers were for death-related events.

The advantages of the investment component were not well and fully understood by customers. Invest Plus assumes the accumulation of resources for future plans, whether it's about paying university studies for children or earning additional income at the retirement age. Customers have a great deal of flexibility in their investment decisions on domestic capital markets or in foreign markets, and if they have additional amounts for future plans, they have the opportunity to increase the value of the investment at any time.

SOLUTIONS AND RECOMMENDATIONS

Based on the case study a better clarification of Invest Plus is required. Also, access to an online platform called e-Customer that allows a high degree of transparency, as customers can quickly see the name of the selected investment program, the number of units, the price of a fund, the amount of the account, the value of the savings benefits with the aim of constantly optimizing the plan.

The granting of bonuses to loyal customers is another necessary recommendation. For example, customers who choose the Invest Plus investment component benefit from loyalty bonuses at the age of 10, 15 and 20 years of contract, and bonuses for happy events such as marriage, childbirth, admission to college, admission of the child to college, silver wedding, etc. This should be clearly stated and communicated to the client. The improvement of the sales staff is accomplished through specialized training, vertical, cross-sectional communication, horizontal between the components of the value chain of the financial insurance supply services on the Romanian market.

FUTURE RESEARCH DIRECTIONS

Based on the objectives set at the beginning of the chapter, I believe that these objectives have been met, addressing both the academic environment and to the business environment particularly interested in this topical theme.By compiling a large amount of information, processing and presenting it synthetically, based on specialized studies about the financial insurance market in Romania, the chosen topic covered a rather extensive area, but there are some segments to future research.In order to complete the presented topic, the specialists and all those interested can open new research directions focused on:

- The comparative analysis of the insurance market in Romania with the other European countries.
- The analysis of the impact of financial audit decisions on the managerial activity of insurance companies.
- The analysis of the possibility of creating new tools for monitoring and measuring the financial performance of financial audit firms.

CONCLUSION

This chapter covers a wide range of topics, starting with the conceptual approaches of financial insurance concepts and audit services, and continuing with the financial analysis of the financial audit firm on the Romanian market. Results have shown that the audit firm's business developed on a sound basis, that is: economic profitability of 20%, financial profitability of 80%, commercial profitability of 9.2% and cost-effectiveness of 10%, in 2017.

At the end of 2017 on the insurance market in Romania there were 31 insurance companies authorized by the financial supervisory authority, of which 17 provided general assurance, 8 offered only life assurance and 6 provided various types of insurance. Concerning the Romanian insurance companies' investments, there were significant increases from year to year, reaching 14234 lei in 2017.

In conclusion, the audit methodology must be applied by a competent team and facilitated by state-of-the-art technology. There is a hypothesis that the development of artificial intelligence will bring a grim future to certain professions, including audit and non-audit service providers.

The Quality Control System (SMC) for our audit and non-audit services is based on the International Quality Control Standard no. 1 - "Quality Control of Firms Performing Audit and Review of Financial Statements, and Other Insurance and Related Assurance Services" (ISQC 1), published by the International Auditing and Assurance Standards Board (IAASB) and standards / norms established by the Chamber of Financial Auditors in Romania.ISQC 1 applies to companies conducting audits of financial statements, reports on investment decisions and providing insurance services for activities of public interest. The objective of ISQC 1 is to establish and maintain a quality control system to provide reasonable assurance that: the firm and its employees comply with professional standards and regulatory and legal requirements.

According to the audit firm, the motivations to purchase a life assurance are related to individual and family protection, protection against unforeseen expenses, savings for the period of retirement, but also a sense of feeling safe offered by a planned long-term protection. The financial audit market is in the process of integration, while the Romanian financial insurance market, which is in the process of consolidation and concentration. The trend is upward and positive with real opportunities for development in Romania by diversifying and personalizing the services offered by specialists at the highest professional and ethical standards.

REFERENCES

Aktas, N., Andries, K., Croci, E., & Ozdakak, A. (2019). Stock market developement and the financing role of IPOs in acquisitions. *Journal of Banking & Finance*, *98*, 25–38. doi:10.1016/j.jbankfin.2018.10.015

Axelsen, M., Green, P., & Ridley, G. (2017). Explaining the information systems auditor role in the public sector financial audit. *International Journal of Accounting Information Systems*, *24*, 15–31. doi:10.1016/j.accinf.2016.12.003

Brooks, C., Fenton, E., Schopohl, L., & Walker, J. (2019). Why does research in finance have so little impact? *Critical Perspectives on Accounting*, *58*, 24–52. doi:10.1016/j.cpa.2018.04.005

Brooks, C., & Schopohl, L. (2018). Topics and trends in finance research: What is published, who publishes it and what gets cited? *The British Accounting Review*, *50*(6), 615–637. doi:10.1016/j.bar.2018.02.001

Bruszas, S., Kaschutzke, B., Maurer, R., & Siegelin, I. (2018). Unisex pricing of German participating life annuities- Boon or bane for customer and insurance company? *Insurance, Mathematics & Economics*, *78*, 230–245. doi:10.1016/j.insmatheco.2017.09.012

Carey, P., Liu, L., & Qu, W. (2017). Voluntary corporate social responsability reporting and financial statement auditing in China. *Journal of Contemporary Accounting & Economics*, *13*(3), 244–262. doi:10.1016/j.jcae.2017.09.002

Chang, C. H. (2018). The dynamic linkage between insurance and banking activities: An analysis on insurance sector assets. *Journal of Multinational Financial Management*, *46*, 36–50. doi:10.1016/j.mulfin.2018.07.001

Chen, A., Nguyen, T., & Stadje, M. (2018). Optimal investment under VaR-Regulation and Minimum Insurance. *Insurance, Mathematics & Economics*, *79*, 194–209. doi:10.1016/j.insmatheco.2018.01.008

Chen, L., Krishnan, G. V., & Yu, W. (2018). The relation between audit fee cuts during the global financial crisis and earnings quality and audit quality. *Advances in Accounting*, *45*, 14–31. doi:10.1016/j.adiac.2018.07.007

Cumming, D., & Groh, A. P. (2018). Entrepreneurial finance: Unifying themes and future directions. *Journal of Corporate Finance*, *50*, 538–555. doi:10.1016/j.jcorpfin.2018.01.011

Dobrin, M., & Tanasescu, P. (2003). Teoria şi Practica Asigurărilor. Ediţia a doua, revizuită şi îmbunătăţită. Editura economic: Bucureşti

Douglas, E., Lont, D., & Scott, T. (2014). Finance company failure in New Zealand during 2006-2009: Predictible failures? *Journal of Contemporary Accounting & Economics*, *10*(3), 277–295. doi:10.1016/j.jcae.2014.10.002

Dutta, G., Rao, H. V., Basu, S., & Tiwari, M. K. (2019). Asset liability management model with decision support system for life assurance companies: Computational results. *Computers & Industrial Engineering*, *128*, 985–998. doi:10.1016/j.cie.2018.06.033

Eling, M., & Jia, R. (2018). Business failure efficiency, and volatility: Evidence from the European insurance industry. *International Review of Financial Analysis*, *59*, 58–76. doi:10.1016/j.irfa.2018.07.007

Eling, M., & Schaper, P. (2017). Under pressure: How the business environment affects productivity and efficienty of European life insurance companies. *European Journal of Operational Research*, *258*(3), 1082–1094. doi:10.1016/j.ejor.2016.08.070

Elliehausen, G., & Hannon, S. M. (2018). The Credit Card Act and consumer finance company leading. *Journal of Financial Intermediation*, *34*, 109–119. doi:10.1016/j.jfi.2018.01.007

Felicio, J. A., & Rodrigues, R. (2015). Organizational factors and customers' motivation effect on insurance companies' performance. *Journal of Business Research*, *68*(7), 1622–1629. doi:10.1016/j.jbusres.2015.02.006

Fernandez, J., Ferreiro-Ferreiro, A. M., Garcia-Rodriguez, J., & Vazquez, C. (2018). GPU parallel implementation for asset-liability management in insurance companies. *Journal of Computational Science*, *24*, 232–254. doi:10.1016/j.jocs.2017.05.010

Fischer, M. (2017). The source of financing in mergers and acquisitions. *The Quarterly Review of Economics and Finance*, *65*, 227–239. doi:10.1016/j.qref.2017.01.003

He, L., Hou, P., & Liang, Z. (2008). Optimal control of the insurance company with proportional reinsurance policy under solvency constraints. *Insurance, Mathematics & Economics*, *43*(3), 474–479. doi:10.1016/j.insmatheco.2008.09.004

International Auditing and Assurance Standards Board. (2017). *Manualul de Reglementări Internaţionale de Control al Calităţii, Audit, Revizuire, Alte Servicii de Asigurare şi Servicii Conexe*. Retrieved from http://mf.gov.md/sites/default/files/legislatie/2015%20IAASB%20Manual%20-%20Volumul%201%20RO_2016_final.pdf

Ionescu, R. (2010). *Economia asigurărilor*. Bucureşti: Editura Universitară.

Johannsdottir, L. (2015). Drives of proactive environmental actions of small, medium and large Nordic non-life insurance companies- and insurers as a driving force of actions. *Journal of Cleaner Production*, *108*, 685–698. doi:10.1016/j.jclepro.2015.06.055

Laptes, R., Popa, A. F., & Dobre, F. (2014). Research of the Evolution of Financial Audit in Romania-Past, Current and Future Trends. *Procedia Economics and Finance*, *15*, 807–814. doi:10.1016/S2212-5671(14)00523-1

Li, X., Castellanos, S., & Maassen, A. (2018). Emeging trends and innovations for electric bus adoption- a comparative case study of contracting and financing of 22 cities in the Americas, Asia-Pacific, and Europe. *Research in Transportation Economics*, *69*, 470–481. doi:10.1016/j.retrec.2018.06.016

Ma, Y. L., Zhu, X., Hu, X., & Chiu, Y. C. (2018). The use of context-sensitive insurance telematics data in auto insurance rate making. *Transportation Research Part A, Policy and Practice*, *113*, 243–258. doi:10.1016/j.tra.2018.04.013

Meda Antal, R., & Şumandea-Simionescu, I. (2015). Possible solutions to the question of insolvency-empirical analysis regarding the degree of expolsure of the solvency of Romanian insurance companies. *Procedia Economics and Finance*, *32*, 376–382. doi:10.1016/S2212-5671(15)01407-0

Narayan, P. K., & Phan, D. H. B. (2019). A sourvey of Islamic banking and finance literature: Issues, chellenges and future directions. *Pacific-Basin Finance Journal*, *53*, 484–496. doi:10.1016/j.pacfin.2017.06.006

Negru, T. (2006). *Asigurări Ghid practic*. Bucureşti: Editura C.H. Beck.

Pagano, A. J., Feofilovs, M., & Romagnoli, F. (2018). The relationship between insurance companies and natural disaster risk reduction: Overview of the key characteristics and mechanisms dealing with climate change. *Energy Procedia*, *147*, 566–572. doi:10.1016/j.egypro.2018.07.072

Pavlovic, R. Z., Bukvic, R. M., & Gajic, A. M. (2016). Internal Sources of Financing Companies on the Basis of Static and Dynamic Indicators: Comparative Analysis. *Procedia: Social and Behavioral Sciences*, *221*, 270–277. doi:10.1016/j.sbspro.2016.05.115

Rizvi, S. L. (2013). When Insurance Companies and Clinicians Pay Attention to Data, Everybody Wins: A Commentary on Koons, O'Rourke, Carter, and Erhardt. *Cognitive and Behavioral Practice*, *20*(3), 325–327. doi:10.1016/j.cbpra.2013.03.003

Santos, M. A., Lopes Favero, L. P., & Distadio, L. F. (2016). Adoption of the International Financial Reporting Standards (IFRS) on companies' financing structure in emerging economies. *Finance Research Letters*, *16*, 179–189. doi:10.1016/j.frl.2015.11.002

Scholtens, B. (2017). Why Finance Should Care about Ecology. *Trends in Ecology & Evolution*, *32*(7), 500–505. doi:10.1016/j.tree.2017.03.013 PMID:28457498

Shahzad, K., Pouw, T., Rubbaniy, G., & El-Temtamy, O. (2018). Audit quality during the global financial crisis: The investors' perspective. *Research in International Business and Finance*, *45*, 94–105. doi:10.1016/j.ribaf.2017.07.137

Sharma, A., Jadi, D. M., & Ward, D. (2018). Evaluating financial performance of insurance companies using rating transition matrices. *Journal of Economic Asymmetries*, *18*, 102. doi:10.1016/j.jeca.2018.e00102

Shi, P., & Frees, E. W. (2010). Long-tail longitudinal modeling of insurance company expenses. *Insurance, Mathematics & Economics*, *47*(3), 303–314. doi:10.1016/j.insmatheco.2010.07.005

Talonen, A. (2016). Systematic literature review of research on mutual insurance companies. *Journal of Co-operative Organization and Management*, *4*(2), 53–65. doi:10.1016/j.jcom.2016.09.003

Tone, K., Kweh, Q. L., Lu, W. M., & Ting, I. W. K. (2018). Modeling investments in the dynamic network performance of insurance companies. *Omega*, 1–11.

Wang, C. W., Huang, H. C., & Hong, D. C. (2013). A feasible natural hedging strategy for insurance companies. *Insurance, Mathematics & Economics*, *52*(3), 532–541. doi:10.1016/j.insmatheco.2013.02.015

Wei, L., Haili, Y., & Yijun, H. (2011). The optimal strategy for insurance company under the influence of terminal value. *Acta Mathematica Scientia*, *31B*(3), 1077–1090.

Yang, Y., Lan, Q., Liu, P., & Ma, L. (2017). Insurance as a market mechanism in managing regional environmental and safety risks. *Resources, Conservation and Recycling*, *124*, 62–66. doi:10.1016/j.resconrec.2017.04.004

Zalata, A. M., Tauringana, V., & Tingbani, I. (2018). Audit committee financial expertise, gender, and earnings management: Does gender of the financial expert matter? *International Review of Financial Analysis*, *55*, 170–183. doi:10.1016/j.irfa.2017.11.002

Zeyneloglu, I. (2018). Fiscal policy effectiveness and the golden rule of public finance. *Central Bank Review*, *18*(3), 85–93. doi:10.1016/j.cbrev.2018.08.001

KEY TERMS AND DEFINITIONS

Financial Accounting: The way to measure, evaluate, knowledge, manage, and control the company's assets, liabilities, and equity.

Financial Audit: Represents the review activity for the financial auditors to express an opinion on the financial statements in accordance with the auditing standards that are in line with international auditing standards and adopted by the Chamber of Financial Auditors of Romania.

Insurance Audit: Consultancy services by which, based on the discussions with the client and the information provided by him/her, understanding the business carried out by the firm or the group of companies to which it belongs, an insurance program is designed to respond best customer protection needs.

Insurance Program: It is made up of several types of policies or may be a single policy that will contain all the insurance lines agreed with the client for the desired insurance protection: property insurance, vehicle damage and theft, RCA, cargo, civil liability, etc.

Life Assurance: That form of insurance on the basis of which the insurer undertakes, in exchange for the sums received from the insured, to pay to the insured or the beneficiary the insurance, a sum of money stipulated in the insurance contract, in case of his death or his survival after exceeding the age stated in the contract.

Quality Audits: Auditors are required to apply a rigorous audit process and quality control procedures in accordance with the applicable laws, regulations, and standards.

Chapter 7
Sustainable Business Practices and Their Influence on Manager Decisions:
Transversal Study

Mirela-Cătălina Turkeş
Dimitrie Cantemir Christian University, Romania

Dan Ioan Topor
1 Decembrie 1918 University, Romania

Sorinel Căpuşneanu
https://orcid.org/0000-0003-3799-3993
Titu Maiorescu University, Romania

Dana Maria Constantin
University of Bucharest, Romania

ABSTRACT

This chapter highlights the results of a transversal study on the influences of managers' decisions on sustainable business models. The objectives of this chapter are presentation of business models and sustainable business models and a study on the influences of managers' decisions on the use of sustainable business models. Based on the internal and international literature, the authors present the concepts of business models and sustainable business models as well as their typology. The types of sustainable business models are presented. The case study is focused on presenting the influences of managerial decisions on the sustainable business models of SMEs. Thus, through the authors' contribution, a new theoretical and empirical framework is created, which facilitates the identification of new ideas, themes, and debates of other aspects encountered in business and sustainable business models.

DOI: 10.4018/978-1-7998-0178-8.ch007

INTRODUCTION

Society and stakeholders cannot guarantee the sustainable use of natural resources without the involvement of qualified institutions and large enterprises or SMEs. In this respect, enterprises become responsible for having the necessary technological and financial basis for the application of sustainable development (Elkington, 1997), while also having an institutional role (Labuschagne et al., 2005). Although there have been divergences in the implementation of the principles of sustainable development, including its conceptual-applicative delimitation (Bolis et al., 2014), most specialists advocate the competitive advantages of corporate social responsibility (Porter & Kramer, 2006), the use of sustainable corporate technology in the long run, the promotion of human values with a direct effect on the progress of society (Porter & Kramer, 2011). Thus, businesses, especially SMEs, face the challenge of incorporating sustainability into their businesses, trying to contribute to global sustainability. Traditional business models are transformed based on innovation and thus give rise to sustainable business models (Boons & Lüdeke-Freund, 2013; Bocken et al., 2014). Starting from the general framework of sustainable development, the main business models and sustainable business models present in the literature are presented and analyzed. It also presents and analyzes a transversal study on the use of sustainable business models in SMEs in Bucharest, Romania, but also the results and conclusions of the authors. The main objectives of this chapter are: (1) *identifying and presenting the main business models and sustainable business models, and* (2) *presenting and analyzing a transversal study on the use of sustainable business models in SMEs in Bucharest, Romania.*

BACKGROUND

Business Models. Conceptual Approaches

The emergence of the business model concept is related to the economic momentum produced by dot-coms of the 1990s, whose economic implications have been studied by specialists (Zott et al., 2011). They tried to define the business model by assigning different meanings such as:

- *Architecture* for products, services and information flows, including a description of the various business actors and their roles, potential benefits for different business actors and their sources of income (Timmers, 1998); its architecture and its network of partners for the creation, marketing and supply of values and services, capital for customer segments to generate profitable and sustainable income streams (Dubosson-Torbay et al., 2002, Osterwalder et al., 2002) or the conceptual and architectural implementation of the business strategy as a foundation for the implementation of business processes (Osterwalder & Pigneur, 2002);
- *A statement* whereby a firm shows how it earns money and supports the flow of profit over time (Stewart & Zhao, 2000);
- *A way of doing business* or a particular concept of the business model that is reflected by the core values of customer propositions whose value network is configured to provide that value consisting of its own strategic capabilities just like other networks of values and capabilities . Capacities for leadership and governance are continuous and support their own reinvention to meet the multiple objectives of stakeholders, including shareholders (Voelpel et al., 2004).

- *Representation* of the way in which an interconnected set of decision variables in the areas of strategy, architecture, and risk economy are designed to create a sustainable competitive edge in defined markets" (Morris et al., 2005) or a representation of the underlying logic of a firms and strategic choices for creating and capturing value in a valuable network (Shafer et al., 2005);
- *Description* of the way (or mechanisms) by which a business can create value by the value it proposes to its customers through its value-added architecture and how it can turn this value into profit (Lehmann-Ortega & Schoettl, 2005; Moingeon & Lehmann -Ortega, 2010);
- *A structural template* of how a firm comes to agreement with local customers, partners and suppliers, how it chooses to connect with these factors and product markets (Zott & Amit, 2008);
- *A conceptual tool* that contains a set of elements and their relationships that allow expression of the business logic of a particular firm (Osterwalder et al., 2005); an integrated model that allows a concise look at the main aspects of interconnection and the logic of value creation between a firm's business over time (Aspara et al., 2013);
- *A set* of structured operations and interdependent relationships between a firm and its customers, suppliers, complementary partners, partners and other stakeholders as well as between its internal units and departments (Doz & Kosonen, 2010);
- *A configuration* of activities and organizational units that are executed inside and outside a design firm to create value in producing/delivering products on sales markets (Santos et al., 2009); a configuration (activity systems) of what activities are doing and what they invest in (resources) based on logics, that bring profit to a specific business (Chatterjee, 2013);
- *Logics* or logical operational center of a value creation organization, indicating activities and approaches that enable it to attract customers, employees and investors, and deliver profitable products and services (Linder & Cantrell, 2000);
- *Design* by which an organization converts a set of strategic choices (about market, customers, processes, architecture, culture, and measurement systems) so as to create and capture this value (Smith et al., 2010);
- *System* manifested in key components (company's network of relationships, operations included in business processes and the company's resource base, company finance and accounting components) and related materials related to cognitive aspects (Tikkanen et al., 2005); a well-defined system of interdependent structures, activities and processes that serve as the organizational logic for creating value (for its customers) and acquiring value (for itself and for its partners) (Sorescu et al., 2011);

The business model has received from the specialists other interpretations such as: (1) the business model consists of interlocking the four elements together (proposal of customer value, profit formula, key resources, key processes) (Johnson et al., 2008) (2) the business model is defined as a revenue-generating approach at reasonable cost and incorporating assumptions about how both could create and capture value (McGahan, 2010); (3) the business model is defined as the way a company processes its own activities to determine the concentration, location and way of doing business (Onetti et al., 2012); (4) the essence of the business model lies in the way the company delivers value to customers, attracting customers to pay value and convert it into profit (Teece, 2010).

Sustainable Business Models. History and Evolution

The first attempts to define the sustainable business model consisted in identifying its main purpose, i.e. integrating the concept of sustainability to reach sustainability by companies and turning them into sustainable economic systems. In other words, a sustainable business model "a model in which the concepts of sustainability are the driving force of the firm and decision-making [so that] the dominant neoclassical model of the firm is transformed, rather than supplemented, by social and environmental priorities" (Stubbs & Cocklin, 2008); a business model for sustainability "would contribute to achieving sustainability [by] respecting major [...] sustainability principles" defined as: resource efficiency, social relevance, location and employment, longevity, ethical supply and enrichment work" (Wells, 2013).

Other definitions made by specialists in the concept of sustainable business model emphasize other features such as: the need for sustainable products and services on the global market (Garetti & Taisch, 2012); determination of inputs, resource flow and results evaluation indicators (Upward & Jones, 2015); the description by means of 5 sentences: "(1) Sustainable value includes economically, socially and environmentally conceived benefits as forms of value; (2) Sustainable business models require a system of sustainable value flows between multiple stakeholders, including the natural environment and society, as key stakeholders; (3) Sustainable business models require a value-added, design and governance network of values; (4) Sustainable business models require a systematic analysis of stakeholders' interests and responsibilities for creating mutual values; (5) The internalization of externalities through product service systems enables innovation to sustainable business models " (Evans et al., 2017).

Most definitions in the literature include in defining the concept of sustainable business model certain characteristics and objectives of the conventional model of the business model. Among these features we can identify: (1) incorporate concepts, principles or goals that aim at sustainability (Schaltegger et al., 2012; Boons & Lüdeke-Freund, 2013; Wells, 2013); (2) integrates the sustainability into their value propositions, value creation and delivery activities and/or mechanisms for capturing value or exchange with various stakeholder categories (Abdelkafi & Tauscher, 2016; Geissdoerfer et al., 2016). A series of archetypes of sustainable business models with additional features have been identified and presented: product and service systems, pyramid base, circular business models (Bocken et al., 2014). Circular business models include both the features of the conventional model of business model (sustainable value, proactive multi-shareholder management, long-term perspective) as well as the features of the sustainable business model (closing, slowing down and narrowing resource loops) (Geissdoerfer et al., 2018). Sustainable business models are those business models that include the proactive management of multiple stakeholders, the creation of monetary and non-monetary values for a wide range of stakeholders and the holding of long-term prospects (Geissdoerfer et al., 2018b).

Sustainable Business Models Based on Innovation

This concept is relatively new and is based on the conceptual essence of the sustainable business model plus the innovation part. According to the opinion of the specialists, the concept of a sustainable business model based on innovation can be perceived as: (1) Adapting the business model to overcome barriers or boundaries within the company and its environment to deliver sustainable processes, innovative products or services to the market (Boons & Lüdeke-Freund, 2013); (2) innovations that create significant positive changes and/or significantly reduce the impact on the environment and/or society in terms of how its organization and its network of values create, give value and create economic value (Bocken et al., 2014); (3) the processes by which new business models are developed by enterprises and their managers so that they contribute to sustainable development (Roome & Louche, 2016); (4) modified and completed business models that can contribute to their integrative and competitive development either by radically reducing negative impacts and/or by creating positive externalities for the natural environment and society (Schaltegger et al., 2016; Rakoş et al., 2018).

Based on the above mentioned, the specialists divided the innovative business models based on innovation into four categories: "(1) sustainable start-ups: a new organization with a sustainable business model; (2) transforming the sustainable business model: the current business model is changed, resulting in a sustainable business model; (3) diversification of the sustainable business model: no major changes in the existing business models of the organization and additionally the sustainable business model is established; 4) acquisition of sustainable business model: an additional, sustainable business model is identified, acquired and integrated within the organization" (Geissdoerfer et al., 2018b). In other words, by innovating the sustainable business model, management wants to use the 4 types of sustainable innovation mentioned above in order to create sustainable long-term values and proactive stakeholder management. Management also wishes to implement one or more strategic sustainable business models or create sustainable business of circular business type (Oncioiu et al., 2018), social enterprises, lower pyramid solutions or product-service systems (Geissdoerfer et al., 2018b).

THE USE OF SUSTAINABLE BUSINESS MODELS IN BUCHAREST MUNICIPALITIY. TRANSVERSAL STUDY

The purpose of quantitative research involves identifying the opinions and behavior of SMEs in Bucharest, Romania regarding the components, benefits and barriers specific to the business model as a result of the inclusion of sustainability considerations.

The main objectives of the research were: (1) identifying the main components that SMEs focus on developing sustainable business models; (2) perceiving sustainable business models as a competitive advantage by SMEs; (3) improving the business model of enterprises as a result of including sustainability; (4) identifying the factors that generate changes in the business model as a result of the inclusion of sustainability considerations; (5) determining changes in SME commitment to sustainability (in terms of management and investment) over the past year; (6) knowledge of the benefits experienced by SMEs following the use of sustainable business model; (7) identify the main obstacles faced by SMEs as a result of using the sustainable business model.

In this respect, a quantitative marketing research was carried out among the SMEs in Bucharest, Romania. This research is extremely important, providing an overview of the benefits and barriers faced by SMEs in developing sustainable business models. The information needed to carry out the marketing research comes exclusively from representatives of SMEs in Bucharest. The sampling method used in this quantitative marketing research was the inquiry by online survey. Between 1 October 2018 and 1 January 2019, the information gathering stage was conducted from the population surveyed. The questionnaire used for data collection included a total of 7 closed queries of the nominal scale type and range. The online questionnaire was distributed by email to the managers of some SMEs in Bucharest. Following the collection process, 120 responses resulted. The collected information was analyzed with the SPPS package using different bivariate analysis methods such as frequency tables and contingency tables. The limiting conditions of this research are primarily related to the size of the sample (120 respondents), which is not characterized by a high degree of representativeness. Although the response rate is low due to the free self-selection process among respondents, the information obtained from them was relevant to the marketing research objectives and offers the opportunity to carry out new marketing research as a step in overcoming these limits.

RESULTS AND DISCUSSIONS

Question 1: What components does your company focus on for developing a sustainable business model?

For the first question a nominal scale was used and the answers were coded with numbers from 1 to 6. Regarding the six components, the respondents reported that the dynamics of the business model components should be taken into account. Most managers pay special attention to "structure" (31.7%) and "processes" (27.5%) when considering the development of a sustainable business.

"Technology" is the third component on which 16.7% of respondents are focused. 9.2% of SMEs claim that broad knowledge and a deep understanding of strategic objectives, vision and values are very important elements for developing a sustainable business model. More moderate attention is given by SME managers to components such as "revenue" and "legal issues" (7.5%), highlighting the need for a different combination of all six components depending on the nature of the company's business object to generate a sustainable business model (Figure 1). The link between the typology of the components on which SMEs are focused and their size and age was highlighted by contingency tables, using both

Figure 1. Share of SME responses regarding the components that are primarily focused on for developing a sustainable business model
Source: Authors representation

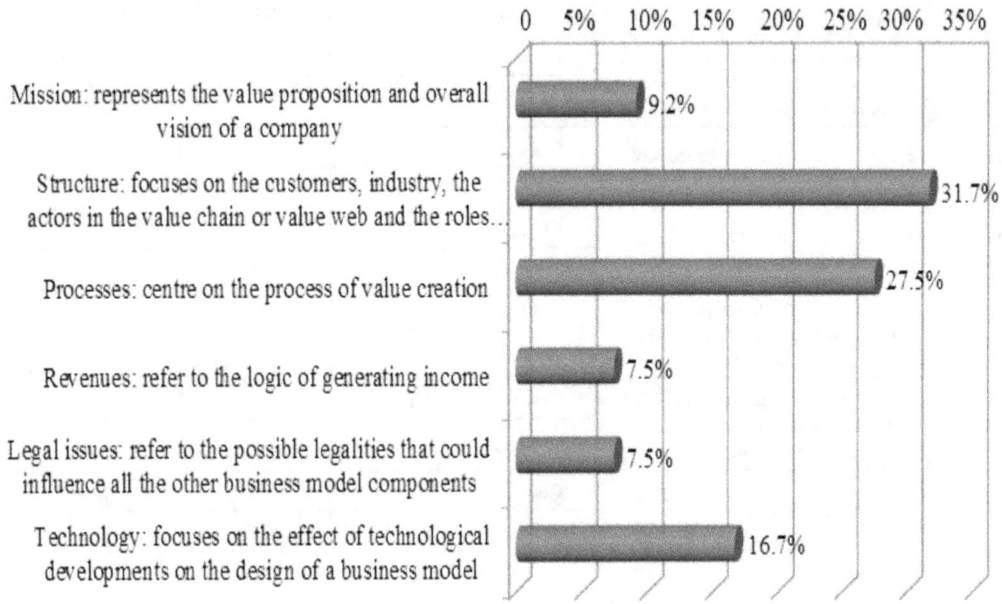

absolute and relative frequencies. Thus, in Table 1 below it can be noticed that 81.7% of the 120 responding SMEs are small (Micro) with up to 9 employees. 12.5% of the entities are small enterprises with between 10-49 employees and the remaining 5.8% are medium-sized enterprises with between 50-249 employees. For the development of the business model, the medium-sized enterprises concentrate equally on three components: "Structure" 1.7%), "Revenues" (1.7%) and "Technology" (1.7%). Medium-sized enterprises have prioritized the components they focus on: "Structure" (5.0%), "Processes" (3.3%) and "Technology" (1.7%). Micro enterprises focus equally on "Structure" (25.0%) and "Processes" (24.2%), followed by "Technology" (13.3%), "Mission" 6.7%) and "Revenue" (5.0%).

5-6 year-old SMEs, for the development of medium enterprises business model focus on components such as: "Processes" (21.7%), "Structure" (20.8%), "Revenues" (1.7%) and "Technology" (14.2%). Although they account for 16.7% of all responding SMEs, enterprises aged 9-14 years focus on the following components: "Structure" (6.7%), "Processes" (3.3%) and "Revenues" 3.3%), when they are considering developing their own business model. Enterprises with more than 15 years of experience on the Bucharest market emphasize components such as: "Structure" (4.2%) and "Processes" (2.5%), "Mission" (1.7%), "Legal issues" and "Revenue" (1.7%) (Table 2).

Question 2: Can sustainable business models be perceived as a competitive advantage?

Table 1. Contingency table regarding the components included by SMEs in business models according to their size (absolute frequencies and percentages)

			Number of employees			Total
			Between 0-9 people	Between 10-49 people	Between 50-249 people	
On what components does your company focus on developing a sustainable business model?	*Mission*: represents the value proposition and overall vision of a company	Count	9	1	1	11
		% of Total	7.5%	0.8%	0.8%	9.2%
	Structure: focuses on the customers, industry, the actors in the value chain or value web and the roles they play	Count	30	6	2	38
		% of Total	25.0%	5.0%	1.7%	31.7%
	Processes: centre on the process of value creation	Count	29	4	0	33
		% of Total	24.2%	3.3%	0.0%	27.5%
	Revenues: refer to the logic of generating income	Count	6	1	2	9
		% of Total	5.0%	0.8%	1.7%	7.5%
	Legal issues: refer to the possible legalities that could influence all the other business model components	Count	8	1	0	9
		% of Total	6.7%	0.8%	0.0%	7.5%
	Technology: focuses on the effect of technological developments on the design of a business model	Count	16	2	2	20
		% of Total	13.3%	1.7%	1.7%	16.7%
Total		Count	98	15	7	120
		% of Total	81.7%	12.5%	5.8%	100.0%

Source: Authors calculation

Table 2. Table of contingency of components included by SMEs in business models according to their age on the national market (absolute frequencies and percentages)

			Year of establishment			Total
			5 - 9 years	9 - 14 years	> 15 years	
On what components does your company focus on developing a sustainable business model?	*Mission*: represents the value proposition and overall vision of a company	Count	8	1	2	11
		% of Total	6.7%	0.8%	1.7%	9.2%
	Structure: focuses on the customers, industry, the actors in the value chain or value web and the roles they play	Count	25	8	5	38
		% of Total	20.8%	6.7%	4.2%	31.7%
	Processes: centre on the process of value creation	Count	26	4	3	33
		% of Total	21.7%	3.3%	2.5%	27.5%
	Revenues: refer to the logic of generating income	Count	3	4	2	9
		% of Total	2.5%	3.3%	1.7%	7.5%
	Legal issues: refer to the possible legalities that could influence all the other business model components	Count	6	1	2	9
		% of Total	5.0%	0.8%	1.7%	7.5%
	Technology: focuses on the effect of technological developments on the design of a business model	Count	17	2	1	20
		% of Total	14.2%	1.7%	0.8%	16.7%
Total		Count	85	20	15	120
		% of Total	70.8%	16.7%	12.5%	100.0%

Source: Authors calculation

For the second question we have coded the answers with numbers 1 to 3 within a nominal scale. 7 out of 10 SME managers have argued that sustainable business models can be perceived as a competitive advantage. Only 20% of respondents said that "No", while 9.2% said "I do not know" (Figure 2).

Of the 81.7% respondent microenterprise who said that sustainable business models could be perceived as a competitive advantage, 58.3% gave an affirmative answer, 15.8% one negative and the remaining 7.5% claimed "I do not know". The same was supported by 8.3% of small enterprises and 4.2% of medium-sized enterprises (Table 3).

Figure 2. Share of SMEs' responses about perceiving sustainable business models as competitive advantages
Source: Authors representation

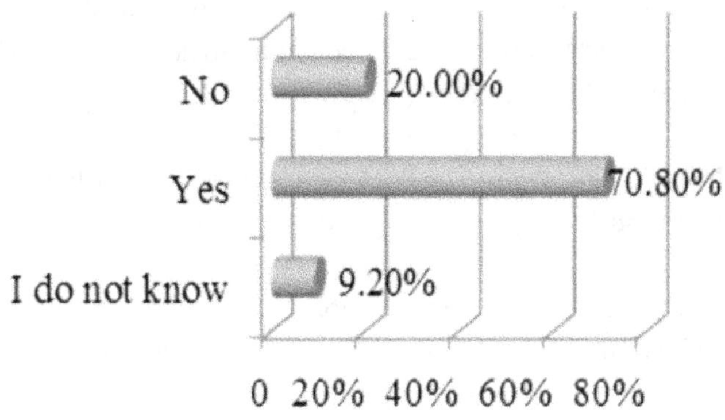

Table 3. Contingency table based on business models perceived as competitive advantages and enterprise size (absolute frequencies and percentages)

			Number of employees			Total
			Between 0-9 people	Between 10-49 people	Between 50-249 people	
Can sustainable business models be perceived as a competitive advantage?	No	Count	19	4	1	24
		% of Total	15.8%	3.3%	0.8%	20.0%
	Yes	Count	70	10	5	85
		% of Total	58.3%	8.3%	4.2%	70.8%
	I do not know	Count	9	1	1	11
		% of Total	7.5%	0.8%	0.8%	9.2%
Total		Count	98	15	7	120
		% of Total	81.7%	12.5%	5.8%	100.0%

Source: Authors calculation

In Table 4 of contingency, we can see that 35.0% of the SME's in the field of "Trade" and "Tourism, travel and restaurants" gave an affirmative answer to the question about perceiving sustainable business models as real competitive advantages.

Out of the 57.4% of SMEs that said that the business model used by the enterprise changed as a result of sustainability, 13.3% came from "Trade" and 10.0% from "Tourism, travel and restaurants". The rest of the SMEs that responded positively come from: "Business/finance/real estate/information services" (6.7%), "Construction" (4.2%), "Transport and utilities, telecommunications" (4.2%), "Manufacturing industry" (4.2%) and "Agriculture/forestry and fishing/mining" (2.5%).

Question 3: Has your organization's business model changed as a result of sustainability?

For the third question a nominal scale was used, the answers being coded with numbers from 1 to 3. 47.5% of the respondents' SMEs stated that the business model used by the enterprise changed as a result of sustainability. The remaining 52.5% of SMEs responded either to "No" (30.0%) or "I do not know" (22.5%) (Figure 3).

Table 5 shows that 16.7% of responding SMEs active in areas such as "Trade" and "Construction" said their business models did not change substantially following the integration of sustainability elements. The same opinion was shared by 13.3% of managers of SMEs operating in areas such as: "Business/finance/real estate/information services" (2.5%), "Manufacturing industry" (3.3%), "Tourism, travel and restaurants "(3.3%), "Transport and utilities, telecommunications" (2.5%), "Agriculture/forestry and fishing/mining" (0.8%) and other activities (0.8%).

Question 4: Which of the following factors has caused changes to your business model as a result of sustainability considerations?

Within the nominal scale used for the fourth question, the answers were coded with numbers from 1 to 11. From the results obtained for this analyzed variable, we can notice that the factors causing changes

Table 4. The contingency table based on business activity and business models perceived as competitive advantages (absolute frequencies and percentages)

			Can sustainable business models be perceived as a competitive advantage?			Total
			No	Yes	I do not know	
Areas of activity	Agriculture/forestry and fishing/ mining	Count	0	5	0	5
		% of Total	0.0%	4.2%	0.0%	4.2%
	Trade	Count	6	30	3	39
		% of Total	5.0%	25.0%	2.5%	32.5%
	Tourism, travel and restaurants	Count	5	12	2	19
		% of Total	4.2%	10.0%	1.7%	15.8%
	Business/finance/ insurance/real estate/ information services	Count	4	11	3	18
		% of Total	3.3%	9.2%	2.5%	15.0%
	Construction	Count	3	8	0	11
		% of Total	2.5%	6.7%	0.0%	9.2%
	Transport and utilities, telecommunications	Count	4	7	0	11
		% of Total	3.3%	5.8%	0.0%	9.2%
	Manufacturing industry	Count	1	10	1	12
		% of Total	.8%	8.3%	0.8%	10.0%
	Other	Count	1	2	2	5
		% of Total	0.8%	1.7%	1.7%	4.2%
Total		Count	24	85	11	120
		% of Total	20.0%	70.8%	9.2%	100.0%

Source: Authors calculation

Figure 3. Share of SMEs' responses about changing the enterprise business model as a result of sustainability
Source: Authors representation

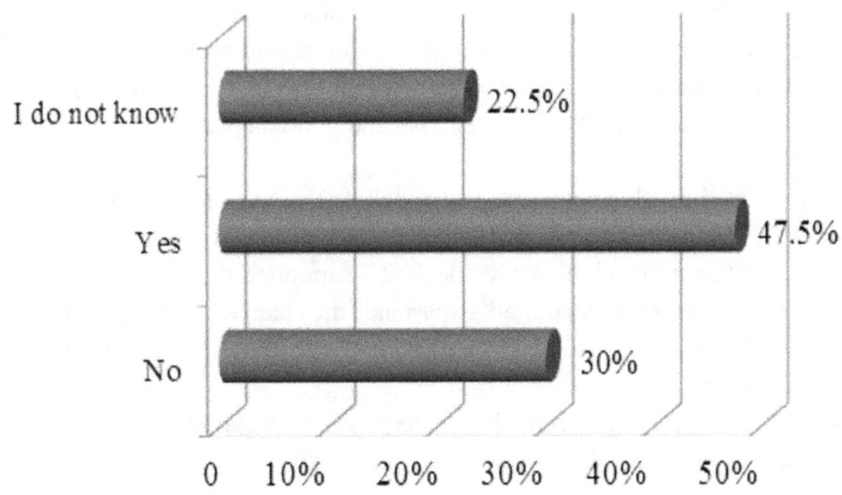

Table 5. The contingency table based on the change in the business model of the enterprise as a result of the sustainability by field of activity (absolute frequencies and percentages)

			Has your organization's business model changed as a result of sustainability?			Total
			No	Yes	I do not know	
Areas of activity	Agriculture/forestry and fishing/mining	Count	1	3	1	5
		% of Total	0.8%	2.5%	0.8%	4.2%
	Trade	Count	15	16	8	39
		% of Total	12.5%	13.3%	6.7%	32.5%
	Tourism, travel and restaurants	Count	4	12	3	19
		% of Total	3.3%	10.0%	2.5%	15.8%
	Business/finance/ insurance/real estate/ information services	Count	3	8	7	18
		% of Total	2.5%	6.7%	5.8%	15.0%
	Construction	Count	5	5	1	11
		% of Total	4.2%	4.2%	0.8%	9.2%
	Transport and utilities, telecommunications	Count	3	5	3	11
		% of Total	2.5%	4.2%	2.5%	9.2%
	Manufacturing industry	Count	4	5	3	12
		% of Total	3.3%	4.2%	2.5%	10.0%
	Other	Count	1	3	1	5
		% of Total	0.8%	2.5%	0.8%	4.2%
Total		Count	36	57	27	120
		% of Total	30.0%	47.5%	22.5%	100.0%

Source: Authors calculation

in the business models of SMEs as a result of sustainability considerations were ranked by respondents as "Customers prefer sustainable products/services" (18.3%), "Meeting demands of existing employees" (13.3%), "Competitors increasing commitment to sustainability" (12.5%), "Maintaining" license to operate "(10.8%)," Strict requirements from partners along the value chain "(10.0%)," Owners' demands for broader value creation (i.e., more than profits)" (6.7%), "Competing for new talent "(6.7%)," Resource scarcity (e.g. increased commodity prices and price volatility)" (5.8%), "Customers willing to pay a premium for sustainable offering" (5.8%), "Legislative and political pressure" (5.8%) and "None of the above" (4.2%) (Table 6).

From the data presented in table below we can conclude that out of the 85 responding enterprises, with a market age of 5-9 years, 36.7% said that their business models did not change substantially following the integration of sustainability elements, while 34.2% supported the opposite. 10.8% of enterprises operating on the market for over 9 years did not experience the change in business models, while 13.4% of them said that the integration of sustainability elements contributed to the substantive improvement of their own business models.

Table 7 shows that managers of medium-sized enterprises have identified three factors that have led to changes in their business models: "Customers prefer sustainable products/services" (2.5%), "Competi-

Table 6. The contingency table based on the change of the business model of the enterprise as a result of the sustainability according to their size (absolute frequencies and percentages)

			Year of establishment			Total
			5 - 9 years	9 - 14 years	> 15 years	
Has your organization's business model changed as a result of sustainability?	No	Count	23	6	7	36
		% of Total	19.2%	5.0%	5.8%	30.0%
	Yes	Count	41	11	5	57
		% of Total	34.2%	9.2%	4.2%	47.5%
	I do not know	Count	21	3	3	27
		% of Total	17.5%	2.5%	2.5%	22.5%
Total		Count	85	20	15	120
		% of Total	70.8%	16.7%	12.5%	100.0%

Source: Authors calculation

tors increasing commitment to sustainability" (12.5%) and "Competing for new talent" (0.8%). 12.5% of small business managers said business models have changed due to factors such as: "Customers prefer sustainable products/services" (3.3%), "Meeting demands of existing employees" (2.5%), "Resource scarcity (e.g., increased commodity prices and price volatility)" (1.7%) and "Owners' demands for broader value creation (i.e., more than profits)" (1.7%).

The factors that influenced business models of microenterprises as a result of sustainability considerations were: "Customers prefer sustainable products/services" (12.5%), "Meeting demands of existing employees" (10.8%), "Competitors increasing commitment to sustainability" (9.2%), "Stricter requirements from partners along the value chain" (9.2%), "Maintaining "license to operate" (10.0%), "Customers willing to pay a premium for sustainable offering" (5.8%), "Legislative *I* political pressure (5.8%), "Owners' demands for broader value creation (i.e., more than profits)" (5.0%), "Resource scarcity (e.g., increased commodity prices and price volatility)" (4.2%), and "None of the above" (4.2%) (Figure 4).

In Table 8 of contingency it can be noticed that enterprises with a market age of more than 15 years have identified 8 factors that have changed their own business models as follows: "Customers willing to pay a premium for sustainable offering" (5.8%), "Meeting demands of existing employees" (2.5%), "Customers prefer sustainable products/services" (1.7%),"Stricter requirements from partners along the value chain" (1.7%), "Competing for new talent" (1.7%), Legislative/political pressure (0.8%), "Competitors increasing commitment to sustainability" (0.8%) and "Maintaining "license to operate" (0.8%).

Among the factors that generated changes at the level of enterprises between the ages of 9-14 years are identified: "Maintaining "license to operate" (5.0%), "Customers prefer sustainable products/services" (4.2%), "Owners' demands for broader value creation (i.e., more than profits)" (1.7%), "Meeting demands of existing employees" (1.7%), "Customers willing to pay a premium for sustainable offering" (0.8%), Legislative/political pressure (0.8%), "Competitors increasing commitment to sustainability" (0.8%) and "Stricter requirements from partners along the value chain" (0.8%).

Among enterprises with a market age of up to 9 years, managers have pointed out that the factors that generated the most extensive changes in their own business models were: "Customers prefer sustainable products/services" (12.5%), "Competitors increasing commitment to sustainability" (10.8%), "Meeting

Table 7. The contingency table regarding the factors that caused changes in the business model as a result of sustainability considerations by size of enterprises (absolute frequencies and percentages)

			Number of employees			Total
			between 0-9 people	between 10-49 people	between 50-249 people	
Which of the following factors have led to changes in your business model as a result of sustainability considerations?	Resource scarcity (e.g., increased commodity prices and price volatility)	Count	5	2	0	7
		% of Total	4.2%	1.7%	.0%	5.8%
	Owners' demands for broader value creation (i.e., more than profits)	Count	6	2	0	8
		% of Total	5.0%	1.7%	.0%	6.7%
	Customers willing to pay a premium for sustainable offering	Count	7	0	0	7
		% of Total	5.8%	.0%	.0%	5.8%
	Legislative I political pressure	Count	7	0	0	7
		% of Total	5.8%	.0%	.0%	5.8%
	Meeting demands of existing employees	Count	13	3	0	16
		% of Total	10.8%	2.5%	.0%	13.3%
	Customers prefer sustainable products I services	Count	15	4	3	22
		% of Total	12.5%	3.3%	2.5%	18.3%
	Competitors increasing commitment to sustainability	Count	11	1	3	15
		% of Total	9.2%	.8%	2.5%	12.5%
	Maintaining "license to operate"	Count	12	1	0	13
		% of Total	10.0%	.8%	.0%	10.8%
	Stricter requirements from partners along the value chain	Count	11	1	0	12
		% of Total	9.2%	.8%	.0%	10.0%
	Competing for new talent	Count	6	1	1	8
		% of Total	5.0%	.8%	.8%	6.7%
	None of the above	Count	5	0	0	5
		% of Total	4.2%	.0%	.0%	4.2%
Total		Count	98	15	7	120
		% of Total	81.7%	12.5%	5.8%	100.0%

Source: Authors calculation

demands of existing employees" (9.2%), "Stricter requirements from partners along the value chain" (7.5%), "Resource scarcity (e.g., increased commodity prices and price volatility)" (5.8%), "Owners' demands for broader value creation (i.e., more than profits)" (5.0%), "Maintaining license to operate" (5.0%), "Legislative/political pressure" (4.2%), "Competing for new talent" (4.2%) and "Customers willing to pay a premium for sustainable offering" (2.5%).

Question 5: How has your organization's commitment to sustainability (in terms of management's attention and investment) changed in the past year?

Figure 4. The share of SMEs' responses regarding the factors that caused changes to the business model of the company as a result of the sustainability considerations
Source: Authors representation

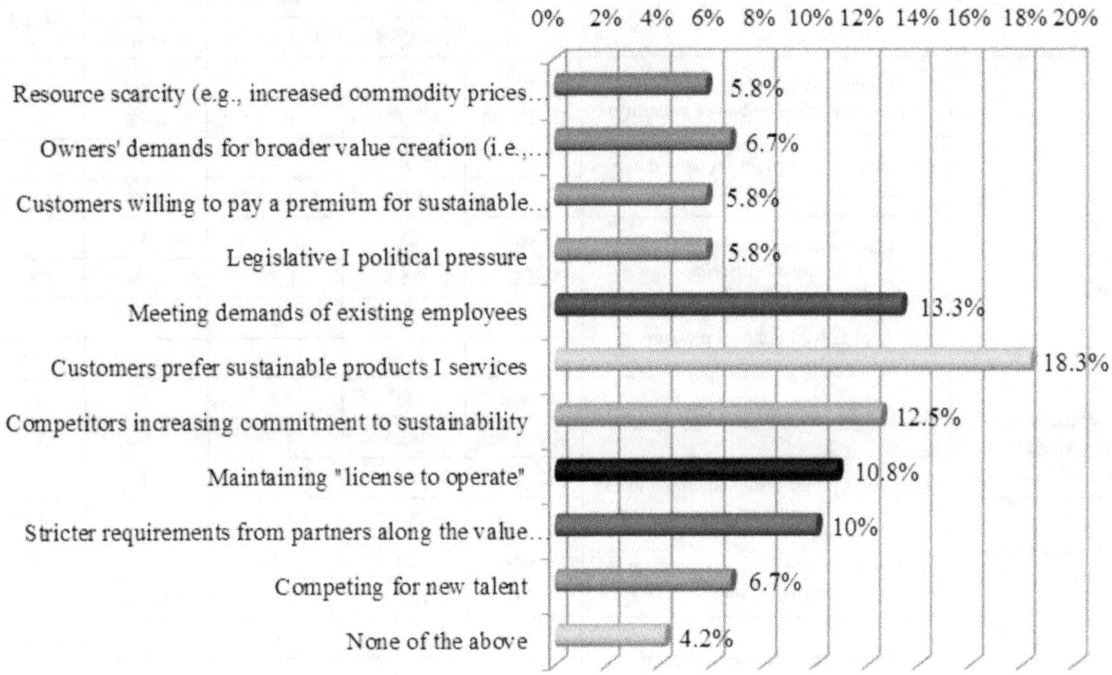

For the fifth question, an ordinal scale of the semantic differentiation type was used, and the answers were coded with numbers from 1 to 6, each code signifying the existence of a higher or lower rank of the ordering criterion. Thus, 1 means "Significant growth" and 5 = "Significantly low". The "I do not know" answers were encoded with number 88. Nearly 70.2% of respondents said that changing business commitment to sustainability in the past year has seen a "Significantly Increased" or "Somewhat Increased". The intermediate level was indicated by 3.3% of the managers who answered this question, while 20.8% of the managers experienced a "Somewhat reduced" or "Significantly reduced" change. There were 10 "I do not know" answers (Table 9).

Frequency distribution shows a concentration of SME managers' responses to the positive side of the scale. In the opinion of more than 75.5% of the respondents, the shift in enterprises' commitment to sustainability in the last year has seen a "Significantly Increased" or "Somewhat Increased" (Figure 5).

As can be seen in Table 10 of descriptive statistics, both the median and the modal value are 2, indicating the "Somewhat Increased" response pattern. The average score was 2.30 points, ranging from "Somewhat increased" to "Business as usual I No changes".

Question 6: What are the greatest benefits for your organization in using the sustainable business model?

Responding managers were asked to express their agreement or disagreement about the first benefit that could be felt following the use of the sustainable business model, namely "Reduction of costs." Over 85.9% of SME managers agree the fact that the cost reduction will be an important benefit for

Table 8. The contingency table regarding the factors that led to changes in the business model as a result of market durability considerations (absolute frequencies and percentages)

			Year of establishment			Total
			5 - 9 years	9 - 14 years	> 15 years	
Which of the following factors have led to changes in your business model as a result of sustainability considerations?	Resource scarcity (e.g., increased commodity prices and price volatility)	Count	7	0	0	7
		% of Total	5.8%	0.0%	0.0%	5.8%
	Owners' demands for broader value creation (i.e., more than profits)	Count	6	2	0	8
		% of Total	5.0%	1.7%	0.0%	6.7%
	Customers willing to pay a premium for sustainable offering	Count	3	1	3	7
		% of Total	2.5%	0.8%	2.5%	5.8%
	Legislative I political pressure	Count	5	1	1	7
		% of Total	4.2%	0.8%	0.8%	5.8%
	Meeting demands of existing employees	Count	11	2	3	16
		% of Total	9.2%	1.7%	2.5%	13.3%
	Customers prefer sustainable products I services	Count	15	5	2	22
		% of Total	12.5%	4.2%	1.7%	18.3%
	Competitors increasing commitment to sustainability	Count	13	1	1	15
		% of Total	10.8%	0.8%	0.8%	12.5%
	Maintaining "license to operate"	Count	6	6	1	13
		% of Total	5.0%	5.0%	0.8%	10.8%
	Stricter requirements from partners along the value chain	Count	9	1	2	12
		% of Total	7.5%	0.8%	1.7%	10.0%
	Competing for new talent	Count	5	1	2	8
		% of Total	4.2%	0.8%	1.7%	6.7%
	None of the above	Count	5	0	0	5
		% of Total	4.2%	0.0%	0.0%	4.2%
Total		Count	85	20	15	120
		% of Total	70.8%	16.7%	12.5%	100.0%

Source: Authors calculation

the enterprise in using the sustainable business model. Nearly 8.3% of respondents provided a "Neither agree or disagree" interim response, while 5.8% do not believe that after using the sustainable business model, costs will not be substantially reduced (Figure 6).

The second benefit included in the questionnaire was - "Enhancing reputation and image of the company". 8 out of 10 SME managers (87.5%) agreed that after using the sustainable business model, both the reputation and the image of the company will be considerably improved. About 8.3% of respondents provided a "Neither agree or disagree" interim response, while 4.1% do not consider that developing a sustainable business model could improve so much the reputation and image of the enterprise (Figure 7).

The third benefit presented to SME managers through the questionnaire was - "Increase in customer satisfaction, awareness and demand". More than two-thirds of SME managers (81.6%) agree that it could increase customer satisfaction, awareness and demand after using the enterprise's sustainable business

Table 9. Frequency table for changing the commitment of SMEs to sustainability in the last year

		Frequency	Percent	Valid Percent	Cumulative Percent
Valid	Significantly increased	32	26.7	29.1	29.1
	Somewhat increased	51	42.5	46.4	75.5
	Business as usual I No changes	4	3.3	3.6	79.1
	Somewhat decreased	8	6.7	7.3	86.4
	Significantly decreased	15	12.5	13.6	100.0
	Total	110	91.7	100.0	
Missing	88	10	8.3		
Total		120	100.0		

Source: Authors calculation

Figure 5. Frequency distribution
Source: Authors representation

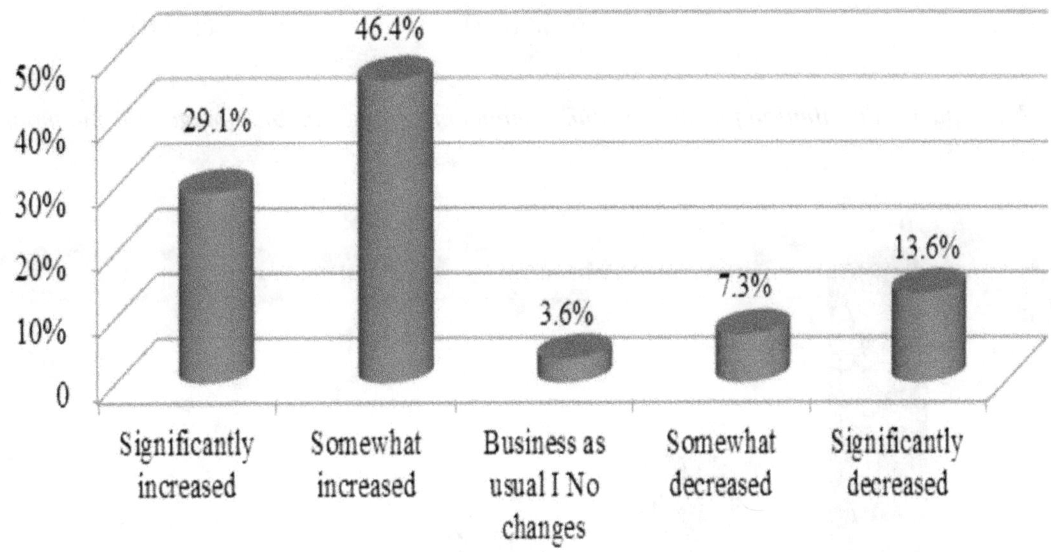

Table 10. Table of Descriptive Statistics for Changing SME Engagement over Sustainability in the Last Year

N	Valid	110
	Missing	10
Mean		2.30
Median		2.00
Mode		2

Source: Authors calculation

Figure 6. Frequency distribution for the variable "Reduction of costs"
Source: Authors representation

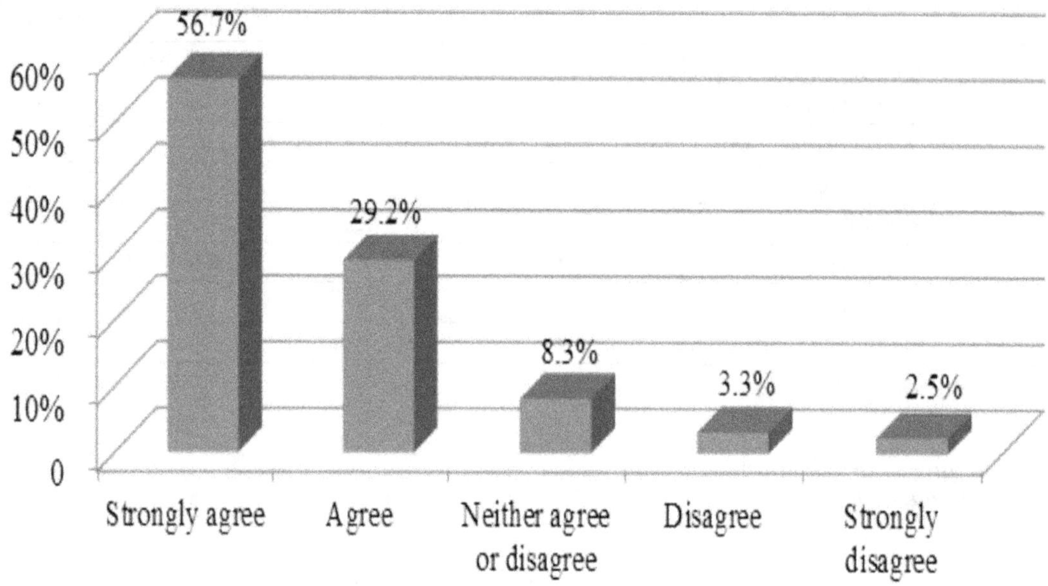

Figure 7. Frequency distribution for the variable "Enhancing reputation and image of the company"
Source: Authors representation

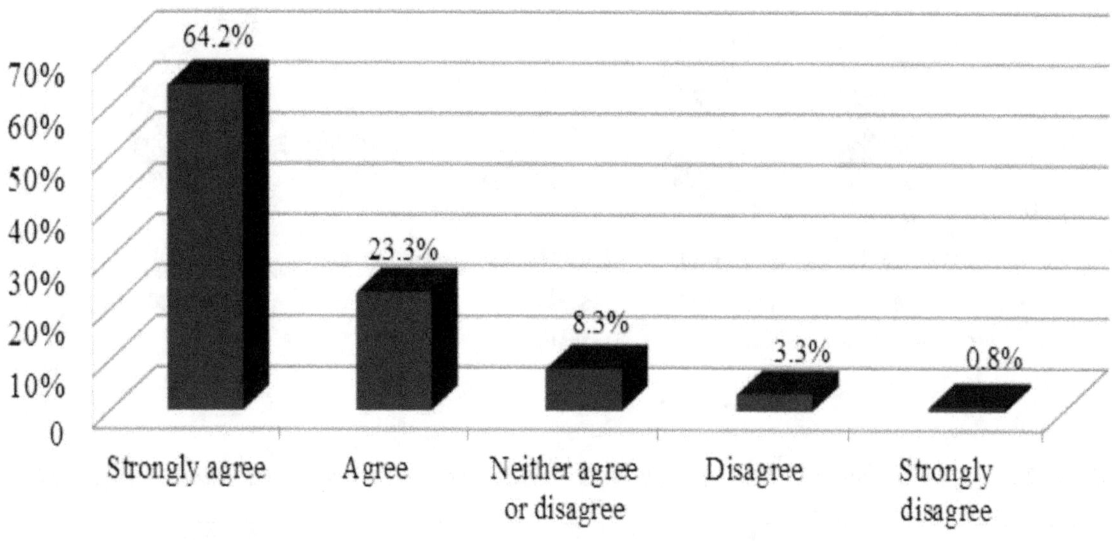

model. 13.3% of respondents gave a "Neither agree or disagree" interim response, while 5.0% do not consider that developing a sustainable business model could lead to an accelerated increase in customer satisfaction and demand (Figure 8).

The fourth benefit exposed to managers for the analysis was - "Reducing negative impacts on social, cultural and ecological environment". 81.6% of respondents agreed that after using the sustainable business model, the negative impact of the enterprise on the social, cultural and environmental environment

Figure 8. Frequency distribution for the variable "Increase in customer satisfaction, awareness and demand"
Source: Authors representation

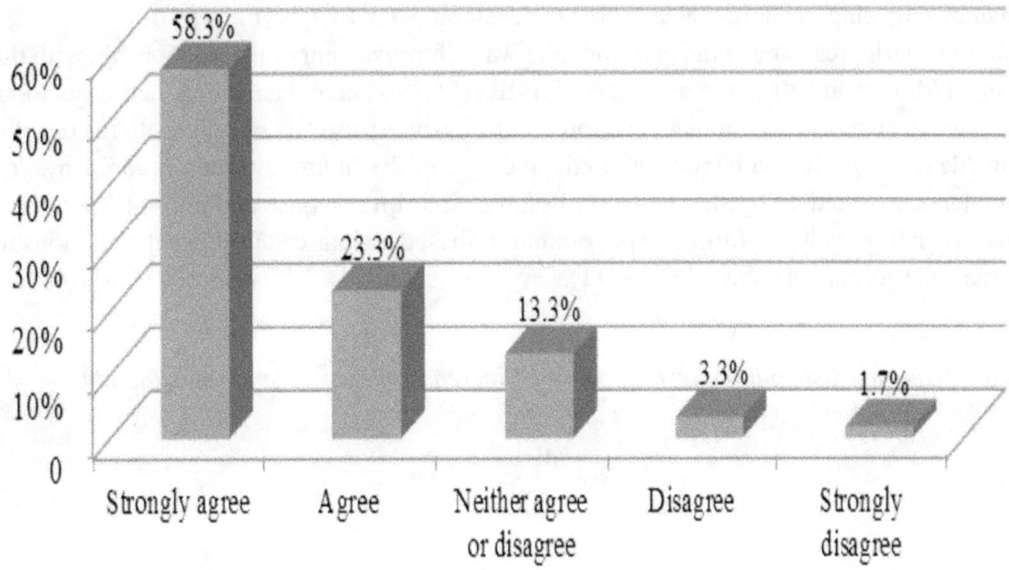

would be considerably reduced. 13.3% of the respondents provided a "Neither agree or disagree" interim response, while 5.0% did not believe that isolated business-only sustainable actions would reduce the negative impact on the social, cultural and ecologic environment in the short term (Figure 9).

The fifth benefit presented in the questionnaire was "Increase in employee job satisfaction". 7 out of 10 SME managers (72.5%) agree that another benefit that can be gained after using the sustainable

Figure 9. Frequency distribution for the variable "Reduction of negative impacts on social, cultural and ecological environment"
Source: Authors representation

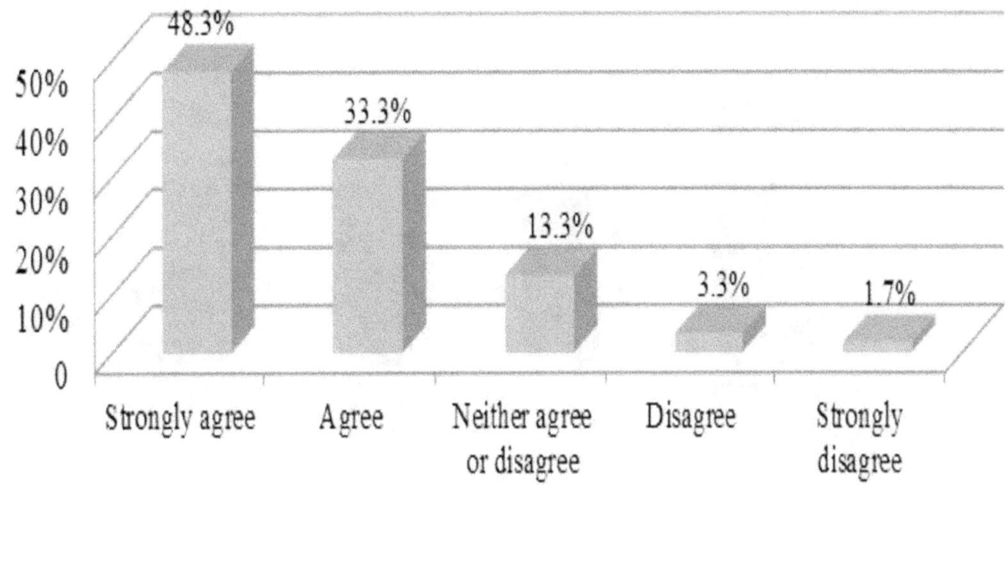

business model within the enterprise could be to increase employee's professional satisfaction. 18.3% of the respondents provided a "Neither agree or disagree" interim response and only 9.2% of managers believe that the increase in employee's professional satisfaction can be ensured by material incentives rather than by engaging in additional sustainable development activities (Figure 10).

The sixth benefit presented in the questionnaire was "Improvement of the relationship with the local community". More than half of the managers of SMEs (61.7%) agree that by conducting socio-cultural actions related to supporting community action groups by enterprises it contributes to the development of sustainable relationships with them and to the increase of the future revenues of company. 26.7% of the respondents provided a "Neither agree or disagree" interim response and only 11.7% of managers do not believe that sporadic performance of community-based actions can improve the relationship with it and some benefits can be gained (Figure 11).

Figure 10. Frequency distribution for the variable "Increase in employee job satisfaction"
Source: Authors representation

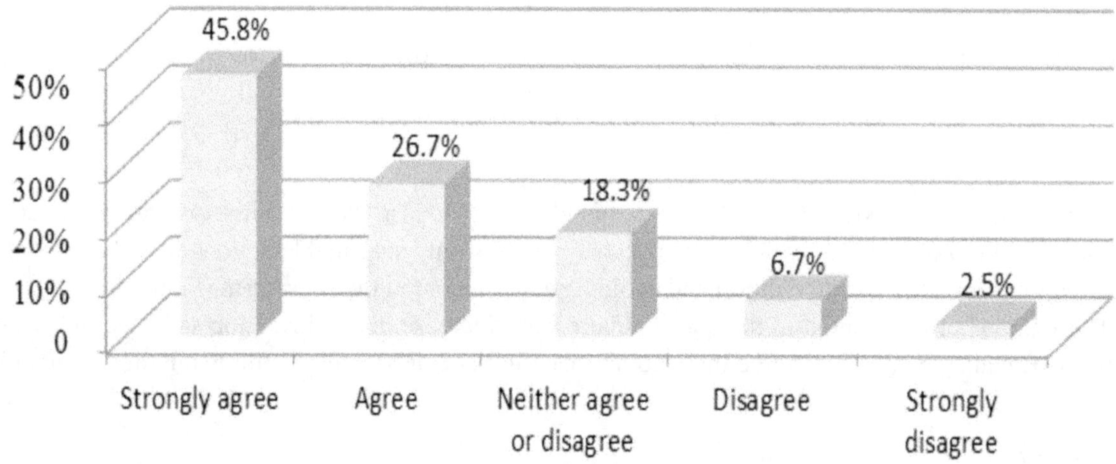

Figure 11. Frequency distribution for the variable "Improving the relationship with the local community"
Source: Authors representation

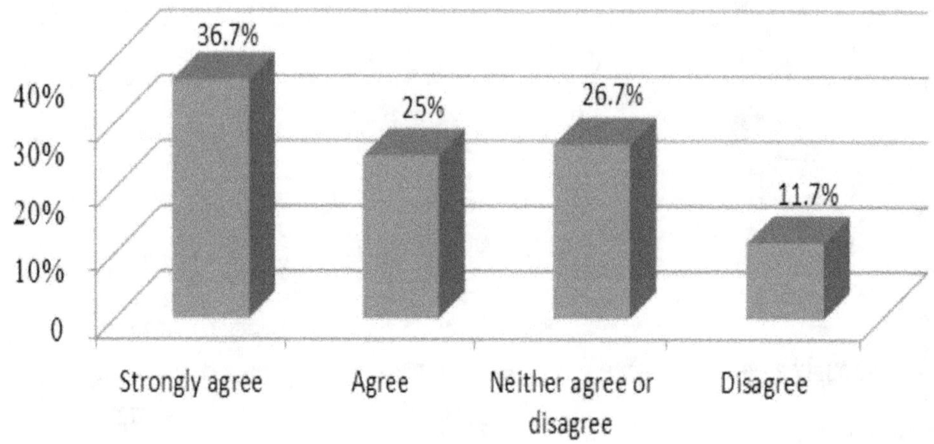

The seventh benefit exposed to SME managers was "Business-or Corporation philosophy." 75.0% of business managers agree that through the implementation of sustainable business practices and through ethical conduct, positive business results can be achieved and their management initiatives and efforts are a new business philosophy and not a growth tool application. 23.3% of the respondents provided a "Neither agree or disagree" interim response and only 1.7% of managers disagree that an enterprise that adopts the concept of sustainability as a business philosophy does so only in good faith and to contribute to environmental protection but on the contrary, it regards the consumer as an income-enhancing tool (Figure 12).

As can be seen in Table 11 of the descriptive statistics, the first three variables record the value 1 both in terms of median and modal value. The average score of these variables is between 1.53 points and 1.67 points, i.e. between the "Strongly Agree" and "Agree" levels. For the last four variables, the median is 2 and the modal value is 1. The average score for these variables is between 1.77 points and 2.13 points, i.e. between the "Strongly Agree" and "Neither agree or disagree" levels.

Figure 12. Frequency distribution for the variable "Business-or Corporation philosophy"
Source: Authors representation

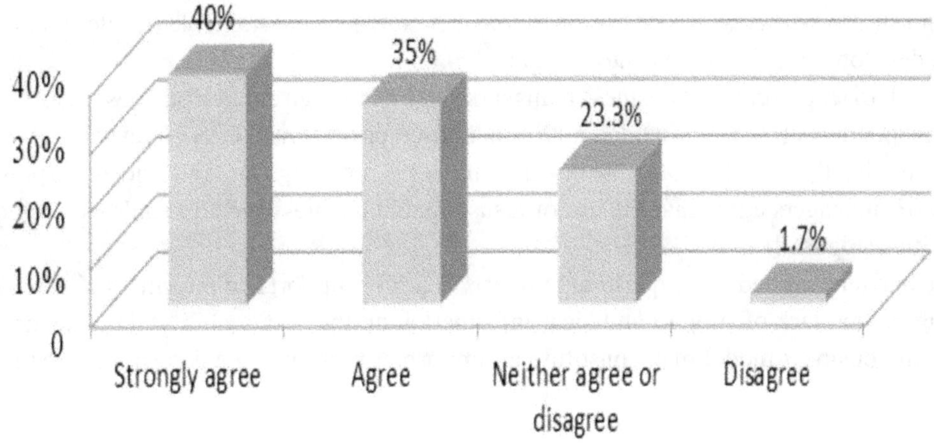

Table 11. Table of descriptive statistics regarding the benefits for SMEs following the use of the sustainable business model

The benefits	N Valid	Mean	Median	Mode
Reduction of costs	120	1.66	1	1
Enhancing reputation and image of the company	120	1.53	1	1
Increase in customer satisfaction, awareness and demand	120	1.67	1	1
Reduction of negative impacts on social, cultural and ecological environment	120	1.77	2	1
Increase in employee job satisfaction	120	1.93	2	1
Improvement of the relationship with the local community	120	2.13	2	1
Business-or Corporation philosophy	120	1.87	2	1

Source: Authors calculation

Question 7: What are your organization's main barriers to using the sustainable business model?

Responding managers were asked to express their opinion on the first barrier included in the questionnaire, namely "The high costs that make the implementation commercially not worthwhile". 58.3% of SME managers agree that high costs are an important barrier for the enterprise to use the sustainable business model. Nearly 24.2% of respondents provided a "Neither agree or disagree" interim response, while 17.5% do not consider costs a barrier when considering business development (Figure 13).

The second barrier included in the questionnaire was "Their complexity which cannot be translated into practical strategies". More than half of the managers of SMEs (55%) agreed that the complexity of the specific elements of the sustainable business model, which cannot be translated into practical strategies, is another important barrier for the enterprise. About 20.8% of the respondents provided a "Neither agree or disagree" interim response, while 24.2% did not consider the complexity of specific business model elements a barrier when considering their own business development (Figure 14).

The third barrier exposed to SME managers was "Too much time and manpower intensive in every day operations". 5 out of 10 SME managers (52.5%) agreed that the implementation of enterprise sustainability activities involved a lot of time and improved workforce, which is why new elements imply new costs, thus a new barrier for enterprises. 22.5% of the respondents provided a "Neither agree or disagree" interim response, while 25% did not consider staffing in sustainable development actions as a barrier to developing their own business (Figure 15).

The fourth barrier presented to business managers was "Not a high enough business priority". Almost half of the respondents (47.5%) provided a "Neither agree or disagree" interim response, while 23.3% of them agreed that the use of sustainable business model is not a high enough priority at present. Only 29.1% of SME managers agree that the use of a sustainable business model should be included in the list of priorities (Figure 16).

The fifth barrier included in the questionnaire was "Lack of support and information". 60.8% of SME managers agree that lack of support and clear information on the sustainability elements needed to be included in the business model may constitute an important barrier to the enterprise. About 23.3% of

Figure 13. Frequency distribution for the variable "The high costs which make the implementation commercially not worthwhile"
Source: Authors representation

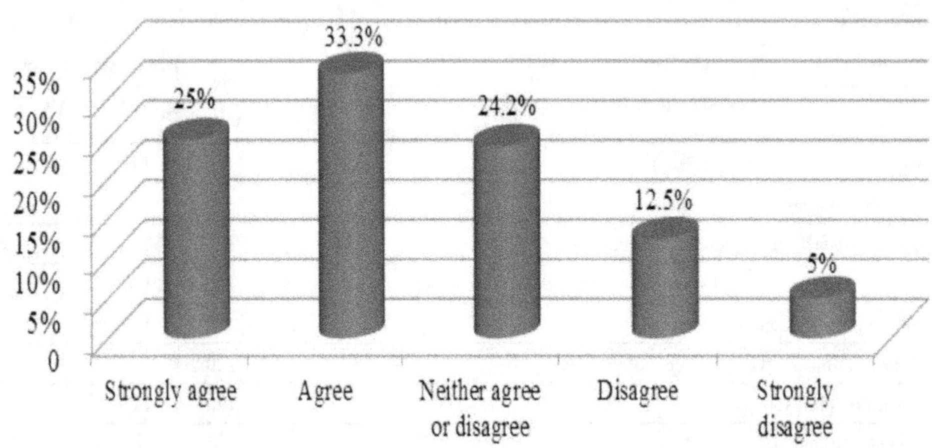

Figure 14. Frequency distribution for the variable "Their complexity which cannot be translated into practical strategies"
Source: Authors representation

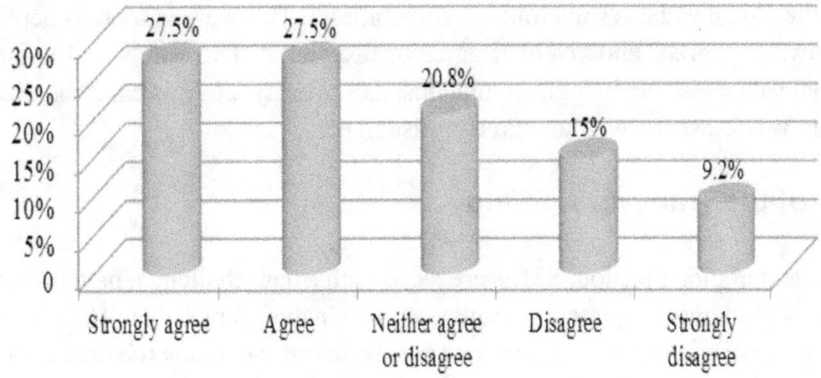

Figure 15. Frequency distribution for the variable "Too much time and manpower intensive in every day operations"
Source: Authors representation

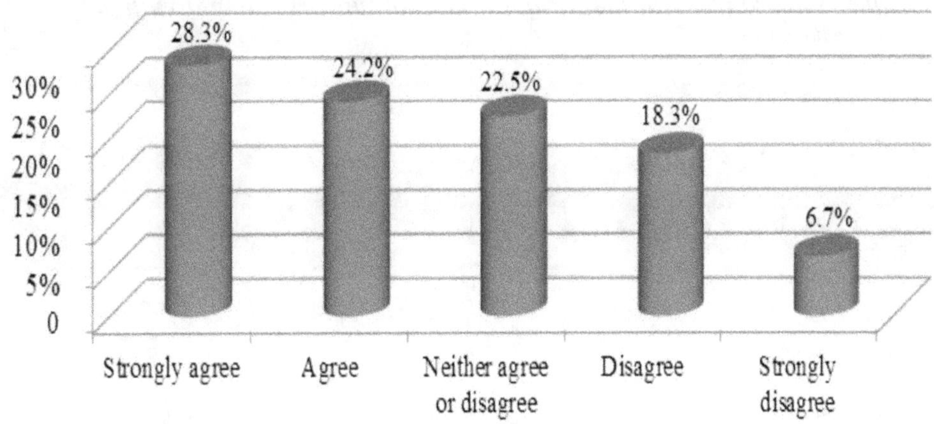

Figure 16. Frequency distribution for the variable "Not a high enough business priority"
Source: Authors representation

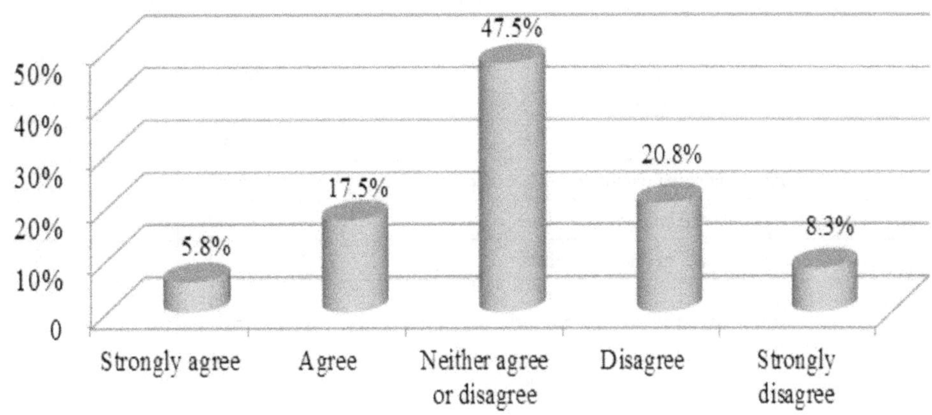

the respondents provided a "Neither agree or disagree" interim response, while 15.8% did not consider the lack of support and sustainability information a barrier to the enterprise (Figure 17).

In Table 12 of the descriptive statistics, for four of the variables analyzed it can be seen that the median is 2 and the modal value is sometimes 1, sometimes 2. The average score is between levels 2.31 and 2.51, i.e. between "Agree" and "Neither agree or disagree ". The only variable that has both the median and modal value 3 is "Not a high enough business priority". In this case, the average score was 3.08 points, being very close to "Neither agree or disagree".

Conclusions of the Transversal Study

In the current context of globalization, SMEs are faced with a new challenge, namely moving from one linear business model to another pattern, circular, as sustainable as possible. These changes are often accompanied by positive and negative actions and events. In order to know the impact of these changes, the perceived benefits and the barriers encountered, a quantitative marketing research was carried out among SMEs in Bucharest, Romania. Taking into account the dynamics of the business model components, research results indicate that respondents attributed particular attention to components such as

Figure 17. Frequency distribution for the variable "Lack of support and information"
Source: Authors representation

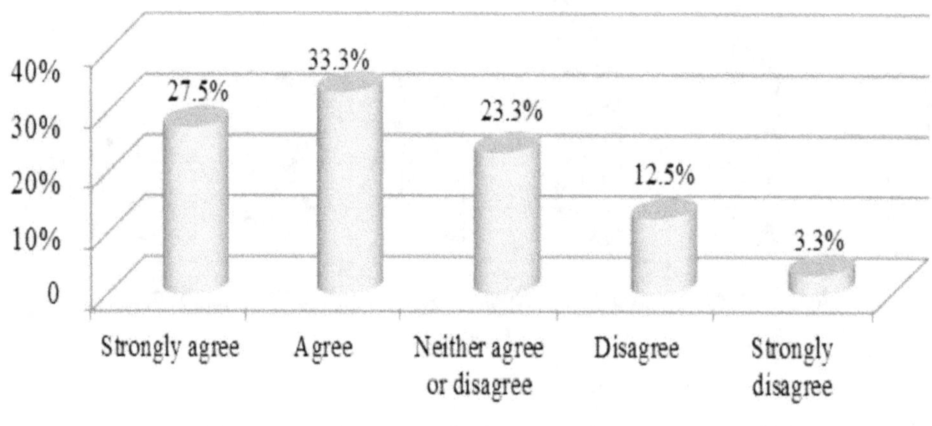

Table 12. Table of descriptive statistics on the main barriers of SMEs in using the sustainable business model

	N Valid	Mean	Median	Mode
The high costs which make the implementation commercially not worthwhile	120	2.39	2	2
Their complexity which cannot be translated into practical strategies	120	2.51	2	1
Too much time and manpower intensive in every day operations	120	2.51	2	1
Not a high enough business priority	120	3.08	3	3
Lack of support and information	120	2.31	2	2

Source: Authors calculation

"Structure" (31.7%), "Processes" (27.5%), "Technology" (16.7%), "Mission" (9.2%), "Revenue "(7.5%) and" Legal Issues "(7.5%). In order to better understand the main components that Romanian companies focus, depending on their size and age on the market, absolute and relative frequencies were calculated using contingency tables based on data provided by respondents. Thus, it was found that medium-sized enterprises focus on three components: "Structure" (1.7%), "Revenues" (1.7%) and "Technology" (1.7%); small businesses consider components such as: "Structure" (5.0%), "Processes" (3.3%) and "Technology" (1.7%); the micro-enterprises focus on "Structure" (25.0%) and "Processes" (24.2%). However, business managers have pointed out that it was necessary to build a mix between all six components of "Structure", "Processes", "Technology", "Mission", "Legal issues" and "Revenues" sustainable.

Furthermore, SMEs with a minimum of 9 years of age, in order to develop the business model, medium-sized enterprises are generally focused on components such as: "Processes" (21.7%) "Structure" (20.8%), "Revenues" %) and "Technology" (14.2%). At the same time, enterprises with a market age of more than 10 years focus mainly on the following components: "Structure" (6.7%), "Processes" (3.3%) and "Revenues" (3.3%). If 70.8% of business managers said sustainable business models could be perceived as a competitive advantage, 29.2% of respondents indicated either the "No" or "Do not know" answers. Given the size of enterprises, 81.7% of the respondent microenterprises said that sustainable business models may be perceived as a competitive advantage, which is also supported by 8.3% of small business managers and 4.2% of medium business managers.

Positive responses to the question about perceiving sustainable business models as real competitive advantages were provided by some SMEs that are active in areas such as "Trade" and "Tourism, travel and restaurants" (35.0%), "Business/finance/insurance/real estate/information services" (9.2%), "Manufacturing industry" (8.3%), "Construction" (6.7%), "Transport and utilities, and fishing/mining" (4.2%). Out of the 20% of SMEs that responded negatively, 5.0% of enterprises came from the "Trade" (5.0%) and "Tourism, travel and restaurants" (4.2%). Over 47.8% of respondents' SMEs said that the business model used by the enterprise changed as a result of sustainability, while the remaining respondents (52.2%) indicated either "No" (30.0%) or "I don't know" (22.5%).

Nearly 2 out of 5 respondents, who said the business model used by the enterprise changed as a result of sustainability, come from the "Trade" or "Tourism, travel and restaurants" domains. The same response was also obtained from managers of SMEs from "Business/finance/real estate/information services" (6.7%), "Construction" (4.2%), "Transport and utilities, telecommunications" (4.2%), "Manufacturing industry" (4.2%) and "Agriculture/forestry and fishing/mining" (2.5%). On the other hand, 29.9% of the analyzed SMEs are active in the fields of: "Trade" and "Construction" (16.7%), "Business/finance/insurance/real estate/information services" (2.5%), "Manufacturing industry" (3.3%), "Tourism, travel and restaurants" (3.3%), "Transport and utilities, telecommunications" (2.5%), "Agriculture/forestry and fishing/mining" (0.8%) and "Other activities" (0.8%) said that their business models did not change substantially following the integration of sustainability elements. Out of the 85 companies surveyed with an age on the Bucharest market of up to 9 years, 41 said that their business models have changed substantially from the integration of the elements of sustainability, while 44 claimed otherwise.

According to the research results, the main factors that led to changes in the business model of the enterprise as a result of sustainability considerations were highlighted by managers in the order of their preferences as follows: "Customers prefer sustainable products/services" (18.3%), "Meeting demands of existing employees" (13.3%), "Competitors increasing commitment to sustainability" (12.5%), "Maintaining "license to operate" (10.8%), "Stricter requirements from partners along the value chain" (10.0%), "Owners' demands for broader value creation (i.e., more than profits)" (6.7%), "Competing for new talent"

(6.7%), "Resource scarcity (e.g., increased commodity prices and price volatility)" (5.8%), "Customers willing to pay a premium for sustainable offering" (5.8%), "Legislative / political pressure (5.8%) and "None of the above" (4.2%). 7 out of 10 respondents said that the change in enterprises' commitment to sustainability in the past year has seen a "Significantly Increased" or "Somewhat Increased", while only 3 managers have responded "Significantly decreased".

Given the managers' responses to the agreement or disagreement on the benefits that could be felt as a result of using the sustainable business model, it was found that the average score of the seven variables was between 1.53-2.13 points, i.e. between the levels of "Strongly Agree" and "Neither agree or disagree" as follows: Enhancing reputation and image of the company (1.53), Reduction of costs (1.66), Increase in customer satisfaction, awareness and demand (1.67), Reduction of negative impacts on social, cultural and ecological environment (1.77), Business-or Corporation philosophy (1.87), Increase in employee job satisfaction (1.93), Improvement of the relationship with the local community (2.13). Regarding the respondents' views on the barriers experienced by using the sustainable business model, it was observed that the average score of the five variables was between levels 2.31 and 3.08, i.e. between "Agree" and "Neither agree or disagree" answers as follows: Lack of support and information (2.31), The high costs which make the implementation commercially not worthwhile (2.39), Their complexity which cannot be translated into practical strategies (2.51), Too much time and manpower intensive in every day operations (2.51), Not a high enough business priority (3.08).

SOLUTIONS AND RECOMMENDATIONS

Taking into consideration the issues discussed in this chapter, we propose to the specialists and all those interested to analyze and improve the following solutions and themes:

- Detailed analysis of the factors that generate changes in business models implemented or under implementation (Türkeş et al., 2014b);
- Analysis of changes in the commitment of enterprises (large and SMEs) to management and investment towards sustainability (Türkeş et al., 2014a; Topor et al., 2016);
- Identifying and analyzing the drivers and barriers encountered in implementing sustainable business models including competitive/non-competitive;
- Identifying other innovation-based sustainable business models and their impact on managerial strategies (Constantin et al., 2019).
- BASED on the studied national and international literature, we would like to recommend to the specialists and those interested in developing sustainable business models the following:
- Carefully analyzing the main components that large businesses and SMEs focus on in developing their business models and influencing their behavior on competitive markets. It is necessary to set up an analysis team that will study all aspects necessary for the adoption and implementation of the sustainable business model (Căpuşneanu et al, 2019).
- Research of literature on the successful adoption and implementation of sustainable business models in large enterprises and SMEs. Identifying viable solutions and guaranteeing the success of implementing a sustainable business model with the help of specialized institutions or experts in the field of sustainability.

- Research of literature on the successful adoption and implementation of sustainable business models in large enterprises and SMEs. Identifying viable solutions and guaranteeing the success of implementing a sustainable business model with the help of specialized institutions or experts in the field of sustainability.

FUTURE RESEARCH DIRECTIONS

Through the launched objectives, which we believe have been achieved throughout this chapter, we have addressed both the business environment and the academic environment in particular. The chosen theme covered a broad segment of knowledge related to the interpretations and composition of business models and sustainable business models. However, we believe that there are still some unseen segments that could contribute to a broader picture of the conceptual-applicative understanding of sustainable business models, including the benefits of its implementation in SMEs in particular. That is why, to complement the subject presented by us, specialists can identify new research directions such as:

- The analysis of the possibility of implementing innovative business models of innovation in large enterprises and SMEs, in particular;
- Analyzing the impact of managerial decisions resulting from the implementation of sustainable business models within large enterprises and SMEs across countries or continents;
- Analyzing the benefits (drivers) or limits (barriers) to adopting or implementing sustainable business models in large enterprises and SMEs.

CONCLUSION

Based on conceptual-applied approaches of business concepts or sustainable business models, this chapter covers a wide range of topics on debate and analysis. A transversal study was also presented on the use of sustainable business models in SMEs in Bucharest, Romania. All these analyzes offer a large amount of information, which can be considered as strong points of the chapter presented by the fact that:

- It presents various conceptual-applicative approaches of the concepts of business models and sustainable business models existing in the literature;
- Completes some existing gaps in the sustainability and application of sustainable business models within companies precisely through interpretations of conceptual approaches and the theories debated, including their advantages;
- Presents the conclusions of a transversal study on the views of the managers of SMEs in Bucharest regarding the use of sustainable business models used.

By contributing to clarifying certain aspects of sustainable business models and their applicability to SMEs in Romania, we believe that the mission has been accomplished. On this occasion, other future research directions have been opened among specialists from business and academia. Through their contributions, we are confident that successful solutions to successful business models in SMEs and beyond will be guaranteed and will bring the desired satisfactions for managers, investors, other stakeholders.

Completing the theoretical-empirical framework of sustainability can be achieved through the development of partnerships between specialized bodies and enterprises, and the collection, processing and analysis of information will help identify the best solutions to guarantee the efficiency of implementing innovative business models based on innovation.

REFERENCES

Abdelkafi, N., & Tauscher, K. (2016). Business models for sustainability from a system dynamics perspective. *Organization & Environment*, *29*(1), 74–96. doi:10.1177/1086026615592930

Aspara, J., Lamberg, J.-A., Laukia, A., & Tikkanen, H. (2013). Corporate Business Model Transformation and InterOrganizational Cognition: The Case of Nokia. *Long Range Planning*, *46*(6), 459–474. doi:10.1016/j.lrp.2011.06.001

Bocken, N. M. P., Short, S. W., Rana, P., & Evans, S. (2014). A literature and practice review to develop sustainable business model archetypes. *Journal of Cleaner Production*, *65*, 42–56. doi:10.1016/j.jclepro.2013.11.039

Bolis, I., Morioka, S. N., & Sznelwar, L. I. (2014). When Sustainable Development Risks Losing its Meaning. Delimiting the Concept with a Comprehensive Literature Review and a Conceptual Model. *Journal of Cleaner Production*, *83*, 7–20. doi:10.1016/j.jclepro.2014.06.041

Boons, F., & Lüdeke-Freund, F. (2013). Business models for sustainable innovation: State-of-the-art and steps towards a research agenda. *Journal of Cleaner Production*, *45*, 9–19. doi:10.1016/j.jclepro.2012.07.007

Chatterjee, S. (2013). Simple Rules for Designing Business Models. *California Management Review*, *55*(2), 97–124. doi:10.1525/cmr.2013.55.2.97

Doz, Y. L., & Kosonen, M. (2010). Embedding strategic agility: A leadership agenda for accelerating business model renewal. *Long Range Planning*, *43*(2-3), 370–382. doi:10.1016/j.lrp.2009.07.006

Dubosson-Torbay, M., Osterwalder, A., & Pigneur, Y. (2002). E-Business Model Design, Classification, and Measurements. *Thunderbird International Business Review*, *44*(1), 5–23. doi:10.1002/tie.1036

Elkington, J. (1997). *Cannibals with Forks: The Triple Bottom Line of the 21st Century Business*. Oxford, UK: New Society Publishers.

Evans, S., Vladimirova, D., Holgado, M., Van Fossen, K., Yang, M., Silva, E., & Barlow, C. (2017). *Business model innovation for sustainability: towards a unified perspective for creation of sustainable business models*. Bus. Strat. Environ. doi:10.1002/bse

Garetti, M., & Taisch, M. (2012). Sustainable manufacturing: Trends and research challenges. *Production Planning and Control*, *23*(2-3), 83–104. doi:10.1080/09537287.2011.591619

Geissdoerfer, M., Bocken, N. M. P., & Hultink, E. J. (2016). Design thinking to enhance the sustainable business modelling process. *Journal of Cleaner Production*, *135*, 1218–1232. doi:10.1016/j.jclepro.2016.07.020

Geissdoerfer, M., Morioka, S. N., de Carvalho, M. M., & Evans, S. (2018a). Business models and supply chains for the Circular Economy. *Journal of Cleaner Production, 190*, 712–721. doi:10.1016/j.jclepro.2018.04.159

Geissdoerfer, M., Vladimirova, D., & Evans, S. (2018b). Sustainable business model innovation: A review. *Journal of Cleaner Production, 198*, 401–416. doi:10.1016/j.jclepro.2018.06.240

Johnson, M. W., Christensen, C. M., & Kagermann, H. (2008, December). Reinventing Your Business Model. *Harvard Business Review*, 50–60.

Labuschagne, C., Brent, A. C., & van Erck, R. P. G. (2005). Assessing the Sustainability Performances of Industries. *Journal of Cleaner Production, 13*(4), 373–385. doi:10.1016/j.jclepro.2003.10.007

Lehmann-Ortega, L., & Schoettl, J.-M. (2005). *From Buzzword to Managerial Tool: The Role of Business Model in Strategic Innovation*. Paper presented at CLADEA, Santiago de Chile, Chile.

Linder, J., & Cantrell, S. (2000). Changing Business Models: Surveying the Landscape. *Accenture Institute for Strategic Change, 34*(2), 1–15.

McGahan, A. (2010). Business Model Innovation and Industry Change. *Rotman Magazine*, 91–94.

Moingeon, B., & Lehmann-Ortega, L. (2010). Creation and Implementation of a New Business Model: A disarming case study. *Management, 13*(4), 266–297.

Morris, M., Schindehutte, M., & Allen, J. (2005). The entrepreneur's business model: Toward a unified perspective. *Journal of Business Research, 58*(6), 726–735. doi:10.1016/j.jbusres.2003.11.001

Onetti, A., Zucchella, A., Jones, M. V., & McDougall-Covin, P. P. (2012). Internationalization, innovation and entrepreneurship: Business models for new technology-based firms. *The Journal of Management and Governance, 16*(3), 337–368. doi:10.100710997-010-9154-1

Osterwalder, A., & Pigneur, Y. (2002). An e-business model ontology for modeling e-business. *15th Bled Electronic Commerce Conference*, 1–12.

Osterwalder, A., Pigneur, Y., & Tucci, C. L. (2005). Clarifying business models: Origins, present, and future of the concept. *Communications of the Association for Information Systems, 15*, 1–40.

Osterwalder, A., Rossi, M., & Dong, M. (2002). *The Business Model Handbook for Developing Countries.* Economics Working Paper Archive at WUSTL, (0202003), 1–10.

Porter, M. E., & Kramer, M. (2006). Strategy and Society. *Harvard Business Review*, 4–6. PMID:17183795

Porter, M. E., & Kramer, M. R. (2011). Creating Shared Value: How to reinvent capitalism - and unleash a wave of innovation and growth. *Harvard Business Review, 89*, 62–77.

Roome, N., & Louche, C. (2016). Journeying toward business models for sustainability: A conceptual model found inside the black box of organisational transformation. *Organization & Environment, 29*(1), 11–35. doi:10.1177/1086026615595084

Santos, J., Spector, B., & Van der Heyden, L. (2009). *Toward a Theory of Business Model Innovation within Incumbent Firms.* INSEAD Working Paper Series, 0–53.

Schaltegger, S., Hansen, E., & Lüdeke-Freund, F. (2012). Business cases for sustainability and the role of business model innovation. *International Journal of Innovation and Sustainable Development*, *6*(2), 95–119. doi:10.1504/IJISD.2012.046944

Schaltegger, S., Hansen, E. G., & Lüdeke-Freund, F. (2016). Business models for sustainability: Origins, present research, and future avenues. *Organization & Environment*, *29*(1), 3–10. doi:10.1177/1086026615599806

Shafer, S. M., Smith, H. J., & Linder, J. C. (2005). The power of business models. *Business Horizons*, *48*(3), 199–207. doi:10.1016/j.bushor.2004.10.014

Smith, W. K., Binns, A., & Tushman, M. L. (2010). Complex business models: Managing strategic paradoxes simultaneously. *Long Range Planning*, *43*(2-3), 448–461. doi:10.1016/j.lrp.2009.12.003

Sorescu, A., Frambach, R. T., Singh, J., Rangaswamy, A., & Bridges, C. (2011). Innovations in Retail Business Models. *Journal of Retailing, 87S*(1), S3–S16.

Stewart, D. W., & Zhao, Q. (2000). Internet Marketing, Business Models, and Public Policy. *Journal of Public Policy & Marketing*, *19*(2), 287–296. doi:10.1509/jppm.19.2.287.17125

Stubbs, W., & Cocklin, C. (2008). Conceptualizing a sustainability business model. *Organization & Environment*, *21*(2), 103–127. doi:10.1177/1086026608318042

Teece, D. J. (2010). Business Models, Business Strategy and Innovation. *Long Range Planning*, *43*(2-3), 172–194. doi:10.1016/j.lrp.2009.07.003

Tikkanen, H., Lamberg, J. A., Parvinen, P., & Kallunki, J. P. (2005). Managerial cognition, action and the business model of the firm. *Management Decision*, *43*(6), 789–809. doi:10.1108/00251740510603565

Timmers, P. (1998). Business Models for Electronic Markets. *Electronic Markets*, *8*(2), 3–8. doi:10.1080/10196789800000016

Upward, A., & Jones, P. (2015). An ontology for strongly sustainable business models defining an enterprise framework compatible with natural and social science. *Organization & Environment*, *29*(1), 97–123. doi:10.1177/1086026615592933

Voelpel, S. C., Leibold, M., & Tekie, E. B. (2004). The wheel of business model reinvention: How to reshape your business model to leapfrog competitors. *Journal of Change Management*, *4*(3), 259–276. doi:10.1080/1469701042000212669

Wells, P. E. (2013). *Business Models for Sustainability*. Cheltenham, UK: Edward Elgar. doi:10.4337/9781781001530

Zott, C., & Amit, R. (2008). The Fit between Product Market Strategy and Business Model: Implications for Firm Performance. *Strategic Management Journal*, *29*(1), 1–26. doi:10.1002mj.642

Zott, C., Amit, R., & Massa, L. (2011). The Business Model: Recent Developments and Future Research. *Journal of Management*, *37*(4), 1019–1042. doi:10.1177/0149206311406265

ADDITIONAL READING

Căpuşneanu, S., Topor, D. I., Türkeş, M. C., & Rakoş, I.-S. (2019). Throughput Accounting: Decisional Informational Support for Optimizing Entity's Profit. In I. Oncioiu (Ed.), Throughput Accounting in a Hyperconnected World, 27-56, Hershey, PA: IGI Global, USA.

Constantin, D. M., Topor, D. I., Căpuşneanu, S., & Anica-Popa, A. (2019). Throughput Accounting and Green Reporting: Decision Support for Enhancing Environmental Performance. In I. Oncioiu (Ed.), Throughput Accounting in a Hyperconnected World, 94-119, Hershey, PA: IGI Global, USA. doi:10.4018/978-1-5225-7712-6.ch005

Oncioiu, I., Căpuşneanu, S., Türkeş, M. C., Topor, D. I., Oprea Constantin, D. M., Marin-Pantelescu, A., & Ştefan Hint, M. (2018). The Sustainability of Romanian SME's and their Involvement in Circular Economy. *Sustainability*, *10*(8), 2761. doi:10.3390u10082761

Rakoş, I.-S., & Căpuşneanu, S., (Oprea) Constantin, D.-M., Topor, D. I., & Bogan, E. (2018). Improve Air Quality Management by Monitoring and Assessing Heavy Metal Emissions. Case Study: Hunedoara County, Romania, *Annals of the University of Petroşani-Mining. Engineering*, *19*, 228–236.

Türkeş, M., Raicu, I., & Vija, I. (2014a). Enhancing the performance of business process in Romanian SMEs through ERP solutions. *Knowledge Horizons Economics*, *6*(4), 30–32.

Türkeş, M., Scarlat, E., Vija, R. I., & Raicu, I. (2014b). Improving the Performance of Business Process Modeling for Small-Medium Sized Companies. *Knowledge Horizons-Economics*, *6*(4), 72–74.

KEY TERMS AND DEFINITIONS

Business Model (BM): A business model that creates a competitive edge with superior customer value and contributes to the sustainable development of society and society.

Sustainability: The current economic and social development without damaging the natural environment.

Sustainability Report: (SR): Report on the environmental situation of a company based on environmental indicators.

Sustainable Business Model (SBM): An enterprise that has a minimal negative impact on the global, local or global environment, community, society, or economy – a business that strives to reach the triple bottom line.

Chapter 8
The Effect of Accounting Manipulation on the Business Performances

Ionica Oncioiu
Titu Maiorescu University, Romania

Cristina Maria Ştefan
Valahia University, Romania

Valentin Radu
Valahia University, Romania

Georgiana Burlacu
Valahia University, Romania

ABSTRACT

The dual nature of creative accounting has been intensely debated since its emergence in the Anglo-Saxon economies. The lack of a common accounting language, different accounting systems at international level, applied in different languages, international legislation harmonized more or less correctly, amidst a turbulent economic environment, left room for multiple interpretations and meanings. This chapter presents the advantages of fair value in manipulating business performances by creative accounting, but there are voices that are challenging this concept because of its volatility and tendency to subjectivism, and also manipulating the models used to evaluate balance-sheet structures or profit and loss account. The results show that fair value was introduced by accounting norms in response to the deterioration of confidence in the financial statements and targets a new system for assessing the entity's assets and liabilities.

DOI: 10.4018/978-1-7998-0178-8.ch008

INTRODUCTION

The interests determined by factors such as intensity of competition or increased pressure on businesses to communicate the „digestible" results, especially from investors and analysts, make the information collected by market valuation experts and accountants mitigate the possible effects of creativity (Chen, Qu & Sun, 2017). If the purpose of creative accounting is to improve the accounts (or the image created for the company), taking advantage of the weaknesses and deficiencies of accounting regulation, the authors consider that this concept is nothing new, because the principle of accounting options has been known for a long time (Holthausen & Watts, 2001; Baker & Bettner, 1997; Caylor, 2010).

The emergence of creative accounting was influenced by the flexibility of international accounting rules (Damayant, 2013). Creative accounting is treated in most cases negatively (negative creation), designed to lead to achieving value for intangible assets able to respond to the wishes of managers on the company's financial position and performance (Doukakis, 2014). Simultaneous treatment of creative accounting as a tool to achieve the interests of accounting and accounting engineering is based on the accounting policies adopted by a patrimonial entity to produce and communicate information (Richardson, 2011; Jackson & Liu, 2010; Ball, Li & Shivakumar, 2015).

Accountants who accept the ethic challenge of creative accounting should be aware of the abuse to both the choice of accounting policies and to the handling of transactions (Byard, Li & Yu, 2011). Such accounting has developed mainly in Anglo-Saxon economies due to the freedom of the accounting profession. It was placed on the edge of the legal form and economic substance of transactions and events (Barth et al., 2014). Discussed in terms of accounting practitioners, creative accounting has facilitated the emergence of basic and alternative treatments used to solve problems (Ahmed, Neel & Wang, 2013; Barth, Landsman & Lang, 2008; Fan, Li & Zheng, 2016). Of course, issues of evaluation of assets are cases of creative accounting practice that involve subjective reasoning as it applies to the professional accountant or expert appraiser. Using creative accounting for intangible assets, for example, especially in its gray area favored by accounting rules, makes it difficult or even impossible to guess the true value of these assets (Li, 2010; Ozkan, Singer & You, 2012; Barth, 2013).

In this context, the following questions arise: will we return to accounting at the initial cost, in which intangible assets are recorded at outdated values and are therefore not relevant or reliable? How important are the psychological factors in accounting measurement? Can a model of assessment ensure the maximum quality of the accounting information on intangible assets? The answer to these questions, as well as various controversial issues of the fair value concept of intangible assets, are presented in the current draft of the International Accounting Standards Board (IASB) and the American Accounting Standards Board (FASB). As a result, today, we perceive an accelerated rate of change, aggressive disruptive phenomena and emerging economies that are rapidly developing against the backdrop of a Digital Era (Chen et al., 2010; He, Pan & Tian, 2017).

BACKGROUND

Theme creative accounting practices are addressed by several disciplines: accounting, information technology, psychology and management, but they have grown tremendously in recent decades throughout the entire spectrum of companies (Brown, 2010). Creative accounting is operating at shade where accusations substantiated by non-compliance with professional or legal norms can be brought, but where common sense logic notifies the presence of a certain dose of „forcing the note" (Bettner & Kate, 2013).

A number of authors have described creative accounting as such:

Parker notices that 'all businesses hide their benefits. The published synthesis documents are based on registers that have been 'delicately' or even substantially altered. The figures presented to the investors have been entirely changed to protect those guilty. This is, in fact, a legitimate scam and is called creative accounting…' (Parker, 2012). The practitioner, Ball, states that 'the accounting process involves operating with different opinions and resolving conflicts between them in order to present the results generated by transactions. Such flexibility facilitates manipulation, deception and distortion. These activities, practiced by some less scrupulous members of the profession, are becoming known as creative accounting… Creative accounting does not violate law and accounting rules. It respects the letter, but obviously not its spirit… There is no doubt about the negative nature of creative accounting. It distorts the results and the financial position of the enterprise, and if we lend credence to the theoreticians, it becomes an increasingly used practice…' (Ball, 2013). Lukka defines creative accounting as a communication technique that aims to improve the information provided to investors (Lukka, 2010). On the same line, Dennis believes that the creative accounting expression describes 'accounting practices, often at the limit of legality, practiced by some businesses that, taking advantage of the normalization limits, seek to embellish their financial position image and economic and financial performance' (Dennis, 2014).

The different methods of recording intangibles through creative accounting can be classified into four categories (Schleicher, Tahoun & Walker, 2010):

- Sometimes accounting rules allow a company to choose between different accounting methods. For example, a company can choose the accounting policy which gives the desired image (it is allowed to choose between treating development costs as expenses when incurred, or to absorb these costs throughout the project life);
- Some accounts of intangible assets involve a degree of estimation, reasoning and prediction, especially when there is no market for that asset. These estimates are usually made in the company or by an expert evaluator and the creative accountant are able to assume a position of caution and optimism in setting the estimate;
- Artificial transactions can be recorded to manipulate intangible amounts on the balance sheet and to transfer profits between accounting periods (sale and lease-back);
- And real transactions involving intangibles can be planned at various times in order to create the desired impression to accounting information users. Property entity management is free to choose the year when they will sell the intangible investment, increasing the profit in the financial statements.

The methods in which some processes reveal creative accounting for intangible assets can be grouped in:

- Processes which have the effect of modeling the result and management decisions;
- Processes and techniques meant to improve the effect of balance sheet information;
- Processes which impact the presentation of the results.

The techniques and practices used for intangible assets having as effect shaping the outcome, the authors mention:

First, an optimistic attitude regarding the chances of success of a development project will lead to the capitalization of development costs, with implications for the size of the result, the capitalization for the year. In future exercises, expenses recording with amortization will impact the result in the sense of decreasing it. If the enterprise has the interest payment of development costs in the profit and loss (expenditure) it will claim that at least one of the conditions stipulated by IAS 38 para. 43 is not met.

Second, undervaluation of assets acquired by the company leads to increased goodwill. Capitalization and amortization of goodwill over its useful life will influence the outcome in future years (goodwill amortization costs lead to diminished results, with consequences on the course of action and competitiveness of competitive stock takeover bids). Charging goodwill on equity to reduce their lead, results in their diminishing, the result of future exercises not being influenced by goodwill amortization expenses (Hou et al., 2015).

RESEARCH METHODOLOGY

The procedures of financial engineering used have at their base the choices permitted by accounting regulation, the possibilities given by the weaknesses and deficiencies of the accounting norms, and the mechanisms through which accounting can intervene: the determination of accounting interpretation of a legally-financial transaction or the elaboration of a legally-financial mechanisms having the purpose the modification of results of financial situations (Florou & Pope, 2012; Allen & Ramanna, 2013).

Table 1 reviews some creative accounting methods, techniques and practices that have some influence on modelling the result:

The opportunity to choose accounting methods may be decreased by reducing the number of permitted accounting methods or by specifying the circumstances in which each method must be used. It is interesting to note that the auditors should step up their efforts to identify possible manipulations of the information provided by the financial statements (Cahan & Sun, 2015). In this respect, the audit function should include an assessment of the company's internal control system to prevent creative accounting or fraud. In order to ensure broader and more rigorous supervision, auditors should be willing to fight against their clients. This could lead to a radical reflection on the nature of the relationship between auditors and managers. It should not be neglected those concepts such as: integrity, objectivity, confidentiality, competence and, last but not least, credibility must be found in the conduct and documents of the work of any professional.

At the same time, the accounting result represents an important component of the value of a share (Andon, Baxter & Chua, 2007). There have been few cases when very Romanian profitable companies have gone into liquidation. That is why the stock market authority should sensitize investors about the indispensability of education and information, but this is a lengthy process.

SOLUTIONS AND RECOMMENDATIONS

As stated above, creative accounting is seen as a particular feature of the Anglo-Saxon approach to accounting, characterized by flexibility and rationality, to the European continental model, characterized by detailed traditions and prescriptions. The continental accounting model, more prescriptive and inflexible, may be an opportunity to reduce abuses in choosing accounting methods and manipulating estimates in accounting (Table 2).

Table 1. Creative accounting methods, techniques and practices

Balance sheet item and / or profit and loss account	Mechanism and impact on result modelling
Fixed assets	The practice of 'subjective depreciation' of assets creates a field conducive to creativity in accounting. Based on the exercise of professional judgment, IAS 36 requires that at each balance sheet date, it is determined whether there is any indication that the asset underwriting has been impaired. If the enterprise's management considers the recoverable amount to be less than the net book value, the asset is considered to be impaired for the difference. In this situation, the result will be affected by recording a depreciation expense.
Development costs	An optimistic attitude regarding the chances of success of a development project will result in the capitalization of development expenditures, with consequences on the size of the result, in the capitalization exercise. In future exercises, the recording of depreciation expense will have an impact on the result to diminish it. If the enterprise has an interest in transferring development expenses to the income statement (at expense), it will be invoked that at least one of the conditions set out in IAS 38, paragraph 43 is not met.
Goodwill	Under-evaluation of the assets of the acquired company leads to the increase of the goodwill. Capitalization of goodwill and its depreciation over its useful life have an impact on the result of future exercises (amortization of goodwill leads to a decrease in the result, with consequences on the stock exchange rate and the competitiveness of competitive bidding). Impairment of goodwill on equity results in the decrease, and the result of future exercises is not influenced by amortization of goodwill.
Stocks	The 'stocks' field provides enough opportunities for subjectivism and creative accounting. A discrepancy found voluntarily in determining the stock size in the estate at the end of the exercise may lead to a "smoothing" of the outcome, meaning that the under-valuation or overestimation of the final stock has a bearing not only on the financial statements of the current exercise, but and those that belong to the next exercise. On the other hand, the inclusion of financial expenses in the cost of inventories has the effect of increasing the result in the year in which the expenditure is included. On the opposite side, if the enterprise's management has a pessimistic view of the outcome, it will apply the result method by treating interest as an expense item of the current exercise.
Provisions for risks and expenses	The practice of provisions (increasing and reducing them) is an effective tool for "smoothing" the outcome. The provisioning of provisions in those years in which the enterprise generates profit leads to a reduction in the result, while the resumption of earnings in provisions in the years when the enterprise records a deficit leads to an increase in the result.
Construction contracts	The choice between the two methods of accounting for construction contracts has the following impact on the profit and loss account: on the basis of the completed contract, the result will be recognized when the contract is finalized; based on the finalization percentage method, the result will be spread over time over the entire duration of the contract. Changing from one method to another also has a significant impact on the profit and loss account.

Source: The authors adaptation based on IFRS

Table 2. Accounting methods and manipulating estimates in accounting

Opportunities for creative accounting	Solutions that come to restrain creative accounting	Accounting traditions, where solutions are easy to apply
Choices regarding accounting methods	Reducing the number of allowed accounting methods	Western accounting model
Trends to estimate	Minimize opportunity for estimates	Western accounting model
Entering into an artificial transaction	'Substance over form'	Anglo-Saxon accounting model
Authentic transactions planning	Prescribing revaluations	Anglo-Saxon accounting model

Source: The authors adaptation based on IFRS

Financial scandals are based either on the discovery of falsehoods (willing submission of false statements or the dissemination of inaccurate information) or the discovery of the use of techniques to disguise the real situation, known as creative accounting. So, professional accountants long caricatured for their lack of imagination and rigid behavior have created the surprise of inventing creative or imaginative accounting.

FUTURE RESEARCH DIRECTIONS

The presented and analyzed issues are a synthesized part of the vast amount of information that has been developed by the authors to create the framework for understanding manipulating business performances by creative accounting. Therefore, there are new directions of future research such as:

- The choice of accounting methods should be diminished by reducing the number of permitted accounting methods or by specifying the situations in which each method should be used. The imposition of consistent methods is useful because a company who chose a method that gives a positive image in a year, will have to use the same method and during the years when the result will be less favorable.
- The abuse of reasoning can be nipped in two ways: by mapping rules to minimize the use of reasoning or by imposing consistency so that if a company chooses an accounting policy that favors one of the years, they will have to apply it during the coming years even if no longer favors them.
- For artificial transactions „the prevalence of substance over form" concept can be invoked, according to which the economic substance rather than the legal form is the one that determines the accounting substance.
- The time of the transaction is clearly a matter of leadership. However, the purpose of their use can be reduced by requiring the regular review of the elements so that gains or losses of values change accounts are recognized in accounts for the years in which they appear (and not entirely in the year are transferred).

All these measures against „fraudulent" accounting practices must have the purpose to ensure a qualitative accounting information that faithfully represents reality and to allow decisions to ensure an optimal allocation between participants in value creation.

CONCLUSION

The manipulation of accounting information can be done within the law and accounting rules or outside them (Li et al., 2017). In the latter case there are witnessing an illegal practice: accounting fraud. Although there is a clear difference between creative accounting and deliberate violation of the law (fraud), there is always a clear demarcation between the situation of creative accounting practices and accounting malpractice. Because the law is a two-tailed sword - a control tool, but also an argumentation base for deviating from the rule - the auditors should step up their efforts to identify possible manipulations of the information provided by the financial statements. In this respect, the audit function should include an assessment of the company's internal control system to prevent creative accounting or fraud. In order to ensure broader and more rigorous supervision, auditors should be willing to fight against their clients. This could lead to a radical reflection on the nature of the relationship between auditors and managers. It should not be neglected those concepts such as: integrity, objectivity, confidentiality, competence and, last but not least, credibility must be found in the conduct and documents of the work of any professional.

The fundamental problem of convergence of accounting is linked to the note of credibility given to accounting. The statement is based on the user confidence to the situation where the same public company, for the same period in different countries has different size images in equity and results, as a result of compliance with the rules in these countries.

Also consider that successful convergence IFRS - U.S. GAAP in practical terms depends on the co-ordination of activity of the IASB and FASB interpretation, because, even if the standards issued by the two bodies will be identical, the financial statements (prepared in accordance with IFRS or U.S. GAAP) will not be comparable (or will be only limited comparable), convergence efforts thus undermined, if the recommendations for the implementation of these standards will also be the same (or comparable).

Europeans are more skeptical of the utility of fair value for other categories of users of accounting information and there are many criticisms about the accounting model. Furthermore, the fair value is unlikely to apply within a Romanian accounting system, all the more so in the context of the loss of confidence in capital markets over the last few years, amplified by the global economic crisis. This is because fair value is an emanation of the capital market (Ramanna, 2008). Even if the benefits of the fair value system, which are in balance with the disadvantages, are discussed, it cannot be said with certainty that it is superior to the historical cost system. The latter has an incontestable advantage - to be known and therefore mastered.

In conclusion, given the trends of globalization, accounting information users prefer to use an accounting system (concepts, principles, and accounting standards) uniform. As a condition of credibility, the information in financial statements must be complete, in terms of two general restrictions: the cost-benefit and materiality. Omissions can cause information to be false or misunderstood, resulting in a decrease in credibility and relevance.

REFERENCES

Ahmed, A., Neel, M., & Wang, D. (2013). Does mandatory adoption of IFRS improve accounting quality? Preliminary evidence. *Contemporary Accounting Research*, *30*(4), 388–423. doi:10.1111/j.1911-3846.2012.01193.x

Ahrens, T. (2008). Overcoming the subjective–objective divide in interpretive management accounting research. *Accounting, Organizations, and Society, 33*(2), 292-297.

Allen, A., & Ramanna, K. (2013). Towards an understanding of the role of standard setters in standard setting. *Journal of Accounting and Economics*, *55*(1), 1–66. doi:10.1016/j.jacceco.2012.05.003

Andon, P., Baxter, J., & Chua, W. F. (2007). Accounting change as relational drifting: A field study of experiments with performance measurement. *Management Accounting Research*, *18*(2), 273–308. doi:10.1016/j.mar.2006.06.007

Baker, C., & Bettner, M. (1997). Interpretive and Critical Research in Accounting: A Commentary on its Absence from Mainstream Research. *Critical Perspectives on Accounting*, *8*(4), 293–310. doi:10.1006/cpac.1996.0116

Ball, R. (2013). Accounting informs investors and earnings management is rife: Two questionable beliefs. *Accounting Horizons*, *27*(4), 847–853. doi:10.2308/acch-10366

Ball, R., Li, X., & Shivakumar, L. (2015). Contractibility and transparency of financial statement information prepared under IFRS: Evidence from debt contracts around IFRS adoption. *Journal of Accounting Research*, *53*(5), 915–963. doi:10.1111/1475-679X.12095

Barth, M., Landsman, W., & Lang, M. (2008). International accounting standards and accounting quality. *Journal of Accounting Research*, *46*(3), 467–498. doi:10.1111/j.1475-679X.2008.00287.x

Barth, M. E. (2013). Global comparability in financial reporting: What, why, how, and when? *China Journal of Accounting Studies*, *1*(1), 2–12. doi:10.1080/21697221.2013.781765

Barth, M. E., Landsman, W. R., Young, D., & Zhuang, Z. (2014). Relevance of Differences between Net Income based on IFRS and Domestic Standards for European Firms. *Journal of Business Finance & Accounting*, *41*(3-4), 297–506. doi:10.1111/jbfa.12067

Bettner, M., & Kate, K. (2013). Changes in annual reporting rituals of financial services firms in periods of market crisis. *International Journal of Critical Accounting*, *5*(6), 577–593. doi:10.1504/IJCA.2013.059027

Brown, J. (2010). Accounting and visual cultural studies: Potentialities, challenges and prospects. *Accounting, Auditing & Accountability Journal*, *23*(4), 482–505. doi:10.1108/09513571011041598

Byard, D., Li, Y., & Yu, Y. (2011). The effect of mandatory IFRS adoption on financial analysts' information environment. *Journal of Accounting Research*, *49*(1), 69–96. doi:10.1111/j.1475-679X.2010.00390.x

Cahan, S. F., & Sun, J. (2015). The effect of audit experience on audit fees and audit quality. *Journal of Accounting, Auditing & Finance*, *30*(1), 78–100. doi:10.1177/0148558X14544503

Caylor, M. L. (2010). Strategic revenue recognition to achieve earnings benchmarks. *Journal of Accounting and Public Policy*, *29*(1), 82–95. doi:10.1016/j.jaccpubpol.2009.10.008

Chen, H., Tang, Q., Jiang, Y., & Lin, Z. (2010). The role of international financial reporting standards in accounting quality: Evidence from the European Union. *Journal of International Financial Management & Accounting*, *21*(3), 220–278. doi:10.1111/j.1467-646X.2010.01041.x

Chen, M., Qu, X., & Sun, X. (2017). Whose cost of equity capital reduces after IFRS convergence and why? Heterogeneity evidence from Chinese stock market. *China Journal of Accounting Studies*, *5*(1), 1–27. doi:10.1080/21697213.2017.1304539

Damayant, T. (2013). Who is afraid of Qualitative Research? A Compromise Accounting Research Failure in Improving Accounting Practices. *International Journal of Advances in Management and Economics*, 2(2), 89-94.

Dennis, I. (2014). *The Nature of Accounting Regulation*. New York: Routledge.

Doukakis, L. C. (2014). The effect of mandatory IFRS adoption on real and accrual-based earnings management activities. *Journal of Accounting and Public Policy*, *33*(6), 551–572. doi:10.1016/j.jaccpubpol.2014.08.006

Fan, J. P. H., Li, J., & Zheng, G. (2016). Revisiting the bright and dark sides of capital flows in business groups. *Journal of Business Ethics*, *134*(4), 509–528. doi:10.100710551-014-2382-6

Florou, A., & Pope, P. (2012). Mandatory IFRS adoption and institutional investment decisions. *The Accounting Review*, *87*(6), 1993–2025. doi:10.2308/accr-50225

He, K., Pan, X., & Tian, G. (2017). Legal liability, government intervention, and auditor behavior: Evidence from structural reform of audit firms in China. *European Accounting Review*, *26*(1), 61–95. doi: 10.1080/09638180.2015.1100547

Holthausen, R. W., & Watts, R. L. (2001). The relevance of the value-relevance literature for financial accounting standard setting. *Journal of Accounting and Economics*, *31*(1-3), 3–75. doi:10.1016/S0165-4101(01)00029-5

Hou, Q., Jin, Q., Yang, R., Yuan, H., & Zhang, G. (2015). Performance commitments of controlling shareholders and earnings management. *Contemporary Accounting Research*, *32*(3), 1099–1127. doi:10.1111/1911-3846.12111

Jackson, S. B., & Liu, X. K. (2010). The allowance for uncollectible accounts, conservatism, and earnings management. *Journal of Accounting Research*, *48*(3), 565–601. doi:10.1111/j.1475-679X.2009.00364.x

Li, L., Qi, B., Tian, G., & Zhang, G. (2017). The contagion effect of low-quality audits at the level of individual auditors. *The Accounting Review*, *92*(1), 137–163. doi:10.2308/accr-51407

Li, S. (2010). Does mandatory adoption of international accounting standards in the European Union reduce the cost of equity capital? *The Accounting Review*, *85*(2), 607–636. doi:10.2308/accr.2010.85.2.607

Lukka, K. (2010). The roles and effects of paradigms in accounting research. *Management Accounting Research*, *21*(2), 110–115. doi:10.1016/j.mar.2010.02.002

Ozkan, N., Singer, Z., & You, H. (2012). Mandatory IFRS adoption and the contractual usefulness of accounting information in executive compensation. *Journal of Accounting Research*, *50*(4), 1077–1107. doi:10.1111/j.1475-679X.2012.00453.x

Parker, L. (2012). Qualitative management accounting research: Assessing deliverables and relevance. *Critical Perspectives on Accounting*, *23*(1), 54–70. doi:10.1016/j.cpa.2011.06.002

Ramanna, K. (2008). The implications of unverifiable fair-value accounting: Evidence from the political economy of goodwill accounting. *Journal of Accounting and Economics*, *45*(2-3), 253–281. doi:10.1016/j.jacceco.2007.11.006

Richardson, A. (2011). Myth, Paradigms and Academic Accounting Research: A Comment on Reading and Understanding Academic Research in Accounting. *Global Perspectives on Accounting Education*, *8*, 67–77.

Schleicher, T., Tahoun, A., & Walker, M. (2010). IFRS adoption in Europe and investment-cash flow sensitivity: Outsider versus insider economies. *The International Journal of Accounting*, *45*(2), 143–168. doi:10.1016/j.intacc.2010.04.007

KEY TERMS AND DEFINITIONS

Accounting Engineering: The process whereby, given the existence of gaps in the rules to manipulate accounting numbers and taking advantage of flexibility, those practices are chosen for measurement and information that allow transforming synthesis documents from what they should be in what managers want.

Convergence of Accounting: The process by which accounting standards are developed in a manner that is able to lead to the same act or purpose, by showing the similarity of national, regional, international.

Corruptible Value: The amount for which an asset could be changed into a balanced transaction between informed and determined parties other than in a forced sale of liquidation.

Creative Accounting: A tool to create a distortion of the quality of financial information, creating uncertainty about the consistency and comparability of information for users, in which case we are dealing with an accounting of intent.

Fair Value: The amount at which an asset is bought or sold in an arm's-length transaction, in which neither party is forced to act.

Financial Engineering: Represents an aggregate of procedures, which have as objective the modification of the level of the results while taking into account the optimization, minimization, or presentation of financial situations.

Chapter 9
Circular Economy and Circular Business Models in the Actual Global Ecological Context:
Various Approaches

Dana Maria Constantin
University of Bucharest, Romania

Sorinel Căpușneanu
https://orcid.org/0000-0003-3799-3993
Titu Maiorescu University, Romania

Dan Ioan Topor
1 Decembrie 1918 University, Romania

Hassan Danial Aslam
The Islamia University of Bahawalpur, Pakistan

ABSTRACT

This chapter aims to synthesize some of the current issues of the circular economy and circular business models. Based on the international literature, the chapter highlights aspects such as the conceptual theoretical approaches of the circular economy and circular business models, interconnecting the principles of the circular economy, the difference between the linear and the circular economy, the circular economy and the sustainable development, the supply chain within the circular economy, possible business models of the circular economy, advantages and limitations in the successful implementation of the circular economy and supporting sustainability, other aspects of the circular economy and sustainability. The covered topics are based on the studies conducted by specialists and also present some author opinions on the sustainable development and circular economy. The chapter ends with the authors' conclusions on the impact of the circular economy and circular business models in the actual ecological context, launching possible future research topics for specialists.

DOI: 10.4018/978-1-7998-0178-8.ch009

INTRODUCTION

Finding viable solutions for the sustainable economic growth has emerged as a result of the demographic growth and environmental pressure. The goal of a circular economy is to reduce the contribution of the raw materials and waste production to the environment by closing the economic and environmental loops of the resources. The urban areas offer the possibility of creating synergies within the economy in order to increase the efficiency of the resources use as a result of the high population density and shareholders. There is a pressing need for a sustainable development of society that protects and preserves the natural environment, and for these purpose economic, social and environmental policies must be tackled synergistically at all levels. Global warming is already highlighted by the analysis of long strata of metrological data, being a cause of both natural factors, variations in the solar radiation spectrum and volcanic activity, as well as anthropogens, by changing the composition of the atmosphere due to human activity. The use of fossil fuels is the core of the climate problem, which has led to an increase in the amount of carbon dioxide in the atmosphere by over 40% compared to the pre-industrial age (IPCC, 2013; Li et al., 2017; Rakoş et al., 2018). Also, the amount of methane doubled as a result of human activity (IPCC, 2013). Between 1880 and 2012, the global average temperature increased by 0.85°C, and for Europe by almost 1°C, with an increasing trend after 1990 (IPCC, 2013). Depending on the different greenhouse gas emission scenarios, global climate change projections for the 21st century have been projected, so that an increase of 1.8°C to 4.0°C is projected for the end of the century as compared to the current period. The society is already experiencing climate change and, in addition to efforts to reduce greenhouse gas emissions, efforts are also needed to adapt to the changes already made. The transition from the linear economy to a circular economy that uses concepts and instruments of industrial ecology (Saavedra et al., 2018) is absolutely necessary in the context of global climate change. Thus, this chapter provides a global perspective on the relationship between the circular economy and sustainability, highlighting some theoretical approaches of this relationship, the interconnection principles and the existing business models with great possibilities for implementation.

In order to unleash this circular economy-sustainability relationship in the actual environmental context, we tried to find answers to the following questions: (1) *What is the circular economy and what are its relationships with sustainability?(2) What are the underlying principles of the circular economy-sustainability relation and what are the interconnections between them? (3) What is the linkage between the circular economy, climate changes, supply chain and sustainability? (4) What are the business models that can be implemented in a circular economy?* (5) *Which are the advantages and limits in the successful implementation of the circular economy and supporting the sustainability?* The research methodology used consisted of: studying the national and international literature, performing comparative analyzes, issuing hypotheses and conclusions based on the investigations of the studied organisms and researchers. The chapter was organized in such a way that it could present answers to the questions under investigation.

BACKGROUND

Theoretical Approaches to Circular Economy and Its Relationship With Sustainability

The emergence of the concept of circular economy is related to a work describing the earth as a closed and circular system with a limited assimilation capacity, and by deducting it came to the idea that the economy and the environment should coexist in equilibrium (Boulding, 1966). This idea has spurred some organizations and specialists in conducting research to introduce and develop the concept of circular economy since the 1970s (Pearce & Turner, 1990; EMF, 2013).

A conceptualization of the loop economy was made by describing industrial strategies for waste prevention, resource efficiency, regional job creation, dematerialization of the industrial economy (Stahel & Reday, 1976). The most relevant business model for a loop-saving economy is to allow industrial companies to obtain profits without externalization the costs and risks associated with waste (Stahel, 1982). Understanding and conceptual development of the circular economy, including its application in practice, has evolved from economic systems and industrial processes to incorporating the different features and contributions of other concepts that share the idea of closed loop: (1) ecology laws (Commoner, 1971); (2) regenerative design (Lyle, 1994); (3) industrial ecology (Graedel & Allenby, 1995); (4) cradle-to-cradle (McDonough & Braungart, 2002); (5) biomimicry (Benius, 2002); (6) the blue economy (Pauli, 2010).

Specialists have attempted to describe how natural resources influence the economy by supplying inputs for production and consumption, as well as a drain sieve for waste resulting from production processes, emphasizing the linear and open features of contemporary economic systems (Andersen, 2007; Ghisellini et al., 2016; Lieder & amp; Rashid, 2016; Su et al., 2013).

Among the definitions of the circular economy are: (1) the circular economy consists in creating a closed loop of material flow in the entire economic system (Geng & Doberstein, 2008); (2) the ring of the circular economy is given by the circular flow of materials and the use of raw materials and energy in several phases (Yuan et al., 2008); (3) an industrial economy consisting of restoration or regeneration by intent and design (EMF, 2013, Bastein et al., 2013) and which aims at minimizing (or eliminating) waste, using renewable energy sources and the phasing out of use of harmful substances (EMF, 2012); (4) the circular economy is a design-restored economy that aims at permanently preserving products, components and materials at their highest utility and value (Bicket et al., 2014, WEF et al., 2014, Webster, 2015); (5) design and strategies of business models that contribute to slowing down, closing and lowering resource loops (Bocken et al., 2016).

Other specialists have conducted specialized studies dedicated to the concept of circular economy and other features associated with it, such as: (1) the closed loop and the supply chains (Wells & Seitz, 2005; & Wassenhove Guide & Stam & Sahamie, 2014; Govindan et al., 2015); (2) circular business models and circular product design (Bakker et al., 2014, Bocken et al., 2016). The pros and cons are presented in the context of the relationship between the concept of circular economy and the concept of sustainability:

- Circularity and service-based systems are a necessary but not sufficient condition for a sustainable system (Nakajima, 2000; EC, 2014), it must be accompanied by a change in lifestyle to achieve long-term sustainability.
- Circularity in business models and supply chains is a precondition for sustainable processing, which is in fact necessary to improve the economic and environmental performance of developing industrialized countries (Rashid et al., 2013).
- Circular economy is an important element of sustainable development, job creation and GDP growth (Läpple, 2007; EC, 2014, Oncioiu et al., 2018) and circularity is absolutely necessary for sustainable economic output (Bakker et al., 2014) or the maintenance of economic growth (UNEP, 2006).
- Circular strategies help to increase efficiency and dematerialisation (Selger, 2007; Evans et al., 2009; Allwood et al., 2012), being an archetype of sustainable business models among others (Bocken et al., 2014).
- The circular economy does not integrate the social dimension (Murray et al., 2015) and the costs of circular systems must be balanced to avoid creating negative values (Andersen, 2007, Alwood, 2014); the efficiency of the materials used and other forms of inputs (inputs) should have a higher priority than the circular economy).

Theoretical Interconnecting the Circular Economy Principles

Principle 1: *Waste design.* It states that when the components of a product are efficiently designed to fit within the biological or technical cycle and are manufactured to allow disassembly and easy renovation in the future, waste becomes non-existent. Biologically, the materials are non-toxic and can simply be returned to the biosphere (through composting or other approaches), while the technical materials are designed to be used again with the minimum amount of energy and retention of the highest quality (Braungart & McDonough, 2002).

Principle 2: *Building resistance through diversity.* This principle reveals that modularity, versatility, and adaptability are the characteristics that create resistance (Pauli, 2010). Diversity must be balanced with efficiency to lead to an efficient system. If the most efficient systems have fewer nodes and connections and more production capacity, they are more vulnerable to the effects of shocks. If efficient systems have multiple nodes, connections, and scales, they are more resilient when subjected to external shocks.

Principle 3: *Based on renewable energy.* This principle implies that in a circular economy, systems should aim at developing on renewable sources that can only be achieved by reducing energy consumption (Braungart & McDonough 2002; Erkman, 2001).

Principle 4: *Thinking in systems.* This principle gives the ability to understand how the parties are influenced within the whole as well as the interdependence of the whole on the parties. This principle underpins the development of circular models (Pauli, 2010) and includes the examination of the elements in relation to their infrastructure, their environment and their social contexts and involves the understanding of the flows and stocks in play.

Principle 5: *Waste is food.* According to this principle, waste is no longer seen as a valueless or low value material for its last user but as a by-product with valuable resources for other actors in the system (Braungart & McDonough, 2002; Erkman, 2001). Biological materials are reintroduced into the biosphere through non-toxic backward loops, while technical materials can be addressed in various ways: either by creating new upcycle products or by circulating secondary products in a network of enterprises (industrial symbiosis).

Principle 6: *Thinking in cascade.* Creating value for biological materials consists in the possibility of extracting added value from products and materials by cascading other applications (Pauli, 2010).

Principle 7: *Action at the local level.* It is about generating value through existing resources. If ecosystems are used only by existing resources, then sustainable businesses must do the same. This means taking advantage of unused resources, taking into account local resources and the full range of outputs (Pauli, 2010).

Principle 8: *Concentration on performance.* It achieves synergies by profitable exploitation of the three objectives of creating value, creating jobs and reducing resource consumption by selling performance instead of goods (Stahel, 2010).

THE CIRCULAR ECONOMY: THE BASIS OF THE SUSTAINABILITY AND THE ALTERNATIVE OF THE LINEAR ECONOMY

In the actual context of the demographic growth, the intensification of urbanization, the increased energy needs, of the technological development and climate change, the need for a sustainable development is becoming more and more intense. The long-term sustainable development means engaging, at all levels, in policy-making, in taking and implementing decisions (WSSD, 2002; Topor et al., 2016). The sustainable development involves four interconnected aspects or dimensions, namely: political, economic, social and environmental (Bălteanu & Şerban, 2005). The assessment of sustainable development can be done on a set of indicators, including: the human capital used in the current economic and financial evaluation; the natural capital represented by air, water, soil, livestock and used for the acquisition of goods and services; the human capital formed by the human resource and the social capital constituted by the institutional component whose functionality is vital in the implementation of the sustainable development (Bălteanu & Şerban, 2005). The integrated assessment of the four categories of capital sets the level of the sustainable development. The strong level of sustainable development means the untouched preservation of each capital.

The waste of raw materials and energy, the use of energy-intensive and polluting technologies, the poor management of waste resulting from manufacturing, the focus of the companies on short-term profit strategies are the basis in the linear economy. In this type of economy, the ecological dimension of management is lacking in all its aspects: strategic, operational, financial and human resources.

In order to eliminate this restriction that severely limits the sustainability process, a new direction of management should be given, in the ecosystemic and adaptive management (Vădineanu, 2004). In order to succeed such an approach, the companies have to ensure an integrated approach, based on the principle of the rational economic growth, medium and long-term sustainable strategies, and by limiting those sectors which damage the environment, in a negative way (Dumitriu, 2003).

Without the implementation, by companies, of an adaptive ecosystemic management, there is a statistically significant decrease in the natural resources used as raw materials in the global economy. We exemplify the use of fossil fuels - coal, oil and gas - mainly used in the energy industry. In 2012, the International Energy Agency predicted that the use of coal for electricity will compete with oil until 2017 (IEA, 2012). These reserves of fossil fuels have formed in tens of millions of years and are consumed in the hundreds of years since 1882, when Thomas Edison opened the first coal-fired power plant (Flannery, 2015). The strong level of sustainable development, in this case, means that the funds obtained from the use of fossil fuels, for energy, to be invested in the production of renewable energy (solar and wind energy). Nowadays, the human society uses natural resources 1.7 times faster than their ability to regenerate, as shown in Figure 1 (Global Footprint Network, 2017).

In order for the sustainable development to reach the strong level, according to the integrated assessment system of the four categories of capital, it is necessary to promote and implement the adaptive ecosystemic based management, which is the basis of the circular economy.

The main difference between the two types of economies is the one which refers to the role of the environment as a simple natural free resource in the linear economy, and as an integral part of the circular economy circuit. In the linear economy, the environment is not part of the macro-economic flows, but rather is an annex (Dumitriu, 2003), being the linear expression of the verbal action "to extract – to produce – to use – to throw" (Berndtsson, 2015; Lakatos et al., 2017), as shown in Figure 2.

The current economic and social linear development has been based on the use of natural resources as raw materials, usually obtaining goods as a single-use, and eliminating them as waste at the end of life cycle (Heshmati, 2015) (Figure 3).

Linear economy has created a series of complex environmental problems that we face, from unsustainable exploitation of natural resources, chemical pollution and climate change, to reducing freshwater resources, acidification of oceans, biodiversity loss, cycle alteration phosphorus and nitrogen and the hole in the ozone layer (Pernigotti, 2017). *Reducing freshwater resources* is the result of increasing the Planetary Ocean by 0.19 m over the entire 20th century (IPCC, 2013) and reducing the regular flow of many rivers, adding drought and diminishing cryosphere. *Acidification of the oceans* is a consequence of air pollution, so that one quarter of the amount of carbon dioxide emitted annually is absorbed by the

Figure 1. The ecological mark of the world linear economy
Source: Global Footprint Network, 2017

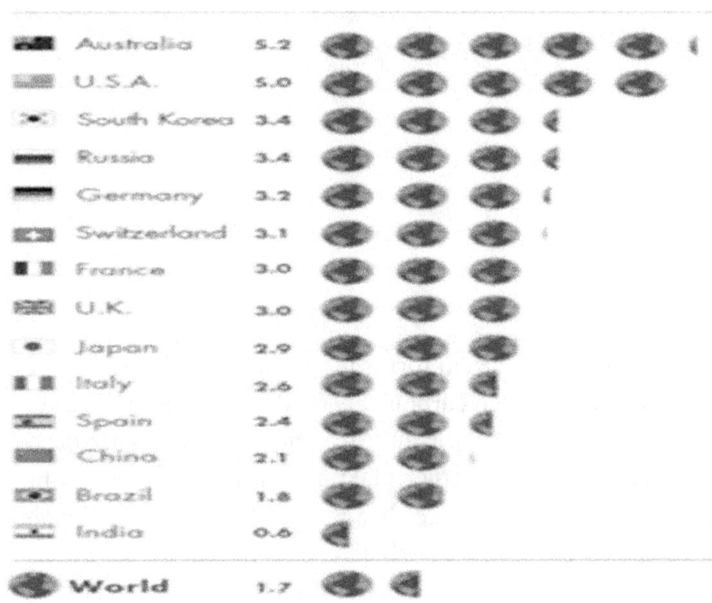

Figure 2. The macro-economic flows in the linear economy
Source: Adapted after Dumitriu (2003)

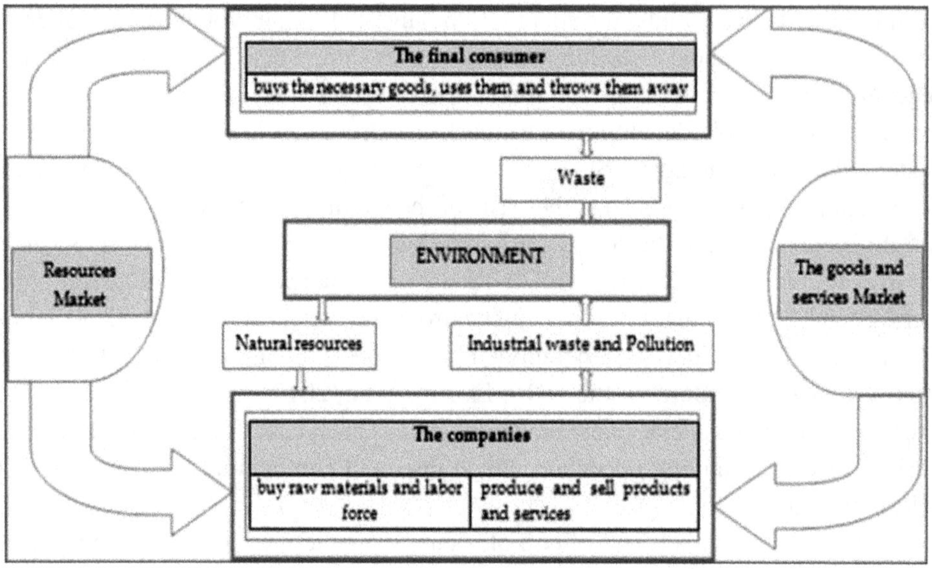

Figure 3. The linear economy
Source: Adapted after Lakatos et al. (2017)

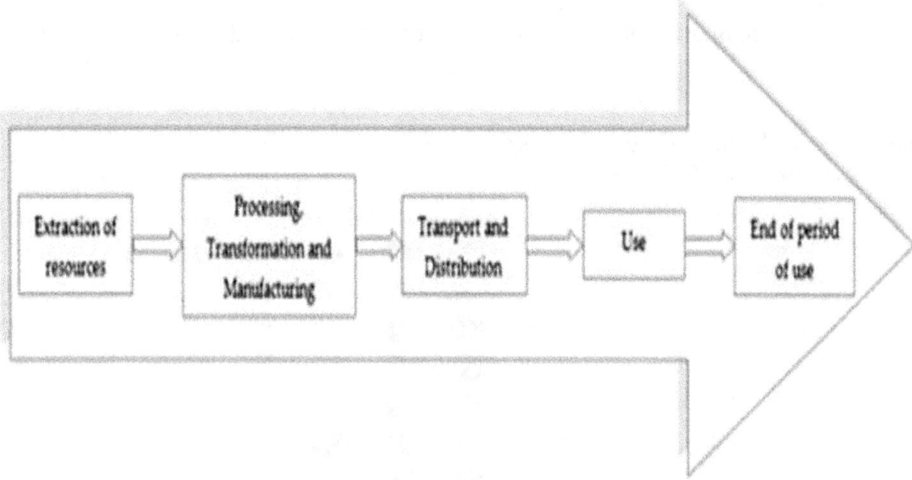

oceans. In reaction with water, carbonic acid forms is accentuating the acidity of the Planetary Ocean, which is reflected in the balance between carbonates, molluscs shells and many organisms, and bicarbonate. *The reduction of biodiversity* is the result of man's extensive land-based control of the land, drastically limiting the space available to other plant and animal species. Anthropogenic pressure on biodiversity is now being magnified by climate change. In a global study of amphibians in 2004, nearly one-third of over 6,000 species were found to be threatened with extinction (Stokstad, 2004). *The alteration of the phosphorus and nitrogen cycle* is the result of soil fertilization in order to stimulate the growth of crops with repercussions in the degradation of the aquifer layers but also of the atmosphere due to the percentage that returns in the form of nitrogen oxides. Alteration of the phosphorus and nitrogen cycle is also reflected in people's health by increasing the phenomenon of obesity as a result of eating disorder. *The ozone hole* located mostly above the Antarctic is the effect of chlorofluorocarbons (CFC), gases composed of halogen substances, such as chlorine and fluoride, spread through spray tubes and refrigeration circuits. This feedback aspect of the linear economy to the environment is being solved by replacing with new substances introduced by technological development for the consumer market, but we are far from returning to the initial condition of the ozone layer. Also, directly or indirectly, ecological problems induced by the linear economy may have multiple consequences on the health of the pollutant. In a World Health Organization (WHO) study of 1996, there has been an increase in the number of cases of disease, especially contagious diseases, as a result of global climate change. Weather conditions will favor the development of bacteria, viruses, and spread vectors, such as insects and rats.

All of these, briefly presented, are the results of a linear economy that meets our needs, but at the same time it aggresses the environment, questioning the good socio-economic functionality of future generations. Environmental damages have the effect of reducing economic performance, and in this respect it can intervene through policies and regulations, but also through the transition to a form of economy that limits aggression to the environment and ensures sustainability.

The opposite of the linear economy is the circular economy, a real pillar of the sustainable development, where the environment is an integral part of the macro-economic flows. In this type of economy, the main concern is the saving of the new economic resources - the environment, through which new measures are adopted, such as: the rational use of deficient natural resources; the reduction of polluting emissions; the reduction of waste quantities and the integrated waste management. The circular economy is the circular expression of the verbal action "to produce – to use – to recycle", as shown in Figure 4. This type of economy is based on the principle of the 3Rs, namely: Reduction, Re-use and Recycling

Figure 4. The circular economy
Source: Adapted after Lakatos et al. (2017)

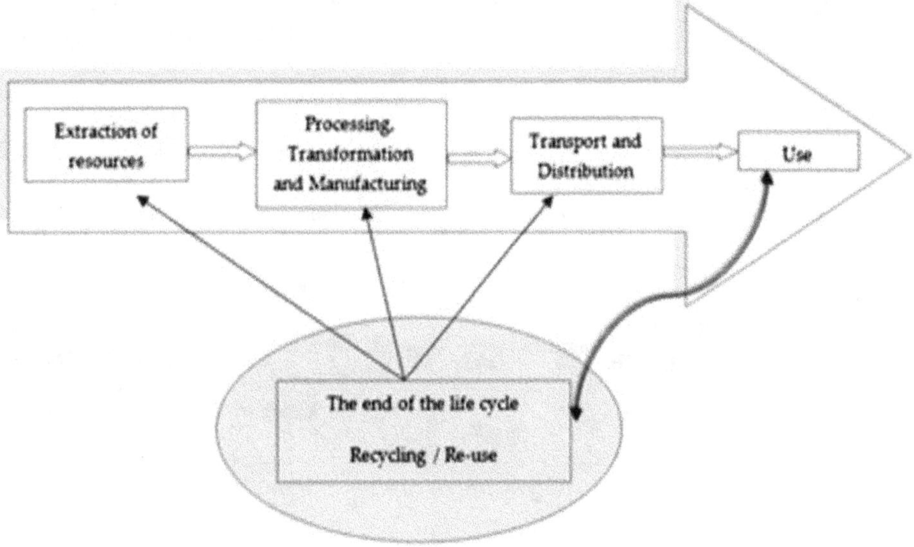

of materials, establishing a relationship of interdependence between the economy and the environment (Heshmati, 2015).

This type of economy has begun to be viable for implementation from the second decade of the 21st century, with the "Manifesto & Policy Recommendations" document of the European Commission, 2012. Implementation precursors of this type of economy were Germany in 1996 and Japan in 2002. Subsequently, in the same direction of the circular economy, other states, such as China, Sweden, France, were also engaged. Following the European Commission's approach, most of the European countries have shown interest in implementing programs and legislation on the circular economy.

Although it presents a series of challenges and limits (Korhonen et al., 2018), the circular economy ensures the resource saving, the recycling of materials and elements in the composition of products, the responsible supply of the raw materials, the change from the non-renewable to renewable energy, the on-going environmental impact assessment and the reduce of the pressure on it. All these lead, ultimately, to reduce the production costs and even create jobs. According to the European Commission (2015), if 95% of the mobile phones were collected and recycled, a reduction in production costs of over 1 billion Euros could be made. Also, if a shift from recycling to vehicle upgrading took place, savings of about 6.4 billion Euros per year and a reduction in energy costs of 140 billion Euros would be generated, besides a decrease of greenhouse gases of 6.3 million tones. The circular economy is the tool that enables waste recycling in order this to become the basis for the second-hand resources resulted from treatment, being the first stage of the supply chain.

We exemplify such a supply chain in the circular economy with the manufacture of the road transport vehicles. There are producers who have chosen to set up dismantling collection networks, so that the re-use and recovery of the vehicles manufactured before January 1st, 1980 can reach at least 75% of the average mass per vehicle and per year (Ministry of Environment, Waters and Forests of Romania, 2017). The diagram in Figure 5 shows the supply chain in the circular economy, for the example above.

In order to promote such a sustainable development, respecting its principles: the mission and priorities of the company; integrated management; continuous improvement; preventive and proactive conduct; employee education; ecological products and services; informing the consumer; research; factories and technologies based on saving resources and energy; caution; suppliers and distributors; crisis strategies; technology transfer; social and environmental responsibility towards the community; performance and compliance with environmental standards (Dumitriu, 2003), it is necessary to develop a new business model based on a circular economy.

Figure 5. The supply chain in the circular economy
Source: Adapted after Ministry of Environment, Waters and Forests of Romania (2017)

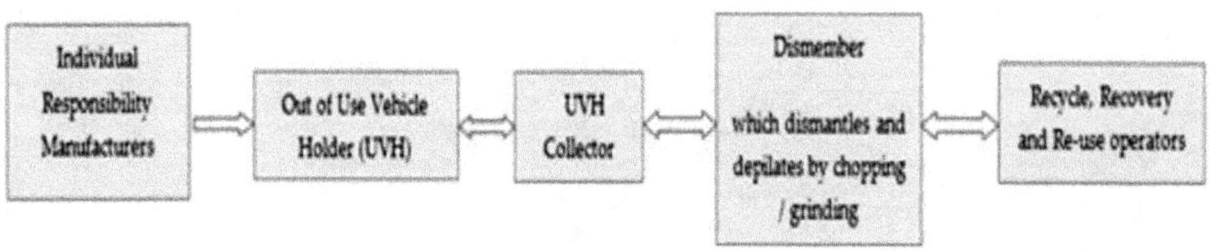

POSSIBLE BUSINESS MODELS OF THE CIRCULAR ECONOMY

The concept of business model and its application was widely debated and explained by specialists (Zott & Amit, 2010; Sawy & Pereira, 2013), but the most widely used approach and recognition (Lewandowski, 2016) where an organization creates, offers and captures value (Osterwalder & Pigneur, 2010). According to this model, the authors identified 9 building blocks whereby a company creates value, captures and offers the value (Osterwalder & Pigneur, 2010): (1) segments of the customer for which value is created; (2) the value proposition that includes services and products to meet the needs of customer segments; (3) distribution channels that are required to deliver, communicate and sell value propositions; (4) customer relationships designed to support communication with each client segment; (5) revenue streams resulting from the sale of value propositions within customer segments; (6) the key resources needed to deliver and deliver value; (7) key activities designed and created to provide value; (8) key partnerships that are realized with the help of networks of suppliers and other partners in order to achieve value; (9) the cost structure that includes all costs associated with the operation of the business model (Figure 6).

The circular business model is the approach to the circular economy but from the perspective of a company that describes the logic behind its creation, delivery, and value capture by closing its resource loops. From the analysis of literature, two approaches to circular business models were selected: (1) ReSOLVE (Ellen MacArthur Foundation et al., 2015); and (2) Resource cycles - slowing, closing and looping loops (Bocken et al., 2016).

The ReSOLVE approach is based on circular economy principles being developed as a tool for generating circular strategies and growth initiatives to help governments and businesses move towards a circular economy and is based on the following elements (Ellen MacArthur Foundation et al., 2015):

Figure 6. Business model based on 9 blocks
Source: Osterwalder & Pigneur (2010)

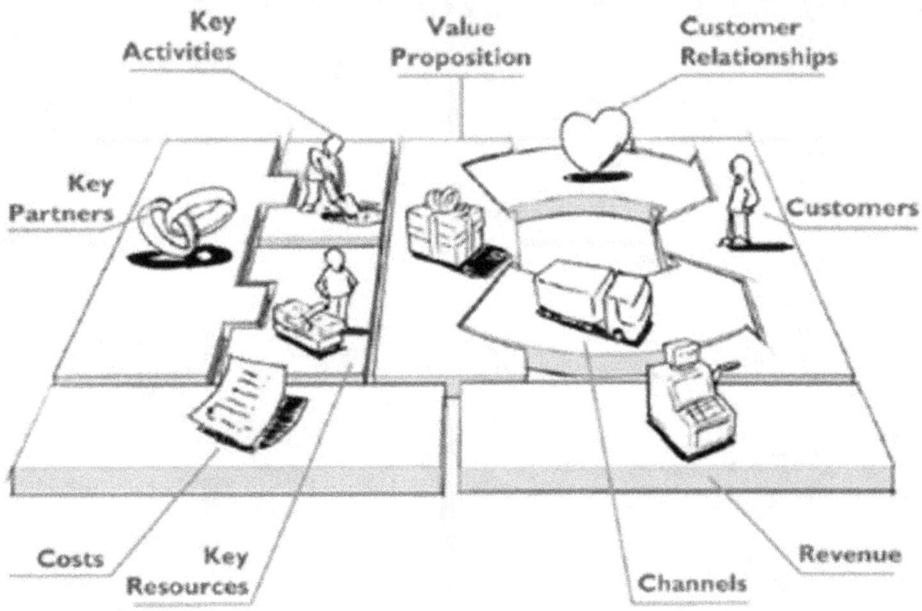

- **Regeneration:** It involves the transition to renewable energy and materials as well as the recovery, retention and regeneration of ecosystem health and the return of biological resources recovered in the biosphere.
- **Division:** It consists in slowing down product loops by maximizing their use by dividing them among different users, reusing them by prolonging their lifetime through maintenance, repairs, and sustainability design.
- **Optimization:** Optimizing a company can be achieved by increasing the performance and efficiency of a product by eliminating waste from the production process and the supply chain and by using large data, automation, remote sensing and direction. These actions take place without changing the product or technology.
- **Loop**: Consists in keeping components and materials in closed loops, giving priority to inner loops.
- **Virtualization:** It consists in the dematerialization of resources by providing practical, direct or indirect utilities.
- **Exchange:** It requires the replacement of old materials with advanced non-renewable materials and the application of new technologies and the selection of new products or services (Figure 7).

The Resource Cycle-slowing, closing, and reduce looping approach is based on how resources, materials, and components flow through a system, with the following strategies being proposed to increase the duration of resource cycles (Bocken et al., 2016):

Figure 7. The ReSOLVE approach with examples
Source: Ellen MacArthur Foundation et al. (2015)

- **Tilt the Resource Loop:** It includes designing long-lasting goods and extending the life span of products as well as increasing the use of a product by prolonging its life span or enhancing its use.
- **Closing the Resource Loop:** It is achieved by re-using materials through recycling, closing the loop between the end of the product life cycle and the production phase.
- **Thin Curls:** Using resource efficiency is intended to use fewer resources per product, a strategy that also works in the linear economy.

Based on this approach, Bocken et al. (2016) and Kraaijenhagen et al. (2016) identified a few examples of business model strategies for a circular economy as presented in Table 1.

DIFFICULTIES IN IMPLEMENTING THE CIRCULAR ECONOMY AND SUSTAINABILITY

The transition to a circular economy has implications for logistics flows at all levels, and therefore the inductors and the difficulties of the circular economy have to be taken into account. Being transversal, logistical difficulties and solutions are relevant at any stage of a value chain. There are several factors whose influence is reciprocal in establishing policy inductors, legal or regulatory frameworks, other social, economic, cultural, technological or infrastructure issues. In the case of infrastructure, support for efficient product collection after use or "reverse cycles" (Ellen MacArthur Foundation, 2012) can be influenced by a number of levers such as: policy tools (landfill tax), extended producer responsibility, models new business etc.

Table 1. Examples of business model strategies for a circular economy

	Business model strategy	Defining
Business model for tilting the resource loop	Functionality, Not Property/ Access Model and Performance	Provide capacity or services to meet the needs of users without the need for their own physical products.
	Expanding product value	Exploitation of the residual value of products - from manufacturing to consumers and then back to production - or the collection of products between distinct economic entities
	Long-lasting classic model	Business models have focused on delivering a long product life, backed by sustainability and repair design
	Encouraging sufficiency	Solutions that actively seek to reduce end-user consumption by principles such as sustainability, upgrading, service, warranties and reparability, and a non-consuming marketing and sales approach
Business model for closing resources loop	Expansion of resources, collection and value of resources	Exploitation of Residual Resource: collecting and supplying "scattered" materials or resources to turn them into new forms of value
	Industrial symbiosis	A process-oriented solution that refers to the use of residual results from a process as raw material for another process that benefits from the geographical proximity of enterprises
Business model for narrowing resource loop	Maximize material and energy efficiency	It is about doing more with fewer resources and generating less waste, emissions and pollution (efficiency and zero-waste policies)

Source: Adaptation by Bocken et al. (2016) and Kraaijenhagen et al. (2016)

The actions taken towards the circular economy have been directed to maximizing value along the value chain and to re-introducing assets into markets. Maintaining customer relationships over several cycles is done by perceiving the material as an investment and customers as users. There are a number of policies that allow business models and value chains to be circular, such as: (1) encouraging manufacturers to develop and develop product lines that respond to customer/user requests without losing resources and taking into account of their real cost; (2) stimulating companies to provide materials from regenerative loops and not from linear flows; (3) development by companies of revenue models generating value in all parts of the value chain; (4) identifying customers/users willing to change their consumption and ownership patterns.

According to the experts' opinion, a number of important difficulties were identified in implementing a circular economy that could be solved if political action would be involved: (1) the absence of internalization of externalities through policies or other economic measures and the lack of pricing, the efficient use of resources or their re-use/recycling; (2) lack of incentives for sustainable procurement for public authorities; (3) lack of investment and innovation in infrastructure and recycling/recovery technologies; (4) lack of skills and investment in product design and circular production; (5) lack of know-how and economic incentives, including for repairs and re-use; (6) lack of consumer information on origins and perishability of products; (7) lack of waste separation at source; (8) the lack of harmonization of transport flows between municipalities, which leads to confusion between shippers and transporters.

SOLUTIONS AND RECOMMENDATIONS

Exceeding the difficulties of implementing the principles of the circular economy could be achieved by adopting the following policies:

Encouraging change in consumer mentality through:

1. Support and promotion of leasing and renting contracts (payments for use instead of ownership) and repairs and reuse of products.
2. Informing consumers of the origin, perishability and validity of the products purchased or the rules for the separation of food and packaging waste from the source.
3. Introducing a differentiated tariff system by charging users depending on the amount and type of waste they generate.
4. Developing obligations for public sector agencies and government departments to acquire effective resources.

Encouraging economic actors to take into account the economic value of their environmental externalities by:

1. Regulatory requirements for the principle of Extended Producer Responsibility (ERP), whereby environmental costs are associated with products throughout their lifetime, encouraging manufacturers to develop eco-friendly products and manage their costs more efficiently. Thus, the costs of recycling products are directly included in the price of the products and local authorities are exempted from additional management costs (Türkeş et al., 2014a).

2. Regulatory requirements for the design and standardization of organic products.
3. Granting economic incentives or fiscal incentives to change the behavior of economic actors and encouraging them to recover resources (raw materials).

Encourage skills development, awareness and investment in circular product design and production through:

1. Support programs for investment in R&D and eco-innovation, as well as the integration of circular design concepts and reusable parts.
2. Expanding information services on raw materials, suppliers, pricing and supply risks, and spreading knowledge about developing new materials.
3. Promoting cleaner production methods by preventing pollution even during product manufacturing processes by conducting analyzes.

Encouraging the improvement of inter-cyclical and inter-sectoral performance by:

1. The development of local Internet-based networks to identify industrial symbiosis opportunities or the development of local/regional counseling programs to identify company resource exchanges for resource management solutions.
2. The creation of planning agencies (public or private) that would deal at territorial level with activities such as: identification and transformation of by-products in raw materials, management of relations with regulatory agencies and brokering agreements with them, shipment of users.

Encouraging investment and innovation in infrastructure and recycling/recovery technologies through:

1. The establishment of long-term recyclable waste collection companies by concluding contracts with companies in the business environment or by offering their own collection services.
2. Supporting investment in regional infrastructure for those companies that develop innovative waste recycling/recovery.
3. Eliminating and harmonizing difficulties with the regulatory arrangements for the use of waste or clarifying certain concepts of re-use or recycling of by-products or products.
4. Providing incentives to suppliers and traders to conclude contracts for the immediate recovery of unsold products.

Encouraging the harmonization of transport flows between municipalities through:

1. Streamlining transport flows and urban distribution through business-to-business or consumer-company concepts.
2. Stepping up cooperation between transport companies.
3. Developing concepts on city logistics through flexible and incentive tenders.

FUTURE RESEARCH DIRECTIONS

This chapter generates topics for further research. Since the circular economy-sustainability relationship has not been thoroughly researched, especially the new business models, it seems that the companies and entities which have put into practice the circular economy have not yet reported the changes and the impacts on their business.

In conclusion, our research has brought a variety of study options that require a deeper reflection at a later stage. Our suggestions for further research are the following: the impact of legislation on the circular economy for a particular branch of industry or agriculture; studying the effect of the reverse supplies in a circular economy; identifying revenue models for the business models of the circular economy; the impact of business models on different companies located in different sectors of the economy and in different geographic areas; the environmental impact beyond the economic and environmental variables.

CONCLUSION

Based on the questions studied, this chapter reflects the main interferences drawn from the theoretical and practical parts and it makes suggestions about what the researchers see as the most current interesting business models of the circular economy, including the advantages and limitations in order to apply the circular economy. The circular economy is that part of the system which has the potential to lead to sustainability, being the opposite to the liniar economy, which was the model of production and consumption since the Industrial Revolution until the beginning of the 21st century, when it became questioning the compromise to satisfy the needs for the future generations.

The strengthening actions based on sustainable policies and information-based tools can help to increase the consumer's awareness on the practices, products and business processes (Türkeş et al., 2014b). This is a serious reason to take into account in the implementation of sustainable business models and of consumers' awareness for the products and processes of the circular economy.

Clarifying some aspect of sustainable business models for the circular economy and applicability for SMEs in Romania, we believe that the goal has been achieved, with further directions being open for specialists from business and academia. In the current environmental context, the business model strategies for a circular economy in SMEs guaranteed and will bring the desired satisfactions for managers, investors, other stakeholders. The development of partnerships between specialized bodies and enterprises ensures the realization of the sustainable process in the socio-economic environment. Also the collection, processing and analysis of information will help identify the best solutions to guarantee the efficiency of implementing innovative business models based on innovation.

REFERENCES

Allwood, J. M. (2014). Squaring the Circular Economy: The Role of Recycling within a Hierarchy of Material Management Strategies. In Handbook of Recycling: State-of-the-Art for Practitioners, Analysts, and Scientists, (pp. 445–477). Academic Press.

Andersen, M. S. (2007). An introductory note on the environmental economics of the circular economy. *Sustainability Science, 2*(1), 133–140. doi:10.100711625-006-0013-6

Bakker, C. A., den Hollander, M. C., van Hinte, E., & Zljlstra, Y. (2014). *Products That Last - Product design for circular business models*. Delft: TU Delft Library.

Băltenu, D., & Şerban, M. (2005). *Global environmental changes. An interdisciplinary assessment of uncertainties*. Bucharest: Coresi.

Benyus, J. M. (2002). *Biomimicry*. New York: Harper Perennial.

Berndtsson, M. (2015). *Circular Economy and Sustainable Development*. Uppsala University.

Bocken, N. M. P., de Pauw, I., Bakker, C., & van der Grinten, B. (2016). Product design and business model strategies for a circular economy. *J. Ind. Prod. Eng., 33*, 308–320.

Bocken, N. M. P., Short, S. W., Rana, P., & Evans, S. (2014). A literature and practice review to develop sustainable business model archetypes. *Journal of Cleaner Production, 65*, 42–56. doi:10.1016/j.jclepro.2013.11.039

Boulding, K. E. (1966). The Economics of the Coming Spaceship Earth. In *Environmental quality in a growing economy: Essays from the sixth RFF forum*. New York: RFF Press.

Braungart, M., & McDonough, W. (2002). *Cradle to Cradle: Remaking the Way We Make Things* (1st ed.). New York: North Point Press.

Commoner, B. (1971). *The closing circle: Nature, man, and technology*. New York: Random House.

Dumitriu, C. (2003). *Environmental management and marketing. A strategic approach*. Iasi: Tehnopress.

El Sawy, O. A., & Pereira, F. (2013). *Business Modelling in the Dynamic Digital Space - An Ecosystem Approach*. New York: Springer Heidelberg. doi:10.1007/978-3-642-31765-1

Ellen MacArthur Foundation. (2012). *Towards the Circular Economy. Economic and business rationale for an accelerated transition*. Ellen MacArthur Foundation.

Ellen MacArthur Foundation. (2013). *Towards the Circular Economy. Opportunities for the consumer goods sector*. Ellen MacArthur Foundation.

Ellen MacArthur Foundation. (2015). *Delivering the Circular Economy: A Toolkit for Policymakers*. Author.

Erkman, S. (2001). Industrial Ecology: a new perspective on the future of the industrial system. In President's lecture, Assemblée annuelle de la Société Suisse de Pneumologie, Geneva, Switzerland.

European Commission (EC). (2012). European resource efficiency platform (EREP). *Manifesto & Policy Recommendations*. Available from: http://ec.europa.eu/environment/ index_en.htm

European Commission (EC). (2014). *Towards a Circular Economy: A Zero Waste Programme for Europe, Communication from the Commission to the European Parliament, the Council, the European Economic and Social Committee and the Committee of the Regions*. Brussels: European Commission.

Evans, S., Gregory, M., Ryan, C., Bergendahl, M., & Tan, A. (2009). *Towards a sustainable industrial system: With recommendations for education, research, industry and policy*. University of Cambridge Institute for Manufacturing and Cranfield University.

Flannery, T. (2015). *Atmosphere of hope. Searching for solutions to the climate crisis*. Melbourne: The Text Publishing Company.

Geng, Y., & Doberstein, B. (2008). Developing the circular economy in China: Challenges and opportunities for achieving "leapfrog development." *International Journal of Sustainable Development and World Ecology*, *15*(3), 231–239. doi:10.3843/SusDev.15.3:6

Ghisellini, P., Cialani, C., & Ulgiati, S. (2016). A review on circular economy: The expected transition to a balanced interplay of environmental and economic systems. *Journal of Cleaner Production*, *114*, 11–32. doi:10.1016/j.jclepro.2015.09.007

Global Footprint Network. (2017). Available from: https://www.footprintnetwork.org/

Govindan, K., Soleimani, H., & Kannan, D. (2015). Reverse logistics and closed loop supply chain: A comprehensive review to explore the future. *European Journal of Operational Research*, *240*(3), 603–626. doi:10.1016/j.ejor.2014.07.012

Graedel, T. E., & Allenby, B. R. (1995). *Industrial ecology*. Englewood Cliffs, NJ: Prentice Hall.

Guide, V. D. R. J. Jr, & Van Wassenhove, L. N. (2009). Or Forum—The Evolution of Closed-Loop Supply Chain Research. *Operations Research*, *57*(1), 10–18. doi:10.1287/opre.1080.0628

Heshmati, A. (2015). *A review of the circular economy and its implementation*. IZA Discussion Paper No. 9611.

Intergovernmental Panel on Climate Change (IPCC). (2013). The physical science basis. Contribution of working group I to the fifth assessment report of the intergovernmental panel on climate change. Cambridge, UK: Cambridge University Press.

International Energy Agency (IEA). (n.d.). Available from: https://www.iea.org/

Korhonen, J., Honkasalo, A., & Seppälä, J. (2018). Circular Economy: The concept and its limitations. *Ecological Economics*, *143*, 37–46. doi:10.1016/j.ecolecon.2017.06.041

Kraaijenhagen, C., van Oppen, C., & Bocken, N. (2016). Circular Business: Collaborate and Circulate. Amsterdam: Ecodrukkers.

Lakatos, E. S., Rusu, T., & Crişan, O. A. (2017). An Effective Alternative to the Linear Economy: Circular Economy. *Stiinta si Inginerie*, *31*(21), 1–8.

Läpple, F. (2007). *Abfall - und kreislaufwirtschaftlicher Transformationsprozess in Deutschland und in China: Analyse, Vergleich, Übertragbarkeit*. Heidelberg, Germany: Universität Heidelberg.

Lewandowski, M. (2016). Designing the Business Models for Circular Economy-Towards the Conceptual Framework. *Sustainability*, *8*(1), 43. doi:10.3390u8010043

Li, H., Dong, L., Xie, Y. T., & Fang, M. (2017). Low-carbon benefit of industrial symbiosis from a scope-3 perspective: A case study in China. *Applied Ecology and Environmental Research, 15*(3), 135–153. doi:10.15666/aeer/1503_135153

Lieder, M., & Rashid, A. (2016). Towards circular economy implementation: A comprehensive review in context of manufacturing industry. *Journal of Cleaner Production, 115*, 36–51. doi:10.1016/j.jclepro.2015.12.042

Lyle, J. T. (1994). *Regenerative design for sustainable development*. New York: John Wiley & Sons.

Ministry of Environment, Waters, and Forests of Romania/Ministerul Mediului, Apelor şi Pădurilor din România (MMAPR). Programul Operaţional Capacitate Administrativă 2014–2020. Asistenţă Tehnică pentru realizarea Planului Naţional de Gestionare a Deşeurilor şi a Planului Naţional de Prevenire a Generării Deşeurilor. (n.d.). Available from: http://www.mmediu.ro

Murray, A., Skene, K., & Haynes, K. (2015). The Circular Economy: An Interdisciplinary Exploration of the Concept and Application in a Global Context. *Journal of Business Ethics*, 1–12.

Nakajima, N. (2000). A Vision of Industrial Ecology: State-of-the-Art Practices for a Circular and Service-Based Economy. *Bulletin of Science, Technology & Society, 20*(1), 54–69. doi:10.1177/027046760002000107

Osterwalder, A., & Pigneur, Y. (2010). Business Model Generation: A Handbook for Visionaries, Game Changers, and Challengers. In T. Clark (Ed.), A handbook for visionaries, game changers, and challengers. Amsterdam: John Wiley & Sons.

Pauli, G. A. (2010). *The blue economy: 10 years, 100 innovations, 100 million jobs*. Taos, NM: Paradigm Publications.

Pearce, D. W., & Turner, R. K. (1990). *Economics of natural resources and the environment*. New York: Harvester Wheatsheaf.

Pernigotti, D. (2017). *Cu apa până la gât/With water to the throat*. Bucharest: Seneca Lucius Annaeus.

Rashid, A., Asif, F. M. A., Krajnik, P., & Nicolescu, C. M. (2013). Resource Conservative Manufacturing: An essential change in business and technology paradigm for sustainable manufacturing. *Journal of Cleaner Production, 57*, 166–177. doi:10.1016/j.jclepro.2013.06.012

Saavedra, M. B. Y., Iritani, R. D., Pavan, L. R. A., & Ometto, R. A. (2018). Theoretical contribution of industrial ecology to circular economy. *Journal of Cleaner Production, 170*, 1514–1522. doi:10.1016/j.jclepro.2017.09.260

Seliger, G. (2007). *Sustainability in manufacturing: Recovery of resources in product and material cycles*. Berlin: Springer. doi:10.1007/978-3-540-49871-1

Stahel, W. (1982). The product life factor. In G. S. Orr (Ed.), *An Inquiry into the Nature of Sustainable Societies. The Role of the Private Sector* (pp. 72–105). Houston, TX: Houston Area Research Centre.

Stahel, W., & Reday, G. (1976). *The potential for substituting manpower for energy*. Report to the Commission of the European Communities.

Stahel, W. R. (2010). *The performance economy*. Basingstoke, UK: Palgrave Macmillan.

Stindt, D., & Sahamie, R. (2014). Review of research on closed loop supply chain management in the process industry. *Flexible Services and Manufacturing Journal, 26*(1-2), 268–293. doi:10.100710696-012-9137-4

Stokstad, E. (2004). Global survey documents puzzling decline of amphibians. *Science, 306*(5695), 391. doi:10.1126cience.306.5695.391a PMID:15486264

Su, B., Heshmati, A., Geng, Y., & Yu, X. (2013). A review of the circular economy in China: Moving from rhetoric to implementation. *Journal of Cleaner Production, 42*, 215–227. doi:10.1016/j.jclepro.2012.11.020

UNEP. (2006). *Circular Economy. An alternative model for economic development*. Paris: United Nations Environment Programme.

Vădineanu, A. (2004). *Development Management. An ecosystem approach*. Bucharest: Ars Docendi.

Webster, K. (2015). *The Circular Economy: A Wealth of Flows*. Isle of Wight, UK: Ellen MacArthur Foundation.

Wells, P., & Seitz, M. (2005). Business models and closed-loop supply chains: A typology. *Supply Chain Management, 10*(4), 249–251. doi:10.1108/13598540510612712

World Health Organization. (1996). Available from: http://www.who.int/en/

WSSD. (2002). *World Summit on Sustainable Development in Johannesburg*. Available from: https://sustainabledevelopment.un.org/milesstones/wssd

Yuan, Z., Bi, J., & Moriguichi, Y. (2008). The Circular Economy: A New Development Strategy in China. *Journal of Industrial Ecology, 10*(1-2), 4–8. doi:10.1162/108819806775545321

Zott, C., & Amit, R. (2010). Business model design: An activity system perspective. *Long Range Planning, 43*(2-3), 216–226. doi:10.1016/j.lrp.2009.07.004

ADDITIONAL READING

Oncioiu, I., Căpuşneanu, S., Türkeş, M. C., Topor, D. I., Oprea Constantin, D. M., Marin-Pantelescu, A., & Ştefan Hint, M. (2018). The Sustainability of Romanian SME's and their Involvement in Circular Economy. *Sustainability, 10*(8), 2761. doi:10.3390u10082761

Türkeş, M., Raicu, I., & Vija, I. (2014a). Enhancing the performance of business process in Romanian SMEs through ERP solutions. *Knowledge Horizons Economics, 6*(4), 30–32.

Türkeş, M., Scarlat, E., Vija, R. I., & Raicu, I. (2014b). Improving the Performance of Business Process Modeling for Small-Medium Sized Companies. *Knowledge Horizons-Economics, 6*(4), 72–74.

KEY TERMS AND DEFINITIONS

Business Model (BM): A business model that creates a competitive edge with superior customer value and contributes to the sustainable development of society and society.

Circular Economy: The economy where the environment is as an integral part of the economic circuit.

Ecosystem: Ensemble formed by biotope and biocenosis, in which close relationships are established between both organisms and between them and abiotic factors.

Environment: All natural and anthropogenic components outside of a living being that influences its existence.

Extended Producer Responsibility: Is a strategy to add all of the environmental costs associated with a product throughout the product life cycle to the market price of that product.

Linear Economy: The economy where the environment is as a simple natural free resource.

Stakeholders: Groups interested in disclosing sustainable information contained in the company's sustainability report.

Sustainability: The current economic and social development without damaging the natural environment.

Sustainable Development: All forms and methods of socio-economic development that focus primarily on ensuring a balance between social, economic and ecological aspects and the elements of natural capital.

Sustainable Use: Using renewable resources in a way to ensure the needs and aspirations of the present and future generations.

Chapter 10
Perceiving the Value of the Company in Managing Business Risks:
Evidence From Finland

Lavinia Essen
University of Lapland, Finland

ABSTRACT

Seen as a reflection of the clear vision of some extreme leaders, the overall performance of the entity is achieved today against the backdrop of the innovation process. The value of the company is necessary to become the key element in any entity development strategy. However, it requires a comparative analysis of the entity with other market players or emerging markets. This chapter analyzes the new research directions at the intersection between accounting and management, with the role of potentiating the important valorization of managerial culture and the implementation of an integrated system of performance indicators to accurately determine the value of a company.

INTRODUCTION

Currently, in all countries, especially in the economically developed ones, with democratic traditions and an important and clear legal system, in which capitalism proves it's obvious advantages, where the market is the sole arbiter of the economy and the private enterprise is encouraged, it is estimated that development is the main way and will continue to be for many decades, with a growing importance of the role and weight of small and medium enterprises in the national economy (Stettina & Hörz, 2015; Akgün, Keskin & Byrne, 2009; Chan, Shaffer & Snape, 2004).

One aspect of great importance to the existence, perpetuation and rise or fall of companies in the economy of any country is their contribution to creating new value, or, in other words, the value added in order to be more relevant, needs to be examined closely, along with the number of employees (Becker & Huselid, 2006; Alhyari, Alazab, Venkatraman, Alazab & Alazab, 2013). Enterprises activity is not

DOI: 10.4018/978-1-7998-0178-8.ch010

confined to any country to production in the strict sense; they participate in both exports and imports in order to achieve the purposes of the owners. In addition, it should be noted that between them, the most important place is micro (Arsenault & Faerman, 2014; Fisher, 2010). Due to its' small size and simpler organizational structures, they can make many changes during their existence, that allow them to operate in conditions of economic efficiency. Another important advantage of small and medium size organizations refers to their innovative potential in the technical, technological and managerial view (Agha, Alrubaiee & Jamhour, 2012).

Value analysis of the company is another technique of organizing and processing the values of individuals and organizational culture (Amagoh, 2008; Taticchi, Tonelli & Cagnazzo, 2010). This method provides information about what people value more or less, about what they value as desirable in correspondence with certain intentions, expectations and ideals. In organizations where employees are more concerned with meeting the basic, elementary needs, their behavioral choices are restricted, which leads to a decrease in their contribution to increasing the efficiency of their work (Deutsch & Silcox, 2003; Ashkanasy, 2011). In strong economic firms, employees have higher aspirations, both spiritually and materially, which leads to their participation in organizational performance (Olson, Slater, Tomas & Hult, 2005; Andriole, 2010).

For the time being, the only alternatives for developing businesses in Finland are: the ability to create new products and services, the ability to improve internal and external relationships so as to favor the creation of competitive advantages that will ensure success in the market. Successful companies increasingly manifest themselves as true open systems, whose position in the market depends not only on their internal resources, but also their relations with configuration and external entities with complementary skills. External network of the company is basically an extension of the internal borders between the two types of networks becoming increasingly difficult to identify.

This chapter analysis the new research directions at the intersection between accounting and management, with the role of potentiating the important valorization of managerial culture and the implementation of an integrated system of performance indicators to accurately determine the value of a company. The theoretical and practical conclusion shows that if the company ceases to expand at a cost under the cost of trading in the market, but equally the cost of organizing the transaction by another firm, both procedures may allow the organization of production at a price below the market. Therefore, the entrepreneur does not seek any specific actions undermining the market economy or business isolation, rather it has clear objectives that are channeled to seize all opportunities of the free market.

BACKGROUND

In the light of the new conditions generated by digital economy, any company, no matter the field it has as operation, rules the principles of effectiveness and efficiency, competitive party, functional and decisional autonomy, and that of developing activities that suit the market requests (Cocca & Alberti, 2010). Consequently, due to changes fever, due to their rapid succession rhythm, companies are compelled to frequently reorganize their structure, to continuous adapt to new trends determined by the contemporary scientific and technical progress, by the intensification of the contest within the national and international level, by human taste development and change in needs.

The display of efficiency in the economical field may take different shapes, as follows: the output increase per man-shift; reducing the consumption of raw materials, fuel and consumables, reducing the freight costs, increase profitability of the enterprises, improving the quality of the products (Hurley, 2002; Ahearne, Lam, Mathieu & Bolander, 2010). Thus, the efficiency is expressed upon case by its multitude of forms and partial aspects, but especially through their reunite series.

Economic efficiency must represent a basis component of the entire economic activity due to the limited character of the resources which have to be wisely managed so as to ensure the economic progress and the improvement of mankind living standards (Davila, 2012). Within a market economy context, the economic efficiency must be viewed both from the micro and macro economical point of view. Furthermore, this should also be viewed from the level of the countries with whom Finland economy interacts, as the improvement of the activities carried out by the parties' leads to better products obtained with less effort input. The economic efficiency, especially the investment and fixed capital, have a foresight character, fact that guarantees a particular importance in taking economic decisions. Decisions shall be taken based on the existence of several project variants, creating the possibility of choosing the most efficient one. The economic efficiency represents the main qualitative factor of the economic growth as it ensures the absolute boost of the effects using the same effort volume input.

The economical efforts should be analyzed from the following points of view; planning in time, financing sources, report of the import investment versus the total investment, degree of availability of certain resources, renewing potential, consequences of these expenses upstream and downstream the activity where they are meant to be used (Cameron & Quinn, 2011). Last but not the least, we have to bear in mind that the consumed resources are expressed in different measuring units (pc, hrs. / man; m^3, tons etc.)

The concept of efficiency has been practically introduced in all socio-human activities, so, we can easily discuss today about economic, social and ecological efficiency (Tallon & Pinsonneault, 2011). From the social prospect, a system is deemed as efficient if it's capable to focalize within the social and economic circuit all the necessary resources, if it is able to optimally distribute them on different fields and branches, to manage them with maximum effectiveness so as to satisfy the social need at her highest point.

Social efforts materialized in educational, cultural, sanitary and social assistance programmers, correlated with the social, individual and collective effects are defining the concept of social efficiency (Behery, Jabeen & Parakandi, 2014). The physical state of the population, degree of civilization, social security and protection, welfare expressed by the living standard and the quality of socio- ecological life are all upshots justifying the distribution of resources for the mankind benefit.

The actual economic efficiency includes natural environment protection and preservation exploiting the resources in order to study the ecological balance, to adopt sets of measures preventing and eliminating negative effects caused by disturbing factors and maintaining a life friendly environment (Behery, Jabeen & Parakandi, 2014; Basten & Haamann, 2018). Feature of the environment protection, the ecological efficiency expresses the attempts that have to be made in order to meet the natural environment parameters with the normal evolution standards, imposed by the ecological balance.

A minute assessment of any economic activity efficiency implies a systemic approach that sets off economic, political, social or ecological aspects, having in mind the multiple set of effects created up and down the specific subject activity.

THE EFFECT IN PERCEIVING THE VALUE OF THE COMPANY: EVIDENCE FROM FINLAND

One of the major tasks of management in perceiving the value of the company is the maintenance of balance for satisfying the investors' interests (shareholders) and workers (personnel). The decisive condition of the improving of current situation for Finland companies is the finding of reasons and resources for the consolidation of the common actions of opponent subjects of the enterprise (Tong & Arvey, 2015).

On the other hand, the specific sensitivity of the company, its distinctiveness and rapid transformation of customers' preferences justifies the systemic and dynamic approach of the efficiency, fact that takes into consideration the premises of a rational use of resources and their preservation in order to maintain the eco balance and the mankind health (Hartnell, Ou & Kinicki, 2011).

Any activity plan, (production, investment, promotion of the technical progress, organizational, purchasing and dispatching) implies several achieving methods (Rowland & Hall, 2014). At its turn, each modality has at its incipit point numerous project variants, characterized by a variety of information regarding efforts, effects, the existing report between, duration of completion, period till achieving the expected socio-economic effects. Next, a system of economic indicators is used to choose the best variant quantitatively and as much as possible qualitative. The need for using a system of indicators is imposed by the complex character of the economic efficiency as each part of it reflects a certain criterion of economic efficiency (Kaplan & Norton, 2006; Tapanainen, 2012).

When the analysis refers to the activity of several companies from Finland, one of the most valuable classifications is that upon the nature of the analysis object, thus: the cluster of general indicators of the entire economic activity; the cluster of the efficiency indicators of the production factors; the cluster of structural indicators of the consumed resources and the achieved results; the cluster of indicators specific to the industry.

The cluster of general indicators of the entire economic activity includes indicators that characterize the broad efficiency of the economic activity, despite the level of achieving (workshop, shop, company, national economy, activity field etc.). The main indicators belonging to this group are the profit arte and the expenses at a 1000 Euro production (income).

This particular indicator helps in reflecting the totality of the final effects (from certain activities), as well as the totality of the resources consumed, no matter their nature– human resource, material or financial – exploited for the welfare of that specific activity. The indicator calculated in this manner perfectly expresses the influence of each factor part of the production process and thus, favored the achieving of that precise profit. It might be calculated for the entire commercial unit as well as for each kind or product individually.

In relation to this indicator it is worth mentioning that for some economic analysis it is taken into account instead of production costs the total volume of the production capital allotted which contains the fixed capital and the working capital of the commercial society.

In order to evaluate the value of the company when exploiting the fixed capital, it is normally used a system of indicators related to: dynamics, structural and functional state of the fixed capital; the extensively and the efficient of the equipment based on the synthetically efficiency indicators.

As the economic efficiency growth calls for supplementary investment, the appraisal methodology of the efficiency within the e industry must follow the accuracy of all investment efforts, especially of the multiple economic effects, direct or indirect. In this view, the evaluation of the economic efficiency is achieved by calling a complex system of indicators, system that includes main indicators in the static and dynamic approach, to which we add a number of indicators specific to the industry.

The Economic Value Added (EVA) method was proposed for the first time Stern Stewart & Co. in 1991, and then developed over 90 years as an internal indicator of business performance measurement for determining the efficiency of capital. EVA "provides a common language for managers in discussions about creating value, and because it is widely accepted and used in financial circles, may increase the legitimacy of a company in financial markets as an indicator of the ability of a company to create value, or, conversely, destroy it during a certain period of time"(Anand & Kodali, 2010).

Stern Stewart has developed this model to help managers incorporate two basic principles in making decisions (Chen & Fu, 2008). The first is that the main financial goal of any company should be to increase shareholder value; the second is that the value of a company depends on the amount by which income exceeds the cost of capital.

EVA is defined in the European Management Journal as "the difference between net sales and the amount of operating expenses, taxes and cost of capital (capital charges), where the cost of capital is calculated as a weighted average cost of capital multiplied by total invested capital. Basically, EVA increases when the average cost of capital is lower than the rate of return on assets (return on net assets), and vice versa" (Alstete & Beutell, 2018).

EVA calculation, based on the following indicators: WACC (Weighted Average Cost of Capital - Weighted average cost of capital) - weighted average cost of debt, after tax and equity (cost of equity); ROIC = ratio of capital invested and at night (which is similar rate ROI).

As shown, EVA model was developed initially as an internal measure of performance used by managers to help them make decisions about investments. In practice has shown that an investment project that causes higher incomes than the net cost of its financing and thus generate profit, not necessarily lead to increased company value (Tapanainen, Hallanoro, Päivärinta & Salmela, 2008). A company should be concerned only those investment projects capable of generating a positive EVA or even increasing, because it will increase shareholder value. Thus, it becomes clear that applying the principles of this method companies should change their priorities.

Creating value for shareholders involves maximizing the difference between the market value of the company and the nominal value of shares (initial investment of shareholders), this difference is called market value added (MVA) - market value added or the present value of EVA, and is essentially the difference between the capital that investors have brought in the original company and the amount of money they can get far by selling shares they hold (Yadav & Sagar, 2013). Maximizing the wealth gap actually increases the company's shareholders. The difference between market value and book value of the company is attributable, as shown before intangible assets that are usually neglected by accounting documents of the company.

Market value added is a measure of external performance, while EVA is an internal performance indicator which measures the firm, in terms of the market (Sarabi, Naghizadeh, Liu & Liu, 2016). EVA was created to remove MVA shortcomings, namely that the latter indicator expresses the company's value based on performance in the previous year and the current situation so that a company can register a positive MVA even if investments made in the current or to be made are bad.

Since the value added measure has not been fully achieved either in this way, due to factors that could not be determined (to establish whether the drive way destroy or create value or measurement of intellectual potential), has developed a new method, VAIC (Value added intellectual coefficient), which was designed to assist managers in determining the potential of their companies, based on current performance (Sementelli, 2016).

Companies have recognized the importance of intellectual capital as a key factor for success, looking for ways to measure and control this factor (Jung, Nam, Lee & Kim, 2016). Financial performance measurement is not sufficient that reflects how the profit is due to intellectual capital. In the knowledge economy, wealth is created through a combination of services and products that generate value. Each company has its unique set of knowledge, skills, values and solutions, all intangible resources. Monitoring and management of these resources can be made with value creation efficiency analysis because it is a priority for managers to obtain and maintain productivity and efficiency in the enterprise. VAIC indicates value creation efficiency of all resources, expressing a firm's intellectual abilities. The more qualitative resources (human and intellectual capital) were used, the higher the value creation efficiency of the company.

VAIC depends on the structure of human capital employed and the results they have achieved in the past (patents, licenses, innovation, customer relationship), the value added (VA = operating profit + depreciation + cost of salaries and depreciation), the costs employees (salaries, bonuses, training) and the value of assets involved in the work (Lin, Peng & Kao, 2008).

VAIC analysis is based on two essential resources: capital employed (physical and financial) and intellectual capital. Both are treated as investments and are creating value. Human capital consists of all employees, their organization and their ability to create value that can assess the market. Performance Monitoring equity and intellectual capital based on VAIC analysis, based on financial results: value added (difference between operating revenue and expenses from outside the enterprise). Expenditure on salaries is not included in the calculation because they are treated as investments.

To calculate the value creation efficiency of the two factors used indicators: EEC (capital employed efficiency = VA / EC) - the efficiency of capital employed, HCE (human capital efficiency = VA / HC) - the efficiency of human capital SCE (structural capital efficiency = SC / VA) - structural capital efficiency. SCE is calculated differently for HCE and the ECA, is inversely proportional to the efficiency of human capital (Schneider & Somers, 2006). These indicators show how much value was created from a monetary unit. If the indicators are aggregated to obtain VAIC, it will be shown the overall effectiveness of a company or intellectual abilities.

Another element that contributes to increasing the value of a company is the quality of the products which represents the final expression of the production processes (Henczel, 2002). It is also synthesizing the technical level, the operational and the economical performances, as well the esthetical ones. In substance, the quality represents the level to which the totality of a certain product properties is made worth. It is the expression of the degree in which the society needs are satisfied, by means of the products technical, economical and esthetical parameters.

For an accurate assessment of the quality we select those properties which significantly determine the degree in which the product satisfies the consumer requirements. That constitutes the quality features.

By measuring or evaluating the quality features that essentially contribute to the way the product is estimated, we obtain the quality indicators (Homburg & Pflesser, 2000). Concluding, the quality indicators of the textile products are grouped in: technical, esthetical, hygienic-sanitary and comfort indicators, utilization and operational ones and nevertheless, the economical ones. Every single one is ascribed in standards, tasks books and specifications.

The quality indicators level of the textile finished products depends upon the designed quality, the quality of raw materials as well as upon the quality of the manufacturing process.

SOLUTIONS AND RECOMMENDATIONS

The degree of increasing the economic efficiency within Finland depends in a high extent on the development enterprises composing the system. Subsequent to retechnologization and revamping projects, the efficiency increment of the Finland enterprises will bring forth favorable results for the entire national economy that becomes in its turn, more and more competitive.

At the same time, managerial culture highlights the needs and aspirations of an entity's managers and reflects the behavior, personality of stakeholders or strong leaders, influencing the decisions and actions of managers on different hierarchical levels. Managers are those who are directly involved in the process of building and developing organizational culture, discovering strong motivation, which leads to the establishment of norms, standards, and codes of conduct in accordance with their values. It is also why they agree to be evaluated and motivated, as do all the actors involved, in relation to established standards.

FUTURE RESEARCH DIRECTIONS

Achieving the main objective within the companies from Finland, increasing the economical efficiency, imply steps like retechnologization and revamping methods, by own efforts or by international technology transfer, so as to face new challenges generated by the globalization phenomenon. Commissioning new production capacities as well as the revamping of the existent ones is a major must for the specialists working in this sensitive economic field.

CONCLUSION

Today, companies develop their activity within an environment which is permanently changing, especially from the technological point of view and due to the market conditions (Basten & Haamann, 2018). In the context of the great changes from the Finland economy, the action of the market contemporary forces determines certain behavior of the companies, which become more and more engaged in the resources, quality, customers and suppliers, in which the top role is played by the top quality management.

The realities brought into light by the present epoch determined the rise of significant concerns from the economical theoreticians and practitioners side in order to increase the companies' efficiency. They have also generated the occurrence of specialized organizations primarily dealing with managing resources and limiting their consumption correlated with human society needs. Their main focusing direction is towards finding out alternative, durable solutions, so as to ensure that the generations to come have at least equal chances of existence, knowledge and development. The classical approach of organizations, without a complex tactic on long and medium term cannot confer them any chance in expanding the business, the main issue being now the survival of the fittest.

REFERENCES

Agha, S., Alrubaiee, L., & Jamhour, M. (2012). Effect of core competence on competitive advantage and organizational performance. *International Journal of Business and Management*, *7*(1), 192–204.

Ahearne, M., Lam, S. K., Mathieu, J. E., & Bolander, W. (2010). Why are some sales people better at adapting to organizational change? *Journal of Marketing*, *74*(3), 65–79. doi:10.1509/jmkg.74.3.065

Akgün, A. E., Keskin, H., & Byrne, J. (2009). Organizational emotional capability, product and process innovation, and firm performance: An empirical analysis. *Journal of Engineering and Technology Management*, *26*(3), 103–130. doi:10.1016/j.jengtecman.2009.06.008

Alhyari, S., Alazab, M., Venkatraman, S., Alazab, M., & Alazab, A. (2013). Performance evaluation of e-government services using balanced scorecard. *Benchmarking: An International Journal*, *20*(4), 512–536. doi:10.1108/BIJ-08-2011-0063

Alstete, J. W., & Beutell, N. J. (2018). Designing learning spaces for management education: A mixed methods research approach. *Journal of Management Development*, *37*(2), 201–211. doi:10.1108/JMD-08-2017-0247

Amagoh, F. (2008). Perspectives on organizational change: Systems and complexity theories. *The Innovation Journal*, *13*(3), 1–14.

Anand, G., & Kodali, R. (2010). A mathematical model for the evaluation of roles and responsibilities of human resources in a lean manufacturing environment. *International Journal of Human Resources Development and Management*, *10*(1), 63–100. doi:10.1504/IJHRDM.2010.029447

Andriole, S. J. (2010). Business impact of Web 2.0 Technologies. *Communications of the ACM*, *53*(12), 67–79. doi:10.1145/1859204.1859225

Arsenault, P., & Faerman, S. R. (2014). Embracing paradox in management: The value of the competing values framework. *Organizational Management Journal*, *11*(3), 147–158. doi:10.1080/15416518.2014.949614

Ashkanasy, N. (2011, February). International happiness; a multilevel perspective. *The Academy of Management Perspectives*, 23–29.

Becker, B. E., & Huselid, M. A. (2006). Strategic human resources management: Where do we go from here? *Journal of Management*, *32*(6), 898–925. doi:10.1177/0149206306293668

Behery, M., Jabeen, F., & Parakandi, M. (2014). Adopting a contemporary performance management system. *International Journal of Productivity and Performance Management*, *63*(1), 22–43. doi:10.1108/IJPPM-07-2012-0076

Cameron, K. S., & Quinn, R. E. (2011). *Diagnosing and Changing Organizational Culture: Based on the Competing Values Framework*. San Francisco, CA: Jossey-Bass.

Chan, L. L., Shaffer, M. A., & Snape, E. (2004). In search of sustained competitive advantage: The impact of organizational culture, competitive strategy and human resource management practices on firm performance. *International Journal of Human Resource Management*, *15*(1), 17–35. doi:10.1080/0958519032000157320

Chen, H. M., & Fu, P. C. (2008). A systematic framework for performance appraisal and compensation strategy. *Human Systems Management*, *27*, 161–175.

Cocca, P., & Alberti, M. (2010). A framework to assess performance measurement in SMEs. *International Journal of Productivity and Performance Management*, *59*(2), 186–200. doi:10.1108/17410401011014258

Davila, A. (2012). New trends in performance measurement and management control. *In Performance Measurement and Management Control. Global Issues (Washington, D.C.)*, *25*, 65–87.

Deutsch, P., & Silcox, B. (2003). Learning from other libraries: Benchmarking to assess library performance. *Information Outlook*, *7*(7), 18–25.

Fisher, C. D. (2010). Happiness at Work. *International Journal of Management Reviews*, *12*(4), 384–412. doi:10.1111/j.1468-2370.2009.00270.x

Hartnell, C. A., Ou, A. Y., & Kinicki, A. (2011). Organizational culture and organizational effectiveness: A meta-analytic investigation of the competing values framework's theoretical suppositions. *The Journal of Applied Psychology*, *96*(4), 677–694. doi:10.1037/a0021987 PMID:21244127

Henczel, S. (2002). Benchmarking – measuring and comparing for continuous improvement. *Information Outlook*, *6*(7), 12–20.

Homburg, C., & Pflesser, C. (2000). A Multiple Layer Model of Market-Oriented Organizational Culture: Measurement Issues and Performance Outcomes. *JMR, Journal of Marketing Research*, *37*(4), 449–462. doi:10.1509/jmkr.37.4.449.18786

Hurley, R. F. (2002). Putting people back into organizational learning. *Journal of Business and Industrial Marketing*, *17*(4), 270–281. doi:10.1108/08858620210431679

Kaplan, R. S., & Norton, D. P. (2006). How to implement a new strategy without disrupting your organization. *Harvard Business Review*, *84*(3), 100. PMID:16515159

Lin, C. H., Peng, C. H., & Kao, D. T. (2008). The innovativeness effect of market orientation and learning orientation on business performance. *International Journal of Manpower*, *29*(8), 752–772. doi:10.1108/01437720810919332

Olson, E. M., Slater, S. F., Tomas, G., & Hult, M. (2005). The performance implications of fit among business strategy, marketing organization structure, and strategic behavior. *Journal of Marketing*, *69*(3), 49–65. doi:10.1509/jmkg.69.3.49.66362

Rowland, C., & Hall, R. (2014). Management learning, performance and reward: Theory and practice revisited. *Journal of Management Development*, *33*(4), 342–356. doi:10.1108/JMD-08-2012-0110

Schneider, M., & Somers, M. (2006). Organizations as complex adaptive systems: Implications of complexity theory for leadership research. *The Leadership Quarterly*, *17*(4), 351–365. doi:10.1016/j.leaqua.2006.04.006

Stettina, C. J., & Hörz, J. (2015). Agile portfolio management: An empirical perspective on the practice in use. *International Journal of Project Management*, *33*(1), 140–152. doi:10.1016/j.ijproman.2014.03.008

Tallon, P. P., & Pinsonneault, A. (2011). Competing Perspectives on the Link Between Strategic Information Technology Alignment and Organizational Agility: Insights from a Mediation Model. *Management Information Systems Quarterly*, *35*(2), 463–486. doi:10.2307/23044052

Tapanainen, T. (2012). *Information Technology (IT) managers' contribution to IT agility in organizations–views from the field. Publications of Turku School of Economics, serie A*. Turku, Finland: Juvenes Print.

Tapanainen, T., Hallanoro, M., Päivärinta, J., & Salmela, H. (2008). Towards an Agile IT Organization: A Review of Prior Literature. In *Proceedings of the 2nd European Conference on Information Management and Evaluation* (pp. 425-432). London, UK: Academic Conferences Limited.

Taticchi, P., Tonelli, F., & Cagnazzo, L. (2010). Performance measurement and management: A literature review and a research agenda. *Measuring Business Excellence*, *14*(1), 4–18. doi:10.1108/13683041011027418

Tong, Y. K., & Arvey, R. D. (2015). Managing complexity via the Competing Values Framework. *Journal of Management Development*, *34*(6), 653–673. doi:10.1108/JMD-04-2014-0029

Yadav, N., & Sagar, M. (2013). Performance measurement and management frameworks. *Business Process Management Journal*, *19*(6), 947–971. doi:10.1108/BPMJ-01-2013-0003

ADDITIONAL READING

Basten, D., & Haamann, T. (2018). Approaches for Organizational Learning: A Literature Review. *SAGE Open*, *8*(3), 1–20. doi:10.1177/2158244018794224

Jung, J., Nam, C., Lee, E., & Kim, S. (2016). Subculture by autonomy and group cohesion and its effect on job satisfaction of R&D professionals in an R&D organization. *Journal of Management & Organization*, *22*(2), 154–172. doi:10.1017/jmo.2015.20

Sarabi, A., Naghizadeh, P., Liu, Y., & Liu, M. (2016). Risky business: Fine-grained data breach prediction using business profiles. *Journal of Cybersecurity*, *2*(1), 15–28. doi:10.1093/cybsec/tyw004

Sementelli, J. (2016). OD, change management, and the a priori: Introducing parrhesia. *Journal of Organizational Change Management*, *29*(7), 1083–1096. doi:10.1108/JOCM-12-2015-0234

KEY TERMS AND DEFINITIONS

Environmental Characteristics: The external factors that may limit or support a company's activities.

Financial Risks: These types of risk may reflect inadequate or unclear definition of strategies and objectives of the organization.

Organizational Performance: Elements affecting company performance such as financial and marketing factors, return on sales, return on investment, etc.

Chapter 11
Importance of Ethics and Education to Understand the Audit Mission

Melinda Timea Fülöp
Babeş-Bolyai University, Romania

George Silviu Cordoş
Babeş-Bolyai University, Romania

Nicolae Măgdaş
Babeş-Bolyai University, Romania

ABSTRACT

The chapter brings forward the discussion of how the level of accounting and audit knowledge has an impact on how stakeholders understand the audit mission, the auditor's responsibilities, and the message conveyed by the audit report, even when considering the new and extended reports. The preliminary results of this analysis indicate that audit education influences the audit expectation gap (the reasonableness gap), and if measures would be taken to upsurge the stakeholder's levels of education in auditing and accounting, combined with new and revised standards, the audit expectation gap can be reduced. In this sense, the International Accounting Education Standards Board (IAESB) is an independent standard-setting body that serves the public interest by establishing standards in the field of professional accounting education that prescribe technical competence and professional skills, values, ethics, and attitudes.

INTRODUCTION

In any liberal profession, and even more in the field of the accountancy profession, due to the nature of its problems, in the context of the globalization of national economies, it is necessary to lay them on fundamental ethical principles meant to ensure the highest standards of professionalism.

DOI: 10.4018/978-1-7998-0178-8.ch011

Globalization has become a topical concept in the last decade in social, economic sciences, and last but not least, it gives new dimensions to the role that the accounting profession plays in combating negative phenomena in national economies.

Accounting is not only an instrument of knowledge and management of the separate patrimonial economic values, but it is also a social phenomenon, crossed by the contradictions of society, becoming a stake for various social protagonists, each trying to take advantage of its interests. The product it delivers can only be the result of a compromise between expectations and multiple exigencies. It does not fully satisfy all users, which, despite all of them, has not yet altered its prestige or authority.

To promote ethical conduct within the profession, the most appropriate protective measures will be taken to eliminate the risks of conflict of interest that would harm the public interest and the role played by this professional category. Therefore any threat that would discredit in any way the profession is required to be neutralized.

Often formal definitions have the undesirable effect of making the precise meaning of some terms obscure. At first glance, it is easy to understand that "ethics" is an area that seeks to clarify the moral issues that are rooted in the work of organizations in a society that embraces the system of a market economy characterized by pluripartitism and pluripropriety.

This refers to principles that define fair, correct and appropriate behaviour. Ethical principles do not always dictate a single course of action but offer means of assessment and decision-making among alternatives.

Thus, on one hand, "ethics is the science that studies the moral principles, their origin, nature, essence, development and content" (Marcu & Maneca, 1978) and, on the other hand, "ethics is the ensemble of rules, values and moral norms that regulate the behavior of individuals in society and / or determine their obligations in general, or in a particular field of activity, in particular "(Gonzalez, 2000).

Since ethics is the science that studies moral principles, we also need to define the concept of morality to highlight the differences between the two concepts. A moral is a form of social consciousness that reflects and fixes ideas, thoughts, beliefs about individual behaviour in society.

Although related, ethical and moral concepts have different origins and substances: ethics is moral theory and science, while moral is the subject of ethics. The ethical name is of Greek origin, while the moral originates in the Latin word mos-moris (morav-moravuri), from which the moralistic term, the modern etimony of the moral term (Grigoraş, 1999) appeared.

One of the theories of ethics is Kohlberg's moral development model (Kohlberg, 1969). It presents moral development as a series of six progressive stages that describe the logic used in decision-making in situations involving ethical components. In Kohlberg's model, the individual level of moral development is at a distinct standard at any given point.

Kohlberg was the first one that introduces a method of assessing moral reasoning, presenting to the subject a series of dilemmas in the form of a series of stories, each of which puts a specific moral problem. Maybe the best known is "Heinz's dilemma":

A woman was on her deathbed. There was one drug that the doctors thought might save her. It was a form of radium that a druggist in the same town had recently discovered. The drug was expensive to make, but the druggist was charging ten times what the drug cost him to produce. He paid $200 for the radium and charged $2,000 for a small dose of the drug. The sick woman's husband, Heinz, went to everyone he knew to borrow the money, but he could only get together about $1,000 which is half of what *it cost. He told the druggist that his wife was dying and asked him to sell it cheaper or let him pay later. But the druggist said: "No, I discovered the drug and I'm going to make money from it." So Heinz got desperate and broke into the man's laboratory to steal the drug for his wife. Should Heinz have broken into the laboratory to steal the drug for his wife? Why or why not? (Kohlberg, 1981)*

After presenting this story, the subject is asked a series of questions: Did Heinz do well when he stole the medicine? What would have happened if he had not loved his wife, or if it were a stranger? Should he do the same?

Based on responses to such dilemmas, Kohlberg concluded that there are three main levels of moral reasoning (Table 1).

Kohlberg's model has been used in many ethical accounting studies, which found that students in accounting and practitioners obtained lower scores than the general population of students and graduates (Dellaportas, 2006; Bean & Bernardi, 2007).

Exposing the theory of single business responsibility through which profit is realized - according to Milton Fridman - refers to the fact that "There is only one responsibility in the business: to use resources and to engage in activities to increase profit" (Bowie & Duska, 1990).

Table 1. Kohlberg's six moral stages

Stage of moral development	Characteristics
Preconvention **1.** Obedience **2.** Instrumental egoism and simple exchange	**Sef centred** Naively egoistic, the concepts of good and bad, right or wrong, are interpreted in terms of pleasant or unpleasant consequences Avoiding punishment or obedience to authority Do what you are told avoid punishment Let's make a deal
Conventional **3.** Interpersonal concordance **4.** Law and duty to the social order	**Conformity** Good person, performing duty, meeting the expectations of the group norms and social conformity Adherence to low and social order Consideration, nice, and kind, you will make friends Everyone is society is obligated to and protected by the law
Post-conventional **5.** consensus-building procedures **6.** Non-arbitrary social co-operation	**Principled** Universal principles of reasoning abstracts of morality, utilitarianism and justice pervade the ethical framework judged by the internalized principles of the individuals You are obligated by the arrangements that are agreed to by due process procedures Morality is defined by how rational and impartial people would ideally organize co-operation

Source: Dellaportas (2006)

THE ETHICAL CODE OF THE ENTITY VS. THE ETHICAL CODE OF THE PROFESSIONAL ACCOUNTANT

Business Ethics aims to clarify, with theoretical means, the sources, meaning and purpose of the values and moral norms that business people must take into account in their current work. We have in mind the selection criteria used in adopting those decisions, strategies and managerial policies that are likely to increase the economic efficiency of long-term organizations in a favourable economic environment. This implies, among other things, the assumption of specific moral responsibilities.

Often formal definitions have the undesirable effect of making the clear meaning of some terms obscure. At first glance, it is easy to understand that "business ethics" is an area that seeks to clarify the moral issues that are currently rooted in the activity of economic agents in a society embracing the system of market economy, but also that of mixed-type savings.

What Is Ethics?

According to the explanatory dictionary of the Romanian language, ethics is the science that deals with the theoretical study of human values and condition from the perspective of moral principles, with their role in social life, bringing together all the norms of moral conduct.

Ethics refers to principles that define fair, correct and appropriate behaviour. Ethical principles do not always dictate the course of action but offer means of assessment and decision-making between alternatives. It is, therefore, appropriate to define the notion of morality.

Milton Friedman, the winner of the 1976 Nobel Prize in Economics, states that "there is but one and only one social responsibility of business - to use its resources and engage in activities designed to increase its profits for as long as it remains within the rules of the game, which is to say, engages in open and free competition, without deception or fraud".

Lewis (1985) defines business ethics as "that set of principles or arguments that should govern conduct in business individually or collectively". The definition given by Lewis highlights what people should do in business. Therefore, we can conclude that, according to Lewis, business ethics delimits its moral norms, indicating to economic agents what they need and what they should not do in their specific activity.

Another definition of business ethics was given by De George (1990) who is considered to be one of the most prominent authors in the field, defining business ethics as "An *ethical perspective*, *either implied* in the *behavior* or stated *explicitly*, of a campaign or of an *individual* who does *business* " By this definition, we may conclude that De George places business ethics at the level of a simple description of what an economic agent declares and does about specific ethical considerations. Thus, we can point out that the two authors emphasize different aspects of business ethics.

Following the recent definitions of business ethics - "business ethics is the study of business situations, activities and decisions that raise issues of good and evil" (Crane & Matten, 2004), we note that, over time, the notion of business ethics is developing and encompassing more and more aspects of the work within the organization.

Within the entities/organizations, core principles and values are contained in the ethical code of the entity/organization concerned.

Thus, all the ethical codes of the entity/organization contain some specific elements. Entities tend to label and classify their code of ethics in many different ways, depending on their unique features, their specific goals and interests. Similarly, the content of the code may vary significantly from one entity to another, depending on the branch in which they operate, the regulations/requirements and the purposes of the code. However, we can not say that this ethical code of the entity encompasses all possible situations that can be found within an entity/organization. These ethical codes are intended to guide the proper conduct of the activity within the entity/organization.

The specific elements of an organization's code of ethics are (Pop Cohuţ, 2008):

1. Employment practices: harassment at the workplace; equal opportunities; diversity; equal treatment of employees; work-family balance; discrimination; illicit drugs and alcohol; use of the property of the organization.
2. Employee, customer and seller information: making company records and maintaining information; respect for privacy and confidentiality; disclosure of information.
3. Public information / communication: advertising and marketing; development and fund-raising; clarity of information; access to information; transparency of information.
4. Conflicts of interest: gifts and gifts; political activity; hiring other agents; family members.
5. Vendor Relations: Supply; negotiating contracts.
6. Environmental issues: protecting the environment; health and safety of employees.
7. Managerial ethical tackles: precision of accounting records; the correct use of the company's assets; protect proprietary information.
8. Hiring practices: the proper exercise of authority; voluntary activities of employees.
9. Conflicts of interest.
10. Political involvement.

In support of these ethical codes, there are also the ethical codes of the liberal profession that are developed by professional bodies at the international level and are applied by all professionals in the field. We will continue to focus on the ethical code of the liberal accountant profession.

Some authors have been concerned about ethical issues in the accounting profession, so the research researches aspects of competence, confidentiality and professional conduct in the context of the ethics code of professional accountants (Morariu, 2007) as well as ethical principles in audit work performed by auditors (Mihăilescu, 2007). Lazar (2008) analyzes the relationship between professionalism and ethics in the accounting profession, while ethical dilemmas are presented by Badea (2008).

The IFAC Code of Ethics for Professional Accountants has been set up to serve the needs of professional accountants, whether employed in public practice or other economic sectors. It lays down standards of conduct for professional accountants and sets out the fundamental principles they must respect to achieve the common objectives. The IFAC Code of Ethics is internationally recognized, and its general principles can be adopted by the accounting profession of any country. All professional accountancy or audit bodies, members of IFAC, must adapt the principles of the IFAC Code of Ethics to the national code (for example, CAFR has fully adopted the IFAC Code of Ethics).

The IFAC Code of Ethics for Professional Accountants focuses on the responsibility of the profession to act in the public interest. The accountancy profession has done its best to maintain its reputation for integrity, objectivity and competence over many years of serving its clients, employers and the general public. Any professional accountant who does not (or does not believe) complex with professional standards, and legal requirements make it difficult to maintain the reputation of this profession. The role of IFAC is to provide guidance, encourage progress and promote convergence towards international standards. IFAC, therefore, believes that member bodies must demonstrate that appropriate programs are in place to provide reasonable assurance that all professional accountants adhere to the highest standards of ethics and conduct.

The ethical code of professional accountants sets out rules of conduct for professional accountants and sets out the basic principles to be followed by professional accountants in pursuit of common objectives. The Code acknowledges that the objectives of the accounting profession are set to meet the highest standards of professionalism, achieve the highest levels of performance and meet the requirements of the public interest. The achievement of these objectives requires the fulfilment of four basic requirements:

1. Credibility (trust) throughout society is a need for credibility in information and information systems.
2. Professionalism there is a need for customers, managers and other stakeholders to be able to clearly identify professional accountants.
3. Services quality it is necessary to ensure that all services obtained from the professional accountant are executed at the highest performance standard.
4. Reliability - users of professional accountancy services, must be able to feel confident that there is a framework of professional ethics governing the provision of these services.

A professional accountant must observe the following fundamental principles (IFAC, 2016):

- **Integrity:** To be straightforward and honest in all professional and business relationships.
- **Objectivity:** Not to compromise professional or business judgments because of bias, conflict of interest or undue influence of others.
- **Professional Competence and Due Care:** Attain and maintain professional knowledge and skill at the level required to ensure that a client or employing organization receives competent professional service, based on current technical and professional standards and relevant legislation; and act diligently and by applicable technical and professional standards.
- **Confidentiality:** To respect the confidentiality of information acquired as a result of professional and business relationships
- **Professional Behavior:** To comply with relevant laws and regulations and avoid any conduct that the professional accountant knows or should know might discredit the profession

ETHICAL PRINCIPLES IN ACCOUNTING PROFESSION: INTERNATIONAL APPROACH

The professional accountant has a very varied field of activity, being imbued with impeccable knowledge in his field, but also a certain amount of creativity, to be allowed to overcome the boundaries of the theoretical bases. At present, the professional accountant has to excel in accounting-related areas and is also prepared for economic and financial analysis, evaluation and control, auditing, IT, management, and exceptionally professional ethics. All this knowledge is necessary to facilitate the professional practice in his / her trade, and cooperation with other specialists in the field. The professional accountant can practice in various spheres of accounting, such as tax accounting, management, expertise, consulting, audit, etc. Dilemmas and ethical issues may arise in any of these spheres, but the professional accountant will have to show good practice, no matter what.

The literature lists two types of responsibilities that the professional accountant carries out in his job (Abbott, 1983). These are the corporate obligations that arise with the service of the company (professional obligations that encourage the use of good practices and the fulfillment of the delegated tasks) and the individual (personal) requirements regarding the social responsibility of the professional, based more on the links established between the professional - client, or professor - colleagues). Both corporate and individual obligations are covered by codes of ethics and professional conduct.

A Code of Ethics and Professional Conduct contains the fundamental principles that must be respected by professionals in a given field and sets out rules of conduct for them (Abbott, 1983). Practically these codes show exactly the behaviour a professional must have in his job. Also, with the rules set out in codes of ethics and professional conduct, a professional will be able to solve the ethical dilemmas emerging in his profession, proving good practices in a problematic situation.

An ethical code can be considered as a traditional method through which a profession communicates to both clients and public the responsibilities existing in the profession in question, thus stating the integrity of practice in the profession and work were done in the public interest (Velayutham, 2003).

Ethical codes are used in companies to create ethical standards, encourage business professionals to ethical behavior, inspire ethical conduct of the company, increase the trust of professionals in both their own skills and ethics, demonstrate to society that the company has moral values, demonstrates the existence of social responsibility in the company, and emphasizes that there are ethical norms in the profession. Because codes of ethics have the mentioned advantages, they can be used as a measure to increase customer confidence in the company through its transparency, to accentuate the social responsibility of the company to the general public and even to attract new customers interested in a company that shows good practices.

To observe the importance of the transparency of ethics codes among shareholders, I will use a survey conducted by Richard A. Bernaldi and Catherine C. Bernaldi and LaCross (2009) for five years (2003-2008), comprising 43 listed companies at NYSE. The study attempted to determine the level of transparency of ethical codes for the companies mentioned.

The issue of adding codes of ethics to companies' websites has been posed for greater transparency for shareholders. Although at the beginning of the study period there were no legislative rules on code transparency, some regulations of this kind emerged in US law during the study. However, the regulations that emerged did not influence the study because the study also attempted to take account of the accessibility of the code on the websites of the companies, which was not provided for in the given directives. At the end of the survey period, no fewer than 36 of the 43 companies (about 83.7%) added ethical codes to companies' websites, and information about the code of ethics could easily be accessed (Bernaldi & LaCross, 2009).

As a result, we can see a substantial increase in company transparency. Along with facilitating access to the code of ethics, a company is responsible for any unethical mistakes/practice. Thus, there is an increase not only in the transparency but also in the responsibility of the company and the respect for its shareholders. Also in the same study were 49 unlisted companies at NYSE. At the end of the study, 23 companies out of 49 (about 46.93%) introduced the code of ethics on the company's virtual page. We can interpret that the 23 companies wanted transparency and informing the general public about ethical standards. In conclusion, a code of ethics made available to shareholders increases the company's responsibility in various ethical dilemmas, forces the company to ethical behaviour, wins the confidence of current / potential customers, and maintains or even increases the company's reputation.

There are five fundamental properties (Abbott, 1983) of codes of ethics and professional conduct:

1. Universal distribution (which implies that each profession has at least a formal code of professional ethics; in the absence of such a code, the boundaries of the obligations and responsibilities of a profession would not be defined);
2. The correlation of codes with professional status (which emphasizes that both the commitment to ethics codes and compliance with the rules of the professional are directly proportional to its professional training);
3. Implementing formal codes of ethics among professionals (professionals must comply with the rules set out in the codes, thus respecting both professional and individual obligations);
4. Individuality of codes (implies that each code can be tailored individually for each professional, for each profession and each model of professional behaviour in part - that is, each code contains the most relevant information depending on the activity being maintained and according to the points of code user interests);
5. Highlighting the obligations of professional colleagues (requires clarification of the delimitation and division of rules, obligations and responsibilities for each category of professionals);

According to the study conducted by Abbott (1983), these five properties are fundamental and common to any ethical code, regardless of the field of activity, the properties listed by it being indispensable to ethical codes.

PRINCIPLES OF ETHICS FOR ACCOUNTING PROFESSIONALS IN THE IFAC VISION

IFAC is a global organization set up to help professional accountants. It aims to serve the public interest by strengthening and fortification the accounting profession and participating in the development of internationally sustainable economies. IFAC includes 179 members (national accounting, auditing, audit institutions, associations and chambers) in 130 countries and jurisdictions around the world. IFAC's mission is to serve the public interest by: contributing to the development of quality standards by facilitating the adoption and implementation of the aforementioned standards, contributing to the development of professional accounting organizations and strong accounting firms, contributing to the development of high quality accounting practices, promoting the value of professional accountants around the world and addressing issues of public interest.

In other words, IFAC is an international organization set up to participate in the improvement and development of the accounting profession, acting for the public interest. The organization has independent councils to set standards for the accounting profession, setting such standards on ethics in accounting, financial audit, accounting education and accounting for the public sector.

Thus, about accounting ethics, we mention IESBA, an independent standard board, under the aegis of IFAC, whose function is to develop, advance and promote ethical standards for professional accountants. Through supervision and guidance from PIOB specialists, the standards set forth by IESBA are always qualitative, of public and topical interest. Hence, IESBA is a competent body in drafting the ethical profile of the contacted professional. Among the activities undertaken by IESBA are the promotion of ethical standards in accounting at the global level, guidance on the implementation of established ethical standards and the compilation of an international database containing issues and ethical dilemmas emerging in practice.

The most important function of IESBA is the elaboration of the "Code of Ethics for Professional Accountants", which sets the appropriate ethical limits for the professional accountant. The Code of Ethics of the Professional Accountant was developed in 2010 and has been implemented since January 1, 2011. The 2013 version presents minor modifications, which will come into force on 1 January 2014. The Code is structured in 3 parts, Part A - General Application of the Code, Part B - Professional Professionals in the Public Environment and Part C - Business Professionals. At the end of the manual, explanatory terms are mentioned, and the exact changes to be made are specified.

PRINCIPLES OF ETHICS IN THE ACCOUNTING PROFESSION IN ROMANIA

With Romania's accession to the European Union, certain laws and principles have been modified to comply with the EU's cohesion policy. This policy wants to eliminate economic and social disparities. It was precisely on this detriment that the European Union approved in 2002 Regulation 1606/2002, which entered into force on 14 September 2002. The most relevant article to state the purpose of the Regulation is Art.2: "(2) To contribute to improving the functioning of the internal market, it is necessary for listed companies to apply a single set of high-quality international accounting standards in their consolidated financial statements. It is also important that the financial reporting standards applied by the Community companies participating in the financial markets are accepted internationally and constitute real-world standards. This implies an increased convergence of accounting standards currently used internationally, the ultimate goal being the achievement of a single set of world accounting standards. "Among the related acts of this regulation, we mention Directive 2003/51 / EC, Decision 2008 / 961 / EC, Regulation (EC) No. Commission Regulation (EC) No 1569/2007 and Regulation (EC) No 1126/2008 of the Commission. Thus, since 2005, all listed companies in the European Union have been obliged to apply international IFRS standards issued by the IASB.

THE FUNDAMENTAL ETHICAL PRINCIPLES OF ACCOUNTING PROFESSIONALS IN THE NATIONAL CONTEXT (CECCAR, CAFR)

Romania, as a EU state thus had to comply with the standardization of accounting. Standardization appears precisely to eliminate disparities, leading to an international equalization of the accounting profession. When it comes to standardizing accounting rules, standardization and uniformity of ethical standards can be observed.

Standardization can be seen, in addition to the legal obligation, Romania has, as a need arising due to economic development. In our country, there can be seen an increase in large companies, which provide international services. Moreover, multinational audit firms (Big 4 companies) now have subsidiaries in Romania as well. Through these types of companies, the Romanian professional is put into the job of working with professionals from other countries with different mentalities and principles. To remove any professional barriers between professional accountants, uniformity of accounting rules and principles is the best solution.

Regarding ethics, most ethical dilemmas could be resolved if, irrespective of nationality or geographical location where a professional is working, he would follow the same principles and norms as other external colleagues. In other words, the development of an Ethics Code applied at international level is the best solution for enhancing moral behaviour among professionals. This is why IESBA strongly encourages the translation of the Code in as many languages as possible, to facilitate the access of practitioners everywhere to the rules issued by them. IESBA also allows the Code to be adapted precisely to emphasize that although universal rules are vital, the small peculiarities of a country are relevant.

Thus, the Code of Ethics existing in Romania is the translation of the Code issued by IESBA. The Code was approved by CECCAR through the "Decision of the Superior Council of the Body of Chartered Accountants and Authorized Accountants in Romania, no.11 / 216 of March 2011, based on the Decision of the National Conference of the accounting experts and authorized accountants no. 10/65 of 2 September 2010 "(CECCAR, 2011). The CAFR also adopted the Code issued by IESBA, which was specifically translated by CAFR, maintaining exactly the structure and content proposed by IESBA.

The current Romanian Code of Ethics is entitled "The National Code of Ethics for Professional Professionals", is the fifth edition, revised and amended according to the code issued by IFAC. The code is translated from the English language, so the content is identical to the one mentioned above in subchapter 1.2.1. We recall that it is made up of three parts: Part A - General application of the code (we mention the sections: Introduction and Fundamental Principles, Integrity, Objectivity, Professional Competence and Prudence, Confidentiality, Professional Conduct), Part B - Accounting Professionals in Public Practice, and Part C - Employed Accountants Professionals. The difference between the Romanian and the standard ethical code is the fact that there is an introduction in the Romanian code, which states the following: the decision that led to the application of the code in Romania, the obligations and responsibilities of the CECCAR as an IFAC member, an introduction explaining how to make better use of the code, the CECCAR Board of Governors' statement on how to implement the code and assimilating ethical requirements.

In conclusion, the National Ethics Code of Professional Accountants guides the Romanian professional and urges him to moral behaviour, militating for solving ethical problems and dilemmas. Considering its standardization and uniformity, the code thus contains essential, logically structured information for a better understanding of concepts.

After presenting some conceptual approaches in this chapter and understanding the importance of ethics in accounting, we can draw some conclusions. Ethics is not just a philosophical topic that addresses existential behavioural problems but can outline a professional's moral profile. The need for ethics in accounting comes precisely from the characteristics of the profession; being a profession in which accountability, transparency, honesty and objectivity are so important, a conceptual framework is needed to establish the most professional behaviour. The need for ethics implies the existence of laws and norms that make up the codes of ethics. These codes are vital in the accountancy profession, as it outlines the context of a specialist's behaviour. In terms of these codes, we do not only understand what is allowed in the workplace, and what is not but what we mean is a professional accountant in the true sense of the word. It is up to each of us to try to comply with the rules set out in the codes of ethics, and not because we feel compelled or forced to do it, but because we should realize that to truly be professionals, we must first give proof of adequate behaviour.

THE INTERNATIONAL EDUCATION STANDARDS FOR AUDITORS

According to ISA standards, the auditor is responsible for redacting the independent"auditor's report, within which the auditor expresses the opinion on the analysed financial statements (the ISA 700 standard). The auditor plans the audit mission (*ISA 300 - Planning an Audit of Financial Statement, IAASB, 2009*) and during the mission the auditor has to comply with the IFAC Code of Ethics for Professional Accountants, drafted by the International Ethics Standards Board for Accountants (IESBA, 2014)."The auditor must also comply with the ISA 220 standard regarding the quality control process for the auditing mission. The first step is to set the prerequisites for the audit mission, by elaborating an engagement letter, as established by ISA 210; this step will confer contextual information regarding the client. Subsequently, the auditor will prepare the audit documentation (ISA 230), will set the materiality threshold (ISA 320) and will convene upon the company's responses to assessed risks (ISA 330). In succession, the auditor will collect audit evidence (according to ISA 500, 501, 505 and ISA 510-580), by testing control mechanisms and operations and by analytical procedures and test of balances in the financial statements.

A great number researchers have analysed the current audit reporting model, in light of proposed changes from the above-mentioned regulators (Church *et al.*, 2008; Turner *et al.*, 2010; Coram *et al.*, 2011; Vanstraelen *et al.*, 2012; Glover *et al.*, 2012; Mock *et al.*, 2013). Some of these academics have been commissioned institutes or research centres to research projects on improving audit reporting: AICPA – Turner *et al.* (2010), ACCA &"Maastricht Accounting, Auditing and Information Management Research Center (MARC)"– Vanstraelen *et al.* (2012).

Not only new regulations are necessary, the importance of ethics and organisational culture is also stressed by some researchers (Barlaup et al., 2009; Sikka et al., 2009; Svanberg & Ohman, 2013). Barlaup et al. (2009) propose an ethical decision-making framework as a tool for businesses and auditors; also, they posit that education is an important aspect - both audit and ethical education. Bobek et al. (2012) also consider that while communication with *those charged with governance* (the Audit Committee, internal audit department, management) is important, audit issues can arise from team interaction of the audit partners as well – if unresolved, these issues lead to audit failures.

The *Public Company Accounting Oversight Board* (PCAOB) is a non-profit organisation established by the Sarbanes-Oxley amendment, with the responsibility to supervise the audits of public companies to achieve better protection of investors' interests by assuring informative, accurate and independent audit reports. The PCAOB is the United States equivalent of the IAASB, given the fact that the U.S. do not *use International Accounting Standards or International Standards* in Auditing. The PCAOB has also pushed for reforms in the audit field, especially with regards to a more informative audit report and more transparency in audit missions. Similarly, the *Public Interest Oversight Board* (PIOB) is the global independent oversight body that seeks to improve the quality of the international standards supported by the IFAC and to direct their focus towards public interest, in the areas of audit and assurance, education, and ethics.

To prove that not only new regulation is necessary, the importance of ethics and organisational culture is also stressed by some researchers (Barlaup et al., 2009; Sikka et al., 2009; Svanberg & Ohman, 2013). Barlaup et al. (2009) posit that education is an important aspect - both audit and ethical education.

The International Accounting Education Standards Board (IAESB) is an independent standard-setting body that serves the public interest by establishing standards in the field of professional accounting education that prescribe technical competence and professional skills, values, ethics, and attitudes. Through its activities, the IAESB enhances education by developing and implementing International Education Standards™ (IES™), which increase the competence of the global accountancy profession—contributing to strengthened public trust (IAESB, 2016). The Board obtains input from it Consultative Advisory Group, but also regulators, IFAC member organizations, other accountancy organizations, and the general public. Being part of the IFAC, all IFAC member organizations can provide input to the regulation the IAESB publishes. One current project of the IAESB is the revision of International Education Standards, Framework for International Education Standards for Professional Accountants and Aspiring Accountants, which has been completed in 2015.

There are eight IES standards, as following (IAESB, 2016).

- **IES 1:** *Entry Requirements to Professional Accounting Education Programs*;
- **IES 2:** *Initial Professional Development – Technical Competence*;
- **IES 3:** *Initial Professional Development – Professional Skills*;
- **IES 4:** *Initial Professional Development – Professional values, Ethics and Attitudes*;
- **IES 5:** *Initial Professional Development – Practical Experience*;
- **IES 6:** *Initial Professional Development – Assessment of Professional Competence*;
- **IES 7:** *Continuing Professional Development*;
- **IES 8:** *Professional Competence of Engagement Partners Responsible for Audits of Financial Statements*.

The first six standards focus on the initial professional development for an aspiring accounting professional, while the last two standards address the continuing professional development of accounting professionals. According to IES 1, an Aspiring professional accountant is "an individual who has commenced a professional accountancy education program as part of Initial Professional Development" (IAESB, 2016). Though the standards mentioned above, the IFAC (via IAESB) prescribes the principles to be used when setting and communicating educational requirements for entry to professional accounting education programs (IAESB IES 1, 2015). What should be pointed out, is the fact that the IAESB allows flexibility for IFAC members to set their entry requirements, to suit different jurisdictions or entry options. An IFAC member body may require aspiring accountants "a prequalification entry requirement", such as university degree or equivalent, but can also allow direct entrance for candidates with relevant practical experience. IES 1 also advances the idea of collaboration between IFAC member bodies and universities, for students to be more easily considered for membership in the IFAC member body (IAESB IES 1, 2015). As stated by IES 1, entry requirements can be an assessment of qualifications or experience, taking certain courses or entry tests.

The Initial Professional Development program is developed by each member body and has to be by the requirements of IES standards. Each IES sets the outcomes for competencies that aspiring professionals are required to demonstrate at the end of the IPD (IAESB IES 2, 2015). While IES 2 sets the Technical competencies, IES 3 sets the Professional Skills and IES4 sets the Professional Values, Ethics and Attitudes to be developed by the trainees. Another component of the IPD is the practical experience that the aspiring professional accountants need to complete by the end of the IPD. The IES 5 standard call this "Initial Professional Experience" and each member body needs to ensure that the practical experience is sufficient and relevant to the needs of the trainees, the regulatory authorities and the public expectations.

When the IPD is finished, and the aspiring accounting professional has also completed their practical experience, the candidate will be assessed by each member body, by IES 6, by different assessment activities (IAESB IES 6, 2015). These include either multi-disciplinary examinations at the end of the IPD or examinations throughout the IPD, either written or oral. The standards are flexible in this concern, so member bodies can choose whatever better suits their needs.

Another essential part of IES standards is the Continuing Professional Development, as set by IES 7. Continuing Professional Development is an Accounting Principle, and the IES standard requires professional accountants to "develop and maintain the professional competence necessary to provide high-quality services" to the public (IAESB IES 7, 2015). The Member Bodies are indispensable in this case, as they foster the environment for lifelong learning, the necessary resources and they adopt requirements prescribed by the IAESB when revisions of standards occur. Each professional accountant should complete professional development activities, and member bodies are responsible for monitoring members in this aspect.

INTERNATIONAL EDUCATION STANDARDS APPLICATION IN PROFESSIONAL MEMBER BODIES

The profession itself is also pushing for ethics education in colleges and universities. In 2005, The National Association of State Boards of Accountancy (NASBA) proposed that three ethics courses be required of students, one being business-specific and one accounting-specific (Bean & Bernardi, 2007).

The Association to Advance Collegiate Schools of Business (AACSB) has been clear in its advocacy for ethics incorporated into accounting education. Gordon (2011) pinpoints the AACSB's reasoning for this stance, which is similar to what Wyatt asserted. As Gordon describes it, professional judgment is an issue that the AACSB is concerned with, as it is "related to ethics and important to the development of accountants and auditors" (Gordon, 2011). Similar to the case Wyatt (2004) made about accounting students learning the importance of accounting in society as a whole, Gordon references the AACSB's recognition that "business and society are interdependent" (Gordon, 2011). Students must be capable of recognizing this as well, of performing their duties with the optimal professional judgment that it requires.

Each country has professional organisations for the accountancy profession and universities that offer accounting and audit specialisations. For instance, in Romania, there are two professional bodies in accountancy, both members of the IFAC:

- The "Chamber of Financial Auditors of Romania", and
- The "Body of Expert and Licensed Accountants of Romania".

The Chamber of Financial Auditors of Romania has the main objective to provide the sustainable development of the audit profession and its strengthening, in accordance with the International Auditing Standards (ISAs) and with the Code of Ethics and professional conduct, by "fully assimilating the International Standards on Auditing and the Code of Ethics issued by the International Federation of Accountants (IFAC), that will allow the Romanian financial auditors to provide high-quality services, for the public interest, in general, and for the business community, in special" (CAFR, 2016). To become a trainee, one has to have graduated an economic university, to have a minimum of 4 years of experience in the financial-accounting activity, to have performed at least three years of practical training in the financial audit activity and to pass the access and final exam of the traineeship.

The Body of Expert and Licensed Accountants of Romania is the representative organism of the accountancy profession in Romania. The Body "supports and promotes high-quality professional practices through particular concern for the competence, abilities and ethics of those involved in the profession. By the activities it carries out, the Body encourages professional accountants to observe the moral values required for this profession, monitors that Romanian professional accountants, through the services they provide, always meet market requirements, business environment requirements and public interest" (CECCAR, 2016). To become a trainee, one has to pass an access examination; then, during three years, the trainee attends accountancy, taxation, commercial law, auditing, accounting expertise and other disciplines; then, the trainee has a final exam, which, if passed, grants the expert accountant title.

Table 2 is a synthesis of the entry and exit requirements of both member bodies for aspiring candidates to become professional accountants, with a checklist on whether mentioned criteria are mentioned within the IES standards.

The trainees of national auditing chambers of professional accounting organizations and bodies are all, in light of the IES standards, aspiring professional accountants. The IAESB Glossary of Terms states that a professional accountancy education program is "programs designed to support aspiring professional accountants to develop the appropriate professional competence [...]. They may consist of formal education delivered through degrees or courses offered by universities, other higher education providers, IFAC member bodies [...]". Consequently, we can also include in the trainee category, college students, attending courses for either a Bachelor, Masters or Doctoral degree in Accounting and Auditing.

Thus, for the analysis of the impact of audit education on the understanding of the responsibilities of the auditor, we believe that a first step is to test whether accounting and audit students (at the Bachelor and Masters) fully and correctly understand the responsibility of the auditor in the audit mission, thus having (or not) an impact on the presence of the audit expectation gap.

CONCLUSION

In this paper, we presented what is meant by the proper behaviour of the professional through ethical norms, what are his obligations and responsibility to the society (the users of accounting information).

First of all, we have presented how vital ethics is in the accounting profession because ethical rules are those that establish proper behaviour from the professional. Because of the importance of ethics, there are standardized International Ethics Codes that dictate the principles and rules that a professional accountant should apply. Thus, we analyzed IFAC's "Ethics Code of Professional Professionals" and "AICPA Code of Professional Conduct". These codes set out the basic principles of a professional accountant and provide conceptual frameworks for the application of these principles by defining threats that can lead to their failure to breach and safety measures to protect the professional from these threats.

We have also highlighted the role of the professional in society because we wanted to emphasize the importance of the professional in the entire community, thus causing a particular responsibility towards the users. Therefore, social responsibility forces professionals to show proper behaviour, respecting clear standards of professional conduct.

We analyze the international accounting education standards, which are the standards that help prepare aspiring accounting professionals for their future career as accounting professionals. By correctly applying these standards, member organisations can contribute to assure that future accounting professionals will respect the provisions of auditing standards and ethical standards, to reduce the deficient performance gap. However, while we have proven that audit education has an impact on users understanding of the auditor's responsibility, the question for future studies is: how can we improve audit education, and who is responsible for this process?

Table 2. Romanian member bodies and IES standards application

Admission Criteria	CAFR	CECCAR	IES Standards
Bachelor Degree in Economics	Yes	Yes	Not necessary, but possible
Experience in financial accounting	4 Years	No	Not necessary, but possible
Entry Examination disciplines	Yes	Yes	Not necessary, but possible
Accountancy		Yes	
Taxation		Yes	
Law		Yes	
Appraisal of Entities		Yes	
Audit	Yes	Yes	
Accounting Expertise		Yes	
Doctrine and Deontology		Yes	
Recognition of previous qualifications	Licensed accountants can be accepted in the 2nd year of training	Economics PhD. ACCA certification	Possible
Cooperation with universities	Yes	Yes	Encouraged
No entry exam for graduates from a specific Master's programme	Yes (if 50% of disciplines are audit-related)	Yes	Possible
Recognition of Masters period as experience	2 years maximum	2 years maximum	Possible
Exit Criteria	**CAFR**	**CECCAR**	**IES Standards**
Completion of an IPD	Yes	Yes	Yes
Examination throughout IPD	Yes	Yes	Possible
Written final exam	Yes	Yes	Possible
Oral/practical final exam	Practical	Oral	Possible
Competence Area			
Financial accounting and reporting	Yes	Yes	Mandatory
Management accounting	Yes	Yes	Mandatory
Finance and financial management	Yes	Yes	Mandatory
Taxation	Yes	Yes	Mandatory
Audit and assurance	Yes	Yes	Mandatory
Governance, risk management and internal control	Yes	Yes	Mandatory
Business laws and regulations	Yes	Yes	Mandatory
Information technology	Yes	Yes	Mandatory
Business and organisational environment	Yes	Yes	Mandatory
Economics	Yes	Yes	Mandatory
Business Strategy	Yes	Yes	Mandatory
Scepticism and professional judgement	Yes	Yes	Mandatory
Ethical principles	Yes	Yes	Mandatory
Commitment to public interest	Yes	Yes	Mandatory

In conclusion, we can emphasize how vital the ethical behaviour of the professional is both for users (broad public, society) and for the company. By respecting ethical norms and principles, a professional will be able to behave appropriately in his profession, being able not only to pursue his professional activity but to practice in the true sense of the word.

REFERENCES

Abbott, A. (1983). Professional Ethics. *American Journal of Sociology*, *88*(5), 855–885. doi:10.1086/227762

Badea, D. (2008). O abordare structurată a dilemelor etice. *Audit Financiar*, *8*(6), 5–30.

Barlaup, K., Dronen, H., & Stuart, I. (2009). Restoring trust in auditing: Ethical discernment and the Adelphia scandal. *Managerial Auditing Journal*, *24*(2), 183–203. doi:10.1108/02686900910924572

Bean, D. F., & Bernardi, R. A. (2007). Ethics education in our colleges and universities: A positive role for accounting practitioners. *Journal of Academic Ethics*, *5*(1), 59–75. doi:10.100710805-007-9038-4

Bernaldi, R. A., & LaCross, C. (2009). Positioning codes of ethics on international corporations' websites: A six-year longitudinal study. *Advances în Accounting, incorporating. Advances in International Accounting*, *25*(1), 75–80. doi:10.1016/j.adiac.2009.02.010

Bobek, D., Daugherty, B., & Radtke, R. (2012). Resolving Audit Engagement Challenges through Communication. *Auditing*, *31*(4), 21–45. doi:10.2308/ajpt-50210

Bowie, N. E., & Duska, R. F. (1990). *Business Ethics* (2nd ed.). Prentice-Hall Inc.

Church, B. K., Davis, S. M., Mc, S. A., & Cracken, S. (2008). The Auditor's Reporting Model: A Literature Overview and Research Synthesis. *Accounting Horizons*, *22*(1), 69–90. doi:10.2308/acch.2008.22.1.69

Coram, P., Mock, T., Turner, J., & Gray, G. (2011). The Communicative Value of the Auditor's Report. *Australian Accounting Review*, *21*(3), 235–252. doi:10.1111/j.1835-2561.2011.00140.x

Dellaportas, S. (2006). Making a difference with a discrete course on accounting ethics. *Journal of Business Ethics*, *65*(4), 391–404. doi:10.100710551-006-0020-7

Glover, H., & Reidenbach, M. (2012). Auditor Reporting Model Modifications: Practical Insights from the Academic Community. *Current Issues in Auditing*, *6*(1), C7–C14. doi:10.2308/ciia-50122

Gonzalez, C. R. (2000). *Diccionario Enciclopedico Nuevo Espasa Ilustrado 2000*. Editorial Espasa Calpe S.A. Madrid.

González, C. R. (2000). *Diccionario Enciclopédico Nuevo Espasa Ilustrado*. Madrid: Editorial Espasa Calpe S.A.

Gordon, I. M. (2011). Lessons to be learned: An examination of Canadian and U.S. financial accounting and auditing textbooks for ethics/governance coverage. *Journal of Business Ethics*, *101*(1), 29–47. doi:10.100710551-010-0706-8

Grigoraş, I. (1999). *Probleme de etică. In Editura Universităţii Al* (p. 3). Iaşi: I. Cuza. Retrieved from https://link.springer.com/article/10.1007/s10551-010-0706-8

Kohlberg, L. (1969). Stage and sequence: the cognitive- developmental approach to socialization. In D. A. Golsin (Ed.), *Handbook of Socialization Theory and Research* (pp. 347–480). Chicago, IL: Rand McNally.

Kohlberg, L. (1976). Moral stages and moralization. In T. Lickona (Ed.), Moral Development and Behavior (pp. 219–240). Academic Press.

Kohlberg, L. (1981). Essays on Moral Development: Vol. I. *The Philosophy of Moral Development*. San Francisco, CA: Harper & Row.

Lazăr, M. (2008). Profesionalism şi etică în profesia contabilă şi de audit. *Audit Financiar, 1*(6), 13–22.

Marcu, F., & Maneca, C. (1978). *Dicţionar de Neologisme, Ediţia a III-a (revăzută şi adăugită)*. Bucureşti: Editura Ştiinţifică.

Mihăilescu, I. (2007). Rigori şi principii de etică ale auditorilor în misiunile de audit. *Audit Financiar, 7*(V), 7–14.

Mock, T., Bedard, J., Coram, P., David, S., Espahbodi, R., & Warne, R. (2013). The Auditor's Reporting Model: Current Research Synthesis and Implications. *Auditing, 32*(1), 323–351. doi:10.2308/ajpt-50294

Morariu, A. (2007). Despre competenţă, confidenţialitate şi comportament profesional în contextul Codului etic. *Audit Financiar, 11*(5), 19–22.

Pop Cohuţ, I. (2008), Introducere în etica afacerilor. Note de curs. Universităţii din Oradea.

Sikka, P., Filling, S., & Liew, P. (2009). The audit crunch: Reforming audit. *Managerial Auditing Journal, 24*(2), 135–155. doi:10.1108/02686900910924554

Svanberg, J., & Ohman, P. (2013). Auditors' time pressure: Does ethical culture support audit quality? *Managerial Auditing Journal, 28*(7), 572–591. doi:10.1108/MAJ-10-2012-0761

Turner, J., Mock, J., Coram, P., & Gray, G. (2010). Improving Transparency and Relevance of Auditor Communications with Financial Statement Users. *Current Issues in Auditing, 4*(1), A1–A8. doi:10.2308/ciia.2010.4.1.A1

Vanstraelen, A., Schelleman, C., Meuwissen, R., & Hofmann, I. (2012). The Audit Reporting Debate: Seemingly Intractable Problems and Feasible Solutions. *European Accounting Review, 21*(2), 193–215. doi:10.1080/09638180.2012.687506

Velayutham, S. (2003). The Accounting Profession's Code of Ethics: Is it a Code of Ethics or a Code of Quality Assurance? *Critical Perspectives on Accounting, 14*(4), 483–503. doi:10.1016/S1045-2354(02)00138-7

Wyatt, A. R. (2004). Accounting professionalism—They just don't get it! *Accounting Horizons, 18*(1), 45–53. doi:10.2308/acch.2004.18.1.45

ADDITIONAL READING

Cordoş, G. S., & Fülöp, M. T. (2013). Analiza relaţiei auditor – client şi efectul asupra independenţei auditorului. *Revista Audit Financiar*, *105*, 1844–8801.

Fülöp, M. T. (2013). To serve the Public Interest. The main characteristic of Accounting Profession. *Journal of Accounting and Management*, *3*, 27–37.

Fülöp, M. T. (2014). Consideraţii privind aspectele eticii profesionale contabile – conflictul de interese. *Audit Financiar*, *6*, 12–21.

Fülöp, M. T. (2014). Why do we need effective corporate governance. *International Advances in Economic Research*, *20*(2), 227–228. doi:10.100711294-013-9430-3

KEY TERMS AND DEFINITIONS

Confidentiality: The state of keeping or being kept secret or private.

Corporate Governance: The processes by which companies are directed and controlled. Levels of disclosure differ worldwide but might include information on board composition and development, accountability and audit and relations with shareholders.

Credibility: The quality of being trusted and believed in the quality of being convincing or believable.

Due Care: Degree of care that an ordinary and reasonable person would normally exercise, over his or her own property or under circumstances likes those at issue.

Ethics: Moral principles that govern a person's behavior or the conducting of an activity the branch of knowledge that deals with moral principles.

Integrity: The quality of being honest and having strong moral principles; the state of being whole and undivided.

Objectivity: The quality of being objective.

Professional Behavior: A series of actions deemed acceptable in the workplace. These methods of interaction are dictated by concepts like courtesy, civility and good taste. Professionalism is specific to the industry's business inhabits, the state where a corporation resides and the people that staff its operations.

Professional Competence: The broad professional knowledge, attitude, and skills required in order to work in a specialized area or profession.

Professionalism: The competence or skill expected of a professional the practicing of an activity, especially a sport, by professional rather than amateur players.

Reliability: The quality of being trustworthy or of performing consistently well the degree to which the result of a measurement, calculation, or specification can be depended on to be accurate.

Service Quality: An assessment of how well a delivered service conforms to the client's expectations.

Chapter 12
Important Managerial Controversies in Conversion of Financial Statements

Alin Eliodor Tănase
Titu Maiorescu University, Romania

Dumitru Alexandru Stoica
Valahia University, Romania

Nicoleta Ileana Trăistaru
Valahia University, Romania

Monika Brigitte Sürgün
Valahia University, Romania

ABSTRACT

Functional currency has been defined as the currency of an entity's main economic environment. A group does not have a functional currency, but the functional currency is set at the level of each group entity. Determining each functional currency at each component of a group is made by looking at several factors. In this chapter, the conversion occurs when the currency in which the financial statements are prepared is different from the presentation, and the important managerial controversies are presented in the conversion of the financial statements. The results show that the conversion of financial statements applies only if the entity whose financial statements are converted has a functional currency that is not a hyperinflationary economy.

INTRODUCTION

The International Accounting Standard (IAS) shall be taken into account when accounting for transactions denominated in foreign currency or when the financial statements are translated into the presentation currency (Ball, Li & Shivakumar, 2015; Iatridis, 2010; Guthrie & Parker, 2016). The conversion occurs when the currency in which the financial statements are prepared is different from the presentation cur-

DOI: 10.4018/978-1-7998-0178-8.ch012

rency (Zéghal, Chtourou & Mnif, 2011; Lobo & Zhou, 2001). With respect to the conversion of financial statements, it should be noted that this standard applies only if the entity whose financial statements are converted has a functional currency that is not a hyperinflationary economy (Jones & Smith, 2012; Watts & Zimmerman, 1978; Richardson, 2011; Ball, Li & Shivakumar, 2015).

In examining whether significant influence does exist, we will take into account the existence and effect of potential voting rights that are currently exercisable or convertible, including potential voting rights held by other entities (Choi, Peasnell & Toniato, 2013; Barth, Landsman & Lang, 2008; Cairns, D., Massoudi, Taplin & Tarca, 2011). Potential voting rights that are currently exercisable or convertible must be taken into account because an entity may own warrants on shares, options to purchase equities, debt or equity securities that are convertible into ordinary shares or other financial instruments - if exercised or converted - and that can lead: either providing an entity that holds more voting rights; or reduce the voting rights of another party's financial and operating policies (i.e. potential voting rights).

It is considered that potential voting rights are not currently exercisable or convertible if they cannot be exercised or converted until a future date or until the occurrence of a future event. If the investor loses the power to participate in decision-making regarding financial and operating policies of the investee entity, then we can say that it has lost significant influence (Allen & Ramanna, 2013; Bozec, 2008; Chen, Tang, Jiang & Lin, 2010; Tendeloo & Vanstrelen, 2005).

A joint venture type of shared commitment where the parties have joint control of the undertaking and also of the rights to the net assets of the undertaking (Daske & Gebhardt, 2006; Marra, Mazzola & Prencipe, 2011). There may be joint commitments which the parties have rights to the assets and obligations for liabilities related to commitment (Ghosh & Olsen, 2008; Landsman, Maydew, & Thornock, 2012). This type of commitment is called joint venture operation and it is not covered by this material, nor do we apply the equity method (Pope & McLeay, 2011; Pieper, Trevor, Weller & Duchon, 2017).

If the overseas operation acts as an extension of the reporting entity (the entity that has the foreign operation as a subsidiary, branch, associate or joint commitment) then its functional currency is the same as the reporting entity (Schleicher, Tahoun & Walker, 2010). The Standard specifies that an entity's functional currency reflects the transactions, events and underlying conditions that are relevant to it (Xiong, 2006; Leuz, Nanda & Wysocki, 2003). Consequently, once determined, the functional currency changes only if there is a change in those transactions, events and underlying conditions.

Foreign currency transactions are those transactions that are denominated or which provide for settlement in foreign currency (Zeghal, Chtourou & Fourati, 2012; Dechow, Sloan & Sweeney, 1996). They include, in accordance with IAS 21, the resulting transactions: when an entity buys or sells goods or services the price of which is denominated in foreign currency; borrows or lends funds when the due amounts are denominated in foreign currency; or otherwise acquires or disables assets, supports or repots debts denominated in foreign currency.

A foreign currency transaction - once the functional currency is established - may be recorded in the functional currency according to the two moments, initial recognition and subsequent recognition, as follows: initial recognition - the foreign currency exchange rate of the functional currency and the foreign currency, at the time of the transaction; the subsequent recognition (at the end of each reporting period) - the items will be converted according to their nature, monetary or non-monetary items (Ahmed, Neel & Wang, 2013; Thong, Ding & Lim, 2008; DeFond, 2010).

The interest in an associate or a joint venture is the carrying amount of the investment in the associate or joint venture established by using the equity method, and any long-term interests that, in fact, part of entity's net investment in the associate or joint venture (Barth, 2013; Kothari, Leone & Wasley,

2005). After the holding entity is reduced to zero, additional losses are accounted for and a liability is recognized only to the extent that the entity has incurred legal or constructive obligations or made payments on behalf of the associate or joint venture. If the associate or joint venture subsequently reports profits, the entity resumes recognizing its share of those profits only after its share of the profits equals the share of losses not recognized.

The main objectives of this chapter were to identify the important managerial controversies and they are presented in the conversion of the financial statements.

BACKGROUND

IFRS 10 Consolidated financial statements, consolidated financial statements are the financial statements of a group presented as if it were a single economic entity (Barth, Landsman & Lang, 2008). It is assumed that the consolidated financial statements are more useful for management, owners and lenders entity acquirer. Separate financial statements are those presented by a parent, an investor in an associate or a venture in a jointly controlled entity, in which investments are accounted rather on the basis of the direct equity than on reported results and net assets of the investee (Alzola, 2017; Houque, Zijl, Dunstan & Karim, 2012; Jeanjean & Stolowy, 2008). A complete set of consolidated financial statements include: consolidated statement of financial position at the end of the period; consolidated statement of comprehensive income in the period; consolidated statement of changes in equity over time; consolidated cash flow period and notes, comprising a summary of significant accounting policies and other explanatory information (Lang, Raedy & Wilson, 2006; Fu, Kraft & Zhang, 2012).

The consolidated financial statements are prepared in accordance with IFRS 10, taking into account the following rules: individual financial statements of the main and its subsidiaries, which are used to prepare consolidated financial statements will be prepared for the same reporting date (Messier, Glover & Prawitt, 2008). If the end of the reporting period of a subsidiary is different from that of the main company, the subsidiary prepares, for consolidation purposes, additional financial statements on the same date as the financial statements of the main unless it is impracticable to do so. In these circumstances, the subsidiary will make some adjustments for the effects of significant transactions or events that occur between that date and the date the financial statements of the main company. However, the difference between the end of the reporting period of the subsidiary and the end of the reporting period of the parent company shall not be less than three months (Fan, Li & Zheng, 2016; Klein, 2002). During the reporting periods and any difference between the endings of the reporting periods shall be the same from period to period.

With regard to non-controlling interests (INC), IFRS 10 makes the following statement: INC will be presented in a consolidated statement of financial position within equity, separately from the equity of the owners of the parent; profit or loss and each component of other comprehensive income are attributed to owners of the parent and non-controlling interests. Total comprehensive income must be attributed to owners of the parent and non-controlling interests even if this results in a deficit balance in the non-controlling interests (Rittenberg & Schwieger, 2005).

If the INC is holding the cumulative preference shares classified as equity owned by a subsidiary, then the main company computes its share of profits or losses after adjusting for the dividends on such shares, whether or not dividends have been declared (Louwers, Ramsay, Sinason & Strawser, 2007).

If modifications in the capital shares of the main company in a subsidiary appear, but it did not result in the loss of control, then like the operations they are accounted like transactions with own capital (meaning transactions with the stockholders). Also, the carrying amounts of controlling interests (ICI) and the non-controlling (INC) should be adjusted to reflect changes related holdings in the subsidiary. Any difference between the amount by which the adjusted non-controlling interests (INC) and the fair value of consideration paid or received is recognized directly in equity and attributed owners of the main company.

A group share an associate or a joint venture - IAS 28 - is given by amount of packages of shares held by the parent company and its subsidiaries in that associate or joint venture (Whittington & Pany 2008; Lin, Riccardi & Wang, 2012). Shareholdings of the group in other associates or joint ventures are not taken into account for this purpose. When an associate or joint venture has subsidiaries, associates or joint ventures, profit or loss, other comprehensive income and net assets taken into account in applying the equity method are those recognized in the financial statements of the associate or joint venture (including share of associate or joint venture of profit or loss and other comprehensive income and net assets of its associates and joint ventures).

On the other hand, the financial asset is investment made by the main company in the net assets of the subsidiary (Iatridis, 2012). The net assets of the subsidiary is equivalent to its equity. Since the elements of assets and debt of the subsidiary are added to those of the main company in the consolidated balance sheet, it is normal to remove the asset representing investment the main company in a subsidiary, in return for the subsidiary's equity to avoid counting double of these assets net (Brüggemann, Hitz & Sellhorn, 2013; Beasley, M.S., Buckless, Glover & Prawitt, 2009). The consolidated financial statements will be included only equity belonging to the main company. Any non-controlling interests (ICN) will be presented separately, separately from the equity of the owners of the main company.

STRENGTHENING FOREIGN ENTITIES AND CONVERTING FINANCIAL STATEMENTS INTO PRESENTATION CURRENCY

The method to be used for converting foreign entities' financial statements and the amount of resulting conversion adjustments depends on the determination of the functional currency (Balachandran & Faff, 2015). Taking into account the three types of coins that may arise in the discussion, such as the local currency in which the foreign entity operates, the functional currency and the presentation currency, there may be the following three cases: Local currency = Functional currency # Presentation currency; Local currency # Functional currency = Presentation currency; Local currency # Functional currency # Presentation currency (Barth, M. E., Landsman, Young & Zhuang, 2014).

Case 1 assumes that the entity carries out its accounting records and keeps its books in local currency, which is the same as the functional currency, and will therefore need to convert - where necessary - those records, expressed as financial statements, into presentation currency. In this case, the method known in the literature will be used as the current course method. Gains or losses resulting from conversion are recognized in other comprehensive income or equity.

Case 2 assumes that the entity carries out its accounting records and keeps its bookkeeping accounts in the local currency, which is different from the functional currency, and recalculates these values into equivalent units of functional currency, the result obtained being - in fact - the same as the currency of presentation because of the fact that the functional currency and the presentation currency are the same.

The recalculation term is used as these values have already been initially calculated in the local currency. This recalculation should provide results comparable to those that would have been obtained if the entity had used its functional currency from the outset when recording its foreign currency operations. In this case, the method known in the literature will be used as a temporal method. Gains or losses resulting from recalculation are recognized in profit or loss for the period.

IAS 21 does not explicitly use these terms, but it can be inferred from their scope of application (Barth & Konchitchki, 2013). Thus, account will be taken of the provisions of the section on how to register at the level of each individual entity, whether or not a member of a group, the foreign currency transactions in its functional currency or how the financial statements denominated in foreign currency are converted into currency functional; the section on the conversion to the presentation currency of financial statements denominated in another currency.

The temporal method treats balancing items by their nature: monetary and non-monetary items that are translated as follows: monetary items (e.g. cash, receivables or trade payables) are translated using the closing rate and the resulting differences in differences are recognized in profit or loss; non-monetary items (e.g. tangible, intangible, etc.) are converted: using the exchange rate at the transaction date if they are valued on the historical cost basis or using the exchange rate from the date they were measured at fair value if valued based on fair value, and the resulting differences in profit or loss are recognized either in profit or loss because, when a gain or loss on a non-monetary asset is recognized in profit or loss, any exchange component of that non- the gain or loss must be recognized in profit or loss; or in other items of the comprehensive income because, when a gain or loss associated with a non-monetary item is recognized in other comprehensive income (e.g. revaluation of assets), any component of that gain or of that loss must be recognized directly in other items of comprehensive income (Chebaane & Othman, 2014).

Regarding non-controlling interests (ICN) standard makes the following statement regarding the fair value at the acquisition date: acquirer may measure a non-controlling interest held in the acquire at fair value at the acquisition date; if available prices in an active market for shares - the acquirer can measure the fair value at the acquisition date of INC given these prices; if not available in an active market prices for shares - the acquirer shall measure the fair value at the acquisition date of INC using other valuation techniques; fair values per share of the acquirer's interest in the acquire and the non-controlling interest calculated per share may be different. It is possible that the main difference is the inclusion of a first control in the fair value per share of the acquirer's interest or, conversely, the inclusion of a discount for lack of control (also called reducing minority) in the fair value per share of interest in controlling.

Sum of the first three components (VJ of the consideration transferred, INC and VJ of acquisition of ownership interest held previously) is the default (VI) in the transaction (Doukakis, 2010).

It should also be borne in mind that the financial statements of previous years should be translated at the exchange rates that were duly applied at the time when the conversion was made. In other words, they will not update at the closing rate or at the current average rate used in the financial statements of prior periods. If this update takes place then these items would have different chair values and if they did not record movements.

The use of exchange rates and income from transaction dates in the case of income and expenditure is quite difficult to achieve (Horton, Serafeim & Serafeim, 2013). Consequently, from practical reasoning, a conversion rate can be used to convert exchange rates from transaction dates, for example, an average of the courses for that period. However, if exchange rates fluctuate significantly, the use of the average rate over a period is inadequate

SOLUTIONS AND RECOMMENDATIONS

The cumulative amount of exchange rate differences is presented in a separate component of equity until the disposal of the foreign operation. If these differences are related to a foreign operation that is not wholly owned (i.e. there are non-controlling interests) and which is reinforced, then the share of these differences for non-controlling interests is recognized as part of the non-controlling interest of the consolidated statement of financial position.

The difference between the involved in the transaction value and the accounting values will be allocated in the purchased assets and assumed liabilities from the acquisition date in order to obtain the fair value of them. The excess is allocated to the commercial background. It is important to bear in mind that this table of allocation will be established only once, at the purchasing date, and will remain unchanged. The revenue and expenses of a subsidiary are included beginning with its date of acquisition and until the date when the mother society doesn't control anymore. It is important to know that the value of the assets and the liabilities from the acquisition date will affect the consolidated result.

When talking about the fixed assets that are not depreciable (land), the values that are reported by the subsidiary don't take into account of the fair values from the acquisition date. The difference between the accounting values and fair values from the business combination date will be reflected only in mother society and in the worksheet that is necessary to obtain the consolidated financial situations. This difference, however, doesn't make any of the objects of an adjustment because the land is not depreciable. Anyway, in the situation in which the land is not sold or it is noticed a temporary depreciation, we must make adjustments in the worksheet as well.

The commercial background registered as a consequence from the business combination won't be registered by any of the entities in the own individual financial situations. The commercial background will appear only in the consolidated financial situations of the mother society for an unlimited period of time.

Its value will be adjusted only if – a consequence of the depreciation test- we will notice depreciation. This depreciation will be registered as expenses, and there will be like a discount of the consolidated result. We observe that in the first year there is no depreciation, unlike the following years where the depreciation is present.

An enterprise should disclose, in its financial statements, information about the exchange differences' value either included in net profit or net loss for the period, or classified as equity. It should also reconcile the opening and closing balance to the cumulative exchange difference recorded as part of equity. Other information on functional currency should be included in the financial statements, including: if the functional currency is different from the currency of the country where the enterprise has its headquarters, the reason for using a different currency should be mentioned; the reason that was considered when making the decision to change the presentation or functional currency; if the financial statements are presented in a currency other than the functional currency, the enterprise must present, together with a description of the method used in the conversion process, the reason for using a different presentation currency and certify that the functional currency reflects the substance economic circumstances and the circumstances underlying this.

FUTURE RESEARCH DIRECTIONS

We reiterate the following explanations regarding the statement of equity and the position of other items of comprehensive income: the cumulative amount of exchange rate differences is presented in a separate component of equity to the disposal of the foreign operation; the position of other elements of the overall result includes adjusting the conversion as an increase or decrease.

It is therefore important to determine and establish relevant indicators, the group of them in specific categories (quantitative or qualitative aspects related to individual company's business - e.g. employees - or macro issues) and not i just put together, and also to assign each category a specific weight in calculating the final result.

Another challenge would be to extend and adapt this research to the specifics of different national economic systems, to generalize the relationship between business combination and company performance and other countries and industries, and not go on forever with examples and studies.

CONCLUSION

Societal groups must keep in mind that their efforts: to apply IFRS changes will be reported by investors - many managers consider confidentially management and consider discovery to be far too far (Mechelli & Cimini, 2014). They also have a positive attitude about the high degree of transparency and comparability that IFRSs apply.

It may be a priority for a group's management team to maintain that confidentiality - such as the progress made in implementing IFRS, on the day-to-day business of societies, more special projects.

Most of the managers interviewed are aware that they are well informed and understand the impact of IFRS. More than three quarters of them know the impact of IFRS on companies in their country and in a similar property are very or sufficiently confidential in terms of understanding the impacts on the companies they invest in.

A summary of the above-mentioned conversion rules on the financial statements of a foreign entity would show: income and expenses are translated to the average exchange rate of the period and thus the converted value of the current period result (profit or loss) ; all assets and liabilities are converted to the closing rate; social capital accounts are converted to the historical exchange rate from the date of acquisition; accounts that comprise accumulated profits: initial balance accrued profits - the amount carried forward from the previous year; dividends - are converted at the exchange rate from the reporting date; the current result of the period (profit or loss); Conversion differences - a distinct category in equity (balance amount of the active equation - debt = equity).

REFERENCES

Allen, A., & Ramanna, K. (2013). Towards an understanding of the role of standard setters in standard setting. *Journal of Accounting and Economics*, *55*(1), 1–66. doi:10.1016/j.jacceco.2012.05.003

Alzola, M. A. (2017). Beware of the watchdog: Rethinking the normative justification of gatekeeper liability. *Journal of Business Ethics*, *140*(4), 705–721. doi:10.100710551-017-3460-3

Balachandran, B., & Faff, R. (2015). Corporate governance, firm value and risk: Past, present, and future. *Pacific-Basin Finance Journal, 35*(A), 1-12.

Ball, R., Li, X., & Shivakumar, L. (2015). Contractibility and transparency of financial statement information prepared under IFRS: Evidence from debt contracts around IFRS adoption. *Journal of Accounting Research, 53*(5), 915–963. doi:10.1111/1475-679X.12095

Barth, M., Landsman, W., & Lang, M. (2008). International accounting standards and accounting quality. *Journal of Accounting Research, 46*(3), 467–498. doi:10.1111/j.1475-679X.2008.00287.x

Barth, M. E. (2013). Global comparability in financial reporting: What, why, how, and when? *China Journal of Accounting Studies, 1*(1), 2–12. doi:10.1080/21697221.2013.781765

Barth, M. E., Konchitchki, Y. L., & Landsman, W. R. (2013). Cost of capital and earnings transparency. *Journal of Accounting and Economics, 55*(2–3), 206–224. doi:10.1016/j.jacceco.2013.01.004

Barth, M. E., Landsman, W. R., & Lang, M. H. (2008). International accounting standards and accounting quality. *Journal of Accounting Research, 43*(3), 467–498. doi:10.1111/j.1475-679X.2008.00287.x

Barth, M. E., Landsman, W. R., Young, D., & Zhuang, Z. (2014). Relevance of Differences between Net Income based on IFRS and Domestic Standards for European Firms. *Journal of Business Finance & Accounting, 41*(3-4), 297–506. doi:10.1111/jbfa.12067

Beasley, M. S., Buckless, F. A., Glover, S. M., & Prawitt, D. F. (2009). *Auditing Cases. An Interactive Learning Approach* (4th ed.). Prentice Hall.

Bozec, Y. (2008). Ownership Concentration, Separation of Voting Rights from Cash Flow Rights, and Earnings Management: An Empirical Study in Canada. *Canadian Journal of Administrative Sciences, 25*(1), 1–15. doi:10.1002/cjas.52

Brüggemann, U., Hitz, J.-M., & Sellhorn, T. (2013). Intended and unintended consequences of mandatory IFRS adoption: A review of extant evidence and suggestions for future research. *European Accounting Review, 22*(1), 1–37. doi:10.1080/09638180.2012.718487

Cairns, D., Massoudi, D., Taplin, R., & Tarca, A. (2011). IFRS fair value measurement and accounting policy choice in the United Kingdom and Australia. *The British Accounting Review, 43*(1), 1–21. doi:10.1016/j.bar.2010.10.003

Chebaane, S., & Othman, H. B. (2014). The Impact of IFRS Adoption on Value Relevance of Earnings and Book Value of Equity: The Case of Emerging Markets in African and Asian Regions. *Procedia: Social and Behavioral Sciences, 145*, 70–80. doi:10.1016/j.sbspro.2014.06.012

Chen, H., Tang, Q., Jiang, Y., & Lin, Z. (2010). The role of international financial reporting standards in accounting quality: Evidence from the European Union. *Journal of International Financial Management & Accounting, 21*(3), 220–278. doi:10.1111/j.1467-646X.2010.01041.x

Choi, Y.-S., Peasnell, K., & Toniato, J. (2013). Has the IASB been successful in making accounting earnings more useful for prediction and valuation? UK evidence. *Journal of Business Finance & Accounting, 40*(7–8), 741–768. doi:10.1111/jbfa.12025

Daske, H., & Gebhardt, G. (2006). International financial reporting standards and experts' perceptions of disclosure quality. *Abacus, 42*(3/4), 461–498. doi:10.1111/j.1467-6281.2006.00211.x

Dechow, P., Sloan, R., & Sweeney, A. (1996). Causes and consequences of earnings manipulation: An analysis of firms subject to enforcement actions by the SEC. *Contemporary Accounting Research, 13*(1), 1–36. doi:10.1111/j.1911-3846.1996.tb00489.x

DeFond, M. L. (2010). Earnings quality research: Advances, challenges and future research. *Journal of Accounting and Economics, 50*(2-3), 402–409. doi:10.1016/j.jacceco.2010.10.004

Doukakis, L. C. (2010). The persistence of earnings and earnings components after the adoption of IFRS. *Managerial Finance, 36*(11), 969–980. doi:10.1108/03074351011081286

Fu, R., Kraft, A., & Zhang, H. (2012). Financial reporting frequency, information asymmetry, and the cost of equity. *Journal of Accounting and Economics, 54*(2–3), 132–149. doi:10.1016/j.jacceco.2012.07.003

Ghosh, A., & Olsen, L. (2008). Environmental uncertainty and managers' use of discretionary accruals. *Accounting, Organizations and Society, 34*(2), 188–205. doi:10.1016/j.aos.2008.07.001

Horton, J., Serafeim, G., & Serafeim, I. (2013). Does mandatory IFRS adoption improve the information environment? *Contemporary Accounting Research, 30*(1), 388–423. doi:10.1111/j.1911-3846.2012.01159.x

Houque, M. N. (2012). The effect of IFRS adoption and investor protection on earnings quality around the world. *The International Journal of Accounting, 47*(3), 333–355. doi:10.1016/j.intacc.2012.07.003

Iatridis, G. (2010). International Financial Reporting Standards and the quality of financial statement information. *International Review of Financial Analysis, 19*(3), 193–204. doi:10.1016/j.irfa.2010.02.004

Iatridis, G. (2012). Hedging and earnings management in the light of IFRS implementation: Evidence from the UK stock market. *The British Accounting Review, 44*(1), 21–35. doi:10.1016/j.bar.2011.12.002

Jeanjean, T., & Stolowy, H. (2008). Do accounting standards matter? An exploratory analysis of earnings management before and after IFRS adoption. *Journal of Accounting and Public Policy, 27*(6), 480–490. doi:10.1016/j.jaccpubpol.2008.09.008

Jones, D. A., & Smith, K. J. (2012). Comparing the value relevance, predictive value, and persistence of other comprehensive income and special items. *The Accounting Review, 86*(6), 2047–2073. doi:10.2308/accr-10133

Klein, A. (2002). Audit committee, board of director characteristics and earnings management. *Journal of Accounting and Economics, 33*(3), 375–400. doi:10.1016/S0165-4101(02)00059-9

Kothari, S. P., Leone, A. J., & Wasley, C. E. (2005). Performance matched discretionary accrual measures. *Journal of Accounting and Economics, 39*(1), 163–197. doi:10.1016/j.jacceco.2004.11.002

Landsman, W. R., Maydew, E. L., & Thornock, J. R. (2012). The information content of annual earnings announcements and mandatory adoption of IFRS. *Journal of Accounting and Economics, 53*(1-2), 34–54. doi:10.1016/j.jacceco.2011.04.002

Lang, M., Raedy, J. S., & Wilson, W. (2006). Earnings management and cross listing: Are reconciled earnings comparable to US earnings? *Journal of Accounting and Economics*, *42*(1-2), 255–283. doi:10.1016/j.jacceco.2006.04.005

Leuz, C., Nanda, D., & Wysocki, P. D. (2003). Earnings management and investor protection: An international comparison. *Journal of Financial Economics*, *69*(3), 505–527. doi:10.1016/S0304-405X(03)00121-1

Lin, S., Riccardi, W., & Wang, C. (2012). Does accounting quality change following a switch from U.S.GAAP to IFRS? Evidence from Germany. *Journal of Accounting and Public Policy*, *31*(6), 641–657. doi:10.1016/j.jaccpubpol.2012.10.006

Lobo, G. L., & Zhou, J. (2001). Disclosure quality and earning management. *Asia-Pacific Journal of Accounting & Economics*, *8*(1), 1–20. doi:10.1080/16081625.2001.10510584

Louwers, T. J., Ramsay, R. J., Sinason, D. H., & Strawser, J. R. (2007). *Auditing and Assurance Services* (2nd ed.). New York: McGraw-Hill Irwin.

Marra, A., Mazzola, P., & Prencipe, A. (2011). Board Monitoring and Earnings Management Pre- and Post-IFRS. *The International Journal of Accounting*, *46*(2), 205–230. doi:10.1016/j.intacc.2011.04.007

Mechelli, A., & Cimini, R. (2014). Is comprehensive income value relevant and does location matter? A European study. *Accounting in Europe*, *16*(25), 1–35.

Messier, W. F., Glover, S. M., & Prawitt, D. F. (2008). *Auditing and Assurance Services. A Systematic Approach* (5th ed.). New York: McGraw-Hill Irwin.

Pope, P., & McLeay, S. (2011). The European IFRS experiment: Objectives, research challenges and some early evidence. *Accounting and Business Research*, *41*(3), 233–266. doi:10.1080/00014788.2011.575002

Richardson, A. (2011). Myth, Paradigms and Academic Accounting Research: A Comment on Reading and Understanding Academic Research in Accounting. *Global Perspectives on Accounting Education*, *8*, 67–77.

Rittenberg, L. E., & Schwieger, B. J. (2005). *Auditing. Concepts for a Changing Environment* (5th ed.). Thomson South-Western.

Schleicher, T., Tahoun, A., & Walker, M. (2010). IFRS adoption in Europe and investment-cash flow sensitivity: Outsider versus insider economies. *The International Journal of Accounting*, *45*(2), 143–168. doi:10.1016/j.intacc.2010.04.007

Tendeloo, B., & Vanstrelen, A. (2005). Earnings management under German GAAP versus IFRS. *European Accounting Review*, *14*(1), 155–180. doi:10.1080/0963818042000338988

Thong, T. Y., Ding, D. K., & Lim, C. Y. (2008). Firm diversification and earning management: Evidence from seasoned equity offerings. *Review of Quantitative Finance and Accounting*, *30*(1), 69–92. doi:10.100711156-007-0043-x

Watts, R., & Zimmerman, J. (1978). Towards a Positive Theory of the Determination of Accounting Standards. *The Accounting Review*, *53*(1), 112–134.

Whittington, O. R., & Pany, K. (2008). *Principles of Auditing & Other Assurance Services* (16th ed.). New York: McGraw-Hill Irwin.

Xiong, Y. (2006). Earning management and its measurement; a theoretical perspective. *The Journal of American Academy of Business, Cambridge*, *9*(1), 214–219.

Zeghal, D., Chtourou, S., & Fourati, M. Y. (2012). The effect of mandatory adoption of IFRS on earning quality: Evidence from the European Union. *Journal of International Accounting Research*, *11*(2), 1–25. doi:10.2308/jiar-10221

Zéghal, D., Chtourou, S., & Mnif, S. Y. (2011). An analysis of the effect of mandatory adoption of IAS/IFRS on earnings Management. *Journal of International Accounting, Auditing & Taxation*, *20*(2), 61–72. doi:10.1016/j.intaccaudtax.2011.06.001

ADDITIONAL READING

Ahmed, A., Neel, M., & Wang, D. (2013). Does mandatory adoption of IFRS improve accounting quality? Preliminary evidence. *Contemporary Accounting Research*, *30*(4), 388–423. doi:10.1111/j.1911-3846.2012.01193.x

Ball, R., Li, X., & Shivakumar, L. (2015). Contractibility and transparency of financial statement information prepared under IFRS: Evidence from debt contracts around IFRS adoption. *Journal of Accounting Research*, *53*(5), 915–963. doi:10.1111/1475-679X.12095

Fan, J. P. H., Li, J., & Zheng, G. (2016). Revisiting the bright and dark sides of capital flows in business groups. *Journal of Business Ethics*, *134*(4), 509–528. doi:10.100710551-014-2382-6

Guthrie, J., & Parker, L. D. (2016). Whither the accounting profession, accountants and accounting researchers? Commentary and projections. *Accounting, Auditing & Accountability Journal*, *29*(1), 2–10. doi:10.1108/AAAJ-10-2015-2263

Pieper, J. R., Trevor, C. O., Weller, I., & Duchon, D. (2017). Referral Hire Presence Implications for Referrer Turnover and Job Performance. *Journal of Management*, *19*, 14–20.

KEY TERMS AND DEFINITIONS

Accounting Estimates: Are often made under uncertainty in terms of determining their value as it involves the use of judgment. As a result, the risk of material misstatement is greater when these estimates are involved and in some cases the auditor may determine that the risk of material misstatement is greater, and it requires special attention in the audit.

Equity: Total debts and owners' rights claimed for a specific period of time.

Fair Value: The amount at which an asset is bought or sold in an arm's-length transaction, in which neither party is forced to act.

Joint Business: Is defined as a transaction or other event in which an acquirer obtains control of one or more businesses. After completion of the combined entity as transferee undertaking and acquire continues its existence as a separate legal entity. In practice, some transactions sometimes called "true mergers" or "mergers between equal entities" are also business combinations.

Performance: The ability of an organization to exploit its environment to access scarce resources.

Chapter 13
Creative Accounting and Its Impact on Financial Statements

Gabriela Claudia Oncioiu
Titu Maiorescu University, Romania

Alina Stanciu
1 Decembrie 1918 University, Romania

ABSTRACT

Creative accounting responds to the same issue faced by the management, but the answer lies at the boundary between the legal and de facto recording of the economic event, leaving accountants to create the entity's economic reality. The manager of the entity can choose from the multitude of accounting treatments and policies, the one that is most convenient and responds best to their own interests, which implies that the outcome may be convenient and not necessarily true. This chapter presents the implications and challenges of creative accounting on financial statements. The results show that the main controversy raised by the standards refers to the need for periodic reassessments and the possibility of choosing a method of measuring the value, which creates premises for the practice of creative accounting.

INTRODUCTION

Creative accounting, operating at shade - area - where accusations substantiated by non-compliance with professional or legal norms can be brought, but where common sense logic notifies the presence of a certain dose of "forcing the note" (Dennis, 2014; Richardson, 2011; Englund & Gerdin, 2018).

Using creative accounting for intangible assets, especially in her gray area favored by accounting rules, makes it difficult or even impossible to guess the true value of these assets (Jackson & Liu, 2010). This manipulation of accounting information can be done within the law and accounting rules or outside them (Florou & Pope, 2012). In the latter case we are witnessing an illegal practice: accounting fraud. Although there is a clear difference between creative accounting and deliberate violation of the law (fraud), "there is always a clear demarcation between the situation of creative accounting practices and accounting malpractice" (Damayant, 2013).

DOI: 10.4018/978-1-7998-0178-8.ch013

Accounting engineering's are defined by some authors as representing "the process whereby, given the existence of gaps in the rules to manipulate accounting numbers and taking advantage of flexibility, those practices are chosen for measurement and information that allow transforming synthesis documents from what they should be in what managers want" or "the process by which transactions are structured in such a way as to allow to produce the desired accounting result (Barth, 2013).

One criticism of the procedures above concerns that they contain a certain "dose" of creative accounting with the character of subjectivity with the realization that they change the presentation of accounts, but are nonetheless the result of an option, when selected from among more methods, which makes us say that they are within the accounting regulations (Baker & Bettner, 1997; Ahmed, Neel & Wang, 2013).

This chapter presents the implications and challenges of creative accounting on performance. The results show that the main controversy raised by the standards refers to the need for periodic reassessments and the possibility of choosing a method of measuring the value, which creates premises for the practice of creative accounting.

BACKGROUND

It is obvious that theorists have had different approaches to the concept of creative accounting. If for some authors the attribute of creativity in accounting is represented by a set of procedures that take into account the change of the level of the result in order to increase or decrease it, or the presentation of the financial statements without these objectives being excluded from each other, for others it represents the aggregation of accounting techniques and operations which, without departing from the accounting rule, allow the managers of an enterprise to change the resulting amount or change the appearance of the accounting documents (Ahrens, 2008; Bettner & Kate, 2013; Lukka, 2010; Ramanna, 2008).

The year 2006 brings new approaches to creative accounting (Brown, 2010). Thus, Holthausen and Watts (2001) argue that the real incentive for creative accounting is represented by the conflicts of interest between different groups: the case of investors and shareholders wishing to obtain more capital gains and dividends, while employees intend to get higher wages and share profit, or target shareholders who are interested in paying lower dividend taxes, while the country's tax authorities would like to collect more taxes.

Following this negative strand, for some time creative accounting has been isolated from other sciences and practices. The one who noticed it from a positive perspective was Doukakis in 2014, who feels that there may be flexibility in accounting, which at the same time provides a true and fair view of the accounts so that they can serve its interests while also taking the form of fraudulent financial reports when used for managing, measuring, and presenting accounts so as to serve the interests of financial statements and fraud, or to give a false picture to the accounts.

The most important definition of creative accounting belongs to Parker (2012), who argues that creative accounting is: (1) the process which allows the transformation of documents by the accounting figures that are being manipulated, given the existence of breaches in the rules, and, taking advantage of the flexibility, synthesizing practices from what they should be into what the managers want them to be; (2) the process where transactions are structured in such a way as to produce the desired accounting result.

We believe that the main reason for the emergence of creative accounting practices is the differences in the information needs of the accounting information users (investors, employees, suppliers, customers, creditors, state and public institutions) and the purposes they have in using this information. In view of the wide range of users of financial accounting information, it is natural for them to be interested in different financial or accounting aspects, and at the same time it is natural that a conflict of interest arises between what internal users want to present to external users.

From the point of view of the accounting practice, the need for an ethical or behavioral code is an obvious matter (Ozkan, Singer & You, 2012). Professional accountants have a delicate position when it comes to the need to provide services that meet high quality standards and serve the public interest, and this is the premise of a need for principles of professional behavior (Vladu, Amat & Cuzdriorean, 2016). Thus, the International Federation of Accountants (IFAC) has formulated a set of ethics standards for the accounting profession, which form the Code of Ethics, and highlight the importance of this profession in influencing the organizational culture. In addition to the Code of Ethics, organizations need continuous management involvement as well as professional accountancy organizations working together to implement ethical principles and increase responsibility. Trust is an essential element in business survival, and major economic and financial scandals have demonstrated the fragility of the public or customer confidence.

THE CREATIVE ACCOUNTING AND ITS IMPLICATIONS ON FINANCIAL STATEMENTS

The most important reason when using creative accounting techniques is to report lower financial results in order to reduce the amounts due on taxes and duties or to reduce tax evasion (Allen & Ramanna, 2013). Another reason is to provide a positive view of the valuation of the entity's activities and to reduce the risk of adverse stock-based signals on the basis of the assessments made by financial analysts. Creative accounting can be used to manipulate profits when there are budgets that have not been reached in real terms and that may affect the managers' performance, or when it is desired to finance the activity through various sources (Byard, Li & Yu, 2011; Andon, Baxter & Chua, 2007; Li, Qi, Tian & Zhang, 2017).

After a brief analysis of the accounting principles - especially those concerning the qualitative characteristics of the accounting information, we can observe the first step in facilitating the exercise of creative accounting, namely the repeated use of the phrase "reasonably" (Hou, Jin, Yang, Yuan & Zhang, 2015). What is reasonable? Who decides what is reasonable and to what? Thus, a degree of subjectivity of the professional accountants is allowed and tolerated, which cannot be normalized and consequently monitored or controlled.

The approaches, interpretations and duality of the concept of creative accounting give rise to hypotheses that have the role of demonstrating ... "how far can the creative accounting practices extend?" (Fan, Li & Zheng, 2016).

The first hypothesis starts from the typology of people who either develop such practices, or encourage them. The practice highlighted two different but equally dangerous typologies: the first typology is represented by young people with no experience that are involuntarily using engineering, without analyzing the risks, just out of a desire to affirm them. As part of the second category, there is a mature person who has experience, knows the entity in which he works, and considers creative accounting as a method of supplementing his own financial income.

The second hypothesis relates to the way an entity practicing financial accounting engineering activities is perceived by the environment in which it operates, by the industry.

The third hypothesis is to deceive potential investors who wish to invest in the entity by presenting financial statements resulting from the application of financial engineering. For a potential investor who has made the decision to invest on the basis of clear justifications in the financial statements, a simple attempt to present elements that may influence the decision, hide the reality of the entity or put it in a different form than it is, is considered to be deception.

The accounting regulatory bodies who wish to limit creative accounting must address these approaches in several ways:

- The choice of accounting methods should be diminished by reducing the number of permitted accounting methods or by specifying the situations in which each method should be used. The imposition of consistent methods is useful because a company who chose a method that gives a positive image in a year, will have to use the same method and during the years when the result will be less favorable.
- The abuse of reasoning can be nipped in two ways: by mapping rules to minimize the use of reasoning or by imposing consistency so that if a company chooses an accounting policy that favors one of the years, they will have to apply it during the coming years even if no longer favors them.
- For artificial transactions "the prevalence of substance over form" concept can be invoked, according to which the economic substance rather than the legal form is the one that determines the accounting substance. Thus, linked transactions must be accounted as one.
- The time of the transaction is clearly a matter of leadership. However, the purpose of their use can be reduced by requiring the regular review of the elements so that gains or losses of values change accounts are recognized in accounts for the years in which they appear (and not entirely in the year are transferred).

All these measures against "fraudulent" accounting practices must have the purpose to ensure a capital accounting information on qualitative intangible asset that faithfully represents reality and to allow decisions to ensure an optimal allocation between participants in value creation (Barth, Landsman, Young & Zhuang, 2014).

The manipulation of accounting values or the practice of creative accounting is possible due to the gaps in the accounting regulations and due to the freedom to choose and decide between the accounting methods allowed for the treatment of different categories of balance sheet items or the profit and loss account (Barth, Landsman & Lang, 2008; Schleicher, Tahoun & Walker, 2010). The risk of misrepresentation of results is not an easy to measure risk, which makes it difficult to compare the results of entities in the same industry or to perform other financial analyzes.

A first effect of creative accounting is hiding fraud and masking financial scandals, as it is very difficult for users of financial statements to analyze the results they are offered in detail - whether they do not have the necessary knowledge or do not have access to the data necessary for the financial statements.

Regardless of the creative accounting method used, the result of its application is aimed at influencing the entities' results and altering the financial statements (Ball, Li & Shivakumar, 2015; Li, 2010).

Balancing accounts is the alteration of the amount of items presented in the financial statements in order to distort the financial position or performance of an entity. Creativity when it comes to account balancing means presenting whichever information is desired without violating any international accounting or reporting standards or legal provisions.

Balancing accounts, even if it is not ethical, cannot be considered an accounting fraud because of the limitation of legality. The main reason for the appearance of account balancing is the conflict of interests of different users of the financial information, which have the same expectations as to the qualitative characteristics of the information, but different purposes when it comes to its use.

One of the main qualitative features of accounting information is credibility, which implies the absence of significant errors, lack of bias and fair and reasonable representation of reality, attributes that exclude the use of creative accounting practices. Neutrality is another qualitative characteristic at the opposite of account balancing.

Other creative accounting techniques used to smooth out the results are: timing the current operations in order to reduce time differences in the tax, timing revenues and expenditures, and changing the classification of items in the profit and loss account (He, Pan & Tian, 2017).

The managers' motivation to smooth revenue is generated by the desire to gain tax advantages, to improve relationships with creditors, employees and investors, to reduce the uncertainty generated by fluctuations in revenue size, to reduce the systematic risk by reducing covariates in return rates, to obtain compensation, to influence the market price of shares, to avoid political costs, etc (Ball, 2013).

The possibility of creating and canceling provisions is another way of diminishing the results when they occur or when the results are overseen when they are canceled (Cahan & Sun, 2015).

For entities carrying out construction work, they may choose from a set of methods when income recognition occurs, which has a different effect on the result of the exercise (recognition of the revenue at the time of completion of the work, versus the gradual recognition of revenue over the course of the work).

On the other hand, International Financial Reporting Standards have been introduced to facilitate the understanding of financial statements and to provide increased transparency but also to limit the possible opportunities offered by a creative accounting (Chen, Tang, Jiang & Lin, 2010). Regarding the International Financial Reporting Standards (IFRS), the main examples of how they attempt to prevent and/or restrict creative accounting refer to the obligation to publish cash flows that can assist in preventing the manipulation of the results (IFRS 1), the need for a transparent disclosure of the relationship between a parent and its subsidiaries, which prevents the disclosure of liabilities or assets in the balance sheet in the financial statements of the subsidiaries or the income statement where the source is not specified (IFRS 2), the obligation to use a form of financial statement that focuses on various elements that contribute not only to the value of the profit, but also to its realization (IFRS 3), presenting financial instruments in a manner that truly reflects the issuer's obligations (IFRS 4), and reporting transactions both economically and legally (IFRS 5).

While the purpose of the standards has been to protect all stakeholders by providing relevant, neutral, credible and verifiable information, certain irregularities are still likely to occur, in particular due to the replacement of the historical cost as a basis for fair value measurement. Even if fair value is aimed at improving the balance sheet value measurement tools and reflecting a relevant and current business valuation, it is the engine for creating prerequisites for creative accounting, especially with regard to asset valuation.

As we can see, creative accounting provides a challenge for the accounting profession and beyond. The problem is internationally, accounting policy choice is a particular problem for the Anglo-American tradition and transactions handling regarding intangible assets are a particular problem the European continental tradition.

SOLUTIONS AND RECOMMENDATIONS

Against the backdrop of these changes in the economic environment, managers need to maintain their reputation, market position, customers, and, ultimately, raise new standards of performance. In a world where the smallest detail differentiates you, where in the race to remain competitive, the only weapon is to improve in the smallest detail the quality of the offered services or products, because the typology of the Digital Era consumer demands excellence. How can an entity retain its reputation? The answer to all these questions is the top managers, the atrocentric leaders who through their inner strength have the full capacity to maintain the entity's performance. And in support of finding these answers, accountants have developed innovative ideas without breaking the law, taking advantage of the differences in its perception and understanding.

And then, at the interdependence between normativism and positivism, the management of the entity notes that the annual financial statements have a double role: on the one hand, to inform the decision makers about the economic situation of the entity, and on the other, to mislead them (Caylor, 2010; Alstete & Beutell, 2018; Chen, Qu & Sun, 2017).

The Yang creative accounting is characterized by the fact that the accounting information is presented within the legal limits and accounting standards and regulations, having a decisive role in substantiating management decisions.

The Yin creative accounting assumes that the accounting information is presented in an uncertain, estimative manner, based on the accountants' self-explanatory reasoning by interpretation and misleading.

There are two types of managerial behavior induced by the financial statements prepared and presented by accountants in order to increase the performance of the entity, perhaps gaining new clients in the portfolio, preserving one's reputation; initiatives that the entity management even supports and encourages: macro-manipulation and micro-manipulation.

- **Macro-Manipulation:** Accountants are aware of the new accounting rules and, being convinced that they are not practical, they engage in lobbying activities to prevent the adoption of these regulations. In this respect, they bring to attention an alternative description of the economic reality in a way that favors them.
- **Micro-Manipulation:** In an entity, this type of manipulation involves presenting the decision-makers of accounting information that present another reality than it is intended to be presented, not the actual reality.

Creative accounting practices are directly related to the causes that have generated them, so their disappearance or limitation depends on these causes. Practitioners and theoreticians in creative accounting make some recommendations for limiting its use:

- Developing a conceptual accounting framework that will be used as a tool for professional accountants to help them understand the accounting rules more thoroughly and analyses complex operations.
- Reducing the number of permitted accounting treatments or clearly establishing the circumstances in which each processing should be applied.

- Reducing the importance of the accounting result and assessing its quality through cash flows. Guiding external users to cash flows could discourage managers from using accounting information handling techniques.
- Creating the possibility to use a competent body for arbitration and / or interpretation, whose mission is to oversee the financial statements of all entities.
- Establishing very clear rules that leave no room for interpretation.

However, creative accounting is based on the same standard accounting practices and techniques, to which different substrates are added or removed, in order to present the entity in a more persuasive perspective from the point of view of performance (Arsenault & Faerman, 2014). The proliferation within the entity of this Yin side of creative accounting determines the occurrence of the fraud phenomenon over time. As long as the creative accounting speculates legal breaches without violating them, the conditions of tax fraud are not met.

FUTURE RESEARCH DIRECTIONS

Beyond the managerial level, the performance of an entity is best reflected in its economic and financial situation as a result of the process organization and the conduct of the financial-accounting activity. That is why the concept of performance can be seen from two different managerial and accounting perspectives. Therefore, there are new directions of future research such as:

- From a management point of view, performance is the result of top managers and the reflection of their entity management process in terms of maximizing the wealth of stakeholders in a constant, linear and natural trend.
- From an accounting point of view, performance can be reflected by applying the formula according to which: Performance = economy + efficiency + effectiveness or in other words procuring resources at the lowest cost in order to maximize the result and minimize the amount of resources for a predictable result to reach forecasts.

Based on these two different perspectives of approaching the concept of performance, we can infer that an entity circulates economic and financial items in the form of accounting information that managers have to understand by their position, and to use them in the processes of making strategic decisions, both on the short-term development of the entity as well as on the prediction process. All this accounting information is found in managerial accounting.

In the future, entities will need to rethink their asset base to understand how and where to create value based on the four digital trends that influence the form of an entity: increasing the automation; increasing transparency and intelligence; lowering transaction costs. The consequence of these trends is that the entity of the future as well as the industry of the future can be remodeled in very significant ways in which the value creation process can be recombined in more efficient and effective ways in delivering value customers. We are witnessing the emergence of different types of entities that appear today and in the future as a result of this. We see platforms that link assets across the industry in ways that create value, whether they are device entities or individual players. And we will see that these platforms play incredibly important roles in different industries.

CONCLUSION

In this chapter, the concept of Creative Accounting is essentially the process used by accountants, especially in more complicated situations, to find at least two out-of-the-crisis solutions at the limit of what is allowed and what is forbidden, based on the use of accounting information that can make decisions with a major impact on the entity's managerial and economic performance.

Entities may use creative accounting tools when listing stocks on their stock market and aiming towards maintaining a stable course of shares when there is an increased volatility in financial and capital markets, which creates a high economic and financial risk when the field of the economic operations is multinational and several regulatory bases are needed to work in harmonization, etc. These are examples of practicing positive creative accounting, but given the very small boundary between the positive and negative nature of using the creative accounting tools, the examples mentioned above can lead to fraud and tax evasion.

From this perspective, I think that the notion of creative accounting used by accountants in the context of achieving performance is very much a matter of Innovation. All the more in 2030, entities need to align their Strategies, Operations, Performance and Actions with the Sustainable Development Goals (SDGs). What contradicts the Yin area of creative accounting is thought to be reflected in the values, attitudes and behaviors of the leader, thus of the managerial culture. In other words, in an entity, the negative aspect of Creative Accounting can be countered only through a strong Managerial Culture developed by a leader who has the necessary skills to know the implications of using accounting information in decision-making processes.

From what has been exposed so far, we can see the multiple implications that managerial accounting has on decision-making, up to the performance of the entity seen at both individual and global levels. However, as any concept has its nuances, accounting seen from the perspective of performance is no exception. How much is Yin and how much is Yang? Theoreticians and practitioners in particular have understood that the external factors of the entity have a great impact on the accuracy of the quality of the transmitted accounting information, especially since the economic environment in which the entities operate is governed by volatility, complexity, uncertainty and ambiguity. Four external forces that are combined can provide a perfect context in which accounting information can be distorted and interpreted, which has deliberately led to the emergence of a new concept of Creative Accounting.

REFERENCES

Ahmed, A., Neel, M., & Wang, D. (2013). Does mandatory adoption of IFRS improve accounting quality? Preliminary evidence. *Contemporary Accounting Research, 30*(4), 388–423. doi:10.1111/j.1911-3846.2012.01193.x

Ahrens, T. (2008). Overcoming the subjective–objective divide in interpretive management accounting research. *Accounting, Organizations and Society, 33*(2), 292–297. doi:10.1016/j.aos.2007.03.002

Allen, A., & Ramanna, K. (2013). Towards an understanding of the role of standard setters in standard setting. *Journal of Accounting and Economics*, *55*(1), 1–66. doi:10.1016/j.jacceco.2012.05.003

Andon, P., Baxter, J., & Chua, W. F. (2007). Accounting change as relational drifting: A field study of experiments with performance measurement. *Management Accounting Research*, *18*(2), 273–308. doi:10.1016/j.mar.2006.06.007

Arsenault, P., & Faerman, S. R. (2014). Embracing paradox in management: The value of the competing values framework. *Organizational Management Journal*, *11*(3), 147–158. doi:10.1080/15416518.2014.949614

Baker, C., & Bettner, M. (1997). Interpretive and Critical Research in Accounting: A Commentary on its Absence from Mainstream Research||. *Critical Perspectives on Accounting*, *8*(4), 293–310. doi:10.1006/cpac.1996.0116

Ball, R. (2013). Accounting informs investors and earnings management is rife: Two questionable beliefs. *Accounting Horizons*, *27*(4), 847–853. doi:10.2308/acch-10366

Barth, M., Landsman, W., & Lang, M. (2008). International accounting standards and accounting quality. *Journal of Accounting Research*, *46*(3), 467–498. doi:10.1111/j.1475-679X.2008.00287.x

Barth, M. E. (2013). Global comparability in financial reporting: What, why, how, and when? *China Journal of Accounting Studies*, *1*(1), 2–12. doi:10.1080/21697221.2013.781765

Barth, M. E., Landsman, W. R., Young, D., & Zhuang, Z. (2014). Relevance of Differences between Net Income based on IFRS and Domestic Standards for European Firms. *Journal of Business Finance & Accounting*, *41*(3-4), 297–506. doi:10.1111/jbfa.12067

Bettner, M., & Kate, K. (2013). Changes in annual reporting rituals of financial services firms in periods of market crisis. *International Journal of Critical Accounting*, *5*(6), 577–593. doi:10.1504/IJCA.2013.059027

Brown, J. (2010). Accounting and visual cultural studies: Potentialities, challenges and prospects. *Accounting, Auditing & Accountability Journal*, *23*(4), 482–505. doi:10.1108/09513571011041598

Byard, D., Li, Y., & Yu, Y. (2011). The effect of mandatory IFRS adoption on financial analysts' information environment. *Journal of Accounting Research*, *49*(1), 69–96. doi:10.1111/j.1475-679X.2010.00390.x

Cahan, S. F., & Sun, J. (2015). The effect of audit experience on audit fees and audit quality. *Journal of Accounting, Auditing & Finance*, *30*(1), 78–100. doi:10.1177/0148558X14544503

Caylor, M. L. (2010). Strategic revenue recognition to achieve earnings benchmarks. *Journal of Accounting and Public Policy*, *29*(1), 82–95. doi:10.1016/j.jaccpubpol.2009.10.008

Chen, H., Tang, Q., Jiang, Y., & Lin, Z. (2010). The role of international financial reporting standards in accounting quality: Evidence from the European Union. *Journal of International Financial Management & Accounting*, *21*(3), 220–278. doi:10.1111/j.1467-646X.2010.01041.x

Damayant, T. (2013). Who is afraid of Qualitative Research? A Compromise Accounting Research Failure in Improving Accounting Practices. *International Journal of Advances in Management and Economics, 2*(2), 89-94.

Dennis, I. (2014). *The Nature of Accounting Regulation*. New York: Routledge.

Doukakis, L. C. (2014). The effect of mandatory IFRS adoption on real and accrual-based earnings management activities. *Journal of Accounting and Public Policy, 33*(6), 551–572. doi:10.1016/j.jaccpubpol.2014.08.006

Fan, J. P. H., Li, J., & Zheng, G. (2016). Revisiting the bright and dark sides of capital flows in business groups. *Journal of Business Ethics, 134*(4), 509–528. doi:10.100710551-014-2382-6

Florou, A., & Pope, P. (2012). Mandatory IFRS adoption and institutional investment decisions. *The Accounting Review, 87*(6), 1993–2025. doi:10.2308/accr-50225

He, K., Pan, X., & Tian, G. (2017). Legal liability, government intervention, and auditor behavior: Evidence from structural reform of audit firms in China. *European Accounting Review, 26*(1), 61–95. doi: 10.1080/09638180.2015.1100547

Holthausen, R. W., & Watts, R. L. (2001). The relevance of the value-relevance literature for financial accounting standard setting. *Journal of Accounting and Economics, 31*(1-3), 3–75. doi:10.1016/S0165-4101(01)00029-5

Hou, Q., Jin, Q., Yang, R., Yuan, H., & Zhang, G. (2015). Performance commitments of controlling shareholders and earnings management. *Contemporary Accounting Research, 32*(3), 1099–1127. doi:10.1111/1911-3846.12111

Jackson, S. B., & Liu, X. K. (2010). The allowance for uncollectible accounts, conservatism, and earnings management. *Journal of Accounting Research, 48*(3), 565–601. doi:10.1111/j.1475-679X.2009.00364.x

Li, S. (2010). Does mandatory adoption of international accounting standards in the European Union reduce the cost of equity capital? *The Accounting Review, 85*(2), 607–636. doi:10.2308/accr.2010.85.2.607

Lukka, K. (2010). The roles and effects of paradigms in accounting research. *Management Accounting Research, 21*(2), 110–115. doi:10.1016/j.mar.2010.02.002

Ozkan, N., Singer, Z., & You, H. (2012). Mandatory IFRS adoption and the contractual usefulness of accounting information in executive compensation. *Journal of Accounting Research, 50*(4), 1077–1107. doi:10.1111/j.1475-679X.2012.00453.x

Parker, L. (2012). Qualitative management accounting research: Assessing deliverables and relevance. *Critical Perspectives on Accounting, 23*(1), 54–70. doi:10.1016/j.cpa.2011.06.002

Ramanna, K. (2008). The implications of unverifiable fair-value accounting: Evidence from the political economy of goodwill accounting. *Journal of Accounting and Economics, 45*(2-3), 253–281. doi:10.1016/j.jacceco.2007.11.006

Richardson, A. (2011). Myth, Paradigms and Academic Accounting Research: A Comment on Reading and Understanding Academic Research in Accounting. *Global Perspectives on Accounting Education*, *8*, 67–77.

Schleicher, T., Tahoun, A., & Walker, M. (2010). IFRS adoption in Europe and investment-cash flow sensitivity: Outsider versus insider economies. *The International Journal of Accounting*, *45*(2), 143–168. doi:10.1016/j.intacc.2010.04.007

Vladu, A. B., Amat, O., & Cuzdriorean, D. D. (2016). Truthfulness in accounting: How to discriminate accounting manipulators from non-manipulators. *Journal of Business Ethics*, *140*(4), 633–648. doi:10.100710551-016-3048-3

ADDITIONAL READING

Alstete, J. W., & Beutell, N. J. (2018). Designing learning spaces for management education: A mixed methods research approach. *Journal of Management Development*, *37*(2), 201–211. doi:10.1108/JMD-08-2017-0247

Ball, R., Li, X., & Shivakumar, L. (2015). Contractibility and transparency of financial statement information prepared under IFRS: Evidence from debt contracts around IFRS adoption. *Journal of Accounting Research*, *53*(5), 915–963. doi:10.1111/1475-679X.12095

Chen, M., Qu, X., & Sun, X. (2017). Whose cost of equity capital reduces after IFRS convergence and why? Heterogeneity evidence from Chinese stock market. *China Journal of Accounting Studies*, *5*(1), 1–27. doi:10.1080/21697213.2017.1304539

Englund, H., & Gerdin, J. (2018). Management accounting and the paradox of embedded agency: A framework for analyzing sources of structural change. *Management Accounting Research*, *38*(1), 1–11. doi:10.1016/j.mar.2017.12.001

Li, L., Qi, B., Tian, G., & Zhang, G. (2017). The contagion effect of low-quality audits at the level of individual auditors. *The Accounting Review*, *92*(1), 137–163. doi:10.2308/accr-51407

KEY TERMS AND DEFINITIONS

Creative Accounting: A tool to create a distortion of the quality of financial information, creating uncertainty about the consistency and comparability of information for users, in which case we are dealing with an accounting of intent.

Decision: A person or group of persons' social and deliberate act defining the purpose and the objectives of a certain action, the directions and the ways to achieve that action, all of them determined, according to a certain need, by a process of obtaining information, deliberation, and assessment of the means and consequences of carrying out that action.

Financial Accounting Standards Board (FASB): Set up and develop generally accepted accounting principles.

Financial Engineering: Represents an aggregate of procedures, which have as objective the modification of the level of the results while taking into account the optimization, minimization, or presentation of financial situations.

Organizational Performance: Elements affecting company performance such as financial and marketing factors, return on sales, return on investment, etc.

Chapter 14
The Concept of Corporate Reporting and Audit Quality

George Silviu Cordoş
Babeş-Bolyai University, Romania

Melinda Timea Fülöp
Babeş-Bolyai University, Romania

Nicolae Măgdaş
Babeş-Bolyai University, Romania

ABSTRACT

The responsibility of auditors is a controversial topic that has brought much debate amongst academics and experts alike in recent years. This chapter's aim is to set the framework in which audit reporting exists: part of the wider landscape of corporate reporting and the final fragment of the sphere of the financial statements audit quality. By using a general-to-specific deductive approach, the authors discuss the international and European perspectives on the process of financial statement audits, as well as the stakeholders or audit and audit reporting, in order to clearly define the regulatory space in which any changes in this field occur. The authors also discuss the theories that explain the process of audit reporting, with an emphasis on the lending credibility theory, the inspired confidence theory, and the sociology of education theory. The authors consider that these theories explain the improvements undertaken to improve the communicative value of the audit quality.

INTRODUCTION

As a consequence of the international financial crisis and financial scandals, the audit report has recently been in the attention of standard setters and regulators, but also under the scrutiny of the public and third-party users. The introduction of revised regulations, focusing on increased disclosure requirements within the audit report has led, in turn, to an increase in the transparency level of the report.

Audit reporting is an important subject for the accounting and audit research field, due to its influence in the decision-making process that involves the stakeholders that rely on audited financial situations.

DOI: 10.4018/978-1-7998-0178-8.ch014

Some stakeholders consider that the auditors could disclose more information that they gather regarding the audited company, within the audit report. Other users of the report consider that the language the auditors use is too standardised and the fact that the reasoning behind the issued opinion is not sufficiently explained is unsettling for stakeholders who consider the auditor should communicate more aspects. These aspects are the reason behind the revision process the IAASB has started, with the purpose of clarifying auditing standards, especially those concerning audit reporting and audit quality. The process comes as a response to stakeholders' expressed needs and hopes to fulfil this necessity. These changes plan on improving and covering any deficiencies, but even so, the usefulness and efficiency of these proposals are being questioned.

THE CONCEPT OF CORPORATE REPORTING

Corporate reporting is the concept that connects the company to its stakeholders. Audit reporting is part of corporate reporting, along with financial reporting, corporate governance, corporate responsibility, integrated reporting and others.

Taking these elements into account, the objective of the chapter is to set the framework of audit reporting, as part of the larger sphere of corporate reporting, while analysing its strong link to corporate governance and, in particular, to the transparency principle. By using a general to specific deductive approach, we start our analysis from the concept of corporate reporting, taking into consideration the insights provided by academic research and professional organisations. Another part of this chapter is to provide a starting point to auditing theories that explain the objectives and outcomes of our research.

Corporate reporting is a company's means of communication with stakeholders, as part of their accountability and stewardship obligations (FEE, 2015). The meaning of corporate reporting is in a continuous transformation, as Professor Mervyn E. King posits: "*corporate reporting is not what is used to be*" (Centre for Tomorrow's Company, 2011). Some possible explanations for this statement are exposed subsequently. The economic world has changed in the last decade. Financial scandals have had an adverse effect on the confidence and perception of the stakeholders regarding the figures provided by reports – financial and audit reports equally. Around 80% of investors are looking for better reporting quality, because the company's reporting quality has an unswerving impact on their investment decisions (PwC, 2014). Thus, although the auditor still focuses on the financial statements, whether they provide a"true and fair view of the company's financial position, the communicative value of the audit report has significantly improved in recent years. And it is all because of the trend of changes in the corporate reporting framework, with the purpose of better fulfilling the needs of stakeholders."

A first step is to define a corporation, the governance process, and corporate governance. Corporations, in a more reduced organisational size from that what they are today, have existed since the beginning of the Medieval ages (Berman, 1983) and then evolved in the 18th and 19th centuries into a more modern organisation, given the rise of classical liberalism (Smith, 1776) and the development of company laws. Followed by a deregulation period, the beginning of the 20th century saw the development of corporate legislation and the evolution into what corporations are today. A corporation can be defined as "*a large company or group of companies authorised to act as a single entity and recognised as such in law*" (Oxford Dictionary). We consider that this definition, while clear, is not sufficient to fully explain what a corporation is, and more importantly, it does not explain its connection to the world in which is exists. A corporation cannot exist without its stakeholders, as it must "relate to society", therefore connect with its stakeholders, provide appropriate information and address the needs of an extensive audience. The corporation is directed by the management, which, in its turn, is overseen by an elected Board of Directors. The way in which the company is managed, is the company's *governance*: "the act, manner or fact of governing, power or control." The noun has Latin roots, *gubernare*, which can be translated into "steering, ruling," suggesting "a direction." Thus, we can conclude that the governance is responsible for the processes and structures, which steer the entity or the society. Therefore, taken together, the concepts of "corporation" and "governance," form the notion of "corporate governance."

In today's economic context, corporate governance plays an important part. Consequently, the topic has been thoroughly researched, and there are differences in opinion regarding a clear definition of this concept. In order to define corporate governance, we have relied on an evolutionary approach, which we consider provides the most appropriate research results.

The first definition of the concept is provided by Adrian Cadbury (1992): "corporate governance can be defined as the system by which companies are directed and controlled". The most important part of this definition is "system": this includes formal and informal structures and associations within the company and not outside the enterprise." The external environment is, of course, critical in the decision-making process, but corporate governance, in Cadbury's view, excludes external elements, and focuses on control from within the company. A second definition is that corporate governance is a "set of laws, rules, regulations and codes of conduct voluntarily implemented, which allow an entity to attract the resources is needs to conduct its activity" (The World Bank, 1998, p.7). This definition brings forward a mention of the external environment of the company because it implies that companies need outside resources in order to conduct their affairs. Another definition of corporate governance is that it "specifies the distribution of rights and responsibilities among the different participants in the organisation – such as the board, managers, shareholders and other stakeholders – and lays down the rules and procedures for decision-making" (OECD, 2004, p. 11). In this definition, the OECD, similar to the World Bank, stresses that the corporation relies on the outside world, the society – the stakeholders. The International Federation of Accountants (IFAC) has set a more universal definition, namely: "Corporate governance is a set of practice of the Board and executive management, which aims to secure strategic direction, the achievement of goals and objectives, the accountability of financial resources and the risk management of the entity." We can notice that the IFAC definition brings the accounting and financial elements of the corporation, in defining the concept.

Corporate governance is an indispensable part of corporations and their stakeholders, for the reason that it assures that the company's resources are protected and cannot be expropriated from the entity. Consequently, an entity demonstrates sustainability if it correcly and consistently applies corporate governance principles (Mallin, 2006, p.3) Over time, there has been interest in improving corporate governance, thus, the concept of corporate governance has evolved into efficient and/or good corporate governance, as first mentioned in the Agency Theory (Berle & Means, 1932). Good corporate governance is the result of the accountability of the management to guarantee the sustainability of the company (Lo et al., 2010). An effective corporate governance is achievable only if the Board of Directors produces instruments for the assessment of internal controls relating to financial reporting, in order to decrease the company's susceptibility to fraud and wrongdoings (Lobo & Whalen, 2007).

In this regard, the demise of Enron or Worldcom has had a great impact on the world economy and corporate governance principles. These companies, according to all published reports (annual reports, transparency, and sustainability, financial statements) stated their compliance with all accounting regulations; however, they were, in fact, misleading their shareholders and stakeholders. Their demise had an impact not only on the stock market, but on the audit and accounting profession as well, and, since then, the audit mission has suffered a period of challenges. This due to the public's perceived auditor responsibility and independence. This misperception appeared not only because of the aforementioned businesses implications in these financial scandals. Auditing firms also had their contribution (i.e. Arthur Andersen, former audit firm), by issuing unqualified audit opinions for Enron's financial statements. These reports certified that Enron's financial situations were clear of any indication of fraud, within reasonable assurance. The auditing firm does not exist anymore, as their reputation suffered immensely after Enron's public demise. Stakeholders could not trust a company that did not detect fraud and was a suspect in covering up the fraud. In this sense, corporate governance is critical in today's business environment because, together with transparency, it plays a major role in the decision-making process.

In order to take action as a consequence of these financial scandals, the Organisation for Economic Cooperation and Development (OECD)"has revised the set of basic principles that guides the functioning of corporate governance (OECD, 2015). A good corporate governance system combines elements of the internal and the external environment of the company, to make the most of the business performance, decrease risk and offer thorough protection of stakeholder interests. The corporate governance principles are aimed at "creating market confidence and business integrity" for companies (OECD, 2015). Having been developed in 1999 and updated in 2004, the current corporate governance principles are presented within six chapters in table 1.

As seen in the table presented above, the principle of disclosure and transparency as a part of good corporate governance should be considered a crucial step to protect stakeholders' interests and to endorse an effective and operational corporate setting within the economic environment. If all information (financial, sustainability, environmental) is readily available for stakeholders, they can easily evaluate the company's management and the company's performance. Corporate transparency involves the widespread accessibility of relevant and reliable statistics regarding an entity's financial and non-financial aspects.

Currently, there is a need to understand corporate governance in a much wider and multifaceted sense; it should be perceived as a structure that guarantees the ideal use of capitals for the advantage of stakeholders (and shareholders), with the purpose of fulfilling society's expectations. Consequently, the aims of good corporate governance should be:

1. To consolidate the responsibilities and accountability of the management and the supervising committee;
2. To attain a management team that is skillful, independent and experienced;
3. To ensure that the management is truthful and reliable;
4. To protect the reliability and truthfulness of the financial reporting process;
5. To ensure a functioning internal control system and to adequately manage risks;
6. To disclose information relevant to the needs of shareholders and stakeholders;
7. To ensure a good cooperation between the Board, the management, the Audit Committee and the stakeholders.
8. To assure that the management is skillful, experienced, independent and in accordance with the company's needs.

Table 1. Corporate governance principles

Table 1: ***Corporate Governance Principles***

Chapters	Concepts
I. Ensuring the basis for an effective corporate governance framework;	Transparent and fair markets; Efficient allocation of resources; Quality and consistency of regulations; Division of responsibilities between authorities; Quality of supervision and enforcement; Role of stock markets in supporting good corporate governance.
II. The rights and equitable treatment of shareholders and key ownership functions;	Shareholder rights – information and participation; Disclosure of control structures; Shareholder participation in the decision of executive remuneration.
III. Institutional investors, stock markets and other intermediaries;	Sound economic incentives throughout the investment chain; Disclosure and minimisation of conflicts of interest; Fair and effective price discovery in stock markets.
IV. The role of stakeholders in corporate governance;	Active cooperation between corporations and stakeholders; Recognition of stakeholders rights; Stakeholders access to information; Actions for violations of stakeholders' rights.
V. Disclosure and transparency;	Financial and operating results; Company objectives; Major share ownership; Remuneration; Related party transactions; Risk Factors; Board members; Non-financial information;
VI. The responsibilities of the board.	Key functions of the Board of Directors; Risk management; Tax planning and internal auditing; Board training and evaluation; Establishment of specialised Board Committees.

Source: OECD Corporate Governance Principles (2015)

The changes in accounting and auditing are aimed at providing protection and assurance to stakeholders, with regards to the confidence in the financial statements. The efficiency and professional conduit of the auditor is necessary for stakeholders to consider the audit mission as being "of quality".

International Standards on Auditing (ISA's) establish that the final stage of a financial statements audit is the audit report, which contains the auditor's opinion on the "true and fair view and present fairly all material aspects" of a company's financial position, with the specified reporting framework (IFRS, IAS, GAAP, national regulations). Based on sufficient audit evidence, the auditor must issue an opinion, and this opinion contains a reasonable level of assurance that there are no misstatements. Because of this level of assurance, even if reasonable and not absolute, the auditor has a great responsibility regarding the provided opinion. This aspect is also a reason for the existance of the audit expectation gap, as stakeholders do not understand the difference between "reasonable" and "absolute". In this sense, the audit reporting reform started by the IAASB plans on covering parts of the audit expectation gap, with new and improved auditing standards.

THE CONCEPT OF FINANCIAL STATEMENTS AUDIT

An International Perspective on Financial Statements Audit

The word "audit" comes from the Latin word "auditus," which translates to "listening" and refers to supporting the integrity of financial reporting and business conduct, and the pursuit of truth. The role of audit in society is critical to maintaining trust in economic processes of the capital markets and the public sector. In the modern sense, the audit has focused on the analysis of public"financial statements that are reported in compliance with generally accepted accounting principles (Percy, 1997).

The concept of the "auditor" comes from the fact that the audit report has been provided as a detailed verbal report; following a series of changes over time, the report has turned into a written report. In the early 1990s, the audit was an unstandardized report, in the form of a certificate, in which the auditor had confirmed that the audited financial statements are accurate. It was not unusual for the audit report to contain one or two sentences, or even just the word "certificate" (Church, Davis & McCracken, 2008).

One of the first definitions of auditing was set by the"American Accounting Association (AAA), a body that defines the process of auditing"as "a systematic process of objectively obtaining and evaluating evidence regarding assertions about economic actions and events, to ascertain the degree of correspondence between those assertions and established criteria and communicating the results to interested users" (AAA, 1973).

At the international level, there are three relevant standard setters in the auditing and assurance field:"The International Auditing and Assurance Standards Board (part of IFAC), the Auditing Standards Board (ASB, part of the American Institute of CPAs) and the"Public Company Accounting Oversight Board."The reason for wanting to present the international standard setters and international standards is because these standards, combined, are applied in the majority of countries worldwide. The standards developed by the ASB and the PCAOB are implemented in the United States, but given the fact that many companies with a global presence are listed on American stock exchanges (the NY stock exchange, for instance), as well as European or Asian, they need to comply with legislation in all parts of the world. Also, the US market is more developed and has the largest share of the worldwide economy, as the World Bank has calculated in their list of countries, by GDP. The US has a GDP (2015) of 17.946.996 mil. $, followed by the EU with 16.229.464 mil. $, China (with 10.866.444 mil. $) and Japan with 4.123.258 mil. $ (World Bank, 2016). Given these numbers, it can be said that a large part of the world economy either uses ISAs as auditing standards or other standards such as the ones developed by the ASB or PCAOB. As such, we consider that for our international perspective on financial statements audit; we will present regulations issued by the IAASB, the ASB, and the PCAOB. Each regulator publishes a set of auditing standards, with different levels of similarity and dissimilarity, when compared with each other. In the following paragraphs we will briefly present an outline of these standards and, as added value, present a brief comparison between the regulations.

IAASB International Auditing Standards

The International Federation of Accountants (IFAC) defines the audit as "an independent examination of the financial statements and relevant financial information of an entity, be it profit oriented or not, regardless of its size or legal form of organization, when the examination is the objective to express an opinion regarding this information" (IAASB, 2015). The"International Auditing and Assurance Standards Board"(referred from here on as IAASB), is the regulating body, part of the IFAC, responsible for the issuing and revision of International Auditing Standards (ISAs). A definition of auditing can be found in the ISA 200 standard –"*Overall Objectives of the Independent Auditor and the Conduct of an Audit in Accordance with International Standards on Auditing* (ISA 200, p.11 (a), (b), 2015):"

obtaining reasonable assurance about whether the financial statements as a whole are free from material misstatement, whether due to fraud or error, thereby enabling the auditor to express an opinion on whether the financial statements are prepared, in all material respects, in accordance with an applicable financial reporting framework; and to report on the financial statements, and communicate as required by the ISAs, in accordance with the auditor's findings.

The International Standards on Auditing (ISAs) were first published in 1991, having been named "guidelines" up until then. The regulating body now known as the IAASB was first titled the"*International Auditing Practices Committee (IAPC)*,"and was created in 1978 by the IFAC, and was later renamed as the IAASB in 2002. Unlike the standards that are issued by the PCAOB and AICPA, the ISAs are applicable to audit missions in all companies, both private and public. After several revisions throughout time, the most notable being the revision process brought by the Clarity Project (2004-2008), which was a joint project with the ASB, the current ISAs comprise of a number of 37 auditing standards (IAASB, 2016).

According to ISA standards, the auditor is responsible for redacting the independent"auditor's report, within which the auditor expresses the opinion on the analysed financial statements (the ISA 700 standard). The auditor plans the audit mission (*ISA 300 - Planning an Audit of Financial Statement, IAASB, 2009*) and during the course of the mission the auditor has to comply with the IFAC Code of Ethics for Professional Accountants, drafted by the International Ethics Standards Board for Accountants (IESBA, 2014)."The auditor must also comply with the ISA 220 standard regarding the quality control process for the auditing mission. The first step is to set the prerequisites for the audit mission, by elaborating an engagement letter, as established by ISA 210; this step will confer contextual information regarding the client. Subsequently, the auditor will prepare the audit documentation (ISA 230), will set the materiality threshold (ISA 320) and will convene upon the company's responses to assessed risks (ISA 330). In succession, the auditor will collect audit evidence (according to ISA 500, 501, 505 and ISA 510-580), by testing control mechanisms and operations and by analytical procedures and test of balances in the financial statements.

At the completion of the audit mission, the auditor will collect final audit evidence, will evaluate the obtained results and will draft the auditor's report, which contains the audit opinion on the financial statements (ISA 700). The auditor's opinion can be unmodified (ISA 700), with or without explanatory paragraphs, modified, contrary or disclaimer of opinion (ISA 705). With the new ISA 701 standard, the auditor is also required to disclose on Key Audit Matters, the matters which, by using their professional judgement, the auditors have determined to be of most significance in the audit mission, based on discussions with *those charged with governance (TCWG)*. In the last step, the auditor delivers the finalised report to the Audit Committee and the management of the audited company.

ISAs are being applied worldwide, being either enforced directly by law or being adopted indirectly by national legislation. There are several jurisdictions in which either generally accepted auditing standards developed by national regulators are applied, such as auditing standards from the AICPA, PCAOB or other regulators. The IFAC has published, through its Compliance Program, the ISA Adoption around the world; some countries are required by law to use IASs, others have adopted ISAs or use ISAs as national standards, while some countries using national auditing standards based on ISAs or similar to them (IFAC, 2012).

ASB Audit and Attest Standards and *PCAOB Auditing Standards*

In the United States, there are two regulating bodies for auditing standards, depending on the type of company. After the 2002 Sarbanes-Oxley Act, the legislation for generally accepted accounting and auditing principles and standards is shared between the"Auditing Standards Board (ASB), a committee of the American Institute of CPAs (AICPA), created in 1978, and the Public Company Accounting Oversight Board (PCAOB),"formed in 2002. For public listed companies, the PCAOB and the Securities Exchange Commission (SEC) are responsible and have authority over auditing practices and regulation for public enterprises. For private companies, the ASB is in authority of "developing, updating and communicating comprehensive standards and practice guidance that enable practitioners to provide high-quality, objective audit and attestation services to non-public companies, in an effective and efficient manner" (AICPA, 2016).

Together with the IAASB, the ASB agreed to redraft auditing standards to converge their standards, through the joint project known as the Clarity Project (2004-2008). The ASB publishes the generally accepted auditing standards as *Audit and Attest Standards*, and they include (AICPA, 2016):"

- Clarified Statements on Auditing Standards (SASs);
- Statements on Standards for Attestation Engagements (SSAEs);
- Statements on Quality Control Standards (SQCSs)."

The Public Company Accounting Oversight Board is a "non-profit corporation established by Congress to protect investors and the public interest by promoting informative, accurate, and independent audit reports and to oversee the audits of public companies and broker-dealers" (PCAOB, 2016). After it had been established, the PCAOB adopted AICPA's Generally Accepted Auditing Standards at their form in 2003. However, since then, both the PCAOB and the AICPA have updated the standards in different manners, resulting in differing guidelines nowadays (Cullinan et al, 2013). The current PCAOB auditing standards have also been redrafted and, similarly to the ISAs drafted by the IAASB, will go into effect as of December 31st, 2016.

We have compared the three sets of regulations between them, and we have found similarities on multiple levels, such as for guidelines regarding auditing procedures, auditing sampling, audit risk and audit evidence and with regards the responsibilities of the auditor and their independence. However, because these standards are regulated by different standards boards, there are differences in regulations which pose challenges for all interested parties, auditing firms, professionals, academia, and others. In time, the divergence between standards has widened (Cullinan et al., 2013), but efforts for convergence are apparent when comparing IAASB standards with AICPA standards.

As stated before, both regulating bodies have worked closely to redraft standards, through the Clarity Project, a project in which the PCAOB was not part of. Alternatively, we understand the differences between the AICPA standards and the PCAOB standards because they address different types of companies (private vs. public), but we do not comprehend why there are dissimilarities between standards drafted by PCAOB and IAASB, given the fact that ISAs are applicable for both public and private entities. Of course, there is a collaboration between the IAASB and PCAOB to align their standards, which can be seen in recent joint efforts of defining the IAASB's *Key Audit Matters* and PCAOB's *Critical Audit Matters* concepts (PCAOB, 2016).

Stakeholders would prefer a single set of standards, to be used in all situation, for all types of companies Based on the US situation, the authors posit that a unique set of standards, such as the ISAs, might be a better solution in the long-term because AICPA standards converge with ISAs. Thus more and more companies will opt for the ISAs indirectly. Still, for the short and medium term, "different auditing standards are likely to continue to exist for the foreseeable future, and a greater divergence among the standards in the future is inevitable" (Cullinan *et. al*, 2013).

The synthesis provided for the above examination is a good starting point for the analysis of audit reporting standards, which are part of the auditing regulation drafted by the IAASB, the AICPA, and the PCAOB.

AN EUROPEAN PERSPECTIVE ON FINANCIAL STATEMENTS AUDIT

Alongside international regulations and regulators in auditing standards, the legislation is completed by the Directives drafted in the"European Union, by the European Parliament, the European Commission and the European Council."All EU-28 member states are required to comply with these regulations, and more recently, the Commission has issued a new regulatory framework for statutory audit in the European Union.

According to the European Commission, the statutory audit is "an audit of annual or consolidated accounts in so far as required by Community law. The role of statutory audit is to certify companies' financial statements, i.e. to provide stakeholders such as investors and shareholders with an opinion on the accuracy of companies' accounts. Hence, statutory audit contributes to the orderly functioning of markets by enhancing the integrity of and the confidence in financial statements" (EC, 2016). The Commission states that the aim of statutory audits is to ensure high-quality audit missions, through the following goals (EC, 2016):

- Consolidating the independence of both statutory audit firms and auditors;
- Improving the communicative value of the audit report to investors;
- Providing "cross-border" audit services of the same quality within the EU;
- Creating a dynamic audit market within the EU;
- Improving the supervisory activities of audit services at national and EU level;
- Protecting and promoting cooperation and convergence with other countries.

Currently, the main regulations for statutory audit in the EU have entered into force on June 16th, 2014, being applicable from June 17th, 2016 and are the following (EC, 2016):

- Directive 2014/46/EU amending Directive"2006/43/EC on statutory audits of annual accounts and consolidated accounts;"
- Regulation 537/2014 on the explicit requirements concerning the"statutory audit of public-interest entities."

In chronological order, at the EU level, the following regulations regarding auditing have been drafted:

1. Fourth Directive 78/660/CEE can be considered the promoter for implementation of mandatory financial audit for companies with certain criteria as their size and number of employees. Other provisions include (Directive 78/660/CEE):
    a. A clear delineation between small and medium size companies, by their turnover, total assets and number of staff (Art. 11);
    b. Rules for the preparation of the balance sheet and structure of financial statements (including the simplified structure) (Art. 27).
2. Seventh Directive 83/349/CEE comes with additional provisions to the Fourth Directive (Directive 83/349/CEE):
    a. The obligation to conduct financial audits of companies that prepare consolidated financial statements (Art. 37);
    b. Provisions related to the consolidation of businesses.
3. Eighth Directive 84/253/CEE is an important step in the auditing sphere in the European Union as it brings additional guidelines related to the qualification of professionals involved and conducting audit missions and the skills they need to acquire to become certified. Other provisions include (Directive 84/253/CEE):
    a. Recognition of professional qualifications between Member States (Art. 12);
    b. The organisation of the certification and examination process (Art. 5);
    c. The organisation of certified individuals (certified individuals, legal entity) (art. 28);
    d. Mandating principles of independence and professional conduct for certified professionals (Section III);
    e. Mandating rules for certified professionals' publicly available information (Section IV).
4. Directive 2006/43/EC sets out as main objectives:
    a. The reliable application of"International Standards on Auditing (ISAs)" within the Member States as regards to statutory audits – "high-level — though not full — harmonisation of statutory audit requirements" (Para. 5);
    b. Adherence to accounting principles and accounting standards – "Statutory auditors should adhere to the highest ethical standards" (Para. 9);
    c. Better cooperation between the Member States, to ensure a degree of "standardisation" of the statutory audit, "to increase comparability between companies applying the same accounting standards" (para. 16);
    d. Improve and "ensure consistently high quality" of statutory audits (para. 13);
    e. The rotation of the statutory audit partner, to warrant auditor independence - to guarantee a certain "restraint" for issuing an unqualified opinion, due to familiarity with the audited client (para. 26)
5. Another European Union regulation on auditing is the Green Paper on Audit Policy. Firstly published in 1996, its aim has been to harmonise statutory audit within the EU space and to initiate a consultation process on this development.

Directive 2014/46/EU amending Directive"2006/43/EC on statutory audits of annual accounts and consolidated accounts and the Regulation 537/2014 on specific requirements regarding statutory audit of public-interest entities"are new legislative packages aimed at reforming audit in the EU. Having been published in June 2015, both the Directive and the Regulation are currently in effect, having been mandatory to be transposed by the Member States by June 17th, 2016. The legislation is applicable in all EU-28 states and also in member countries of the European Economic Area (Ernst & Young, 2015). The main provisions of the new regulations are relating to the statutory audits of Public Interest Entities, mandatory audit firm rotation, the list of prohibited non-audit services that are assured by the same auditor.

The most important provisions of the new European auditing regulations are (Directive 2014/46/EU, Regulation 537/2014):

- An improvement of the"communicative value of the auditor's report,"by including additional relevant information (Directive Art. 28);
- Limit the duration of the audit engagement to 10 years in the case of audit partner (Regulation Art. 17 Para. 2), and 20 years in the case of the audit firm (Regulation Art. 17 Para. 4);
- Exclusion of providing non-audit provided services to audit clients (Regulation Art. 5);
- Composition requirements of the Audit Committee, which now must include at least one member with auditing/accounting competencies, an independent chairman and a majority of independent members (Directive Art. 39);
- Auditors "are required to issue an additional report to the Audit Committee"(Regulation Art. 11).

One final observation regarding the European auditing provisions is the fact that, under the Company Law Directive on statutory audit, the"International Standards on Auditing (ISAs) are applied in the"EU. The Directive states that "audits of annual accounts or consolidated accounts required under Community law shall be carried out in accordance with these standards adopted by the Commission" (EC, 2016). The provisions drafted by the"European Commission, the European Parliament and the European Council"are not standards per-se, but they rely on ISAs; the European auditing regulation is drafted to warrant a consistent and undeviating application of auditing standards, rules and procedures across the EU-28 member states.

AN EXPLANATION OF AUDIT REPORTING THROUGH AUDIT THEORIES

Theories on the mandate for auditing provide a general framework for auditing, or at least for understanding it. In this sense Mautz & Sharaf (1961) define the purpose of theory as: "One reason, then, for a serious and substantial investigation into the opportunity and nature of auditing theory is the hope that it will provide us with solutions or, at least, clues to solutions, of problems which we now find difficult". Based on the current published literature, we consider that auditing can be explained by more than one theory, as such, the aim of this chapter is to expose the most important audit theories that may account for the need for audit services.

A theory is a "set of systematically interrelated concepts, definitions, and propositions that are advanced to explain and predict phenomena" (Cooper & Schindler, 1998) and in this sense, we consider that the premises for an auditing theory are existent. Auditing is used as a means to demonstrate and test accountability in case of the financial statements, and by comparing the statements with a set of predefined reporting framework (IFRS, US GAAP, and others) the auditor generates "economic and social benefits" (Flint, 1988). Auditing is considered as being an activity that has always been present in the economic life:

The origin of auditing goes back to times scarcely less remote than that of accounting... Whenever the advance of civilization brought about the necessity of one man being entrusted to some extent with the property of another the advisability of some kind of check upon the fidelity of the former would become apparent. (Richard Brown (ed), A History of Accounting and Accountants, T.T. and E.C. Jack, 1905, page 75)

With regards to other auditing theories, besides the general theory of auditing, the literature is a fair starting point to determine which audit theories are best suited for our doctoral research. In this sense, we start will a brief synthesis of relevant auditing theories, and then we will explain how each relates, more or less, to the objectives of our research. Figure 1 offers a presentation of auditing theories.

Figure 1. Important audit theories, as present in published literature on audit

Policeman theory

- The auditor focuses on the accuracy of operations and to fraud detection and prevention

Inspired confidence theory

- Audit services are necessary as a consequence of the needs of stakeholders from the entity. The management is accountable to stakeholders, as a return for the stakeholder's involvement in the company.

Lending credibility theory

- This theory suggests that the audit adds credibility to the financial statements.

Agency theory

- The entity is viewed as the result of its relationships with several groups of stakeholders. The auditor is appointed to protect the interests of stakeholders and the management.

Assurance theory

- By providing assurance to the financial statements, the auditors increases the quality of information relevant to the decision-making process.

Stakeholder Theory

- It came up as an argument against the premise that not only investors have interests in the organization, as such, the role of the auditors is to ensure that all who have stake in the business are protected, by acting as watchdogs to the activities of management

Source: Author's projection, according to Limpberg (1932), Jensen & Meckling (1976), (Freeman, 1984), Hayes (1999), Carmichael (2004), Akinbuli (2010)

In relation to the seven postulates Flint (1988) states regarding auditing as a theory, we consider that auditing can be itself a theory because of the following reasons. Given the relationship between auditing and accountability, it is impossible to demonstrate accountability without some form of inquiring, some form of an audit. In this sense, the audit activity requires independence, to set the premises for being able to explain and test accountability. The conclusions of the auditing activity are backed-up by evidence and the auditors rely on their professional judgement, and with regards to what a theory accomplished, auditing provides a solution to an issue: the question of "whether the financial statements are compliant with a set of reporting standards and whether they are free from misstatements and/or fraud. Because of this outcome, we consider that auditing can be the base of a theory of auditing, as it produces an economic and social outcome to interested stakeholders."

The Policeman Theory states that the job of the auditor is to focus on the accuracy of financial statements and fraud detection, thus considering the auditor a "policeman" responsible of detecting fraud. This theory was widely used in the middle of the 20th century (Hayes et al., 1999). According to this theory, the auditor must focus on mathematical procedures that can uncover any errors the financial statements might have. But, given the fact that the auditor cannot verify all operations, as the auditor relies on sampling, this theory is not used anymore. Similarly, the auditor cannot be held responsible for detecting fraud at an absolute assurance, given the fact that the management is responsible for fraud prevention, by setting the correct mechanisms for internal controls in these regards. The auditor applies a level of materiality in the audit mission and if material misstatements or irregularities are found (either errors or fraud), the auditor will report on these matters. As such, it seems like the general premises of this theories have faded in today's environment, and we do not consider that the auditor nowadays solely relies on fraud detection. Of course, the auditor does analyse the compliance of the financial statements and whether they are free from misstatements, however detecting fraud is not the primary objective.

The Agency theory has usually been used in this subject area of auditing (Eilifsen & Messier, 2000; Gerayli et al., 2011, Sharma et al., 2008; Law, 2011; Quick et al., 2013). The agency theory is the most prominent theory on auditing for the reason that it offers an explanation of audit services as the means of communication between companies and the setting in which they activate. The audit process serves as a method of providing confidence in the financial information provided by the management. A central question discussed in the literature, is: "What happens when shareholders feel that the auditors do not accomplish their role?" According to Guénin-Paracini & Gendron (2010), the auditing profession has claimed that the auditor is always regarded as the "scapegoat," given the fact that if their issued opinion proves to be unreal, they can be held liable, despite the fact that their assurance is only reasonable. In this regard, Martin Hagen, the former"president of the"*Institute of Chartered Accountants in England and Wales* (ICAEW)"notes that he "remains adamant that the auditors are not to blame" (Beattie, 2009). To guarantee that the interests of management are aligned with those of shareholders, monitoring mechanisms must be put in place, such as the internal control system, but another important control instrument in this sense is the external auditor (Sharma *et al.*, 2008). In the Agency theory, Jensen & Meckling (1976) state that the company presents a "black box", and describe"an agency relationship as a pact between parts, the principal, and the agent;"one individual has to achieve some facility (in our case auditors) on their behalf (the company), which includes the delegating of some of the decision-making expertise to the agent. The auditor provides assurance services to the business: their management, the Board, the stakeholders. Eisenhardt (1989) notes: "Overall, the domain of agency theory is relationships that mirror the basic agency structure of a principal and an agent who are engaged in the cooperative behavior, but have differing goals and differing attitudes towards risk." The business environment features four conditions, which create the prerequisites of an"independent audit: the conflict of interest; the consequence; the complexity and the remoteness (Campbell, 1984, p.13).

The Inspired Confidence Theory (Limperg, 1932) represents a fundamental theory of the auditor's purpose and stresses that the auditor has a social responsibility. Carmichael (2004), the chief auditor of the Public Company Accounting Oversight Board (PCAOB),"stresses the public liability of the independent auditor by the results of the audit report to meet society's needs. Carmichael's attention focused on the role that the PCAOB has and its performances in reestablishing the trust of stakeholders in the independent auditors report. According to the researcher, the values of Limperg's model are of particular importance in the evolution of the audit function: "We have a particular need in our current environment to try to understand and appreciate the social significance of auditing and the implications for how an audit should be performed" (Carmichael, 2004). Limperg describes the function of the auditor and his responsibility as follows: "The auditor-confidential agent derives his general function in society from the need for expert and independent examination and the need for an expert and independent opinion based on this review. The role is rooted in the confidence that society places in the effectiveness of the audit and in the view of the accountant. This trust is consequently a condition for the existence of that function; if the confidence is betrayed, the function, too, is destroyed, since it becomes useless" (Limperg Institute, 1985).

In our view, the *Key Audit Matters* section will prove useful to users as it will contain pertinent information, useful in the decision-making process and to test management provided information as to being subjective or not. This is consistent with the theory mentioned above, as the KAM section is meant, as IAASB has stated, to assist users even if what it only accomplishes is to highlight matters which the auditor considers to be relevant regarding the financial statements of the entity (Cordoş & Fülöp, 2015). Given the recent reform of the audit reporting process, we consider this theory an important part of our doctoral research, as it explains why the auditor opinion is vital to stakeholders. The theory is also an explanation for stakeholders need of more relevant information from the auditor, therefore the increase of the communicative value of the report.

The Lending Credibility Theory, according to Akinbuli (2010), reflects that the audited financial statements can improve the stakeholders' confidence in the data the management provides. In this sense, the lending credibility theory is similar to the agency theory and recommends that the principal purpose of the auditor is to add trustworthiness to the financial reports of a company. In this view, the service that the auditors are selling to the clients is credibility (Hayes et al. 2005). This is also a central theory in our research, because the accounting profession has been in the blame for the financial scandals, and has tried to rebuild the public trust. Consequently, the Lending Credibility Theory is directly applicable to the audit reporting process, as the auditor now also presents Key Audit Matters of the audit process, in which, using professional judgement, the auditor tests how the company has dealt with matters found relevant in the audit of the company's financial statement; if the company's response to that particular risk has been adequate, the auditor will backup the management's decisions, thus adding credibility, and providing an economic and social outcome.

The Assurance theory, related to the agency theory, states that the auditing professional issues an judgement on the financial statements to ascertain whether the statements can be regarded as reliable or not (Cosserat, 2009). Similar to the agency theory and lending credibility theory, the assurance theory consists of a service provided by a part, towards another part, in our case the assurance services provided by the auditors to the company. Elder et al. (2010) consider that an "assurance service is regarded as an autonomous specialised service that increases the quality of data" that is available stakeholders in the decision-making process.

The Stakeholder Theory can also be considered as a variation of the agency theory. The theory appeared as an argument in contrast to the premises that it is not only shareholders who have interests in an organization, but also other stakeholders as well, and as such, the role of the auditors is to ensure that all who have stake in the business are protected by acting as watchdogs to the activities of management (Freeman, 1984). This theory explains who the stakeholders of the auditor report are, and more on the applicability of this theory will be discussed in the following subchapter.

Given the fact that the audit report has a number of different stakeholders, with diverse backgrounds, we also consider that the differences in their understanding of the audit report conclusion can be explained by the sociology of education theory (Marshall, 1998). In this sense, this theory is relevant to explain how students, used as proxies for stakeholders, have a different understanding of the auditor's responsibility, based on their accounting and auditing educational level – so based on how the institutions (educational) affect their education and the outcomes of their education, with the curricula aligned to international accounting education standards.

In our view, we consider that the best-suited theories to explain the improvements undertaken to "improve the communicative value of the audit report, are the following:" Limperg's Inspired Confidence Theory and the Lending Credibility Theory (or Assurance theory). All these theories explain the reform of improving the stakeholders' confidence in management's provided data, by the auditor's providing more relevant information in the audit report, thus improving its informative values. The stakeholders of the audit report are explained through the stakeholder theory, and the different levels of the stakeholder's education can be explained by the sociology of education.

STAKEHOLDERS OF AUDIT REPORTING

As we have seen in the previous sub-chapters, auditors are assigned by the Audit Committee to provide an opinion on the financial statements, as to whether they provide "a true and fair view of the company's financial position. The report is then submitted to the Audit Committee and the management, so one might assume that the stakeholders of the Audit Report are the Committee and management. However, this is a false assumption, because when we are discussing the audit of a public company, automatically the audit is serving a higher purpose, with a higher audience. The stakeholder theory explains who the stakeholders of a company are, and the fact that all a company must strive to meet the expectations of all interested parties.

The Oxford dictionary defines a *stakeholder* as "a person with an interest or concern in something, especially a business." The OECD considers that good corporate governance ensures that "corporations take into account that interests of a wide range of constituents" (OECD, 2015), not just that the shareholders of the company.

We have started from the presumption that a corporation cannot exist without its stakeholders, as it must "relate to society," thus connect with its stakeholders, provide appropriate information and address the needs of a wider stakeholder audience. Consequently, the audited financial statements and the auditor's report are a part of the company, providing assurance to the issued financial statements. Therefore, they also "connect" with the company's stakeholders, directly, and indirectly, the audit service connects to the society. Auditors, while being a stakeholder in the company, are also providers to the business;

at the same time, auditors are also providers to other stakeholders, so we can conclude that they play multiple parts in the auditing stakeholder theory (see Figure 2).

Consequently, the stakeholders of a company are also the stakeholders of the audited financial statements. Sachs, Rühli, & Kern (2009) provide a list of company stakeholders, based on their association to different systems: the company, the economic system, and the societal system. The researchers consider that by mapping stakeholders based on their association with these systems can help the company identify their strategically relevant stakeholders.

The Agency Theory explains the aim of auditing services in communicating between entities and their environment, between the companies and their stakeholders. In this case, the audit mission serves a fundamental purpose in endorsing assurance in the provided financial information. However, imagine that the outcome of the audit mission is the auditor's report, a document with several pages (usually one page, when previous standards were in use) in which the auditor issues an opinion, and, more recently, provides information regarding key audit matters. This document has to be sufficient for a number of different stakeholders, with different professional backgrounds, different accounting and auditing education levels and different interests. Consequently, meeting stakeholder expectations is quite difficult, especially because of the diversity within the stakeholder groups. The communicative value of the audit report has significantly improved in recent years, but users of the audit report consider that more enhancements need to be made.

Figure 2. Stakeholders of a company

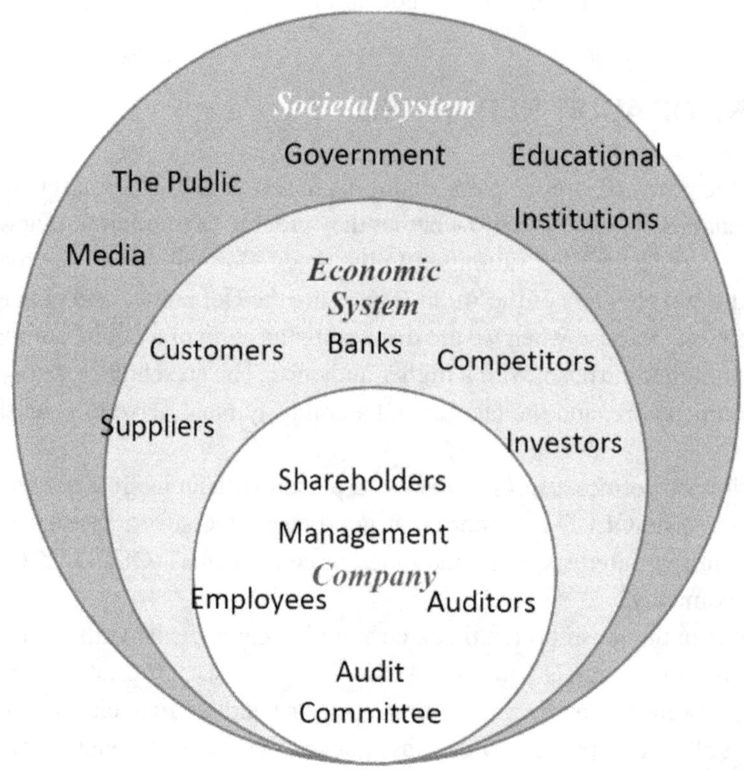

Source: Author's projection of Sachs, Rühli and Kern (2009)

The majority of investors are looking for better reporting quality because the company's reporting quality has a direct impact on their investment decisions (PwC, 2014). There is also a debate on the likelihood of audit reports carrying additional value if they offered more information that users of the report find necessary and relevant (ACCA, 2010). Moreover, Deloitte (2015) confirms that investors, audit committee members and financial statement preparers would like auditors to focus not only on the financial statements but on other details as well. However, auditing standards clearly state the auditor's responsibility in an audit mission, consequently, in order to meet the expectations of one stakeholder, another's interests are put aside, in this case, the auditor's interests.

An additional issue is the level of accounting education of stakeholders. The public's confidence in the audit and accounting profession was shattered after the financial scandals, and interested parties demanded that auditors and accounting professionals should take responsibility for their involvement. Within the auditing profession, the concept of the audit expectation gap has been discussed on numerous occasions; the audit expectation gap is the difference between what auditors consider their responsibility to be, and what the actual responsibility of the auditors is, as set by regulations and auditing standards. The public also demands more facts, relevant information, to be disclosed within the auditor's report. However, certain stakeholders might not know the difference between reasonable and absolute assurance. Moreover, the same public might not have sufficient knowledge to understand the meaning of what is being disclosed; thus, by disclosing more, the expectation gap only deepens.

CONCLUSION

In this chapter we the purpose to setting the framework of audit reporting, as part of the larger sphere of corporate reporting. Taking into consideration the insights provided by academic research and professional organisations, we accomplished to highlight the international and European perspectives on financial statements audit, but also the most important auditing theories that explain the objectives. Last but not least, we have underlined the stakeholders of the audit reporting process, and how their different perspectives have an influence on their understanding of the audit mission. Therefore, we propose to end this chapter with an open question: is it possible for an audit report to suit the needs and be considered useful for, and agreed upon by all interested parties?

REFERENCES

AAA. (1973). *A Statement of Basic Auditing Concepts*. Retrieved from https://www.worldcat.org/title/statement-of-basic-auditing-concepts/oclc/701015

ACCA. (2010). *Accountancy Futures: Reshaping the audit for the new global economy*. Retrieved from http://www2.accaglobal.com/pdfs/international/singapore/RA.pdf

ACCA, MARC. (2011). *A framework for Extended Audit Reporting, Final report, commissioned by ACCA and executed by MARC members*. Author.

Akinbuli, S. F. (2010). The effect of audit expectation gap on the work of auditors, the profession and users of financial information. *Niger Accountant*, *43*(4), 37–47.

Beattie, E. (2009). Don't blame the accountants. *Accountancy, 143*(1390), 38–39.

Berle, A., & Means, G. (1932). *The Modern Corporation and Private Property*. Transaction Publishers.

Berman, H. J. (1983). Law and Revolution: Vol. 1. *The Formation of the Western Legal Tradition*. Cambridge, MA: Harvard University Press.

Brown, R. (2009). Revisiting the expectations gaps after 15 years. *Journal of Applied Accounting Research, 10*(2), 92–95. doi:10.1108/09675420910984655

Campbell, L. G. (1984). *International Auditing: A Comparative Study of Professional Requirements in Australia*. Springer.

Carmichael, D. R. (2004). The PCAOB and the social responsibility of the auditor. *Accounting Horizons, 18*(2), 127–133. doi:10.2308/acch.2004.18.2.127

Carmichael, F. (2014). Reflections on the Establishment of the PCAOB and Its Audit Standards-Setting Role. *Accounting Horizons, 28*(4), 901–915. doi:10.2308/acch-50851

Church, B. K., Davis, S. M., & McCracken, S. A. (2008). The Auditor's Reporting Model: A Literature Overview and Research Synthesis. *Accounting Horizons, 22*(1), 69–90. doi:10.2308/acch.2008.22.1.69

Cooper, F., & Schindler, I. (1998). *Business Research Methods*. Irwin/McGraw-Hill.

Cordoş, G. S., & Fülöp, M. T. (2015). Understanding audit reporting changes: Introduction of Key Audit Matters. *Journal of Accounting and Management Information Systems, 14*(1), 128–152.

Cosserat, G. W., & Rodda, N. (2009). *Modern auditing* (3rd ed.). John Wiley & Sons Ltd.

Cullinan, C. P., Earley, C. E., & Roush, P. B. (2013). Multiple auditing standards and standard setting: Implications for practice and education. *Current Issues in Auditing, 7*(1), C1–C10. doi:10.2308/ciia-50344

Deloitte. (2015). *Audit of the Future*. Retrieved from https://www2.deloitte.com/us/en.html

DirectiveE. U. 2014/56/EU. (n.d.). Retrieved from https://publications.europa.eu/en/publication-detail/-/publication/39de2648-e657-11e3-8cd4-01aa75ed71a1/language-en

Eilifsen, A., Messier, W. F., Glover, S. M., & Prawitt, D. W. (2010). Auditing and assurance services (2nd ed.). McGraw-Hill Education.

Elder, R. J., Beasley, M. S., & Arens, A. A. (2010). *Auditing and assurance services: an integrated approach: global edition* (13th ed.). Englewood Cliffs, N.J.: Prentice-Hall.

Flint, D. (1988). *Philosophy and principles of auditing: an introduction*. Basingstoke, UK: Macmillan Education.

Freeman, R. E. (1984). *Strategic Management: A stakeholder approach*. Boston: Pitman.

Gerayli, M. S., Yanesari, A. M., & Ma'atoofi, A. R. (2011). Impact of Audit Quality on Earnings Management: Evidence from Iran. *International Research Journal of Finance and Economics, 66*, 77–84.

Guénin-Paracini, H., & Gendron, Y. (2010). Auditors as modern pharmakoi: Legitimacy paradoxes and the production of economic order. *Critical Perspectives on Accounting, 21*(2), 134–158. doi:10.1016/j.cpa.2009.11.003

Hayes, R., Schilder, A., Dassen, R., & Wallage, P. (1999). *Principles of Auditing: An International Perspective*. London: McGraw Hill.

IFAC. (2012). *IFAC Member Body Compliance Program*. Retrieved from http://www.ifac.org/publications-resources/2012-ifac-annual-report

International Auditing and Assurance Standards Board (IAASB). (2012). *Improving the Auditor's Report. Invitation to Comment*. Retrieved from http://www.ifac.org/publications-resources/2012-ifac-annual-report

International Auditing and Assurance Standards Board (IAASB). (2013). *Reporting on Audited Financial Statements: Proposed New and Revised International Standards on Auditing*. Retrieved from http://goo.gl/mVRmNB

Law, P. (2011). Audit regulatory reform with a refined stakeholder model to enhance corporate governance: Hong Kong evidence. *Corporate Governance, 11*(2), 123–135. doi:10.1108/14720701111121001

Limperg Institute. (1985). *The social responsibility of the auditor. A basic theory on the auditor's function*. Retrieved from http://goo.gl/5ILFWH

Lo, A., Wong, R., & Firth, M. (2010). Can corporate governance deter management from manipulating earnings? Evidence from related-party sales transactions in China. *Journal of Corporate Finance, 16*(2), 225–235. doi:10.1016/j.jcorpfin.2009.11.002

Lobo, G. J., & Whalen, D. J. (2007). Does good corporate governance reduce information asymmetry around quarterly earnings announcements? *Journal of Accounting and Public Policy, 26*(4), 497–522. doi:10.1016/j.jaccpubpol.2007.05.003

Mallin, C. (2006). *Handbook on International Corporate Governance Country Analyses*. Edward Elgar.

Marshall, G. (1998). *A dictionary of sociology*. Oxford University Press.

Mautz, R. K., & Sharaf, H. A. (1961). *The Philosophy of Auditing*. Sarasota, FL: American Accounting Association.

OECD. (2015). *Corporate Governance Principles*. Retrieved from http://www.oecd.org/corporate/principles-corporate-governance.htm

PCAOB (2016). The Auditor's Report on an Audit of Financial Statements When the Auditor Expresses an Unqualified Opinion ("reproposed standard" or "reproposal"); IESBA. *Code of Ethics for Professional Accountants*.

Percy, J. P. (1997). Auditing and corporate governance: A look forward into the 21st century. *International Journal of Auditing*, *1*(1), 3–12.

Public Company Accounting Oversight Board. (2011). *Improving the Transparency of Audits: Proposed Amendments to PCAOB Auditing Standards and Form 2*. Retrieved from http://goo.gl/j4Obtu

PwC. (2014). *Corporate performance – What do investors what to know?* Retrieved from https://www.pwc.fr/fr/publications/communication-financiere/corporate-performance-what-do-investors-want-to-know.html

Quick, R., Sattler, M., & Wiemann, D. (2013). Agency conflicts and the demand for non-audit services. *Managerial Auditing Journal*, *28*(4), 323–344. doi:10.1108/02686901311311927

Regulation No, E. U. 537/2014. (n.d.). Retrieved from https://publications.europa.eu/en/publication-detail/-/publication/567809be-e656-11e3-8cd4-01aa75ed71a1/language-en

Sachs, S., Rühli, E., & Kern, I. (2009). *Sustainable Success with Stakeholders – The Untapped Potential*. London: Palgrave. doi:10.1057/9780230271746

Sharma, D. S., Boo, E., & Sharma, V. D. (2008). The impact of non-mandatory corporate governance on auditors' client acceptance, risk and planning judgements. *Accounting and Business Research*, *38*(2), 105–120. doi:10.1080/00014788.2008.9663324

Smith, A. (1776). *An Inquiry into the Nature and Causes of the Wealth of Nations*.

The IAASB, International Standards of Auditing. (n.d.). Retrieved from http://goo.gl/3q9TjO

ADDITIONAL READING

Cordoş, G. S., & Fülöp, M. T. (2013). Consideraţii privind preferinţa entităţilor cotate la bursa de valori pentru a fi auditate de companii mari de audit. *Audit Financiar*, *106*(10), 17–23.

Cordoş, G. S., & Fülöp, M. T. (2013). Analiza relaţiei auditor – client şi efectul asupra independenţei auditorului. *Audit Financiar*, *105*(9), 3–11.

Cordoş, G. S., & Fülöp, M. T. (2015). New audit reporting challenges: Auditing the going concern basis of accounting. *Procedia Economics and Finance Emerging Markets Queries in Finance and Business*, *2*, 216–224.

Cordoş, G. S., & Fülöp, M. T. (2015). Understanding audit reporting changes: Introduction of Key Audit Matters. *Journal of Accounting and Management Information Systems*, *14*(1), 128–152.

KEY TERMS AND DEFINITIONS

Corporate Governance: The processes by which companies are directed and controlled. Levels of disclosure differ worldwide but might include information on board composition and development, accountability and audit and relations with shareholders.

Corporate Reporting: Is the concept that connects the company to its stakeholders. Audit reporting is part of corporate reporting, along with financial reporting, corporate governance, corporate responsibility, integrated reporting, and others.

Financial Reporting: At the core of the corporate reporting model is the financial reporting model, consisting of financial statements and accompanying notes that comply with generally accepted accounting principles (GAAP).

Financial Statement Audit: Is the examination of an entity's financial statements and accompanying disclosures by an independent auditor.

Financial Statements: Are written records that convey the business activities and the financial performance of a company.

Key Audit Matters (KAM): Those matters that, in the auditor's professional judgment, were of most significance in the audit of the financial statements of the current period. Key audit matters are selected from matters communicated with those charged with governance.

Chapter 15
Implementation of Time-Driven Activity-Based Costing System in the Manufacturing Industry:
Evidence From Turkey

Ahmet Özcan
Adana Alparslan Türkeş Science and Technology University, Turkey

ABSTRACT

In the current business environment, the costing system used within the firms has prominent impact on strategic decisions. High-quality cost data significantly increases the quality of firms' strategic decisions. The activity-based costing system has failed to satisfy the needs of firms operating in the competitive economic environment. The time-driven activity-based costing system is the developed version of activity-based costing system. Time-driven activity-based costing system is one of the most sophisticated costing systems that enable firms to accurately calculate the cost of goods and services. Time-equations are used in time-driven activity-based costing system to estimate the time consumed by each activity. This chapter aims to discuss main dynamics of time-driven activity-based costing system and provides an illustration of this costing system in the manufacturing industry. The case study demonstrates that time-driven activity-based costing system is useful in calculating idle capacity cost.

INTRODUCTION

Firms are required to adopt an effective costing system so as to gain competitive advantage. In today's business world, there is a huge need for accurate cost data. Cost knowledge plays a key role in the relationship among suppliers, manufacturers and customers. Firms increasingly need a costing system that excels in identifying, classifying, allocating and analysing costs. Without detail analysing of actual costs of goods and services, the quality of strategic decisions made by the firm management significantly decreases (Dejnega, 2011).

DOI: 10.4018/978-1-7998-0178-8.ch015

The selection of appropriate costing system has always been a significant challenge for the management of firms. The management of firms should analyse the strengths and weaknesses of available costing systems. It is worth mentioning that the costing system implemented by the firms should integrate into firms' objectives.

Before 1980, costing systems used by firms adopted a different approach. Those systems did not sufficiently support decision making process, management, planning and defining objectives (Johnson and Kaplan, 1987). As the business world is becoming much more globalized than before, traditional costing systems have failed to deal with the changing needs of firms. Traditional costing systems have become obsolete in the manufacturing industry (Öker & Özyapıcı, 2013). Traditional costing systems were criticized for misallocating overhead costs. Consequently, the cost of goods and services is inaccurately calculated under traditional costing systems.

In the beginning of 1980s, activity based costing system has been developed to solve these problems. However, the implementation of activity based costing system has become impractical for many firms in the late years. Kaplan, the founder of activity based costing system, agreed with the opinion that the implementation of activity based costing system is difficult for firms to maintain.

Time-driven activity based costing system has emerged to resolve drawbacks of activity based costing system. Time-driven activity based costing system developed by Kaplan and Anderson (2004) aims to simplify the calculation of costs and avoid time-consuming and expensive implementation processes. Time-driven activity based costing system is a simplified version of activity based costing system. Kaplan and Anderson (2007) state that time-driven activity based costing system provides prominent competitive advantages to firms operating in the competitive economic environment.

This book chapter is structured as follows. First section presents primary features of time-driven activity based costing system. Second section discusses the advantages of time-driven activity based costing system. Third section compares the results of time-driven activity based costing system with activity based costing system. Fourth section presents literature review. Fifth section provides the implementation of time-driven activity based costing system in the manufacturing firm. Last section concludes the chapter and provides suggestions for future studies.

FEATURES OF TIME-DRIVEN ACTIVITY BASED COSTING SYSTEM

In this section, the main features of time-driven activity based costing System are discussed. Along with the development of technology, the nature and dynamics of costing systems have changed. In today's business environment, the cost structure is highly complex. Traditional costing systems are ineffective in dealing with complex cost structure. This can lead to ineffective decision making process.

Previous studies demonstrated that time-driven activity based costing system is fit for ever-changing market conditions. In today's business climate, firms' management wants to employ a costing system that can produce accurate results for complex operations. An advanced software can make it possible.

Kaplan and Anderson (2007) state that time-driven activity based costing system is simple and one of the effective ways to get detailed information about costs incurred in production process. In the firms using time-driven activity based costing system, the consumption time of activity plays a vital role in the costing of goods and services. Inaccurate estimation of activity time could cause misleading results. Time-driven activity based costing system employs time equations for assigning the resource costs (Kaplan & Anderson, 2007).

The implementation of time-driven activity based costing system is simpler and cheaper than other costing systems. Moreover, time-driven activity based costing system can be effectively integrated into the firms' operations. Everaert et al. (2012) stated that many firms regardless of complexity of operations, product segments and channels can apply time-driven activity based costing system. Time-driven activity based costing system has two important parameters; the unit cost of resource used and time consumed to complete an activity (Monroy et al., 2014).

ADVANTAGES OF USING TIME-DRIVEN ACTIVITY BASED COSTING SYSTEM

There are some important benefits of using time-driven activity based costing system. Kaplan and Anderson (2007) listed these benefits below.

- It enhances the quality of cost data.
- It provides detailed information that enables firm management to identify the root causes of problems.
- It is inexpensive to maintain and update if needed.
- It enables firm management to effectively manage capacity and analyse capacity utilization. Therefore, firms can establish an effective capacity planning through time-driven activity based costing.
- Firms operating in any industry can employ time-driven activity based costing system.
- It enables firms to have enhanced control over costs.
- The measurements of time-driven activity based costing system are taken by employee surveys, interviews, direct observations and information collected from business process management. In the activity based costing system, employee surveys and interviews take too much time. The cost and time spent in conducting survey and interviews discourage firms from adopting activity based costing system.
- It enables firms to accurately forecast resource demands for future periods.
- With the help of time- equations created in time-driven activity based costing system, firms can determine which operational activities demand more time.
- Operational efficiency can be improved by reducing resource waste.

THE COMPARISON OF ACTIVITY BASED COSTING SYSTEM AND TIME-DRIVEN ACTIVITY BASED COSTING SYSTEM

This section of the book chapter aims to compare general characteristics of activity based costing system and time-driven activity based costing system. Figure 1 presents an activity based costing system. Four different resource costs are identified in the activity based costing model. These four resource costs are linked to four activity pools. In the Activity Based Costing model, firms firstly allocate resource costs to the four activity pool and then activities' costs are allocated to products. A single cost driver rate is used for each activity in activity based costing system.

Activity based costing system needs too much data (Balakrishnan et al., 2012). A large number of cost drivers is used in activity based costing system. In the activity based costing system, employees'

Figure 1. Activity based costing system

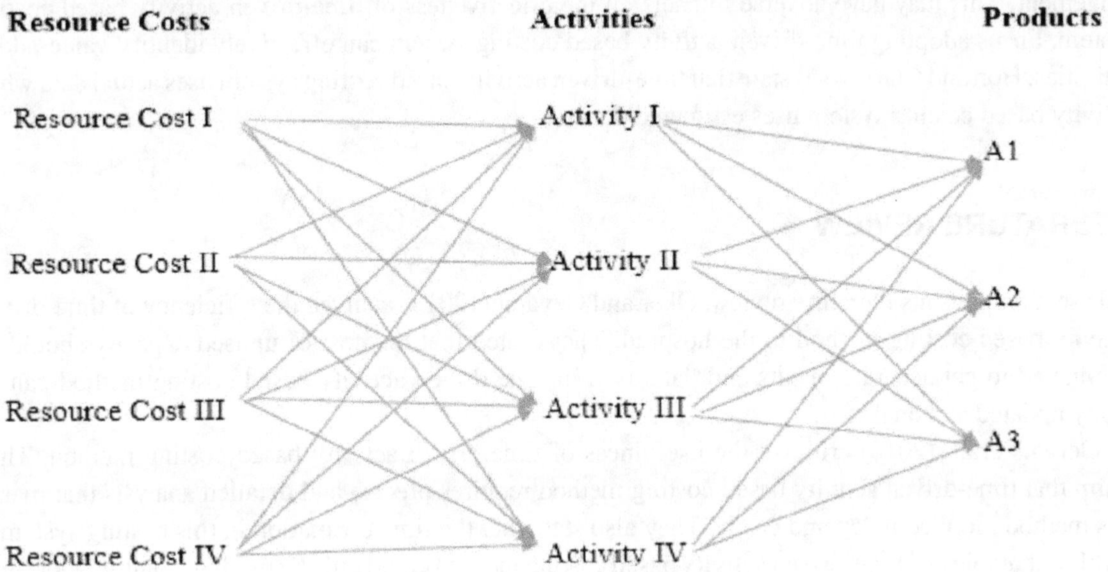

surveys and interviews are so expensive and time- consuming (Stout & Propri, 2011; Demeere et al., 2009; Kaplan & Anderson; 2007).

Figure 2 presents time-driven activity based costing system. Time-driven activity based costing system appears to be as activity based costing system. Both systems have same cost pools, activities and cost objects. In time-driven activity based costing system, resource costs are directly linked with cost objects via resource activity cost drivers (Kaplan & Anderson, 2007). There is an independent link between resource cost and cost object.

Figure 2. Time-Driven activity based costing system

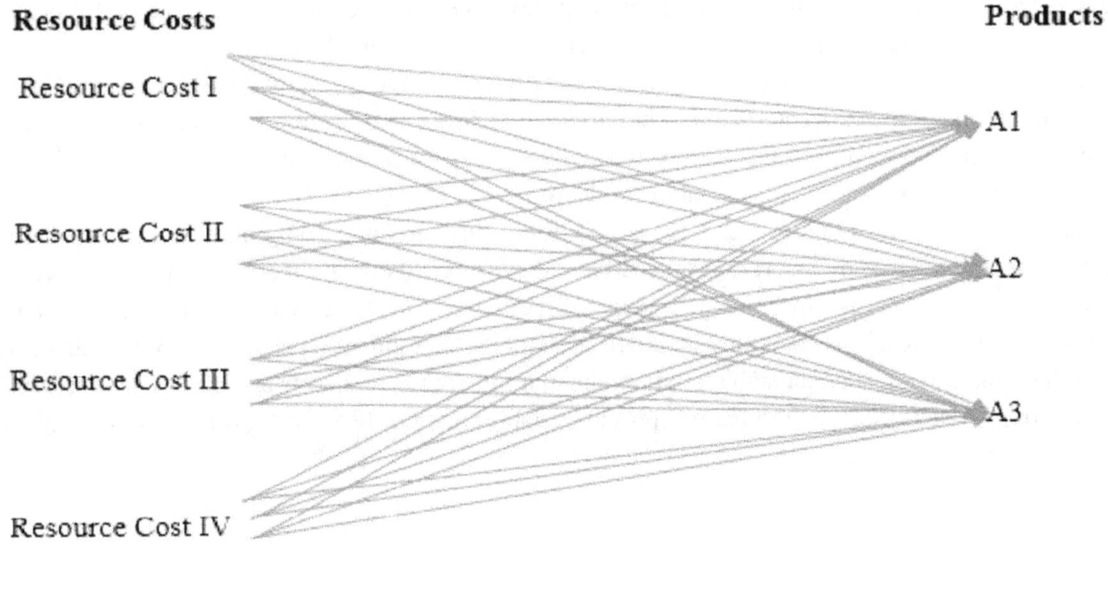

In time-driven activity based costing system, time-estimation is based on employees' subjective judgement. This may have adverse impacts on the effectiveness of time-driven activity based costing system. Firms adopting time-driven activity based costing system can effectively identify value-added activities. Hon and Chu (2015) state that time-driven activity based costing system uses actual data while activity based costing system uses estimated data.

LITERATURE REVIEW

This section presents literature review. Öker and Özyapıcı (2013) analyze the efficiency of time-driven activity based costing method in the hospital. They stated that the cost of unused capacity should be eliminated to get accurate results and data used in time-driven activity based costing method can be easily updated and analyzed.

Gervais et al. (2010) criticize the usefulness of time-driven activity based costing method. They claim that time-driven activity based costing method requires precise and detailed analysis that makes this method more complex and costly. They also state that the time estimation in this costing system is highly debatable and time-driven activity based costing method could only be used to monitor labor time.

Yun et al. (2016) use time-driven activity based costing method in emergency department. They state that time-driven activity based costing method should be used to improve processes in emergency department and hospital leadership should provide strong support for the implementation of time-driven activity based costing method.

Everaert et al. (2008) apply time-driven activity based costing method to a firm operating in logistic industry. They found that time-driven activity based costing system has significant positive impacts on profit management and reporting and the level of acceptance of the model can soar with accurate time equations.

Öker and Adıgüzel (2010) apply time-driven activity based costing method to a manufacturing firm and state that capacity utilization analysis through time-driven activity based costing method enables firms to compute excess capacity. They support the assertion that it is much easier for service firms to apply time-driven activity based costing method than for manufacturing firms. Tse and Gong (2009) state that service firms that have information technology resources and standardized operational processes can get prominent benefits from time-driven activity based costing method.

Meriç and Gersil (2018) analyze the effectiveness of time-driven activity based costing method in the small and medium sized enterprises. They found that firms using time-driven activity based costing method can accurately set sales targets and selling prices for products and determine the optimum number of production that maximizes labor productivity.

Barros and Costa (2017) investigate the suitability of time-driven activity based costing method in a manufacturing firm. They assert that time-driven activity based costing method is more complex for manufacturing firms. When machinery time and direct labor time are consumed by some production processes, two different time equations should be built for these production processes. Souza et al. (2010) found that time equations under stable production environment are relatively accurate. Therefore, time-driven activity based costing method cannot provide reliable output in the volatile production environment.

THE CASE STUDY

A case study is presented in this section. Case study research enables us to explore and deeply understand the complex issues (Zainal, 2007). The case study is conducted on a firm called Mediterranean Corporation that has operated for over 50 years. Mediterranean Corporation is selected for the case study since this corporation is one of the first corporation that have used Time-driven activity based costing system.

Mediterranean Corporation is one of the export-oriented corporations in Turkey. Mediterranean Corporation manufactures three different products: A1, A2 and A3. The data used in the case study is collected from employee surveys, interviews and accounting information systems.

As stated before, time-driven activity based costing system directly allocates resource costs to cost objects. Table 1 indicates information on resource costs. Four resource costs, depreciation, energy, maintenance and repairs and supervision are identified in the cost model. It is worth mentioning that resource costs should be meticulously determined by firms. As can be seen from table 1, depreciation is the highest resource cost and supervision is the lowest resource cost.

There are four different resource drivers; square meter, kilowatt, maintenance and repair hours and the number of supervision hours. Resource drivers' quantities for each activity are presented in Table 2. Activities were determined through production process analysis. These activities are presented in Table 2. These activities consist of machine setup, assembly, painting and quality control.

In table 3, activity drivers are identified for the allocation of costs collected in the activity pools to the products. Table 3 also shows the activity drivers and the use of product groups for each activity. For example, unit of production is the activity driver for assembly and painting.

Table 4 presents resource costs per hour. Resource cost per hour is calculated by dividing resource costs by capacity per year. The capacity of each resources is determined through observations, interviews, system database and accounting information systems.

Table 5 reveals the data on time spent for each activity. The total time for each activity was determined by multiplying the time per unit of activity by the number of units. As can be seen from table,

Table 1. Resource costs and drivers

Resource	Costs	Resource Driver
Depreciation	$561,000	Square meter
Energy	$360,000	Kilowatt
Maintenance and Repairs	$142,000	Maintenance and repair hours
Supervision	$80,000	Number of supervision hours

Table 2. Quantities of resource drivers

Resource Driver	Machine Setup	Assembly	Painting	Quality Control
Square meter	1,000	2,000	3,000	2,000
Kilowatt	20,000	40,000	20,000	10,000
Maintenance and repair hours	150	250	200	150
Number of supervision hours	100	250	200	250

Table 3. Activity drivers

Activity	Activity Driver	A1	A2	A3
Machine Setup	Setups	1000	2000	2000
Assembly	Unit of production	1000	2500	2500
Painting	Unit of production	1000	2500	2500
Quality Control	Inspection	100	200	300

Table 4. Resource costs per hour

Resource	Capacity per year (hours)	Cost Per Hour
Depreciation	93,500	$6.00
Energy	90,000	$4.00
Maintenance and Repairs	94,667	$1.50
Supervision	96,385	$0.83

Table 5. Duration of activities

Activity	Product Line	Time per Unit (hours)	Number of Units	Total Time (hours)
Machine Setup	A1	1.5	1,000	1,500
	A2	2	2,000	4,000
	A3	3	2,000	6,000
Assembly	A1	5	1,000	5,000
	A2	10	2,500	25,000
	A3	10	2,500	25,000
Painting	A1	3	1,000	3,000
	A2	4	2,500	10,000
	A3	4	2,500	10,000
Quality Control	A1	0.5	100	50
	A2	1	200	200
	A3	2	300	600
Total				90,350

the amount of time spent to produce a unit in each product is different. Time per unit of activity was determined through time studies obtained during visits to the firm in September 2018. Table 5 indicates that assembly activity consumes much more time than other activities and quality control activity takes the shortest time.

Table 6-9 shows the allocation of resource costs (depreciation, energy, maintenance and repairs, supervision) to the product lines. The difference between the total resource cost and the committed resource cost is the cost of idle capacity.

Table 6. Allocation of depreciation costs to products

Product	Activity	Activity Drivers	Unit of Activity	Allocated Cost
A1	Machine Setup	$9.00 ($6.00*1.5)	1000	$9.000
A1	Assembly	$30.00 ($6.00*5)	1000	$30.000
A1	Painting	$18.00 ($6.00*3)	1000	$18.000
A1	Quality Control	$3.00 ($6.00*0.5)	100	$300
A2	Machine Setup	$12.00 ($6.00*2)	2000	$24.000
A2	Assembly	$60.00 ($6.00*10)	2500	$150.000
A2	Painting	$24.00 ($6.00*4)	2500	$60.000
A2	Quality Control	$6.00 ($6.00*1)	200	$1.200
A3	Machine Setup	$18.00 ($6.00*3)	2000	$36.000
A3	Assembly	$60.00 ($6.00*10)	2500	$150.000
A3	Painting	$24.00 ($6.00*4)	2500	$60.000
A3	Quality Control	$12.00 ($6.00*2)	300	$3.600
Total Cost				$542.100

Table 7. Allocation of energy costs to products

Product	Activity	Activity Drivers	Unit of Activity	Allocated Cost
A1	Machine Setup	$6.00 ($4.00*1.5)	1000	$6.000
A1	Assembly	$20.00 ($4.00*5)	1000	$20.000
A1	Painting	$12.00 ($4.00*3)	1000	$12.000
A1	Quality Control	$2.00 ($4.00*0.5)	100	$200
A2	Machine Setup	$8.00 ($4.00*2)	2000	$1.600
A2	Assembly	$40.00 ($4.00*10)	2500	$100.000
A2	Painting	$16.00 ($4.00*4)	2500	$40.000
A2	Quality Control	$4.00 ($4.00*1)	200	$800
A3	Machine Setup	$12.00 ($4.00*3)	2000	$24.000
A3	Assembly	$40.00 ($4.00*10)	2500	$100.000
A3	Painting	$16.00 ($4.00*4)	2500	$40.000
A3	Quality Control	$8.00 ($4.00*2)	300	$2.400
Total Cost				$347.000

Table 10 shows product costs under time-driven activity based costing system. The distribution of total costs to product line is computed as $1.101.659. It is revealed that product A3 consumes the majority of resources. The cost of product A1 is roughly 11% of total cost under time-driven activity based costing system.

Table 8. Allocation of maintenance and repairs costs to products

Product	Activity	Activity Drivers	Unit of Activity	Allocated Cost
A1	Machine Setup	$2.25 ($1.50*1.5)	1000	$2.250
A1	Assembly	$7.50 ($1.50*5)	1000	$7.500
A1	Painting	$4.50 ($1.50*3)	1000	$4.500
A1	Quality Control	$0.75 ($1.50*0.5)	100	$750
A2	Machine Setup	$3.00 ($1.50*2)	2000	$6.000
A2	Assembly	$15.00 ($1.50*10)	2500	$37.500
A2	Painting	$6.00 ($1.50*4)	2500	$15.000
A2	Quality Control	$1.5 ($1.50*1)	200	$300
A3	Machine Setup	$4.50 ($1.50*3)	2000	$10.000
A3	Assembly	$15.00 ($1.50*10)	2500	$37.500
A3	Painting	$6.00 ($1.50*4)	2500	$15.000
A3	Quality Control	$3.00 ($1.50*2)	300	$900
Total Cost				$137.200

Table 9. Allocation of supervision costs to products

Product	Activity	Activity Drivers	Unit of Activity	Allocated Cost
A1	Machine Setup	$1.24 ($0.83*1.5)	1000	$1.240
A1	Assembly	$4.15 ($0.83*5)	1000	$4.150
A1	Painting	$2.49 ($0.83*3)	1000	$2.490
A1	Quality Control	$4.15 ($0.83*0.5)	100	$415
A2	Machine Setup	$1.66 ($0.83*2)	2000	$3.320
A2	Assembly	$8.3 ($0.83*10)	2500	$20.750
A2	Painting	$3.32 ($0.83*4)	2500	$8.300
A2	Quality Control	$0.83 ($0.83*1)	200	$166
A3	Machine Setup	$2.49 ($0.83*3)	2000	$4.980
A3	Assembly	$8.30 ($0.83*10)	2500	$20.750
A3	Painting	$3.32 ($0.83*4)	2500	$8.300
A3	Quality Control	$1.66 ($0.83*2)	300	$498
Total Cost				$75.359

Table 11 reveals that resource costs incurred in time-driven activity based costing system are not fully allocated to product lines. Time-driven activity based costing system enables us to analyse idle capacity. This is the most distinctive and superior property of time-driven activity based costing system. The gap of $41.341 is the idle capacity amounting 3.61%. This firm should improve assembly activity that takes the longest time in order to mitigate idle capacity cost. Generally speaking, firms should try to reduce idle capacity cost in order to become more competitive in the business environment.

Table 10. Total costs calculated for products

Activities	A1	A2	A3
Machine Setup	$18.490	$34.920	$74.980
Assembly	$61.650	$308.250	$308.250
Painting	$36.990	$123.300	$123.300
Quality Control	$1.665	$2.466	$7.398
Total Cost	$118.795	$468.936	$513.928

Table 11. Calculation of idle resource

Resource	Estimated Cost	Allocated Cost	Idle Resource
Depreciation	$561.000	$542.100	$18.900
Energy	$360.000	$347.000	$13.000
Maintenance and Repairs	$142.000	$137.200	$4.800
Supervision	$80.000	$75.359	$4.641
Total	$1.143.000	$1.101.659	$41.341

CONCLUDING REMARKS

Cost data plays a vital role in firms' strategic decisions. Firms need high-quality cost data in order to boost the quality of strategic decisions. Activity based costing system was one of the contemporary methods used in the calculation of product costs. However in the later years, activity based costing system has failed to integrate into the organizational information systems. Additionally, it is highly costly to update activity based costing system according to changing needs of firms. Time-driven activity based costing has emerged to eliminate these weaknesses.

In today's competitive business environment, time-driven activity based costing system has been widely employed by firms to enhance operational efficiency and helps the management of firms make more rational and accurate decisions about pricing, the allocation of resources and pricing. Time-driven activity based costing enables the management of firms to focus more on profitable customers.

A case study is selected as a research method. This method is selected as it analyses the usefulness of time-driven activity based costing system from different perspectives. Case study presented by this study reveals that time-driven activity based costing system provides detailed information about idle capacity. Therefore, the management of firms can accurately calculate the cost of idle capacity. Firms using time-driven activity based costing system eliminate unused capacity to enhance their productivity. Time-driven activity based costing system enables the management of firms to use cost information quickly and efficiently.

It is worth mentioning that implementation of time-driven activity based costing method takes too much time to collect the costs of capacity and resources used. Additionally, time-driven activity based costing method may fail to provide reliable cost data in the unstable production environment. Taken together, firms should select appropriate costing method that fits firms' operational processes.

REFERENCES

Balakrishnan, R., Labro, E., & Sivaramakrishnan, K. (2011). Product costs as decision aids: An analysis of alternative approaches (Part 1). *Accounting Horizons*, *26*(1), 1–20. doi:10.2308/acch-50086

Barros, R. S., & Ferreira, A. M. D. S. D. C. (2017). Time-driven activity-based costing: Designing a model in a Portuguese production environment. *Qualitative Research in Accounting & Management*, *14*(1), 2–20. doi:10.1108/QRAM-10-2015-0095

Dejnega, O. (2011). Method time driven activity-based costing. *Journal of Applied Economic Sciences*, *6*(15), 7–15.

Demeere, N., Stouthuysen, K., & Roodhooft, F. (2009). Time-driven activity-based costing in an outpatient clinic environment: Development, relevance and managerial impact. *Health Policy (Amsterdam)*, *92*(2-3), 296–304. doi:10.1016/j.healthpol.2009.05.003 PMID:19505741

Everaert, P., Bruggeman, W., Sarens, G., Anderson, S. R., & Levant, Y. (2008). Cost modeling in logistics using time-driven ABC: Experiences from a wholesaler. *International Journal of Physical Distribution & Logistics Management*, *38*(3), 172–191. doi:10.1108/09600030810866977

Everaert, P., Cleuren, G., & Hoozée, S. (2012). Using time-driven ABC to identify operational improvements: A case study in a university restaurant. *Cost and Management*, *26*(2), 41–48.

Gervais, M., Levant, Y., & Ducrocq, C. (2010). Time-driven activity-based costing (TDABC): An initial appraisal through a longitudinal case study. *Journal of Applied Management Accounting Research*, *8*(2), 1–20.

Hon, J. S., & Chu, S. J. (2015). Mechanics and application of time-driven activity-based costing system: A case study of Taiwan aerospace factory. *Int. J. Mech. Eng. Autom*, *2*(2), 69–78.

Kaplan, R. S., & Anderson, S. R. (2004). Time-driven activity-based costing. *Harvard Business Review*, *82*(11), 131–138. PMID:15559451

Kaplan, R. S., & Anderson, S. R. (2007). The innovation of time-driven activity-based costing. *Journal of Cost Management*, *21*(2), 5–15.

Kaplan, R. S., & Johnson, H. T. (1987). *Relevance lost: the rise and fall of management accounting*. Boston: Harvard Business School.

Meric, E., & Gersil, M. (2018). Usability of time driven activity-based costing methods in the budgeting process of SMEs. *Business and Economics Research Journal*, *9*(4), 961–978. doi:10.20409/berj.2018.134

Monroy, C. R., Nasiri, A., & Peláez, M. Á. (2014). Activity based costing, time-driven activity based costing and lean accounting: Differences among three accounting systems' approach to manufacturing. In *Annals of Industrial Engineering 2012* (pp. 11–17). London: Springer. doi:10.1007/978-1-4471-5349-8_2

Öker, F., & Adigüzel, H. (2010). Time-driven activity-based costing: An implementation in a manufacturing company. *Journal of Corporate Accounting & Finance*, *22*(1), 75–92. doi:10.1002/jcaf.20646

Öker, F., & Özyapici, H. (2013). A new costing model in hospital management: Time-driven activity-based costing system. *The Health Care Manager*, *32*(1), 23–36. doi:10.1097/HCM.0b013e31827ed898 PMID:23364414

Souza, A. A., Avelar, E. A., Boina, T. M., & Raimundini, S. L. (2010). Análise da aplicabilidade do time-driven activity-based costing em empresas de produção por encomenda. *Revista Universo Contábil*, *6*(1), 67–84.

Stout, D. E., & Propri, J. M. (2011). Implementing time-driven activity-based costing at a medium-sized electronics company. *Management Accounting Quarterly*, *12*(3), 1–11.

Tse, M., & Gong, M. (2009). Recognition of idle resources in time-driven activity-based costing and resource consumption accounting models. *Journal of Applied Management Accounting Research*, *7*(2), 41–54.

Yun, B. J., Prabhakar, A. M., Warsh, J., Kaplan, R., Brennan, J., Dempsey, K. E., & Raja, A. S. (2016). Time-driven activity-based costing in emergency medicine. *Annals of Emergency Medicine*, *67*(6), 765–772. doi:10.1016/j.annemergmed.2015.08.004 PMID:26365921

Zainal, Z. (2007). Case study as a research method. *Jurnal Kemanusiaan*, *5*(1), 1–6.

Compilation of References

AAA. (1973). *A Statement of Basic Auditing Concepts*. Retrieved from https://www.worldcat.org/title/statement-of-basic-auditing-concepts/oclc/701015

Abbott, A. (1983). Professional Ethics. *American Journal of Sociology*, *88*(5), 855–885. doi:10.1086/227762

Abdelkafi, N., & Tauscher, K. (2016). Business models for sustainability from a system dynamics perspective. *Organization & Environment*, *29*(1), 74–96. doi:10.1177/1086026615592930

ACCA, MARC. (2011). *A framework for Extended Audit Reporting, Final report, commissioned by ACCA and executed by MARC members*. Author.

ACCA. (2010). *Accountancy Futures: Reshaping the audit for the new global economy*. Retrieved from http://www2.accaglobal.com/pdfs/international/singapore/RA.pdf

Afonso, A., Schuknecht, L., & Tanzi, V. (2008). *Income Distribution Determinants and Public Spending Efficiency,* ECB Working Paper no. 861.

Agha, S., Alrubaiee, L., & Jamhour, M. (2012). Effect of core competence on competitive advantage and organizational performance. *International Journal of Business and Management*, *7*(1), 192–204.

Ahearne, M., Lam, S. K., Mathieu, J. E., & Bolander, W. (2010). Why are some sales people better at adapting to organizational change? *Journal of Marketing*, *74*(3), 65–79. doi:10.1509/jmkg.74.3.065

Ahmed, A., Neel, M., & Wang, D. (2013). Does mandatory adoption of IFRS improve accounting quality? Preliminary evidence. *Contemporary Accounting Research*, *30*(4), 388–423. doi:10.1111/j.1911-3846.2012.01193.x

Ahrens, T. (2008). Overcoming the subjective–objective divide in interpretive management accounting research. *Accounting, Organizations and Society, 33*(2), 292-297.

Ahrens, T. (2008). Overcoming the subjective–objective divide in interpretive management accounting research. *Accounting, Organizations, and Society, 33*(2), 292-297.

Ahrens, T. (2008). Overcoming the subjective–objective divide in interpretive management accounting research. *Accounting, Organizations and Society*, *33*(2), 292–297. doi:10.1016/j.aos.2007.03.002

Akbas, H. E. (2014). Company Characteristics and Environmental Disclosure: An Empirical Investigation on Companies Listed on Borsa Istanbul 100 Index. *Muhasebe ve Finansman Dergisi*, (62).

Akgün, A. E., Keskin, H., & Byrne, J. (2009). Organizational emotional capability, product and process innovation, and firm performance: An empirical analysis. *Journal of Engineering and Technology Management*, *26*(3), 103–130. doi:10.1016/j.jengtecman.2009.06.008

Akhtaruddin, M., Hossain, M. A., Hossain, M., & Yao, L. (2009). Corporate governance and voluntary disclosure in corporate annual reports of Malaysian listed firms. *Journal of Applied Management Accounting Research*, *7*(1), 1.

Akinbuli, S. F. (2010). The effect of audit expectation gap on the work of auditors, the profession and users of financial information. *Niger Accountant*, *43*(4), 37–47.

Aktas, N., Andries, K., Croci, E., & Ozdakak, A. (2019). Stock market developement and the financing role of IPOs in acquisitions. *Journal of Banking & Finance*, *98*, 25–38. doi:10.1016/j.jbankfin.2018.10.015

Al Amosh, H. A. M., & Mansor, N. (2018). Sustainability and corporate reporting: A review on environmental and social accounting disclosure, International Journal of Accounting. *Finance and Business*, *3*(8), 78–87.

Albawwat, A. H. (2015). Corporate governance and voluntary disclosure of interim financial reporting in Jordan. *Journal of Public Administration and Governance*, *5*(2), 100-127.

Albu, N., & Albu, C. (2003). Instrumente de management al performanţei: Vol. 2. Control de gestiune. Economica Publishing.

Alcouffe, S., Berland, N., & Levant, Y. (2008). Actor-networks and the diffusion of management accounting innovations: A comparative study. *Management Accounting Research*, *19*(1), 1–17. doi:10.1016/j.mar.2007.04.001

Alhazaimeh, A., Palaniappan, R., & Almsafir, M. (2014). The impact of corporate governance and ownership structure on voluntary disclosure in annual reports among listed Jordanian companies. *Procedia: Social and Behavioral Sciences*, *129*, 341–348.

Alhazmi, A. N. A. S. (2017). *Exploring the factors and effects of Corporate Social Responsibility Disclosure in Saudi Arabia (in the area of accounting and finance)* (Doctoral dissertation). Nottingham Trent University.

Alhyari, S., Alazab, M., Venkatraman, S., Alazab, M., & Alazab, A. (2013). Performance evaluation of e-government services using balanced scorecard. *Benchmarking: An International Journal, 20*(4), 512–536. doi:10.1108/BIJ-08-2011-0063

Allen, A., & Ramanna, K. (2013). Towards an understanding of the role of standard setters in standard setting. *Journal of Accounting and Economics, 55*(1), 1–66. doi:10.1016/j.jacceco.2012.05.003

Allwood, J. M. (2014). Squaring the Circular Economy: The Role of Recycling within a Hierarchy of Material Management Strategies. In Handbook of Recycling: State-of-the-Art for Practitioners, Analysts, and Scientists, (pp. 445–477). Academic Press.

Alstete, J. W., & Beutell, N. J. (2018). Designing learning spaces for management education: A mixed methods research approach. *Journal of Management Development, 37*(2), 201–211. doi:10.1108/JMD-08-2017-0247

Alzola, M. A. (2017). Beware of the watchdog: Rethinking the normative justification of gatekeeper liability. *Journal of Business Ethics, 140*(4), 705–721. doi:10.100710551-017-3460-3

Amagoh, F. (2008). Perspectives on organizational change: Systems and complexity theories. *The Innovation Journal, 13*(3), 1–14.

Ameer, R., & Othman, R. (2012). Sustainability Practices and Corporate Financial Performance: A Study Based on the Top Global Corporations. *Journal of Business Ethics, 108*(1), 61–79.

Anand, G., & Kodali, R. (2010). A mathematical model for the evaluation of roles and responsibilities of human resources in a lean manufacturing environment. *International Journal of Human Resources Development and Management, 10*(1), 63–100. doi:10.1504/IJHRDM.2010.029447

Andersen, M. S. (2007). An introductory note on the environmental economics of the circular economy. *Sustainability Science, 2*(1), 133–140. doi:10.100711625-006-0013-6

Andon, P., Baxter, J., & Chua, W. F. (2007). Accounting change as relational drifting: A field study of experiments with performance measurement. *Management Accounting Research, 18*(2), 273–308. doi:10.1016/j.mar.2006.06.007

Andriole, S. J. (2010). Business impact of Web 2.0 Technologies. *Communications of the ACM, 53*(12), 67–79. doi:10.1145/1859204.1859225

Antheaume, N. (2004). Valuing external costs – from theory to practice: Implications for full cost environmental accounting. *European Accounting Review, 13*(3), 443–464. doi:10.1080/0963818042000216802

Anthony, R. (1965). Planning and Control Systems: A Framework for Analysis, Division of Research. Harvard Business School.

Anthony, R., & Govindarajan, V. (2007). *Management Control Systems*. Chicago: Mc-GrawHill Irwin.

Antwi-Agyei, P., Dougill, A., & Stringer, L. (2017). Assessing Coherence between Sector Policies and Climate Compatible Development: Opportunities for Triple Wins. *Sustainability*, *9*(11), 2130.

Arsenault, P., & Faerman, S. R. (2014). Embracing paradox in management: The value of the competing values framework. *Organizational Management Journal*, *11*(3), 147–158. doi:10.1080/15416518.2014.949614

Ashkanasy, N. (2011, February). International happiness; a multilevel perspective. *The Academy of Management Perspectives*, 23–29.

Aspara, J., Lamberg, J.-A., Laukia, A., & Tikkanen, H. (2013). Corporate Business Model Transformation and InterOrganizational Cognition: The Case of Nokia. *Long Range Planning*, *46*(6), 459–474. doi:10.1016/j.lrp.2011.06.001

Axelsen, M., Green, P., & Ridley, G. (2017). Explaining the information systems auditor role in the public sector financial audit. *International Journal of Accounting Information Systems*, *24*, 15–31. doi:10.1016/j.accinf.2016.12.003

Azzone, G., Brophy, M., Noci, G., Welford, R., & Young, W. (1997). A Stakeholders' View of Environmental Reporting. *Long Range Planning*, *30*(5), 699–709.

Azzone, G., Noci, G., Manzini, R., Welford, R., & Young, C. W. (1996). Defining Environmental Performance Indicators: An Integrated Framework. *Business Strategy and the Environment*, *5*(2), 69–80.

Badea, D. (2008). O abordare structurată a dilemelor etice. *Audit Financiar*, *8*(6), 5–30.

Baker, C., & Bettner, M. (1997). Interpretive and Critical Research in Accounting: A Commentary on its Absence from Mainstream Research||. *Critical Perspectives on Accounting*, *8*(4), 293–310. doi:10.1006/cpac.1996.0116

Bakker, C. A., den Hollander, M. C., van Hinte, E., & Zljlstra, Y. (2014). *Products That Last - Product design for circular business models*. Delft: TU Delft Library.

Balachandran, B., & Faff, R. (2015). Corporate governance, firm value and risk: Past, present, and future. *Pacific-Basin Finance Journal, 35*(A), 1-12.

Balakrishnan, R., Labro, E., & Sivaramakrishnan, K. (2011). Product costs as decision aids: An analysis of alternative approaches (Part 1). *Accounting Horizons*, *26*(1), 1–20. doi:10.2308/acch-50086

Ball, R. (2013). Accounting informs investors and earnings management is rife: Two questionable beliefs. *Accounting Horizons*, *27*(4), 847–853. doi:10.2308/acch-10366

Ball, R., Li, X., & Shivakumar, L. (2015). Contractibility and transparency of financial statement information prepared under IFRS: Evidence from debt contracts around IFRS adoption. *Journal of Accounting Research, 53*(5), 915–963. doi:10.1111/1475-679X.12095

Băltenu, D., & Şerban, M. (2005). *Global environmental changes. An interdisciplinary assessment of uncertainties*. Bucharest: Coresi.

Bani-Khalid, T., Kouhy, R., & Hassan, A. (2017). The Impact of Corporate Characteristics on Social and Environmental Disclosure (CSED): The Case of Jordan. Journal of Accounting and Auditing: Research & Practice.

Barako, D. G., Hancock, P., & Izan, H. Y. (2006). Factors influencing voluntary corporate disclosure by Kenyan companies. *Corporate Governance, 14*(2), 107–125.

Barlaup, K., Dronen, H., & Stuart, I. (2009). Restoring trust in auditing: Ethical discernment and the Adelphia scandal. *Managerial Auditing Journal, 24*(2), 183–203. doi:10.1108/02686900910924572

Barros, R. S., & Ferreira, A. M. D. S. D. C. (2017). Time-driven activity-based costing: Designing a model in a Portuguese production environment. *Qualitative Research in Accounting & Management, 14*(1), 2–20. doi:10.1108/QRAM-10-2015-0095

Barth, M. E. (2013). Global comparability in financial reporting: What, why, how, and when? *China Journal of Accounting Studies, 1*(1), 2–12. doi:10.1080/21697221.2013.781765

Barth, M. E., Konchitchki, Y. L., & Landsman, W. R. (2013). Cost of capital and earnings transparency. *Journal of Accounting and Economics, 55*(2–3), 206–224. doi:10.1016/j.jacceco.2013.01.004

Barth, M. E., Landsman, W. R., Young, D., & Zhuang, Z. (2014). Relevance of Differences between Net Income based on IFRS and Domestic Standards for European Firms. *Journal of Business Finance & Accounting, 41*(3-4), 297–506. doi:10.1111/jbfa.12067

Barth, M., Landsman, W., & Lang, M. (2008). International accounting standards and accounting quality. *Journal of Accounting Research, 46*(3), 467–498. doi:10.1111/j.1475-679X.2008.00287.x

Bayoud, N. S., Kavanagh, M., & Slaughter, G. (2012a). Corporate Social Responsibility Disclosure and Corporate Reputation in Developing Countries: The Case of Libya. *Journal of Business and Policy Research, 7*(1), 131–160.

Bayoud, N. S., Kavanagh, M., & Slaughter, G. (2012b). Factors influencing levels of corporate social responsibility disclosure Libyan firms: A mixed study. *International Journal of Economics and Finance, 4*(4), 13–29.

Bean, D. F., & Bernardi, R. A. (2007). Ethics education in our colleges and universities: A positive role for accounting practitioners. *Journal of Academic Ethics, 5*(1), 59–75. doi:10.100710805-007-9038-4

Beasley, M. S., Buckless, F. A., Glover, S. M., & Prawitt, D. F. (2009). *Auditing Cases. An Interactive Learning Approach* (4th ed.). Prentice Hall.

Beattie, E. (2009). Don't blame the accountants. *Accountancy, 143*(1390), 38–39.

Becker, B. E., & Huselid, M. A. (2006). Strategic human resources management: Where do we go from here? *Journal of Management, 32*(6), 898–925. doi:10.1177/0149206306293668

Behery, M., Jabeen, F., & Parakandi, M. (2014). Adopting a contemporary performance management system. *International Journal of Productivity and Performance Management, 63*(1), 22–43. doi:10.1108/IJPPM-07-2012-0076

Bellantuono, N., Pontrandolfo, P., & Scozzi, B. (2016). Capturing the Stakeholders' View in Sustainability reporting: A novel approach. *Sustainability, 8*, 379.

Bennett, M., Bouma, J. J., & Wolters, T. (2002). The Development of Environmental Management Accounting: General Introduction and Critical Review. In M. Bennett & J. J. Bouma (Eds.), *Environmental Management Accounting: Informational and Institutional Developments. Eco-Efficiency in Industry and Science* (Vol. 9). Dordrecht: Springer.

Bennett, M., & James, P. (1997). Environment related management accounting: Current practice and future trends. *Greener Management International, 17*, 33–51.

Bennett, M., Rikhardson, P., & Schaltegger, S. (2003). *Enviromental Management Accounting- Purpose and Progress*. Kluwer Academic Publishers. doi:10.1007/978-94-010-0197-7

Benyus, J. M. (2002). *Biomimicry*. New York: Harper Perennial.

Berle, A., & Means, G. (1932). *The Modern Corporation and Private Property*. Transaction Publishers.

Berman, H. J. (1983). Law and Revolution: Vol. 1. *The Formation of the Western Legal Tradition*. Cambridge, MA: Harvard University Press.

Bernaldi, R. A., & LaCross, C. (2009). Positioning codes of ethics on international corporations' websites: A six-year longitudinal study. *Advances în Accounting, incorporating. Advances in International Accounting, 25*(1), 75–80. doi:10.1016/j.adiac.2009.02.010

Berndtsson, M. (2015). *Circular Economy and Sustainable Development*. Uppsala University.

Bettner, M., & Kate, K. (2013). Changes in annual reporting rituals of financial services firms in periods of market crisis. *International Journal of Critical Accounting, 5*(6), 577–593. doi:10.1504/IJCA.2013.059027

Bieker, T. (2002). Sustainability Management with the Balanced Scorecard. *Corporate Sustainability, 5th International Summer Academy on Technology Studies, Deutschlandsberg, Austria, July 13–19, 2003, Conference Proceedings*, 17–34.

Bieker, T., & Gminder, C. U. (2001). Towards A Sustainability Balanced Scorecard. *Oikos PhD Summer Academy*. Retrieved from http://www.oikos-stiftung.unisg.ch/

Bieker, T., & Waxenberger, B. (2002). Sustainability Balanced Scorecard and Business Ethics: Developing a Balanced Scorecard for Integrity Management. In *Conference proceeding 10th Conference of the Greening of Industry Network*. Göteborg, Sweden: Greening of Industry Network.

Birch, C. (2000). *Future Success*. Prentice Hall.

Bobek, D., Daugherty, B., & Radtke, R. (2012). Resolving Audit Engagement Challenges through Communication. *Auditing*, *31*(4), 21–45. doi:10.2308/ajpt-50210

Bocken, N. M. P., de Pauw, I., Bakker, C., & van der Grinten, B. (2016). Product design and business model strategies for a circular economy. *J. Ind. Prod. Eng.*, *33*, 308–320.

Bocken, N. M. P., Short, S. W., Rana, P., & Evans, S. (2014). A literature and practice review to develop sustainable business model archetypes. *Journal of Cleaner Production*, *65*, 42–56. doi:10.1016/j.jclepro.2013.11.039

Boerrigter, S. (2015). *The use of the Sustainability Balanced Scorecard Framework for Dutch SMEs as a tool for measuring the performance of their sustainability strategy*. 5th IBA Bachelor Thesis Conference, Enschede, The Netherlands.

Bolis, I., Morioka, S. N., & Sznelwar, L. I. (2014). When Sustainable Development Risks Losing its Meaning. Delimiting the Concept with a Comprehensive Literature Review and a Conceptual Model. *Journal of Cleaner Production*, *83*, 7–20. doi:10.1016/j.jclepro.2014.06.041

Boons, F., & Lüdeke-Freund, F. (2013). Business models for sustainable innovation: State-of-the-art and steps towards a research agenda. *Journal of Cleaner Production*, *45*, 9–19. doi:10.1016/j.jclepro.2012.07.007

Botnari, N., & Nedelcu, A. (2015). Evaluarea performanţei financiare a întreprinderilor industriale prin prisma dimensiunilor de profitabilitate, rentabilitate şi creştere. *Economica*, *3*(93), 49–59.

Boulding, K. E. (1966). The Economics of the Coming Spaceship Earth. In *Environmental quality in a growing economy: Essays from the sixth RFF forum*. New York: RFF Press.

Bouma, J. J. (2000). Environmental Management Systems and Audits as AlternativePolicy Instruments. In C. Knill & A. Lenschow (Eds.), *Implementing EU Environmental Policy*. Manchester, UK: Manchester University Press.

Bouquin, H. (2006). *Comptabilité de gestion* (3rd ed.). Paris: Economia.

Bouquin, H. (2004). *Contabilitate de gestiune*. Iaşi: TipoMoldova Publishing.

Bouquin, H. (2008). *Contrôle de gestion*. Paris: Presses Universitaires de France.

Bowen, F., & Wittneben, B. (2011). Carbon accounting. Negotiating accuracy, consistency and certainty across organisational fields. *Accounting, Auditing & Accountability Journal, 24*(8), 1022–1036. doi:10.1108/09513571111184742

Bowie, N. E., & Duska, R. F. (1990). *Business Ethics* (2nd ed.). Prentice-Hall Inc.

Bozec, Y. (2008). Ownership Concentration, Separation of Voting Rights from Cash Flow Rights, and Earnings Management: An Empirical Study in Canada. *Canadian Journal of Administrative Sciences, 25*(1), 1–15. doi:10.1002/cjas.52

Braungart, M., & McDonough, W. (2002). *Cradle to Cradle: Remaking the Way We Make Things* (1st ed.). New York: North Point Press.

Briciu, S., Căpuşneanu, S., Rof, L. M., & Topor, D. (2010). *Accounting and management control. Tools for performance evaluation entity*. Alba Iulia: Aeternitas Publishing.

Brooks, C., Fenton, E., Schopohl, L., & Walker, J. (2019). Why does research in finance have so little impact? *Critical Perspectives on Accounting, 58*, 24–52. doi:10.1016/j.cpa.2018.04.005

Brooks, C., & Schopohl, L. (2018). Topics and trends in finance research: What is published, who publishes it and what gets cited? *The British Accounting Review, 50*(6), 615–637. doi:10.1016/j.bar.2018.02.001

Brown, J. (2010). Accounting and visual cultural studies: Potentialities, challenges and prospects. *Accounting, Auditing & Accountability Journal, 23*(4), 482–505. doi:10.1108/09513571011041598

Brown, R. (2009). Revisiting the expectations gaps after 15 years. *Journal of Applied Accounting Research, 10*(2), 92–95. doi:10.1108/09675420910984655

Brüggemann, U., Hitz, J.-M., & Sellhorn, T. (2013). Intended and unintended consequences of mandatory IFRS adoption: A review of extant evidence and suggestions for future research. *European Accounting Review, 22*(1), 1–37. doi:10.1080/09638180.2012.718487

Bruszas, S., Kaschutzke, B., Maurer, R., & Siegelin, I. (2018). Unisex pricing of German participating life annuities- Boon or bane for customer and insurance company? *Insurance, Mathematics & Economics, 78*, 230–245. doi:10.1016/j.insmatheco.2017.09.012

Burlaud, A., & Simon, C. (2003). Comptabilité de Gestion. Vuibert.

Burritt, R. L., Hahn, T., & Schaltegger, S. (2002). Towards a comprehensive framework for Environmental Management Accounting - Links between business actors and environmental management accounting tools. *Australian Accounting Review, 12*(2), 39–50. doi:10.1111/j.1835-2561.2002.tb00202.x

Burritt, R. L., Herzig, C., & Tadeo, B. D. (2009). Environmental management accountingfor cleaner production: The case of a Philippine rice mill. *Journal of Cleaner Production*, *17*(4), 431–439. doi:10.1016/j.jclepro.2008.07.005

Burritt, R. L., & Saka, C. (2006). Environmental management accounting applications and eco-efficiency: Case studies from Japan. *Journal of Cleaner Production*, *14*(14), 1262–1275. doi:10.1016/j.jclepro.2005.08.012

Burritt, R., & Schaltegger, S. (2001). Eco-efficiency incorporate budgeting. *Environmental Management and Health*, *12*(2), 158–174. doi:10.1108/09566160110389924

Buys, P., Oberholzer, M., & Andrikopoulos, P. (2011). An investigation of the economic performance of sustainability reporting companies versus non-reporting companies: A South African perspective. *Journal of Social Sciences*, *29*(2), 151–158.

Byard, D., Li, Y., & Yu, Y. (2011). The effect of mandatory IFRS adoption on financial analysts' information environment. *Journal of Accounting Research*, *49*(1), 69–96. doi:10.1111/j.1475-679X.2010.00390.x

Cahan, S. F., & Sun, J. (2015). The effect of audit experience on audit fees and audit quality. *Journal of Accounting, Auditing & Finance*, *30*(1), 78–100. doi:10.1177/0148558X14544503

Cairns, D., Massoudi, D., Taplin, R., & Tarca, A. (2011). IFRS fair value measurement and accounting policy choice in the United Kingdom and Australia. *The British Accounting Review*, *43*(1), 1–21. doi:10.1016/j.bar.2010.10.003

Cameron, K. S., & Quinn, R. E. (2011). *Diagnosing and Changing Organizational Culture: Based on the Competing Values Framework*. San Francisco, CA: Jossey-Bass.

Campbell, L. G. (1984). *International Auditing: A Comparative Study of Professional Requirements in Australia*. Springer.

Căpuşneanu, S. (2006). *Contabilitate de gestiune. Studii aplicative şi teste-grilă*. Bucharest: Economică Publishing.

Caraiani, C., & Dumitrana, M. (n.d.). *Contabilitate de gestiune & Control de gestiune*. Bucuresti: Ed. InfoMega.

Carey, P., Liu, L., & Qu, W. (2017). Voluntary corporate social responsability reporting and financial statement auditing in China. *Journal of Contemporary Accounting & Economics*, *13*(3), 244–262. doi:10.1016/j.jcae.2017.09.002

Carmichael, D. R. (2004). The PCAOB and the social responsibility of the auditor. *Accounting Horizons*, *18*(2), 127–133. doi:10.2308/acch.2004.18.2.127

Carmichael, F. (2014). Reflections on the Establishment of the PCAOB and Its Audit Standards-Setting Role. *Accounting Horizons*, *28*(4), 901–915. doi:10.2308/acch-50851

Casian, A. (2013). *Dezvoltarea sistemului de audit intern în instituțiile publice din Republica Moldova. In 60 de ani de învățămînt economic superior în Republica Moldova prin inovare și competitivitate spre progres economic. Materialele conferinței științifice internaționale* (pp. 35–38). Chișinău: ASEM.

Caylor, M. L. (2010). Strategic revenue recognition to achieve earnings benchmarks. *Journal of Accounting and Public Policy*, *29*(1), 82–95. doi:10.1016/j.jaccpubpol.2009.10.008

Chandler, A. D. (1990). *The Managerial Revolution in Americas Business. Scale and Scope: The Dynamics of Industrial Capitalism*. Cambridge, UK: Belknap Press.

Chang, C. H. (2018). The dynamic linkage between insurance and banking activities: An analysis on insurance sector assets. *Journal of Multinational Financial Management*, *46*, 36–50. doi:10.1016/j.mulfin.2018.07.001

Chang, W., Tung, Y., Huang, C., & Yang, M. (2008). Performance improvement after implementing the Balanced Scorecard: A large hospitals experience in Taiwan. *Total Quality Management & Business Excellence*, *19*(11), 1143–1154. doi:10.1080/14783360802323560

Chan, L. L., Shaffer, M. A., & Snape, E. (2004). In search of sustained competitive advantage: The impact of organizational culture, competitive strategy and human resource management practices on firm performance. *International Journal of Human Resource Management*, *15*(1), 17–35. doi:10.1080/0958519032000157320

Chan, Y. C. L. (2004). Performance measurement and adoption of balanced scorecards: A survey of municipal governments in the USA and Canada. *International Journal of Public Sector Management*, *17*(3), 204–211. doi:10.1108/09513550410530144

Chatterjee, S. (2013). Simple Rules for Designing Business Models. *California Management Review*, *55*(2), 97–124. doi:10.1525/cmr.2013.55.2.97

Chebaane, S., & Othman, H. B. (2014). The Impact of IFRS Adoption on Value Relevance of Earnings and Book Value of Equity: The Case of Emerging Markets in African and Asian Regions. *Procedia: Social and Behavioral Sciences*, *145*, 70–80. doi:10.1016/j.sbspro.2014.06.012

Chen, A., Nguyen, T., & Stadje, M. (2018). Optimal investment under VaR-Regulation and Minimum Insurance. *Insurance, Mathematics & Economics*, *79*, 194–209. doi:10.1016/j.insmatheco.2018.01.008

Chen, H. M., & Fu, P. C. (2008). A systematic framework for performance appraisal and compensation strategy. *Human Systems Management*, *27*, 161–175.

Chen, H., Tang, Q., Jiang, Y., & Lin, Z. (2010). The role of international financial reporting standards in accounting quality: Evidence from the European Union. *Journal of International Financial Management & Accounting*, *21*(3), 220–278. doi:10.1111/j.1467-646X.2010.01041.x

Chen, L., Krishnan, G. V., & Yu, W. (2018). The relation between audit fee cuts during the global financial crisis and earnings quality and audit quality. *Advances in Accounting*, *45*, 14–31. doi:10.1016/j.adiac.2018.07.007

Chen, M., Qu, X., & Sun, X. (2017). Whose cost of equity capital reduces after IFRS convergence and why? Heterogeneity evidence from Chinese stock market. *China Journal of Accounting Studies*, *5*(1), 1–27. doi:10.1080/21697213.2017.1304539

Choi, Y.-S., Peasnell, K., & Toniato, J. (2013). Has the IASB been successful in making accounting earnings more useful for prediction and valuation? UK evidence. *Journal of Business Finance & Accounting*, *40*(7–8), 741–768. doi:10.1111/jbfa.12025

Christ, L. K., & Burritt, R. L. (2013). Environmental management accounting: The significance of contingent variables for adoption. *Journal of Cleaner Production*, *41*, 163–173. doi:10.1016/j.jclepro.2012.10.007

Christmann, P. (2000). Effects of "Best Practices" of environmental management on cost advantage: The roleof complementary assets. *Academy of Management Journal*, *43*(4), 663–680.

Church, B. K., Davis, S. M., Mc, S. A., & Cracken, S. (2008). The Auditor's Reporting Model: A Literature Overview and Research Synthesis. *Accounting Horizons*, *22*(1), 69–90. doi:10.2308/acch.2008.22.1.69

Ciubotaru, M., & Hîncu, V. (2015). Evaluarea performanțelor bugetare din perspectiva ajustării managementului finanțelor publice din Republica Moldova la principiile europene. In *Rolul investițiilor în asigurarea dezvoltării economice durabile în contextul integrării europene. Materialele conferinței științifice internaționale* (pp. 28–36). Chișinău: ASEM.

Clarkson, M. B. E. (1995). A stakeholder framework for analysing and evaluating corporate social performance. *Academy of Management Review*, *20*(1), 92–117.

Cocca, P., & Alberti, M. (2010). A framework to assess performance measurement in SMEs. *International Journal of Productivity and Performance Management*, *59*(2), 186–200. doi:10.1108/17410401011014258

Collins, E., Lawrence, S., Roper, J., & Haar, J. (2011). Sustainability and the role of the management accountant. *Research Executive Summary Series, 7*(14), 1-11.

Commoner, B. (1971). *The closing circle: Nature, man, and technology*. New York: Random House.

Constantin (Oprea), D. M., Topor, D. I., Căpușneanu, S., Barbu, C.M., & Bogan, E. (2016). The monitoring of carbon monoxide air pollutant, as part of the air quality management. Case study: Olt County, Romania. *Annales Universitatis Apulensis Series Oeconomica*, *2*(18), 27–34.

Constantin (Oprea), D.M. (2013). Relaţia climă – poluarea mediului înconjurător în arealul municipiului Slatina, Colecţia Pământul–Casa Noastră. Editura Universitară, Bucureşti.

Cooper, F., & Schindler, I. (1998). *Business Research Methods*. Irwin/McGraw-Hill.

Coram, P., Mock, T., Turner, J., & Gray, G. (2011). The Communicative Value of the Auditor's Report. *Australian Accounting Review*, *21*(3), 235–252. doi:10.1111/j.1835-2561.2011.00140.x

Cordoş, G. S., & Fülöp, M. T. (2015). Understanding audit reporting changes: Introduction of Key Audit Matters. *Journal of Accounting and Management Information Systems*, *14*(1), 128–152.

Cosserat, G. W., & Rodda, N. (2009). *Modern auditing* (3rd ed.). John Wiley & Sons Ltd.

Criado-Jimenez, I., Fernandez-Chulian, M., Larrinage-Gonzalez, C., & Husillos-Carques, F. J. (2008). Compliance with mandatory environmental reporting in financial statements: The case of Spain (2001–2003). *Journal of Business Ethics*, *79*(3), 245–262. doi:10.100710551-007-9375-7

Cullen, D., & Whelan, C. (2006). Environmental mamangement accounting: The state of play. *Journal of Business & Economics Research*, *4*(10), 1–4.

Cullinan, C. P., Earley, C. E., & Roush, P. B. (2013). Multiple auditing standards and standard setting: Implications for practice and education. *Current Issues in Auditing*, *7*(1), C1–C10. doi:10.2308/ciia-50344

Cumming, D., & Groh, A. P. (2018). Entrepreneurial finance: Unifying themes and future directions. *Journal of Corporate Finance*, *50*, 538–555. doi:10.1016/j.jcorpfin.2018.01.011

Curkovic, S., & Sroufe, R. (2007). Total QualityEnvironmental Management and Total Cost Assessment: An exploratory study. *J. Production Economics*, *105*(2), 560–579. doi:10.1016/j.ijpe.2006.04.021

Damayant, T. (2013). Who is afraid of Qualitative Research? A Compromise Accounting Research Failure in Improving Accounting Practices. *International Journal of Advances in Management and Economics, 2*(2), 89-94.

Darnall, N., & Edwards, D. Jr. (2006). Predicting the cost of environmental management system adoption: The role of capabilities, resources and ownership structure. *Strategic Management Journal*, *27*(4), 301–320. doi:10.1002mj.518

Daske, H., & Gebhardt, G. (2006). International financial reporting standards and experts' perceptions of disclosure quality. *Abacus*, *42*(3/4), 461–498. doi:10.1111/j.1467-6281.2006.00211.x

Davila, A. (2012). New trends in performance measurement and management control. *In Performance Measurement and Management Control. Global Issues (Washington, D.C.)*, *25*, 65–87.

De Beer, P., & Friend, F. (2006). Environmental accounting: A management tool for enhancing corporate environmental and economic performance. *Ecological Economics*, *58*(3), 548–600. doi:10.1016/j.ecolecon.2005.07.026

de Klerk, M., & de Villiers, C. (2012). The value relevance of corporate responsibility reporting: South African evidence. *Meditari Accountancy Research, 20*(1).

De Palma, R., & Csutora, M. (2001). *Introducing Environmental Management Accounting (EMA) At Enterprise Level – Methodology and Case Studies From Central and Eastern Europe - A contribution of the UNIDO project "Transfer of Environmentally Sound Technology (TEST) in the Danube River Basin"*. Retrieved from http://unipub.lib.unicorvinus.hu/223/1/Robertacsutora.pdf

De Palma, R., & Dobes, V. (2010). An integrated approach towards a sustainable entrepreneurship – Experience from the TEST project in transitional economies. *Journal of Cleaner Production, 18*(18), 1807–1821. doi:10.1016/j.jclepro.2010.07.025

Dechow, P., Sloan, R., & Sweeney, A. (1996). Causes and consequences of earnings manipulation: An analysis of firms subject to enforcement actions by the SEC. *Contemporary Accounting Research, 13*(1), 1–36. doi:10.1111/j.1911-3846.1996.tb00489.x

Deegan, C. (2000). *Financial Accounting Theory*. Beijing: Mc Graw Hill.

DeFond, M. L. (2010). Earnings quality research: Advances, challenges and future research. *Journal of Accounting and Economics*, *50*(2-3), 402–409. doi:10.1016/j.jacceco.2010.10.004

Dejnega, O. (2011). Method time driven activity-based costing. *Journal of Applied Economic Sciences*, *6*(15), 7–15.

Dellaportas, S. (2006). Making a difference with a discrete course on accounting ethics. *Journal of Business Ethics*, *65*(4), 391–404. doi:10.100710551-006-0020-7

Deloitte Touche Tohmatsu International (DTTI). (1993). *Coming clean - Corporate environmental reporting*. London: International Institute for Sustainable Development.

Deloitte. (2015). *Audit of the Future*. Retrieved from https://www2.deloitte.com/us/en.html

Demeere, N., Stouthuysen, K., & Roodhooft, F. (2009). Time-driven activity-based costing in an outpatient clinic environment: Development, relevance and managerial impact. *Health Policy (Amsterdam)*, *92*(2-3), 296–304. doi:10.1016/j.healthpol.2009.05.003 PMID:19505741

Dennis, I. (2014). *The Nature of Accounting Regulation*. New York: Routledge.

Detre, J. D., & Gunderson, M. A. (2011). The Triple Bottom Line: What is the Impact on the Returns to Agribusiness? *The International Food and Agribusiness Management Review*, *14*(4), 165–178.

Deutsch, P., & Silcox, B. (2003). Learning from other libraries: Benchmarking to assess library performance. *Information Outlook*, *7*(7), 18–25.

Dhaliwal, D. S., Li, O. Z., Tsang, A., & Yang, Y. G. (2011). Voluntary non-financial disclosure and the cost of equity capital: The initiation of corporate social responsibility reporting. *The Accounting Review*, *86*(1), 59–100.

Diamond, J. (2006). *Budget System Reform in Emerging Economies: The Challenges and the Reform Agenda*. International Monetary Fund. Retrieved from https://www.imf.org/External/Pubs/ NFT/op/245/op245.pdf

Dibia, N. O., & Onwuchekwa, J. C. (2015). Determinants of Environmental Disclosures in Nigeria: A Case Study of Oil and Gas Companies. *International Journal of Finance and Accounting*, *4*(3), 145–152.

Dillard, J., Brown, D., & Marshall, R. S. (2005). An environmentally enlightened accounting. *Accounting Forum*, *29*(1), 77–101. doi:10.1016/j.accfor.2004.12.001

DirectiveE. U. 2014/56/EU. (n.d.). Retrieved from https://publications.europa.eu/en/publication-detail/-/publication/39de2648-e657-11e3-8cd4-01aa75ed71a1/language-en

Dixon, R., Mousa, G. A., & Woodhead, A. D. (2004). The necessary characteristics of environmental auditors:a review of the contribution of the financial auditing profession. *Accounting Forum*, *28*(2), 119–138. doi:10.1016/j.accfor.2004.01.001

Dobrin, M., & Tanasescu, P. (2003). Teoria şi Practica Asigurărilor. Ediţia a doua, revizuită şi îmbunătăţită. Editura economic: Bucureşti

Dobrin, C., & Badea, F. (2006). *Gestiunea bugetară a sistemelor de producţie*. Bucharest: Economică Publishing.

Donaldson, T., & Preston, L. E. (1995). The Stakeholder Theory of the Corporation: Concepts, Evidence, and Implications. *Academy of Management Review*, *20*, 65–91.

Douglas, E., Lont, D., & Scott, T. (2014). Finance company failure in New Zealand during 2006-2009: Predictible failures? *Journal of Contemporary Accounting & Economics*, *10*(3), 277–295. doi:10.1016/j.jcae.2014.10.002

Doukakis, L. C. (2010). The persistence of earnings and earnings components after the adoption of IFRS. *Managerial Finance*, *36*(11), 969–980. doi:10.1108/03074351011081286

Doukakis, L. C. (2014). The effect of mandatory IFRS adoption on real and accrual-based earnings management activities. *Journal of Accounting and Public Policy*, *33*(6), 551–572. doi:10.1016/j.jaccpubpol.2014.08.006

Doz, Y. L., & Kosonen, M. (2010). Embedding strategic agility: A leadership agenda for accelerating business model renewal. *Long Range Planning*, *43*(2-3), 370–382. doi:10.1016/j.lrp.2009.07.006

Dragomirescu, S. (2010). *Controlul de gestiune în economia modern* (Doctoral thesis). Iaşi.

Dragomirescu, S. (2008). *Controlul de gestiune - coordonator al organizaţiilor descentralizate. Volumul "Convergenţa economică şi rolul cunoaşterii în condiţiile integrării în Uniunea Europeană, Universităţii "Alexandru Ioan Cuza"*. Iaşi: Publishing.

Dubosson-Torbay, M., Osterwalder, A., & Pigneur, Y. (2002). E-Business Model Design, Classification, and Measurements. *Thunderbird International Business Review*, *44*(1), 5–23. doi:10.1002/tie.1036

Dumitriu, C. (2003). *Environmental management and marketing. A strategic approach*. Iasi: Tehnopress.

Dutta, G., Rao, H. V., Basu, S., & Tiwari, M. K. (2019). Asset liability management model with decision support system for life assurance companies: Computational results. *Computers & Industrial Engineering*, *128*, 985–998. doi:10.1016/j.cie.2018.06.033

Eccles, R. G., Ioannou, I., & Serafeim, G. (2012). *The impact of a corporate culture of sustainability on corporate behavior and performance (No. w17950)*. National Bureau of Economic Research.

Eckerson, W. W. (2006). *Performance Dashboards: Measuring, Monitoring, and Managing Your Business*. John Wiley & Sons.

Eilifsen, A., Messier, W. F., Glover, S. M., & Prawitt, D. W. (2010). Auditing and assurance services (2nd ed.). McGraw-Hill Education.

El Sawy, O. A., & Pereira, F. (2013). *Business Modelling in the Dynamic Digital Space - An Ecosystem Approach*. New York: Springer Heidelberg. doi:10.1007/978-3-642-31765-1

Elder, R. J., Beasley, M. S., & Arens, A. A. (2010). *Auditing and assurance services: an integrated approach: global edition* (13th ed.). Englewood Cliffs, N.J.: Prentice-Hall.

Elfeky, M. I. (2017). The extent of voluntary disclosure and its determinants in emerging markets: Evidence from Egypt. *The Journal of Finance and Data Science*, 1–15.

Eling, M., & Jia, R. (2018). Business failure efficiency, and volatility: Evidence from the European insurance industry. *International Review of Financial Analysis*, *59*, 58–76. doi:10.1016/j.irfa.2018.07.007

Eling, M., & Schaper, P. (2017). Under pressure: How the business environment affects productivity and efficienty of European life insurance companies. *European Journal of Operational Research*, *258*(3), 1082–1094. doi:10.1016/j.ejor.2016.08.070

Elkington, J. (1997). *Cannibals with Forks: The Triple Bottom Line of the 21st Century Business*. Oxford, UK: New Society Publishers.

Elkington, J. (1998). *Cannibals with forks*. Gabriola Island, BC, Canada: New Society Publishers.

Ellen MacArthur Foundation. (2012). *Towards the Circular Economy. Economic and business rationale for an accelerated transition*. Ellen MacArthur Foundation.

Ellen MacArthur Foundation. (2013). *Towards the Circular Economy. Opportunities for the consumer goods sector*. Ellen MacArthur Foundation.

Ellen MacArthur Foundation. (2015). *Delivering the Circular Economy: A Toolkit for Policymakers*. Author.

Elliehausen, G., & Hannon, S. M. (2018). The Credit Card Act and consumer finance company leading. *Journal of Financial Intermediation*, *34*, 109–119. doi:10.1016/j.jfi.2018.01.007

Epstein, M. J., & Rejc Buhovac, A. (2014). Making Sustainability Work: Best Practices in Managing and Measuring Corporate Social, Environmental, and Economic Impacts (2nd ed.). San Francisco: Greenleaf Publishing Ltd.

Epstein, M. J., & Wisner, P.S. (2001a). Good Neighbors: Implementing Social and Environmental Strategies with the BSC. In *Balanced Scorecard Report* (pp. 5-6). Boston: Harvard Business School Publishing and Balanced Scorecard Collaborative.

Epstein, M. J., & Manzoni, J. F. (1998). Implementing Corporate Strategy: From Tableaux de Bord to Balanced Scorecards. *European Management Journal*, *16*(2), 190–203. doi:10.1016/S0263-2373(97)00087-X

Epstein, M. J., & Wisner, P. S. (2001b). Using a balanced scorecard to implement sustainability. *Environmental Quality Management*, *11*(2), 1–10. doi:10.1002/tqem.1300

Erkman, S. (2001). Industrial Ecology: a new perspective on the future of the industrial system. In President's lecture, Assemblée annuelle de la Société Suisse de Pneumologie, Geneva, Switzerland.

Eugénio, T., Lourenco, C. I., & Morais, A. I. (2010). Recent developments in social and environmental accounting research. *Social Responsibility Journal*, *6*(2), 286–305. doi:10.1108/17471111011051775

European Commission (EC). (2012). European resource efficiency platform (EREP). *Manifesto & Policy Recommendations*. Available from: http://ec.europa.eu/environment/ index_en.htm

European Commission (EC). (2014). *Towards a Circular Economy: A Zero Waste Programme for Europe, Communication from the Commission to the European Parliament, the Council, the European Economic and Social Committee and the Committee of the Regions*. Brussels: European Commission.

Evans, S., Gregory, M., Ryan, C., Bergendahl, M., & Tan, A. (2009). *Towards a sustainable industrial system: With recommendations for education, research, industry and policy*. University of Cambridge Institute for Manufacturing and Cranfield University.

Evans, S., Vladimirova, D., Holgado, M., Van Fossen, K., Yang, M., Silva, E., & Barlow, C. (2017). *Business model innovation for sustainability: towards a unified perspective for creation of sustainable business models*. Bus. Strat. Environ. doi:10.1002/bse

Everaert, P., Bruggeman, W., Sarens, G., Anderson, S. R., & Levant, Y. (2008). Cost modeling in logistics using time-driven ABC: Experiences from a wholesaler. *International Journal of Physical Distribution & Logistics Management, 38*(3), 172–191. doi:10.1108/09600030810866977

Everaert, P., Cleuren, G., & Hoozée, S. (2012). Using time-driven ABC to identify operational improvements: A case study in a university restaurant. *Cost and Management, 26*(2), 41–48.

Fan, J. P. H., Li, J., & Zheng, G. (2016). Revisiting the bright and dark sides of capital flows in business groups. *Journal of Business Ethics, 134*(4), 509–528. doi:10.100710551-014-2382-6

Felicio, J. A., & Rodrigues, R. (2015). Organizational factors and customers' motivation effect on insurance companies' performance. *Journal of Business Research, 68*(7), 1622–1629. doi:10.1016/j.jbusres.2015.02.006

Fernandez, J., Ferreiro-Ferreiro, A. M., Garcia-Rodriguez, J., & Vazquez, C. (2018). GPU parallel implementation for asset-liability management in insurance companies. *Journal of Computational Science, 24*, 232–254. doi:10.1016/j.jocs.2017.05.010

Fernando, A., Albuquerque, F., & Almeida, M. (2010). As Matérias Ambientais, as Licenças de Emissão de Gases com Efeito Estufa e os Normativos Aplicáveis em Portugal. *Jornal de Contabilidade, 395*, 31–38.

Ferreira, A., Moulang, C., & Hendro, B. (2010). Environmental management accounting and innovation: An exploratory analysis. *Accounting, Auditing & Accountability Journal, 23*(7), 920–948. doi:10.1108/09513571011080180

Figge, F., Hahn, T., Schaltegger, S., & Wagner, M. (2002b). The Sustainability Balanced Scorecard – Theory and Application of a Tool for Value-Based Sustainability Management. *Center for Sustainability Management.* Retrieved on February 12, 2008, http://www.strategyguide.org/

Figge, F., Hahn, T., Schaltegger, S., & Wagner, M. (2002a). The sustainability balanced scorecard – linking sustainability management to business strategy. *Business Strategy and the Environment, 11*(5), 269–284. doi:10.1002/bse.339

Fineman, S., & Clarke, K. (1996). Green stakeholders: Industry interpretations and response. *Journal of Management Studies, 33*(6), 715–730.

Fischer, M. (2017). The source of financing in mergers and acquisitions. *The Quarterly Review of Economics and Finance*, *65*, 227–239. doi:10.1016/j.qref.2017.01.003

Fisher, C. D. (2010). Happiness at Work. *International Journal of Management Reviews*, *12*(4), 384–412. doi:10.1111/j.1468-2370.2009.00270.x

Flannery, T. (2015). *Atmosphere of hope. Searching for solutions to the climate crisis*. Melbourne: The Text Publishing Company.

Flint, D. (1988). *Philosophy and principles of auditing: an introduction*. Basingstoke, UK: Macmillan Education.

Florou, A., & Pope, P. (2012). Mandatory IFRS adoption and institutional investment decisions. *The Accounting Review*, *87*(6), 1993–2025. doi:10.2308/accr-50225

Freeman, R. E. (1984). *Strategic Management: A Stakeholder Approach*. London: Financial Times Prentice Hall.

Freeman, R. E. (1984). *Strategic Management: A stakeholder approach*. Boston: Pitman.

Freeman, R. E. (1984). *Strategic Management: A Stakeholder Perspective*. Boston, MA: Pitman.

Freeman, R. E. (2010). *Strategic Management: A Stakeholder Approach*. Cambridge, UK: Cambridge University Press.

Frost, G., & Wilmshurst, T. D. (2000). The Adoption of Environment-related Management Accounting: An Analysis of Corporate Environmental Sensitivity. *Accounting Forum*, *24*(4), 344–361. doi:10.1111/1467-6303.00045

Fu, R., Kraft, A., & Zhang, H. (2012). Financial reporting frequency, information asymmetry, and the cost of equity. *Journal of Accounting and Economics*, *54*(2–3), 132–149. doi:10.1016/j.jacceco.2012.07.003

Fussel, L., & Georg, S. (2000). The institutionalization of Environmental Concerns - Making the Environment Perform. *International Studies of Management & Organization*, *30*(3), 41–58. doi:10.1080/00208825.2000.11656794

Gadenne, D. L., Kennedy, J., & McKeiver, C. (2009). An empirical study of environmental awareness andpractices in SMEs. *Journal of Business Ethics*, *84*(1), 45–63. doi:10.100710551-008-9672-9

Garetti, M., & Taisch, M. (2012). Sustainable manufacturing: Trends and research challenges. *Production Planning and Control*, *23*(2-3), 83–104. doi:10.1080/09537287.2011.591619

Geissdoerfer, M., Bocken, N. M. P., & Hultink, E. J. (2016). Design thinking to enhance the sustainable business modelling process. *Journal of Cleaner Production*, *135*, 1218–1232. doi:10.1016/j.jclepro.2016.07.020

Geissdoerfer, M., Morioka, S. N., de Carvalho, M. M., & Evans, S. (2018a). Business models and supply chains for the Circular Economy. *Journal of Cleaner Production*, *190*, 712–721. doi:10.1016/j.jclepro.2018.04.159

Geissdoerfer, M., Vladimirova, D., & Evans, S. (2018b). Sustainable business model innovation: A review. *Journal of Cleaner Production*, *198*, 401–416. doi:10.1016/j.jclepro.2018.06.240

Geng, Y., & Doberstein, B. (2008). Developing the circular economy in China: Challenges and opportunities for achieving "leapfrog development." *International Journal of Sustainable Development and World Ecology*, *15*(3), 231–239. doi:10.3843/SusDev.15.3:6

Gerayli, M. S., Yanesari, A. M., & Ma'atoofi, A. R. (2011). Impact of Audit Quality on Earnings Management: Evidence from Iran. *International Research Journal of Finance and Economics*, *66*, 77–84.
Guénin-Paracini, H., & Gendron, Y. (2010). Auditors as modern pharmakoi: Legitimacy paradoxes and the production of economic order. *Critical Perspectives on Accounting*, *21*(2), 134–158. doi:10.1016/j.cpa.2009.11.003

Gervais, M., Levant, Y., & Ducrocq, C. (2010). Time-driven activity-based costing (TDABC): An initial appraisal through a longitudinal case study. *Journal of Applied Management Accounting Research*, *8*(2), 1–20.

Ghisellini, P., Cialani, C., & Ulgiati, S. (2016). A review on circular economy: The expected transition to a balanced interplay of environmental and economic systems. *Journal of Cleaner Production*, *114*, 11–32. doi:10.1016/j.jclepro.2015.09.007

Ghosh, A., & Olsen, L. (2008). Environmental uncertainty and managers' use of discretionary accruals. *Accounting, Organizations and Society*, *34*(2), 188–205. doi:10.1016/j.aos.2008.07.001

Gibson, K. C., & Martin, B. A. (2004). Demonstrating value through the use ofenvironmental management accounting. *Environmental Quality Management*, *13*(3), 45–52. doi:10.1002/tqem.20003

Global Footprint Network. (2017). Available from: https://www.footprintnetwork.org/

Global Reporting Initiative. (2011). *Sustainability Reporting Guidelines*. Global Reporting Initiative.

Glover, H., & Reidenbach, M. (2012). Auditor Reporting Model Modifications: Practical Insights from the Academic Community. *Current Issues in Auditing*, *6*(1), C7–C14. doi:10.2308/ciia-50122

Godschalk, S. (2008). Does Corporate Environmental Accounting Make Business Sense. *Ecoefficiency in Industry and Science*, *24*, 249–265. doi:10.1007/978-1-4020-8913-8_13

Gonzalez, C. R. (2000). *Diccionario Enciclopedico Nuevo Espasa Ilustrado 2000*. Editorial Espasa Calpe S.A. Madrid.

González, C. R. (2000). *Diccionario Enciclopédico Nuevo Espasa Ilustrado*. Madrid: Editorial Espasa Calpe S.A.

Gordon, I. M. (2011). Lessons to be learned: An examination of Canadian and U.S. financial accounting and auditing textbooks for ethics/governance coverage. *Journal of Business Ethics*, *101*(1), 29–47. doi:10.100710551-010-0706-8

Gottlieb, G. (2008). Moving from performance measurement to strategy management at Brighamand Women's/Faulkner Hospital. *Balanced Scorecard Report*, *10*(2), 11–13.

Govindan, K., Soleimani, H., & Kannan, D. (2015). Reverse logistics and closed loop supply chain: A comprehensive review to explore the future. *European Journal of Operational Research*, *240*(3), 603–626. doi:10.1016/j.ejor.2014.07.012

Graedel, T. E., & Allenby, B. R. (1995). *Industrial ecology*. Englewood Cliffs, NJ: Prentice Hall.

Gray, R. (2010). Is accounting for sustainability actually accounting for sustainability and how would we know? An exploration of narratives of organisations and the planet. *Accounting, Organizations and Society*, *35*(1), 47–62. doi:10.1016/j.aos.2009.04.006

Gray, R. (2010). Is accounting for sustainability actually accounting for sustainability. And how would we know? An exploration of narratives of organizations and the planet. *Accounting, Organizations and Society*, *35*(1), 47–62.

Gray, R., Javad, M., Power, D. M., & Sinclair, C. D. (2001). Social and environmental disclosure and corporate characteristics: A research note and extension. *Journal of Business Finance & Accounting*, *28*(3-4), 327–356.

Grecco, M. C. P., Milani Filho, M. A. F., Segura, L. C., Sanchez, I. M. G., & Dominguez, L. R. (2013). The voluntary disclosure of sustainable information: a comparative analysis of Spanish and Brazilian companies. *Revista de Contabilidade e Organizações*, *7*(17).

Grigoraş, I. (1999). *Probleme de etică. In Editura Universităţii Al* (p. 3). Iaşi: I. Cuza. Retrieved from https://link.springer.com/article/10.1007/s10551-010-0706-8

Guide, V. D. R. J. Jr, & Van Wassenhove, L. N. (2009). Or Forum—The Evolution of Closed-Loop Supply Chain Research. *Operations Research*, *57*(1), 10–18. doi:10.1287/opre.1080.0628

Guidry, R. P., & Patten, D. M. (2010). Market reactions to the first-time issuance of corporate sustainability reports: Evidence that quality matters. *Sustainability Accounting, Management and Policy Journal*, *1*(1), 33–50.

Hahn, T., & Wagner, M. (2001). *Sustainability Balanced Scorecard Von der Theorie zur Umsetzung*. Centre for Sustainability Management.

Hammer, M. (2001). *The Agenda: What Every Business Must Do to Dominate the Decade*. Crown Business.

Harmon, J., Fairfield, K. D., & Wirtenberg, J. (2010). Missing an opportunity: HR leadership and sustainability. *People and Strategy, 33*, 16-21.

Hartnell, C. A., Ou, A. Y., & Kinicki, A. (2011). Organizational culture and organizational effectiveness: A meta-analytic investigation of the competing values framework's theoretical suppositions. *The Journal of Applied Psychology*, *96*(4), 677–694. doi:10.1037/a0021987 PMID:21244127

Hayes, R., Schilder, A., Dassen, R., & Wallage, P. (1999). *Principles of Auditing: An International Perspective*. London: McGraw Hill.

He, K., Pan, X., & Tian, G. (2017). Legal liability, government intervention, and auditor behavior: Evidence from structural reform of audit firms in China. *European Accounting Review*, *26*(1), 61–95. doi:10.1080/09638180.2015.1100547

He, L., Hou, P., & Liang, Z. (2008). Optimal control of the insurance company with proportional reinsurance policy under solvency constraints. *Insurance, Mathematics & Economics*, *43*(3), 474–479. doi:10.1016/j.insmatheco.2008.09.004

Henczel, S. (2002). Benchmarking – measuring and comparing for continuous improvement. *Information Outlook*, *6*(7), 12–20.

Hendro, B., Ferreira, A., & Moulang, C. (2008). Does the use of environmentalmanagement accounting affect innovation? An exploratory analysis. *31st AnnualCongress of the European Accounting Association*.

Henriques, I., & Sadorsky, P. (1999). The relationship between environmental commitment and managerial perceptions of stakeholder importance. *Academy of Management Journal*, *42*(1), 87–99.

Heshmati, A. (2015). *A review of the circular economy and its implementation*. IZA Discussion Paper No. 9611.

Holthausen, R. W., & Watts, R. L. (2001). The relevance of the value-relevance literature for financial accounting standard setting. *Journal of Accounting and Economics*, *31*(1-3), 3–75. doi:10.1016/S0165-4101(01)00029-5

Homburg, C., & Pflesser, C. (2000). A Multiple Layer Model of Market-Oriented Organizational Culture: Measurement Issues and Performance Outcomes. *JMR, Journal of Marketing Research*, *37*(4), 449–462. doi:10.1509/jmkr.37.4.449.18786

Hon, J. S., & Chu, S. J. (2015). Mechanics and application of time-driven activity-based costing system: A case study of Taiwan aerospace factory. *Int. J. Mech. Eng. Autom*, *2*(2), 69–78.

Hopwood, A. G., Unerman, J., & Fries, J. (2010). *Accounting for sustainability: Practical insights*. Abingdon, UK: Earthscan. doi:10.4324/9781849776332

Hopwood, A., & Miller, P. (1994). *Accounting as Social and Institutional Practice*. Cambridge, UK: University Press.

Horngren, C. T., Forster, G., Rajan, M., Ittner, C., & Datar, S. M. (Eds.). (2010). *Cost Accounting: a managerial emphasis*. American Accounting Association.

Horton, J., Serafeim, G., & Serafeim, I. (2013). Does mandatory IFRS adoption improve the information environment? *Contemporary Accounting Research*, *30*(1), 388–423. doi:10.1111/j.1911-3846.2012.01159.x

Hou, Q., Jin, Q., Yang, R., Yuan, H., & Zhang, G. (2015). Performance commitments of controlling shareholders and earnings management. *Contemporary Accounting Research*, *32*(3), 1099–1127. doi:10.1111/1911-3846.12111

Houque, M. N. (2012). The effect of IFRS adoption and investor protection on earnings quality around the world. *The International Journal of Accounting*, *47*(3), 333–355. doi:10.1016/j.intacc.2012.07.003

Humphrey, J. E., Lee, D. D., & Shen, Y. (2012). The Independent Effects of Environmental, Social and Governance Initiatives on the Performance of UK Firms. *Australian Journal of Management*, *37*(2), 135–151.

Hurley, R. F. (2002). Putting people back into organizational learning. *Journal of Business and Industrial Marketing*, *17*(4), 270–281. doi:10.1108/08858620210431679

Iatridis, G. (2010). International Financial Reporting Standards and the quality of financial statement information. *International Review of Financial Analysis*, *19*(3), 193–204. doi:10.1016/j.irfa.2010.02.004

Iatridis, G. (2012). Hedging and earnings management in the light of IFRS implementation: Evidence from the UK stock market. *The British Accounting Review*, *44*(1), 21–35. doi:10.1016/j.bar.2011.12.002

ICV (Internationaler Controller Verein). (2011). *Internationaler Controller Verein e.V.* Green Controlling.

IFAC. (2012). *IFAC Member Body Compliance Program*. Retrieved from http://www.ifac.org/publications-resources/2012-ifac-annual-report

IISD (International Institute for Sustainable Development). (1997). *Website of the International Institute for Sustainable Development "Instruments for Change" project – a collaborativeproject of IISD and the United Nations Division for Sustainable Development (UNDSD).* Retrieved from http://www.iisd.ca/susprod/ compendium.htm

IISD. (2010). The State of Sustainability Initiatives Review 2010: Sustainability and Transparency. Berne, Switzerland: IISD.

Inamdar, N., Kaplan, R., & Reynolds, K. (2002). Applying the balanced scorecard in healthcare provider organizations. *Journal of Healthcare Management, 47*(3), 179–195. doi:10.1097/00115514-200205000-00008 PMID:12055900

Intergovernmental Panel on Climate Change (IPCC). (2013). The physical science basis. Contribution of working group I to the fifth assessment report of the intergovernmental panel on climate change. Cambridge, UK: Cambridge University Press.

Intergovernmental Panel on Climate Change (IPCC). (2018). *Special Report: Global Warming of 1.5°C.* Retrieved from https://www.ipcc.ch/site/assets/uploads/sites/2/2019/02/SR15_Chapter5_Low_Res.pdf

International Auditing and Assurance Standards Board (IAASB). (2012). *Improving the Auditor's Report. Invitation to Comment.* Retrieved from http://www.ifac.org/publications-resources/2012-ifac-annual-report

International Auditing and Assurance Standards Board (IAASB). (2013). *Reporting on Audited Financial Statements: Proposed New and Revised International Standards on Auditing.* Retrieved from http://goo.gl/mVRmNB

International Auditing and Assurance Standards Board. (2017). *Manualul de Reglementări Internaţionale de Control al Calităţii, Audit, Revizuire, Alte Servicii de Asigurare şi Servicii Conexe.* Retrieved from http://mf.gov.md/sites/default/files/legislatie/2015%20IAASB%20Manual%20-%20Volumul%201%20RO_2016_final.pdf

International Energy Agency (IEA). (n.d.). Available from: https://www.iea.org/

Ionescu, R. (2010). *Economia asigurărilor.* Bucureşti: Editura Universitară.

Ittner, C. D., & Larcker, D. F. (1998). Innovations in performance measurement: Trends and research implications. *Journal of Management Accounting Research, 10*, 205–238.

Jackson, S. B., & Liu, X. K. (2010). The allowance for uncollectible accounts, conservatism, and earnings management. *Journal of Accounting Research, 48*(3), 565–601. doi:10.1111/j.1475-679X.2009.00364.x

Jalil, M. H., Abar, M. N., & Dadashian, F. (2016). Environmental Management Accounting Model on the Basis of Environmental Management System in Leather Industry. *International Journal of Environmental Sciences and Development, 7*(1), 52–58. doi:10.7763/IJESD.2016.V7.740

Jasch, C. (2003). The use of Environmental Management Accounting (EMA) for identifying environmental costs. *Journal of Cleaner Production, 11*(6), 667–676. doi:10.1016/S0959-6526(02)00107-5

Jasch, C. (2006). How to perform an environmental management cost assessment in one day. *Journal of Cleaner Production, 14*(14), 1194–1213. doi:10.1016/j.jclepro.2005.08.005

Jasch, C., Ayres, D., & Bernaudat, L. (2010). Environmental Management Accounting (EMA) CaseStudies in Honduras An Integrated UNIDO Project. *Social and Environmental Accounting, 4*(2), 89–103. doi:10.22164/isea.v4i2.48

Jeanjean, T., & Stolowy, H. (2008). Do accounting standards matter? An exploratory analysis of earnings management before and after IFRS adoption. *Journal of Accounting and Public Policy, 27*(6), 480–490. doi:10.1016/j.jaccpubpol.2008.09.008

Johannsdottir, L. (2015). Drives of proactive environmental actions of small, medium and large Nordic non-life insurance companies- and insurers as a driving force of actions. *Journal of Cleaner Production, 108*, 685–698. doi:10.1016/j.jclepro.2015.06.055

Johansson, A., & Larson, L. (2015). *A Standalone Sustainability Balanced Scorecard.* Institutionen för industriell ekonomi Blekinge Tekniska Högskola.

Johnson, H. T., & Kaplan, R. S. (1987). *Relevance lost: the rise and fall of management accounting.* Boston, MA: Harvard Business Press.

Johnson, M. W., Christensen, C. M., & Kagermann, H. (2008, December). Reinventing Your Business Model. *Harvard Business Review*, 50–60.

Jonäll, P. (2008). *Environmental Management Accounting (EMA), Management Accounting including Environmental Management – a literature review* (Master's thesis). University of Goteborg.

Jones, D. A., & Smith, K. J. (2012). Comparing the value relevance, predictive value, and persistence of other comprehensive income and special items. *The Accounting Review, 86*(6), 2047–2073. doi:10.2308/accr-10133

Juhmani, O. I. (2013). Ownership structure and corporate voluntary disclosure: Evidence from Bahrain. *International Journal of Accounting and Financial Reporting, 3*(2), 133.

Kaizer, M. (2017). *The suitability of Environment Management Accounting (EMA) models applied by the German Mittelstand* (Doctoral thesis). The University of Gloucestershire.

Kaplan, R. S. (2010). *Conceptual Foundations of the Balanced Scorecard.* Working paper. Boston: Harvard Business School.

Kaplan, R. S., & Norton, D. P. (2002). *Partnering and the Balanced Scorecard.* HBS Working Knowledge. Retrieved from http:/hbswk.hbs.edu/item/3231.html

Kaplan, R.S., & Norton, D.P. (1992, January). The Balanced Scorecard – Measures that drive performance. *Harvard Business Review.*

Kaplan, R. S. (1984). The evolution of management accounting. *The Accounting Review*, *59*, 390–418.

Kaplan, R. S., & Anderson, S. R. (2004). Time-driven activity-based costing. *Harvard Business Review*, *82*(11), 131–138. PMID:15559451

Kaplan, R. S., & Anderson, S. R. (2007). The innovation of time-driven activity-based costing. *Journal of Cost Management*, *21*(2), 5–15.

Kaplan, R. S., & De Pinho, R. R. (2007). *Amanco: Developing the Sustainability Scorecard.* Boston: Harvard Business School.

Kaplan, R. S., & Norton, D. P. (1996a). Using the Balanced Scorecard as a Strategic Management System. *Harvard Business Review*, *74*(1-2), 75–85.

Kaplan, R. S., & Norton, D. P. (1996b). *The Balanced Scorecard: Translating Strategy into Action.* Boston: Harvard Business School Press.

Kaplan, R. S., & Norton, D. P. (2004). *Strategy Maps.* Boston: Harvard Business School Press.

Kaplan, R. S., & Norton, D. P. (2006). How to implement a new strategy without disrupting your organization. *Harvard Business Review*, *84*(3), 100. PMID:16515159

Keating, B., Quazi, A., Kriz, A., & Coltman, T. (2008). In pursuit of a sustainable supply chain: Insights from Westpac Banking Corporation. *Supply Chain Management*, *13*(3), 175–179. doi:10.1108/13598540810871217

Kerzner, H. (2001). *Project Management; Systems Approach to Planning, Scheduling and Controlling.* New York: John Wesley and Sons.

Khaveh, A., Nikhasemi, S. R., Haque, A., & Yousefi, A. (2012). Voluntary Sustainability Disclosure, Revenue, and Shareholders Wealth-A Perspective from Singaporean Companies. *Business Management Dynamics*, *1*(9), 6–12.

King, M. E. (2002). *King Report on Corporate Governance for South Africa 2002.* Institute of Directors in Southern Africa.

Klein, A. (2002). Audit committee, board of director characteristics and earnings management. *Journal of Accounting and Economics*, *33*(3), 375–400. doi:10.1016/S0165-4101(02)00059-9

Kocakülâh, M., & Austill, D. (2007). Balanced Scorecard Application in the Health Care Industry: A Case Study. *Journal of Health Care Finance*, *34*(1), 72–99. PMID:18972988

Kohlberg, L. (1976). Moral stages and moralization. In T. Lickona (Ed.), Moral Development and Behavior (pp. 219–240). Academic Press.

Kohlberg, L. (1969). Stage and sequence: the cognitive- developmental approach to socialization. In D. A. Golsin (Ed.), *Handbook of Socialization Theory and Research* (pp. 347–480). Chicago, IL: Rand McNally.

Kohlberg, L. (1981). Essays on Moral Development: Vol. I. *The Philosophy of Moral Development*. San Francisco, CA: Harper & Row.

Korhonen, J., Honkasalo, A., & Seppälä, J. (2018). Circular Economy: The concept and its limitations. *Ecological Economics*, *143*, 37–46. doi:10.1016/j.ecolecon.2017.06.041

Kothari, S. P., Leone, A. J., & Wasley, C. E. (2005). Performance matched discretionary accrual measures. *Journal of Accounting and Economics*, *39*(1), 163–197. doi:10.1016/j.jacceco.2004.11.002

Kraaijenhagen, C., van Oppen, C., & Bocken, N. (2016). Circular Business: Collaborate and Circulate. Amsterdam: Ecodrukkers.

Kreuze, J.G., & Newell, G.E. (1994, February). ABC and life cycle costing for environmentexpenditures. *Management Accounting*, 38-42.

Kuk, G., Fokeer, S., & Hung, W. (2005). Strategic Formulation and Communication of Corporate Environmental Policy Statements: UK Firms' Perspective. *Business Ethics (Oxford, England)*, *58*, 375–385.

Kumpulainen, A., & Pohjola, T. (2008). Success factors in developing EMA- Experiences from four follow-up case studies in Finland. *Environmental Management Accounting for Cleaner Production, Eco-Efficiency in Industry and Science*, *24*, 477–490. doi:10.1007/978-1-4020-8913-8_27

Labuschagne, C., Brent, A. C., & van Erck, R. P. G. (2005). Assessing the Sustainability Performances of Industries. *Journal of Cleaner Production*, *13*(4), 373–385. doi:10.1016/j.jclepro.2003.10.007

Lakatos, E. S., Rusu, T., & Crişan, O. A. (2017). An Effective Alternative to the Linear Economy: Circular Economy. *Stiinta si Inginerie*, *31*(21), 1–8.

Landsman, W. R., Maydew, E. L., & Thornock, J. R. (2012). The information content of annual earnings announcements and mandatory adoption of IFRS. *Journal of Accounting and Economics*, *53*(1-2), 34–54. doi:10.1016/j.jacceco.2011.04.002

Lang, M., Raedy, J. S., & Wilson, W. (2006). Earnings management and cross listing: Are reconciled earnings comparable to US earnings? *Journal of Accounting and Economics*, *42*(1-2), 255–283. doi:10.1016/j.jacceco.2006.04.005

Lansiluoto, A., & Jarvenpaa, M. (2010). Greening the balanced scorecard. *Business Horizons, 53*(4), 385–395. doi:10.1016/j.bushor.2010.03.003

Läpple, F. (2007). *Abfall - und kreislaufwirtschaftlicher Transformationsprozess in Deutschland und in China: Analyse, Vergleich, Übertragbarkeit.* Heidelberg, Germany: Universität Heidelberg.

Laptes, R., Popa, A. F., & Dobre, F. (2014). Research of the Evolution of Financial Audit in Romania-Past, Current and Future Trends. *Procedia Economics and Finance, 15*, 807–814. doi:10.1016/S2212-5671(14)00523-1

Laszlo, C. (2005). *The Sustainable Company.* Washington, DC: Island Press.

Laszlo, C., & Zhexembayeva, N. (2011). *Embedded sustainability: The next big competitive advantage.* Sheffield, UK: Greenleaf Publishing.

Law, P. (2011). Audit regulatory reform with a refined stakeholder model to enhance corporate governance: Hong Kong evidence. *Corporate Governance, 11*(2), 123–135. doi:10.1108/14720701111121001

Lawrie, G., & Cobbold, I. (2004). 3rd Generation Balanced Scorecard: Evolution of an effective strategic control tool. *International Journal of Productivity and Performance Management, 53*(7), 611–623. doi:10.1108/17410400410561231

Lazăr, M. (2008). Profesionalism şi etică în profesia contabilă şi de audit. *Audit Financiar, 1*(6), 13–22.

Lehmann-Ortega, L., & Schoettl, J.-M. (2005). *From Buzzword to Managerial Tool: The Role of Business Model in Strategic Innovation.* Paper presented at CLADEA, Santiago de Chile, Chile.

Leuz, C., Nanda, D., & Wysocki, P. D. (2003). Earnings management and investor protection: An international comparison. *Journal of Financial Economics, 69*(3), 505–527. doi:10.1016/S0304-405X(03)00121-1

Lewandowski, M. (2016). Designing the Business Models for Circular Economy-Towards the Conceptual Framework. *Sustainability, 8*(1), 43. doi:10.3390u8010043

Lieder, M., & Rashid, A. (2016). Towards circular economy implementation: A comprehensive review in context of manufacturing industry. *Journal of Cleaner Production, 115*, 36–51. doi:10.1016/j.jclepro.2015.12.042

Li, H., Dong, L., Xie, Y. T., & Fang, M. (2017). Low-carbon benefit of industrial symbiosis from a scope-3 perspective: A case study in China. *Applied Ecology and Environmental Research, 15*(3), 135–153. doi:10.15666/aeer/1503_135153

Li, L., Qi, B., Tian, G., & Zhang, G. (2017). The contagion effect of low-quality audits at the level of individual auditors. *The Accounting Review, 92*(1), 137–163. doi:10.2308/accr-51407

Limperg Institute. (1985). *The social responsibility of the auditor. A basic theory on the auditor's function*. Retrieved from http://goo.gl/5ILFWH

Lin, C. H., Peng, C. H., & Kao, D. T. (2008). The innovativeness effect of market orientation and learning orientation on business performance. *International Journal of Manpower*, *29*(8), 752–772. doi:10.1108/01437720810919332

Lindblom, C. K. (1993). *The Implication of Organization Legitimacy for Corporate Social Performance and Disclosure*. Paper presented at the Critical Perspectives in Accounting Conference, New York, NY.

Linder, J., & Cantrell, S. (2000). Changing Business Models: Surveying the Landscape. *Accenture Institute for Strategic Change*, *34*(2), 1–15.

Lin, S., Riccardi, W., & Wang, C. (2012). Does accounting quality change following a switch from U.S.GAAP to IFRS? Evidence from Germany. *Journal of Accounting and Public Policy*, *31*(6), 641–657. doi:10.1016/j.jaccpubpol.2012.10.006

Lipe, M. G., & Salterio, S. E. (2000). The balanced scorecard; Judgmental effects of common and unique performance measures. *The Accounting Review*, *3*(3), 283–298. doi:10.2308/accr.2000.75.3.283

Li, S. (2010). Does mandatory adoption of international accounting standards in the European Union reduce the cost of equity capital? *The Accounting Review*, *85*(2), 607–636. doi:10.2308/accr.2010.85.2.607

Li, X., Castellanos, S., & Maassen, A. (2018). Emeging trends and innovations for electric bus adoption- a comparative case study of contracting and financing of 22 cities in the Americas, Asia-Pacific, and Europe. *Research in Transportation Economics*, *69*, 470–481. doi:10.1016/j.retrec.2018.06.016

Llena, F., Moneva, J. M., & Hernandez, B. (2007). Environmental disclosures and compulsory accounting standards: The case of spanish annual reports. *Business Strategy and the Environment*, *16*(1), 50–63. doi:10.1002/bse.466

Lo, A., Wong, R., & Firth, M. (2010). Can corporate governance deter management from manipulating earnings? Evidence from related-party sales transactions in China. *Journal of Corporate Finance*, *16*(2), 225–235. doi:10.1016/j.jcorpfin.2009.11.002

Lobo, G. J., & Whalen, D. J. (2007). Does good corporate governance reduce information asymmetry around quarterly earnings announcements? *Journal of Accounting and Public Policy*, *26*(4), 497–522. doi:10.1016/j.jaccpubpol.2007.05.003

Lobo, G. L., & Zhou, J. (2001). Disclosure quality and earning management. *Asia-Pacific Journal of Accounting & Economics*, *8*(1), 1–20. doi:10.1080/16081625.2001.10510584

Lopez, M. V., Garcia, A., & Rodriguez, L. (2007). Sustainable development and corporate performance: A study based on the Dow Jones Sustainability Index. *Journal of Business Ethics*, *75*(3), 285–300.

Louwers, T. J., Ramsay, R. J., Sinason, D. H., & Strawser, J. R. (2007). *Auditing and Assurance Services* (2nd ed.). New York: McGraw-Hill Irwin.

Lubin, D., Longsworth, A., & Russell, R. (2011). Sustainability Strategy Transforms the Enterprise. *Balanced Scorecard Report*, *13*(6), 1–6.

Lukka, K. (2010). The roles and effects of paradigms in accounting research. *Management Accounting Research*, *21*(2), 110–115. doi:10.1016/j.mar.2010.02.002

Lyle, J. T. (1994). *Regenerative design for sustainable development*. New York: John Wiley & Sons.

Mallin, C. (2006). *Handbook on International Corporate Governance Country Analyses*. Edward Elgar.

Malmi, T. (2001). Balanced scorecards in Finnish companies: A research note. *Management Accounting Research*, *12*(2), 207–220. doi:10.1006/mare.2000.0154

Man, M., & Rakoş, I.-S. (2015). Cost-Based Budgeting - A Relevant Instrument for the Improvement of Mining Companies' Performances. *Proceedings of the 25th IBIMA Conference*, 2444-2458.

Mansor, N., Jamil, A., & Bahari, A. (2017). Integrated Waqf Reporting System. *International Journal of Accounting*. *Finance and Business*, *2*(6), 155–166.

Marcu, F., & Maneca, C. (1978). *Dicţionar de Neologisme, Ediţia a III-a (revăzută şi adăugită)*. Bucureşti: Editura Ştiinţifică.

Marra, A., Mazzola, P., & Prencipe, A. (2011). Board Monitoring and Earnings Management Pre- and Post-IFRS. *The International Journal of Accounting*, *46*(2), 205–230. doi:10.1016/j.intacc.2011.04.007

Marshall, G. (1998). *A dictionary of sociology*. Oxford University Press.

Marston, C. L., & Shrives, P. J. (1991). The use of disclosure indices in accounting research: A review article. *The British Accounting Review*, *23*(3), 195–210.

Masanet-Llodra, M. J. (2006). Environmental management accounting: A case study research on innovative strategy. *Journal of Business Ethics*, *68*(4), 393–408. doi:10.100710551-006-9029-1

Mathur, V. N., Afionis, S., Paavola, J., Dougill, A. J., & Stringer, L. C. (2014). Experiences of host communities with carbon market projects: Towards multi-level climate justice. *Climate Policy*, *14*(1), 42–62.

Mautz, R. K., & Sharaf, H. A. (1961). *The Philosophy of Auditing*. Sarasota, FL: American Accounting Association.

Ma, Y. L., Zhu, X., Hu, X., & Chiu, Y. C. (2018). The use of context-sensitive insurance telematics data in auto insurance rate making. *Transportation Research Part A, Policy and Practice*, *113*, 243–258. doi:10.1016/j.tra.2018.04.013

McGahan, A. (2010). Business Model Innovation and Industry Change. *Rotman Magazine*, 91–94.

Mechelli, A., & Cimini, R. (2014). Is comprehensive income value relevant and does location matter? A European study. *Accounting in Europe*, *16*(25), 1–35.

Meda Antal, R., & Şumandea-Simionescu, I. (2015). Possible solutions to the question of insolvency-empirical analysis regarding the degree of expolsure of the solvency of Romanian insurance companies. *Procedia Economics and Finance*, *32*, 376–382. doi:10.1016/S2212-5671(15)01407-0

Medley, P. (1997). Environmental accounting – what does it mean to professional accountants? *Accounting, Auditing & Accountability Journal*, *10*(4), 594–600. doi:10.1108/09513579710180833

Meric, E., & Gersil, M. (2018). Usability of time driven activity-based costing methods in the budgeting process of SMEs. *Business and Economics Research Journal*, *9*(4), 961–978. doi:10.20409/berj.2018.134

Messier, W. F., Glover, S. M., & Prawitt, D. F. (2008). *Auditing and Assurance Services. A Systematic Approach* (5th ed.). New York: McGraw-Hill Irwin.

Mihăilescu, I. (2007). Rigori şi principii de etică ale auditorilor în misiunile de audit. *Audit Financiar*, *7*(V), 7–14.

Miller, M. (1994). Accounting as social and institutional practice: An introduction. In A. G. Hopwood & P. Miller (Eds.), *Accounting as Social and Institutional Practice* (pp. 1–39). Cambridge, UK: Cambridge University Press.

Milne, M., & Patten, D. (2001). Securing organizational legitimacy: an experimental decision case examining the impact of ED. *APIRA Conference*, 1-44.

Ministry of Environment, Waters, and Forests of Romania/Ministerul Mediului, Apelor şi Pădurilor din România (MMAPR). Programul Operațional Capacitate Administrativă 2014–2020. Asistență Tehnică pentru realizarea Planului Național de Gestionare a Deşeurilor şi a Planului Național de Prevenire a Generării Deşeurilor. (n.d.). Available from: http://www.mmediu.ro

Mitchell, R. K., Agle, B. R., & Wood, D. J. (1997). Toward a theory of stakeholder identification and salience: Defining the principle of who and what really. *Academy of Management Review*, *22*, 853–886.

Mock, T., Bedard, J., Coram, P., David, S., Espahbodi, R., & Warne, R. (2013). The Auditor's Reporting Model: Current Research Synthesis and Implications. *Auditing*, *32*(1), 323–351. doi:10.2308/ajpt-50294

Moingeon, B., & Lehmann-Ortega, L. (2010). Creation and Implementation of a New Business Model: A disarming case study. *Management*, *13*(4), 266–297.

Moller, A., & Schaltegger, S. (2005). The sustainability balanced scorecard as a framework for eco-efficiency analyses. *Journal of Industrial Ecology*, *9*(4), 73–83. doi:10.1162/108819805775247927

Moneva, J. M., & Ortas, E. (2010). Corporate environmental and financial performance: A multivariate approach. *Industrial Management & Data Systems*, *110*(2), 193–210. doi:10.1108/02635571011020304

Monroy, C. R., Nasiri, A., & Peláez, M. Á. (2014). Activity based costing, time-driven activity based costing and lean accounting: Differences among three accounting systems' approach to manufacturing. In *Annals of Industrial Engineering 2012* (pp. 11–17). London: Springer. doi:10.1007/978-1-4471-5349-8_2

Monteiro, S. M., & Aibar-Guzman, B. (2010). The influence of the Portuguese environmental accounting standard on the environmental disclosures in the annual reports of large companies operating in Portugal: A first view (2002-2004). *Management of Environmental Quality*, *21*(4), 414–435. doi:10.1108/14777831011049070

Morariu, A. (2007). Despre competență, confidențialitate și comportament profesional în contextul Codului etic. *Audit Financiar*, *11*(5), 19–22.

Morris, M., Schindehutte, M., & Allen, J. (2005). The entrepreneur's business model: Toward a unified perspective. *Journal of Business Research*, *58*(6), 726–735. doi:10.1016/j.jbusres.2003.11.001

Munkøe, L., & Jasch, C. (2008). Waste reduction program based on IFAC's EMA Guideline. *Environmental Management Accounting for CleanerProduction. Eco-Efficiency in Industry and Science*, *24*, 379–394. doi:10.1007/978-1-4020-8913-8_21

Murray, A., Skene, K., & Haynes, K. (2015). The Circular Economy: An Interdisciplinary Exploration of the Concept and Application in a Global Context. *Journal of Business Ethics*, 1–12.

Nakajima, N. (2000). A Vision of Industrial Ecology: State-of-the-Art Practices for a Circular and Service-Based Economy. *Bulletin of Science, Technology & Society*, *20*(1), 54–69. doi:10.1177/027046760002000107

Narayan, P. K., & Phan, D. H. B. (2019). A sourvey of Islamic banking and finance literature: Issues, chellenges and future directions. *Pacific-Basin Finance Journal*, *53*, 484–496. doi:10.1016/j.pacfin.2017.06.006

Nawaiseh, M. E., Boa, S. S. A., & El-shohnah, R. A. Z. Y. (2015). Influence of Firm Size and Profitability on Corporate Social Responsibility Disclosures by Banking Firms (CSRD): Evidence from Jordan. *Journal of Applied Finance and Banking*, *5*(6), 97.

Neely, A. (1999). The performance measurement revolution: Why now and what next? *International Journal of Operations & Production Management*, *19*(2), 206–228. doi:10.1108/01443579910247437

Neely, A. (2002). *Business Performance Measurement: Theory and Practice*. Cambridge, UK: Cambridge University Press. doi:10.1017/CBO9780511753695

Negru, T. (2006). *Asigurări Ghid practic*. Bucureşti: Editura C.H. Beck.

Nguyen, L. S., Tran, M. D., Nguyen, T. X. H., & Le, Q. H. (2017). Factors Affecting Disclosure Levels of Environmental Accounting Information: The Case of Vietnam. *Accounting and Finance Research*, *6*(4), 255.

Ngwakwe, C. C. (2009). Environmental responsibility and firm performance: Evidence from Nigeria. *International Journal of Humanities and Social Science*, *3*(2), 97–103.

Nilsson, F., & Olve, N.-G. (2001). Control Systems in Multibusiness Companies: From Performance Management to Strategic Management. *European Management Journal*, *19*(4), 344–358. doi:10.1016/S0263-2373(01)00036-6

OECD. (2015). *Corporate Governance Principles*. Retrieved from http://www.oecd.org/corporate/principles-corporate-governance.htm

Okcabol, F. (2007). Corporate and Government Accountability for Sustainable Environments: The Balanced Scorecard Approach. *Advances in Public Interest Accounting*, *13*, 151–175. doi:10.1016/S1041-7060(07)13007-8

Öker, F., & Adigüzel, H. (2010). Time-driven activity-based costing: An implementation in a manufacturing company. *Journal of Corporate Accounting & Finance*, *22*(1), 75–92. doi:10.1002/jcaf.20646

Öker, F., & Özyapici, H. (2013). A new costing model in hospital management: Time-driven activity-based costing system. *The Health Care Manager*, *32*(1), 23–36. doi:10.1097/HCM.0b013e31827ed898 PMID:23364414

Olalekan, I. O., & Jumoke, O. O. (2017). Identifying barriers to environmental management accounting practices: A comparative study of Nigeria and South Africa. *The Business and Management Review*, *9*(1), 168–179.

Olson, O., Guthrie, J., & Humphrey, C. (1998). *Growing Accustomed to Other Faces: The Global Themes and Warnings of Our Project*. Osaka: Second Asian Pacific Interdisciplinary Research in Accounting Conference.

Olson, E. M., Slater, S. F., Tomas, G., & Hult, M. (2005). The performance implications of fit among business strategy, marketing organization structure, and strategic behavior. *Journal of Marketing*, *69*(3), 49–65. doi:10.1509/jmkg.69.3.49.66362

Olve, N.-G., Roy, J., & Wtter, M. (1999). *Performance Drivers: A Practical Guide to Using the Balanced Scorecard*. New York: John Wiley & Sons.

Onetti, A., Zucchella, A., Jones, M. V., & McDougall-Covin, P. P. (2012). Internationalization, innovation and entrepreneurship: Business models for new technology-based firms. *The Journal of Management and Governance*, *16*(3), 337–368. doi:10.100710997-010-9154-1

Osterwalder, A., & Pigneur, Y. (2010). Business Model Generation: A Handbook for Visionaries, Game Changers, and Challengers. In T. Clark (Ed.), A handbook for visionaries, game changers, and challengers. Amsterdam: John Wiley & Sons.

Osterwalder, A., Rossi, M., & Dong, M. (2002). *The Business Model Handbook for Developing Countries*. Economics Working Paper Archive at WUSTL, (0202003), 1–10.

Osterwalder, A., & Pigneur, Y. (2002). An e-business model ontology for modeling e-business. *15th Bled Electronic Commerce Conference*, 1–12.

Osterwalder, A., Pigneur, Y., & Tucci, C. L. (2005). Clarifying business models: Origins, present, and future of the concept. *Communications of the Association for Information Systems*, *15*, 1–40.

Özbirecikli, M. (2007). A Review on How CPAs Should Be Involved in Environmental Auditing and Reporting for the Core Aim of It. *Problems and Perspectives in Management*, *5*(2), 113–126.

Ozkan, N., Singer, Z., & You, H. (2012). Mandatory IFRS adoption and the contractual usefulness of accounting information in executive compensation. *Journal of Accounting Research*, *50*(4), 1077–1107. doi:10.1111/j.1475-679X.2012.00453.x

Pagano, A. J., Feofilovs, M., & Romagnoli, F. (2018). The relationship between insurance companies and natural disaster risk reduction: Overview of the key characteristics and mechanisms dealing with climate change. *Energy Procedia*, *147*, 566–572. doi:10.1016/j.egypro.2018.07.072

Paladino, R.E. (2001). *Integrating EVA and ABM with the Balanced Scorecard*. In Balanced Scorecard European Summit 2001, Nice, France.

Parker, L. (2012). Qualitative management accounting research: Assessing deliverables and relevance. *Critical Perspectives on Accounting*, *23*(1), 54–70. doi:10.1016/j.cpa.2011.06.002

Patten, D. M. (1992). Intra-industry environmental disclosures in response to the Alaskan oil spill: A note on legitimacy theory. *Accounting, Organizations and Society*, *17*(5), 471–475.

Pauli, G. A. (2010). *The blue economy: 10 years, 100 innovations, 100 million jobs*. Taos, NM: Paradigm Publications.

Pavlovic, R. Z., Bukvic, R. M., & Gajic, A. M. (2016). Internal Sources of Financing Companies on the Basis of Static and Dynamic Indicators: Comparative Analysis. *Procedia: Social and Behavioral Sciences*, *221*, 270–277. doi:10.1016/j.sbspro.2016.05.115

PCAOB (2016). The Auditor's Report on an Audit of Financial Statements When the Auditor Expresses an Unqualified Opinion ("reproposed standard" or "reproposal"); IESBA. *Code of Ethics for Professional Accountants*.

Pearce, D. W., & Turner, R. K. (1990). *Economics of natural resources and the environment*. New York: Harvester Wheatsheaf.

Percy, J. P. (1997). Auditing and corporate governance: A look forward into the 21st century. *International Journal of Auditing*, *1*(1), 3–12.

Pernigotti, D. (2017). *Cu apa până la gât/With water to the throat*. Bucharest: Seneca Lucius Annaeus.

Persson, K., & Vingren, T. (2017). *Factors affecting the sustainability disclosures in Swedish State-Owned Enterprises as hybrid organizations* (Master thesis). Kristianstad University.

Pop Cohuţ, I. (2008), Introducere în etica afacerilor. Note de curs. Universităţii din Oradea.

Pope, P., & McLeay, S. (2011). The European IFRS experiment: Objectives, research challenges and some early evidence. *Accounting and Business Research*, *41*(3), 233–266. doi:10.1080/00014788.2011.575002

Porter, M. E., & Kramer, M. (2006). Strategy and Society. *Harvard Business Review*, 4–6. PMID:17183795

Porter, M. E., & Kramer, M. R. (2011). Creating Shared Value: How to reinvent capitalism - and unleash a wave of innovation and growth. *Harvard Business Review*, *89*, 62–77.

Post, J. E., Preston, L. E., & Sachs, S. (2002). Managing the extended enterprise: The new stakeholder view. *California Management Review*, *45*, 6–28.

Public Company Accounting Oversight Board. (2011). *Improving the Transparency of Audits: Proposed Amendments to PCAOB Auditing Standards and Form 2*. Retrieved from http://goo.gl/j4Obtu

PwC. (2014). *Corporate performance – What do investors what to know?* Retrieved from https://www.pwc.fr/fr/publications/communication-financiere/corporate-performance-what-do-investors-want-to-know.html

Quick, R., Sattler, M., & Wiemann, D. (2013). Agency conflicts and the demand for non-audit services. *Managerial Auditing Journal*, *28*(4), 323–344. doi:10.1108/02686901311311927

Radcliffe, M. (1999). Using Balanced Scorecard to develop Metrics for Sustainable Development. In *Conference Proceedings of Eighth International Conference of Greening of Industry Network: Sustainability: Ways of Knowing/Ways of Acting*. Chapel Hill, NC: The Greening of Industry Network.

Ramanna, K. (2008). The implications of unverifiable fair-value accounting: Evidence from the political economy of goodwill accounting. *Journal of Accounting and Economics*, *45*(2-3), 253–281. doi:10.1016/j.jacceco.2007.11.006

Rashid, A., Asif, F. M. A., Krajnik, P., & Nicolescu, C. M. (2013). Resource Conservative Manufacturing: An essential change in business and technology paradigm for sustainable manufacturing. *Journal of Cleaner Production*, *57*, 166–177. doi:10.1016/j.jclepro.2013.06.012

Regulation No, E. U. 537/2014. (n.d.). Retrieved from https://publications.europa.eu/en/publication-detail/-/publication/567809be-e656-11e3-8cd4-01aa75ed71a1/language-en

Richardson, A. (2011). Myth, Paradigms and Academic Accounting Research: A Comment on Reading and Understanding Academic Research in Accounting. *Global Perspectives on Accounting Education*, *8*, 67–77.

Rittenberg, L. E., & Schwieger, B. J. (2005). *Auditing. Concepts for a Changing Environment* (5th ed.). Thomson South-Western.

Rizvi, S. L. (2013). When Insurance Companies and Clinicians Pay Attention to Data, Everybody Wins: A Commentary on Koons, O'Rourke, Carter, and Erhardt. *Cognitive and Behavioral Practice*, *20*(3), 325–327. doi:10.1016/j.cbpra.2013.03.003

Robinson, M. (2007). *Performance Budgeting Models and Mechanisms*. Retrieved from http://www.focusintl.com/RBM137-0230553567.pdf

Robkob, P., & Ussahawanitchakit, P. (2009). Antecedents and consequences of voluntary disclosureof environmental accounting: An empirical study of foodsand beverage firms in Thailand. *Review of Business Research*, *9*(3), 1–30.

Roome, N., & Louche, C. (2016). Journeying toward business models for sustainability: A conceptual model found inside the black box of organisational transformation. *Organization & Environment*, *29*(1), 11–35. doi:10.1177/1086026615595084

Rouf, A. (2011). Corporate characteristics, governance attributes and the extent of voluntary disclosure in Bangladesh. *African Journal of Business Management*, *5*(19), 7836–7845.

Rowland, C., & Hall, R. (2014). Management learning, performance and reward: Theory and practice revisited. *Journal of Management Development*, *33*(4), 342–356. doi:10.1108/JMD-08-2012-0110

Saavedra, M. B. Y., Iritani, R. D., Pavan, L. R. A., & Ometto, R. A. (2018). Theoretical contribution of industrial ecology to circular economy. *Journal of Cleaner Production*, *170*, 1514–1522. doi:10.1016/j.jclepro.2017.09.260

Sachs, S., Rühli, E., & Kern, I. (2009). *Sustainable Success with Stakeholders – The Untapped Potential.* London: Palgrave. doi:10.1057/9780230271746

SAM Research, & Robeco Quantitative Strategies. (2011). *SAM White Paper: Alpha from Sustainability.* SAM Sustainability Investing. Retrieved from http://www.robecosam.com/images/Alpha_from_Sustainability_e.pdf

Samaha, K., Khlif, H., & Hussainey, K. (2015). The impact of board and audit committee characteristics on voluntary disclosure: A meta-analysis. *Journal of International Accounting, Auditing & Taxation*, *24*, 13–28.

Sánchez, R. G., Bolívar, M. P. R., & Hernández, A. M. L. (2017). Corporate and managerial characteristics as drivers of social responsibility disclosure by state-owned enterprises. *Review of Managerial Science*, 1–27.

Santos, J., Spector, B., & Van der Heyden, L. (2009). *Toward a Theory of Business Model Innovation within Incumbent Firms.* INSEAD Working Paper Series, 0–53.

Santos, M. A., Lopes Favero, L. P., & Distadio, L. F. (2016). Adoption of the International Financial Reporting Standards (IFRS) on companies' financing structure in emerging economies. *Finance Research Letters*, *16*, 179–189. doi:10.1016/j.frl.2015.11.002

Scavone, G. M. (2006). Challenges in internal environmental management reporting in Argentina. *Journal of Cleaner Production*, *14*(14), 1276–1285. doi:10.1016/j.jclepro.2005.08.011

Schadewitz, H., & Niskala, M. (2010). Communication via responsibility reporting and its effect on firm value in Finland. *Corporate Social Responsibility and Environmental Management*, *17*(2), 96–106.

Schaltegger, S., Bennett, M., Burritt, R. L., & Jasch, C. (2010). *Eco-efficiency in industry and science. Environmental Management Accounting for Cleaner Production* (5th ed.). Springer Science and Business Media.

Schaltegger, S., & Burritt, R. L. (2000). *Contemporary environmental accounting – Issues, concepts and practice.* Sheffield, UK: Greenleaf Publishing.

Schaltegger, S., Burritt, R., & Petersen, H. (2003). *An introduction to corporate environmental management: Striving for sustainability.* Greenleaf Publishing.

Schaltegger, S., Hansen, E. G., & Lüdeke-Freund, F. (2016). Business models for sustainability: Origins, present research, and future avenues. *Organization & Environment*, *29*(1), 3–10. doi:10.1177/1086026615599806

Schaltegger, S., Hansen, E., & Lüdeke-Freund, F. (2012). Business cases for sustainability and the role of business model innovation. *International Journal of Innovation and Sustainable Development*, *6*(2), 95–119. doi:10.1504/IJISD.2012.046944

Schaltegger, S., & Müller, K. (1997). Calculating the true profitability of pollution prevention. *Greener Management International*, *17*, 53–68.

Schleicher, T., Tahoun, A., & Walker, M. (2010). IFRS adoption in Europe and investment-cash flow sensitivity: Outsider versus insider economies. *The International Journal of Accounting*, *45*(2), 143–168. doi:10.1016/j.intacc.2010.04.007

Schneider, M., & Somers, M. (2006). Organizations as complex adaptive systems: Implications of complexity theory for leadership research. *The Leadership Quarterly*, *17*(4), 351–365. doi:10.1016/j.leaqua.2006.04.006

Scholtens, B. (2017). Why Finance Should Care about Ecology. *Trends in Ecology & Evolution*, *32*(7), 500–505. doi:10.1016/j.tree.2017.03.013 PMID:28457498

Sciulli, N. (2009). Sustainability reporting by local councils in coastal regions: An Australian study. *Asian Journal of Finance & Accounting.*, *1*(1), 76–86.

Seliger, G. (2007). *Sustainability in manufacturing: Recovery of resources in product and material cycles*. Berlin: Springer. doi:10.1007/978-3-540-49871-1

Seuring, S. A. (2001). Green supply chain costing: Joint cost management in the polyester linings supply chain. *GMI*, *33*(Spring), 71–80.

Shafer, S. M., Smith, H. J., & Linder, J. C. (2005). The power of business models. *Business Horizons*, *48*(3), 199–207. doi:10.1016/j.bushor.2004.10.014

Shahzad, K., Pouw, T., Rubbaniy, G., & El-Temtamy, O. (2018). Audit quality during the global financial crisis: The investors' perspective. *Research in International Business and Finance*, *45*, 94–105. doi:10.1016/j.ribaf.2017.07.137

Sharma, A., Jadi, D. M., & Ward, D. (2018). Evaluating financial performance of insurance companies using rating transition matrices. *Journal of Economic Asymmetries*, *18*, 102. doi:10.1016/j.jeca.2018.e00102

Sharma, D. S., Boo, E., & Sharma, V. D. (2008). The impact of non-mandatory corporate governance on auditors' client acceptance, risk and planning judgements. *Accounting and Business Research*, *38*(2), 105–120. doi:10.1080/00014788.2008.9663324

Shi, P., & Frees, E. W. (2010). Long-tail longitudinal modeling of insurance company expenses. *Insurance, Mathematics & Economics*, *47*(3), 303–314. doi:10.1016/j.insmatheco.2010.07.005

Sikka, P., Filling, S., & Liew, P. (2009). The audit crunch: Reforming audit. *Managerial Auditing Journal*, *24*(2), 135–155. doi:10.1108/02686900910924554

Simionescu, M. (2015). *Analiza financiară a afacerii*. Retrieved from http://cantemir.ro/cursuriudc/1sem1/Master/

Simons, R. (1995). *Levers of control: How Managers Use Innovative Control Systems to Drive Strategic Renewal*. Boston: Harvard Business School Press.

Singh, G., & Joshi, M. (2009). Environment managementand disclosure practices of Indian companies. *International Journal of Business Research*, *9*(2), 116–128.

Smith, A. (1776). *An Inquiry into the Nature and Causes of the Wealth of Nations.*

Smith, M. (2005). *The balanced scorecard, Financial Management*. Caspian Publishing.

Smith, W. K., Binns, A., & Tushman, M. L. (2010). Complex business models: Managing strategic paradoxes simultaneously. *Long Range Planning*, *43*(2-3), 448–461. doi:10.1016/j.lrp.2009.12.003

Soltani, B. (2014). The anatomy of corporate fraud: A comparative analysis of high profile American and European corporate scandals. *Journal of Business Ethics*, *120*(2), 251–274. doi:10.100710551-013-1660-z

Sorescu, A., Frambach, R. T., Singh, J., Rangaswamy, A., & Bridges, C. (2011). Innovations in Retail Business Models. *Journal of Retailing*, *87S*(1), S3–S16.

Souza, A. A., Avelar, E. A., Boina, T. M., & Raimundini, S. L. (2010). Análise da aplicabilidade do time-driven activity-based costing em empresas de produção por encomenda. *Revista Universo Contábil*, *6*(1), 67–84.

Spence, C., Husillos, J., & Correa-Ruiz, C. (2010). Cargo cult science and the death of politics: A critical review of social and environmental accounting research. *Critical Perspectives on Accounting*, *21*(1), 76–89. doi:10.1016/j.cpa.2008.09.008

Stahel, W., & Reday, G. (1976). *The potential for substituting manpower for energy*. Report to the Commission of the European Communities.

Stahel, W. (1982). The product life factor. In G. S. Orr (Ed.), *An Inquiry into the Nature of Sustainable Societies. The Role of the Private Sector* (pp. 72–105). Houston, TX: Houston Area Research Centre.

Stahel, W. R. (2010). *The performance economy*. Basingstoke, UK: Palgrave Macmillan.

Staniškis, J. K., & Stasiškienė, Z. (2006). Environmental management accounting in Lithuania: Exploratory study of current practices, opportunities and strategic intents. *Journal of Cleaner Production*, *14*(14), 1252–1261. doi:10.1016/j.jclepro.2005.08.009

Staniškis, J., & Stasiškienė, Ž. (2003). Environmental Management Accounting for CP Investment Project Development. *Environmental Research, Engineering and Management*, *1*(23), 60–69.

Stettina, C. J., & Hörz, J. (2015). Agile portfolio management: An empirical perspective on the practice in use. *International Journal of Project Management*, *33*(1), 140–152. doi:10.1016/j.ijproman.2014.03.008

Stewart, D. W., & Zhao, Q. (2000). Internet Marketing, Business Models, and Public Policy. *Journal of Public Policy & Marketing*, *19*(2), 287–296. doi:10.1509/jppm.19.2.287.17125

Stindt, D., & Sahamie, R. (2014). Review of research on closed loop supply chain management in the process industry. *Flexible Services and Manufacturing Journal*, *26*(1-2), 268–293. doi:10.100710696-012-9137-4

Stokstad, E. (2004). Global survey documents puzzling decline of amphibians. *Science*, *306*(5695), 391. doi:10.1126cience.306.5695.391a PMID:15486264

Stout, D. E., & Propri, J. M. (2011). Implementing time-driven activity-based costing at a medium-sized electronics company. *Management Accounting Quarterly*, *12*(3), 1–11.

Stratulat, O. (2002). Principii de optimizare a cheltuielilor pe verigile sistemului bugetar. In Simpossia Professorum. Chişinău: ULIM.

Stubbs, W., & Cocklin, C. (2008). Conceptualizing a sustainability business model. *Organization & Environment*, *21*(2), 103–127. doi:10.1177/1086026608318042

Su, B., Heshmati, A., Geng, Y., & Yu, X. (2013). A review of the circular economy in China: Moving from rhetoric to implementation. *Journal of Cleaner Production*, *42*, 215–227. doi:10.1016/j.jclepro.2012.11.020

Svanberg, J., & Ohman, P. (2013). Auditors' time pressure: Does ethical culture support audit quality? *Managerial Auditing Journal*, *28*(7), 572–591. doi:10.1108/MAJ-10-2012-0761

Tabără, N. (2009). *Control de gestiune-delimitări conceptuale, metode, aplicații*. Iași: Editura Tipo Moldova.

Tallon, P. P., & Pinsonneault, A. (2011). Competing Perspectives on the Link Between Strategic Information Technology Alignment and Organizational Agility: Insights from a Mediation Model. *Management Information Systems Quarterly*, *35*(2), 463–486. doi:10.2307/23044052

Talonen, A. (2016). Systematic literature review of research on mutual insurance companies. *Journal of Co-operative Organization and Management*, *4*(2), 53–65. doi:10.1016/j.jcom.2016.09.003

Tanzi, V. (1974). Redistributing Income through the Budget in Latin America. *Quarterly Review. Indexes - Banca Nazionale del Lavoro*, *27*(108), 65–87.

Tapanainen, T., Hallanoro, M., Päivärinta, J., & Salmela, H. (2008). Towards an Agile IT Organization: A Review of Prior Literature. In *Proceedings of the 2nd European Conference on Information Management and Evaluation* (pp. 425-432). London, UK: Academic Conferences Limited.

Tapanainen, T. (2012). *Information Technology (IT) managers' contribution to IT agility in organizations– views from the field. Publications of Turku School of Economics, serie A*. Turku, Finland: Juvenes Print.

Taticchi, P., Tonelli, F., & Cagnazzo, L. (2010). Performance measurement and management: A literature review and a research agenda. *Measuring Business Excellence*, *14*(1), 4–18. doi:10.1108/13683041011027418

Teece, D. J. (2010). Business Models, Business Strategy and Innovation. *Long Range Planning*, *43*(2-3), 172–194. doi:10.1016/j.lrp.2009.07.003

Tendeloo, B., & Vanstrelen, A. (2005). Earnings management under German GAAP versus IFRS. *European Accounting Review*, *14*(1), 155–180. doi:10.1080/0963818042000338988

The IAASB, International Standards of Auditing. (n.d.). Retrieved from http://goo.gl/3q9TjO

Thong, T. Y., Ding, D. K., & Lim, C. Y. (2008). Firm diversification and earning management: Evidence from seasoned equity offerings. *Review of Quantitative Finance and Accounting*, *30*(1), 69–92. doi:10.100711156-007-0043-x

Tikkanen, H., Lamberg, J. A., Parvinen, P., & Kallunki, J. P. (2005). Managerial cognition, action and the business model of the firm. *Management Decision*, *43*(6), 789–809. doi:10.1108/00251740510603565

Timmers, P. (1998). Business Models for Electronic Markets. *Electronic Markets*, *8*(2), 3–8. doi:10.1080/10196789800000016

Tone, K., Kweh, Q. L., Lu, W. M., & Ting, I. W. K. (2018). Modeling investments in the dynamic network performance of insurance companies. *Omega*, 1–11.

Tong, Y. K., & Arvey, R. D. (2015). Managing complexity via the Competing Values Framework. *Journal of Management Development*, *34*(6), 653–673. doi:10.1108/JMD-04-2014-0029

Trencansky, D., & Tsaparlidis, D. (2014). *The effects of company´ s age, size and type of industry on the level of CSR: The development of a new scale for measurement of the level of CSR* (Master Thesis). Umea University.

Tse, M., & Gong, M. (2009). Recognition of idle resources in time-driven activity-based costing and resource consumption accounting models. *Journal of Applied Management Accounting Research*, *7*(2), 41–54.

Turner, J., Mock, J., Coram, P., & Gray, G. (2010). Improving Transparency and Relevance of Auditor Communications with Financial Statement Users. *Current Issues in Auditing*, *4*(1), A1–A8. doi:10.2308/ciia.2010.4.1.A1

UNDSD (United Nations Division for Sustainable Development). (2000). *ImprovingGovernments' Role in the Promotion of Environmental Managerial Accounting*. Report and meeting document of First Expert Working Group Meeting, Washington, DC.

UNDSD. (2001). United Nations. Division for Sustainable Development, Environmental management accounting procedures and principles. New York: UNDSD.

UNEP. (2006). *Circular Economy. An alternative model for economic development*. Paris: United Nations Environment Programme.

United Nations. (2001). *Environmental Management Accounting: Policies and Linkages. Economic & Social Affairs*. New York: United Nations.

United States Environmental Protection Agency. (1995). *Federal Facility PollutionPrevention Project Analysis: A Primer for Applying Life Cycle and Total CostAssessment Concepts*. EPA.

United States Environmental Protection Agency. (2000). *The Lean and Green SupplyChain: A Practical Guide for Materials Managers and Supply Chain managers to Reduce Costs and Improve Environmental Performance*. Washington, DC: Author.

Upward, A., & Jones, P. (2015). An ontology for strongly sustainable business models defining an enterprise framework compatible with natural and social science. *Organization & Environment*, *29*(1), 97–123. doi:10.1177/1086026615592933

Vădineanu, A. (2004). *Development Management. An ecosystem approach*. Bucharest: Ars Docendi.

Van Der Woerd, F., & van den Brink, T. (2004). Feasibility of a Responsive Business Scorecard - a pilot study. *Journal of Business Ethics*, *55*(2), 173–186. doi:10.100710551-004-1900-3

Vấn, H. (2012). *Environmental benefits and its statement in Environmental Management Accounting* (Doctoral thesis). University of Szeged.

Vanstraelen, A., Schelleman, C., Meuwissen, R., & Hofmann, I. (2012). The Audit Reporting Debate: Seemingly Intractable Problems and Feasible Solutions. *European Accounting Review*, *21*(2), 193–215. doi:10.1080/09638180.2012.687506

Velayutham, S. (2003). The Accounting Profession's Code of Ethics: Is it a Code of Ethics or a Code of Quality Assurance? *Critical Perspectives on Accounting*, *14*(4), 483–503. doi:10.1016/S1045-2354(02)00138-7

Venanzi, D. (2012). *Social Ratings and Financial Performance: An Instrumental Approach*. Available at SSRN 2188859.

Veveriță, E. (2013). Bugetarea pe programe în cadrul Ministerului Economiei şi Ministerului Agriculturii şi Industriei Alimentare. *Chişinău: Centrul analitic independent "Expert-Grup"*, 23.

Viere, T., Schaltegger, S., & Enden, J. V. (2007). Supply chaininformation in environmental management accounting–the case of a Vietnamese coffee exporter. *Social and Environmental Accounting*, *1*(2), 296–310. doi:10.22164/isea.v1i2.19

Vladu, A. B., Amat, O., & Cuzdriorean, D. D. (2016). Truthfulness in accounting: How to discriminate accounting manipulators from non-manipulators. *Journal of Business Ethics*, *140*(4), 633–648. doi:10.100710551-016-3048-3

Voelpel, S. C., Leibold, M., & Tekie, E. B. (2004). The wheel of business model reinvention: How to reshape your business model to leapfrog competitors. *Journal of Change Management*, *4*(3), 259–276. doi:10.1080/1469701042000212669

Wagner, A. (1883). Finanzwissenschaft. *Erst Thail, Leipzig*, *1883*, 221.

Wang, C. W., Huang, H. C., & Hong, D. C. (2013). A feasible natural hedging strategy for insurance companies. *Insurance, Mathematics & Economics*, *52*(3), 532–541. doi:10.1016/j.insmatheco.2013.02.015

Warren, J., & Thomsen, M. (2012). *The Case for Corporate Responsibility Reporting: Valuing and Communicating the Intangibles*. White Paper. OneReport, Inc.

Watts, R., & Zimmerman, J. (1978). Towards a Positive Theory of the Determination of Accounting Standards. *The Accounting Review*, *53*(1), 112–134.

Waweru, N. M. (2010). The origin and evolution of management accounting: A review of the theoretical framework. *Problems and Perspectives in Management*, *8*(3), 165–182.

Webster, K. (2015). *The Circular Economy: A Wealth of Flows*. Isle of Wight, UK: Ellen MacArthur Foundation.

Wei, L., Haili, Y., & Yijun, H. (2011). The optimal strategy for insurance company under the influence of terminal value. *Acta Mathematica Scientia*, *31B*(3), 1077–1090.

Wells, P. E. (2013). *Business Models for Sustainability*. Cheltenham, UK: Edward Elgar. doi:10.4337/9781781001530

Wells, P., & Seitz, M. (2005). Business models and closed-loop supply chains: A typology. *Supply Chain Management*, *10*(4), 249–251. doi:10.1108/13598540510612712

Wheeler, D., & Sillanpää, M. (1997). *The Stakeholder Corporation*. London, UK: Pitman.

Whittington, O. R., & Pany, K. (2008). *Principles of Auditing & Other Assurance Services* (16th ed.). New York: McGraw-Hill Irwin.

World Health Organization. (1996). Available from: http://www.who.int/en/

WSSD. (2002). *World Summit on Sustainable Development in Johannesburg*. Available from: https://sustainabledevelopment.un.org/milesstones/wssd

Wyatt, A. R. (2004). Accounting professionalism—They just don't get it! *Accounting Horizons*, *18*(1), 45–53. doi:10.2308/acch.2004.18.1.45

Xiong, Y. (2006). Earning management and its measurement; a theoretical perspective. *The Journal of American Academy of Business, Cambridge*, *9*(1), 214–219.

Yadav, N., & Sagar, M. (2013). Performance measurement and management frameworks. *Business Process Management Journal*, *19*(6), 947–971. doi:10.1108/BPMJ-01-2013-0003

Yang, Y., Lan, Q., Liu, P., & Ma, L. (2017). Insurance as a market mechanism in managing regional environmental and safety risks. *Resources, Conservation and Recycling*, *124*, 62–66. doi:10.1016/j.resconrec.2017.04.004

Yuan, Z., Bi, J., & Moriguichi, Y. (2008). The Circular Economy: A New Development Strategy in China. *Journal of Industrial Ecology*, *10*(1-2), 4–8. doi:10.1162/108819806775545321

Yun, B. J., Prabhakar, A. M., Warsh, J., Kaplan, R., Brennan, J., Dempsey, K. E., & Raja, A. S. (2016). Time-driven activity-based costing in emergency medicine. *Annals of Emergency Medicine*, *67*(6), 765–772. doi:10.1016/j.annemergmed.2015.08.004 PMID:26365921

Zainal, Z. (2007). Case study as a research method. *Jurnal Kemanusiaan*, *5*(1), 1–6.

Zalata, A. M., Tauringana, V., & Tingbani, I. (2018). Audit committee financial expertise, gender, and earnings management: Does gender of the financial expert matter? *International Review of Financial Analysis*, *55*, 170–183. doi:10.1016/j.irfa.2017.11.002

Zeghal, D., Chtourou, S., & Fourati, M. Y. (2012). The effect of mandatory adoption of IFRS on earning quality: Evidence from the European Union. *Journal of International Accounting Research*, *11*(2), 1–25. doi:10.2308/jiar-10221

Zéghal, D., Chtourou, S., & Mnif, S. Y. (2011). An analysis of the effect of mandatory adoption of IAS/IFRS on earnings Management. *Journal of International Accounting, Auditing & Taxation*, *20*(2), 61–72. doi:10.1016/j.intaccaudtax.2011.06.001

Zeyneloglu, I. (2018). Fiscal policy effectiveness and the golden rule of public finance. *Central Bank Review*, *18*(3), 85–93. doi:10.1016/j.cbrev.2018.08.001

Ziegler, A., Rennings, K., & Schroder, M. (2002). *The effect of environmental and social performance on the shareholder value of European stock corporations*. Centre for European Economic Research (ZEW). Retrieved from http://www.eea-esem.com/papers/eea-esem/2003/342/paper.pdf

Zingales, F., O'Rourke, A., & Hockerts, K. (2002). *Balanced Scorecard and Sustainability State of the Art Review*. Working Papers (65). Fontainbleu: CMER.

Zott, C., & Amit, R. (2008). The Fit between Product Market Strategy and Business Model: Implications for Firm Performance. *Strategic Management Journal*, *29*(1), 1–26. doi:10.1002mj.642

Zott, C., & Amit, R. (2010). Business model design: An activity system perspective. *Long Range Planning*, *43*(2-3), 216–226. doi:10.1016/j.lrp.2009.07.004

Zott, C., Amit, R., & Massa, L. (2011). The Business Model: Recent Developments and Future Research. *Journal of Management*, *37*(4), 1019–1042. doi:10.1177/0149206311406265

Related References

To continue our tradition of advancing information science and technology research, we have compiled a list of recommended IGI Global readings. These references will provide additional information and guidance to further enrich your knowledge and assist you with your own research and future publications.

Abtahi, M. S., Behboudi, L., & Hasanabad, H. M. (2017). Factors Affecting Internet Advertising Adoption in Ad Agencies. *International Journal of Innovation in the Digital Economy*, *8*(4), 18–29. doi:10.4018/IJIDE.2017100102

Agrawal, S. (2017). The Impact of Emerging Technologies and Social Media on Different Business(es): Marketing and Management. In O. Rishi & A. Sharma (Eds.), *Maximizing Business Performance and Efficiency Through Intelligent Systems* (pp. 37–49). Hershey, PA: IGI Global. doi:10.4018/978-1-5225-2234-8.ch002

Alnoukari, M., Razouk, R., & Hanano, A. (2016). BSC-SI: A Framework for Integrating Strategic Intelligence in Corporate Strategic Management. *International Journal of Social and Organizational Dynamics in IT*, *5*(2), 1–14. doi:10.4018/IJSODIT.2016070101

Alnoukari, M., Razouk, R., & Hanano, A. (2016). BSC-SI, A Framework for Integrating Strategic Intelligence in Corporate Strategic Management. *International Journal of Strategic Information Technology and Applications*, *7*(1), 32–44. doi:10.4018/IJSITA.2016010103

Altındağ, E. (2016). Current Approaches in Change Management. In A. Goksoy (Ed.), *Organizational Change Management Strategies in Modern Business* (pp. 24–51). Hershey, PA: IGI Global. doi:10.4018/978-1-4666-9533-7.ch002

Alvarez-Dionisi, L. E., Turner, R., & Mittra, M. (2016). Global Project Management Trends. *International Journal of Information Technology Project Management*, *7*(3), 54–73. doi:10.4018/IJITPM.2016070104

Anantharaman, R. N., Rajeswari, K. S., Angusamy, A., & Kuppusamy, J. (2017). Role of Self-Efficacy and Collective Efficacy as Moderators of Occupational Stress Among Software Development Professionals. *International Journal of Human Capital and Information Technology Professionals*, *8*(2), 45–58. doi:10.4018/IJHCITP.2017040103

Aninze, F., El-Gohary, H., & Hussain, J. (2018). The Role of Microfinance to Empower Women: The Case of Developing Countries. *International Journal of Customer Relationship Marketing and Management, 9*(1), 54–78. doi:10.4018/IJCRMM.2018010104

Arsenijević, O. M., Orčić, D., & Kastratović, E. (2017). Development of an Optimization Tool for Intangibles in SMEs: A Case Study from Serbia with a Pilot Research in the Prestige by Milka Company. In M. Vemić (Ed.), *Optimal Management Strategies in Small and Medium Enterprises* (pp. 320–347). Hershey, PA: IGI Global. doi:10.4018/978-1-5225-1949-2.ch015

Aryanto, V. D., Wismantoro, Y., & Widyatmoko, K. (2018). Implementing Eco-Innovation by Utilizing the Internet to Enhance Firm's Marketing Performance: Study of Green Batik Small and Medium Enterprises in Indonesia. *International Journal of E-Business Research, 14*(1), 21–36. doi:10.4018/IJEBR.2018010102

Atiku, S. O., & Fields, Z. (2017). Multicultural Orientations for 21st Century Global Leadership. In N. Baporikar (Ed.), *Management Education for Global Leadership* (pp. 28–51). Hershey, PA: IGI Global. doi:10.4018/978-1-5225-1013-0.ch002

Atiku, S. O., & Fields, Z. (2018). Organisational Learning Dimensions and Talent Retention Strategies for the Service Industries. In N. Baporikar (Ed.), *Global Practices in Knowledge Management for Societal and Organizational Development* (pp. 358–381). Hershey, PA: IGI Global. doi:10.4018/978-1-5225-3009-1.ch017

Ávila, L., & Teixeira, L. (2018). The Main Concepts Behind the Dematerialization of Business Processes. In M. Khosrow-Pour, D.B.A. (Ed.), Encyclopedia of Information Science and Technology, Fourth Edition (pp. 888-898). Hershey, PA: IGI Global. doi:10.4018/978-1-5225-2255-3.ch076

Bartens, Y., Chunpir, H. I., Schulte, F., & Voß, S. (2017). Business/IT Alignment in Two-Sided Markets: A COBIT 5 Analysis for Media Streaming Business Models. In S. De Haes & W. Van Grembergen (Eds.), *Strategic IT Governance and Alignment in Business Settings* (pp. 82–111). Hershey, PA: IGI Global. doi:10.4018/978-1-5225-0861-8.ch004

Bashayreh, A. M. (2018). Organizational Culture and Organizational Performance. In W. Lee & F. Sabetzadeh (Eds.), *Contemporary Knowledge and Systems Science* (pp. 50–69). Hershey, PA: IGI Global. doi:10.4018/978-1-5225-5655-8.ch003

Bedford, D. A. (2018). Sustainable Knowledge Management Strategies: Aligning Business Capabilities and Knowledge Management Goals. In N. Baporikar (Ed.), *Global Practices in Knowledge Management for Societal and Organizational Development* (pp. 46–73). Hershey, PA: IGI Global. doi:10.4018/978-1-5225-3009-1.ch003

Benmoussa, F., Nakara, W. A., & Jaouen, A. (2016). The Use of Social Media by SMEs in the Tourism Industry. In I. Lee (Ed.), *Encyclopedia of E-Commerce Development, Implementation, and Management* (pp. 2159–2170). Hershey, PA: IGI Global. doi:10.4018/978-1-4666-9787-4.ch155

Berger, R. (2016). Indigenous Management and Bottom of Pyramid Countries: The Role of National Institutions. In U. Aung & P. Ordoñez de Pablos (Eds.), *Managerial Strategies and Practice in the Asian Business Sector* (pp. 107–123). Hershey, PA: IGI Global. doi:10.4018/978-1-4666-9758-4.ch007

Bharwani, S., & Musunuri, D. (2018). Reflection as a Process From Theory to Practice. In M. Khosrow-Pour, D.B.A. (Ed.), Encyclopedia of Information Science and Technology, Fourth Edition (pp. 1529-1539). Hershey, PA: IGI Global. doi:10.4018/978-1-5225-2255-3.ch132

Bhatt, G. D., Wang, Z., & Rodger, J. A. (2017). Information Systems Capabilities and Their Effects on Competitive Advantages: A Study of Chinese Companies. *Information Resources Management Journal, 30*(3), 41–57. doi:10.4018/IRMJ.2017070103

Bhushan, M., & Yadav, A. (2017). Concept of Cloud Computing in ESB. In R. Bhadoria, N. Chaudhari, G. Tomar, & S. Singh (Eds.), *Exploring Enterprise Service Bus in the Service-Oriented Architecture Paradigm* (pp. 116–127). Hershey, PA: IGI Global. doi:10.4018/978-1-5225-2157-0.ch008

Bhushan, S. (2017). System Dynamics Base-Model of Humanitarian Supply Chain (HSCM) in Disaster Prone Eco-Communities of India: A Discussion on Simulation and Scenario Results. *International Journal of System Dynamics Applications, 6*(3), 20–37. doi:10.4018/IJSDA.2017070102

Biswas, A., & De, A. K. (2017). On Development of a Fuzzy Stochastic Programming Model with Its Application to Business Management. In S. Trivedi, S. Dey, A. Kumar, & T. Panda (Eds.), *Handbook of Research on Advanced Data Mining Techniques and Applications for Business Intelligence* (pp. 353–378). Hershey, PA: IGI Global. doi:10.4018/978-1-5225-2031-3.ch021

Bücker, J., & Ernste, K. (2018). Use of Brand Heroes in Strategic Reputation Management: The Case of Bacardi, Adidas, and Daimler. In A. Erdemir (Ed.), *Reputation Management Techniques in Public Relations* (pp. 126–150). Hershey, PA: IGI Global. doi:10.4018/978-1-5225-3619-2.ch007

Bureš, V. (2018). Industry 4.0 From the Systems Engineering Perspective: Alternative Holistic Framework Development. In R. Brunet-Thornton & F. Martinez (Eds.), *Analyzing the Impacts of Industry 4.0 in Modern Business Environments* (pp. 199–223). Hershey, PA: IGI Global. doi:10.4018/978-1-5225-3468-6.ch011

Buzady, Z. (2017). Resolving the Magic Cube of Effective Case Teaching: Benchmarking Case Teaching Practices in Emerging Markets – Insights from the Central European University Business School, Hungary. In D. Latusek (Ed.), *Case Studies as a Teaching Tool in Management Education* (pp. 79–103). Hershey, PA: IGI Global. doi:10.4018/978-1-5225-0770-3.ch005

Campatelli, G., Richter, A., & Stocker, A. (2016). Participative Knowledge Management to Empower Manufacturing Workers. *International Journal of Knowledge Management, 12*(4), 37–50. doi:10.4018/IJKM.2016100103

Căpusneanu, S., & Topor, D. I. (2018). Business Ethics and Cost Management in SMEs: Theories of Business Ethics and Cost Management Ethos. In I. Oncioiu (Ed.), *Ethics and Decision-Making for Sustainable Business Practices* (pp. 109–127). Hershey, PA: IGI Global. doi:10.4018/978-1-5225-3773-1.ch007

Carneiro, A. (2016). Maturity in Health Organization Information Systems: Metrics and Privacy Perspectives. *International Journal of Privacy and Health Information Management*, *4*(2), 1–18. doi:10.4018/IJPHIM.2016070101

Chan, R. L., Mo, P. L., & Moon, K. K. (2018). Strategic and Tactical Measures in Managing Enterprise Risks: A Study of the Textile and Apparel Industry. In K. Strang, M. Korstanje, & N. Vajjhala (Eds.), *Research, Practices, and Innovations in Global Risk and Contingency Management* (pp. 1–19). Hershey, PA: IGI Global. doi:10.4018/978-1-5225-4754-9.ch001

Chandan, H. C. (2016). Motivations and Challenges of Female Entrepreneurship in Developed and Developing Economies. In N. Baporikar (Ed.), *Handbook of Research on Entrepreneurship in the Contemporary Knowledge-Based Global Economy* (pp. 260–286). Hershey, PA: IGI Global. doi:10.4018/978-1-4666-8798-1.ch012

Charlier, S. D., Burke-Smalley, L. A., & Fisher, S. L. (2018). Undergraduate Programs in the U.S: A Contextual and Content-Based Analysis. In J. Mendy (Ed.), *Teaching Human Resources and Organizational Behavior at the College Level* (pp. 26–57). Hershey, PA: IGI Global. doi:10.4018/978-1-5225-2820-3.ch002

Chaudhuri, S. (2016). Application of Web-Based Geographical Information System (GIS) in E-Business. In U. Panwar, R. Kumar, & N. Ray (Eds.), *Handbook of Research on Promotional Strategies and Consumer Influence in the Service Sector* (pp. 389–405). Hershey, PA: IGI Global. doi:10.4018/978-1-5225-0143-5.ch023

Choudhuri, P. S. (2016). An Empirical Study on the Quality of Services Offered by the Private Life Insurers in Burdwan. In U. Panwar, R. Kumar, & N. Ray (Eds.), *Handbook of Research on Promotional Strategies and Consumer Influence in the Service Sector* (pp. 31–55). Hershey, PA: IGI Global. doi:10.4018/978-1-5225-0143-5.ch002

Dahlberg, T., Kivijärvi, H., & Saarinen, T. (2017). IT Investment Consistency and Other Factors Influencing the Success of IT Performance. In S. De Haes & W. Van Grembergen (Eds.), *Strategic IT Governance and Alignment in Business Settings* (pp. 176–208). Hershey, PA: IGI Global. doi:10.4018/978-1-5225-0861-8.ch007

Damnjanović, A. M. (2017). Knowledge Management Optimization through IT and E-Business Utilization: A Qualitative Study on Serbian SMEs. In M. Vemić (Ed.), *Optimal Management Strategies in Small and Medium Enterprises* (pp. 249–267). Hershey, PA: IGI Global. doi:10.4018/978-1-5225-1949-2.ch012

Daneshpour, H. (2017). Integrating Sustainable Development into Project Portfolio Management through Application of Open Innovation. In M. Vemić (Ed.), *Optimal Management Strategies in Small and Medium Enterprises* (pp. 370–387). Hershey, PA: IGI Global. doi:10.4018/978-1-5225-1949-2.ch017

Daniel, A. D., & Reis de Castro, V. (2018). Entrepreneurship Education: How to Measure the Impact on Nascent Entrepreneurs. In A. Carrizo Moreira, J. Guilherme Leitão Dantas, & F. Manuel Valente (Eds.), *Nascent Entrepreneurship and Successful New Venture Creation* (pp. 85–110). Hershey, PA: IGI Global. doi:10.4018/978-1-5225-2936-1.ch004

David, F., van der Sijde, P., & van den Besselaar, P. (2016). Enterpreneurial Incentives, Obstacles, and Management in University-Business Co-Operation: The Case of Indonesia. In J. Saiz-Álvarez (Ed.), *Handbook of Research on Social Entrepreneurship and Solidarity Economics* (pp. 499–518). Hershey, PA: IGI Global. doi:10.4018/978-1-5225-0097-1.ch024

David, R., Swami, B. N., & Tangirala, S. (2018). Ethics Impact on Knowledge Management in Organizational Development: A Case Study. In N. Baporikar (Ed.), *Global Practices in Knowledge Management for Societal and Organizational Development* (pp. 19–45). Hershey, PA: IGI Global. doi:10.4018/978-1-5225-3009-1.ch002

Delias, P., & Lakiotaki, K. (2018). Discovering Process Horizontal Boundaries to Facilitate Process Comprehension. *International Journal of Operations Research and Information Systems*, *9*(2), 1–31. doi:10.4018/IJORIS.2018040101

Denholm, J., & Lee-Davies, L. (2018). Success Factors for Games in Business and Project Management. In *Enhancing Education and Training Initiatives Through Serious Games* (pp. 34–68). Hershey, PA: IGI Global. doi:10.4018/978-1-5225-3689-5.ch002

Deshpande, M. (2017). Best Practices in Management Institutions for Global Leadership: Policy Aspects. In N. Baporikar (Ed.), *Management Education for Global Leadership* (pp. 1–27). Hershey, PA: IGI Global. doi:10.4018/978-1-5225-1013-0.ch001

Deshpande, M. (2018). Policy Perspectives for SMEs Knowledge Management. In N. Baporikar (Ed.), *Knowledge Integration Strategies for Entrepreneurship and Sustainability* (pp. 23–46). Hershey, PA: IGI Global. doi:10.4018/978-1-5225-5115-7.ch002

Dezdar, S. (2017). ERP Implementation Projects in Asian Countries: A Comparative Study on Iran and China. *International Journal of Information Technology Project Management*, *8*(3), 52–68. doi:10.4018/IJITPM.2017070104

Domingos, D., Martinho, R., & Varajão, J. (2016). Controlled Flexibility in Healthcare Processes: A BPMN-Extension Approach. In M. Cruz-Cunha, I. Miranda, R. Martinho, & R. Rijo (Eds.), *Encyclopedia of E-Health and Telemedicine* (pp. 521–535). Hershey, PA: IGI Global. doi:10.4018/978-1-4666-9978-6.ch040

Domingos, D., Respício, A., & Martinho, R. (2017). Reliability of IoT-Aware BPMN Healthcare Processes. In C. Reis & M. Maximiano (Eds.), *Internet of Things and Advanced Application in Healthcare* (pp. 214–248). Hershey, PA: IGI Global. doi:10.4018/978-1-5225-1820-4.ch008

Dosumu, O., Hussain, J., & El-Gohary, H. (2017). An Exploratory Study of the Impact of Government Policies on the Development of Small and Medium Enterprises in Developing Countries: The Case of Nigeria. *International Journal of Customer Relationship Marketing and Management*, *8*(4), 51–62. doi:10.4018/IJCRMM.2017100104

Durst, S., Bruns, G., & Edvardsson, I. R. (2017). Retaining Knowledge in Smaller Building and Construction Firms. *International Journal of Knowledge and Systems Science*, *8*(3), 1–12. doi:10.4018/IJKSS.2017070101

Edvardsson, I. R., & Durst, S. (2017). Outsourcing, Knowledge, and Learning: A Critical Review. *International Journal of Knowledge-Based Organizations*, *7*(2), 13–26. doi:10.4018/IJKBO.2017040102

Edwards, J. S. (2018). Integrating Knowledge Management and Business Processes. In M. Khosrow-Pour, D.B.A. (Ed.), Encyclopedia of Information Science and Technology, Fourth Edition (pp. 5046-5055). Hershey, PA: IGI Global. doi:10.4018/978-1-5225-2255-3.ch437

Ejiogu, A. O. (2018). Economics of Farm Management. In *Agricultural Finance and Opportunities for Investment and Expansion* (pp. 56–72). Hershey, PA: IGI Global. doi:10.4018/978-1-5225-3059-6.ch003

Ekanem, I., & Abiade, G. E. (2018). Factors Influencing the Use of E-Commerce by Small Enterprises in Nigeria. *International Journal of ICT Research in Africa and the Middle East*, *7*(1), 37–53. doi:10.4018/IJICTRAME.2018010103

Ekanem, I., & Alrossais, L. A. (2017). Succession Challenges Facing Family Businesses in Saudi Arabia. In P. Zgheib (Ed.), *Entrepreneurship and Business Innovation in the Middle East* (pp. 122–146). Hershey, PA: IGI Global. doi:10.4018/978-1-5225-2066-5.ch007

El Faquih, L., & Fredj, M. (2017). Ontology-Based Framework for Quality in Configurable Process Models. *Journal of Electronic Commerce in Organizations*, *15*(2), 48–60. doi:10.4018/JECO.2017040104

El-Gohary, H., & El-Gohary, Z. (2016). An Attempt to Explore Electronic Marketing Adoption and Implementation Aspects in Developing Countries: The Case of Egypt. *International Journal of Customer Relationship Marketing and Management*, *7*(4), 1–26. doi:10.4018/IJCRMM.2016100101

Entico, G. J. (2016). Knowledge Management and the Medical Health Librarians: A Perception Study. In J. Yap, M. Perez, M. Ayson, & G. Entico (Eds.), *Special Library Administration, Standardization and Technological Integration* (pp. 52–77). Hershey, PA: IGI Global. doi:10.4018/978-1-4666-9542-9.ch003

Faisal, M. N., & Talib, F. (2017). Building Ambidextrous Supply Chains in SMEs: How to Tackle the Barriers? *International Journal of Information Systems and Supply Chain Management*, *10*(4), 80–100. doi:10.4018/IJISSCM.2017100105

Fernandes, T. M., Gomes, J., & Romão, M. (2017). Investments in E-Government: A Benefit Management Case Study. *International Journal of Electronic Government Research*, *13*(3), 1–17. doi:10.4018/IJEGR.2017070101

Fouda, F. A. (2016). A Suggested Curriculum in Career Education to Develop Business Secondary Schools Students' Career Knowledge Management Domains and Professional Thinking. *International Journal of Technology Diffusion*, *7*(2), 42–62. doi:10.4018/IJTD.2016040103

Gallardo-Vázquez, D., & Pajuelo-Moreno, M. L. (2016). How Spanish Universities are Promoting Entrepreneurship through Your Own Lines of Teaching and Research? In L. Carvalho (Ed.), *Handbook of Research on Entrepreneurial Success and its Impact on Regional Development* (pp. 431–454). Hershey, PA: IGI Global. doi:10.4018/978-1-4666-9567-2.ch019

Gao, S. S., Oreal, S., & Zhang, J. (2018). Contemporary Financial Risk Management Perceptions and Practices of Small-Sized Chinese Businesses. In I. Management Association (Ed.), Global Business Expansion: Concepts, Methodologies, Tools, and Applications (pp. 917-931). Hershey, PA: IGI Global. doi:10.4018/978-1-5225-5481-3.ch041

Garg, R., & Berning, S. C. (2017). Indigenous Chinese Management Philosophies: Key Concepts and Relevance for Modern Chinese Firms. In B. Christiansen & G. Koc (Eds.), *Transcontinental Strategies for Industrial Development and Economic Growth* (pp. 43–57). Hershey, PA: IGI Global. doi:10.4018/978-1-5225-2160-0.ch003

Gencer, Y. G. (2017). Supply Chain Management in Retailing Business. In U. Akkucuk (Ed.), *Ethics and Sustainability in Global Supply Chain Management* (pp. 197–210). Hershey, PA: IGI Global. doi:10.4018/978-1-5225-2036-8.ch011

Giacosa, E. (2016). Innovation in Luxury Fashion Businesses as a Means for the Regional Development. In L. Carvalho (Ed.), *Handbook of Research on Entrepreneurial Success and its Impact on Regional Development* (pp. 206–222). Hershey, PA: IGI Global. doi:10.4018/978-1-4666-9567-2.ch010

Giacosa, E. (2018). The Increasing of the Regional Development Thanks to the Luxury Business Innovation. In L. Carvalho (Ed.), *Handbook of Research on Entrepreneurial Ecosystems and Social Dynamics in a Globalized World* (pp. 260–273). Hershey, PA: IGI Global. doi:10.4018/978-1-5225-3525-6.ch011

Gianni, M., & Gotzamani, K. (2016). Integrated Management Systems and Information Management Systems: Common Threads. In P. Papajorgji, F. Pinet, A. Guimarães, & J. Papathanasiou (Eds.), *Automated Enterprise Systems for Maximizing Business Performance* (pp. 195–214). Hershey, PA: IGI Global. doi:10.4018/978-1-4666-8841-4.ch011

Gianni, M., Gotzamani, K., & Linden, I. (2016). How a BI-wise Responsible Integrated Management System May Support Food Traceability. *International Journal of Decision Support System Technology*, *8*(2), 1–17. doi:10.4018/IJDSST.2016040101

Glykas, M., & George, J. (2017). Quality and Process Management Systems in the UAE Maritime Industry. *International Journal of Productivity Management and Assessment Technologies*, *5*(1), 20–39. doi:10.4018/IJPMAT.2017010102

Glykas, M., Valiris, G., Kokkinaki, A., & Koutsoukou, Z. (2018). Banking Business Process Management Implementation. *International Journal of Productivity Management and Assessment Technologies*, *6*(1), 50–69. doi:10.4018/IJPMAT.2018010104

Gomes, J., & Romão, M. (2017). The Balanced Scorecard: Keeping Updated and Aligned with Today's Business Trends. *International Journal of Productivity Management and Assessment Technologies*, *5*(2), 1–15. doi:10.4018/IJPMAT.2017070101

Gomes, J., & Romão, M. (2017). Aligning Information Systems and Technology with Benefit Management and Balanced Scorecard. In S. De Haes & W. Van Grembergen (Eds.), *Strategic IT Governance and Alignment in Business Settings* (pp. 112–131). Hershey, PA: IGI Global. doi:10.4018/978-1-5225-0861-8.ch005

Grefen, P., & Turetken, O. (2017). Advanced Business Process Management in Networked E-Business Scenarios. *International Journal of E-Business Research, 13*(4), 70–104. doi:10.4018/IJEBR.2017100105

Haider, A., & Saetang, S. (2017). Strategic IT Alignment in Service Sector. In S. Rozenes & Y. Cohen (Eds.), *Handbook of Research on Strategic Alliances and Value Co-Creation in the Service Industry* (pp. 231–258). Hershey, PA: IGI Global. doi:10.4018/978-1-5225-2084-9.ch012

Haider, A., & Tang, S. S. (2016). Maximising Value Through IT and Business Alignment: A Case of IT Governance Institutionalisation at a Thai Bank. *International Journal of Technology Diffusion, 7*(3), 33–58. doi:10.4018/IJTD.2016070104

Hajilari, A. B., Ghadaksaz, M., & Fasghandis, G. S. (2017). Assessing Organizational Readiness for Implementing ERP System Using Fuzzy Expert System Approach. *International Journal of Enterprise Information Systems, 13*(1), 67–85. doi:10.4018/IJEIS.2017010105

Haldorai, A., Ramu, A., & Murugan, S. (2018). Social Aware Cognitive Radio Networks: Effectiveness of Social Networks as a Strategic Tool for Organizational Business Management. In H. Bansal, G. Shrivastava, G. Nguyen, & L. Stanciu (Eds.), *Social Network Analytics for Contemporary Business Organizations* (pp. 188–202). Hershey, PA: IGI Global. doi:10.4018/978-1-5225-5097-6.ch010

Hall, O. P. Jr. (2017). Social Media Driven Management Education. *International Journal of Knowledge-Based Organizations, 7*(2), 43–59. doi:10.4018/IJKBO.2017040104

Hanifah, H., Halim, H. A., Ahmad, N. H., & Vafaei-Zadeh, A. (2017). Innovation Culture as a Mediator Between Specific Human Capital and Innovation Performance Among Bumiputera SMEs in Malaysia. In N. Ahmad, T. Ramayah, H. Halim, & S. Rahman (Eds.), *Handbook of Research on Small and Medium Enterprises in Developing Countries* (pp. 261–279). Hershey, PA: IGI Global. doi:10.4018/978-1-5225-2165-5.ch012

Hartlieb, S., & Silvius, G. (2017). Handling Uncertainty in Project Management and Business Development: Similarities and Differences. In Y. Raydugin (Ed.), *Handbook of Research on Leveraging Risk and Uncertainties for Effective Project Management* (pp. 337–362). Hershey, PA: IGI Global. doi:10.4018/978-1-5225-1790-0.ch016

Hass, K. B. (2017). Living on the Edge: Managing Project Complexity. In Y. Raydugin (Ed.), *Handbook of Research on Leveraging Risk and Uncertainties for Effective Project Management* (pp. 177–201). Hershey, PA: IGI Global. doi:10.4018/978-1-5225-1790-0.ch009

Hassan, A., & Privitera, D. S. (2016). Google AdSense as a Mobile Technology in Education. In J. Holland (Ed.), *Wearable Technology and Mobile Innovations for Next-Generation Education* (pp. 200–223). Hershey, PA: IGI Global. doi:10.4018/978-1-5225-0069-8.ch011

Hassan, A., & Rahimi, R. (2016). Consuming "Innovation" in Tourism: Augmented Reality as an Innovation Tool in Digital Tourism Marketing. In N. Pappas & I. Bregoli (Eds.), *Global Dynamics in Travel, Tourism, and Hospitality* (pp. 130–147). Hershey, PA: IGI Global. doi:10.4018/978-1-5225-0201-2.ch008

Hawking, P., & Carmine Sellitto, C. (2017). Developing an Effective Strategy for Organizational Business Intelligence. In M. Tavana (Ed.), *Enterprise Information Systems and the Digitalization of Business Functions* (pp. 222–237). Hershey, PA: IGI Global. doi:10.4018/978-1-5225-2382-6.ch010

Hawking, P., & Sellitto, C. (2017). A Fast-Moving Consumer Goods Company and Business Intelligence Strategy Development. *International Journal of Enterprise Information Systems, 13*(2), 22–33. doi:10.4018/IJEIS.2017040102

Hawking, P., & Sellitto, C. (2017). Business Intelligence Strategy: Two Case Studies. *International Journal of Business Intelligence Research, 8*(2), 17–30. doi:10.4018/IJBIR.2017070102

Haynes, J. D., Arockiasamy, S., Al Rashdi, M., & Al Rashdi, S. (2016). Business and E Business Strategies for Coopetition and Thematic Management as a Sustained Basis for Ethics and Social Responsibility in Emerging Markets. In M. Al-Shammari & H. Masri (Eds.), *Ethical and Social Perspectives on Global Business Interaction in Emerging Markets* (pp. 25–39). Hershey, PA: IGI Global. doi:10.4018/978-1-4666-9864-2.ch002

Hee, W. J., Jalleh, G., Lai, H., & Lin, C. (2017). E-Commerce and IT Projects: Evaluation and Management Issues in Australian and Taiwanese Hospitals. *International Journal of Public Health Management and Ethics, 2*(1), 69–90. doi:10.4018/IJPHME.2017010104

Hernandez, A. A. (2018). Exploring the Factors to Green IT Adoption of SMEs in the Philippines. *Journal of Cases on Information Technology, 20*(2), 49–66. doi:10.4018/JCIT.2018040104

Hernandez, A. A., & Ona, S. E. (2016). Green IT Adoption: Lessons from the Philippines Business Process Outsourcing Industry. *International Journal of Social Ecology and Sustainable Development, 7*(1), 1–34. doi:10.4018/IJSESD.2016010101

Hollman, A., Bickford, S., & Hollman, T. (2017). Cyber InSecurity: A Post-Mortem Attempt to Assess Cyber Problems from IT and Business Management Perspectives. *Journal of Cases on Information Technology, 19*(3), 42–70. doi:10.4018/JCIT.2017070104

Igbinakhase, I. (2017). Responsible and Sustainable Management Practices in Developing and Developed Business Environments. In Z. Fields (Ed.), *Collective Creativity for Responsible and Sustainable Business Practice* (pp. 180–207). Hershey, PA: IGI Global. doi:10.4018/978-1-5225-1823-5.ch010

Ilahi, L., Ghannouchi, S. A., & Martinho, R. (2016). A Business Process Management Approach to Home Healthcare Processes: On the Gap between Intention and Reality. In M. Cruz-Cunha, I. Miranda, R. Martinho, & R. Rijo (Eds.), *Encyclopedia of E-Health and Telemedicine* (pp. 439–457). Hershey, PA: IGI Global. doi:10.4018/978-1-4666-9978-6.ch035

Iwata, J. J., & Hoskins, R. G. (2017). Managing Indigenous Knowledge in Tanzania: A Business Perspective. In P. Jain & N. Mnjama (Eds.), *Managing Knowledge Resources and Records in Modern Organizations* (pp. 198–214). Hershey, PA: IGI Global. doi:10.4018/978-1-5225-1965-2.ch012

Jabeen, F., Ahmad, S. Z., & Alkaabi, S. (2016). The Internationalization Decision-Making of United Arab Emirates Family Businesses. In N. Zakaria, A. Abdul-Talib, & N. Osman (Eds.), *Handbook of Research on Impacts of International Business and Political Affairs on the Global Economy* (pp. 1–22). Hershey, PA: IGI Global. doi:10.4018/978-1-4666-9806-2.ch001

Jain, P. (2017). Ethical and Legal Issues in Knowledge Management Life-Cycle in Business. In P. Jain & N. Mnjama (Eds.), *Managing Knowledge Resources and Records in Modern Organizations* (pp. 82–101). Hershey, PA: IGI Global. doi:10.4018/978-1-5225-1965-2.ch006

Jamali, D., Abdallah, H., & Matar, F. (2016). Opportunities and Challenges for CSR Mainstreaming in Business Schools. *International Journal of Technology and Educational Marketing*, *6*(2), 1–29. doi:10.4018/IJTEM.2016070101

James, S., & Hauli, E. (2017). Holistic Management Education at Tanzanian Rural Development Planning Institute. In N. Baporikar (Ed.), *Management Education for Global Leadership* (pp. 112–136). Hershey, PA: IGI Global. doi:10.4018/978-1-5225-1013-0.ch006

Janošková, M., Csikósová, A., & Čulková, K. (2018). Measurement of Company Performance as Part of Its Strategic Management. In R. Leon (Ed.), *Managerial Strategies for Business Sustainability During Turbulent Times* (pp. 309–335). Hershey, PA: IGI Global. doi:10.4018/978-1-5225-2716-9.ch017

Jean-Vasile, A., & Alecu, A. (2017). Theoretical and Practical Approaches in Understanding the Influences of Cost-Productivity-Profit Trinomial in Contemporary Enterprises. In A. Jean Vasile & D. Nicolò (Eds.), *Sustainable Entrepreneurship and Investments in the Green Economy* (pp. 28–62). Hershey, PA: IGI Global. doi:10.4018/978-1-5225-2075-7.ch002

Jha, D. G. (2016). Preparing for Information Technology Driven Changes. In S. Tiwari & L. Nafees (Eds.), *Innovative Management Education Pedagogies for Preparing Next-Generation Leaders* (pp. 258–274). Hershey, PA: IGI Global. doi:10.4018/978-1-4666-9691-4.ch015

Joia, L. A., & Correia, J. C. (2018). CIO Competencies From the IT Professional Perspective: Insights From Brazil. *Journal of Global Information Management*, *26*(2), 74–103. doi:10.4018/JGIM.2018040104

Juma, A., & Mzera, N. (2017). Knowledge Management and Records Management and Competitive Advantage in Business. In P. Jain & N. Mnjama (Eds.), *Managing Knowledge Resources and Records in Modern Organizations* (pp. 15–28). Hershey, PA: IGI Global. doi:10.4018/978-1-5225-1965-2.ch002

K., I., & A, V. (2018). Monitoring and Auditing in the Cloud. In K. Munir (Ed.), *Cloud Computing Technologies for Green Enterprises* (pp. 318-350). Hershey, PA: IGI Global. doi:10.4018/978-1-5225-3038-1.ch013

Kabra, G., Ghosh, V., & Ramesh, A. (2018). Enterprise Integrated Business Process Management and Business Intelligence Framework for Business Process Sustainability. In A. Paul, D. Bhattacharyya, & S. Anand (Eds.), *Green Initiatives for Business Sustainability and Value Creation* (pp. 228–238). Hershey, PA: IGI Global. doi:10.4018/978-1-5225-2662-9.ch010

Kaoud, M. (2017). Investigation of Customer Knowledge Management: A Case Study Research. *International Journal of Service Science, Management, Engineering, and Technology*, *8*(2), 12–22. doi:10.4018/IJSSMET.2017040102

Kara, M. E., & Fırat, S. Ü. (2016). Sustainability, Risk, and Business Intelligence in Supply Chains. In M. Erdoğdu, T. Arun, & I. Ahmad (Eds.), *Handbook of Research on Green Economic Development Initiatives and Strategies* (pp. 501–538). Hershey, PA: IGI Global. doi:10.4018/978-1-5225-0440-5.ch022

Katuu, S. (2018). A Comparative Assessment of Enterprise Content Management Maturity Models. In N. Gwangwava & M. Mutingi (Eds.), *E-Manufacturing and E-Service Strategies in Contemporary Organizations* (pp. 93–118). Hershey, PA: IGI Global. doi:10.4018/978-1-5225-3628-4.ch005

Khan, M. A. (2016). MNEs Management Strategies in Developing Countries: Establishing the Context. In M. Khan (Ed.), *Multinational Enterprise Management Strategies in Developing Countries* (pp. 1–33). Hershey, PA: IGI Global. doi:10.4018/978-1-5225-0276-0.ch001

Khan, M. A. (2016). Operational Approaches in Organizational Structure: A Case for MNEs in Developing Countries. In M. Khan (Ed.), *Multinational Enterprise Management Strategies in Developing Countries* (pp. 129–151). Hershey, PA: IGI Global. doi:10.4018/978-1-5225-0276-0.ch007

Kinnunen, S., Ylä-Kujala, A., Marttonen-Arola, S., Kärri, T., & Baglee, D. (2018). Internet of Things in Asset Management: Insights from Industrial Professionals and Academia. *International Journal of Service Science, Management, Engineering, and Technology*, *9*(2), 104–119. doi:10.4018/IJSSMET.2018040105

Klein, A. Z., Sabino de Freitas, A., Machado, L., Freitas, J. C. Jr, Graziola, P. G. Jr, & Schlemmer, E. (2017). Virtual Worlds Applications for Management Education. In L. Tomei (Ed.), *Exploring the New Era of Technology-Infused Education* (pp. 279–299). Hershey, PA: IGI Global. doi:10.4018/978-1-5225-1709-2.ch017

Kożuch, B., & Jabłoński, A. (2017). Adopting the Concept of Business Models in Public Management. In M. Lewandowski & B. Kożuch (Eds.), *Public Sector Entrepreneurship and the Integration of Innovative Business Models* (pp. 10–46). Hershey, PA: IGI Global. doi:10.4018/978-1-5225-2215-7.ch002

Kumar, J., Adhikary, A., & Jha, A. (2017). Small Active Investors' Perceptions and Preferences Towards Tax Saving Mutual Fund Schemes in Eastern India: An Empirical Note. *International Journal of Asian Business and Information Management*, *8*(2), 35–45. doi:10.4018/IJABIM.2017040103

Lassoued, Y., Bouzguenda, L., & Mahmoud, T. (2016). Context-Aware Business Process Versions Management. *International Journal of e-Collaboration*, *12*(3), 7–33. doi:10.4018/IJeC.2016070102

Lavassani, K. M., & Movahedi, B. (2017). Applications Driven Information Systems: Beyond Networks toward Business Ecosystems. *International Journal of Innovation in the Digital Economy*, *8*(1), 61–75. doi:10.4018/IJIDE.2017010104

Lazzareschi, V. H., & Brito, M. S. (2017). Strategic Information Management: Proposal of Business Project Model. In G. Jamil, A. Soares, & C. Pessoa (Eds.), *Handbook of Research on Information Management for Effective Logistics and Supply Chains* (pp. 59–88). Hershey, PA: IGI Global. doi:10.4018/978-1-5225-0973-8.ch004

Lederer, M., Kurz, M., & Lazarov, P. (2017). Usage and Suitability of Methods for Strategic Business Process Initiatives: A Multi Case Study Research. *International Journal of Productivity Management and Assessment Technologies, 5*(1), 40–51. doi:10.4018/IJPMAT.2017010103

Lee, I. (2017). A Social Enterprise Business Model and a Case Study of Pacific Community Ventures (PCV). In V. Potocan, M. Ünğan, & Z. Nedelko (Eds.), *Handbook of Research on Managerial Solutions in Non-Profit Organizations* (pp. 182–204). Hershey, PA: IGI Global. doi:10.4018/978-1-5225-0731-4.ch009

Lee, L. J., & Leu, J. (2016). Exploring the Effectiveness of IT Application and Value Method in the Innovation Performance of Enterprise. *International Journal of Enterprise Information Systems, 12*(2), 47–65. doi:10.4018/IJEIS.2016040104

Lee, Y. (2016). Alignment Effect of Entrepreneurial Orientation and Marketing Orientation on Firm Performance. *International Journal of Customer Relationship Marketing and Management, 7*(4), 58–69. doi:10.4018/IJCRMM.2016100104

Leon, L. A., Seal, K. C., Przasnyski, Z. H., & Wiedenman, I. (2017). Skills and Competencies Required for Jobs in Business Analytics: A Content Analysis of Job Advertisements Using Text Mining. *International Journal of Business Intelligence Research, 8*(1), 1–25. doi:10.4018/IJBIR.2017010101

Leu, J., Lee, L. J., & Krischke, A. (2016). Value Engineering-Based Method for Implementing the ISO14001 System in the Green Supply Chains. *International Journal of Strategic Decision Sciences, 7*(4), 1–20. doi:10.4018/IJSDS.2016100101

Levy, C. L., & Elias, N. I. (2017). SOHO Users' Perceptions of Reliability and Continuity of Cloud-Based Services. In M. Moore (Ed.), *Cybersecurity Breaches and Issues Surrounding Online Threat Protection* (pp. 248–287). Hershey, PA: IGI Global. doi:10.4018/978-1-5225-1941-6.ch011

Levy, M. (2018). Change Management Serving Knowledge Management and Organizational Development: Reflections and Review. In N. Baporikar (Ed.), *Global Practices in Knowledge Management for Societal and Organizational Development* (pp. 256–270). Hershey, PA: IGI Global. doi:10.4018/978-1-5225-3009-1.ch012

Lewandowski, M. (2017). Public Organizations and Business Model Innovation: The Role of Public Service Design. In M. Lewandowski & B. Kożuch (Eds.), *Public Sector Entrepreneurship and the Integration of Innovative Business Models* (pp. 47–72). Hershey, PA: IGI Global. doi:10.4018/978-1-5225-2215-7.ch003

Lhannaoui, H., Kabbaj, M. I., & Bakkoury, Z. (2017). A Survey of Risk-Aware Business Process Modelling. *International Journal of Risk and Contingency Management, 6*(3), 14–26. doi:10.4018/IJRCM.2017070102

Li, J., Sun, W., Jiang, W., Yang, H., & Zhang, L. (2017). How the Nature of Exogenous Shocks and Crises Impact Company Performance?: The Effects of Industry Characteristics. *International Journal of Risk and Contingency Management*, *6*(4), 40–55. doi:10.4018/IJRCM.2017100103

Lu, C., & Liu, S. (2016). Cultural Tourism O2O Business Model Innovation-A Case Study of CTrip. *Journal of Electronic Commerce in Organizations*, *14*(2), 16–31. doi:10.4018/JECO.2016040102

Machen, B., Hosseini, M. R., Wood, A., & Bakhshi, J. (2016). An Investigation into using SAP-PS as a Multidimensional Project Control System (MPCS). *International Journal of Enterprise Information Systems*, *12*(2), 66–81. doi:10.4018/IJEIS.2016040105

Malega, P. (2017). Small and Medium Enterprises in the Slovak Republic: Status and Competitiveness of SMEs in the Global Markets and Possibilities of Optimization. In M. Vemić (Ed.), *Optimal Management Strategies in Small and Medium Enterprises* (pp. 102–124). Hershey, PA: IGI Global. doi:10.4018/978-1-5225-1949-2.ch006

Malewska, K. M. (2017). Intuition in Decision-Making on the Example of a Non-Profit Organization. In V. Potocan, M. Üngan, & Z. Nedelko (Eds.), *Handbook of Research on Managerial Solutions in Non-Profit Organizations* (pp. 378–399). Hershey, PA: IGI Global. doi:10.4018/978-1-5225-0731-4.ch018

Maroofi, F. (2017). Entrepreneurial Orientation and Organizational Learning Ability Analysis for Innovation and Firm Performance. In N. Baporikar (Ed.), *Innovation and Shifting Perspectives in Management Education* (pp. 144–165). Hershey, PA: IGI Global. doi:10.4018/978-1-5225-1019-2.ch007

Martins, P. V., & Zacarias, M. (2017). A Web-based Tool for Business Process Improvement. *International Journal of Web Portals*, *9*(2), 68–84. doi:10.4018/IJWP.2017070104

Matthies, B., & Coners, A. (2017). Exploring the Conceptual Nature of e-Business Projects. *Journal of Electronic Commerce in Organizations*, *15*(3), 33–63. doi:10.4018/JECO.2017070103

McKee, J. (2018). Architecture as a Tool to Solve Business Planning Problems. In M. Khosrow-Pour, D.B.A. (Ed.), Encyclopedia of Information Science and Technology, Fourth Edition (pp. 573-586). Hershey, PA: IGI Global. doi:10.4018/978-1-5225-2255-3.ch050

McMurray, A. J., Cross, J., & Caponecchia, C. (2018). The Risk Management Profession in Australia: Business Continuity Plan Practices. In N. Bajgoric (Ed.), *Always-On Enterprise Information Systems for Modern Organizations* (pp. 112–129). Hershey, PA: IGI Global. doi:10.4018/978-1-5225-3704-5.ch006

Meddah, I. H., & Belkadi, K. (2018). Mining Patterns Using Business Process Management. In R. Hamou (Ed.), *Handbook of Research on Biomimicry in Information Retrieval and Knowledge Management* (pp. 78–89). Hershey, PA: IGI Global. doi:10.4018/978-1-5225-3004-6.ch005

Mendes, L. (2017). TQM and Knowledge Management: An Integrated Approach Towards Tacit Knowledge Management. In D. Jaziri-Bouagina & G. Jamil (Eds.), *Handbook of Research on Tacit Knowledge Management for Organizational Success* (pp. 236–263). Hershey, PA: IGI Global. doi:10.4018/978-1-5225-2394-9.ch009

Mnjama, N. M. (2017). Preservation of Recorded Information in Public and Private Sector Organizations. In P. Jain & N. Mnjama (Eds.), *Managing Knowledge Resources and Records in Modern Organizations* (pp. 149–167). Hershey, PA: IGI Global. doi:10.4018/978-1-5225-1965-2.ch009

Mokoqama, M., & Fields, Z. (2017). Principles of Responsible Management Education (PRME): Call for Responsible Management Education. In Z. Fields (Ed.), *Collective Creativity for Responsible and Sustainable Business Practice* (pp. 229–241). Hershey, PA: IGI Global. doi:10.4018/978-1-5225-1823-5.ch012

Muniapan, B. (2017). Philosophy and Management: The Relevance of Vedanta in Management. In P. Ordóñez de Pablos (Ed.), *Managerial Strategies and Solutions for Business Success in Asia* (pp. 124–139). Hershey, PA: IGI Global. doi:10.4018/978-1-5225-1886-0.ch007

Muniapan, B., Gregory, M. L., & Ling, L. A. (2016). Marketing Education in Sarawak: Looking at It from the Employers' Viewpoint. In B. Smith & A. Porath (Eds.), *Global Perspectives on Contemporary Marketing Education* (pp. 112–130). Hershey, PA: IGI Global. doi:10.4018/978-1-4666-9784-3.ch008

Murad, S. E., & Dowaji, S. (2017). Using Value-Based Approach for Managing Cloud-Based Services. In A. Turuk, B. Sahoo, & S. Addya (Eds.), *Resource Management and Efficiency in Cloud Computing Environments* (pp. 33–60). Hershey, PA: IGI Global. doi:10.4018/978-1-5225-1721-4.ch002

Mutahar, A. M., Daud, N. M., Thurasamy, R., Isaac, O., & Abdulsalam, R. (2018). The Mediating of Perceived Usefulness and Perceived Ease of Use: The Case of Mobile Banking in Yemen. *International Journal of Technology Diffusion*, *9*(2), 21–40. doi:10.4018/IJTD.2018040102

Naidoo, V. (2017). E-Learning and Management Education at African Universities. In N. Baporikar (Ed.), *Management Education for Global Leadership* (pp. 181–201). Hershey, PA: IGI Global. doi:10.4018/978-1-5225-1013-0.ch009

Naidoo, V., & Igbinakhase, I. (2018). Opportunities and Challenges of Knowledge Retention in SMEs. In N. Baporikar (Ed.), *Knowledge Integration Strategies for Entrepreneurship and Sustainability* (pp. 70–94). Hershey, PA: IGI Global. doi:10.4018/978-1-5225-5115-7.ch004

Nayak, S., & Prabhu, N. (2017). Paradigm Shift in Management Education: Need for a Cross Functional Perspective. In N. Baporikar (Ed.), *Management Education for Global Leadership* (pp. 241–255). Hershey, PA: IGI Global. doi:10.4018/978-1-5225-1013-0.ch012

Ndede-Amadi, A. A. (2016). Student Interest in the IS Specialization as Predictor of the Success Potential of New Information Systems Programmes within the Schools of Business in Kenyan Public Universities. *International Journal of Information Systems and Social Change*, *7*(2), 63–79. doi:10.4018/IJISSC.2016040104

Nedelko, Z., & Potocan, V. (2016). Management Practices for Processes Optimization: Case of Slovenia. In G. Alor-Hernández, C. Sánchez-Ramírez, & J. García-Alcaraz (Eds.), *Handbook of Research on Managerial Strategies for Achieving Optimal Performance in Industrial Processes* (pp. 545–561). Hershey, PA: IGI Global. doi:10.4018/978-1-5225-0130-5.ch025

Nedelko, Z., & Potocan, V. (2017). Management Solutions in Non-Profit Organizations: Case of Slovenia. In V. Potocan, M. Üngan, & Z. Nedelko (Eds.), *Handbook of Research on Managerial Solutions in Non-Profit Organizations* (pp. 1–22). Hershey, PA: IGI Global. doi:10.4018/978-1-5225-0731-4.ch001

Nedelko, Z., & Potocan, V. (2017). Priority of Management Tools Utilization among Managers: International Comparison. In V. Wang (Ed.), *Encyclopedia of Strategic Leadership and Management* (pp. 1083–1094). Hershey, PA: IGI Global. doi:10.4018/978-1-5225-1049-9.ch075

Nedelko, Z., Raudeliūnienė, J., & Črešnar, R. (2018). Knowledge Dynamics in Supply Chain Management. In N. Baporikar (Ed.), *Knowledge Integration Strategies for Entrepreneurship and Sustainability* (pp. 150–166). Hershey, PA: IGI Global. doi:10.4018/978-1-5225-5115-7.ch008

Nguyen, H. T., & Hipsher, S. A. (2018). Innovation and Creativity Used by Private Sector Firms in a Resources-Constrained Environment. In S. Hipsher (Ed.), *Examining the Private Sector's Role in Wealth Creation and Poverty Reduction* (pp. 219–238). Hershey, PA: IGI Global. doi:10.4018/978-1-5225-3117-3.ch010

Nycz, M., & Pólkowski, Z. (2016). Business Intelligence as a Modern IT Supporting Management of Local Government Units in Poland. *International Journal of Knowledge and Systems Science*, *7*(4), 1–18. doi:10.4018/IJKSS.2016100101

Obaji, N. O., Senin, A. A., & Olugu, M. U. (2016). Supportive Government Policy as a Mechanism for Business Incubation Performance in Nigeria. *International Journal of Information Systems and Social Change*, *7*(4), 52–66. doi:10.4018/IJISSC.2016100103

Obicci, P. A. (2017). Risk Sharing in a Partnership. In *Risk Management Strategies in Public-Private Partnerships* (pp. 115–152). Hershey, PA: IGI Global. doi:10.4018/978-1-5225-2503-5.ch004

Obidallah, W. J., & Raahemi, B. (2017). Managing Changes in Service Oriented Virtual Organizations: A Structural and Procedural Framework to Facilitate the Process of Change. *Journal of Electronic Commerce in Organizations*, *15*(1), 59–83. doi:10.4018/JECO.2017010104

Ojasalo, J., & Ojasalo, K. (2016). Service Logic Business Model Canvas for Lean Development of SMEs and Start-Ups. In N. Baporikar (Ed.), *Handbook of Research on Entrepreneurship in the Contemporary Knowledge-Based Global Economy* (pp. 217–243). Hershey, PA: IGI Global. doi:10.4018/978-1-4666-8798-1.ch010

Ojo, O. (2017). Impact of Innovation on the Entrepreneurial Success in Selected Business Enterprises in South-West Nigeria. *International Journal of Innovation in the Digital Economy*, *8*(2), 29–38. doi:10.4018/IJIDE.2017040103

Okdinawati, L., Simatupang, T. M., & Sunitiyoso, Y. (2017). Multi-Agent Reinforcement Learning for Value Co-Creation of Collaborative Transportation Management (CTM). *International Journal of Information Systems and Supply Chain Management*, *10*(3), 84–95. doi:10.4018/IJISSCM.2017070105

Ortner, E., Mevius, M., Wiedmann, P., & Kurz, F. (2016). Design of Interactional Decision Support Applications for E-Participation in Smart Cities. *International Journal of Electronic Government Research, 12*(2), 18–38. doi:10.4018/IJEGR.2016040102

Pal, K. (2018). Building High Quality Big Data-Based Applications in Supply Chains. In A. Kumar & S. Saurav (Eds.), *Supply Chain Management Strategies and Risk Assessment in Retail Environments* (pp. 1–24). Hershey, PA: IGI Global. doi:10.4018/978-1-5225-3056-5.ch001

Palos-Sanchez, P. R., & Correia, M. B. (2018). Perspectives of the Adoption of Cloud Computing in the Tourism Sector. In J. Rodrigues, C. Ramos, P. Cardoso, & C. Henriques (Eds.), *Handbook of Research on Technological Developments for Cultural Heritage and eTourism Applications* (pp. 377–400). Hershey, PA: IGI Global. doi:10.4018/978-1-5225-2927-9.ch018

Parry, V. K., & Lind, M. L. (2016). Alignment of Business Strategy and Information Technology Considering Information Technology Governance, Project Portfolio Control, and Risk Management. *International Journal of Information Technology Project Management, 7*(4), 21–37. doi:10.4018/IJITPM.2016100102

Pashkova, N., Trujillo-Barrera, A., Apostolakis, G., Van Dijk, G., Drakos, P. D., & Baourakis, G. (2016). Business Management Models of Microfinance Institutions (MFIs) in Africa: A Study into Their Enabling Environments. *International Journal of Food and Beverage Manufacturing and Business Models, 1*(2), 63–82. doi:10.4018/IJFBMBM.2016070105

Patiño, B. E. (2017). New Generation Management by Convergence and Individual Identity: A Systemic and Human-Oriented Approach. In N. Baporikar (Ed.), *Innovation and Shifting Perspectives in Management Education* (pp. 119–143). Hershey, PA: IGI Global. doi:10.4018/978-1-5225-1019-2.ch006

Pawliczek, A., & Rössler, M. (2017). Knowledge of Management Tools and Systems in SMEs: Knowledge Transfer in Management. In A. Bencsik (Ed.), *Knowledge Management Initiatives and Strategies in Small and Medium Enterprises* (pp. 180–203). Hershey, PA: IGI Global. doi:10.4018/978-1-5225-1642-2.ch009

Pejic-Bach, M., Omazic, M. A., Aleksic, A., & Zoroja, J. (2018). Knowledge-Based Decision Making: A Multi-Case Analysis. In R. Leon (Ed.), *Managerial Strategies for Business Sustainability During Turbulent Times* (pp. 160–184). Hershey, PA: IGI Global. doi:10.4018/978-1-5225-2716-9.ch009

Perano, M., Hysa, X., & Calabrese, M. (2018). Strategic Planning, Cultural Context, and Business Continuity Management: Business Cases in the City of Shkoder. In A. Presenza & L. Sheehan (Eds.), *Geopolitics and Strategic Management in the Global Economy* (pp. 57–77). Hershey, PA: IGI Global. doi:10.4018/978-1-5225-2673-5.ch004

Pereira, R., Mira da Silva, M., & Lapão, L. V. (2017). IT Governance Maturity Patterns in Portuguese Healthcare. In S. De Haes & W. Van Grembergen (Eds.), *Strategic IT Governance and Alignment in Business Settings* (pp. 24–52). Hershey, PA: IGI Global. doi:10.4018/978-1-5225-0861-8.ch002

Perez-Uribe, R., & Ocampo-Guzman, D. (2016). Conflict within Colombian Family Owned SMEs: An Explosive Blend between Feelings and Business. In J. Saiz-Álvarez (Ed.), *Handbook of Research on Social Entrepreneurship and Solidarity Economics* (pp. 329–354). Hershey, PA: IGI Global. doi:10.4018/978-1-5225-0097-1.ch017

Pérez-Uribe, R. I., Torres, D. A., Jurado, S. P., & Prada, D. M. (2018). Cloud Tools for the Development of Project Management in SMEs. In R. Perez-Uribe, C. Salcedo-Perez, & D. Ocampo-Guzman (Eds.), *Handbook of Research on Intrapreneurship and Organizational Sustainability in SMEs* (pp. 95–120). Hershey, PA: IGI Global. doi:10.4018/978-1-5225-3543-0.ch005

Petrisor, I., & Cozmiuc, D. (2017). Global Supply Chain Management Organization at Siemens in the Advent of Industry 4.0. In L. Saglietto & C. Cezanne (Eds.), *Global Intermediation and Logistics Service Providers* (pp. 123–142). Hershey, PA: IGI Global. doi:10.4018/978-1-5225-2133-4.ch007

Pierce, J. M., Velliaris, D. M., & Edwards, J. (2017). A Living Case Study: A Journey Not a Destination. In N. Silton (Ed.), *Exploring the Benefits of Creativity in Education, Media, and the Arts* (pp. 158–178). Hershey, PA: IGI Global. doi:10.4018/978-1-5225-0504-4.ch008

Radosavljevic, M., & Andjelkovic, A. (2017). Multi-Criteria Decision Making Approach for Choosing Business Process for the Improvement: Upgrading of the Six Sigma Methodology. In J. Stanković, P. Delias, S. Marinković, & S. Rochhia (Eds.), *Tools and Techniques for Economic Decision Analysis* (pp. 225–247). Hershey, PA: IGI Global. doi:10.4018/978-1-5225-0959-2.ch011

Radovic, V. M. (2017). Corporate Sustainability and Responsibility and Disaster Risk Reduction: A Serbian Overview. In M. Camilleri (Ed.), *CSR 2.0 and the New Era of Corporate Citizenship* (pp. 147–164). Hershey, PA: IGI Global. doi:10.4018/978-1-5225-1842-6.ch008

Raghunath, K. M., Devi, S. L., & Patro, C. S. (2018). Impact of Risk Assessment Models on Risk Factors: A Holistic Outlook. In K. Strang, M. Korstanje, & N. Vajjhala (Eds.), *Research, Practices, and Innovations in Global Risk and Contingency Management* (pp. 134–153). Hershey, PA: IGI Global. doi:10.4018/978-1-5225-4754-9.ch008

Raman, A., & Goyal, D. P. (2017). Extending IMPLEMENT Framework for Enterprise Information Systems Implementation to Information System Innovation. In M. Tavana (Ed.), *Enterprise Information Systems and the Digitalization of Business Functions* (pp. 137–177). Hershey, PA: IGI Global. doi:10.4018/978-1-5225-2382-6.ch007

Rao, Y., & Zhang, Y. (2017). The Construction and Development of Academic Library Digital Special Subject Databases. In L. Ruan, Q. Zhu, & Y. Ye (Eds.), *Academic Library Development and Administration in China* (pp. 163–183). Hershey, PA: IGI Global. doi:10.4018/978-1-5225-0550-1.ch010

Ravasan, A. Z., Mohammadi, M. M., & Hamidi, H. (2018). An Investigation Into the Critical Success Factors of Implementing Information Technology Service Management Frameworks. In K. Jakobs (Ed.), *Corporate and Global Standardization Initiatives in Contemporary Society* (pp. 200–218). Hershey, PA: IGI Global. doi:10.4018/978-1-5225-5320-5.ch009

Renna, P., Izzo, C., & Romaniello, T. (2016). The Business Process Management Systems to Support Continuous Improvements. In W. Nuninger & J. Châtelet (Eds.), *Handbook of Research on Quality Assurance and Value Management in Higher Education* (pp. 237–256). Hershey, PA: IGI Global. doi:10.4018/978-1-5225-0024-7.ch009

Rezaie, S., Mirabedini, S. J., & Abtahi, A. (2018). Designing a Model for Implementation of Business Intelligence in the Banking Industry. *International Journal of Enterprise Information Systems, 14*(1), 77–103. doi:10.4018/IJEIS.2018010105

Riccò, R. (2016). Diversity Management: Bringing Equality, Equity, and Inclusion in the Workplace. In J. Prescott (Ed.), *Handbook of Research on Race, Gender, and the Fight for Equality* (pp. 335–359). Hershey, PA: IGI Global. doi:10.4018/978-1-5225-0047-6.ch015

Romano, L., Grimaldi, R., & Colasuonno, F. S. (2017). Demand Management as a Success Factor in Project Portfolio Management. In L. Romano (Ed.), *Project Portfolio Management Strategies for Effective Organizational Operations* (pp. 202–219). Hershey, PA: IGI Global. doi:10.4018/978-1-5225-2151-8.ch008

Rostek, K. B. (2016). Risk Management: Role and Importance in Business Organization. In D. Jakóbczak (Ed.), *Analyzing Risk through Probabilistic Modeling in Operations Research* (pp. 149–178). Hershey, PA: IGI Global. doi:10.4018/978-1-4666-9458-3.ch007

Rouhani, S., & Savoji, S. R. (2016). A Success Assessment Model for BI Tools Implementation: An Empirical Study of Banking Industry. *International Journal of Business Intelligence Research, 7*(1), 25–44. doi:10.4018/IJBIR.2016010103

Ruan, Z. (2016). A Corpus-Based Functional Analysis of Complex Nominal Groups in Written Business Discourse: The Case of "Business". *International Journal of Computer-Assisted Language Learning and Teaching, 6*(2), 74–90. doi:10.4018/IJCALLT.2016040105

Ruhi, U. (2018). Towards an Interdisciplinary Socio-Technical Definition of Virtual Communities. In M. Khosrow-Pour, D.B.A. (Ed.), Encyclopedia of Information Science and Technology, Fourth Edition (pp. 4278-4295). Hershey, PA: IGI Global. doi:10.4018/978-1-5225-2255-3.ch371

Ryan, J., Doster, B., Daily, S., & Lewis, C. (2016). A Case Study Perspective for Balanced Perioperative Workflow Achievement through Data-Driven Process Improvement. *International Journal of Healthcare Information Systems and Informatics, 11*(3), 19–41. doi:10.4018/IJHISI.2016070102

Safari, M. R., & Jiang, Q. (2018). The Theory and Practice of IT Governance Maturity and Strategies Alignment: Evidence From Banking Industry. *Journal of Global Information Management, 26*(2), 127–146. doi:10.4018/JGIM.2018040106

Sahoo, J., Pati, B., & Mohanty, B. (2017). Knowledge Management as an Academic Discipline: An Assessment. In B. Gunjal (Ed.), *Managing Knowledge and Scholarly Assets in Academic Libraries* (pp. 99–126). Hershey, PA: IGI Global. doi:10.4018/978-1-5225-1741-2.ch005

Saini, D. (2017). Relevance of Teaching Values and Ethics in Management Education. In N. Baporikar (Ed.), *Management Education for Global Leadership* (pp. 90–111). Hershey, PA: IGI Global. doi:10.4018/978-1-5225-1013-0.ch005

Sambhanthan, A. (2017). Assessing and Benchmarking Sustainability in Organisations: An Integrated Conceptual Model. *International Journal of Systems and Service-Oriented Engineering*, *7*(4), 22–43. doi:10.4018/IJSSOE.2017100102

Sambhanthan, A., & Potdar, V. (2017). A Study of the Parameters Impacting Sustainability in Information Technology Organizations. *International Journal of Knowledge-Based Organizations*, *7*(3), 27–39. doi:10.4018/IJKBO.2017070103

Sánchez-Fernández, M. D., & Manríquez, M. R. (2018). The Entrepreneurial Spirit Based on Social Values: The Digital Generation. In P. Isaias & L. Carvalho (Eds.), *User Innovation and the Entrepreneurship Phenomenon in the Digital Economy* (pp. 173–193). Hershey, PA: IGI Global. doi:10.4018/978-1-5225-2826-5.ch009

Sanchez-Ruiz, L., & Blanco, B. (2017). Process Management for SMEs: Barriers, Enablers, and Benefits. In M. Vemić (Ed.), *Optimal Management Strategies in Small and Medium Enterprises* (pp. 293–319). Hershey, PA: IGI Global. doi:10.4018/978-1-5225-1949-2.ch014

Sanz, L. F., Gómez-Pérez, J., & Castillo-Martinez, A. (2018). Analysis of the European ICT Competence Frameworks. In V. Ahuja & S. Rathore (Eds.), *Multidisciplinary Perspectives on Human Capital and Information Technology Professionals* (pp. 225–245). Hershey, PA: IGI Global. doi:10.4018/978-1-5225-5297-0.ch012

Sarvepalli, A., & Godin, J. (2017). Business Process Management in the Classroom. *Journal of Cases on Information Technology*, *19*(2), 17–28. doi:10.4018/JCIT.2017040102

Satpathy, B., & Muniapan, B. (2016). Ancient Wisdom for Transformational Leadership and Its Insights from the Bhagavad-Gita. In U. Aung & P. Ordoñez de Pablos (Eds.), *Managerial Strategies and Practice in the Asian Business Sector* (pp. 1–10). Hershey, PA: IGI Global. doi:10.4018/978-1-4666-9758-4.ch001

Saygili, E. E., Ozturkoglu, Y., & Kocakulah, M. C. (2017). End Users' Perceptions of Critical Success Factors in ERP Applications. *International Journal of Enterprise Information Systems*, *13*(4), 58–75. doi:10.4018/IJEIS.2017100104

Saygili, E. E., & Saygili, A. T. (2017). Contemporary Issues in Enterprise Information Systems: A Critical Review of CSFs in ERP Implementations. In M. Tavana (Ed.), *Enterprise Information Systems and the Digitalization of Business Functions* (pp. 120–136). Hershey, PA: IGI Global. doi:10.4018/978-1-5225-2382-6.ch006

Seidenstricker, S., & Antonino, A. (2018). Business Model Innovation-Oriented Technology Management for Emergent Technologies. In M. Khosrow-Pour, D.B.A. (Ed.), Encyclopedia of Information Science and Technology, Fourth Edition (pp. 4560-4569). Hershey, PA: IGI Global. doi:10.4018/978-1-5225-2255-3.ch396

Senaratne, S., & Gunarathne, A. D. (2017). Excellence Perspective for Management Education from a Global Accountants' Hub in Asia. In N. Baporikar (Ed.), *Management Education for Global Leadership* (pp. 158–180). Hershey, PA: IGI Global. doi:10.4018/978-1-5225-1013-0.ch008

Sensuse, D. I., & Cahyaningsih, E. (2018). Knowledge Management Models: A Summative Review. *International Journal of Information Systems in the Service Sector*, *10*(1), 71–100. doi:10.4018/IJISSS.2018010105

Sensuse, D. I., Wibowo, W. C., & Cahyaningsih, E. (2016). Indonesian Government Knowledge Management Model: A Theoretical Model. *Information Resources Management Journal*, *29*(1), 91–108. doi:10.4018/irmj.2016010106

Seth, M., Goyal, D., & Kiran, R. (2017). Diminution of Impediments in Implementation of Supply Chain Management Information System for Enhancing its Effectiveness in Indian Automobile Industry. *Journal of Global Information Management*, *25*(3), 1–20. doi:10.4018/JGIM.2017070101

Seyal, A. H., & Rahman, M. N. (2017). Investigating Impact of Inter-Organizational Factors in Measuring ERP Systems Success: Bruneian Perspectives. In M. Tavana (Ed.), *Enterprise Information Systems and the Digitalization of Business Functions* (pp. 178–204). Hershey, PA: IGI Global. doi:10.4018/978-1-5225-2382-6.ch008

Shaikh, A. A., & Karjaluoto, H. (2016). On Some Misconceptions Concerning Digital Banking and Alternative Delivery Channels. *International Journal of E-Business Research*, *12*(3), 1–16. doi:10.4018/IJEBR.2016070101

Shams, S. M. (2016). Stakeholder Relationship Management in Online Business and Competitive Value Propositions: Evidence from the Sports Industry. *International Journal of Online Marketing*, *6*(2), 1–17. doi:10.4018/IJOM.2016040101

Shamsuzzoha, A. (2016). Management of Risk and Resilience within Collaborative Business Network. In R. Addo-Tenkorang, J. Kantola, P. Helo, & A. Shamsuzzoha (Eds.), *Supply Chain Strategies and the Engineer-to-Order Approach* (pp. 143–159). Hershey, PA: IGI Global. doi:10.4018/978-1-5225-0021-6.ch008

Shaqrah, A. A. (2018). Analyzing Business Intelligence Systems Based on 7s Model of McKinsey. *International Journal of Business Intelligence Research*, *9*(1), 53–63. doi:10.4018/IJBIR.2018010104

Sharma, A. J. (2017). Enhancing Sustainability through Experiential Learning in Management Education. In N. Baporikar (Ed.), *Management Education for Global Leadership* (pp. 256–274). Hershey, PA: IGI Global. doi:10.4018/978-1-5225-1013-0.ch013

Shetty, K. P. (2017). Responsible Global Leadership: Ethical Challenges in Management Education. In N. Baporikar (Ed.), *Innovation and Shifting Perspectives in Management Education* (pp. 194–223). Hershey, PA: IGI Global. doi:10.4018/978-1-5225-1019-2.ch009

Sinthupundaja, J., & Kohda, Y. (2017). Effects of Corporate Social Responsibility and Creating Shared Value on Sustainability. *International Journal of Sustainable Entrepreneurship and Corporate Social Responsibility*, *2*(1), 27–38. doi:10.4018/IJSECSR.2017010103

Škarica, I., & Hrgović, A. V. (2018). Implementation of Total Quality Management Principles in Public Health Institutes in the Republic of Croatia. *International Journal of Productivity Management and Assessment Technologies*, *6*(1), 1–16. doi:10.4018/IJPMAT.2018010101

Smuts, H., Kotzé, P., Van der Merwe, A., & Loock, M. (2017). Framework for Managing Shared Knowledge in an Information Systems Outsourcing Context. *International Journal of Knowledge Management*, *13*(4), 1–30. doi:10.4018/IJKM.2017100101

Soares, E. R., & Zaidan, F. H. (2016). Information Architecture and Business Modeling in Modern Organizations of Information Technology: Professional Career Plan in Organizations IT. In G. Jamil, J. Poças Rascão, F. Ribeiro, & A. Malheiro da Silva (Eds.), *Handbook of Research on Information Architecture and Management in Modern Organizations* (pp. 439–457). Hershey, PA: IGI Global. doi:10.4018/978-1-4666-8637-3.ch020

Sousa, M. J., Cruz, R., Dias, I., & Caracol, C. (2017). Information Management Systems in the Supply Chain. In G. Jamil, A. Soares, & C. Pessoa (Eds.), *Handbook of Research on Information Management for Effective Logistics and Supply Chains* (pp. 469–485). Hershey, PA: IGI Global. doi:10.4018/978-1-5225-0973-8.ch025

Spremic, M., Turulja, L., & Bajgoric, N. (2018). Two Approaches in Assessing Business Continuity Management Attitudes in the Organizational Context. In N. Bajgoric (Ed.), *Always-On Enterprise Information Systems for Modern Organizations* (pp. 159–183). Hershey, PA: IGI Global. doi:10.4018/978-1-5225-3704-5.ch008

Steenkamp, A. L. (2018). Some Insights in Computer Science and Information Technology. In *Examining the Changing Role of Supervision in Doctoral Research Projects: Emerging Research and Opportunities* (pp. 113–133). Hershey, PA: IGI Global. doi:10.4018/978-1-5225-2610-0.ch005

Studdard, N., Dawson, M., Burton, S. L., Jackson, N., Leonard, B., Quisenberry, W., & Rahim, E. (2016). Nurturing Social Entrepreneurship and Building Social Entrepreneurial Self-Efficacy: Focusing on Primary and Secondary Schooling to Develop Future Social Entrepreneurs. In Z. Fields (Ed.), *Incorporating Business Models and Strategies into Social Entrepreneurship* (pp. 154–175). Hershey, PA: IGI Global. doi:10.4018/978-1-4666-8748-6.ch010

Sun, Z. (2016). A Framework for Developing Management Intelligent Systems. *International Journal of Systems and Service-Oriented Engineering*, *6*(1), 37–53. doi:10.4018/IJSSOE.2016010103

Swami, B., & Mphele, G. T. (2016). Problems Preventing Growth of Small Entrepreneurs: A Case Study of a Few Small Entrepreneurs in Botswana Sub-Urban Areas. In N. Baporikar (Ed.), *Handbook of Research on Entrepreneurship in the Contemporary Knowledge-Based Global Economy* (pp. 479–508). Hershey, PA: IGI Global. doi:10.4018/978-1-4666-8798-1.ch020

Tabach, A., & Croteau, A. (2017). Configurations of Information Technology Governance Practices and Business Unit Performance. *International Journal of IT/Business Alignment and Governance*, *8*(2), 1–27. doi:10.4018/IJITBAG.2017070101

Talaue, G. M., & İqbal, T. (2017). Assessment of e-Business Mode of Selected Private Universities in the Philippines and Pakistan. *International Journal of Online Marketing*, *7*(4), 63–77. doi:10.4018/IJOM.2017100105

Tam, G. C. (2017). Project Manager Sustainability Competence. In *Managerial Strategies and Green Solutions for Project Sustainability* (pp. 178–207). Hershey, PA: IGI Global. doi:10.4018/978-1-5225-2371-0.ch008

Tambo, T. (2018). Fashion Retail Innovation: About Context, Antecedents, and Outcome in Technological Change Projects. In I. Management Association (Ed.), Fashion and Textiles: Breakthroughs in Research and Practice (pp. 233-260). Hershey, PA: IGI Global. doi:10.4018/978-1-5225-3432-7.ch010

Tambo, T., & Mikkelsen, O. E. (2016). Fashion Supply Chain Optimization: Linking Make-to-Order Purchasing and B2B E-Commerce. In S. Joshi & R. Joshi (Eds.), *Designing and Implementing Global Supply Chain Management* (pp. 1–21). Hershey, PA: IGI Global. doi:10.4018/978-1-4666-9720-1.ch001

Tandon, K. (2016). Innovative Andragogy: The Paradigm Shift to Heutagogy. In S. Tiwari & L. Nafees (Eds.), *Innovative Management Education Pedagogies for Preparing Next-Generation Leaders* (pp. 238–257). Hershey, PA: IGI Global. doi:10.4018/978-1-4666-9691-4.ch014

Tantau, A. D., & Frăţilă, L. C. (2018). Information and Management System for Renewable Energy Business. In *Entrepreneurship and Business Development in the Renewable Energy Sector* (pp. 200–244). Hershey, PA: IGI Global. doi:10.4018/978-1-5225-3625-3.ch006

Teixeira, N., Pardal, P. N., & Rafael, B. G. (2018). Internationalization, Financial Performance, and Organizational Challenges: A Success Case in Portugal. In L. Carvalho (Ed.), *Handbook of Research on Entrepreneurial Ecosystems and Social Dynamics in a Globalized World* (pp. 379–423). Hershey, PA: IGI Global. doi:10.4018/978-1-5225-3525-6.ch017

Trad, A., & Kalpić, D. (2016). The E-Business Transformation Framework for E-Commerce Architecture-Modeling Projects. In I. Lee (Ed.), *Encyclopedia of E-Commerce Development, Implementation, and Management* (pp. 733–753). Hershey, PA: IGI Global. doi:10.4018/978-1-4666-9787-4.ch052

Trad, A., & Kalpić, D. (2016). The E-Business Transformation Framework for E-Commerce Control and Monitoring Pattern. In I. Lee (Ed.), *Encyclopedia of E-Commerce Development, Implementation, and Management* (pp. 754–777). Hershey, PA: IGI Global. doi:10.4018/978-1-4666-9787-4.ch053

Trad, A., & Kalpić, D. (2018). The Business Transformation Framework, Agile Project and Change Management. In M. Khosrow-Pour, D.B.A. (Ed.), Encyclopedia of Information Science and Technology, Fourth Edition (pp. 620-635). Hershey, PA: IGI Global. doi:10.4018/978-1-5225-2255-3.ch054

Trad, A., & Kalpić, D. (2018). The Business Transformation and Enterprise Architecture Framework: The Financial Engineering E-Risk Management and E-Law Integration. In B. Sergi, F. Fidanoski, M. Ziolo, & V. Naumovski (Eds.), *Regaining Global Stability After the Financial Crisis* (pp. 46–65). Hershey, PA: IGI Global. doi:10.4018/978-1-5225-4026-7.ch003

Turulja, L., & Bajgoric, N. (2018). Business Continuity and Information Systems: A Systematic Literature Review. In N. Bajgoric (Ed.), *Always-On Enterprise Information Systems for Modern Organizations* (pp. 60–87). Hershey, PA: IGI Global. doi:10.4018/978-1-5225-3704-5.ch004

van Wessel, R. M., de Vries, H. J., & Ribbers, P. M. (2016). Business Benefits through Company IT Standardization. In K. Jakobs (Ed.), *Effective Standardization Management in Corporate Settings* (pp. 34–53). Hershey, PA: IGI Global. doi:10.4018/978-1-4666-9737-9.ch003

Vargas-Hernández, J. G. (2017). Professional Integrity in Business Management Education. In N. Baporikar (Ed.), *Management Education for Global Leadership* (pp. 70–89). Hershey, PA: IGI Global. doi:10.4018/978-1-5225-1013-0.ch004

Vasista, T. G., & AlAbdullatif, A. M. (2017). Role of Electronic Customer Relationship Management in Demand Chain Management: A Predictive Analytic Approach. *International Journal of Information Systems and Supply Chain Management, 10*(1), 53–67. doi:10.4018/IJISSCM.2017010104

Vergidis, K. (2016). Rediscovering Business Processes: Definitions, Patterns, and Modelling Approaches. In P. Papajorgji, F. Pinet, A. Guimarães, & J. Papathanasiou (Eds.), *Automated Enterprise Systems for Maximizing Business Performance* (pp. 97–122). Hershey, PA: IGI Global. doi:10.4018/978-1-4666-8841-4.ch007

Vieru, D., & Bourdeau, S. (2017). Survival in the Digital Era: A Digital Competence-Based Multi-Case Study in the Canadian SME Clothing Industry. *International Journal of Social and Organizational Dynamics in IT, 6*(1), 17–34. doi:10.4018/IJSODIT.2017010102

Vijayan, G., & Kamarulzaman, N. H. (2017). An Introduction to Sustainable Supply Chain Management and Business Implications. In M. Khan, M. Hussain, & M. Ajmal (Eds.), *Green Supply Chain Management for Sustainable Business Practice* (pp. 27–50). Hershey, PA: IGI Global. doi:10.4018/978-1-5225-0635-5.ch002

Vlachvei, A., & Notta, O. (2017). Firm Competitiveness: Theories, Evidence, and Measurement. In A. Vlachvei, O. Notta, K. Karantininis, & N. Tsounis (Eds.), *Factors Affecting Firm Competitiveness and Performance in the Modern Business World* (pp. 1–42). Hershey, PA: IGI Global. doi:10.4018/978-1-5225-0843-4.ch001

von Rosing, M., Fullington, N., & Walker, J. (2016). Using the Business Ontology and Enterprise Standards to Transform Three Leading Organizations. *International Journal of Conceptual Structures and Smart Applications, 4*(1), 71–99. doi:10.4018/IJCSSA.2016010104 von Rosing, M., & von Scheel, H. (2016). Using the Business Ontology to Develop Enterprise Standards. *International Journal of Conceptual Structures and Smart Applications*, *4*(1), 48–70. doi:10.4018/IJCSSA.2016010103

Walczak, S. (2016). Artificial Neural Networks and other AI Applications for Business Management Decision Support. *International Journal of Sociotechnology and Knowledge Development*, *8*(4), 1–20. doi:10.4018/IJSKD.2016100101

Wamba, S. F., Akter, S., Kang, H., Bhattacharya, M., & Upal, M. (2016). The Primer of Social Media Analytics. *Journal of Organizational and End User Computing*, *28*(2), 1–12. doi:10.4018/JOEUC.2016040101

Wang, C., Schofield, M., Li, X., & Ou, X. (2017). Do Chinese Students in Public and Private Higher Education Institutes Perform at Different Level in One of the Leadership Skills: Critical Thinking?: An Exploratory Comparison. In V. Wang (Ed.), *Encyclopedia of Strategic Leadership and Management* (pp. 160–181). Hershey, PA: IGI Global. doi:10.4018/978-1-5225-1049-9.ch013

Wang, F., Raisinghani, M. S., Mora, M., & Wang, X. (2016). Strategic E-Business Management through a Balanced Scored Card Approach. In I. Lee (Ed.), *Encyclopedia of E-Commerce Development, Implementation, and Management* (pp. 361–386). Hershey, PA: IGI Global. doi:10.4018/978-1-4666-9787-4.ch027

Wang, J. (2017). Multi-Agent based Production Management Decision System Modelling for the Textile Enterprise. *Journal of Global Information Management*, *25*(4), 1–15. doi:10.4018/JGIM.2017100101

Wiedemann, A., & Gewald, H. (2017). Examining Cross-Domain Alignment: The Correlation of Business Strategy, IT Management, and IT Business Value. *International Journal of IT/Business Alignment and Governance*, *8*(1), 17–31. doi:10.4018/IJITBAG.2017010102

Wolf, R., & Thiel, M. (2018). Advancing Global Business Ethics in China: Reducing Poverty Through Human and Social Welfare. In S. Hipsher (Ed.), *Examining the Private Sector's Role in Wealth Creation and Poverty Reduction* (pp. 67–84). Hershey, PA: IGI Global. doi:10.4018/978-1-5225-3117-3.ch004

Wu, J., Ding, F., Xu, M., Mo, Z., & Jin, A. (2016). Investigating the Determinants of Decision-Making on Adoption of Public Cloud Computing in E-government. *Journal of Global Information Management*, *24*(3), 71–89. doi:10.4018/JGIM.2016070104

Xu, L., & de Vrieze, P. (2016). Building Situational Applications for Virtual Enterprises. In I. Lee (Ed.), *Encyclopedia of E-Commerce Development, Implementation, and Management* (pp. 715–724). Hershey, PA: IGI Global. doi:10.4018/978-1-4666-9787-4.ch050

Yablonsky, S. (2018). Innovation Platforms: Data and Analytics Platforms. In *Multi-Sided Platforms (MSPs) and Sharing Strategies in the Digital Economy: Emerging Research and Opportunities* (pp. 72–95). Hershey, PA: IGI Global. doi:10.4018/978-1-5225-5457-8.ch003

Yusoff, A., Ahmad, N. H., & Halim, H. A. (2017). Agropreneurship among Gen Y in Malaysia: The Role of Academic Institutions. In N. Ahmad, T. Ramayah, H. Halim, & S. Rahman (Eds.), *Handbook of Research on Small and Medium Enterprises in Developing Countries* (pp. 23–47). Hershey, PA: IGI Global. doi:10.4018/978-1-5225-2165-5.ch002

Zanin, F., Comuzzi, E., & Costantini, A. (2018). The Effect of Business Strategy and Stock Market Listing on the Use of Risk Assessment Tools. In *Management Control Systems in Complex Settings: Emerging Research and Opportunities* (pp. 145–168). Hershey, PA: IGI Global. doi:10.4018/978-1-5225-3987-2.ch007

Zgheib, P. W. (2017). Corporate Innovation and Intrapreneurship in the Middle East. In P. Zgheib (Ed.), *Entrepreneurship and Business Innovation in the Middle East* (pp. 37–56). Hershey, PA: IGI Global. doi:10.4018/978-1-5225-2066-5.ch003

About the Contributors

Ionica Oncioiu holds a Ph.D. in economy and accounting. Her research interests include the development of SMEs innovation, Project Management, Accounting Information Systems, Asset Management and E-Commerce Marketing. She has had more than 15 years of experience in this area and has published 10 text books and more than 70 papers in scholarly peer reviewed international journals.

Gary Cokins is an internationally recognized expert, speaker, and author in enterprise and corporate performance management improvement methods and business analytics. He is the founder of Analytics-Based Performance Management, an advisory firm located in Cary, North Carolina at www.garycokins.com. Gary received a BS degree in Industrial Engineering/Operations Research from Cornell University in 1971. He received his MBA from Northwestern University's Kellogg School of Management in 1974. Gary began his career as a strategic planner with FMC's Link-Belt Division and then served as Financial Controller and Operations Manager. In 1981 Gary began his management consulting career first with Deloitte consulting, and then in 1988 with KPMG consulting. In 1992 Gary headed the National Cost Management Consulting Services for Electronic Data Systems (EDS) now part of HP. From 1997 until 2013 Gary was a Principal Consultant with SAS, a leading provider of analytics software. His two most recent books are Performance Management: Integrating Strategy Execution, Methodologies, Risk, and Analytics, and Predictive Business Analytics. His books are published by John Wiley & Sons.

Sorinel Căpuşneanu is a PhD associate professor at Titu Maiorescu University of Bucharest. Also, he is the Editor in Chief of Academic Journal of Economic Studies. His research focus is the area of Management Accounting, Management Performance, Management Information Systems, Audit and Controlling, and Business Ethics. He is the author of the following books: Elements of Cost Management, Economica Publishing House (2008) and Management Accounting. Performance Assessment Tool, University Publishing House (2013) and co-author of Ethics and Decision-Making for Sustainable Business Practices (Chapter 7 Business Ethics and Cost Management in SME's. Theories of Business Ethics and Cost Management Ethos) published by IGI-Global (USA, 2017). He has participated in numerous national and international conferences and has made a remarkable contribution to managerial accounting by publishing several articles.

Dan Ioan Topor is a PhD lecturer at the 1 Decembrie 1918 University of Alba-Iulia, Faculty of Economic Sciences. His research focus is the area of Management Accounting, Management Performance and Management Information Systems, Audit and Controlling, and Business Ethics. He is the author of the following books: New dimensions of cost-related cost information for winemaking (2014) and Basics of Accounting (2016). He has published numerous articles on Managerial Accounting and Management Control and has participated in numerous national and international conferences.

* * *

Hassan Danial Aslam is Assistant Professor in Faculty of Management at the Islamia University of Bahawalpur, Pakistan where he is performing his duties by conducting various researches and teaching human resource development subjects like learning and development, organizational learning, education management etc. He is author in the field of Business Management, Human Resource Management research and Educational learning. He has published three international books which include "Dissertation Writing Skills", "Performance Issues of Teachers in Higher Education" and "Offshore Risk Mitigation model". Along with international published books he is author of various research papers in international refereed journals which include the critical areas of performance evaluation & development of teachers in higher education of Pakistan, student learning achievement, formal and non-formal education, academic leadership and individual to organizational learning. He is serving as managing editor of two international journals (International Journal of Academic Research in Business and Social Sciences) having well-known repute among international publishing societies. He has been working as education consultant and human resource adviser in various institutes of Asia and Middle-East. His major contribution to the research field includes projects like "District literacy survey 2010" in Pakistan and "Academic Performance Learning difficulties and learning environment for Saudi students" which proved to be a major policy document in Government think tanks of Pakistan and Saudi Arabia.

Cristian-Marian Barbu, PhD, is a graduate of the Academy of Economic Studies in Bucharest, Romania, and after passing the Bachelor exam in 1997, he received the degree of Economist. He received his PhD degree in Economics from the Academy of Economic Studies in Bucharest in 2005 with the dissertation entitled "Agricultural sustainable economic development in the mountain areas in Romania". After graduation, he took the academic career and started working in higher education in 1998, in "ARTIFEX" University of Bucharest. He held the positions of instructor, starting with 1998, teaching assistant starting with 2000, lecturer starting with 2003, associate professor starting with 2008, and University professor starting with 2017. His expertise in teaching and research, as tenured teaching staff in higher education, since 2003, in Political Economics, Microeconomics, Macroeconomics, Prices and Competition, Economic Policies, made him allocate time to research and the dissemination of the findings, which resulted into books, monographs, studies, and articles published, as well as participation in national and international conferences, and research grants. In his capacity of tenured teaching staff in higher education, he wrote specialized handbooks, as author and co-author, which have been aids for students and enriched the data in the field. During his academic career, he has been involved in research in national research projects and in partnerships with economic agents (contracts with the business companies). He also disseminated his findings in specialized /ISI indexed journals, and during national and international scientific events. The topics of the books, articles, papers and studies published by Mr. Cristian-Marian Barbu reflect his preoccupation about micro and macroeconomics, economic balance, analysis of correlations between the result indicators and the effort indicators, agriculture – a major sector of national economy, economic policies, macroeconomic studies and analyses, comparative analyses regarding the agricultural potential of Romania, analyses regarding various segments of national economy at various moments in time, analyses regarding the cost and /or performance in economic entities, aspects regarding the economic-financial crisis, the need of a paradigm to return to nature and to good sense, price and price policy in the strategic planning of the enterprise, environment and monitoring of prejudice to the economic environment etc. The recognition and the appreciation of his prestige in research and scientific activity are translated in the membership in editorial/scientific boards of IDB indexed journals and conferences editorial boards.

Georgiana Burlacu is PhD student at Valahia University.

Traian Ovidiu Calotă holds a Ph.D. in accounting and had more than 15 years of experience in this area.

Dana Maria (Oprea) Constantin is a PhD in Geography at University of Bucharest, Faculty of Geography. She works at Department of Meteorology and Hidrology. Also, she is the Editor in Chief of International Journal of Academic Research in Environment and Geography (IJAREG). In the past she managed the school network of National Geographic Magazine, Romanian Edition. At present she leads the Students` Scientific Club of Climatology and Air-Environment Protection. Her research focus is the area of Geography, Environmental Economics, Meteorology, Climatology and Environmental Education. Dana Constantin is the author of three books and over fifty articles. She has participated in numerous national and international conferences and research projects.

Lavinia Essen is a student in Lapland University where her major is management in the Faculty of Social Science.

Melinda Timea Fülöp is a Lecturer at the Faculty of Economics and Business Administration in the Babeş-Bolyai University, Cluj-Napoca, Romania. She holds a PhD in Audit and her teaching and research fields are audit profession and ethics, the tripartite function of audit in the context of corporate governance and financial accounting and auditing.

Nicolae Măgdaş is a PhD student in the field of Auditor-client negotiation relationship at the Faculty of Economics and Business Administration in the Babeş-Bolyai University, Cluj-Napoca, Romania. His research interest is in the audit area with a specific focus on audit -client relationship and audit negotiation.

Alexandru Lucian Manole is a graduate of the Bucharest University of Economic Studies, The Faculty of Accounting and Management Information Systems (1999). He is teaching various IT in economics disciplines at the "ARTIFEX" University of Bucharest, The Faculty of Finances and Accounting, The Department of Financial and Accounting. He holds a PhD in Accounting, granted in 2007. As a Professor, he teaches subjects such as database management systems, decision support systems, programming etc. He published articles in scientific journals, two books on databases and decision support systems, co-authored several books and his main interests are the applications of information technology in accounting and finance.

Andreea Marin-Pantelescu is a graduate of the Bucharest University of Economic Studies, The Faculty of Commerce, the specialization Tourism-Services (2002) and of the postgraduate program in International Tourism (2003). In February 2007, she becomes a teacher in the Bucharest University of Economic Studies, The Faculty of Commerce, The Department of Tourism-Services. She obtains her PhD in Economics in the year 2008 with a thesis in services, and in 2010 a Master's Degree in the domain Economics and International Business. As a Lecturer in the Department of Tourism and Geography, the Faculty of Business and Tourism, the Bucharest University of Economic Studies, she teaches subjects like the technique of tourism operations, the technique of hotels operations, development strategies for the tertiary sector, services economy, business ethics, etc. She writes articles published in scientific journals and her research interests are in the field of services, tourism and booking systems (Amadeus and Travelport). Currently, she is focused on the services economy course and conducts research in the domain of creative services. She is a founding member of the Academic Association for Research in Tourism and Services (CACTUS). Editor Journal of Environmental Management and Tourism and CACTUS Academic Journal Organizer member of the 22 RESER International Conference: Services and Economic Development. Local and Global Challenges (2012) CESMAA Award (2009): Best Presentation within the 3rd International Conference on "Further Challenges for a Competitive Management", Craiova, Romania, 23- 24 October 2009 Expert in research projects: "Innovative partnerships between universities and businesses".

Gabriela Claudia Oncioiu has a B.Sc. degree in Social Science. Her research interest resides mainly within the area of corporate governance.

Ahmet Özcan is a faculty member of Faculty of Business at Adana Alparslan Türkeş Science and Technology University. He received his Ph.D. in accounting and finance from Marmara University in 2014. His research interests include auditing, IFRS and cost accounting.

Valentin Radu is teaching at the Valahia University of Targoviste, with over 10 years of teaching activity.

Ileana-Sorina Rakos is a PhD. lecturer at the University of Petrosani, Department of Economic Sciences. Her research focus is the area of Finance and Accounting. She is the author of the book: Management of public institutions. Theoretical and Applied Fundamentals (2018). She has published numerous articles on Finance and Accounting, and she has participated in numerous national and international conferences.

Sorin-Adrian Robu is PhD candidate, Doctoral School within the Academy of Economic Studies – Bucharest.

Alina-Georgiana Solomon is a PhD lecturer at the Dimitrie Cantemir Christian University, Department of Finance and Banking. Her research focus is the area of Finance, Fiscality and Budgeting. She is the author of the books: Fiscal-Budgetary Policy and the Euro Area (2015) and The Public Budget. Elements of Fiscality and Coordination of Economic Policies (2015). She has published numerous articles on Finance, Fiscality and Banking and she has participated in numerous national and international conferences.

Alina Stanciu is a highly skilled professional with extended expertise in Management and Public Relation gained in multinational environment in the past 10 years. Experienced in Business 2 Business Strategy and New Business with a strong understanding of management concepts, leadership, business policies and talent acquisition, having solid track record in building and motivating strong teams. Involved in external relations with business organizations, persuasive and empathic character with strong communication skills.

Cristina Maria Ştefan is teaching at the Valahia University of Targoviste, with over 10 years of teaching activity.

Mihaela Stefan Hint is a PhD student at 1 Decembrie 1918 University, Alba-Iulia.

Dumitru Alexandru Stoica is PhD student at Valahia University.

Monika Brigitte Sürgün is PhD student at Valahia University.

Melinda Timea Fülöp is a Lecturer at the Faculty of Economics and Business Administration in the Babeş-Bolyai University, Cluj-Napoca, Romania. She holds a PhD in Audit and her teaching and research fields are audit profession and ethics, the tripartite function of audit in the context of corporate governance and financial accounting and auditing.

Nicoleta Ileana Trăistaru is PhD student at Valahia University.

Mirela Catalina Turkes is a PhD lecturer at the Dimitrie Cantemir Christian University of Bucharest, Department of Finance, Banking and Accountancy. Her research focus is the area of Marketing and Communications. She is the author of the following books: The Marketing of Financial-Banking Services (2014), Another Way to Learn Marketing (2016) and The Basics of Marketing (2017). She has published numerous articles on Marketing and has participated in numerous national and international conferences.

Index

S

T

V

www.ingramcontent.com/pod-product-compliance
Lightning Source LLC
LaVergne TN
LVHW062121300926
849161LV00010B/2512